MANAGERIAL ACCOUNTING

DECISION MAKING AND PERFORMANCE MANAGEMENT

Fourth Edition

Ray Proctor

With contributions from
Nigel Burton, Adrian Pierce and Gary Burmiston

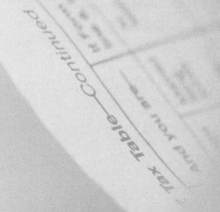

PEARSON

Harlow, England · London · New York · Boston · San Francisco · Toronto · Sydney
Auckland · Singapore · Hong Kong · Tokyo · Seoul · Taipei · New Delhi
Cape Town · São Paulo · Mexico City · Madrid · Amsterdam · Munich · Paris · Milan

Pearson Education Limited
Edinburgh Gate
Harlow
Essex CM20 2JE
England

and Associated Companies throughout the world

Visit us on the World Wide Web at:
www.pearson.com/uk

First published 2002
Second edition published 2006
Third edition published 2009
Fourth edition published 2012

© Pearson Education Limited 2002, 2006, 2009, 2012

ISBN: 978-0-273-76448-9

British Library Cataloguing-in-Publication Data
A catalogue record for this book is available from the British Library

Library of Congress Cataloging-in-Publication Data
A catalog record for this book is available from the Library of Congress

10 9 8 7 6 5 4 3 2
16 15 14

Typeset in 10.5/12.5pt Minion by 35
Printed and bound by Ashford Colour Press., Gosport

MANAGERIAL ACCOUNTING

Visit the *Managerial Accounting: Decision Making and Performance Improvement, fourth edition*, Companion Website at **www.pearsoned.co.uk/proctor** to find valuable **student** learning material including:

- Multiple choice questions to test your understanding
- Extensive links to valuable resources on the web
- Flashcards to explain key terms
- An online glossary to explain key terms

BPP Professional Education
32-34 Colmore Circus
Birmingham B4 6BN
Phone: 0121 345 9843

I dedicate this book to my wife, Sara, who has endured many periods of solitude during its writing, with little or no complaint. Without her support, the book would not have reached completion. I welcome this opportunity to thank her publicly.

Brief Contents

Contents

Part 3
DECISION MAKING   101

5 Variable costing and breakeven analysis   103

6 Short-term decisions using variable costing   134

7 Short-term decisions using relevant costing   158

8 Capital investment appraisal for long-term decisions   179

Part 4
PRODUCT COSTING AND PRICING 221

9 Product costs using absorption costing 223

10 Product costs using activity-based costing 245

11 Comparison of profits under absorption and variable costing 274

12 Pricing your products 294

Supporting resources

Visit **www.pearsoned.co.uk/proctor** to find valuable online resources

Companion Website for students
- Multiple choice questions to test your understanding
- Extensive links to valuable resources on the web
- Flashcards to explain key terms
- An online glossary to explain key terms

For instructors
- Complete, downloadable Instructor's Manual
- PowerPoint slides to assist lecture preparation
- Testbank of question material

Also: The Companion Website provides the following features:

- Search tool to help locate specific items of content
- E-mail results and profile tools to send results of quizzes to instructors
- Online help and support to assist with website usage and troubleshooting

For more information please contact your local Pearson Education sales representative or visit **www.pearsoned.co.uk/proctor**

Part 4
PRODUCT COSTING AND PRICING 221

9 Product costs using absorption costing 223

10 Product costs using activity-based costing 245

11 Comparison of profits under absorption and variable costing 274

12 Pricing your products 294

measured in the same units. These units are the currency used by the organization. In the UK, this unit is usually the pound sterling; in the USA it is the dollar, etc.

The numbers are merely the medium through which the value of these things, and changes to them, are expressed. When a credit sale changes stock into a debtor, all three items are measured in the same units. A sale of £80 may change stock valued at £50 into a debtor of £80. Competence at arithmetic is very useful in accountancy, knowledge of higher mathematics is less so. The ability to estimate answers mentally is very valuable as this enables a check to be performed on the broad accuracy of the detailed calculations. These estimates give ballpark figures approximating to the accurate answers and, for some purposes, are sufficient in themselves.

You probably realize from what you have read so far that you, the reader, are being addressed as a manager, present or future. You *may* also be, or become, a management accountant but the emphasis of this book is *management* (rather than accounting). Of course, the accounting skills covered are important but please remember that they are a means to an end and not an end in themselves. A few years ago, the Chartered Institute of Management Accountants changed the name of its monthly magazine from *Management Accounting* to *Financial Management*. This change of name reinforces the primary objective of management accounting: it is to help managers do their work better. Much of this involves using quantitative information already captured by the existing management information system.

This objective clearly differentiates management accounting from financial accounting. Financial accounts attempt to tell the story of what has happened in the business during a period now ended and what it looks like at the end of that period; it is all about the *past*. In contrast, management accounting is about helping the business to perform better in the *future*. Also, unlike periodic management accounts which are for internal use only, the statutory annual report and accounts are available to the public at large. They are a legal requirement rather than a management tool. They are not designed to help managers perform better.

The book's emphasis on management is reinforced by the inclusion of a section at the end of each chapter called 'The manager's point of view'. These are mostly by Nigel Burton who has been a high-level manager for many years (*not an academic*). He started his business career as a qualified accountant and rose to become managing director. After the chapter has covered the problems and how to tackle them, Nigel discusses the practical aspects based on his long experience of using them. I find these sections very interesting and insightful; as a future manager, I hope you do too.

What is included in this book

The main areas covered by this book are:

- decision making using relevant, variable (a.k.a. marginal) costing;
- fixed asset investment appraisal for long-term decision making;
- product costing and pricing, internally and externally;
- controlling operations through the use of budgets;
- alternative approaches to performance management.

These areas cover a wide range of complex problems. The knowledge and techniques in this book will help you to solve these. Each chapter discusses the problems, explains the techniques available for solving them, encourages you to practise these techniques and *points out their limitations*. It is important for managers to understand the limitations of the techniques they use. Each one is based on a financial model which makes assumptions. For example, calculating a 'payback period' for a proposed purchase of fixed assets assumes that business cash flows are perfectly even with the same amount of money flowing in and out every day! How many businesses do you know where this happens? I do not know of any but this technique is very widely adopted.

A consequence of this is that your calculations produce estimates rather than precise numbers. **An answer given to five decimal places may be very precise but that does not mean to say that it is accurate!** Due to the assumptions built into the models, all the decimal places, and even some numbers to the left of the decimal point, may be worthless as well as misleading. It is important to remember this.

The book also gives an introduction to basic cost behaviour and explains the difference between profit and cash. If you are not confident of your understanding of these, it would be sensible to look at them before moving on to the main body of the book. It also has a section on ratio analysis and working capital management. These two connected topics form a bridge between financial and management accounting. They are included because they use information provided directly by the financial accounts to help managers improve the future performance of their organizations.

The last part of the book includes an important new (to this fourth edition) chapter on performance improvement techniques. Helping their organizations to improve is becoming a more and more popular role for management accountants. Unfortunately, there is a plethora of alternative techniques in existence and their meanings are often obscured by an unnecessarily high degree of management-speak. This chapter should prove useful to both managers and students alike as it outlines how 15 of the most popular techniques work. Also, I highly recommend this chapter's insightful 'Manager's point of view' written by Gary Burmiston; it has a particularly important message, especially for practising managers.

Much thought has been given to the order of the contents. The topics are presented in a logical sequence but not a unique one. Any chapter can be studied without reference to other chapters but they are easier to understand in the light of the other chapters in the same part. For example, the two chapters on budgets are best read consecutively and the five chapters on costing and pricing are best read in conjunction with each other. The order in which Parts 2, 3, 4 and 5 are studied is not so important.

I strongly recommend that you attempt the self-assessment questions as you come across them. This gives an active, rather than passive, understanding of the subject matter and aids comprehension of the following sections. It is easy to believe you understand what you have just read, but attempting these questions will test this and reinforce your understanding of the subject matter.

Summary

The objective of this book is to make you a better manager by enabling you to understand and apply managerial accounting techniques effectively. By knowing the assumptions and approximations on which these financial models are constructed, you will be aware of their limitations and the danger of applying their results without wider consideration of their business context. Most business decisions are too important to be left solely to accountants. Use the information provided by them as a starting point for your deliberations, not as a prescribed course of action.

Organizational activities are not scientifically deterministic. If they were, there would be little or no need for managers. Managing is more of an art than a science. Information provided by accountants is important but it is not sufficient in itself. You also need a good intuitive feeling for how your customers, suppliers, markets and regulatory environment will behave in different situations. This comes from experience rather than academic learning. However, if I did not believe that the contents of this book could help you be a better manager, I would not have made the effort to write it. I wish you success in your management careers.

Introduction to the book for lecturers

Rationale

Is there really a need for yet another book on management accounting? There are many texts currently available on this subject. They tend to fall into one of two categories. First, those aimed at students aiming to become qualified accountants and, second, those aimed at students of business and management who do not intend to be accountants.

This book falls firmly into the second category. But the question still remains: is another book of this type needed? As an experienced teacher of business and management students, I believe it is. My justification is as follows.

Management accounting books for business and management students go into less technical detail than those aimed at professional accountancy students. This is sensible and I also take this approach. However, in my opinion, this only goes partway to fulfilling these students' needs. They also need to know the practicalities of how the techniques are actually used in business. Without this, they will end up as foundation-level accountancy students instead of what they wish to be, i.e. effective business managers.

Management emphasis

The reluctance of some students to embrace management accounting has arisen due to the emphasis being misplaced on accounting rather than management. All too often, assessment of students has tested mathematical proficiency rather than ability to apply appropriate techniques to business situations. This book is different in that it has a **strong management approach**. This is especially evident in 'The manager's point of view' sections at the end of each chapter which are written by practising managers. These unique features use actual examples from the world of business to place the theory into its practical context. Their objective is to remind students that management accounting is a means to an end and not an end in itself.

Market

This introductory book is particularly suitable for students of business and management who have no previous knowledge of management accounting. Provided this condition applies, it is suitable for both undergraduate and MBA students. It is also relevant and useful to practising managers.

Many readers will work in the service sector rather than manufacturing so I have used examples from the service sector wherever I can to reflect this.

Accounting and managerial accounting

Accounting is not about numbers; it is about organizations, what they do and the things they use. Sales, equipment, remuneration, purchases, debtors, owners' investments and many other items all fall within this description. In order to express the relationships between them, they are all measured in the same units. These units are the currency used by the organization. In the UK this unit is usually the pound sterling; in the USA it is the dollar, etc.

The numbers are merely the medium through which the value of these things, and changes to them, are expressed. When a credit sale changes stock into a debtor, all three items are measured in the same units. A sale of £80 may change stock valued at £50 into a debtor of £80. Competence at arithmetic is very useful in accountancy, knowledge of higher mathematics is less so. The ability to estimate answers mentally is very valuable as this enables a check to be performed on the broad accuracy of the detailed calculations. These estimates give ballpark figures approximating to the accurate answers and, for some purposes, are sufficient in themselves.

Financial accounting is essentially orientated towards the past. Its rules are intended to ensure that the statements of performance for a financial year, and the position at the end of that year, give a true and fair view of the organization. Financial accounts can only be completed after the financial year has ended.

Management accounting is orientated towards the future. It is primarily concerned with the provision of information to managers to help them plan, evaluate and control activities. It is essentially a service function: a means to an end rather than an end in itself. Managerial accounting also fits this description but the use of the word 'managerial' emphasizes the service role. This may seem obvious but, for much of the twentieth century, management accounting was used mainly to serve the needs of financial accounting rather than to assist managers in their tasks. (This theme is discussed further in the chapter on balanced scorecards.) **Managerial accounting is about improving the future performance of organizations.**

Structure of the book

The structure of this book is summarized by the table of contents. It is split into five parts preceded by this introduction for lecturers as well as an introduction for students and followed by a glossary and an index. Each chapter starts with a detailed list of contents and an introduction to give the readers a framework for their study. The main topics are then discussed in a logical order. Many illustrative examples are given to show how each technique is applied, followed by an invitation to the readers to attempt a similar question to test their understanding. Answers to these self-assessment questions are given at the end of each chapter.

One important feature appearing in each chapter is the section on the limitations of the techniques discussed. It is very important for students to appreciate that these techniques are financial models of business activity and that no model can ever be as rich as the reality it attempts to represent. In simple terms, the answers produced by the calculations are approximations and not exactitudes. An answer given to five decimal places may be very precise but that does not mean to say that it is accurate! Due to the assumptions built into the models, all the decimal places, and even some numbers to the left of the decimal point, may be worthless as well as misleading.

Next comes 'The manager's point of view'. These sections are written by three qualified accountants: Nigel Burton, Adrian Pierce and Gary Burmiston, each with many years of practical experience (see the 'About the authors' section). I am indebted to them for willingly sharing their knowledge with us. Even if you read nothing else in this book, you would benefit greatly from reading their 'Manager's points of view'; I highly recommend them to you.

After this section is a 'summary' of the main points covered by the chapter. This is to help the readers review the material and make connections between the various items discussed. This is similar to the complete picture emerging from the correct placing of all the pieces of a jigsaw. (It can also serve the useful function of a summary 'revision list' for examinations.)

Following this, the chapter is concluded by a section concerning assessment. First, the answers are given to the self-assessment questions contained within the chapter.

Next, an extensive case study is presented (the answer is given in the Lecturer's Guide). These cases are holistic in that they attempt to bring together many of the different aspects discussed within the chapter. They are suitable for either individual students or groups of students. It is impossible to be exact but these case studies are unlikely to take less than two hours to complete.

Finally, several additional questions are presented for extra practice. The answers to some of these are given at the end of the book. The answers to the remaining questions are given in the Lecturer's Guide, which will also contain masters of overhead transparencies, etc. Supplementary material can be downloaded from: http://www.booksites.net/proctor

In summary, each chapter:

- sets the context;
- introduces the subject;
- explains the principles and techniques in easy steps;
- encourages the readers to practise the techniques immediately;
- explains the limitations of the financial models;
- gives the manager's point of view;
- gives a summary of the main points;
- gives answers to self-assessment questions;
- has a comprehensive case study;
- has additional practice questions.

Much thought was given by the author to the order of the contents. The topics are presented in a logical sequence but not a unique one. Any chapter can be studied without reference to other chapters but they are easier to understand in the light of the other chapters in the same part. For example, the two chapters on budgets are best read consecutively and the five chapters on costing and pricing are best read in conjunction with each other. The order in which Parts 2, 3, 4 and 5 are read is not so important.

Students should be encouraged to attempt the self-assessment questions as they come across them. This gives an active, rather than passive, understanding of the subject matter and aids comprehension of the following sections. It is easy for them to believe that they understand what they have just read, but attempting these questions will test this and reinforce their understanding of the subject matter.

Writing style

The writing style attempts to be concise and unambiguous. The overriding objective is **clarity**. Diagrams, many of them original, are included wherever they can aid understanding. Explanations are kept as simple as possible in order not to confuse. Intermediate steps in the solutions to questions have been included to ensure students can follow them. However, unnecessary algebra has been omitted in favour of a common-business-sense approach. My experience is that students appreciate this approach and learn faster. Much of the text is purposely written in a 'friendly' style to engage readers and put them at their ease. It is consistently practical in its approach, often referring to real situations.

Summary

The objective of this book is to make students into effective managers by enabling them to understand and apply managerial accounting techniques effectively. By knowing the assumptions and approximations on which these financial models are constructed, they will be aware of their limitations and the danger of applying their results without wider consideration of their business context. Most business decisions are too important to be left solely to the accountants. The information provided by the accountants should be used as a starting point for deliberations, not as a prescribed course of action. My hope is that this book will play a small part in raising the standard of management wherever it is used.

About the authors

Ray Proctor started his career as an auditor. He then worked as a management accountant for a UK subsidiary of a multinational company in the food business. After this he became the accountant for a touring caravan manufacturer where his role embraced all aspects of financial and management accounting. On leaving this firm, he and his wife started their own business manufacturing and selling weaving equipment. At the same time as this venture, he began to teach accounting on a part-time basis. He was encouraged to qualify as a teacher and, upon achieving this objective, became a full-time teacher in further education. Having established himself in this role, he gained a Warwick University MBA by distance learning in his spare time. He then moved into higher education, joining the staff of Coventry University in 1996 as senior lecturer in accounting. He also acts as a tutor on the Management Accounting module of the Warwick University MBA and teaches on various courses run by Warwick and Oxford Brookes universities. In addition to his accounting and management experience in the commercial world, he has more than 30 years' experience of teaching accounting.

Nigel Burton has written 'The manager's point of view' sections for most chapters. These are not only authoritative and knowledgeable, but also interesting and informative – no mean feat when writing about accountancy! He qualified as a chartered accountant in 1976 with a London firm, Tansley Witt & Co. After two years of post-qualification experience, he opted for a life in industry, and became financial accountant of the UK subsidiary of a large American chemical corporation. Here he remained for the next 21 years. His initial stint as financial accountant was followed by a three-year term in a European financial capacity, before becoming chief accountant, and then financial director, in the UK. He was appointed managing director after a reorganization in 1992, and in 1996 assumed additional responsibility for one of the European business groups. His extensive experience of life in a manufacturing environment has been seen from not only the financial, but also the administrative and business perspectives. Throughout this period, he has been fully involved in the management of change within his organization, reflecting the rapid technological and managerial advances taking place in the business world. He is, therefore, admirably placed to comment on the contribution that managerial accounting can make to a company's development.

Adrian Pierce co-authored the chapter on working capital management. Ray Proctor contributed some of the theoretical content to the latter but Adrian wrote the majority of the text, including many practical aspects of the day-to-day 'juggling' of working capital which is unavoidable when organizations do not have sufficient cash to enable their operations to run smoothly. Ability in these areas can literally mean the difference between life and death for a business. Ray Proctor knows of no one more skilled than

Adrian in this field and thanks him for taking some of his valuable time to share his knowledge with us. He started his career as an auditor in a 'Big Six' audit firm, before becoming the accountant for a small UK manufacturing company in the outdoor leisure industry. He began as assistant management accountant but soon progressed to the all-embracing role of company accountant. In this senior position, he gained valuable management experience in addition to developing his financial and management accounting abilities. Also, during this time, he qualified as a chartered management accountant. He remained with this company for several years, during which it experienced sustained growth in a fiercely competitive market. He then moved on to become the financial accountant for a high-profile public sector organization. After a couple of years he was also appointed as company secretary. As part of this multiple role, he has gained much experience in the submission of claims to key funding partners. This particular activity has given him significant insight into the extra dimensions of not-for-profit organizations. He currently occupies a senior management role in a not-for-profit organization and has more than 18 years' experience of accounting and management.

Gary Burmiston has written 'The manager's point of view' sections for the chapters on beyond budgeting and balanced scorecards. He qualified as a Chartered Management Accountant with British Gas in 1995. Since that time he has held a number of roles in a variety of business sectors. After qualifying with British Gas he left to join Axa Sun Life as a sales accountant. He remained there for a couple of years before joining Bass Brewers as a commercial finance manager responsible for a number of production sites. After four years he left to join Capital One Bank, eventually becoming CFO (Infrastucture), responsible for the cost base of the European business. He has since returned to the utility sector where he works for a major energy provider in the role of operations finance manager, responsible for the cost base of the retail business. As part of his wide-ranging experience of managing costs in large blue-chip organizations he has been responsible for introducing and managing a number of cost reduction programmes and introducing performance monitoring systems – both used to drive improvements in the cost base of businesses. In addition, he has been responsible for evaluating 'Beyond Budgeting' at a number of organizations and speaking at the Beyond Budgeting Round Table meetings, giving him significant insight into performance management tools and techniques.

Overview

I personally accept full responsibility for the complete contents of this edition. Every single piece of text is there because I want it to be; any errors are mine. I hope these are few and far between but please let me know if you find any. Indeed, I welcome and encourage feedback. My hope is that you find the book informative and helpful.

Acknowledgements

I would like to take this opportunity to thank my co-writers, Nigel Burton, Adrian Pierce and Gary Burmiston, for their encouragement, enthusiasm and willingness to share their experience with the rest of us. This book would be significantly lacking without their contributions. I find their writing interesting, insightful and helpful; I have learned more than a little from them. I am sure readers will also benefit from their unique insights.

I would like to thank the staff of Pearson Education, the publishers of this book. In particular, I would like to thank my original acquisitions editor, Paula Harris, for her belief in this text and in me. I would also like to thank Katie Rowland, Matthew Smith, Amanda McPartlin, Tim Parker, Mary Lince, Jacqueline Senior and Alison Stanford for guiding me through this project over the years. They, and their assistants, have always been helpful and courteous to me, a first-time author who did not 'know the ropes'.

My colleagues at Coventry University also deserve my thanks for their advice, constructive criticism and help with the end-of-chapter questions and cases, particularly David Blight, Steward Hughes, John Panther, Keith Redhead, Graham Sara and Stan Smith. My thanks also go to Adam Byford, Bob Evans, Robin Fraser, Ivan Proctor and Geoff Rayner for reviewing certain sections of the text.

Thanks also to my wife, Sara, and my sister, Rita, for help with proofreading, indexing, scanning and administration. My students also deserve my thanks for the searching questions they have asked me over the years, challenging my understanding and helping me to learn more about my subject. I would also like to thank those of my friends who willingly helped with the arduous task of proofreading.

Finally, I would like to thank the Chartered Institute of Management Accountants for allowing me to reproduce definitions from *Management Accounting Official Terminology* to construct an authoritative glossary.

Publisher's acknowledgements

We are grateful to the following for permission to reproduce copyright material:

Figures

Figure 4.4 after *Corporate Finance: Principles and Practice*, 3 ed., Financial Times/Prentice Hall (Watson, D. and Head, A. 2004) With permission from Pearson Education; Figure 8.7 after *Management Accounting: An Active Learning Approach*, Blackwell Publications Ltd. (Atrill, P. and McLaney, E. 1994) With permission; Figures 10.1 and 10.2 after *Cost and Effect: Using Integrated Cost Systems to Drive Profitability and Performance*, Harvard Business School Press (Kaplan, S. and Cooper, R. 1998) Reprinted by permission of Harvard Business School Press. Copyright © 1998 by the Harvard Business School Publishing Corporation, all rights reserved.; Figures 16.5, 16.6, 16.7 and 16.8 from 'Beyond Budgeting Round Table' (BBRT), reproduced by kind permission of BBRT; Figure 16.9 from 'Toyota motors ahead as Detroit's dinosaurs get left behind', *The Business*, 28/04/2007 (Ashworth, J.), Reprinted with permission of the Press Holdings Media Group (The Spectator), London, UK; Figure 18.6 from *Performance Management – Integrating Strategy, Execution, Methodologies, Risk and Analytics*, John Wiley & Sons, Inc. (Cokins, G. 2009) Copyright © 2009 John Wiley & Sons. Reproduced with permission of John Wiley & Sons, Inc.; Figure 18.13 from Maskell, B. and Baggaley, B. (2005) 'Lean Accounting: What's It All About? Target® Magazine [online] L1-L9 available from http://www.maskell.com/lean_accounting/subpages/lean_accounting/la_ppt.html reproduced with permission; Figure 18.14 from *Performance Dashboards – Measuring, Monitoring and Managing your Business* 2 ed., John Wiley & Sons, Inc. (Eckerson, W. 2011) Copyright (c) 2011 John Wiley & Sons. Reproduced with permission of John Wiley & Sons, Inc.

Text

Extract on pages 540–541 from 'If you want to create more jobs, don't put your faith in startups', *The Observer*, 11/09/2011 (Naughton, John), Copyright Guardian News & Media Ltd. 2011.

In some instances we have been unable to trace the owners of copyright material, and we would appreciate any information that would enable us to do so.

FOUNDATIONS

Part 1 comprises

1 Cost behaviour
2 The difference between profit and cash

Part 1 covers the basic information that will help readers understand the rest of the book. An understanding of the different ways in which costs can behave when the volume of activity changes is of fundamental importance to managers. Cost control will always be an important managerial activity.

Just as important is the need for managers to have a clear understanding of the difference between profit and cash. Many companies that go into liquidation are profitable! They cease to trade because they have run out of cash. Cash is the life-blood of organizations. Without it, they cannot function and pursue their objectives. The information in the rest of this book will be of little use to you if your business fails to survive. Understanding the difference between profit and cash is fundamentally important.

Cost behaviour

Introduction

As a manager, you might find yourself asking your accountant for the cost of one of your products. The answer you expect to be given is probably a specific amount of money, e.g. £49.55. If your accountant replies 'Why do you want to know?' you may think he (or she) is being unnecessarily awkward and assume that he is in a bad mood for some reason or other. However, the accountant's reply is actually very sensible, even though it would have been better for him to reply 'The answer depends on why you want to know.' At first, this may seem very strange to you but a product has several different costs, each of which serves a different purpose. As you will see in the next few chapters of this book, there are several different costing systems in existence, each giving a different answer to your original question.

The absorption costing system gives the absorption cost; the variable costing system gives the variable cost; and the activity-based costing system gives the activity-based cost. They all give the correct cost in the context of their own system. Each system is a financial model based on its own rules and assumptions. Different rules and assumptions result in different numerical answers. For example, the product in question may have an absorption cost of £49.55, a variable cost of £20.95 and an activity-based cost of £142.00. **Each of these three answers is correct.**

The word 'cost' is a general word and is often used in a general sense. However, when a manager asks an accountant for the cost of a product, the manager usually has a specific purpose in mind. The reason why the accountant replied 'Why do you want to know?' is that he wanted to determine the manager's specific purpose so that he could give the right answer. He was actually trying to be helpful rather than awkward! In this chapter, we will look at the different ways in which costs can behave and see how some of these form the bases of the different costing systems.

Learning objectives	**Having worked through this chapter you should be able to:**

Having worked through this chapter you should be able to:

- explain the difference between manufacturing, trading and providing services;
- explain the difference between product and period costs;
- explain the difference between variable and fixed costs;
- explain what semi-variable costs and stepped fixed costs are;
- find fixed and variable elements of semi-variable costs using the high–low method;
- draw a scattergraph based on periodic cost and output data and interpret it;
- explain **in outline** what regression analysis is;
- explain the difference between direct and indirect costs;
- compare variable cost analysis with absorption cost analysis;
- explain the basis for analysing activity-based costs;
- say what relevant costs are used for.

Types of business

There are three main categories of businesses: manufacturers, traders and service businesses. Manufacturers make the goods they sell by converting raw materials into finished products. Traders buy in goods and sell them without altering them in any significant way (they may be repackaged and re-presented). Service businesses create intangible products – for example, banks, accountants, lawyers, financial advisers, freight companies, railways, theatrical agents, education and training institutions. So costs can be described as manufacturing costs, trading costs or service costs.

It is worth noting that the type of organization affects the format of the financial accounts. Gross profit is meaningful for a manufacturer or trader but much less so for a

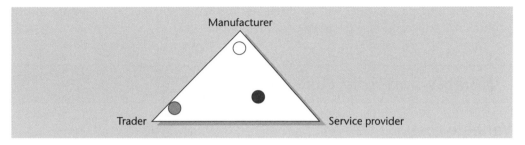

Figure 1.1 Business orientations

service business. Production accounts (to calculate the cost of production) are essential for manufacturers but not applicable to traders or service businesses. However, it is wise not to be too pedantic about this as services tend to be mainly intangible but often include minor tangible items such as chequebooks, sets of accounts, property deeds, share certificates, bills of lading, rail tickets, contracts of employment and degree certificates. In these cases you would probably agree that gross profit is inappropriate.

On the other hand, manufacturers often include a small service element in their products. When you buy a new car, the first two services may be free of charge and there may be a three-year warranty. The price of a new computer usually includes the right to use a selection of software applications for word processing, spreadsheets, databases, etc.

But what about pubs, restaurants and clubs? Are they manufacturers, traders or service providers? The answer is, of course, that they can be all three. The meals are created on the premises, the drinks are bought in and waiting at table, pouring drinks, etc., are pure services. The same applies to residential health clubs and activity holidays where you learn to produce something tangible such as a painting or a piece of pottery.

Figure 1.1 illustrates the relationship between these different types of organization. The darker-coloured circle shows the approximate position of a restaurant. The empty circle represents firms such as furniture makers, and the lighter-coloured circle could represent a national chain of off-licences.

Product and period costs

There are two ways of including costs in the profit and loss account. First, they can be included as part of the production cost of the products made. The production cost of all goods sold in the period gives the total *cost of sales* figure, which is deducted from *sales revenue* to give *gross profit*. Closing stock of finished goods is also valued at production cost. This is how production costs of goods unsold at the year-end are carried forward to the year in which they are sold. (This complies with the accounting rule/concept of realization.) These costs are known as *product costs*.

Second, the full amount of non-production overheads for marketing, administration, etc., appears directly in the profit and loss account of the period in which they were incurred. No attempt is made to apportion them to different financial years. These costs are known as *period costs*.

Product and period costs will be discussed further in Chapter 11, 'Comparison of profits under absorption and variable costing'.

Variable and fixed costs

Variable costs

These are costs which vary **in total** with a measure of activity – for example, the total cost of raw materials increases as output increases (see Figure 1.2b). Take the example of a business making furniture – if the number of chairs produced doubles then the cost of raw materials also doubles.

Note that direct labour is always a variable cost when calculating product costs. However, when looking at the overall total costs of a business, it is often thought of as a fixed cost (provided operatives are employed on a 'permanent' basis, e.g. paid monthly).

Fixed costs

These are costs incurred for a period of time, which, within a given range of production and/or sales activity, do not change (see Figure 1.2c). Continuing the furniture-making example above, if the number of chairs produced doubles, the business rates on the premises do **not** change.

Note that variable costs can be calculated per unit of output but that fixed costs refer to the business as a whole. Variable costing assumes that the variable cost **per unit** stays the same over a range of activity (see Figure 1.2a). This means that **total** variable costs increase linearly with activity (see Figure 1.2b).

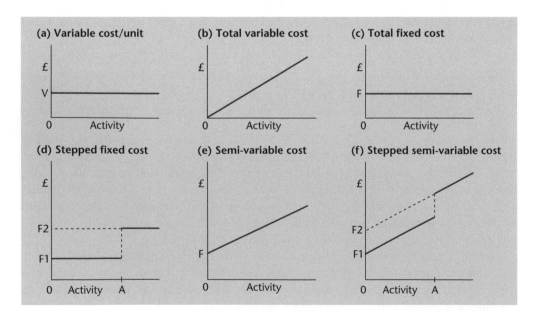

Figure 1.2 Patterns of variable and fixed cost behaviour

Great care must be taken if *fixed cost per unit* is used in calculations. This measure will change every time the number of units changes, i.e. fixed cost per unit is **not** fixed!

Stepped fixed costs

When a certain level of production and/or sales activity is reached, there is a sudden increase in fixed costs from F1 to F2 (see Figure 1.2d). For example, when output increases significantly, it may be necessary to put on an extra work shift. This occurs at activity level A and entails extra costs for items such as supervision, security, heating and lighting, etc.

Semi-variable costs

Although there are several costs which are either purely variable or purely fixed, many costs are semi-variable. The utilities, such as telephone and electricity, often have a fixed cost element such as line rental or a standing charge which has to be paid irrespective of usage. In addition, there is also a cost per unit used. The graph of the semi-variable cost (see Figure 1.2e) combines the features of graphs (b) and (c).

If the semi-variable cost covers a range of activity including a stepped fixed cost, it would behave as shown in graph (f). This graph is obtained by combining graphs (b) and (d).

Try the following question for yourself (answer at the end of the chapter).

Match each of the following graphs to the appropriate descriptions.

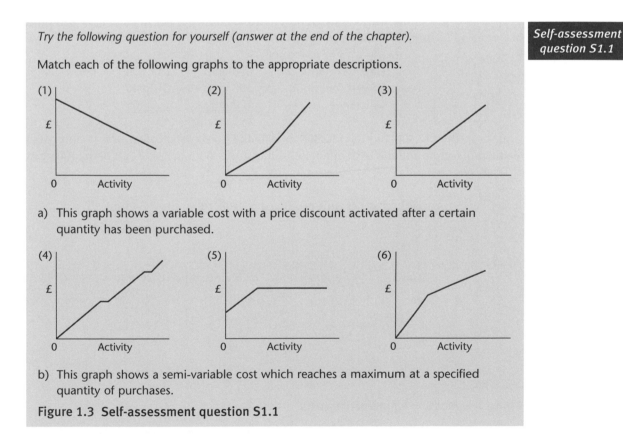

a) This graph shows a variable cost with a price discount activated after a certain quantity has been purchased.

b) This graph shows a semi-variable cost which reaches a maximum at a specified quantity of purchases.

Figure 1.3 Self-assessment question S1.1

c) This graph shows a variable cost with 10 free units for every 100 bought.
d) This graph shows the fixed cost per unit.
e) This graph shows a variable cost which has a minimum charge.
f) This graph shows the variable cost of a scarce item. When local supplies have been exhausted, it has to be purchased abroad, entailing extra transport costs.

Analysis of semi-variable costs into their fixed and variable elements

It is not just the utilities that have semi-variable costs. Many other costs, such as security and maintenance, also follow this pattern. Often, only the **total** amounts of these semi-variable costs are known and the fixed and variable elements have to be worked out mathematically. Three alternative ways of doing this are shown below.

The high–low method

Figure 1.4 shows the machine maintenance costs and the output level of products for the first six monthly periods of the year.

Only two sets of monthly information are used, one from the highest-output month (month 3 = 600 units) and the other from the lowest-output month (month 6 = 500 units).

	Highest (month 3)	600 units	£12,400
Less:	Lowest (month 6)	500 units	£12,000
	Difference	100 units	£400

Since both the £12,400 and the £12,000 include the fixed cost element, this is eliminated by the subtraction and the £400 difference is due solely to the variable cost of the 100 units difference.

Variable cost per unit produced = £400/100 units = £4/unit

Month	Output (units)	Maintenance cost (£)
1	586	12,340
2	503	11,949
3	600	12,400
4	579	12,298
5	550	12,075
6	500	12,000

Figure 1.4 Monthly maintenance costs

Using this in month 6,

$$\text{Variable cost of 500 units} = 500 \times £4 = £2,000$$
$$\text{Total cost of 500 units} = £12,000$$
$$\text{Therefore, fixed cost of 500 units} = £10,000$$

These cost elements can be checked by applying them to the other month used, month 3:

$$\text{Variable cost of 600 units} = 600 \times £4 = £2,400$$
$$\text{Fixed cost of 600 units} = £10,000$$
$$\text{Therefore, total cost of 600 units} = £12,400$$

This shows the calculations to be correct. However, if any of the other months **not** used in the calculation is chosen to test the results, it will probably not work! This is because the high–low method uses the information from only two months. It ignores all the other information. It assumes that the relationship between the cost and production output is a linear one, i.e. if all the monthly points were plotted on a graph, they would all be points on the same straight line. In fact, this is not so, as you can probably see from Figure 1.4. For instance, month 2 has a higher output (503 units) than month 6 (500 units) but a lower maintenance cost.

It can be seen that the high–low method is a fairly crude way of estimating the fixed and variable cost elements of a semi-variable cost. However, its advantage is that it is easy to understand and easy to calculate.

Scattergraphs

If the monthly information shown above (in the high–low method) was plotted on a graph it would look like Figure 1.5.

The line of best fit is drawn on the graph by eye. The intersection of this line and the vertical cost axis gives the fixed cost element. This is **read** from the graph and should be close to £10,000.

The slope of the line

$$\frac{\text{Change in cost}}{\text{Change in output}} = 2,384/600 = £3.97$$

gives the variable cost per unit. You may remember that the equation for a straight line is

$$y = a + bx$$

where a is the intersection with the vertical axis and b is the slope of the line. In this context, the fixed cost is a and the variable cost per unit is b.

The disadvantage of this method is that drawing the line of best fit by eye is subjective and different individuals will produce slightly different lines. However, it does have the advantage of using all the available information and, like the high–low method, a scattergraph will give a workable estimate and is easy to understand.

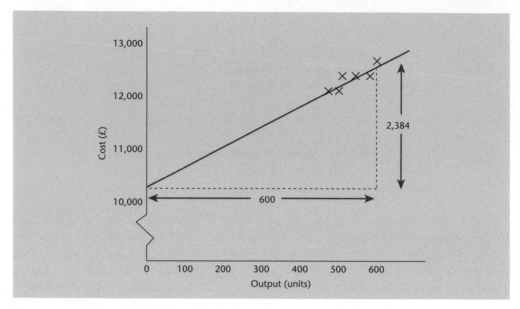

Figure 1.5 A scattergraph

Regression analysis

This method is similar to the scattergraph but the line of best fit is not drawn by eye. The equation for the line is calculated by a statistical technique called *regression analysis*. It is sometimes known as *least squares regression*. It is more precise than the other two methods but it is much more complex mathematically. The technique of regression analysis is not covered by this book. It is sufficient for you to know of its existence and availability if needed.

The most important thing to remember is that, although it is more precise than the high–low and scattergraph methods, it still only gives an estimate of the fixed and variable cost elements. The extra complexity involved may not be worth the improvement in accuracy gained.

Self-assessment question S1.2

Try the following question for yourself (answer at the end of the chapter).

As the manager of an Indian restaurant with a take-away service, you have been asked to prepare a detailed budget for next year. To help you with this, you need to know the fixed and variable cost elements of your delivery cost to customers' homes.

The following information is available from the monthly accounts. Calculate the fixed and variable cost elements using the *high–low* method.

Month	No. of deliveries	Total delivery cost (£)
July	403	662.70
August	291	561.90
September	348	613.20
October	364	627.60
November	521	768.90
December	387	648.30

Absorption costs: direct and indirect

Direct cost

This is expenditure which can be economically identified with, and specifically **measured** in, a product.

Consider an advertising agency specializing in the production of television adverts. The cost of hiring a celebrity to appear in one such advert is a measurable direct cost of that advert. Similarly, if the company is a furniture manufacturer, the cost of materials used to make a chair and the pay of the operative assembling it are measurable direct costs of that chair.

Indirect cost (or overhead)

This is expenditure which **cannot** be economically identified with, and specifically **measured** in, a product.

There are many, many different overheads including expenses such as the supervisor's pay, depreciation of fixed assets, business rates and insurance. Somehow, a proportion of these non-measurable expenses has to be included in the total product cost. Absorption costing is one way of doing this. It is based on the assumption that costs can be analysed into their 'direct' and 'indirect' components. For each product, the direct cost is measured but the indirect cost is estimated.

$$\text{Absorption cost} = \text{direct cost} + \text{indirect cost}$$

The estimates of indirect costs are usually based on some connection or correlation between the cost and a measure such as machine hours used, direct labour hours used or total cost of direct materials used. Absorption costing is the subject of Chapter 9.

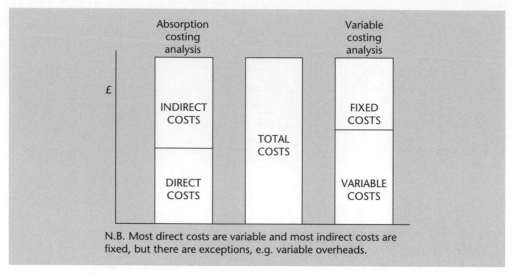

Figure 1.6 **Alternative cost analysis**

Comparison of alternative cost analyses

Variable costing analyses total costs into fixed and variable components. Absorption costing analyses total costs into direct and indirect components. In itself, this is not problematical as these two systems of costing, variable and absorption, are independent financial models. However, it is not unusual to be confused by these terms and how they interrelate. The aim of Figure 1.6 is to clarify these relationships.

Cost analysis by activity

This analysis is based on the principle that costs are **caused** by activities and that activities are caused by products or services. The activity-based cost of a product is a result of determining the costs of all the activities caused by that product. This principle is fundamentally different from the correlation principle used in absorption costing.

Activities are identified and their costs calculated before being attached to products via a measure of the activity called a *cost driver*. Activity-based costing gives significantly more accurate product costs than absorption costing but it has difficulties of its own and does not give 100% accurate costs. This subject is discussed at length in Chapter 10.

Relevant and irrelevant costs

This analysis of costs is very useful in decision making. In brief, it differentiates between those costs which affect a decision (i.e. relevant costs) and those that do not (irrelevant costs). This approach to decision making is discussed further in Chapter 7.

Summary

- Each product can have several different costs.
- The cost of a product depends on the purpose for which this information is required.
- Business types can be divided into three categories: manufacturing, trading and providing services.
- Period costs are written off to the profit and loss account of the period for which they were incurred.
- Product costs are built into the production cost of manufactured items and are either accounted for by the cost of sales figure for the year in which they were incurred or carried forward to the next period in the closing stock valuation figure.
- Total cost can be analysed into variable and fixed cost elements.
- Semi-variable costs have both variable and fixed cost elements.
- Fixed costs are stable only up to a certain level of activity; above this, they step up to a higher level.
- There are three ways of analysing semi-variable costs into their fixed and variable components: the high–low method, scattergraphs and regression analysis.
- Total cost can be analysed into direct and indirect cost elements.
- Costs can be analysed causally according to production activities and activities can be analysed causally by products.
- As an aid to decision making, costs can be analysed into relevant and irrelevant types.
- Direct and indirect costs are similar to, but different from, variable and fixed costs.

Further reading

Anderson, M. C., Banker, R. D. and Janakiraman, S. N. (2003) 'Are selling, general, and administrative costs "sticky"?', *Journal of Accounting Research*, Vol. 41, Issue 1, March.

Drury, C. (2004) *Management and Cost Accounting*, 6th edition, Thomson Learning, London. See chapter 'An introduction to cost terms and concepts'.

Horngren, C., Bhimani, A., Datar, S. and Foster, G. (2002) *Management and Cost Accounting*, Prentice Hall Europe, Harlow. See chapter 'Determining how costs behave'.

Liu, L. and Robinson, J. (2002) 'Double measure', *Financial Management (CIMA)*, October.

Upchurch, A. (2003) *Management Accounting, Principles and Practice*, 2nd edition, Financial Times/Prentice Hall, Harlow. See chapter 'Cost estimation'.

Weetman, P. (2002) *Management Accounting, an Introduction*, 3rd edition, Financial Times/ Prentice Hall, Harlow. See chapter 'Classification of costs'.

Answers to self-assessment questions

S1.1 Cost behaviour graphs

a) Graph 6
b) Graph 5
c) Graph 4
d) Graph 1
e) Graph 3
f) Graph 2

S1.2 Indian take-away delivery costs

Only two sets of monthly information are used, one from the highest-activity month (November = 521 deliveries) and the other from the lowest-activity month (August = 291 deliveries):

	Highest (November)	521 deliveries	£768.90
Less:	Lowest (August)	291 deliveries	£561.90
	Difference	230 deliveries	£207.00

Variable cost per delivery = £207.00/230 = £0.90/delivery

Using this in November,

Variable cost of deliveries = 521 × £0.90 = £468.90
Total cost of 521 deliveries = £768.90
Therefore, Fixed cost of 521 deliveries = £300.00

These cost elements can be checked by applying them to the other month used, August:

Variable cost of 291 deliveries = 291 × £0.90 = £261.90
Fixed cost of 291 deliveries = £300.00
Therefore, Total cost of 291 deliveries = £561.90

Review questions

1 Explain the difference between manufacturing, trading and providing services.
2 Explain the difference between product costs and period costs.
3 Explain the difference between variable and fixed costs.
4 Explain what semi-variable costs and stepped fixed costs are.
5 Describe the advantages and disadvantages of finding the fixed and variable elements of semi-variable costs using the high–low method.
6 Describe the advantages and disadvantages of finding the fixed and variable elements of semi-variable costs using a scattergraph.
7 Explain **in outline** what regression analysis is.
8 Explain the difference between direct and indirect costs.
9 Compare variable cost analysis with absorption cost analysis.
10 Explain the underlying theory of activity-based costing.
11 Explain the difference between relevant and irrelevant costs.

The answers to all these questions can be found in the text of this chapter.

CHAPTER 7

The difference between profit and cash

Introduction

There are many people, including some business people, who think that profit is the same thing as cash. They use the two words interchangeably, believing there to be no difference in their meaning. They are mistaken.

Profit is **not** the same as cash.

As a manager, it is vital that you understand this. If you do not, studying the many other useful topics in this book may prove to be a waste of time!

Cash is the money that individuals and organizations use to exchange things of value. It consists of bank notes, coins and bank account balances.

Profit is the excess of income over expenditure (incurred to produce that income) in a specified period of time. There are many accounting rules, principles and concepts governing the way profit is calculated. They can be very complex (because business is very complex) and are sometimes controversial.

MG Rover, which collapsed in April 2005, is a good example of a complex organization. The holding company, Phoenix Venture Holdings (PVH), was at the top of a web of 15 or so other companies which were connected to each other in complicated ways. Some of these immediately went into administration when the Shanghai Automotive Industry Corporation (SAIC) of China pulled out of talks to buy a significant part of the UK operation, but others remained trading as solvent entities. In the emotional aftermath of the collapse which resulted in many thousands of people losing their jobs, it was reported in the press that there was a possible 'black hole' in PVH's accounts into which £452 million of cash had disappeared. This figure was the difference between the £1,563 million paid into the company since it started in 2000 and the £1,111 million of capital expenditure and losses during most of that period. This so-called black hole is pure speculation as its calculation mixes together cash flows and profit/losses; these are fundamentally different concepts and cannot be combined in this way. Its creators either do not understand this difference or are mischievously ignoring it.

You may have heard of 'creative accounting' where profits shown by audited company accounts have been manipulated (usually increased) by the dubious, but legal, application of accounting rules. Every few years there is a major court case to test whether a company has gone too far and broken the rules rather than just bent them. This situation is partly due to the way in which the world of business is constantly changing, while the rules lag behind until suitably amended.

One result of creative accounting over the years is that many people do not now trust reported profit figures as much as they used to. They are aware that there are many ways in which profit figures can be manipulated. Also, they acknowledge that to understand published accounts fully, a high degree of accounting knowledge is needed.

Take the example of a new road haulage firm that has bought a small fleet of lorries for £500,000. Reducing balance depreciation at 40% a year will give a depreciation charge of £200,000 (£500,000 × 40%). This gives a net profit of £50,000 (see Figure 2.1a). However, if the owner had told his bank that first-year profits would be in the region of £100,000, he might decide to change the depreciation method to straight line over five years. This would give a depreciation charge of £100,000 (£500,000/5) and a profit of £150,000 (see Figure 2.1b). Note that for exactly the same set of business transactions in the year, two different **legitimate** profits have been produced without breaking any accounting rules! This example of creative accounting (which can be extremely complex) has been kept very simple in order to illustrate the point.

a) Reducing balance depreciation at 40% p.a.

	£
Sales revenue	640,000
Depreciation (500,000 × 40%)	200,000
All other expenses	390,000
Total expenses	590,000
Net profit	**50,000**

b) Straight-line depreciation over five years

	£
Sales revenue	640,000
Depreciation (500,000/5)	100,000
All other expenses	390,000
Total expenses	490,000
Net profit	**150,000**

Note: No physical change but profits tripled!

Figure 2.1 **Creative accounting in a road haulage firm**

The published accounts contain three major statements: the balance sheet, the profit and loss account and the cash flow statement. Many professional people who use accounts in their work now believe that the cash flow statement is just as important as the profit and loss account, if not more so. They know that, although profits can be manipulated, cash cannot.

Every figure making up the balance sheet totals is subject, to some extent, to subjective opinion, **except cash**. Cash can be, and is, counted and verified for audit purposes. 'The Pizza Wagon' example below illustrates the difference between profit and cash and shows just how critical this difference can be. It can be literally a matter of life or death for a business.

Learning objectives	**Having worked through this chapter you should be able to:**

Having worked through this chapter you should be able to:

- define what is meant by 'cash';
- define what is meant by 'profit';
- explain the importance of cash flow statements;
- convert profits into cash flows (and vice versa);
- reconcile total profit to total cash flow over the lifetime of a business;
- explain the importance of understanding the difference between profit and cash.

Example 2.1	# The Pizza Wagon

Olive Napoloni has recently lost her job as a result of her employer going into liquidation and ceasing to trade. She is approaching her 57th birthday but will not be able to access her private pension until she is 60 in three years' time. Because Olive is an active woman with a positive attitude to life, she wants to work for the next three years but in a different way from her last 30 years of office work.

Over the years she has helped a friend run a local business providing the catering for one-off events such as weddings and anniversary parties. She enjoys the catering business but would like to work outdoors and to have the opportunity of meeting new people as well. After much careful thought, she decides to start a business of her own offering a mobile catering facility at outdoor events such as pop festivals, fairs and sporting events. She has always been able to make good pizzas and decides to capitalize on this strength. Her business will be called 'The Pizza Wagon' and will be run from a specially converted parcel van.

The final cost of this van, including all alterations, has been quoted at £19,500. However, after three years' heavy use she believes it will not be worth very much and, to be on the safe side, decides to assume it will be worth nothing at all. Her pre-liminary costings show that the ingredients for one good-sized pizza will be £1.00 and she decides to sell them for £4.00 each. Her budgeted accounts for the three financial years and for the three-year period as a whole are as follows.

	Year 1	Year 2	Year 3	Three-year period
No. of pizzas sold	15,000	20,000	25,000	60,000
	£	£	£	£
Sales revenue	60,000	80,000	100,000	240,000
Cost of ingredients	15,000	20,000	25,000	60,000
Gross profit	45,000	60,000	75,000	180,000
Van depreciation	6,500	6,500	6,500	19,500
Van running costs	9,000	9,000	9,000	27,000
Site fees	11,000	14,000	19,000	44,000
Advertising	5,000	4,000	4,000	13,000
Administration	3,500	3,500	3,500	10,500
Total overheads	35,000	37,000	42,000	114,000
Net profit	10,000	23,000	33,000	66,000

Olive is very pleased with these projections, especially as she will avoid making a loss in her first year and need not bother asking her bank for a loan to pay herself a salary. Although the £10,000 in year 1 is only about two-thirds of what she is earning now, she believes she will be able to manage on that for one year if she is very careful with her personal expenditure.

However, because she has no track record in business, she is unable to buy her van on credit terms and has to pay the full £19,500 at the start of her first year of trading. Fortunately, she has been able to arrange an overdraft facility to cover this and other business costs by pledging her home as security. She knows it will be a hard three years but is pleased to be in a position to give this new venture a try.

Unfortunately there is a major flaw in Olive's logic. Can you see what it is?

She is assuming that the profit and the net cash inflow for The Pizza Wagon are the same thing. But there is one legitimate item on the budgeted accounts which does not translate into an equivalent cash movement. The sales revenue figures result in cash inflows of those amounts. The cost of ingredients and the overhead expenses translate into cash outflows with the exception of one item, **depreciation**.

Depreciation is a non-cash expense. In Olive's case, the accounts show straight-line depreciation over three years with a zero residual value for the van. Because she has to pay for it in full at the beginning, the cash outflow for the van in year 1 is £19,500 not £6,500. The cash outflow is £13,000 more than the depreciation for year 1, so the profit of £10,000 translates into a net cash **outflow** of £3,000 (see below).

Olive will not receive £10,000 in cash in year 1. In fact, during that year she will have to put **an extra £3,000** into her business. And what is she going to live on? How is she going to pay for her food, electricity, clothes, etc.? She may or may not be able to arrange a loan from some source to cover the £13,000 difference and provide her with adequate living expenses. But unless she understands the difference between profit and cash, her business and personal life will turn into a financial disaster!

Having looked carefully at year 1, let us consider what happens in years 2 and 3. The depreciation in these years (correctly shown in the accounts) does not translate into any cash flows at all. The financial effect of this is shown below.

	Year 1 £	Year 2 £	Year 3 £	Three-year period £
Net profit	10,000	23,000	33,000	66,000
Adjustment	−13,000	+6,500	+6,500	–
Net cash flow	−3,000	+29,500	+39,500	+66,000

So it is not all bad news for Olive. Although her cash flow is negative in year 1, in years 2 and 3 it is not only positive but greater than she expected. The figures show a timing difference between profit and cash. Timing differences are what the accruals accounting concept is all about. Accruals and prepayments are part of this jigsaw and so are provisions such as depreciation and doubtful debts. The above example has been kept very simple in order to illustrate the principle involved. However, in practice detailed cash budgets must be prepared and monitored for the business to survive. Many, many, many **profitable** businesses have had to cease trading due to insufficient cash resources. Lack of cash is one – if not the major – reason for business insolvency.

The lifetime view

Remember that business is about money, i.e. cash. Profit, on the other hand, is the result of an arbitrary set of rules set by people in government, accountancy associations and committees. It is an intangible concept. The financial year is, to some extent, an irrelevant time period imposed upon businesses. Companies are not created specifically to trade for exactly one year. The vast majority of them wish to trade continuously into the future and would be very happy to prepare published audited accounts only every few years instead of every year. Some businesses, like The Pizza Wagon above, are created for a specific purpose and have a set life span. These organizations tend to view financial years as artificial divisions of their existence. They are much more interested in the outcome of the project over its whole life than its annual profits.

Looking at The Pizza Wagon figures above, you can see that, **over the whole lifetime of a business, the total of profit exactly equals the total of cash** (£66,000 in this case). This principle is just as true for the many continuing businesses all around us even though it is far from obvious.

Self-assessment question S2.1

Try the question for yourself (answer at the end of the chapter).

The Bourton Trading Company existed for four years only before being wound up. Its financial record is shown below in the form of summary annual profit and loss accounts.

	Year 1 £000	Year 2 £000	Year 3 £000	Year 4 £000
Sales revenue	400	375	440	380
Cost of sales	225	200	250	220
Gross profit	175	175	190	160
Increase/(decrease)				
in doubtful debt provision	20	(5)	(5)	(10)
Training expenses	–	3	4	13
Inf'n system depreciation	10	10	10	10
Other admin expenses	45	40	45	50
Co. vehicle depreciation	40	32	26	22
Marketing expenses	25	30	40	35
Bank interest	35	25	30	20
Total overheads	175	135	150	140
Net profit	0	40	40	20

Notes:

1 £10,000 of the £40,000 marketing expenses in year 3 were actually paid in year 2 in order to secure advertising space for a campaign run early in year 3.
2 In order to help the business establish itself, the bank allowed it to defer the payment of 40% of the interest charges it incurred in year 1 until year 2. The profit and loss accounts show the full amounts of interest incurred in each year.
3 In order to get the best discounts, the company always bought its fixed assets for cash with a lump-sum payment.
4 The information system cost £40,000 and was obsolete and worthless when the company closed.
5 The company vehicles cost £140,000 in total. At the end of year 4 they were sold for £20,000 cash.

Tasks:

a) Calculate the net cash flow for each of the four years.
b) Compare the total of profit to the net cash flow for the four-year period as a whole.

The manager's point of view (written by Nigel Burton)

It is an enduring fact of life that you never have enough money to do everything you want. This is as true of companies as it is of individuals. Cash is a company's most precious resource and its stewardship in the best interests of the business is central to the art of management.

Every company has to re-invest in order to survive. If a company were to pay out 100% of its profits in dividends, it would run out of cash in short order. Even a static business will need to spend on renovating or renewing old plant, training replacement staff, and seeking out new customers to replace those that inevitably get lost. Standing still is never an option. And if your company has to change, it may as well become bigger and stronger.

All companies therefore pursue the holy grail of growth. Even Olive in the above example is expecting her little business to show some impressive expansion. Growth demands injections of cash in many different areas: new product developments, new plant on which to manufacture them, new markets into which to sell them, broader infrastructure to support the growing business, and increased working capital to allow the company to operate on a day-to-day basis. It may be several years before even profitable ventures reach the stage of cash-generation rather than cash-consumption.

In the 1980s, our company was one of a number developing components for use in airbag safety systems for motor cars. Here was a product, which, if successful, would quickly become a standard part in every new car. Even with strong competition, the opportunities were clearly enormous. Within just a few years, sales went from zero to multiples of millions. The real challenge to management was to ensure that the plant capacity and administrative infrastructure were continuously upgraded in advance of the ever-growing demand. This meant that every penny generated, together with a good deal of additional outside financing, was ploughed back into the business, and the shareholders, sitting on a hugely profitable venture, saw plenty of capital growth, but precious little cash return in their dividends.

This was, of course, an exceptional circumstance, yet I doubt if there are many companies whose profit projections do not anticipate continuous future growth. How often do we see the 'hockey-stick' graph of a company's projected performance, where actual profits in recent years have remained flat, but future projections show a sharply upward trend? Managers would be accused of, at best, lack of ambition, and, at worst, lack of competence, if their input was not expected to bring improved company results. But how many companies actually achieve these forecasts? If a business fails to make its expected profits, the first casualty may well be cash flow. Budgets are often set as targets, designed to stretch sales efforts and encourage cost savings. Truly realistic estimates might indicate a need for rather higher cash requirements.

So it is easy to overestimate the amount of cash which will become available. Take capital projects for example. In a large, diverse organization, there is always competition between the various businesses for the available capital funds. Senior management will support those projects which give both the greatest rate of return and the quickest payback on their investment. There is pressure on those preparing the supporting documentation to ensure that their project looks attractive, so optimistic salesmen are likely to over-pitch the sales forecasts, while over-confident engineers underestimate the total costs of construction. The result is that the project is far less profitable than forecast, takes much longer to pay back the investment, and in the worst circumstances could pull the entire company down. A business obtaining capital funds on such an unsound basis will almost certainly come unstuck. Every capital investment is, to some degree, a gamble, but the risks can be minimized if a realistic approach to the cash flow requirements is taken.

Perhaps the most common source of liquidity problems today is the failure of management to control working capital, i.e. stocks and debtors, less creditors. This represents the amount of cash needed to oil the wheels of the business, as opposed to investment in capital projects, and is an area which can swallow up large chunks of cash, if it is not properly managed. In fact, it is so frequently neglected, particularly by smaller companies, that the topic warrants a chapter of its own in this book (see Chapter 4).

Sometimes there are external factors which can have a dramatic impact on cash flow. In the early 1970s, a huge increase in the price of oil led to unprecedented levels of inflation, which drove many companies towards insolvency. With inflation in excess of 20% a year, much of the cash generated was needed simply to keep the company standing still. It required 20% more cash than in the previous year to purchase replacement stock, pay the employees wages, or repair a piece of plant. These increases could, of course, be recovered in selling prices, but this was usually too late, as many of the higher costs would be incurred well before the customer had paid up. Any company which was unable to keep pace with the ever increasing cash requirement had to make up the difference through borrowings, which, in turn, hurt profits with continually rising interest costs. During this period, cash generation, rather than profit, became the critical factor to the survival of many companies.

Accounts based on historical costs ceased to give a sufficiently accurate picture of a company's health, so the concept of 'Current Cost Accounting' was introduced. This required balance sheet items to be revalued at their replacement cost, in order to give a better view of the company's solvency and its ability to continue trading on a going-concern basis. This is why the cash flow statement is of such importance. The company may be full of clever people, all pursuing excellent projects which push the overall profits higher and higher, but the sum of their efforts might be bankruptcy. Therefore, a wise manager will always keep an eye on the cash implication of everything he (or she) does.

Finally, a comment on creative accountancy: it is certainly true that there are many different ways of accounting for business activities. Over the years I have had many discussions with the auditors over depreciation rates, accruals, levels of bad debt and obsolete stock reserves, and provisions for other identifiable expenses. There are many areas in a set of accounts where judgement must be applied. But I have never argued for an **increase** in profit unless the underlying circumstances clearly supported it. The prudence concept should be the guiding star for accountants. To anticipate profits, i.e. to take in sales too early, or to underprovide for expenses, is dangerous, irresponsible, unprofessional, does no service to the business, and will get you fired! To be conservative, however, would be regarded as prudent, pragmatic and farsighted. All businesses have to cope with unexpected items of expenditure, such as a bad debt, major repair, exchange loss, etc., and in my experience, managing directors expect their accountants to hold a few 'pots of money', i.e. conservative provisions, which can be released to offset unexpected hits to profit.

The rule is therefore: Keep some provisions up your sleeve for a rainy day, but never, ever, conceal your losses.

Summary

- Cash consists of notes, coins and bank balances.
- Profit is an intangible concept measured by the application of accounting rules.
- Cash is not the same as profit.
- Annual accounts contain many timing differences.
- Timing differences include non-cash expenses, provisions, accruals, prepayments.
- Profits can be manipulated, cash cannot.
- The cash flow figures are at least as important as the profit and loss figures.
- Understanding the difference between profit and cash is vital.
- Many profitable businesses have ceased trading due to lack of cash.
- Over the complete lifetime of a business, total profits equal total net cash flow.

Further reading

Arnold, J. and Turley, S. (1996) *Accounting for Management Decisions*, 3rd edition, Financial Times/Prentice Hall, London. See Chapter 2, 'Accounting and decision making', *section 2.5*: 'The issue of measurement'.

Harrison, W. and Horngren, C. (2001) *Financial Accounting*, 4th edition, Prentice Hall, Englewood Cliffs, NJ. See Chapter 3, 'Accrual accounting and the financial statements', *section*: 'Accrual-basis accounting versus cash-basis accounting'.

Weetman, P. (2002) *Financial Accounting, an Introduction*, 3rd edition, Financial Times/Prentice Hall, Harlow. See chapter 'Who needs accounting', *supplement*: 'Introduction to the terminology of business transactions'.

Answer to self-assessment question

S2.1 The Bourton Trading company

a) Calculate the net cash flow for each of the four years.

	Year 1 £000	Year 2 £000	Year 3 £000	Year 4 £000
Net profit	0	40	40	20
Increase/(decrease) adjustments:				
1 Doubtful debt provision	20	(5)	(5)	(10)
2 Prepaid advertising	–	(10)	10	–
3 Deferred bank interest	14	(14)	–	–
4 Inf'n system depreciation	(30)	10	10	10
5 Co. vehicle depreciation	(100)	32	26	42
Cash in/(out)flow	(96)	53	81	62

Note: The £42,000 vehicle depreciation adjustment in year 4 consists of the £22,000 depreciation charge plus the £20,000 cash received for the sale of the vehicles.

b) Compare the total of profit to the net cash flow for the four-year period as a whole.

Year	Profit	Cash flow
1	0	(96)
2	40	53
3	40	81
4	20	62
Total	100	100

Review questions

1 Define what is meant by 'cash'.
2 Define what is meant by 'profit'.
3 Explain the importance of cash flow statements.
4 Convert profits into cash flows (and vice versa).
5 Reconcile total profit to total cash flow over the lifetime of a business.
6 Explain the importance of understanding the difference between profit and cash.

The answers to all these questions can be found in the text of this chapter.

FINANCIAL MANAGEMENT

Part 2

Part 2 comprises

3 Ratio analysis and financial management
4 Working capital management

Part 2 is about creating a financial 'infrastructure' within which business activities can flourish. These activities include developing, making, buying, selling and delivering products and services to customers. They do not happen in a vacuum; for example, manufacturers must have sufficient cash resources to fund their purchases of raw materials while waiting for their credit customers to pay up. The amount of interest paid on short- and long-term finance should not be so great that it puts a strain on the working capital. A healthy gross profit margin can be erased by allowing the overheads to get out of control.

A wise company will monitor the effects of trading on its own financial infrastructure. It may also take a proactive approach to designing this infrastructure in order to improve its profitability. Note that it is possible to enlarge profits in this non-trading way. A company that reduces the amount of money tied up in working capital will pay less interest on its overdraft or have surplus funds to invest elsewhere. Actively managing a company's financial infrastructure is a 'second string' to its profit-making bow.

CHAPTER
3

Ratio analysis and financial management

Chapter contents

Introduction

All companies produce an annual set of accounts consisting of a balance sheet, profit and loss account and a cash flow statement. Most of these companies also produce interim sets of accounts during the year, usually on a monthly or quarterly basis. These interim accounts are called 'management accounts' and are not available to people outside the company. As their name implies, they are for the company's managers only, enabling them to monitor progress on a regular basis. To do this, ratio analysis can be used.

Managers need to know how well they are performing now to enable them to make their businesses perform better in the future. They need to know the baseline from which their performance as a manager will be measured. An awareness of the current business performance and position will help them to focus their efforts. The analysis of the financial statements enables current performance to be evaluated and this evaluation can be used to determine future action.

Learning objectives

Having worked through this chapter you should be able to:

- evaluate a company's financial position by calculating appropriate liquidity ratios;
- determine a company's financial structure by calculating appropriate gearing ratios;
- evaluate a company's profitability by calculating appropriate profitability ratios;
- evaluate a company's management of working capital by calculating appropriate management efficiency ratios;
- explain the limitations of ratio analysis in evaluating business performance and position.

Financial statements and ratio analysis

The balance sheet is a 'position' statement; it summarizes the financial position at the year-end. The profit and loss account is a 'performance' statement; it tells the story of the year's activities. The cash flow statement also tells a performance story, that of where the cash has come from and how it has been used. Accounts are historical in nature; they describe what has happened and where the business was at the end of a financial period. Sets of accounts are notoriously difficult to understand but, fortunately, the technique of ratio analysis is available to help.

A mathematical ratio compares one (or more) numbers with each other. For example, the gradient of a road may be expressed as '1:4', meaning that for every 4 metres you travel horizontally, you will go up (or down) 1 metre. This is the vertical change compared with the horizontal change. It can also be expressed as a percentage: 1:4 is equivalent to 25%.

If we define a ratio as the comparison of two numbers, how many different ratios can be calculated from a single set of accounts? The answer could easily be *over 1 million!* But almost all of these comparisons are meaningless. For example, what use would it be to compare the cost of new fixed assets purchased with the amount of year-end debtors, or the value of debentures with the provision for obsolete stock?

However, there are a few ratios that **are** meaningful; these are the ones that create the additional information that helps us understand how the business has been performing. An example of this would be the 'profit margin' (which is usually expressed as a percentage). If the profit divided by the sales revenue equals 12%, this can be interpreted as the company making a profit *on average* of 12 pence for every pound of sales it achieves. This average figure gives business managers an estimate of how much profit they will make when selling different amounts of products. A basic set of no more than 20 ratios will enable you to interpret the accounts of a business.

When these ratios have been calculated, they can be compared *with each other* in three different ways to tell us three different things. Continuing the example used above, the *actual* profit margin can be compared with the profit margin calculated from the *budgeted* figures. This tells us if the business is as profitable as it was planned to be. Second, this year's actual profit margin can be compared with the profit margins of competitors for the same time period or thereabouts (usually only possible for annual published accounts). This type of 'industry' comparison is a form of 'benchmarking', identifying best practice in order to emulate it. Third, the actual profit margin for this year can be compared with the equivalent figure for previous years. This may exhibit a trend or it may show fluctuating margins over the years. (Be careful about extrapolating any identified trend into the future as this assumes that neither the business environment nor the internal processes will change.) The following sections of this chapter use ratios in the third of these three ways, comparing them with the equivalent figure for previous years.

To learn how financial statements are interpreted, a simplified set of accounts for a firm called Devah plc will be used – see Figure 3.1. If a real set of accounts were used, the wealth of detail would detract from the understanding of basic principles. In published annual reports, the accounts cover about 5 pages and the notes to the accounts can cover up to 20 pages or more!

Performance ratios: profitability

Performance is about how well the company has been doing. Is it producing a lot of profit or only a little? Is the annual profit improving, deteriorating or staying about the same? To get a feeling for this, it is not a bad idea to compare profits for recent years. But which profit figure should be used? If you look at Devah's accounts, you will see that there are several different profits shown: gross profit, profit before tax, profit after tax and profit retained after dividends. (In reality, it gets even more complicated due to items like 'profit before extraordinary activities'.) The answer depends on why you are carrying out your analysis; in other words, it depends on your 'point of view'. If you are a shareholder, you may be most interested in the 'profit before dividends' as that is what is left for you after the banks and the Inland Revenue have taken the interest and tax due to them.

Devah plc: Balance sheet as at 31 December

(All figures in £m)			**2012**			**2011**
	Cost	Depn	NBV	Cost	Depn	NBV
Fixed assets:						
Land & buildings	860	0	860	780	0	780
Equipment	540	220	320	440	150	290
	1,400	220	1,180	1,220	150	1,070
Current assets:						
Stocks	530			382		
Debtors	156			102		
Cash at bank	0			30		
		686			514	
Less: Current liabilities:						
Creditors	312			242		
Tax due	44			58		
Dividends due	54			60		
Overdraft	18			0		
		428			360	
Net current assets			258			154
Net total assets			1,438			1,224
Less: Debentures (10%)			500			400
			938			824
Financed by:						
Ordinary shares of £1		700			600	
Retained earnings		238			224	
			938			824

Devah plc: Profit and loss accounts for y/e 31 December

(All figures in £m)		2012		2011
Sales		3,646		3,136
Cost of sales		2,482		2,068
Gross profit		**1,164**		**1,068**
Admin & marketing expenses	1,002		884	
Debenture interest	50		40	
		1,052		924
Profit before tax		**112**		**144**
Taxation		44		58
Profit after tax		**68**		**86**
Dividends		54		60
Retained profit for the year		**14**		**26**

Figure 3.1 The accounts of Devah plc

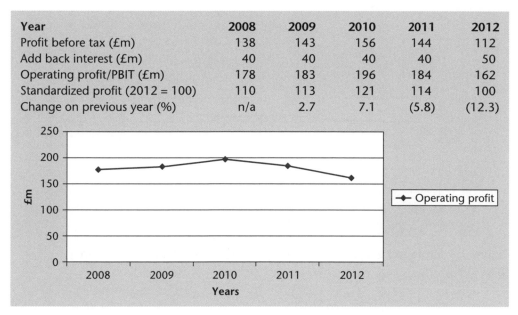

Year	2008	2009	2010	2011	2012
Profit before tax (£m)	138	143	156	144	112
Add back interest (£m)	40	40	40	40	50
Operating profit/PBIT (£m)	178	183	196	184	162
Standardized profit (2012 = 100)	110	113	121	114	100
Change on previous year (%)	n/a	2.7	7.1	(5.8)	(12.3)

Figure 3.2 Table and graph of Devah's operating profits showing changes from previous years

If you are a manager, you are probably most interested in the profits arising from manufacturing and trading activities. This is normally referred to as the 'operating profit' and is defined as the 'profit before interest and tax' (PBIT). As this book is about management, the analysis of performance will be from the manager's point of view.

Figure 3.2 refers to Devah plc; profits are shown for the five most recent years along with the annual changes. Also shown is a list of profits in a standardized form which sets the profit for the most recent year at 100 and all other profits as a percentage of this. This can be useful for comparison purposes. To help get an idea as to the trend (if any), it is a good idea to create a graph of the profits. This type of information is communicated so much better by a graph than by a series of numbers.

It is also worthwhile repeating this exercise for sales revenue; Figure 3.3 illustrates this. Be aware that changes in revenue can be caused by changes in volume, changes in price or, more usually, a combination of both. (Unless there has been a significant change in the profit margin percentage, it is not worth doing a similar analysis of sales *volume* as this will give the same picture. Additionally, this may be distorted by changes in sales mix for multi-product firms and it would be impossible to do for competitors as the necessary information would be confidential.)

An alternative is to display both operating profit and sales revenue on the same chart, but a single scale causes some loss of clarity (see Figure 3.4).

However, a more informative comparison of these two items is given by using their standardized values, taking 2012 as 100 (see Figure 3.5).

The first three of these graphs indicates how the company is performing in absolute terms but the fourth displays the situation in relative terms. This 'relative' approach (showing how one item behaves relative to another) is continued below by looking at three important ratios: return on capital employed, profit margin and asset utilization.

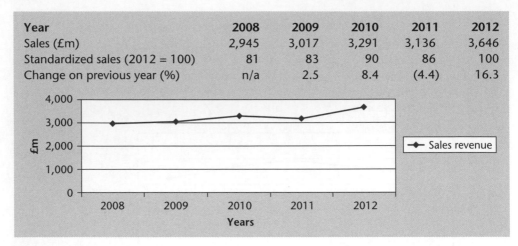

Year	2008	2009	2010	2011	2012
Sales (£m)	2,945	3,017	3,291	3,136	3,646
Standardized sales (2012 = 100)	81	83	90	86	100
Change on previous year (%)	n/a	2.5	8.4	(4.4)	16.3

Figure 3.3 Table and graph of Devah's sales revenue showing changes from previous years

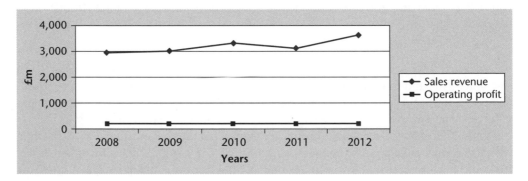

Figure 3.4 Devah's operating profit and sales revenue

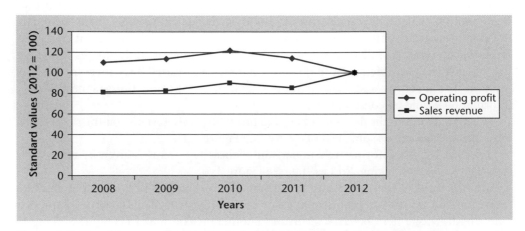

Figure 3.5 Devah's operating profit and sales revenue using standard values

Return on capital employed

If you put money into a savings account, you expect it to earn interest; if you invest money in a business, you also expect it to earn a return for you. The return on capital employed (ROCE) ratio is expressed as a percentage and tells you the rate at which the business is earning profit relative to the amount of money invested:

$$\text{ROCE} = \frac{\text{operating profit}}{\text{total capital employed}} = \frac{\text{operating profit}}{\text{share capital} + \text{reserves} + \text{loan capital}}$$

But what is meant by 'operating profit' and where is it found? A brief examination of Devah's profit and loss account shows that four of its ten lines are labelled as 'profit', so which one is the operating profit? Actually, none of them are; of the four choices, 'net profit before tax' is the nearest. The calculation and payment of taxation and dividends are obviously not a direct part of a business's trading activities.

'Net profit before tax' takes account of all trading income and costs but it is not considered to be the precise definition of 'operating profit' because 'interest' has been deducted in its calculation. 'Interest' is the cost of borrowing rather than trading so it is not included in the 'operating profit' which is defined as 'profit before interest' or, more commonly, 'profit before interest and tax'. So,

$$\text{ROCE} = \frac{\text{profit before interest and tax}}{\text{share capital} + \text{reserves} + \text{loan capital}}$$

For Devah plc (2011):

$$\text{ROCE} = \frac{(144 + 40)}{600 + 224 + 400} = \frac{184}{1,224} = 15.0\%$$

Try the following question for yourself (answer at the end of the chapter).

Calculate the ROCE ratio for Devah plc for 2012 and comment on your findings.

Self-assessment question S3.1

Profit margin

The profit margin expresses the operating profit as a percentage of sales revenue. It can be thought of as the amount of profit for every £100 of sales:

$$\text{Profit margin} = \frac{\text{operating profit}}{\text{sales revenue}}$$

For Devah plc (2011):

$$\text{Profit margin} = \frac{184}{3,136} = 5.87\%$$

This means that, on average, it makes £5.87 operating profit on every £100 of sales turnover.

Self-assessment question S3.2

Try the following question for yourself (answer at the end of the chapter).

Calculate the profit margin for Devah plc for 2012 and comment on your findings.

Asset utilization

This ratio indicates how efficiently the assets of the business are being used to generate sales:

$$\text{Asset utilization} = \frac{\text{sales revenue}}{\text{net total assets}}$$

Another way of expressing the same idea would be to measure how efficiently managers are using the total capital employed in the business to generate sales:

$$\text{Capital utilization} = \frac{\text{sales revenue}}{\text{total capital employed}}$$

These two ratios will have identical answers because the value of 'net total assets' is always equal to the value of 'total capital employed'. This equality is the fundamental basis of the balance sheet; it is why it balances!

For Devah plc (2011):

$$\text{Asset utilization} = \frac{\text{sales revenue}}{\text{net total assets}} = \frac{3,136}{1,224} = 2.56 \text{ times}$$

The managers are using the assets to create 2.6 times their value in sales revenue.

Self-assessment question S3.3

Try the following question for yourself (answer at the end of the chapter).

Calculate the asset utilization ratio for Devah plc for 2012 and comment on your findings.

Relationship between the three ratios

At this point, it is useful to look at the relationship between the three profitability ratios examined so far. ROCE is the profitability ratio of primary importance but it can be analysed into its two constituent parts as shown below:

$$\frac{\text{Operating profit}}{\text{Total capital employed}} = \frac{\text{operating profit}}{\text{sales revenue}} \times \frac{\text{sales revenue}}{\text{total capital employed}}$$

$$\frac{\text{Operating profit}}{\text{Total capital employed}} = \frac{\text{operating profit}}{\text{sales revenue}} \times \frac{\text{sales revenue}}{\text{net total assets}}$$

$$\text{ROCE} = \text{profit margin} \times \text{asset utilization}$$

For Devah plc (2011):

$$15.03\% = 5.87\% \times 2.56 \text{ times}$$

Try the following question for yourself (answer at the end of the chapter). Check that this relationship holds good for Devah plc for 2012. (You will probably need to use two decimal places to be sure the arithmetic is consistent.)	**Self-assessment question S3.4**

The relationship merits further discussion:

$$\text{ROCE} = \text{profit margin} \times \text{asset utilization}$$

Obviously, the ROCE will be high if both the profit margin and asset utilization ratios are high. Also, it will be middle range if both the profit margin and asset utilization ratios are middle range (as for Devah plc above). But a middle-range ROCE can also come from a high profit margin combined with a low utilization of assets or a low profit margin combined with a high utilization of assets:

$$\text{(A) high profit margin} \times \text{low asset utilization} = \text{mid-range ROCE}$$
$$20\% \times 0.8 \text{ times} = 16\%$$

$$\text{(B) low profit margin} \times \text{high asset utilization} = \text{mid-range ROCE}$$
$$2.5\% \times 6.0 \text{ times} = 15\%$$

Example (A) could be a business with relatively few premium-priced sales at the top end of the quality market, whereas example (B) could be a 'pile-them-high–sell-them-cheap' business. These are two well-known business strategies.

Gross margin and cost control

If the ratio analysis shows that the profit margin has gone down, it means that the amount of operating profit has reduced relative to the amount of sales revenue. One possible cause of this is that costs are increasing, indicating a need for management attention.

But which costs should be investigated – the direct ones or the overheads? One way to find out is to calculate the 'gross profit margin' and compare it with that of the last period. This ratio shows whether the direct costs (such as raw materials) are under control:

$$\text{Gross margin} = \frac{\text{gross profit}}{\text{sales revenue}} = \frac{(\text{sales revenue} - \text{direct cost of sales})}{\text{sales revenue}}$$

A decrease in gross margin indicates that direct costs are increasing at a greater rate than sales revenue. An investigation should reveal whether corrective action is possible. For example, if raw material prices have increased, it may be possible to change suppliers. On the other hand, if the increase has been caused by a worldwide increase in oil prices, there may not be any remedy.

Alternatively, if the gross margin is holding steady or improving, any decrease in profit margin will be due to an increase in overhead costs. This can be quantified by calculating either of the following ratios:

$$\frac{\text{overheads}}{\text{sales revenue}} \quad \text{or} \quad \frac{\text{overheads}}{\text{total costs}}$$

Either of these will indicate any disproportionate increase in overhead costs. As the sales revenue figure is easier to find, the first ratio is recommended. Note that, because operating profit is before the deduction of interest, the figure for total overheads should not include any interest costs.

For Devah plc (2011):

$$\text{Gross margin} = \frac{1,068}{3,136} = 34.1\%$$

$$\frac{\text{Overheads}}{\text{Sales revenue}} = \frac{884}{3,136} = 28.2\%$$

Cost control is an important management task necessary to maintain and improve business performance.

Self-assessment question S3.5

Try the following question for yourself (answer at the end of the chapter).

Self-assessment question S3.2 shows the following profit margins: 2011 = 5.87%, 2012 = 4.44%. Explain this decline in performance by calculating the gross margin and overheads/revenue ratios for Devah plc for 2012.

Performance ratios: working capital

All businesses need to control their working capital; the importance of this is discussed at length in the chapter on working capital elsewhere in this book. Appropriate control will result in the overall value of working capital being kept to a minimum. In turn, this will have a positive effect on the primary ratio, ROCE; the smaller the total capital employed (including working capital), the greater the ratio. So, minimizing working capital will improve profitability, provided that any reductions do not affect sales revenue in any way.

Working capital is formally known as 'net current assets' (current assets minus current liabilities) and the management of each of its constituents can be assessed by the use of an appropriate ratio. However, the critical asset of 'cash' will be discussed further on in this chapter in the section on liquidity ratios. Stock, debtors and creditors will now be examined. The constituent ratios are:

- stock turnover period;
- debtors collection period;
- creditors payment period.

Stock turnover ratio

This ratio gives the average amount of time for which stock is held before being sold. (A more descriptive title is 'stock-holding period'.)

$$\text{Stock turnover} = \frac{\text{year-end stock}}{\text{average daily cost of sales}}$$

To be more precise, this formula estimates the amount of time the year-end stock will take to sell. It can only be an estimate because it uses the *average* daily cost of sales. It is unlikely to give a very accurate answer but it may give a reasonable indication of the stock-holding period, depending on the degree of seasonality of the sales. (For example, if the financial year-end occurs during a peak selling time, this ratio will overestimate the length of the stock turnover period.) Note that the answer to this formula will be a number of *days*; if the average cost of sales were expressed in weeks, the answer would also be given in weeks etc. In order to calculate the stock turnover, the average daily cost of sales is needed but this information is not given in the accounts. Only the annual cost of sales is given; this is divided by 365 to give a daily average and the formula changes as follows:

$$\text{Stock turnover} = \frac{\text{year-end stock}}{\text{annual cost sales}/365}$$

Mathematically, this is the same as

$$\text{Stock turnover} = \frac{\text{year-end stock}}{\text{annual cost of sales}} \times 365$$

For Devah plc (2011):

$$\text{Stock turnover} = \frac{382}{2,068} \times 365 = 67 \text{ days}$$

This indicates that the company's money is tied up in stocks for just over two months. If this is longer than in the last period, stock control is deteriorating, but if it is shorter, it is improving.

Self-assessment question S3.6	*Try the following question for yourself (answer at the end of the chapter).* Calculate the stock turnover ratio for Devah plc for 2012 and comment on your findings.

So far in this section, it has been assumed that the business being analysed is a retail trading business. These organizations buy products and resell them with little or no conversion work. But if the business manufactures the products it sells, the above formula for the stock turnover ratio needs adjusting. This is because manufacturers have three types of stock rather than just one: raw materials, work-in-progress and finished goods. Three formulae are now needed:

$$\text{Raw materials turnover} = \frac{\text{year-end stock of raw materials}}{\text{annual cost of raw materials used}} \times 365$$

$$\text{Work-in-progress turnover} = \frac{\text{year-end work-in-progress}}{\text{annual cost of production}} \times 365$$

$$\text{Finished goods turnover} = \frac{\text{year-end stock of finished goods}}{\text{annual cost of sales}} \times 365$$

These show the average length of time that cash is tied up in raw materials, work-in-progress and finished goods stock respectively. If you work for a manufacturing business and are analysing its accounts, you should be able to access the values of the three different types of stock. But if you are analysing another manufacturer, possibly a competitor, it is very unlikely that you will be able to do this. Accounts published in the public domain usually show just a single figure for the value of stocks. In this case, the best you can do is to calculate a single 'stock turnover' period; for a manufacturer this will be an average across the three different types of stock and will lack the detail available from internal management accounts.

Debtor collection period

When stock is sold, either cash is received immediately or, if the customer is given a period of credit in which to pay, a debtor is created:

$$\text{Debtor collection period} = \frac{\text{year-end debtors}}{\text{average daily credit sales}}$$

Again, the daily figure is not available but the annual one is (provided the sales turnover figure in the profit and loss account is assumed to consist totally of credit sales). So the daily amount can be calculated as above and the formula becomes

$$\text{Debtor collection period} = \frac{\text{year-end debtors}}{\text{annual credit sales}} \times 365$$

This gives an estimate of how long it will take for the year-end debtors to pay up.

For Devah plc (2011):

$$\text{Debtor collection period} = \frac{102}{3,136} \times 365 = 12 \text{ days}$$

This indicates that the company's money is tied up in debtors for nearly two weeks. If this is longer than in the last period, credit control is deteriorating, but if it is shorter, it is improving.

Try the following question for yourself (answer at the end of the chapter).

Calculate the debtor collection period for Devah plc for 2012 and comment on your findings.

Self-assessment question S3.7

Creditor payment period

This ratio is a mirror image of the debtor collection period, 'the other side of the same coin'. Businesses usually buy their supplies from other businesses on credit terms, paying for items many days after they have received them. This time, they are freeing up their money for the length of time they take to pay. This works in favour of their liquidity rather than against it (as for stock and debtors).

$$\text{Creditor payment period} = \frac{\text{year-end creditors}}{\text{average daily credit purchases}}$$

Once again, the daily amount is not usually available so the 'divide the annual by 365' device is employed. But there is a bigger problem here. Published sets of accounts do not show 'purchases' for any period of time; the nearest they get to it is the figure for the annual cost of sales. However, if the figures for the opening and closing stocks are known, the amount of the purchases can be calculated by using the following relationship:

$$Cost\ of\ sales = opening\ stock + purchases - closing\ stock$$

So,

$$Purchases = cost\ of\ sales + closing\ stock - opening\ stock$$

Of course, if you are analysing the accounts of the company you work for, you should have access to the annual total of purchases.

For Devah plc (2011):
Devah's accounts at the beginning of this chapter contain sufficient information to calculate the creditor payment period for 2012 but not for 2011. For the purpose of this illustration, it will be assumed that the stock at the start of 2011 had a value of £290 million.

$$Purchases = cost\ of\ sales + closing\ stock - opening\ stock$$
$$= 2,068 + 382 - 290$$
$$= 2,160$$

$$Creditor\ payment\ period = \frac{year\text{-}end\ creditors}{average\ daily\ credit\ purchases}$$

$$= \frac{242}{2,260} \times 365$$

$$= 41\ days$$

This indicates that the company is using its supplier's money for about six weeks. If this is shorter than in the last period, control is deteriorating, but if it is longer, it is improving.

Self-assessment question S3.8	*Try the following question for yourself (answer at the end of the chapter).* Calculate the creditor payment period for Devah plc for 2012 and comment on your findings.

The cash cycle

The above three ratios can be combined to give the average length of time it takes for the business to get back the cash it spends on the purchase of stock. This period is called the 'cash cycle' and is illustrated in Figure 4.10 in the chapter on working capital management. It is defined as follows:

Cash cycle = (stock turnover − creditor payment period) + debtor collection period

Notice that the bracketed term above represents the length of time money is tied up in stock. For example, if stock is held for 10 weeks and suppliers are paid 6 weeks after goods are received, money would be tied up in stock for 4 weeks.

For Devah plc (2011):

$$\text{Cash cycle} = (67 \text{ days} - 41 \text{ days}) + 12 \text{ days} = 26 \text{ days} + 12 \text{ days} = 38 \text{ days}$$

(In the case of a manufacturing organization, the stock turnover period consists of the three types of stock turnover as explained a few pages above.)

The shorter the cash cycle, the less cash is needed by the business; the smaller amount is compensated for by its faster 'velocity of circulation'. The longer the cycle, the more cash is needed by the business. When cash is a scarce resource (which is the case for many businesses) it is vital that it is managed efficiently. The most common cause for organizations going out of business is insufficient cash; this is despite the fact that most of them were making profits at the time of their demise!

Try the following question for yourself (answer at the end of the chapter).

Calculate the cash cycle for Devah plc for 2012 and comment on your findings.

Self-assessment question S3.9

Position ratios: liquidity

It is important to consider whether the business is likely to survive in the immediate future. As the key to survival is having an adequate amount of cash, it is important to know the liquidity position of the business. The following two liquidity ratios will be calculated for Devah plc:

$$\text{Current ratio} = \frac{\text{current assets}}{\text{current liabilities}}$$

$$\text{Liquid ratio} = \frac{\text{liquid assets}}{\text{current liabilities}}$$

The current ratio shows how many times the current liabilities are covered by the current assets and is usually expressed in the form of a mathematical ratio. For example, a ratio of 1.5:1.0 can be interpreted as the current liabilities being covered one-and-a-half times. This means that there is £1.50 of current assets to pay for every £1.00 of current liability.

The liquid ratio (often called the acid test ratio) is a *sharper* measure of liquidity in that it seeks to exclude any current assets that are not very liquid. For many businesses, 'stock' would come under this heading as it may yet have to be converted into saleable goods, stored and sold on credit terms before it could be described as liquid. In this case, the formula would be

$$\text{Liquid ratio} = \frac{\text{current assets} - \text{stock}}{\text{current liabilities}}$$

However, in some businesses, stock could reasonably be considered to be liquid. This would be so where the stock-holding period is similar to or less than the debtors collection period.

For Devah plc (2011):

$$\text{Current ratio} = \frac{\text{current assets}}{\text{current liabilities}} = \frac{514}{360} = 1.4{:}1.0$$

$$\text{Liquid ratio} = \frac{\text{current assets} - \text{stock}}{\text{current liabilities}} = \frac{514 - 382}{360} = 0.4{:}1.0$$

Self-assessment question S3.10	*Try the following question for yourself (answer at the end of the chapter).* Calculate the current and liquid ratios for Devah plc for 2012 and comment on them.

Position ratios: gearing/capital structure

A different aspect of position is that of how the business is financed at the end of the accounting period. Where has the money to run the business come from? Who has provided the capital employed?

There are three basic sources of company funds: shareholders (who own the business), lenders (like banks) and profits retained within the business. As the profits ultimately belong to the shareholders, there are really only two sources: owners and non-owners. (Non-owners are sometimes referred to as 'third parties' to differentiate them from the company itself and the company's owners.) The 'gearing' ratio examines the relationship between these two sources of funds and its implications. It is commonly expressed in two different ways:

$$\text{Gearing} = \frac{\text{funds from third parties}}{\text{total funds}}$$

$$= \frac{\text{funds from third parties}}{\text{shareholder funds} + \text{funds from third parties}}$$

$$= \frac{\text{loan capital}}{(\text{shareholder capital} + \text{reserves}) + \text{loan capital}}$$

This is calculated as a percentage and identifies the proportion of total funds provided by non-owners. A ratio of 75% means that 75% of funds are provided from 'outside' the company and 25% from 'inside'; the higher the percentage, the higher the gearing.

Alternatively,

$$\text{Gearing} = \frac{\text{funds from third parties}}{\text{shareholder funds}}$$

$$= \frac{\text{loan capital}}{\text{shareholder capital} + \text{reserves}}$$

This alternative ratio is a direct comparison of the amounts provided by the two sources and is expressed simply as a number. A ratio of 3.0 means that third parties provide £3 of funds for every £1 provided by shareholders. This describes the identical financial structure as in the 75% ratio shown above. So, a business with a gearing of 3.0 has the same financial structure as one with a gearing of 75%.

For Devah plc (2011):

$$\text{Gearing} = \frac{\text{loan capital}}{\text{shareholder capital} + \text{reserves} + \text{loan capital}}$$

$$= \frac{400}{600 + 224 + 400} = \frac{400}{1,224} = 32.7\%$$

Try the following question for yourself (answer at the end of the chapter).

Calculate the gearing ratio for Devah plc for 2012 and comment on your answer.

Self-assessment question S3.11

The basic idea of 'gearing' is to transform an input into a higher or lower output. Consider a business which has exactly half its £2 million of funds provided by shareholders and half by a bank in the form of a £1 million debenture bearing interest at the rate of 10% a year. The business is producing a return of 15% a year on its total capital employed. The £1 million provided by the bank is earning a return to the company of £150,000 a year but the company is paying only £100,000 of this to the bank in interest. The other £50,000 earned by the loan goes to the shareholders. Their own £1 million capital is earning £150,000 and they also get £50,000 return on the loan capital. So they get a total return of £200,000 on an investment of £1 million; this is a return of 20%. In effect, their investment is *geared up* to 20%. (Of course, all shareholders' earnings are subject to tax but, for the sake of clarity, we will ignore taxation in this explanation.)

Unfortunately, gearing is not always advantageous to the shareholder. If the company's trading activities are earning at a rate greater than it is paying on its loans, the shareholder benefits. However, when the company is earning at a rate less than it is paying on its loans, the shareholder suffers. For example, if the loan in the above case was subject to interest at 25% a year (instead of 10%), the shareholder would get a return of only 5%. (The company's activities produce a return of 15% on £2 million = £300,000. The bank receives 25% of £1 million = £250,000 in interest. This leaves only £50,000 for the shareholders, which is a return of 5% on their investment of £1 million.)

Gearing is a 'two-edged sword' – it cuts both ways! It **amplifies** the return to the shareholders irrespective of whether that return is positive or negative relative to its rate of earning. The consensus of opinion is that it is advantageous to shareholders to have some level of gearing in their company but that too much gearing is a bad thing; the higher the gearing, the greater the risk. The Channel Tunnel Company (Eurotunnel) is a prime example of a very highly geared company; at one time its ratio was approximately 99%! For every £1 provided by shareholders, a consortium of banks provided around £99 in loans. In order to reduce this, some debt has been converted to share capital but it is still very highly geared.

A few years ago, Eurotunnel's creditors were asked to write off £4 billion out of their total £6.4 billion debt! Not surprisingly, they refused. However, the company faced a liquidity crisis in 2006 when interest payments became more onerous and guaranteed minimum payments received from rail operators ceased. Eurotunnel was also due to repay some of the loan capital to the creditor banks but this proved impossible without further financial restructuring and the company became bankrupt, hence its earlier request to write off £4 billion of debt. Early in 2007, the French courts agreed a 'safeguard plan' which financially restructured the company. The total debt was reduced from £6.2 billion to £2.84 billion. This means that, although Eurotunnel's gearing is still high, it now stands a reasonable chance of paying its loan interest out of trading profits.

This is a prime example of a company with far too much gearing, causing the shareholders to suffer. Because interest has to be paid before dividends can be declared, the shareholders have had very little, if any, return on their investment in recent years.

Self-assessment question S3.12

Try the following question for yourself (answer at the end of the chapter).

Devah's ROCE is 15.0% for 2011 (see above); this is greater than the interest rate of 10.0% on its debenture. For this year, the return on shareholders' funds (ROSF) is 17.5% (ignoring taxation).

$$\text{ROSF} = \frac{\text{profit before tax}}{\text{total shareholders' funds}} = \frac{144}{824} = 17.5\%$$

Suppose the debenture had been for £400 million more and the ordinary share capital for £400 million less. The 10% debenture would have been for £800 million (instead of £400 million), the ordinary share capital would have totalled £200 million (instead of £600 million) and the gearing ratio would have doubled from 32.7% (see above) to 65.4% as follows:

$$\text{Gearing} = \frac{800}{200 + 224 + 800} = \frac{800}{1,224} = 65.4\%$$

What effect would this have had on the ROSF?

Although it is useful for a manager to have a good understanding of gearing and its effects on shareholders, the manager will be more directly concerned with the business's ability to pay the required amounts of interest on the loans (as well as the repayment of the loan capital itself) when they become due. The 'interest cover' ratio gives some insight into this; its objective is to calculate the number of times the interest on third-party loans can be paid for by the operating profit. This gives an idea of the sensitivity and criticality of these payments. A company whose operating profit is only 1.5 times as big as the amount of interest due would be much more concerned than one whose profit was 7.5 times as big. (Third-party loans are also known as 'debt capital', 'long-term indebtedness' or just 'debt'; this can be confusing until you get used to it.)

$$\text{Interest cover} = \frac{\text{operating profit}}{\text{interest payable}}$$

If the operating profit is £5.5 million and the interest on loan capital is £500,000, the interest is covered '11 times'.

Consider a company with no third-party loans (i.e. zero gearing) which has made a 'profit before tax' of £1 million. If, instead of zero gearing, part of that company's finance had been provided by a £2 million 10% debenture, its 'profit before tax' would have been £800,000 (£1,000,000 profit – £200,000 interest). 'Profit before tax' depends on both the trading performance and the financial structure of the company. 'Profit before interest' depends only on the trading activities and can correctly be described as 'operating profit'.

For Devah plc (2011):

$$\text{Interest cover} = \frac{\text{profit before tax} + \text{interest}}{\text{interest}} = \frac{144 + 40}{40} = 4.6 \text{ times}$$

Whether this is considered to be good or bad depends on the volatility of profits. Small variations on this would not concern a stable company but if profits fluctuate violently from one year to the next, 4.6 could easily turn into 1.6 and that would cause concern.

Try the following question for yourself (answer at the end of the chapter).

Calculate the interest cover ratio for Devah plc for 2012 and comment on your answer.

Self-assessment question S3.13

Limitations of ratio analysis

The introduction to this chapter stressed that managers need to know the current position of the business in order to measure future improvements. Ratio analysis enables this position to be established – but how accurate is the picture it paints? This is not an easy question to answer; each of the following factors impacts on the reliability of the analysis.

Financial scandals such as Enron, WorldCom and Parmalat are evidence that annual accounts are sometimes nearer to fiction than fact, even when they have been given a clean bill of health by their auditors! Creative accounting is alive and well in the twenty-first century. **Ratios are only as good as the data they use.**

Normal application of accounting conventions can sometimes give misleading information. For example, when inflation is significant, the historic cost convention means that the value of assets on the balance sheet may seriously understate the total of resources being used by the company and, therefore, the amount of capital it employs.

When two competing companies are compared, it is assumed that they have adopted identical accounting policies. It is unlikely that this is absolutely true, which means that like is not being compared with like and the comparison is invalid to some extent. For example, one company may use straight-line depreciation whilst the other uses the reducing-balance method. If they had exactly the same assets purchased for the same money at the same time, it would mean that they had different amounts of capital employed. The fact that no two businesses are ever exactly alike weakens the comparative analysis approach.

Ratio analysis is sometimes used to predict future performance. This assumes that neither the business environment nor the internal processes of the business will change significantly for the period being forecast. However, due to the accelerating rate of change, this assumption is becoming less and less reliable with the passing of time. It is increasingly risky to assume past performance to be a good indicator of future performance.

Ratios may be able to quantify **what** has happened but they often offer no explanation as to **why** it has happened. Also, ratios can only provide information on those aspects of business that can be expressed in numbers. They cannot throw any light on important factors such as 'intellectual capital' or 'employee goodwill'.

The manager's point of view (written by Nigel Burton)

A set of accounts can, at first, seem nothing more than a dry statement of financial data. If you do not have a detailed knowledge of the company, which will always be the case unless the business is your own, you will need to apply ratio analysis to this data, in an attempt to throw a little light on the reality behind the figures. In your own company, of course, you will already be fully conversant with the background, but ratio analysis can still perform a key, if somewhat different, role.

The single most important ratio, by far, is the Return on Capital Employed. Nothing else really matters. Is your company making good use of the money invested in it, or would the shareholders be better off investing elsewhere, or, indeed, leaving the money sitting securely in the bank? A satisfactory ROCE will show an acceptable performance in comparison with previous years, a return which contrasts favourably with rival companies, and a profit sufficiently large to compensate shareholders for the perceived risks they are taking. If the ROCE is running at the right level, and the company's cash position is adequate, it hardly matters what else the accounts may be telling you. All the other ratios are aids which can help you keep the ROCE on track.

In my company, the ROCE became an issue only once a year, during the budget preparation. The worldwide corporation had a target ROCE of 20%, and we were all under pressure to edge up our own individual performances, to enable this global target to be achieved. Our own ROCE in the UK was already in excess of this, which helped to compensate for the younger businesses elsewhere which still fell some way short. There was no question of our being able to rest on our laurels, though, and at budget time the impact of our own proposals on the global position was closely scrutinized. The usual detailed budget discussions were held, followed by endless tweaking, until we had honed it down to a set of figures which we all felt were achievable, and which met the requirements of profits growth, profit margins and ROCE. This process may have included some other ratio checks, but, with a satisfactory ROCE target, we could now set out to achieve the individual budget numbers, in the knowledge that they would automatically lead to the desired statistics.

During the year, we tended to use only three financial ratios. The first was Direct Profit Margin, i.e. net sales, less direct costs of material, labour and overhead, expressed as a percentage of net sales. This was potentially the most variable item in the income statement. You cannot control the customers. They may buy more or less than you anticipated, or buy different products at different times, thereby changing the mix; you may not get the price increase you were hoping for, or suffer from cost increases which you cannot recover in time. All these will have an impact on the Direct Profit Margin. However, if you can achieve the budgeted target here, you know you will have a good chance of achieving both the Net Profit and ROCE targets, as all the other items in the accounts are more or less within the company's control. Concentration on the profit margin will instantly highlight variations from the expected pattern, and allow you to take early remedial action. If the variations produce a higher profit margin than planned, you can look forward to the excess falling straight through to the bottom line, assuming that overheads are kept under control.

The other two ratios used on a regular basis were Debtor Collection Period and the Stock Turnover Period. These were used in setting up the balance sheet budget at the beginning of the year, and were usually set at the same level, or slightly tighter, than the actual performance in the previous year. In this way, they were used as targets for the credit and stock control functions, and, as investment in Working Capital is an important element of Total Capital Employed, a good performance here could have a positive impact on the ROCE achievement. They were monitored on a monthly basis, and were considered sufficiently important to warrant inclusion in our company's list of key performance indicators.

Ratio analysis is perhaps a more valuable tool when investigating companies with which you are considering entering into trading commitments. You will need to examine the accounts of not only new customers, to ensure that they are sufficiently financially sound to pay their future bills, but also new vendors, to check that they are viable companies who will be able to meet their supply obligations over the longer term.

The contents of a company's annual accounts are prescribed by a series of Companies Acts introduced over many decades, which have required ever greater disclosure of company activities. In return for the comfortable safety net of limited liability, companies are required to place specified information in the public domain, for the benefit of potential trading partners. Yet the accounts can still fall frustratingly short of divulging the full picture.

The more financial detail a company makes available, the better you will be able to judge its performance. But at the same time, any information which helps you, as a pro-spective partner, will also be of considerable interest to the company's competitors. Consequently, there is a great temptation for companies to obey the letter and, for the most part, the spirit of the law, but in such a way as to reveal as little really useful information as possible. For example, a geographical analysis of sales provides an interesting snapshot of a company's business, but knowledge of a company's market penetration could be invaluable to competitors. My company used to overcome this particular problem in its accounts by aggregating the numbers for completely different businesses within our chemicals portfolio, rendering them impenetrable to competitors.

Extensive ratio analysis, however, can reveal information which is not immediately apparent. Accounts, and particularly the Notes to the Accounts, are full of nuggets of information, which can add unexpected colour to a drab set of numbers. You may wish to calculate sales and profit per employee, compare capital spending with depreciation, or dividends with profit. When looked at over a period of years, this information can be very revealing. It may not prove anything conclusively, but such trends may shed light on the direction the company is travelling, and flag up potential problems down the line.

Conversely, steady trends in the right direction may reflect the competence of the company's management, and allow you to enter into financial arrangements with the company in greater confidence. History, of course, is no guarantee of future success, but a good track record is as good a reassurance as one can expect in business.

Whilst the dissection of published accounts can yield interesting facts, this, too, will usually stop short of giving you the complete picture, so some educated guesswork is usually necessary. But in doing this, some further caveats should be borne in mind. Companies can play the same sort of games with published accounts as we saw with budgets. This is known as window dressing, and is normally resorted to by unsound companies desperate to show their financial position at the year-end in the best possible light. This can take the form of anything from convoluted schemes for off-balance-sheet financing to simply delaying the payment of creditors. Running stocks down to artificially low levels and conducting major purges on outstanding debts are other common year-end tactics. These will tend to improve the company's apparent cash position, so it is important to consider the balance sheet and notes in total, instead of focusing just on a single item like cash.

You should also bear in mind that the accounts you are looking at may be considerably out of date. Companies can submit their accounts up to 10 months after their year-end. The latest accounts available therefore will probably relate to the year before last. So, in the absence of current information, you may have to rely on historical trends to predict the future.

Finally, always remember to check the audit report. Although current audit reports are heavily hedged around by disclaimers as to the extent and purpose of their work, the auditors' final view that the accounts show a true and fair view is still a source of comfort. A qualified audit report should set all the alarm bells ringing. After all, the basic purpose of using published accounts is to look for indications of anything that might be going wrong with the company. So, any warning signs, whether explicit in the audit report, or emerging from your ratio analysis, should make you stop and think, 'Is this a risk I am prepared to accept?'

Summary

- Ratios can compare actual performance with budget.
- Ratios can compare a business with its competitors.
- Ratios can compare one year with previous years.
- Business performance can be evaluated by profitability ratios.
- ROCE can be analysed into profit margin and asset utilization.
- Management performance can be evaluated by working capital ratios.
- The cash cycle is the combination of the stock, debtors and creditors ratios.
- Liquidity ratios evaluate financial position and indicate survival chances.
- Gearing ratios show what proportion of finance is provided by third parties.
- Gearing can amplify the returns to shareholders, both positive and negative.
- The interest cover ratio highlights the criticality of interest payments.
- Ratios are only as good as the accounts they use.
- Accounting conventions and policies can distort intercompany comparisons.
- Trends revealed by ratio analysis must be extrapolated with great care.
- Ratios tell you what has happened but not why it has happened.

Summary of ratio formulae

a) *Profitability:*

$$\text{Return on capital employed, ROCE} = \frac{\text{profit before interest and tax}}{\text{shareholder capital} + \text{reserves} + \text{loan capital}}$$

$$\text{Profit margin} = \frac{\text{profit before interest and tax}}{\text{sales}}$$

$$\text{Asset utilization} = \frac{\text{sales}}{\text{fixed assets} + \text{current assets} - \text{current liabilities}}$$

$$\text{Gross profit margin} = \frac{\text{gross profit}}{\text{sales}}$$

b) *Working capital control:*

$$\text{Stock turnover} = \frac{\text{year-end stock}}{\text{average daily cost of sales}}$$

$$\text{Debtor collection period} = \frac{\text{year-end debtors}}{\text{average daily credit sales}}$$

$$\text{Creditor payment period} = \frac{\text{year-end creditors}}{\text{average daily credit purchases}}$$

c) *Liquidity:*

$$\text{Current ratio} = \frac{\text{current assets}}{\text{current liabilities}}$$

$$\text{Liquid ratio} = \frac{\text{current assets} - \text{stock}}{\text{current liabilities}}$$

d) *Capital structure:*

$$\text{Gearing} = \frac{\text{loan capital}}{\text{shareholder capital} + \text{reserves} + \text{loan capital}}$$

$$\text{Interest cover} = \frac{\text{profit before interest and tax}}{\text{interest payable}}$$

Further reading

Atrill, P. and McLaney, E. (2004) *Accounting and Finance for Non-Specialists*, 4th edition, Pearson Education, Harlow. See Chapter 6, 'Analysing and interpreting financial statements'.

Halkos, G. E. and Salamouris, D. S. (2004) 'Efficiency measurement of the Greek commercial banks with the use of financial ratios: a data envelopment analysis approach', *Management Accounting Research*, Vol. 15, Issue 2, June.

Horngren, C., Sundem, G. and Stratton, W. (2005) *Introduction to Management Accounting*, 13th edition, Pearson Education, Englewood Cliffs, NJ. See Chapter 17, 'Understanding and analysing consolidated financial statements'.

Answers to self-assessment questions

S3.1 For Devah plc (2012)

$$\text{ROCE} = \frac{\text{profit before interest and tax}}{\text{share capital} + \text{reserves} + \text{loan capital}}$$

$$= \frac{(112 + 50)}{700 + 238 + 500}$$

$$= \frac{162}{1{,}438} = 11.3\%$$

This shows that there has been a very sharp drop in the ROCE from 15.0% to 11.3%, a fall of about one-quarter. It is imperative for management to find out why this has occurred and, if possible, to correct this trend over the coming year.

S3.2 For Devah plc (2012)

$$\text{Profit margin} = \frac{162}{3,646} = 4.44\%$$

This shows that the profit margin has reduced by about a quarter, from 5.87% to 4.44%. This is a significant change and should be corrected if possible.

S3.3 For Devah plc (2012)

$$\text{Asset utilization} = \frac{\text{sales revenue}}{\text{net total assets}} = \frac{3,646}{1,438} = 2.54 \text{ times}$$

This shows that there has been no significant change in the utilization of assets (2005 = 2.56 times).

S3.4 For Devah plc (2012)

$$\text{ROCE} = \text{profit margin} \times \text{asset utilization}$$
$$11.3\% = 4.44\% \times 2.54 \text{ times}$$

This confirms the accuracy of the calculations and it also shows that the drastic fall in the ROCE is almost entirely due to the fall in the profit margin.

S3.5 For Devah plc (2011, 2012)

		2012	2011
Profit margin	=	4.44%	5.87%
Gross margin $= \dfrac{1,164}{3,646} =$		31.93%	34.06%
$\dfrac{\text{Overheads}}{\text{Sales revenue}} = \dfrac{1,002}{3,646} =$		27.48%	28.19%

This shows that the overheads are a smaller proportion of sales revenue in 2012 than they were in 2011, indicating that they have been well controlled. However, the gross margin has declined from 34% to 32%, indicating that there has been a disproportionate increase in the direct cost of sales. So management attention should be focused on direct costs rather than overheads.

S3.6 For Devah plc (2012)

$$\text{Stock turnover} = \frac{530}{2{,}482} \times 365$$

$$= 78 \text{ days}$$

This shows that the management of stock has worsened over the year; stock days have increased from 67 to 78, a deterioration of 16%.

S3.7 For Devah plc (2012)

$$\text{Debtor collection period} = \frac{156}{3{,}646} \times 365$$

$$= 16 \text{ days}$$

This shows that the management function of 'credit control' is being performed much less well than last year. Debtor days have increased by one-third, from 12 to 16.

S3.8 For Devah plc (2012)

$$\text{Purchases} = \text{cost of sales} + \text{closing stock} - \text{opening stock}$$
$$= 2{,}482 + 530 - 382$$
$$= 2{,}630$$

$$\text{Creditor payment period} = \frac{\text{year-end creditors}}{\text{average daily credit purchases}}$$

$$= \frac{312}{2{,}630} \times 365$$

$$= 43 \text{ days}$$

This shows a very slight improvement in creditor days, from 41 to 43.

S3.9 For Devah plc (2012)

$$\text{Cash cycle} = (\text{stock turnover} - \text{creditor payment period}) + \text{debtor collection period}$$
$$= (78 \text{ days} - 43 \text{ days}) + 16 \text{ days}$$
$$= 35 \text{ days} + 16 \text{ days}$$
$$= 51 \text{ days}$$

This shows that the cash cycle has increased by about one-third over the year, from 38 days to 51 days. This significant deterioration indicates inefficient management of working capital. It is important for this trend to be reversed as soon as possible.

S3.10 For Devah plc (2012)

$$\text{Current ratio} = \frac{\text{current assets}}{\text{current liabilities}} = \frac{686}{428} = 1.6{:}1.0$$

$$\text{Liquid ratio} = \frac{\text{current assets} - \text{stock}}{\text{current liabilities}} = \frac{686 - 530}{428} = 0.4{:}1.0$$

This shows that, although the current ratio has improved slightly compared with last year, the liquid ratio has not changed.

S3.11 For Devah plc (2012)

$$\text{Gearing} = \frac{\text{loan capital}}{\text{shareholder capital} + \text{reserves} + \text{loan capital}}$$

$$= \frac{500}{700 + 238 + 500} = \frac{500}{1{,}438} = 35\%$$

This shows that there has been a slight increase (of two percentage points) in gearing compared with the previous year.

S3.12 For Devah plc (2011)

	£m	£m
Gross profit		1,068
Admin & marketing expenses	884	
Debenture interest @ 10%	80	
		964
Profit before tax		104

$$\text{ROSF} = \frac{\text{PBT}}{\text{TSF}} = \frac{104}{200 + 224} = \frac{104}{424} = 24.5\%$$

The doubling of the gearing has increased the ROSF from 17.5% to 24.5%. (Although this is a very significant increase, note that the ROSF has not doubled.) In this case, the shareholders are considerably wealthier due to the increase in gearing.

S3.13 For Devah plc (2012)

$$\text{Interest cover} = \frac{\text{profit before tax} + \text{interest}}{\text{interest}} = \frac{112 + 50}{50} = 3.2 \text{ times}$$

Although this does not represent any imminent danger, the interest cover has reduced by about a quarter to 3.2 times (from 4.6 times). Further borrowing will worsen this position.

This case study shows how ratio analysis can be used by managers to help them improve the performance of their business.

JRP Ltd is a large wholesaler of electrical goods formed four years ago by the amalgamation of two smaller companies. Extracts from its annual accounts are shown below.

Early in year 4, one of JRP's most important suppliers insisted that all future deliveries should be paid for on or before delivery. As a result of this, JRP decided not to use this supplier and to source its goods elsewhere.

Management was aware that sales were significantly down in year 4 and had taken the prudent step of drastically reducing JRP's overheads. Staffing levels had been reduced at each of the depots and in every department at head office, including marketing and accounting. Due to cost cutting, JRP's 'quarterly' catalogue, from which most of its sales originate, had been revised only once during the year.

The accounts section lost one-third of its staff and could not keep up with the demand for information. The staff usually produced management accounts on a quarterly basis but the last set produced was for the first quarter and these were not completed until the middle of month 5. The chief accountant made a positive decision to concentrate on cash management in order to keep the business afloat.

Early in the year, the chief accountant realized that the company was going to breach its overdraft limit of £110,000. He approached JRP's bank who agreed to increase this to £120,000. But just before the end of the year, he had no choice but to ask the bank for a further increase of £25,000. Very reluctantly, the bank agreed to this, but only on a temporary basis for three months.

As soon as the accounts for year 4 were approved by the auditors, the management team held a meeting to discuss the results. They were aware that, due mainly to a downturn in the house-building market, year 3 had been disappointing compared with year 2. It had been assumed that its results would be worse than those of the previous year but when the pre-tax loss of £40,000 was announced, the directors were shocked.

It seemed to them that the drastic cost-cutting exercise of last year had been in vain. They could not see any other overheads that could be reduced without directly harming the business – all the 'fat' had been dispensed with. In fact, they knew that there were certain areas which were in desperate need of more money being spent on them rather than less. They realized that immediate remedial action was necessary, but they did not know what to do or where to start.

Task:

Analyse the company's performance and advise management on the action it should take to restore this to the levels achieved in previous years.

(Assume that the stock at the start of year 1 was valued at £50,000.)

Extracts from profit and loss account (all figures in £000)

	Year 1	Year 2	Year 3	Year 4
Sales	1,090	1,950	1,480	1,040
Cost of sales	650	1,190	899	748
Gross profit	440	760	581	292
Admin & marketing costs	375	654	509	320
Debenture interest	10	10	12	12
Profit before tax	55	96	60	−40
Taxation	15	38	18	0
Profit after tax	40	58	42	−40
Dividends	20	30	20	0
Retained profit for the year	20	28	22	−40

Extracts from balance sheet (all figures in £000)

	Year 1	Year 2	Year 3	Year 4
Net fixed assets	280	290	340	270
Current assets – stock	60	115	135	160
– debtors	210	393	385	265
Total	270	508	520	425
Current liabilities – creditors	55	240	297	165
– overdraft	100	107	105	140
– dividends	10	15	10	0
– taxation	15	38	18	0
Total	180	400	430	305
Net current assets	90	108	90	120
Total net assets	370	398	430	390
Debentures	50	50	60	60
Total	320	348	370	330
Financed by:				
Share capital	300	300	300	300
Retained earnings	20	48	70	30
Shareholders' funds	320	348	370	330

Questions

An asterisk * on a question number indicates that the answer is given at the end of the book. Answers to the other questions are given in the Lecturer's Guide.

Q3.1* Panther plc

Tasks:

1 Calculate the profitability ratios for each of the three years.
2 Calculate the working capital ratios for each of the three years.
3 Calculate the liquidity ratios for each of the three years.
4 Calculate the capital structure ratios for each of the three years.
5 Interpret your findings by describing the company's trading history over the three-year period and evaluate its performance.

Profit and loss accounts for year ended 31 December (all figures in £m)

	2013	2012	2011
Sales	23,093	17,931	14,345
Cost of sales	17,394	14,572	11,358
Gross profit	**5,699**	**3,359**	**2,987**
Indirect costs	4,172	2,522	2,224
Debenture interest	93	59	44
Profit before tax	**1,434**	**778**	**719**
Taxation	410	278	241
Profit after tax	**1,024**	**500**	**478**
Dividends	477	229	172
Retained profit for the year	547	271	306

Balance sheet as at 31 December (all figures in £m)

	2013	2012	2011
Fixed assets (NBV)	**5,100**	**4,458**	**4,678**
Current assets:			
Stocks	2,850	2,177	1,790
Debtors	2,711	2,260	2,356
	5,561	4,437	4,146
Less: Current liabilities:			
Creditors	3,216	2,980	2,474
Tax due	540	278	241
Dividends due	368	133	92
Overdraft	491	605	1,447
	4,615	3,996	4,254
Net current assets	**946**	**441**	**–108**
Net total assets	**6,046**	**4,899**	**4,570**

	2013	2012	2011
Less: Debentures	1,564	964	906
	4,482	**3,935**	**3,664**
Financed by:			
Share capital	2,666	2,666	2,666
Retained earnings	1,816	1,269	998
	4,482	**3,935**	**3,664**

(Assume opening stock for 2011 = 1,689.)

Q3.2* The Wholesale Textile Company Ltd

The annual accounts of the Wholesale Textile Company Ltd have been summarized for 2011 and 2012 as follows:

	2011		2012	
	£	£	£	£
Sales				
Cash	60,000		64,000	
Credit	540,000	600,000	684,000	748,000
Cost of sales		472,000		596,000
Gross profit		128,000		152,000
Expenses				
Warehousing		26,000		28,000
Transport		12,000		20,000
Administration		38,000		38,000
Selling		22,000		28,000
Debenture interest		–		4,000
		98,000		118,000
Net profit		**30,000**		**34,000**

	31 December 2011		31 December 2012	
	£	£	£	£
Fixed assets (net book value)		60,000		80,000
Current assets				
Stock	120,000		188,000	
Debtors	100,000		164,000	
Cash	20,000	240,000	14,000	366,000
Less: Current liabilities				
Trade creditors		100,000		152,000
Net current assets		140,000		214,000
		200,000		294,000
Less: Debenture		–		60,000
		200,000		**234,000**
Financed by:				
Share capital		150,000		150,000
Reserves and undistributed profit		50,000		84,000
		200,000		**234,000**

You are informed that:

1 All sales were from stocks in the company's warehouse.
2 The range of merchandise was not changed and buying prices remained steady throughout the two years.
3 Budgeted total sales for 2012 were £780,000.
4 The debenture loan was received in 1 January 2012, and additional fixed assets were purchased on that date.

Task:

Perform a ratio analysis to assist the management of the company to measure the efficiency of its operation, including its use of capital. Your answer should name the ratios and give the figures (calculated to one decimal place) for 2011 and 2012. Discuss possible reasons for changes in the ratios over the period. (Ratios relating to capital employed should be based on the capital at the year-end. Ignore taxation.)

Q3.3* Chonky Ltd

Chonky Ltd is a private company manufacturing and supplying spares to the motor trade. The following is a summary of the results of the business for the last four years together with year-end balance sheets.

Summary trading and profit and loss accounts (£000)

	2011		2012		2013		2014
Cash sales	280		340		450		500	
Credit sales	120		160		350		500	
Total sales		400		500		800		1,000
Opening stock	20		24		26		74	
Purchases	244		307		568		732	
	264		331		594		806	
Less: Closing stock	24		26		74		126	
Cost of goods sold		240		305		520		680
Gross profit		160		195		280		320
Operating expenses	120		144		210		260	
Depreciation on plant	10		11		12		14	
Debenture interest	–		–		3		6	
		130		155		225		280
Net profit before tax		30		40		55		40
Taxation		12		15		21		16
Net profit after tax		18		25		34		24
Proposed dividend		8		10		14		12
Retained profit		10		15		20		12

Balance sheets as at 31 December (£000)

	2011		2012		2013		2014
Freehold property		100		100		140		140
Plant less depreciation		50		66		70		92
Fixed assets		150		166		210		232
Stocks in hand		24		26		74		126
Debtors		11		15		35		54
Investments		10		10		2		–
Cash at bank		12		14		–		–
Total assets		207		231		231		412
Creditors	22		26		50		92	
Proposed dividend	8		10		14		12	
Taxation accrued	12		15		21		16	
Bank overdraft	–		–		6		20	
Current liabilities		42		51		91		140
Net total assets		165		180		230		272
Less: Debentures		–		–		30		60
		165		180		200		212
Financed by:								
Ordinary shares		100		100		100		100
Retained earnings		65		80		100		112
		165		180		200		212

Note: There were no sales of fixed assets during the four-year period.

Task:

Comment on Chonky's liquidity, capital structure, profitability and working capital management during the four-year period. (State any assumptions you make.)

Q3.4 Digby plc

The following are extracts from the profit and loss accounts and balance sheets of Digby plc:

Profit and loss account (£m)

	2012	2011	2010
Sales	3,000	2,000	1,000
Cost of goods sold	1,950	1,240	600
Gross profit	1,050	760	400
Operating expenses	760	590	330
Debenture interest	16	13	8
Net profit before tax	274	157	62
Taxation	96	55	22
Profit after tax	178	102	40
Preference dividend	10	10	10
Equity dividend	60	30	10
Retained profit	108	62	20

Balance sheet at 31 December (£m)

	2012	2011	2010
Fixed assets	330	302	250
Stock	250	170	120
Debtors	190	140	80
Cash	20	10	20
Liabilities < 12 months	140	110	70
Net capital employed	650	512	400
Less: Debentures 10%	160	130	80
Net assets employed	490	382	320
Financed by:			
Equity capital	200	200	200
Retained profits	190	82	20
Preference shares	100	100	100
	490	382	320

Task:

Comment on Digby's liquidity, capital structure, profitability and working capital management during the three-year period. (State any assumptions you make.)

Q3.5 Shoes Ltd

Shoes Ltd has operated in the retail sector for the past eight years. A summary of its financial statements for the year just ended is given below:

Trading and profit and loss account

	£000
Sales	1,200
Cost of sales	740
Gross profit	460
Expenses	390
Interest	12
Net profit	**58**

Balance sheet

	£000	£000
Fixed assets (at WDV)		700
Current assets:		
Stock	240	
Debtors	10	
	250	
Less: Current liabilities:		
Creditors	50	
Taxation	14	
Dividends	35	
Bank overdraft	14	
	113	

	£000	£000
Net current assets		<u>137</u>
Net total assets		837
Debentures		<u>98</u>
		<u>**739**</u>
Financed by:		
Equity capital		100
Reserves		<u>639</u>
		<u>**739**</u>

Task:

You are required to calculate the following ratios and, by comparing them with the industry averages shown below, comment upon the financial state of the company, particularly with regard to liquidity, profitability and working capital management. (Assume the opening stock for the year was £220,000 and that only 20% of sales are made on credit terms.)

	Industry average
1 ROCE	9.5%
2 Gross profit margin	55%
3 Net profit margin	8%
4 Asset utilization	1.6 times
5 Stock turnover period	87 days
6 Debtors collection period	7 days
7 Creditor payment period	46 days
8 Current ratio	1.5:1.0
9 Liquid ratio	0.3:1.0

Review questions

1 Explain how to evaluate a company's cash position by calculating appropriate liquidity ratios.
2 Explain how to determine a company's financial structure by calculating appropriate gearing ratios.
3 Explain how to evaluate a company's performance by calculating appropriate profitability ratios.
4 Explain how to evaluate a company's management of working capital by calculating appropriate management efficiency ratios.
5 Explain the limitations of ratio analysis in evaluating business performance and position.

The answers to all these questions can be found in the text of this chapter.

Working capital management

(Written by Adrian Pierce and Ray Proctor)

Introduction

All businesses need resources to function. Some resources are of a long-term nature (buildings, machinery, vehicles, etc.) whilst others are short-term (stocks, debtors, cash, etc.). This chapter concentrates on the short-term resources used for conducting day-to-day business operations; these are normally referred to jointly as the *working capital* of the business. Just because these resources are short-term, it does not mean that they are small compared with their long-term equivalents. Typically, the investment in working capital is between 40% and 60% of the total investment in the business.

Working capital consists of cash and other items that can be quickly converted into cash or cash equivalents. Of course, businesses also have short-term liabilities which are normally paid for with these short-term assets. An example of this is a payment out of the business's bank account to a supplier of raw materials. Cash is the asset which typifies working capital for most managers as it is the most easily applied of its components;

in other words, it is the most 'liquid'. It is worth pointing out that 'cash' usually means the combination of 'cash-in-hand' and 'cash-at-bank'. Cash can be thought of as being 100.0% liquid and cash-at-bank as 99.9% liquid; in practical terms, they are both as instantaneously applicable as each other.

The majority of businesses also have stock, debtors and creditors and these are often larger in amount than their cash balance, especially when the business is running a bank overdraft. (Overdrafts are actually a liability rather than an asset as they are money owing by the business to the bank.) Of course, there are exceptions – supermarkets, for example, would have a far larger amount of cash than debtors, though their creditors may well be of a similar size to 'non-cash' businesses in different economic sectors.

The control and management of working capital directly influences an organization's ability to survive. To illustrate this, consider the fact that many organizations that go out of business are profitable! The reason they can no longer function is that that they have run out of cash; if they cannot pay their creditors on time they are not going to receive any further supplies on credit terms. If they cannot get their supplies, they cannot produce their goods and services; if they cannot do this, they have nothing to sell! If they have nothing to sell, their cash position will deteriorate rapidly and everything will soon grind to a halt. If you were employed by such a company, how long would you continue to work for no pay?

Learning objectives

Having worked through this chapter you should be able to:

- define working capital;
- calculate economic order quantities for stock;
- rank stock items according to the ABC system;
- discuss the just-in-time system of stock control;
- explain 'buffer stock';
- describe how computers can improve stock control;
- explain the importance of regular physical stock counts;
- list the advantages and disadvantages of holding stock;
- describe a standard credit control system;
- explain 'factoring' and 'invoice discounting';
- decide if debt insurance is appropriate;
- discuss alternative policies for dealing with multi-currency debts;
- define 'cash' and 'liquid funds';
- appreciate the fundamental importance of operating cash budgets;
- compare leasing and buying fixed assets;
- describe the difference between an operating lease and a finance lease;
- explain the importance of good supplier relationships;
- explain when alternative suppliers should be used;
- compare and contrast the working capital cycle with the cash cycle;
- define 'overtrading' and 'overcapitalization';
- appreciate the limitations of various techniques used to control working capital.

Definition of working capital

If you look at a balance sheet, you will see that working capital has a section of its own where each of its components is itemized. It will look similar to Figure 4.1.

Notice that the current assets are shown in the order of reverse liquidity with the most liquid being shown last. (This is traditional and the balance sheet would still balance if the order was changed.) Stock sold on credit terms creates debtors and these debts have to be collected to convert the asset into cash. So stock is the least liquid of the current assets with debtors coming between stock and cash.

All these items can, and should, be controlled. However, due to their nature, managers do not usually spend time trying to control 'prepayments' and 'accruals'. Prepayments are very similar to debtors; debtors are *money* owed to the business whereas prepayments are usually *services* owed to the business. An example would be an annual insurance premium for cover commencing one-third of the way through a financial year. At the year-end, the invoice for the full 12 months would have been entered in the accounting records but there would still be 4 months of insurance cover (the service) owing to the business. (One way of 'controlling' this is to pay by instalments; this action is also a good example of cash control which is discussed later in the chapter.)

Similarly, accruals are amounts owed for goods or services received in the year which have not been recorded in the books of account at the year-end. This is usually due to the appropriate invoices not having been received from the supplier, so an estimate of the cost involved has to be made. If the year-end is December 31 and the last invoice from the electricity supplier was for the quarter ended November 30, the next invoice would not be due until early March of the following year. As the accounts would normally have to be produced and audited by then, the creation of an accrual for the electricity used in December is essential. So managers spend much more of their time chasing debtors and fending off creditors than trying to control prepayments and accruals.

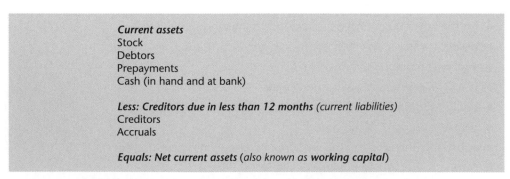

Current assets
Stock
Debtors
Prepayments
Cash (in hand and at bank)

Less: Creditors due in less than 12 months (current liabilities)
Creditors
Accruals

Equals: Net current assets (also known as **working capital**)

Figure 4.1 Balance sheet extract showing the structure of working capital

Objectives of working capital management

There are two main objectives of working capital management:

1 to maintain sufficient liquidity for the business to function effectively and efficiently;
2 to improve the profitability of the business.

Unfortunately, these objectives tend to conflict with one another. The greater the amount of working capital, the more likely the business is to run smoothly, but this will reduce its profitability. Consider the effect on the *return on capital employed* ratio:

$$\text{ROCE} = \frac{\text{operating profit}}{\text{total capital employed}}$$

$$= \frac{\text{operating profit}}{\text{fixed capital} + \text{working capital} + \text{loan capital}}$$

Any increase in working capital will increase the denominator of the fraction which will result in a smaller ROCE. The interrelationship of ratios is shown in Figure 4.2.

Those businesses which choose to actively reduce the amount of working capital in order to improve profitability can be described as 'proactive'; those that do not employ this strategy, as 'passive'. The effects are shown in Figure 4.3.

If the firm is performing well and is 'cash-rich', it may maintain a high level of working capital (almost by default) which helps the trading operations to run smoothly. On the other hand, if it is undergoing a survival crisis and desperately short of cash, it may have no choice but to operate with an inadequate amount of working capital investment. This leads to turbulent day-to-day operations causing management and accounts staff much extra work. However, provided nothing goes wrong, it will improve the ROCE percentage. The necessary 'juggling' of resources has the potential for upsetting both

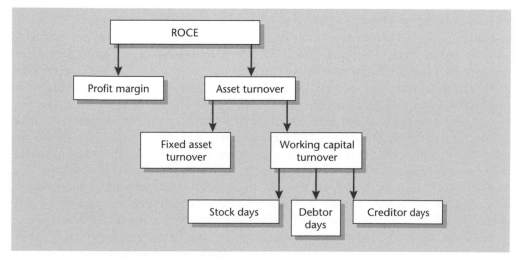

Figure 4.2 The interrelationships of ratios

Summarized balance sheet		
	Passive	**Proactive**
	£m	**£m**
Net fixed assets	80	80
Working capital	45	40
Total net assets	**125**	**120**
Total capital employed (TCE)	**125**	**120**
Profitability calculations:		
PBIT	12	12
ROCE (= PBIT/TCE)	*9.6%*	*10.0%*

Figure 4.3 Effect of working capital size on profitability

suppliers and customers as well as the bank manager; a vicious circle may ensue, causing things to continually worsen to the point of insolvency.

Effect of working capital financing policies on profitability

It makes sense to finance fixed assets by long-term funds as this matches up the life spans of the two entities. This implies that working capital (a.k.a. net *current* assets) should be financed by short-term funds. However, a little thought will show that a certain amount of working capital is continuously needed on a long-term basis. The total of working capital will fluctuate between a minimum and a maximum amount. The 'minimum' amount is needed on a permanent basis but amounts above this are temporary in nature. Therefore, it is logical and consistent to finance the permanent part of working capital by long-term funds. This leaves only the temporary part to be financed by short-term funds such as an overdraft (see Figure 4.4a – the *matching* policy).

However, some businesses will decide to adopt the low-risk approach of financing part of the temporary working capital with long-term funds (see Figure 4.4b – the *conservative* policy). Others will choose the high-risk approach of financing all of their working capital and some of their fixed assets (permanent capital) by short-term funds (see Figure 4.4c – the *aggressive* policy).

The 'risk' referred to above comes from the uncertainty of interest rates payable when rolling over short-term funds on a regular basis compared with the fixed rates of interest available on long-term finance. Compare the renewal of a one-year short-term loan for ten consecutive years (at rates as yet unknown) with a single ten-year loan at one fixed rate of interest. Because there is less risk and uncertainty associated with long-term loans, they tend to cost more than short-term ones. Thus, adoption of an aggressive policy should result in less interest being paid, which will improve profitability *after interest*.

However, the conservative policy carries a risk of a different type as part of the temporary working capital is financed by the more expensive long-term funds. If there is a reduction in the amount of working capital needed in total, the short-term element will

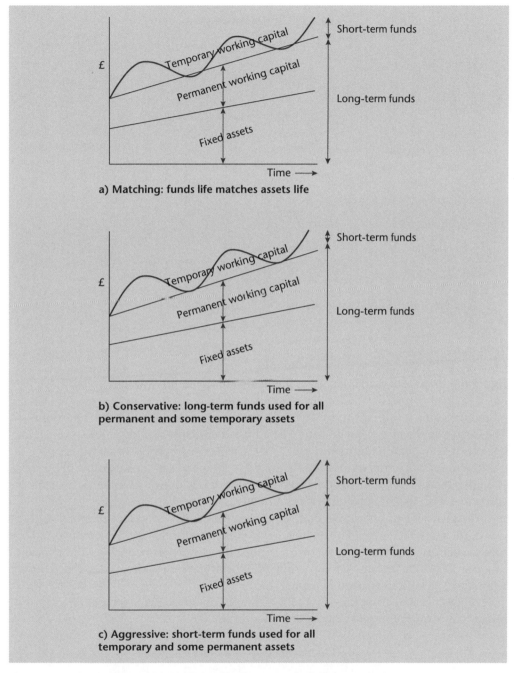

Figure 4.4 Three alternative policies for financing working capital
Source: after D. Watson and A. Head (2004) *Corporate Finance – Principles and Practice,* 3rd edition, Financial Times/Prentice Hall, Harlow

Summarized balance sheet			
	Conservative £m	Matching £m	Aggressive £m
Net fixed assets	80	80	80
Working capital	40	40	40
Total net assets	**120**	**120**	**120**
Share capital	60	60	60
L-T loans (10%)	40	30	20
Share capital + L-T loans	100	90	80
S-T funds (7%)	20	30	40
Total capital employed (TCE)	**120**	**120**	**120**
Profitability calculations:			
PBIT	12	12	12
Interest @ 10%	4.0	3.0	2.0
Interest @ 7%	1.4	2.1	2.8
Total interest	5.4	5.1	4.8
Profit before tax (= PBIT − total interest)	6.6	6.9	7.2
PBT/TCE	*5.5%*	*5.8%*	*6.0%*
NB: ROCE (= PBIT/TCE)	*10.0%*	*10.0%*	*10.0%*

Figure 4.5 Impact of working capital financing choice on profitability

be reduced and it will cost more to fund as more interest will be paid proportionately. The long-term finance element cannot be adjusted until it is due for renewal, which may be several years into the future.

Note that these terms should only be used for companies in the same line of business. It is not valid to say that the working capital policy of a retailing organization is aggressive compared with that of an engineering company.

If the provision of both long- and short-term funds cost the same (i.e. bore the same rate of interest), there would be no 'financing' effect on profitability. However, long-term funds, such as debentures, tend to cost more than short-term ones so the choice of funding will have an impact on profitability *after interest* (sometimes called 'profit before tax'). This is illustrated by Figure 4.5.

Having considered working capital as a single entity, the management of each of its individual components will now be discussed in detail.

Stock

Economic order quantity (EOQ)

Holding goods in stock has a cost; if a business did not need stock it would not need to pay for a storekeeper or storage facilities. The less stock it holds, the less it costs to store it. This argument points towards ordering small quantities on a frequent basis, say, every week. However, this means a very active 'purchase ordering' department with lots of work to do. If larger orders were placed less frequently, fewer resources would be needed to run the purchasing section. This illustrates the dilemma between the cost of holding stock and the cost of ordering it. So is there a happy medium? Is there a specific ordering quantity for each stock item which will keep the combination of these costs to a minimum? Traditional theory says there is such a quantity and calls it the 'economic order quantity'.

If:
h = holding cost of one unit for one year
d = annual demand in units
p = average cost of making one purchase order

$$EOQ = \sqrt{(2pd/h)}$$

(This formula can be derived from first principles by the use of calculus but it is not necessary to be able to do this in order to use it!)

For example, if
$h = £5$
$d = 50,000$ units
$p = £200$

$$EOQ = \sqrt{(2 \times 200 \times 50,000/5)}$$
$$= \sqrt{(20,000,000/5)}$$
$$= \sqrt{4,000,000}$$
$$= 2,000 \text{ units}$$

So, it would be most economical if this particular stock item was ordered in quantities of 2,000 units.

Try the following question for yourself (answer at the end of the chapter).

Self-assessment question S4.1

What is the EOQ for a stock item whose annual demand is 45,000 units if the holding cost of one unit is £10 a year and the average cost of placing a single order is £1,000?

It should be pointed out that the EOQ is of limited practical use. First, consider the difficulty in calculating the three numbers involved. Any calculation of the holding cost of stock (h) or the cost of making a purchase order (p) involves many estimations and averages as this information is not readily available. Also, annual demand is a forecast rather than a certainty. This formula will give a precise mathematical answer but its result should be treated very much as an estimate rather than an accurate figure. (This concept is known as 'spurious accuracy'.) For the EOQ to be genuinely useful, the business would have to be in a very stable economic environment where the predictability of transactions is high. In the twenty-first century, there are very few businesses with an environment like this.

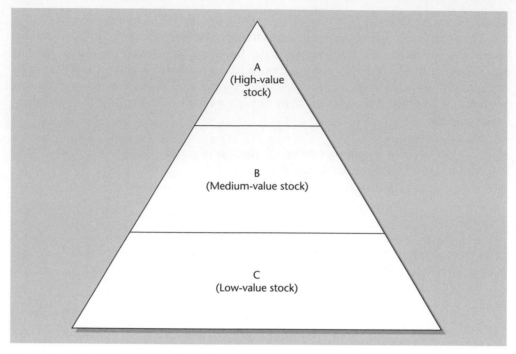

Figure 4.6 The ABC system of stock control

The ABC ranking system of stock control

A traditional method of classifying stock is known as the 'ABC system'. This method of control offers management a tool for sorting stock into three broad categories (in terms of their monetary value) to help concentrate resources on the higher-value items. This is a sensible approach as it is not efficient to spend a lot of time on the maintenance of minor stock items at the expense of securing and maintaining stocks critical to your products. For example, if you were making wheel braces for the motor vehicle industry, sandpaper would be a grade 'C' item but high-grade steel would be grade 'A'.

Figure 4.6 shows the majority of stock items being of low value (C), a smaller mid-range group of medium-value items (B) and a smaller still proportion of high-value stock items (A). This classification provides a simple tool that managers can apply to make the most efficient use of their resources according to the relative value of stock elements.

Although the ABC stock ranking system is a useful management tool, it is not without its problems. For example, there is often a grey area as to where to draw meaningful monetary boundaries for classification, or finding that items regularly move from one category to another as a result of constant price changes in the marketplace.

Just in time (JIT)

This approach to stock control is often used due to the highly competitive cost-oriented environment in which businesses now operate. It requires dialogue and appreciation of the timeliness of deliveries on the part of both supplier and recipient. The main principle of JIT is the reduction in required stock-holding levels due to the guaranteed delivery of stock at the time it is needed for production. Although JIT can be applied to most repetitive production processes, it is most suitable for those businesses with high predictability of demand which use predetermined supply-chain scheduling.

The process can be applied externally in defining the supplier–customer delivery mechanism or internally by considering each sub-division within a production process as an 'internal supplier/internal customer unit' within the same organization. The goal of JIT is the delivery of the exact amount required, on time, to specification and within cost. Such is the power of control available with this system that customers may require more than one delivery in a day.

It is the supplier's responsibility to ensure that the appropriate product is available to the customer exactly when required. The supplier may also use a JIT system in its own supply chain, thereby reducing its stock-holding costs, freeing up space for alternative use and reducing insurance premiums due to lower stock levels. The principle of JIT, although now widely adopted in industry, has been used on individual projects as long ago as 1930 for the construction of the Empire State Building, New York. Due to the limited storage space on the building site, the 60,000 tons of steel girders had to be delivered in small batches when they were needed by the construction workers. It would have been impossible to store them all without demolishing several adjacent buildings! In this sense, JIT can be seen as part of a project management procurement approach.

The JIT principle uses a stock reorder system known as the '*kanban*' or **two-bin system**. Two 'bins' (any device for storing a small amount of stock) are used, both full at the start of the production activity. The contents of bin 'A' are reordered immediately it becomes empty, for delivery just before bin 'B' becomes empty. This is a simple but effective method of stock control as the empty bin itself acts as the trigger for stock replenishment. JIT applications range from ones as simple as this to highly sophisticated electronic versions controlled by spreadsheets or bespoke software which take account of minimum stock levels, anticipated lead times and appropriate reorder levels.

Consider the scenario of a fish and chip shop: the opening of its last drum of frying oil can be used as a trigger to place an order for another drum to avoid running out of stock. However, it would probably require a higher level of 'buffer' stock so as not to run out completely if it experienced an unexpected increase in sales. It may prefer to have a stock of two drums of oil rather than one; this would be a three-bin system with the third oil drum being the 'buffer stock' bin.

Buffer stock

When buffer stock is held internally, the holder incurs the cost of ownership. Alternatively, suppliers may be persuaded to hold a comfortable level of 'reserve' stock to assist you in calling off purchase requirements quickly, so avoiding costly delays arising from stock-outs and delivery lead times. The benefit to the purchaser is that less working capital is tied up in stock and the benefit to the supplier is a guaranteed sale immediately the stock is required. In this situation, a supplier may be able to minimize its risk by retaining stocks in a semi-finished state from which it could effect last-minute finishing operations to convert them to the required specification. At the same time, this approach will minimize its own stock-holding costs.

Computers and stock control

Computers can be a great help in controlling stock; the greater the number of stock items, the greater the potential benefits. Supermarkets typically carry more than 50,000 different stock items and would find it almost impossible to control their stock without the help of sophisticated information systems. When customers pay for their purchases at the checkout, the details of every item they buy are used to update the theoretical quantities remaining in stock. This is done by the electronic point of sale system (EPOS), an integrated information system with many different functions. When the stock level reaches the preset reorder level, a 'reorder' instruction is generated automatically; some systems also automatically send an order to the supplier for replacement goods. Provided that reorder levels are reviewed from time to time in the light of historical purchasing data, such systems are very effective in the retail environment. A periodic physical stock check will also be necessary to adjust the computer stock to that physically present as 'shrinkage' may occur, for example, through theft.

Computers can also be very useful to manufacturers. The information system called 'Material Requirements Planning' creates a list of all the components needed to meet a given production schedule and this is used to ensure adequate stocks are available when needed. This system is particularly useful where the product is complex such as vehicles or jet engines. There are also many other less sophisticated systems, within a wide price range, that help to control stock. Businesses should be careful to choose one with an appropriate capability, at a reasonable price. Sometimes, for small businesses, a chalk mark on a wall in the stores can be more effective than a computerized stock control system.

Physical stock counts

Although physically checking the amount of stock held is a very basic procedure, businesses avoid this aspect of stock control at their peril. It is essential that stock is counted (and examined) on a regular basis. This should be at least once a year but, preferably, more frequently. For example, all important, high-value items (category A items) could be counted every month and other items only counted every three months on a rotational basis. The reason that stock counts are so important is that the condition and existence of the stock directly affects its value and its value affects profits on a pound-for-pound basis. Stock is subject to damage, deterioration, theft and obsolescence. As it is often a significant item on the balance sheet, an incorrect stock value may give a misleading impression of the business's performance. Physically counting the stock is an important and necessary reality check for any business.

Advantages and disadvantages of holding stock

The arguments in favour of holding and not holding stock are considered below but, ultimately, management must decide what level of stock-holding best suits the production processes and market conditions.

Advantages:

- minimized risk of stock-outs and consequential lost sales due to inability to supply demand;
- reduced order costs as able to purchase less often;
- ability to benefit from quantity discounts for buying in bulk;
- reduced set-up costs as a result of ability to perform longer production runs;
- potential 'investment' value, in cases of likelihood of the purchase price increasing in the near future;
- ability to maintain the continuity of supply to own customers.

Disadvantages:

- higher demands on physical space requirements;
- increased costs of insurance and other storage costs;
- greater risk of damage, deterioration, theft and obsolescence;
- missing out on possible future price reductions;
- internal 'systems' costs such as recording and maintaining stock records;
- tying up money in working capital!

As can be seen, there is no quick solution that will suit every business and consideration of the above factors will have to be given before a decision is made. With regard to the type of stock, the optimal level held is likely to vary depending on the nature of the stock items and their importance to the business. Stock represents money which cannot be used elsewhere in the business; it is important that no more than is necessary is tied up in this way.

Debtors

Debtors result from selling goods or services on credit. They are often called 'trade debtors' but this narrow definition would not include debts arising as a result of, for example, the sale of fixed assets, investments or even a whole business. Trade debt is likely to be more liquid than non-trade debt as it is usually dealt with according to widely accepted, standardized terms of trading as opposed to being tightly defined in specific, legal transactions of which payment may form only one of many conditions to be met. There is also the benefit of being able to put pressure on trade debtors to pay by temporarily withholding supplies (known as putting them 'on stop') – an option clearly not available in the case of a one-off sale of a fixed asset.

Standard credit control

Debtors are created by a business granting credit to its customers; so the activity of collecting debts is known as 'credit control'. Most businesses operate a standard credit control system similar to the one shown in Figure 4.7.

The quality of the debts receivable should be regularly reviewed, at least every time a set of accounts is prepared and preferably on a monthly basis. The usual way of doing this

Step	Action
1	Grant credit status on the basis of bank and trade references, published accounts, visits to customer's premises or by using a professional credit-rating agency
2	Determine an appropriate credit period – this is usually in accordance with the company's standard terms of trading, say, 30 days
3	Send a monthly statement to customers reminding them how much they owe and when it is due
4	If money not received by due date, send a first 'reminder' letter
5	If money still not received after another week, phone debtor asking for payment
6	If money still not received after another week, send second 'reminder' letter
7	If money still not received after another week, phone again
8	If money still not received after another week, send final letter threatening legal action
9	When debt is two months overdue, put it in the hands of a solicitor or professional collection agency

Figure 4.7 An example of a standard credit control process

Customer	Total debt £	1–30 days £	31–60 days £	61–90 days £	More than 90 days £
Hanwing Co.	80,500	80,000			500
Pitson Ltd	145,000	95,000	50,000		
Jewse Ltd	31,000		16,500	14,500	
Contro Inc.	54,500		54,500		
Quinit Ltd	125				125
Wim & Co.	30,000				30,000
Totals	341,125	175,000	121,000	14,500	30,625

Figure 4.8 A debtors age analysis

is by analysing them according to their age. Figure 4.8 shows a simplified example of a typical age analysis. Hanwing Co. appears to be a good customer although it disputes the £500 which is several months old. Pitson Ltd seems to be a reasonable customer, although it is a slow payer which exceeds its 30-day credit limit. Jewse Ltd presents a real danger as it has exceeded its credit period by one month and two months and has not taken delivery of any items in the most recent month. Is it still trading? Priority should be given to recovering these debts as soon as possible. The oldest part of £14,500 should be put into solicitors' hands if this has not already been done. Although its debt is not as old, Contro Inc. is overdue for the large amount of £54,500 and should also be chased as a priority. It should be put into solicitors' hands without hesitation at the appropriate time. Quinit Ltd appears to have ceased trading with the business and is in dispute over an old debt of £125; this may have to be written off, as solicitors' fees to collect it would probably exceed this amount. The £30,000 owed by Wim & Co. should already be with the solicitors for legal action. It is a large amount and is over three months old.

Collecting debts is a time-consuming activity so it is worthwhile thinking about ways of encouraging prompt payment. One well-known method is to offer a discount for early settlement. For example, a discount of 5% could be offered to customers who pay on receipt of goods or services. An invoice of £1,000 could be cleared by a cheque for £950 sent to the supplier on the same day as the goods were received. The supplier may be very happy to suffer the £50 discount in order to improve the cash flow of the business. The theoretical cost of this can be calculated. If the supplier is operating on an overdraft bearing 12% a year interest, the early receipt of the £950 will save it £9.50 (£950 × 12% × 1/12). But the cost of this saving is £50 so the transaction seems very bad from the company's point of view, resulting in a deficit of £40.50 (50.00 − 9.50).

However, this theoretical comparison does not tell the whole story. Whilst debts exist, there is always a chance that they will go bad and not be collectable; money in the bank has a definite advantage over the promise of money in the future. More importantly, if the business is desperate for cash to ensure its survival (a situation not as unusual as you might think) the £40.50 may be worth every penny.

Factoring and invoice discounting

Normally, businesses perform their own credit control, from invoicing to collection of cash. However, there are alternatives and these may suit certain businesses which can more profitably invest their time and resources elsewhere. For example, a company may decide to outsource its invoicing in circumstances where the large volume of transactions makes it profitable to do so. This can be done as a single service, or it can also involve the sale of the debts arising from the invoices; this is known as '**factoring**'. The originating company would receive an immediate cash injection equal to the value of the debt sold less the fee charged by the factoring company. The arrangement may be '*factoring with recourse*', where the purchaser of the debt has the right to resell it back to the originating company if the debt cannot be recovered within a certain predetermined time period. Alternatively, it may be '*factoring without recourse*', where the purchaser of the debt has no come-back on the seller and so must pursue the debtor until ultimately the debt is paid or written off. The second of these two options is likely to be more expensive to the original vendor of debt as the risk is higher to the purchaser. Both methods offer an immediate injection of cash into the originator's working capital thereby allowing the earlier reinvestment of resources into the business. However, it will be fairly obvious to the debtor that it now owes money to a third party and not the original supplier of the goods.

Another option is for a company to sell its debts receivable but continue to collect the debts itself. This is known as '**invoice discounting**' and also provides the company with the benefit of an immediate cash injection, typically set at 75% of the total invoiced value. It also eventually receives the 'balance' of 25% less the deduction of an operational percentage and other small charges levied by the finance company. In this case, the discounting provider would typically protect itself from bad debt in two ways: first, by applying individual 'capping limits' to the credit covered on more risky debtors and, second, by operating an overall 'retention' comprising not only the 25% not yet paid, but also a percentage of the overall book debt calculated with respect to its ageing.

Invoice discounting is done on a 'confidential' basis leaving the purchaser totally unaware of the fact that the seller has raised cash through the sale of its debts to a third party. In practice, the only clue is that a new bank account will suddenly appear as the one into which payments have to be made; this is often explained as necessary for 'administrative purposes'. The perceived benefit to the selling company of the 'confidential' route is that its customers know of no change of ownership of the debt and, correspondingly, of no external debt financing, which could be perceived as a weakening in the position of a company's finance structure.

In addition, where the primary seller–buyer relationship is split via the use of a separate third party, the purchaser's loyalty and goodwill towards its supplier can easily be reduced. For example, when dealing with a separate body in terms of payment, it becomes easier to distance the accounts payable function from the purchasing department in order to 'stretch' an otherwise tightly controlled relationship, as the vendor has no immediate incentive to chase the debt. Consequently, although likely to be slightly more expensive, it may be preferable to choose the 'confidential invoice discounting' route as opposed to an otherwise transparent sale of debt route, such as factoring.

Debt insurance

Sometimes, to safeguard its assets, a company will choose to insure some or all of the amounts owing by its trade debtors. This may arise where security is required for a bank loan giving the bank 'first charge' on its current assets. To cover itself as much as possible, the bank may insist that the company insures its debts receivable. Even without this external influence, a manager may decide that to insure the company's trade debt is a wise decision. Of course, in practice this would depend upon the perceived risk of non-payment; a company with a 'blue-chip' customer base may perceive the risk to be so low as not to merit any such form of insurance. This situation would effectively leave the seller in a position of managing the risk internally or 'self-insuring' its debt. This option is often adopted by large suppliers with good credit control systems and a wide statistical spread of customer debt.

As with all control systems, management should periodically review the policy in use, its appropriateness and its effectiveness as circumstances can quickly change in the business environment. A mixed policy may also be appropriate, such as deciding to insure only the overseas debt when considering the associated costs and benefits. It is usually far easier and cheaper to recover debts from businesses based in the same country as the seller, either directly or through solicitors, than it would be for a foreign-based debt. The decision to insure the debts receivable should be taken in the light of the costs of doing so.

Multi-currency debts

In the worldwide marketplace of today, it is not unusual for a company to have some of its debts in a foreign currency. One policy for dealing with these is for it to invoice everything in its own currency, thereby eliminating all exchange risk. The reduction of exchange risk resulting from this inflexible policy must be compared with the reduction in potential trading opportunities where customers are not prepared to be invoiced in this currency. Less extreme policies must address whether the company is going to collect the debt itself or use overseas agents. It may choose to have multi-currency bank accounts or simply have the debt payments converted into its home currency; it must decide how to manage its cash balances through multi-currency treasury management.

Of course, a potential benefit of invoicing in a foreign currency, especially a common one such as the euro or US dollar, is that the paid debt provides a readily available pool of funds (free of conversion costs) from which to pay your own foreign currency creditors. This makes the whole process simple and quick and is especially beneficial for the smaller organization which does not have its own dedicated treasury department. The 'opportunistic' value of holding cash can be vital; it may be that a business deal can be clinched simply by having the funds readily available in the right currency at the right time.

Cash

'Cash' usually means the combination of 'cash-in-hand' and 'cash-at-bank'. Cash in the form of notes and coins can be thought of as being 100.0% liquid and bank current accounts as 99.9% liquid; in practical terms, they are both as easily convertible as each other. (There are also numerous types of investment or deposit accounts whose liquidity is inversely proportional to their notice periods. Any notice period of more than a week or so would indicate that the asset should be listed as a short-term investment rather than cash.) Cash is the most liquid of funds due to its inherent portable nature: it can usually be used to secure purchases of all types. It is so readily acceptable because it can be reused by the recipient without any difficulty.

However, there are exceptions to the universal acceptability of cash; for example, where the physical volume of notes and coins would be large enough to cause concern to the recipient over its security. Imagine paying for a new car in this way! This would be an obvious opportunity to make use of the bank account and pay by cheque. More importantly, in a period of unstable inflation where the value of money itself was rapidly falling, it would be preferable to be paid in a more stable medium such as gold. Foreign currency deposits are relatively common in today's global business environment. With the growth of desktop computer banking, these are becoming more common and are almost as easy to use as the 'home' currency.

As stated in the introduction to this chapter, businesses need cash to survive; if they cannot pay their creditors on time they are not going to receive any further supplies on credit. If they cannot get their supplies, they cannot produce their goods and services; if they cannot do this, they have nothing to sell! If they have nothing to sell, their cash position will deteriorate rapidly and everything will soon grind to a halt.

Cash budgets

Using cash budgets to actively manage cash is one of the most important tasks performed by finance managers. It is especially important for start-up businesses and those that find themselves struggling to build up or maintain working capital in a difficult competitive marketplace. Of course, there are longer-term matters that are of equal significance in the battle to survive and grow, such as ensuring costs are driven down and sales levels achieved, but none is as time-critical to a business's survival as the effective short-term management of cash. Businesses do not suddenly go under as a result of poor profit margins; they cease trading due to a lack of cash and the resulting inability to pay their debts.

No cash means no more credit from suppliers and no access to goods/services needed for the production process. A creditor is not usually interested in its customers' profit margins but it is very interested in their ability to pay their debts. However, in the case of an unpaid debt of sufficient minimum value, it can go to the extreme of petitioning the courts for a winding-up order in the event of continued non-payment.

Cash budgets are used to monitor cash flow on a regular basis, usually monthly, weekly or daily. However, in the event of a cash crisis, the monitoring can be done on an hourly basis to deal with events and changes occurring throughout the day. An important point to realize is that, whereas budgets for revenue, expenses and profits are usually subject to variance analysis (see Chapter 15) on a monthly, historical basis, the cash budget will normally be used much more frequently on a proactive, 'real-time' basis. Although time-consuming, this task may be partly devolved to junior staff by giving them control over expenditure within reasonable preset limits and tasking them to produce regular summaries for senior management. (The creation and use of cash budgets is also covered in Chapter 14.)

It is useful to think of cash as the lubrication of the machinery of business itself; the machinery needs constant maintenance and must not be allowed to stop!

Purchase of fixed assets: lease or buy?

From time to time, businesses need to purchase fixed assets such as buildings, vehicles and computer systems. This raises the question of how they will pay for them. If they are 'cash-rich', they can pay with cash; alternatively, they may decide to pay by raising a loan from their bank or even to issue some new shares if the asset is very expensive. But if the business is short of cash it may make more sense to *hire* the asset and pay a monthly rent rather than buy it outright for the full purchase price. This type of arrangement is usually done through a 'lease'; the *owner* of the asset is called the 'lessor' and the *user* is called the 'lessee'. A lease is a legal contract by which the lessor retains ownership but allows the lessee to use the asset for a specified period of time in return for a series of rental payments on specific dates.

There are two common types of lease, an *operating* lease and a *finance* (or *capital*) lease. **Operating leases** are where the user hires the asset for a given purpose and returns it when that purpose has been fulfilled. This is the same idea as people hiring tools, such as concrete mixers, from a plant hire company for a specific job and returning them when it is finished. The lessor bears the maintenance costs of the asset. Alternatively, a **finance lease** is where the user acts as though it also owns the asset; the hire period is usually equivalent to its economic lifetime and the user may bear the maintenance costs. With a finance lease, the lessee pays for the asset by instalments over its lifetime, which is better for the company's cash flow than paying its total cost at the date of acquisition.

Leasing is very useful to businesses which have liquidity problems or find it difficult to raise loans; they are also flexible with mid-term cancellation options. Operating leases also have the advantages of minimizing asset obsolescence and avoiding maintenance costs. They also create 'off-balance-sheet' finance (see below) but finance leases do not.

If a company buys its fixed assets, they appear on the balance sheet under that heading. On the other hand, if it hires its fixed assets on operating leases, they do not appear on

	Cash purchase		Operating lease	
	£m	£m	£m	£m
BALANCE SHEET				
Fixed assets	80		60	
Net current assets	30		50	
Total capital employed		110		110
Less: long-term loans		20		20
		90		90
Share capital and reserves		90		90
PROFIT and LOSS				
Gross profit		60		60
Depreciation	20		15	
Lease payments	–		2	
Other overheads	30		30	
		50		47
Operating profit		10		13
ROCE		9.1%		11.8%

Figure 4.9 The effect of an operating lease on the ROCE

the balance sheet. The leasing costs are shown as overheads on the profit and loss account but no entry is made on the balance sheet as the assets are not owned by the business. One of the advantages of this off-balance-sheet finance is that it makes the company's financial performance look better; the ROCE ratio will increase as the asset base will be smaller. Also, by not borrowing large sums to purchase fixed assets, the business avoids increasing its gearing ratio.

However, where the hire contract is judged to be a finance lease, International Accounting Standard 17 (IAS 17) requires that the assets and their related finance be shown on the balance sheet (as fixed assets and long-term liabilities) as though they were owned by the business. The aim is to prevent showing a distorted picture to the users of published accounts due to the inclusion of misleading information.

Figure 4.9 shows the effect on its ROCE of a company using an operating lease instead of a cash purchase for 25% of its fixed assets. Note that leasing £20m of fixed assets means that the cash balance is £20m higher than it would otherwise have been. The only difference between the two scenarios is the lease/purchase decision; in all other respects, trading is identical but the ROCE has increased by nearly one-third from 9.1% to 11.8%!

Self-assessment question S4.2

Try the following question for yourself (answer at the end of the chapter).

The extract below from the accounts for Akro's first year of trading shows that the business owns £300m of fixed assets. If Akro had hired one-third of these on operating leases instead of purchasing them, how would this affect its ROCE? Assume that the depreciation charge would reduce by one-third and that the annual leasing costs would be £10m.

Akro Ltd

	£m	£m
BALANCE SHEET		
Fixed assets	300	
Net current assets	70	
		370
Less: Long-term loans	50	
		320
Share capital & reserves		**320**
PROFIT & LOSS		
Gross profit		
Depreciation	45	
Lease payments	–	
Other overheads	135	
		180
Operating profit		**40**
ROCE		**10.8%**

Businesses ignore the fundamentally important task of cash control at their peril. At best, they may be unable to take advantage of unexpected opportunities due to lack of available cash and, at worst, they could go out of business.

Creditors

Credit and the supplier relationship

When businesses first start to trade, they are very unlikely to be offered credit by their suppliers. Before this happens, they have to establish a 'track record' of cash on delivery in order to convince suppliers, and their credit insurers, of their reliability and trustworthiness. Trading on credit terms is not an automatic right; it must be earned. And once it has been earned, it must be maintained.

The establishment of good supplier relationships is an important part of an effective supply chain. This involves 'give-and-take' when things do not go exactly to plan; tolerance and a constructive approach to putting things right build the relationship over time. Accepting a delivery schedule change, proposed at short notice by a supplier, may help when you ask the supplier, at a future date, to allow you an extra month's credit for a particular payment.

This example illustrates how creditors can be used to manage working capital. Taking longer to pay creditors increases the amount of cash available. However, the relationship should not be put under too much strain or it may break down altogether. Great care must be taken to avoid suppliers putting a 'stop' on deliveries, as the consequences of a 'stock-out' can be extremely serious. For example, the non-payment of a supplier's invoice for £8,000 could result in the non-delivery of a vital stock item. This, in turn, could cause a production line stoppage costing the manufacturer £60,000 a day!

Communication is fundamentally important in avoiding such a breakdown. The supplier may refuse your request for an extra month's credit but may suggest weekly stage payments instead. This kind of compromise is common in day-to-day dealings between businesses. Ideally, the purchaser – supplier relationship should be viewed as a partnership by both sides; after all, they both stand to gain from it.

Alternative suppliers

One strategy for managing a continuous flow of materials is for a business to source stock items from at least two different suppliers. If, for any reason, one of the suppliers cannot deliver as planned, the other supplier(s) can be asked to increase their delivery quantities to meet the shortfall. By buying identical goods from multiple sources, the purchaser is able to manage the risk of stock-outs. This approach is particularly useful to businesses which use JIT stock control or something close to it.

Early-settlement discounts

If a business is in the happy position of having more than an adequate amount of cash available, it could choose to take advantage of any early-settlement discounts offered by suppliers. Of course, it should first calculate whether it is worthwhile to do so. Suppose a supplier is offering a 2.5% discount for payment on or before delivery as an alternative to the normal credit period of one month. The discount on goods invoiced at £1,000 is £25 (£1,000 × 2.5%). If the buyer is operating on an overdraft bearing interest at 12% a year, the early payment will cost it £10 (£1,000 × 12% × 1/12). So, in this case, the discount should be taken as it will save the buyer £15. Of course, it will also cost the supplier £15 (assuming it also operated on an overdraft at 12% a year). As discussed above under 'debtors', the reason a supplier is willing to suffer this cost is to ensure an adequate supply of cash flows into its business.

Try the following question for yourself (answer at the end of the chapter).

A business, which operates an overdraft at 15% a year, is about to receive goods costing £18,000 from one of its regular suppliers. Is it worth taking advantage of a 2.5% cash discount offered for cash on delivery if the supplier's normal trading terms are 'payment two months after delivery'?

Self-assessment question S4.3

Cycles and ratios

The 'operating cycle' is the average time (usually measured in days) for raw materials and/or products for resale to be received into stock, converted into output, the output sold and the money received. The period from receiving stock to that stock being sold, possibly in a converted form, is known as the 'stock-holding' or 'stock turnover' period.

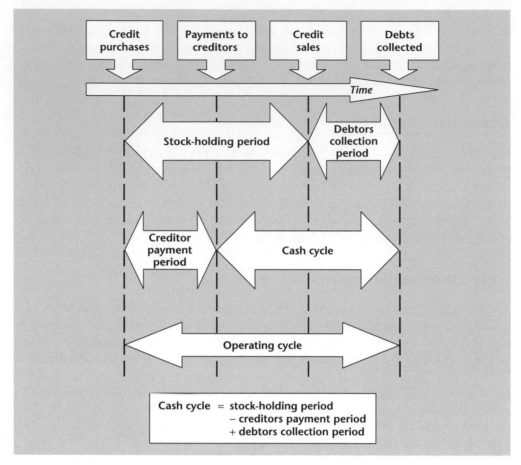

Figure 4.10 The operating and cash cycles

The 'cash cycle' is the average number of days between the time the purchased stocks are paid for and the time the sales revenue is received. The cash cycle may be reduced by maximizing the time taken to pay creditors (creditor days); the operating cycle can be reduced by minimizing the stock-holding and production times and minimizing the debt collection period. These cycles are illustrated in Figure 4.10 and the methods for calculating the periods involved are given in Chapter 3 on ratio analysis.

In today's competitive world, reducing the average time for which cash is tied up, i.e. the cash cycle, is a key management task. Usually, the first step in achieving this is to extend the creditors payment period as this is the easiest to achieve. However, when doing this, due consideration must be given to the supplier–customer relationship (as well as government and business regulations concerning interest charges and creditor protection). If the supplier feels it is being unduly taken advantage of, it may refuse to supply further goods until overdue payments have been made. Even worse, if the creditor thinks that the extended non-payment is a sign of deteriorating liquidity, it may impose more stringent terms of trading; for example, it could insist on being paid in advance for future supplies.

The other side of the same coin is to tighten up on credit control to reduce the debtors collection period. Giving debtors more frequent reminders may do the trick, at least with some of them. But the manager's opposite number in the customer's business probably knows the game just as well because he plays the same game. This highlights the 'two-faced' nature of working capital management, chasing debtors for earlier payment while taking longer to pay creditors. It is not unknown for managers to have two lists, one giving excuses for late payment to creditors and the other listing the counter-arguments to the same points! For example, the creditor payment list may include 'the cheque signatory is ill and absent from work at the moment' and the credit control list may state 'all businesses should anticipate this occurrence and have deputy signatories'.

Overtrading and overcapitalization

Overtrading occurs when a business has insufficient working capital to support its trading activities. This is often associated with rapid expansion of trading such as when the economy is recovering from a recession. More sales means more money tied up in stock and production, more debtors and more overheads. Increased trading activity requires increased working capital. Unfortunately, ignorance of this can, and does, lead to businesses being wound up even though they are making profits. This can be seen as 'a problem of success' but it is crucial that working capital is expanded at the same time as sales; *the bigger the engine, the more lubrication it requires!*

At the other end of the scale, a business may have too much working capital. Whilst not as serious as overtrading, this *overcapitalization* means that the business is not making the best use of its money. Too much stock, debtors and cash means that excessive funds are tied up in short-term assets when they could be used to finance long-term projects such as opening another branch of the business or developing a new version of an existing project. Overcapitalization is evidenced by excessive liquidity ratios and stock-holding periods.

Limitations

Taking capital management as a whole, a major limitation can be the lack of time to do it. This is particularly true when the business is having a cash crisis. Not being able to pay creditors on time will result in their chasing up their money. This will cause extra work and take up extra time. For example, an officer of the court may appear unannounced and demand a list of all business assets on the premises. This will take a significant amount of management time which would be better spent on activities such as chasing debtors to improve cash flow so that creditors can be paid and raw materials purchased. Managers in this situation find themselves in a 'vicious circle' which is very difficult to break.

'When you are desperately trying to stop alligators biting your backside, it is very difficult to plan the best way to drain the swamp.' It usually takes some major intervention to break these destructive loops, e.g. a large injection of new cash, possibly by deciding to factor your debtors. The workload on accountants and their staff can spiral out of control. All the unscheduled work done to keep the company afloat means that routine tasks like producing monthly accounts have to be postponed, at least until the bank insists on seeing an up-to-date set of accounts before it will even consider lending more money to the business!

The manager's point of view (written by Nigel Burton)

Controlling working capital is a bit like going to the gym. Excess stocks and debtors act like a heavy weight on a company, locking up cash which might otherwise be used in more productive areas. Stocks and debtors need constant work to reduce them to the minimum possible levels. A company with low levels of non-cash working capital is fit, lean and healthy, with cash in the bank providing flexibility and opportunity. It is probably true to say that, in most companies, working capital does not receive the attention it deserves, as management prefers to focus on profit generation. Yet, this is an area which can cripple a business perhaps more quickly than any other.

First, let us consider stocks. The difficulty here is that nearly everyone in the company wants a high level of stock-on-hand. Salespeople want product available to sell off the shelf, as quick delivery times will give them an edge over the competition. Production staff like high levels of both raw materials and finished goods, so that they can plan their production schedules with the greatest efficiency. The purchasing department, too, like the keener prices that bulk-buying offers, together with the reduced risk of panic buying to avoid stock-outs. On the other side of the scales sit the accountants, whose interests are in keeping to a minimum the amount of cash locked up in stock. I once asked a salesman to specify the sales department's optimum stock levels for finished products; he produced a requirement which was four times the existing level, a financial impossibility for the company. These conflicting positions can lead to some interesting discussions. Management must put all the variables into a pot, and come up with a stock-holding policy which strikes an acceptable mean between the various demands. Then the position needs to be watched on a continuous basis, as each element is constantly variable, and the policy can swiftly become outdated.

I advocate a strict write-off policy for ageing stock. My company's products generally had a long shelf life, and could have remained in a saleable state in our warehouse for years. However, in order to ensure that our book stocks did not become overburdened with slow- or non-moving items, we made a provision against anything which had not moved for a year. This length of time will of course vary considerably from company to company, depending on its type of product, but the important thing is to place a time limit so that all old stock is ultimately dealt with. Then there is the question of physically disposing of the stock. It may seem extravagant to dispose of perfectly good saleable stock when a customer for it may appear at any time. As a chemical company, disposal of the stock was also an expensive operation. But the danger is that the warehouse will become clogged with obsolete material, increasing stock-holding costs, and reducing efficiency. The long-awaited customer may never appear. Better, in my view, to take the hit for producing unwanted stock, and keep the company lean.

Debtors can lead to similar problems. It is always very tempting to offer the customer extended credit terms as a final incentive. This is especially attractive to salespeople, as the cost will be lost somewhere in interest charges, and therefore well outside their own area of responsibility. Once again, cash tied up for lengthy periods in debtors acts like dead weight upon the company.

Credit control is a vital function, and it always surprises me that many companies, even quite large ones, do not have a dedicated credit control function. In our company, the credit controller carried considerable power. He was required to approve all new business, and to sanction all business which exceeded existing credit limits. This naturally led to disagreements with the sales department, resolved through an appeals process, which led ultimately to the managing director's office.

Of course, his principal activity was the timely collection of debts. We did send out statements and reminder letters, but in my view these were of limited value, as reluctant payers came to recognize the pattern, and wait until the second reminder before paying up. We also avoided the use of discounts for prompt payment; customers will tend to take these anyway, whether they pay on time or not, leaving you with the problem of collecting irritatingly small balances which may not be worth chasing. A far more effective approach was to build a working relationship with the customer's payables department. This frequently allowed us to expedite payments, probably at the expense of other, less rigorous, suppliers. Another productive strategy was to ensure close liaison between credit control and salespeople on the status of outstanding debts, so that the appropriate pressure could be applied during sales negotiations.

The credit controller's ultimate weapon was to place a stop on all business with a customer who had overdue balances, an extremely effective method of recovering outstanding amounts. It is a fallacy to believe that strict application of credit terms will frighten customers away. Invariably the reaction of a purchaser who is prevented from placing an order is to give an earful to his accounting department for failing to pay invoices on time. I do not believe we lost a single customer as a result of our strong credit control policy.

We once took over a company which had a six-figure debt with its principal customer, representing around 18 months' trading. On investigation, we found that this customer had minimal capital employed, and no loans or overdrafts. We were financing their entire operation, on an interest-free basis. With a certain amount of encouragement and threat from us, they managed to bring their business onto a more conventional financial footing and paid off their outstanding debt to us over the next few months. Thereafter, we traded with them on a normal and completely satisfactory basis.

In some industries, and in some parts of the world, extended credit terms are simply a fact of business life. We used to trade on 180-day terms with customers in the Middle East and South America. Such lengthy credit periods are a concern, as so much time will pass before you get any inkling of any bad debt problems. You may even have made further shipments to the customer in the meantime. There are ways of laying off the risks through insurance or factoring without recourse, but these are expensive. They may, however, be essential if the debt is of critical importance to your company. Until we had established a satisfactory track record with a customer, we preferred to operate with a confirmed letter of credit, where a bank guarantees the debt on the basis of their knowledge of the customer's financial soundness. Thereafter, we would operate on open account, and I'm pleased to say that our bad debt experience was negligible.

On the other side of the coin, you can always improve cash flow by delaying payments to creditors. We tried this only once, when our finance director embarked on a project to reduce the company's interest costs. Our overdraft balances certainly decreased, but the action generated a huge number of telephone calls from irate suppliers. Our purchasers found that they were on the defensive when trying to negotiate prices, and at times were unable to obtain material at all, putting production schedules at risk. Failure to pay on time damages the reputation of the company, and raises the suspicion that the company may be heading into financial difficulties. All in all, it was a disastrous experiment, and is not to be recommended.

So, even without manipulating creditors, there is plenty of mileage in the control of stocks and debtors to release valuable amounts of cash back into the business.

Summary

- Working capital consists of current assets and current liabilities.
- Working capital objectives and policies should be clear and explicit.
- Working capital policy can be conservative, matching or aggressive.
- Conservative policy is low-risk; aggressive policy is high-risk.
- Conservative policy reduces profit; aggressive policy increases it.
- Cash is the only 100% liquid asset.
- The most economic quantity for ordering stock can be calculated.
- Stock items can be ranked according to their monetary value and more attention can be paid to high-value stocks.
- Stock-holdings can be kept to a minimum by adopting a 'just-in-time' approach to supplies of raw material stocks.
- Persuading suppliers to hold stocks until you need them minimizes your investment in stock; buffer stocks are also minimized.
- Stock items can be reordered automatically by using a computerized stock control system (e.g. EPOS).
- The cost of using computerized stock control systems needs to be carefully evaluated.
- Regular physical stock counts are essential for verifying the quantity and quality of stock.
- Holding stocks has both advantages and disadvantages.
- The amount of money owed to the company by customers can be controlled by a systematic 'credit control' process.
- The total debtors figure can be analysed by customer and by age to help prioritize debts for collection.
- When companies are short of cash, they should be prepared to pay (e.g. offer cash discounts) to ensure that debts are collected promptly.
- Debts can be sold or 'factored' to another company which specializes in their collection; customers may or may not be aware of the situation.
- 'Invoice discounting' is similar but the original company continues to perform its debt collection activities on behalf of the new owners of the debt; debtors are totally unaware of the situation.
- Debts can be insured if thought appropriate, on a piecemeal basis if required.
- Companies should have policies regarding foreign debts, e.g. the currency in which debts should be paid and the country where they should be paid.
- Businesses will not survive if they do not have adequate amounts of cash, no matter how profitable they are.
- Monthly cash budgets are a good way of monitoring cash; in a crisis, they can be done weekly or daily.
- Operating leases are where the user hires the asset for a given purpose and returns it when that purpose has been fulfilled.

- A finance lease is where the user acts as though it also owns the asset; the hire period is usually equivalent to its economic lifetime and the user may bear the maintenance costs. With a finance lease, the lessee pays for the asset by instalments over its lifetime, which is better for the company's cash flow than paying its total cost on acquisition.

- Relationships with suppliers/creditors are very important. Trading on credit terms is not an automatic right; it must be earned and maintained.

- By buying identical goods from more than one supplier, the purchaser is able to manage the risk of stock-outs.

- If a business has an adequate amount of cash available, it could choose to take advantage of any early-settlement discounts offered by suppliers.

- The 'working capital cycle' is the average time (usually measured in days) for raw materials and/or products for resale to be received into stock, converted into output, the output sold and the money received. The working capital cycle can be reduced by minimizing the stock-holding and production times and minimizing the debt collection period.

- The period from receiving stock to that stock being sold, maybe in a converted form, is known as the 'stock-holding' or 'stock turnover' period.

- The 'cash cycle' is the average number of days between the time the purchased stocks/products are paid for and the time the final sales revenue is received. The cash cycle may be reduced by maximizing the time taken to pay creditors (creditor days).

- Overtrading occurs when a business has insufficient working capital to support its trading activities.

- Overcapitalization occurs when a business has too much working capital. Too much stock, debtors and cash means that excessive funds are tied up in short-term assets when they could be used to finance long-term projects such as opening another branch of the business or developing a new version of an existing project.

Further reading

Antanies, J. (2002) 'Recognising the effects of uncertainty to achieve working capital efficiency', *Pulp & Paper*, July.

Arnold, G. (2005) *Corporate Financial Management*, 3rd edition, Financial Times/Prentice Hall, Harlow. See Chapter 13.

Atrill, P. and McLaney, E. (2004) *Management Accounting for Decision Makers*, 4th edition, Financial Times/Prentice Hall, Harlow. See Chapter 9.

Bridge, M. and Moss, I. (2003) 'COSO back in the limelight', *Perspectives on Financial Services*, April.

Committee of Sponsoring Organizations of the Treadway Commission (COSO) (1994) *Internal Control-Integrated Framework*, COSO, New York.

Cotis, L. (2004) 'Lean working capital management', *Business Credit*, January.

Deloof, M. (2003) 'Does working capital management affect profitability of Belgian firms?', *Journal of Business Finance & Accounting*, Vol. 30, Issue 3/4, April.

Hall, C. (2002) 'Total working capital management', *Treasury and Cash Management*, November/December.

Howorth, C. and Westhead, P. (2003) 'The focus of working capital management in UK small firms', *Management Accounting Research*, Vol. 14, Issue 2, June.

Pike, R. and Neale, B. (2002) *Corporate Finance and Investment*, 4th edition, Prentice Hall International, Harlow.

Samuels, J., Wilkes, F. and Brayshaw, R. (1999) *Financial Management and Decision Making*, International Business Press, London. See Chapter 18.

Stokes, J. R. (2005) 'Dynamic cash discounts when sales volume is stochastic', *Quarterly Review of Economics & Finance*, Vol. 45, Issue 1, February.

Watson, D. and Head, A. (2004) *Corporate Finance – Principles and Practice*, 3rd edition, Financial Times/Prentice Hall, Harlow.

(2002) 10 Blunders to Avoid. *Financial Executive*, Vol. 18, Issue 6, September, p. 41.

http://www.coso.org/index.htm

http://www.planware.org/workcap.htm#1

http://www.sbap.org/resources/CashFlowManagement.pdf

Answers to self-assessment questions

S4.1

What is the EOQ for a stock item whose annual demand is 45,000 units if the holding cost of one unit is £10 a year and the average cost of placing a single order is £1,000?

$$h = £10$$
$$d = 45,000 \text{ units}$$
$$p = £1,000$$

$$\text{EOQ} = \sqrt{(2 \times 1,000 \times 45,000/10)}$$
$$= \sqrt{(90,000,000/10)}$$
$$= \sqrt{9,000,000}$$
$$= \textbf{3,000 units}$$

So, it would be most economical if this particular stock item was ordered in quantities of 3,000.

S4.2

	Cash £m	Purchase £m	Operating £m	Lease £m
BALANCE SHEET				
Fixed assets	300		200	
Net current assets	70		170	
		370		370
Less: Long-term loans	50		50	
		320		**320**
Share capital and reserves		**320**		**320**
PROFIT & LOSS				
Gross profit		220		220
Depreciation	45		30	
Lease payments	–		10	
Other overheads	135		135	
		180		175
Operating profit		**40**		**45**
ROCE		**10.8%**		**12.2%**

Note that, even though none of the trading activities changed due to the lease, the ROCE has improved significantly, implying that the business is performing better. Indeed, the reduction in overhead cost shows that the business is performing better (in a financial sense) but it should not be assumed that its trading performance has improved.

S4.3

$$\text{Saving:} \quad \text{discount} = £18,000 \times 2.5\% \qquad = £450$$
$$\text{Cost:} \quad \text{interest} = £18,000 \times 15.0\% \times 2/12 = £450$$
$$\text{Net saving} = \text{zero}$$

The cash discount offers no financial advantage.

Kindorm Ltd

Kindorm Ltd manufactures a variety of metal and plastic fasteners for other businesses. Its summarized accounts for 2012 are shown below. In 2013, it plans to increase its sales turnover by 20% by extending the length of time it allows its customers to pay. The average credit period will increase by 14 days. Administration and marketing costs are expected to rise by 10% but debenture interest will be unchanged at £50,000. Annual taxation will be £75,000 and dividends will total £80,000, both payable in full in 2008.

It expects the cost of goods sold and the value of year-end creditors also to increase by 20%. At the same time, it intends to improve its stock control and reduce the length of time for which stock is held. This should enable it to limit the increase in the value of stock to 10%. Any additional necessary expansion in working capital is to be provided by the overdraft. The current overdraft limit of £25,000 was only recently negotiated and the bank is unlikely to welcome any request for a further increase without the provision of additional security. However, all the available security has been set against the debenture.

All Kindorm's purchases and sales are made on credit terms. No new issue or redemption of share capital or debentures is expected in 2013. The annual accounts for 2012 are shown below.

Kindorm Ltd: Balance sheet as at 31 December 2012

	£000 Cost	£000 Depn	£000 NBV
Fixed assets:			
Land & buildings	860	0	860
Equipment	540	220	320
	1,400	220	1,180
Current assets:			
Stocks	530		
Debtors	156		
Cash at bank	0		
		686	
Less: Current liabilities:			
Creditors	312		
Tax due	44		
Dividends due	54		
Overdraft	18		
		428	

	£000	£000	£000
	Cost	Depn	NBV
Net current assets			258
Net total assets			1,438
Less: Debentures			500
			938
Financed by:			
Ordinary shares of £1		700	
Retained earnings		238	
			938

Kindorm Ltd: Profit & loss account for y/e 31 December 2012

	£000	£000
Sales		3,646
Cost of sales		2,482
Gross profit		**1,164**
Admin & marketing expenses	1,002	
Debenture interest	50	
		1,052
Profit before tax		**112**
Taxation		44
Profit after tax		**68**
Dividends		54
Retained profit for the year		**14**

Tasks:

(You are advised to work to the nearest £000 in your calculations.)

A. Calculate the size of the resulting overdraft at the end of 2013 (assume the current ratio remains the same as it was in 2012).

(15 marks)

B. Calculate the length of the cash cycle at the end of 2013 and compare it with 2012 (assume the value of stock at the end of 2011 was £382,000).

(15 marks)

C. Calculate the operating profit and the retained profit 2013.

(15 marks)

D. Calculate the profitability ratios for 2012 and 2013.

(15 marks)

E. Evaluate Kindorm's expansion strategy and advise the company regarding any actions it needs to take to ensure its success.

(40 marks)
(Total 100 marks)

Questions

An asterisk * on a question number indicates that the answer is given at the end of the book. Answers to the other questions are given in the Lecturer's Guide.

Q4.1* Worthy Ltd

It is 30 January 2013 and Worthy Ltd's board of directors is meeting to discuss the 2012 accounts (summarized below together with those of 2011). Worthy Ltd is a manufacturing business and all its sales and purchases are made on credit terms. During 2012, it adopted an expansion strategy led by an across-the-board reduction in its selling prices. Its overdraft limit is £1.6 million but, towards the end of 2012, the bank reluctantly agreed to increase this to £2.0 million on a temporary basis. The directors are due to meet their bank next week to present a report analysing the causes of the cash shortage and outlining the action they intend to take in order to improve the situation. It is very likely that the bank will give notice that the temporary overdraft extension will be terminated in the near future. (Worthy's stock at 1 June 2010 was £230,000.)

	2011 £000	2012 £000
P & L A/C for year ended 31 May		
Sales revenue	3,000	4,600
Cost of sales	(1,650)	(2,700)
Gross profit	1,350	1,900
Distribution costs	(300)	(450)
Administrative expenses	(750)	(1,000)
Profit before taxation	350	450
Taxation	(75)	(85)
Profit after taxation	275	365
Dividends	(80)	(80)
Transferred to reserves	195	285
Balance sheets at 31 May		
Fixed assets at cost	2,300	3,000
Less: Accumulated depreciation	250	300
	2,050	2,700
Current assets:		
Stocks	370	1,200
Trade debtors	440	810
Cash	80	140
	890	2,150

	2011 £000	2012 £000
Current liabilities:		
Bank overdraft	(900)	(1,950)
Trade creditors	(450)	(950)
Taxation	(75)	(100)
Dividend	(80)	(80)
	1,505	3,080
Net current assets	(615)	(930)
Net total assets	**1,435**	**1,770**
Financed by:		
Share capital	250	250
Profit and loss account	1,235	1,520
Total capital employed	**1,435**	**1,770**

Task:

Prepare a report for the board of directors of Worthy Ltd examining the financial performance of the company during the two-year period to 31 May 2012. The report should also include advice as to how the company could reduce its overdraft to below the original limit of £1.6 million.

Q4.2* BKZ Ltd

BKZ Ltd is a new company about to launch its business-to-business service on the Internet. The launch will take place in April and it hopes to achieve monthly sales of £100,000 in only four months! Most of its sales will be on credit terms and, based on their experience, its directors expect customers to pay as follows: 30% in the month of sale, 50% one month after sale, 15% two months after sale with 5% lost as bad debts.

BKZ does not carry any stock and it intends to pay all its expenses in the month they are incurred. At the beginning of April, after paying for its fixed assets, it will have a positive bank balance of only £2,000. However, its bank has agreed to give it an overdraft (secured against its assets) with a limit of £40,000.

Extracts from its budget for the first six months of trading are shown below (all figures in £000). Depreciation of £13,000 a month is included in the expenses figures.

Month	April	May	June	July	August	September
Sales	20	40	60	100	100	100
Expenses	63	53	57	63	63	63

Tasks:

1 Based on the information given above, what will the overdraft be at the end of each month? Comment on your answer.
2 The financial director suggests offering a cash discount of 10% to customers paying on the day of sale. He believes this will be sufficient to attract many customers who would otherwise pay after one month. Customers are now expected to pay as follows: 60% in

the month of sale, 20% one month after sale, 15% two months after sale with 5% lost as bad debts. What will the overdraft be at the end of each month? Advise BKZ how it could manage its working capital to solve its problems.

Q4.3* Rogers Motor Parts

Vic Rogers is a sole trader running a vehicle parts business for the motor trade. All his sales are on credit terms. During 2011, he reduced his selling prices in order to increase the volume of sales. His objective was to make his business bigger, stronger and more profitable. To facilitate this expansion, he had to build an extra storeroom and purchase more storage bins. However, during 2011, he was surprised that he had to ask his bank for an overdraft. He was originally granted £5,000 but had to apply for a further £5,000 a few months later. The bank reluctantly agreed to his request but made it clear that it would not consider any further increase until 2013. It also insisted that the whole £10,000 overdraft be secured against his private residence. But even with this facility, some of his suppliers are very unhappy with the length of time Vic is taking to pay them. At the moment, he is relying heavily on their goodwill for continued supplies of stock items.

Summarized balance sheets as at 31 December 2010 and 2011 (£000)

		2011		2010
Fixed assets at net book value		43		33
Current assets:				
Stock	18		7	
Debtors	36		12	
Bank	0		1	
Current liabilities:				
Creditors	37		15	
Overdraft	10		0	
Working capital		7		5
Net total assets		**50**		**38**
Owner's capital:				
Opening balance	38		21	
Annual profit	35		30	
Less: Drawings	23		13	
Total capital employed		**50**		**38**

Trading results for the years to 31 December 2010 and 2011 (£000)

	2011	2010
Sales	200	120
Cost of sales	150	80
Gross profit	50	40
Overheads	15	10
Net profit	35	30

Tasks:

1 Calculate the following ratios for both years:
   - Percentage mark-up on cost of sales
   - Gross profit margin
   - Return on capital employed
   - Debtor collection period
   - Stock turnover days
   - Creditors payment period (stock at 1 January 2010 = £5,000)
   - Current ratio
   - Liquid ratio.
2 Discuss how the profitability and liquidity have been affected by the increase in sales and advise Vic on the running of his business in 2012.

Q4.4 Alborg Co. Ltd

The Alborg Company Ltd manufactures and sells doors and window frames to the building trade. It has been expanding rapidly over the last two years, experiencing an annual growth rate of 25%. The board is looking at the draft results for 2013 together with a forecast for 2014 (see below). Although the company wishes to continue growing rapidly, it is uncertain whether it will be able to finance this due to the size of the forecast overdraft.

The overdraft at the end of 2013 is £245,000 compared with a positive bank balance of £25,000 one year earlier when the overdraft limit was £125,000. During 2013, the bank had agreed a temporary increase to £250,000 but has now written to say that this increase can no longer be allowed, and must be reduced to £125,000 by the end of March 2014, i.e. within the next three months.

The board observes from the forecast that, without corrective action, the predicted overdraft in 12 months' time will be £605,000. Currently, there are no alternative sources of finance available and the board is now considering how it might resolve the problem.

Alborg Co. Ltd
Income statements for y/e 31 December

		2012			2013			2014 forecast
		£000			£000			£000
Sales		2,000			2,500			3,000
Costs:								
Materials used	750			950			1,125	
Other production costs	500			600			700	
Depreciation	200			300			400	
Cost of goods sold		1,450			1,850			2,225	
Admin and selling		100	1,550		150	2,000		200	2,425
Profit before tax			450			500			575
Taxation			125			150			200
Profit after tax			325			350			375
Dividends			195			210			225
Retained profit			130			140			150

Balance sheets at 31 December

Fixed assets (net book value)			1,000			1,200			1,475		
Current assets											
Stocks: Raw materials		175			275			375			
Finished goods		325			475			575			
Debtors		150			225			375			
Bank		25			0			0			
		675			975			1,325			
Less: Current liabilities											
Trade creditors	150			225			275				
Tax due	125			150			200				
Dividends due	195			210			225				
Overdraft	0	470	205	245	830	145	605	1,305	20		
			1,205			1,345			1,495		
Financed by:											
Issued share capital			500			500			500		
Retained profits			705			845			995		
			1,205			1,345			1,495		

Tasks:

1 Using a cash flow statement for 2013, explain why the cash position has deteriorated during that year.
2 Comment on the company's management of working capital by commenting on the operating and cash cycles for all three years and suggest ways in which the company might improve its working capital position. (You are aware that the 2012 position is typical of the industry in which Alborg operates.)
3 By looking at your suggestions to improve working capital and at the expected cash flow over the next three months, advise the company how (if at all) the overdraft can be reduced to £125,000 by the end of March 2014.

Q4.5 Charlesworth plc

Charlesworth plc is a distributor of tiles to the building trade. The vast majority of these tiles are purchased in Eastern Europe and South-East Asia. It has been quite successful since it was set up 10 years ago with sales growing, on average, at the rate of 10% a year.

Amy Backson has recently taken over as managing director to oversee a planned expansion of about 20% in the coming year. Amy is satisfied that the expansion can be managed from a logistical point of view as £11 million is planned to be spent on new vehicles and warehousing facilities. The old vehicles being replaced will be sold at auction and are expected to raise £250,000 which is also their net book value at the end of the current year. (The £21 million forecast for expenses includes £5 million for depreciation.)

However, the first draft of the forecast for next year is causing some concern as it predicts a substantial overdraft. The summarized accounts of Charlesworth plc have just been completed in draft form for the current year together with a forecast for next year (see below). Amy has been told by the bank that the overdraft limit has just been doubled to £1 million but no further increases will be granted for the foreseeable future. Charlesworth pays interest at 10% a year on its overdraft and loans.

Amy wants to have these matters discussed at the board meeting next week and has asked you for some help in preparing the necessary figures setting out some options.

Balance sheets as at 31 December (£000)

	Current year			Next year's forecast	
Fixed assets (at NBV)		30,000			35,750
Stocks	8,000			12,000	
Debtors	8,000			11,000	
Bank	300			0	
	16,300			23,000	
Creditors	2,900		3,500		
Overdraft	0		5,800		
Tax due	3,000		2,500		
Dividends due	4,000	9,900	4,200	16,000	
Working capital		6,400			7,000
		36,400			42,750
Less: Loan @ 10%		4,000			7,000
		32,400			35,750
Financed by:					
Share capital	10,000			10,000	
Reserves	22,400	32,400		25,750	35,750

Profit and loss accounts for year ended 31 December

	Current year			Next year's forecast	
Sales		52,000			61,000
Opening stock	5,000			8,000	
Purchases	30,000			33,000	
	35,000			41,000	
Less: Closing stock	8,000			12,000	
Cost of goods sold		27,000			29,000
Gross profit		25,000			32,000
Less:					
Expenses	17,000			21,000	
Interest – O/D	0			250	
Interest – loan	400	17,400		700	21,950
Net profit		7,600			10,050
Tax		3,000			2,500
Profit after tax		4,600			7,550
Dividends		4,000			4,200
Retained in year		600			3,350

Tasks:

1 Create a cash flow statement for next year explaining why the cash position deteriorates during that year.

2 Comment on the company's management of working capital by examining the operating and cash cycles for both years and suggest ways in which the company might improve its working capital position.

3 In what other ways could Charlesworth achieve its planned expansion while not breaching the overdraft limit of £1 million?

Review questions

1 Define working capital.
2 Explain the just-in-time system of stock control.
3 Explain 'buffer stock'.
4 Describe how computers can improve stock control.
5 Explain the importance of regular physical stock counts.
6 List the advantages and disadvantages of holding stock.
7 Describe a standard credit control system.
8 Explain 'factoring' and 'invoice discounting'.
9 Describe alternative policies for dealing with multi-currency debts.
10 Define 'cash' and 'liquid funds'.
11 Explain the fundamental importance of operating cash budgets.
12 Compare leasing and buying fixed assets.
13 Describe the difference between an operating lease and a finance lease.
14 Explain the importance of good supplier relationships.
15 Explain when alternative suppliers should be used.
16 Compare and contrast the working capital cycle with the cash cycle.
17 Define 'overtrading' and 'overcapitalization'.

The answers to all these questions can be found in the text of this chapter.

DECISION MAKING

Part 3 comprises

5 Variable costing and breakeven analysis
6 Short-term decisions using variable costing
7 Short-term decisions using relevant costing
8 Capital investment appraisal for long-term decisions

When Henry Mintzberg performed his analysis of what managers actually spent their time doing, he found that making decisions did not take up very much of their time. However, when managers do have to make decisions, it is important that they get them right. Management accounting is a source of help on these occasions.

Some decisions will have an immediate, short-term effect but others will impact on the business for many years to come. Contribution analysis (Chapters 5 and 6) is a simple yet powerful technique to help you make correct decisions. Basically, it concentrates on the costs and revenues that will change because of the decision and ignores those that will not. If absorption costing were used in these situations, the wrong decision would often be made as it takes account of *all* the costs associated with the product, whether or not they will change. Relevant costing continues along the same lines as contribution analysis but widens the scope of consideration to include the indirect effects of decisions as well as the direct ones. For example, if a decision to cease production of one particular product meant that 10 employees would become redundant, the redundancy pay arising (say, £100,000) would be included as a cost arising from the decision. Chapters 5, 6 and 7 should be read in sequence as they reflect increasing degrees of reality.

Capital investment appraisal concerns decisions which will affect company performance for many years. Essentially, they are about deciding which fixed assets to buy. The more expensive the fixed assets, the more relevant the use of capital investment appraisal techniques. Typically, large sums of money are tied up for long periods of time. Make the wrong decision and either you will have to live with it for a long time or it will be *very* expensive to correct. Although there are many qualitative factors to consider, any help from management accounting techniques is very welcome when such important decisions have to be made.

Variable costing and breakeven analysis

Introduction

Sometimes there are ways of doing things which are so simple they seem almost too easy, too good to be true. Variable costing is one of these. But do not be fooled by its simplicity – it is a very powerful technique. It is used mainly for short-term decision making and calculating the effect of production and sales levels on profitability. Short-term decision making is the subject of the next chapter. This chapter concentrates on the relationship between profit and activity (i.e. production and sales), commonly known as breakeven analysis.

At some point in your life you will probably think seriously about starting your own business. If the type of business you have in mind involves providing the same item for many different customers, breakeven analysis will be very useful to you. Suppose you decide to open a driving school, offering lessons to learner drivers. After much careful thought you will be able to estimate your total annual cost. Dividing this amount by the number of lessons (**estimated conservatively**) will give you the cost per lesson. But what are you going to charge your customers for each lesson? How do you know if you will make a profit or a loss? And how much is it likely to be? These are very important questions for anyone going into business on their own. Breakeven analysis is the financial model designed to answer these questions.

Note that variable costing is also known as *marginal costing and cost–volume–profit (CVP) analysis.*

Learning objectives

Having worked through this chapter you should be able to:

- differentiate between variable and fixed costs;
- define contribution;
- explain the relationship between contribution, fixed costs and net profit;
- calculate contribution;
- calculate breakeven point;
- draw traditional and contribution breakeven charts;
- define and calculate the margin of safety;
- evaluate different cost structures in terms of their operational gearing;
- calculate the activity level to produce a target profit;
- draw and use a profit–volume chart;
- discuss the assumptions and limitations of breakeven analysis.

Cost behaviour

This section is a brief revision of Chapter 2. Variable costing is based on the difference between fixed and variable costs, which are defined as follows and illustrated in Figure 5.1.

Variable costs – Costs which vary with output (e.g. raw materials)
Fixed costs – Costs which do not change when output changes (e.g. business rates)
Semi-variable costs – Costs which are partly fixed and partly variable (e.g. telephone)

Although there are several costs which are either purely variable or purely fixed, many costs are semi-variable. The utilities, such as telephone and electricity, often have a fixed

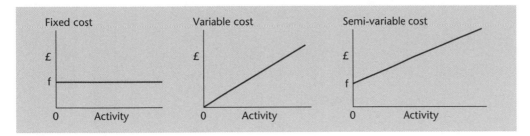

Figure 5.1 Patterns of cost behaviour

cost element, such as line rental or a standing charge, which has to be paid irrespective of usage. In addition, there is also a cost per unit used. The graph of the semi-variable cost combines the features of the other two graphs. Sometimes, only the total amounts of semi-variable costs are known for successive periods and the fixed and variable elements have to be worked out. (One way of doing this is the 'high–low method' as detailed in Chapter 1, on cost behaviour.)

Contribution

In the introduction to this chapter, it was pointed out that ignoring fixed costs is sometimes the correct thing to do. As fixed costs cannot be changed **in the short term**, there is no point considering them for short-term decision making. This approach results in something that is like 'profit' but is not 'profit'. To avoid confusion, this new entity is called 'contribution'.

Contribution is defined as the excess of sales revenue over the variable costs.

It can be thought of as the contribution towards paying for the fixed costs. Once all fixed costs have been covered, any further contribution is all net profit, as shown in Figure 5.2.

Contribution calculations

The Grubsteaks restaurant sells 18,000 meals a year at a standard selling price of £5. If each meal has a variable cost of £2, what annual contribution is earned? If the fixed costs are £30,000 in total, what is the net profit?

£

Sales revenue = 90,000   (18,000 × £5)
Variable costs = <u>36,000</u>   (18,000 × £2)
Contribution = 54,000
Fixed costs = <u>30,000</u>
Net profit = <u>24,000</u>

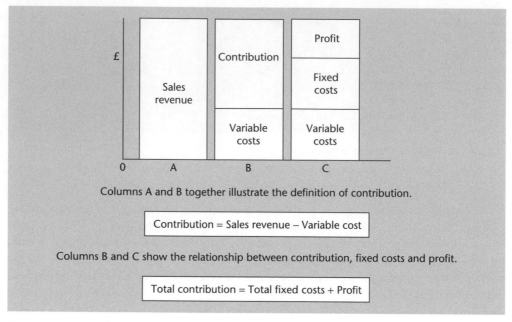

Columns A and B together illustrate the definition of contribution.

Contribution = Sales revenue − Variable cost

Columns B and C show the relationship between contribution, fixed costs and profit.

Total contribution = Total fixed costs + Profit

Figure 5.2 Contribution relationships

Alternatively, the contribution per unit could have been calculated first to give £3 (= £5 − £2). Multiplying this by 18,000 meals gives the total contribution of £54,000.

Self-assessment question S5.1	*Try the following question for yourself (answer at the end of the chapter).* The Good Health drinks tent at a local horse-race meeting sells all its drinks at £2.50 each. The variable cost of each drink is £1.00 and the fixed cost for the one-day event is £2,700. If 4,000 drinks are sold in the day, what is (a) the total contribution, and (b) the net profit?

Breakeven point

Definition and calculation

The total contribution increases as more units are sold. A point will come when the total contribution is just enough to cover the fixed costs. At this precise level of sales, all the costs have been covered and the next unit sold will produce the first profits for the business. This critical point, where the business makes neither a profit nor a loss, is known as the *breakeven point* (BEP). This is a useful concept for planning and control purposes.

At BEP, Total contribution = total fixed costs

Continuing with the example used above, the Grubsteaks restaurant sells 18,000 meals a year at a standard selling price of £5 and a variable cost of £2 with fixed costs of £30,000; how many meals will it need to sell to break even?

Let breakeven occur when N meals have been sold – in other words, when N lots of unit contributions have been received.

$$\text{Total contribution} = \text{total fixed costs}$$
$$N \times \text{unit contribution} = \text{total fixed costs}$$
$$N \times (5 - 2) = 30,000$$
$$N = 30,000/3$$
$$N = \textbf{10,000 meals}$$

The relationship between costs and revenues can be illustrated graphically by *breakeven charts*. Figure 5.3 gives the basic structure; this is then added to in two alternative ways in Figures 5.4 and 5.5. It is these two alternatives that are normally seen and used in practice.

Figure 5.4 shows the total cost broken down into its fixed and variable elements.

Figure 5.5 also shows the fixed and variable elements, but with their positions reversed. This enables the contribution to be clearly illustrated by the shaded area. (This is not possible on the traditional breakeven chart.)

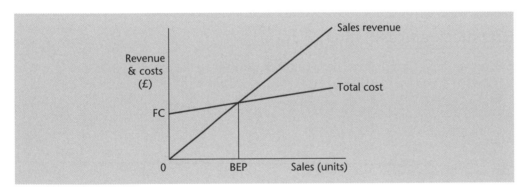

Figure 5.3 Fundamental structure

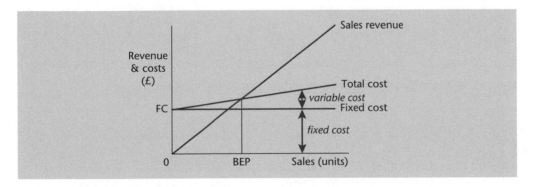

Figure 5.4 Traditional breakeven chart

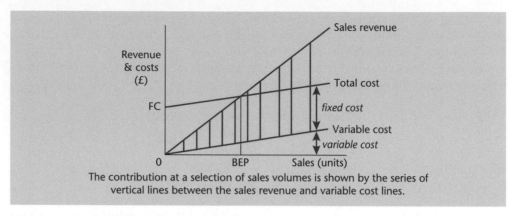

The contribution at a selection of sales volumes is shown by the series of vertical lines between the sales revenue and variable cost lines.

Figure 5.5 Contribution breakeven chart

Try the following question for yourself (answer at the end of the chapter).

Continuing with S5.1 above, the Good Health drinks tent at a local horse-race meeting sells all its drinks at £2.50 each. The variable cost of each drink is £1.00 and the fixed cost for the one-day event is £2,700. How many drinks does it need to sell to break even?

Graphical representation

The restaurant example used above can be illustrated by the chart in Figure 5.6.

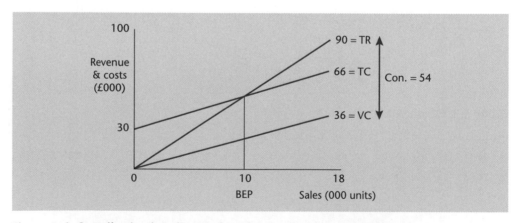

Figure 5.6 Contribution breakeven chart for the Grubsteaks restaurant

Try the following question for yourself (answer at the end of the chapter).

Using your answers from S5.1 and S5.2 above, draw a contribution breakeven chart (to scale) for the Good Health drinks tent.

Margin of safety

This is a measure of the amount by which sales can fall before profit turns to loss, i.e. the excess of actual sales over breakeven sales. This can be expressed as a number of units or as a percentage of sales and is illustrated by Figure 5.7.

For the Grubsteaks restaurant example:

$$\text{Actual number of meals sold} = 18,000$$
$$\text{Breakeven level of sales} = \underline{10,000}$$
$$\text{Margin of safety} = \underline{8,000} \text{ meals}$$

or

$$\frac{\text{Margin of safety in units}}{\text{Actual sales in units}} \times 100 = \frac{8,000}{18,000} \times 100 = 44\% \text{ of sales}$$

So sales could fall by 44% before losses occurred.

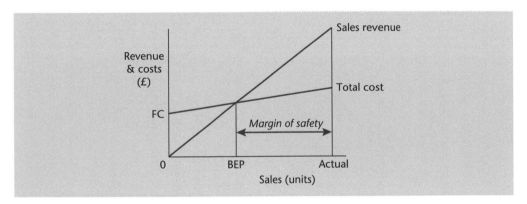

Figure 5.7 Margin of safety

Try the following question for yourself (answer at the end of the chapter).

Calculate the margin of safety for the Good Health drinks tent example in S5.3, (a) in units, and (b) as a percentage of sales.

Self-assessment question S5.4

Operational gearing

Operational gearing describes the relationship between fixed costs and total costs. The greater the amount of fixed costs, expressed as a percentage of total costs, the greater the operational gearing. The greater the operational gearing, the greater the effect of changes in sales volume on contribution and profit. The following formula expresses this numerically:

$$\text{Operational gearing} = \frac{\text{change in contribution or profit}}{\text{change in output}}$$

Consider the following situation where two separate businesses make and sell the same item at the same price. They both make cardboard 'outer' boxes to contain, for example, 48 packets of cereal. These large outers are used to transport large volumes of goods around the country.

Business A keeps fixed costs to a minimum but has a high proportion of variable costs. It uses simple bending and gluing devices operated by 12 employees and buys in large sheets of ready-made cardboard as its raw material. On the other hand, business B has invested heavily in automated machinery whose first process is to make its own cardboard sheet. This needs only two people to operate but causes a much larger amount of depreciation (i.e. fixed cost) than in business A. Its raw material is shredded recycled paper and other fibres which are much cheaper to buy than ready-made cardboard. Consequently, business B has a much higher proportion of fixed costs than variable costs compared with A. (See Figure 5.8 and notice the change in slope of the total cost line.)

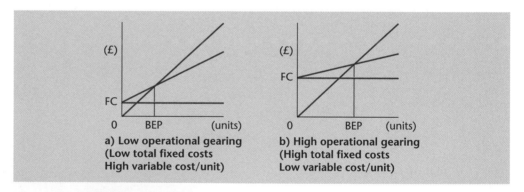

Figure 5.8 Operational gearing

As an example, for one outer:

	A	B
	£	£
Selling price	5	5
Variable cost	3	1
Contribution	2	4
Annual fixed cost	£100,000	£300,000

If there is a new order for 3,000 outers the profit will increase by £6,000 (3,000 × £2) for business A but by £12,000 (3,000 × £4) for business B. B will do better than A.

However, if a customer decides to purchase its outers elsewhere and cancels an order for 3,000 outers, the profit will decrease by £6,000 (3,000 × £2) for business A but by £12,000 (3,000 × £4) for business B. This time, A will do better than B.

The greater the operational gearing, the greater the effect of changes in sales volume on profit. In other words, the greater the operational gearing, the greater the risk.

When starting a new business, and sales are not very predictable, low operational gearing is preferable to high operational gearing. Low gearing means that there are fewer fixed costs to be covered before reaching profitability. This strategy helps to minimize risk.

On the other hand, as shown in the above example, provided the business is making profits, high gearing gives a greater increase in profit for each extra item sold.

Activity levels for target profits

Another useful calculation is to determine the number of items that has to be sold to achieve a given net profit. Figure 5.2 at the start of this chapter illustrates the following relationship:

Total contribution = total fixed costs + profit

If the unit contribution, the total fixed cost and the target profit are known, the activity level can be calculated. Suppose you were given the following information:

	£/unit
Direct materials	4
Direct labour	7
Variable overhead	3
Selling price	24
Total fixed cost	£5,000

How many items need to be sold for the business to make a profit of £10,000?

$$\text{Unit contribution} = \text{sales revenue} - \text{variable costs}$$
$$= 24 - (4 + 7 + 3) = 10$$

Let the number of items needed $= N$. Then

$$\text{Total contribution} = \text{total fixed costs} + \text{profit}$$
$$N \times 10 = 5,000 + 10,000$$
$$10N = 15,000$$
$$N = 1,500$$

Therefore

1,500 items need to be sold to achieve a profit of £10,000

Try the following question for yourself (answer at the end of the chapter).

A new style of electric bass guitar is about to be launched by a well-known instrument company. The materials for each guitar total £25 and 2.5 hours of labour (paid at £12/hour) are needed to assemble one. Variable overheads are charged at £2/labour hour and the associated fixed costs are £600 per month. If the selling price is set at £160, how many guitars need to be sold to achieve an annual profit of £20,000?

Profit–volume relationships

Sometimes it is preferable to bypass the details of sales and costs and compare profit directly with the volume of activity. The profit–volume chart shown in Figure 5.9 has the same horizontal axis as the breakeven chart but the vertical axis is for profit only. The breakeven point is where the profit line crosses the horizontal axis.

In order to draw a profit–volume graph, two points are needed to determine the position of the profit line. One of these points is easy to find. When activity is zero, the loss being made is exactly equal to the total of fixed costs. For the other point, a calculation is needed. The following relationship is used (see Figure 5.2):

$$\text{Total contribution} = \text{total fixed costs} + \text{profit}$$

Assuming the total of fixed costs is given, the amount of profit can be calculated for a chosen activity level if the total contribution at that level can be found.

The Grubsteaks restaurant example earlier in this chapter showed the application of this formula. At the activity level of 18,000 meals a year the profit was calculated to be £24,000 (see Figure 5.10).

The advantage of the profit–volume chart over the breakeven chart is that the profit can be determined for any level of activity within the range of the graph. This is done simply by reading the graph.

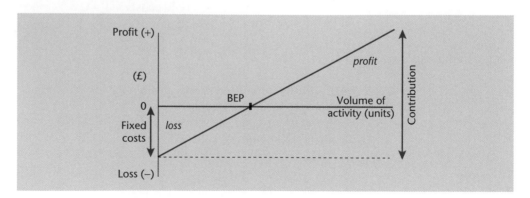

Figure 5.9 Profit–volume chart

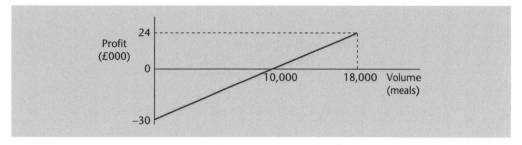

Figure 5.10 Profit–volume chart for the Grubsteaks restaurant

Try the following question for yourself (answer at the end of the chapter).

Using the answer to S5.1, draw a profit–volume graph for the Good Health drinks tent. From this graph, **read** the profit for sales of (a) 1,200 drinks and (b) 2,500 drinks.

Effect of alternative sales mixes

The vast majority of businesses sell more than one product and many of these sell lots of different products. As different products tend to have different unit contributions and no one knows for sure the sales mix that will occur in the next period, it is impossible to determine the breakeven level of output for the whole business. Different sales mixes will have different breakeven points. However, if the sales mix tends not to change much, it is possible to make an estimate with some degree of reliability.

Consider a business with just two products, As and Bs. Product B has a higher price and unit contribution, but a lower volume, than product A. The current sales mix is three As are sold for every B (A:B = 3:1).

Product	A	B	Total
Sales price	10	18	
Variable cost	4	9	
Unit contribution	6	9	
Quantities	30,000	10,000	40,000
Total contribution	180,000	90,000	270,000
Total fixed costs			148,500
Profit			121,500

To calculate the breakeven point, let N = number of Bs sold at BEP:

$$\text{Total contribution} = \text{total fixed cost}$$
$$3N(6) + N(9) = 148{,}500$$
$$27N = 148{,}500$$
$$N = 5{,}500$$

At BEP, 16,500 As and 5,500 Bs are sold (22,000 units in total)

But if the sales mix is changed to 2:1 (= A:B),

$$\text{Total contribution} = \text{total fixed cost}$$
$$2N(6) + N(9) = 148{,}500$$
$$21N = 148{,}500$$
$$N = 7{,}071$$

At BEP, 14,142 As and 7,071 Bs are sold (21,243 units in total)

Note that this is 757 items less in total than the previous sales mix.

What if the original volume was sold in total (40,000 units) but in the new sales mix of 2:1?

Product	A	B	Total
Sales price	10	18	
Variable cost	4	9	
Unit contribution	6	9	
Quantities	26,667	13,333	40,000
Total contribution	160,002	119,998	280,000
Total fixed costs			148,500
Profit			131,500

Note that this is £10,000 greater than with the original sales mix.

Self-assessment question S5.7

Try the following question for yourself (answer at the end of the chapter).

Hoffman Limited makes and sells only two types of portable cooking stove, the Lightweight (L) and the Megarange (M). The Megarange is more sophisticated and sells for more than twice as much as the Lightweight which is very popular. Consequently, nine Ls are sold for every M. The selling prices for Ls and Ms respectively are £8.20 and £19.40; their variable costs are £3.70 and £10.90. The budget for next year shows 50,000 stoves sold altogether with fixed overheads costing £150,000 in total.

For next year, calculate:

1 Profit if sales mix remains L:M = 9:1.
2 Breakeven point if sales mix remains L:M = 9:1.
3 Breakeven point if sales mix becomes L:M = 15:1.
4 Profit if sales mix becomes L:M = 15:1.

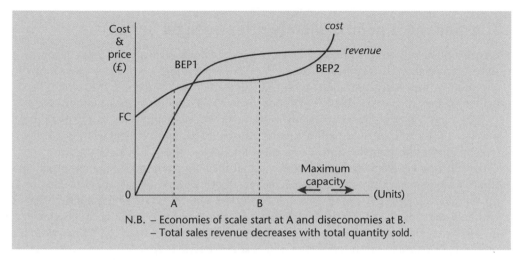

Figure 5.11 Economist's cost–volume chart

Limitations of variable costing

The relationship between sales income and quantity sold may not be linear. Beyond a certain point, it may be necessary to reduce the selling price in order to achieve further sales. The previously straight sales revenue line starts to curve beyond this point. (See Figure 5.11.)

The relationship between total costs and quantity produced may not be linear. The greater the quantity of units produced, the lower may be the price per unit of materials purchased. The straight total cost line also turns into a curve. (See Figure 5.11.)

Contribution analysis can be unreliable outside the relevant range (the range of activity levels for which the curves approximate to straight lines). At very high (close to maximum capacity) and very low activity levels, costs and revenues may not be representative of normal values (see Figure 5.11).

Breakeven analysis is not very useful for multi-product businesses as different break-even points are produced for different sales mixes. Because different products have different unit contributions, different sales mixes for the same overall activity will have different breakeven points.

It is difficult to measure activity for 'jobbing' businesses, where every item produced is different. Breakeven calculations and charts are applicable to firms which make large volumes of the same product. They are of no use to firms which make only one or a few of each item. This would include civil engineering firms producing public buildings and boatyards producing to customer specification only.

It is assumed that all the items made are sold, i.e. there is no increase or decrease in stock levels over the period. But stock levels may change over a financial period. When this is the case, the production activity will not be the same as the sales activity. Which of these two activity levels should be used for breakeven purposes? As breakeven is based on contribution (sales revenue – variable cost), the sales activity level should be used. 'Variable cost' is the variable cost of the items sold, not the items made.

The manager's point of view (written by Nigel Burton)

Breakeven analysis can provide vital financial information, particularly for small, relatively simple companies. It also has a role to play in larger, more complex organizations, although its potential applications tend to be limited. In all companies, however, it can help managers to understand the cost/price/volume relationships in their businesses.

The main use of breakeven analysis in single-product companies is to calculate the number of items to be sold before a profit can be made. Most small businesses know exactly where this point is, and it becomes one of the driving forces of the business. Once this point is reached, managers know that they are starting to generate profit. A small businessman of my acquaintance reckons that he works on Mondays to pay the taxman, Tuesdays to pay the VAT man, Wednesdays and Thursdays to pay his suppliers, and only starts working for himself on Fridays. He knows nothing about accounting, and his logic may be slightly suspect, but his little joke demonstrates that, even if he doesn't realize it, he has grasped the principles of breakeven analysis!

The same basic technique is employed for various purposes in large companies. It is commonly used, in conjunction with other measurements, in capital appraisals. All formal proposals for capital projects will be accompanied by supporting financial data, which will inevitably demonstrate that a satisfactory rate of return and payback period can be expected. But are the numbers reasonable? It is possible that the underlying assumptions about projected sales, capital expenditure and operating costs are all at their most optimistic limits, and could spell disaster if just one of them failed to materialize. To test the figures, therefore, it is useful to carry out a sensitivity analysis, calculating the impact on the rate of return of, say, a 10% reduction in sales, or a 20% overspend in capital expenditure. One of the key calculations here is the breakeven point, which represents the 'least acceptable' position. What level of inaccuracy in the numbers will bring the project down to its breakeven level? This neatly puts all the alternative scenarios into context and allows management to assess the robustness of the proposed figures.

Some years ago, breakeven principles played an important part in another type of major project, this time the sale of a business. We were instructed by our American parent company to shed a particular product line, and achieve a specified net gain for the company. The matter was greatly complicated when the favoured purchaser decided to buy only the trading assets, i.e. customer lists, product know-how and working capital, but not the fixed assets, i.e. land, buildings and plant. As a result, we were obliged to close down the factory, leading to significant expenditure which had not been envisaged when the sale of the business had first been authorized. This included decommissioning of the plant, building demolition, environmental testing, land remediation, and redundancy, among many others. Against these we had several unforeseen items of revenue, such as sale of plant and the disposal of the land. Our job was to ensure that the ultimate sale of the land covered all the net expenditure, leaving the American parent company with the profit it expected from the sale of the business. We used a breakeven model to monitor progress on this project, initially using estimated figures, and replacing them with the actual numbers as they became confirmed. In this way we were able to monitor constantly the proceeds required from the sale of the land to break even, and keep an eye on the property market to see if this level was achievable. Unfortunately, when we were ready to sell, the property market was in a slump, so we retained the land for a further five years until the market had recovered sufficiently to enable us to reach our breakeven point.

These examples will hopefully illustrate that breakeven principles can be used in a variety of different ways, even if the determination of sales volume, especially in small companies, remains its most common application. However, in large companies, the breakeven point of individual items is rather muddied by the multiplicity of products being sold; if you sell more of Product A than you expected, thus recovering a higher level of overhead, the breakeven point on Product B may go down. That is why we found ourselves concentrating more on the overall level of marginal income being generated by groups of products, and the contribution that they made towards fixed costs. The concept of contribution is a useful way of focusing on profit, and analysing the elements which are causing you to over- or underachieve the profit target. By increasing volume, or by changing the mix of sales towards the higher margin products, more marginal income will be generated. This additional contribution should fall straight through to the bottom line profit, assuming that the fixed costs remain fixed. In practice, of course, they rarely do. There are always spending variances to be managed, but this merely demonstrates another opportunity for effective profit generation. If you can reduce the level of fixed costs, at the same time as increasing marginal income, the gearing effect on the profit line can be significant.

Finally, the concept of contribution can sometimes show expenditure in a startling light. For instance, how big a deal do your American salespeople have to make, in order to pay for the managing director's first-class flight to New York to sign the final contract? The contribution calculation will tell you this, although you may not wish to point it out to the MD! Perhaps a more relevant question is: 'Will the contribution generated by the New York sale cover all the costs associated with it, and still leave a satisfactory profit?' Consider not only the variable costs of materials, labour, variable overhead and freight, but also other related costs, such as warehousing, export documentation, currency risks from $ invoicing, extended credit terms and bank charges, as well as the cost of customer visits and technical support. The MD's visit could be the final straw which pushes this piece of business into loss!

Summary

- Costs can be analysed into variable and fixed.
- Contribution is sales revenue minus variable cost, either per unit or in total.
- Total contribution equals total fixed cost plus profit.
- At breakeven point (profit = 0) total contribution equals total fixed cost.
- There are two types of breakeven charts, traditional and contribution.
- The margin of safety shows how far above breakeven point a firm is operating.
- Operational gearing affects the amount of profit due to changes in sales volume.
- Activity levels can be calculated for target profits.
- The profit–volume chart is an alternative to the breakeven chart.

Further reading

Horngren, C. T. (2004) 'Management accounting: some comments', *Journal of Management Accounting Research*, Vol. 16, 207–211.

Horngren, C., Bhimani, A., Datar, S. and Foster, G. (2002) *Management and Cost Accounting*, 2nd edition, Prentice Hall Europe, Harlow. See Chapter 8, 'Cost–volume–profit relationships'.

Upchurch, A. (2003) *Management Accounting, Principles and Practice*, 2nd edition, Financial Times/Prentice Hall, Harlow. See Chapter 6, 'Cost/volume/profit analysis'.

Weetman, P. (2002) *Management Accounting, an Introduction*, 3rd edition, Financial Times/Prentice Hall, Harlow. See chapter 'Profit measurement and short-term decision making'.

Answers to self-assessment questions

S5.1 Good Health drinks tent

$$
\begin{array}{rl}
& £ \\
\text{Sales revenue} = & 2.50/\text{unit} \\
\text{Variable costs} = & \underline{1.00}/\text{unit} \\
\text{Unit contribution} = & 1.50/\text{unit} \\
\text{Number of units} = & \underline{4,000} \\
\text{Total contribution} = & 6,000 \\
\text{Fixed costs} = & \underline{2,700} \\
\text{Net profit} = & \underline{\underline{3,300}}
\end{array}
$$

a) Total contribution = £6,000
b) Net profit = £3,300

S5.2 Good Health drinks tent

Let BEP occur when B drinks have been sold.

$$
\begin{array}{c}
\text{Total contribution} = \text{total fixed costs} \\
B \times \text{unit contribution} = \text{total fixed costs} \\
B \times (2.50 - 1.00) = 2,700 \\
B = 2,700/1.50 \\
\text{Breakeven point, } B = 1,800 \text{ drinks}
\end{array}
$$

S5.3 Contribution breakeven chart for the drinks tent

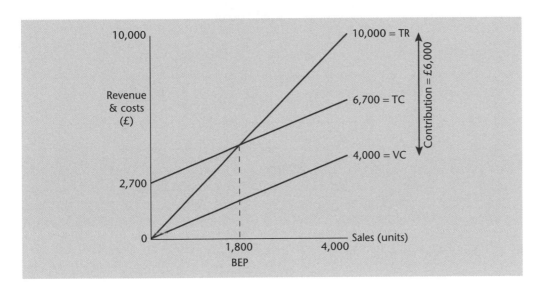

S5.4 For the Good Health drinks tent example

a) Actual number of drinks sold $= 4,000$
Breakeven level of sales $= \underline{1,800}$
Margin of safety $= \underline{2,200}$ drinks

b) $\dfrac{\text{Margin of safety in units}}{\text{Actual sales in units}} \times 100 = \dfrac{2,200}{4,000} \times 100 = 55\%$

So, sales could fall by 55% before losses occurred.

S5.5 Variable costs

Materials	25	
Labour	30	(2.5×12)
Overheads	5	(2.5×2)
Total	60	
Sales price	160	
Unit contribution	100	

Let the number of items needed $= N$
Total contribution $=$ total fixed costs $+$ profit
$N \times 100 = (600 \times 12) + 20,000$
$N = 27,200/100$
$N = 272$

So, 272 bass guitars need to be sold to create a net profit of £20,000.

S5.6 Profit–volume chart for the Good Health drinks tent

a) If 1,200 drinks are sold, a **loss** of £900 would occur.

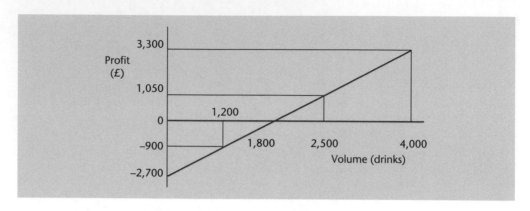

b) If 2,500 drinks are sold, a **profit** of £1,050 would occur.

S5.7 Hoffman Ltd

The current sales mix is 9 Ls are sold for every M (L:M = 9:1).

Product	L	M	Total
Sales price	8.20	19.40	
Variable cost	3.70	10.90	
Unit contribution	4.50	8.50	
Quantities	45,000	5,000	50,000
Total contribution	202,500	42,500	245,000
Total fixed costs			150,000
Profit			95,000

To calculate the breakeven point, let N = number of Bs sold at BEP:

$$\text{Total contribution} = \text{total fixed cost}$$
$$9N(4.50) + N(8.50) = 150,000$$
$$49N = 150,000$$
$$N = 3,061$$

At BEP, 27,549 Ls and 3,062 Ms are sold (30,611 stoves in total)

But if the sales mix changed to 15:1 (= L:M),

$$\text{Total contribution} = \text{total fixed cost}$$
$$15N(4.50) + N(8.50) = 150,000$$
$$76N = 150,000$$
$$N = 1,974$$

At BEP, 29,610 Ls and 1,974 Ms are sold (31,584 stoves in total)

Note that this is 973 stoves more in total than the previous sales mix.

What if the original volume was sold in total (50,000 stoves) but in the new sales mix of 15:1?

Product	L	M	Total
Sales price	8.20	19.40	
Variable cost	3.70	10.90	
Unit contribution	4.50	8.50	
Quantities	46,875	3,125	50,000
Total contribution	210,937	26,563	237,500
Total fixed costs			150,000
Profit			87,500

Note that this is £8,000 less than with the original sales mix.

The Hutton Vinification Company

HVC Ltd is based in north Somerset and has a financial year starting on 1 August. It produces wine from bulk grape juice bought from vineyards in southern England. In 2012/13 it made and sold 90,000 litres of wine in standard-sized 750 millilitre bottles to customers located throughout the UK. The maximum annual output of its plant is estimated to be 98,000 litres. Demand has grown steadily over the last 10 years in step with increased interest in, and knowledge of, wine in the UK. Home market production has been encouraged by the recent gradual warming of the climate.

However, the number of complaints received by HVC Ltd has risen sharply over the last two years and, if nothing is done to correct this, sales and profits are expected to fall next year. The directors attribute the complaints to the difficulty in controlling the quality of the 'must' (bought-in grape juice). The managing director has suggested that it would be easier to control the quality of harvested grapes rather than processed must. This means that HVC Ltd would have to acquire wine-pressing equipment to process the purchased grapes. Despite the extra temporary labour involved in pressing the grapes, the resulting self-pressed must is expected to have a variable cost equal to only 60% of bought-in must. The necessary grape-pressing machinery will cost £440,000 and will last 10 years before being scrapped (at zero value).

The managing director's remuneration is £42,000 p.a. and the sales director's is £38,000 p.a. In addition to the two directors, HVC Ltd has five full-time employees, whose pay in 2012/13 totalled £89,000. This included £25,000 annual salary for the production manager and basic annual pay of £10,000 for each of four operatives. This remuneration is considered to be a fixed cost but the remainder, which was earned as overtime by the four operatives, is considered to be a variable cost.

The total cost of must purchased in 2012/13 was £45,000. The average cost of the bottle, cork and label is £0.20 a bottle and delivery costs average £0.10 a bottle. HVC Ltd has a policy of having zero stocks at the end of July (this is also the company's financial year-end). Apart from a negligible amount, it has managed to achieve this for the last few years.

With effect from 1 August 2013 the directors will be entitled to a profit-related bonus dependent on the annual increase in net profit. Naturally, they are both very keen to earn a good bonus. With this in mind, the managing director has analysed the costs for 2012/13 (which was a typical year) as follows:

Fixed costs	£	Variable costs	£
Salaries and wages	145,000	Must	45,000
Depreciation	88,000	Overtime pay	24,000
Production costs	47,000	Bottle, cork and label	24,000
Selling costs	33,000	Delivery	12,000
Administration costs	29,000		£105,000
Interest	8,000		
	£350,000		

The sales director is not entirely convinced that the managing director's idea is the best solution. She thinks it would be better to go further south than at present, into central France, in order to purchase better-quality must. She believes that the effect of this would be to increase the must cost by 25% but this would be more than covered by her proposed 5% increase in the sales price.

HVC Ltd: Profit and loss account for y/e 31 July 2013

	£000	£000
Sales		504
Must	45	
Operatives' wages	64	
Bottles, corks and labels	24	
Production depreciation	53	
Other production costs	47	
Manufacturing costs of goods sold		233
Gross profit		271
Salaries	105	
Depreciation	35	
Selling costs	33	
Delivery costs	12	
Administration costs	29	
Bank interest	8	
Total overheads		222
Net profit		49

Tasks:

1 For 2012/13:
   a) Calculate the breakeven point in litres.
   b) Calculate the net profit if HVC Ltd had made and sold 95,000 litres.
   c) How many litres would have to be sold to increase net profit by 50%?

   (20 marks)

2 If the MD's plan to buy and press grapes (instead of purchasing grape must) is put into operation for 2013/14 and output increases to 95,000 litres and the selling price increases by 5%:
   a) What would the revised breakeven point be?
   b) What would the revised profit be?

   (20 marks)

3 Alternatively, if the sales director's plan to buy better-quality grape must is put into operation for 2013/14 and output increases to 95,000 litres and the selling price increases by 5%:
   a)   What would the revised breakeven point be?
   b)   What would the revised profit be?

(20 marks)

4 Evaluate the directors' plans and recommend a course of action for 2013/14. You may wish to use chart(s) to illustrate your answer.

(40 marks)
(Total 100 marks)

The Muesli Company

The Muesli Company (TMC) is a small business which makes and sells muesli. It was started two years ago by Rosemary Helms on the basis of her family's liking for the homemade mixture of cereals, nuts and dried fruits she had created for personal consumption. When a new farm shop opened nearby, she enquired if it would be interested in selling her muesli. The shop agreed to give it a try and found that it sold sufficient quantities to justify a permanent place in the shop. Rosemary now has five outlets and is considering selling her muesli on the Internet.

The business has reached a point where decisions have to be made concerning product type and distribution channel. The original recipe used nine different ingredients which were sourced from supermarkets and local shops. However, in recent months, Rosemary has created a new simplified recipe which uses only organic ingredients. Her idea is to appeal to the growing health food market which is willing to pay premium prices for organic foods. However, she has discovered that, if she wishes to use the word 'organic' on the label, she must register with the Soil Association and pay an annual fee of £440. As the business is just starting up, she is undecided as to whether this cost is worthwhile. She could continue with the current labels (omitting the word 'organic') while still using the organic ingredients to improve the taste.

While searching for organic materials, she discovered a wholesaler based 25 miles (40 km) away which delivers direct to its customers. The minimum quantities purchased are much higher but the prices are significantly lower than local shops. Rosemary now saves time and effort by using this supplier for all her ingredients. The supplier has pointed out that she could get even better prices if she ordered in greater quantities (about five times what she orders now). Although she is tempted by these low prices, she is not sure if she should buy her ingredients in these quantities.

Her son, who is something of a computer expert, has suggested creating a website to sell the muesli over the Internet. She is not too sure about this but is investigating the possibility and thinking about the consequences. How much would it cost to set up? What would the minimum delivery size have to be? How much extra would customers be prepared to pay for postage and packing? Could she cope if demand surged? How much would she need to sell to break even? Are there any 'hidden' costs?

In a two-and-a-half-hour session, she makes 12 kg of muesli. The product is packed in individual 500 g bags and special scales are needed to ensure that the weight is accurate. (To ensure that no bag is underweight, each one is slightly overfilled.) The Internet orders would be for a 'parcel' of seven bags. She thinks the website would last for about five years before a complete overhaul would be necessary. Although it is a few years old, she could use her present computer, but she would need to purchase broadband access.

The current selling price is £2.00 a bag to her retail outlets who sell it to their customers for £3.00 a bag. For the Internet business, direct to the consumer, she thinks she will charge £21.00 a parcel (7 bags @ £3.00).

While doing this exercise, Rosemary realizes that she does not know what her current breakeven point is and decides to calculate it. Also, it will serve as a useful comparison with the proposed Internet business. She does not use a computer for the local farm shop business and she uses her own car to deliver orders. It is difficult to be precise but she estimates that her average delivery is 12 bags, takes one hour and costs her £1.80 in petrol. She has recently purchased scales and a bag-sealing machine. Her costs are shown below.

For all sales:	£
Cereals	0.20/500 g bag
Nuts	0.45/500 g bag
Dried fruits	0.50/500 g bag
Plastic bags and sealing tape	0.01/500 g bag
Labels	0.05/500 g bag
Bag-sealing machine	45.00
Weighing scales	235.00
For Internet sales only:	
Creation of website	250.00
Maintenance of website	50.00 per month
Internet payment company charges	30.00 per month
Broadband access	20.00 per month
Packing materials	0.42/parcel of 3.5 to 4.0 kg
Postage	7.21/parcel of 3.5 to 4.0 kg

At the moment she is only selling about 12 bags a week and wants to expand in order to create more income. Her objective is to make a profit of approximately £10,000 a year by working no more than 20 hours a week for 50 weeks a year on her muesli business.

Tasks:

Without the use of 'organic' labels – Soil Association fee not paid:

1 Calculate the breakeven point of her current 'farm shop' business (in numbers of bags). Assume all sales are through farm shops and Internet sales are zero.

(15 marks)

2 If Internet sales caused the volume to increase sufficiently, the bulk purchase of edible ingredients would be justified, giving a 25% saving on current costs. Calculate the breakeven point (in numbers of bags) if this was so. Assume all sales are over the Internet and farm shop sales are zero.

(15 marks)

3 Assuming the 25% bulk saving was in operation, how many bags would Rosemary need to sell in order to make a profit of £10,000 a year? Assume all sales are over the Internet and farm shop sales are zero.

(15 marks)

With the use of 'organic' labels only – Soil Association fee paid:

4 Repeat task 1.

(5 marks)

5 Repeat task 2.

(5 marks)

6 Repeat task 3.

(5 marks)

General

7 Advise Rosemary about the possible expansion of her business to achieve her desired level of profit.

(40 marks)
(Total 100 marks)

Questions

An asterisk * on a question number indicates that the answer is given at the end of the book. Answers to the other questions are given in the Lecturer's Guide.

Q5.1* Bodgit Ltd

Bodgit Ltd makes 200 wooden kitchen chairs every month and sells them for £50 each. Fixed monthly overheads are £3,000 and the standard cost of one chair is as follows:

	£
Materials	15
Direct labour	8
Variable overheads	7

Tasks:

1 Calculate for one month:
   a) the variable cost of one chair;
   b) the breakeven point;
   c) the profit if 200 chairs are sold;
   d) the number of chairs sold to give a profit of £4,000.
2 In an attempt to boost sales, Bodgit plans to reduce the selling price to £48, improve the quality by spending 20% more on materials and increase its advertising by £1,000 a month.
      Calculate:
   a) the new breakeven point;
   b) the profit if 350 chairs are sold;
   c) the margin of safety (expressed as a % of sales) if 350 chairs are sold;
   d) the number of chairs sold to give a profit of £4,000.
3 Explain why your answers to the above questions should be seen as estimates rather than exact answers.

Q5.2* Concord Toy Company

The Concord Toy Company has two separate strategic business units. A draft plan, incorporating a target return on capital employed (ROCE) of 20% per annum, has been created by the managing director. Aware that the toy industry is a volatile one, the board of directors wishes to review the flexibility of the profit forecast shown by the plan. In preparation for the board meeting to discuss the plan, certain questions have been posed for each operating unit (see below).

Operating Unit 1 – novelty pens

This unit produces novelty pens. Most of these are based on popular cartoon characters. Variable costs are taken as raw materials and royalties. All other costs are assumed to be fixed in the short term. The following forecasts have been made:

Selling price per pen	£2
Variable cost per pen	£1.50
Sales revenue	£800,000
Average capital employed	£300,000

Within the output range 300,000 to the maximum capacity of 450,000 pens, the fixed costs are £150,000.

Operating Unit 2 – dolls' accessories

This unit produces three main products – a doll's buggy, a doll's scooter and a doll's MP3 player. In the past, the company has exported most of its products but, in its drive to develop home sales, it has recently obtained a contract to supply a national chain store. The store's toy buyer has requested the company to supply a doll's convertible car in addition to its existing products.

Forecast accounts

Product	Buggy	Scooter	MP3 player	Total
Selling price	£20	£10	£10	
Unit sales (000)	100	100	100	
Sales (£000)	2,000	1,000	1,000	4,000
Variable costs (£000)	600	200	400	1,200
Contribution (£000)	1,400	800	600	2,800
Fixed costs (£000)	700	700	700	2,100
Profit/loss (£000)	700	100	(100)	700

Fixed costs are apportioned on the basis of unit sales. The average capital employed is estimated at £3.6 million. To make a doll's convertible car would require new plant, financed in full by a bank loan.

Tasks re Unit 1:

1 What is the breakeven point in sales volume and value?
2 What is the margin of safety shown by the forecast?
3 Will the operating unit achieve a 20% return on capital employed?
4 What will be the profit if production output increases to maximum capacity? Qualify your answer.
5 How many pens must be sold to make a profit of £60,000?
6 What actions can be taken to improve profitability?

Tasks re Unit 2:

1 Will this operating unit achieve a 20% return on capital employed on the existing sales forecast?

2 If the sales mix remains at equal volumes of the three products, what is the breakeven point in sales volume and value?

3 What will the operating profit be if the sales volume on each product falls
   a) 10% below forecast?
   b) 20% below forecast?

4 Should Concord stop producing and selling the MP3 player?

5 Should the selling price of the MP3 player be increased to £12 to cover the full costs?

6 What further information is required to decide whether or not to make a doll's convertible car?

Q5.3* Rover's 'last chance saloon'

The following comments were broadcast on a television news programme in the first week of February 1999:

> Rover's future depends on the success of their latest model, codename R75. They intend to attract buyers away from Audi and Volvo to what they describe as the best car they have ever built. They claim to have paid more attention to detail than ever before on this upmarket saloon car. This may be why the launch has been put back from autumn 1998 to the summer of 1999.
>
> Selling prices will be a crucial element in their battle for market share and are expected to range from £18,000 to £26,000. Rover say they need to sell 140,000 cars a year to break even and acknowledge that this is a significant challenge. However, this is one test they cannot afford to fail. It is no coincidence that the R75 has been nicknamed 'the last chance saloon'!

Investigation

Assume:

> The retail selling price is £22,000 (average of £18,000 and £26,000).
> The trade selling price is 75% of the retail price.
> The total cost is 80% of the trade selling price.
> The variable cost is X% of the total cost.

Tasks:

1 Calculate the total fixed costs for the R75 project if X is
   a) 50%
   b) 65%
   c) 80%.
   As well as an annual total, express your answers in £/day.

2 Assuming the variable cost is 65% of total cost, how many R75s need to be sold for profit to be £100 million?

3 If 200,000 R75s were sold in the year, assuming the variable cost is 65% of total cost, how much profit would they make?

4 If the total capital employed on the R75 project is £10,000 million and Rover's owners wanted a 20% return on capital employed (ROCE), how many cars would have to be sold?

Q5.4 SACCUS

SACCUS is a local charity which decides to hold an outdoors fund-raising event in mid-summer. The secretary has a connection with an entertainments company which puts on musical laser light shows for the public. For charities, it charges a reduced rate of £375 all-inclusive. The venue would be provided free of charge by a local farmer. A barbecue would be put on and the food and drink would be included in the ticket price. It is estimated that the food would cost £2 a head and the drink £1 a head. Also, a special licence for the sale of alcohol would be needed at a cost of £25. Based on the experience of similar events, SACCUS expects to sell 500 tickets at £5 each.

However, the treasurer (who has a degree in business studies) is a little concerned about this plan and proposes an alternative. She suggests hiring a nationally known West Indian steel band at the special rate of £100 plus £50 transport costs. The ticket price would remain at £5 and food would be provided as before. However, no drink would be provided, the audience being invited to bring their own. The number of people attending is expected to be half that for the laser show.

Tasks:

1 Advise SACCUS as to which event it should stage.
2 Illustrate your answer by sketching a contribution breakeven chart for each event.

Q5.5 Royal Hotel

Jim Culf is the manager of the Royal Hotel, Bigtown-on-Sea. In anticipation of preparing next year's budget, he has analysed his recent costs and income. His findings are summarized below.

	£/week
Staff salaries	2,000
Head office charge	400
Depreciation of equipment and fittings	875
Heating	425

For each guest the average variable cost of food, drink, linen and sundries totals £100 per week. Jim considers all other overheads to be semi-variable and has produced the following data from his records:

Week no.	Occupancy (no. of guests)	Other overheads (£)
13	75	7,050
14	94	8,200
15	70	6,980
16	61	6,500
17	57	6,350
18	83	7,590
19	85	7,700

The average price charged for a week's stay is £240 per guest. Since it is a seaside hotel, the vast majority of its customers stay for either one or two weeks at a time.

Tasks:

1 Calculate the average number of guests needed each week to avoid making a loss.
2 The hotel can accommodate a maximum of 120 people. How much is the weekly profit if the average occupancy level is:
   a) 70%?
   b) 80%?
   c) 90%?
3 Jim has been invited by an international tour company to quote a competitive price for a group of 20 Japanese tourists who wish to stay in the area for two weeks. They are due to arrive in 10 days' time.
   a) Calculate the lowest price Jim can quote if he is to avoid making a loss on the tour. (Assume that the hotel is currently 70% booked for the two weeks in question.)
   b) If Jim wants to make a profit of £2,000 from this tour, what price should he quote?

Q5.6 Hughes Healthfoods

Hughes Healthfoods makes and sells two types of diet supplement, Slim Quick (SQ) and Healthy Living (HL). It has a single production line on which the two products are made alternately in batches. Some details from next year's budget are shown below:

Product	Unit selling price (£)	Unit variable cost (£)	Annual sales volume (units)
SQ	5.00	2.00	800,000
HL	9.00	4.00	200,000

The annual total fixed cost is £2.9 million and the production facility has an absolute maximum capacity of 1.1 million units a year.

Tasks:

1 Calculate the budgeted profit.
2 Determine the breakeven point. (Assume the budgeted sales mix is stable throughout the year.)
3 Is it possible for the business to double its profit while maintaining the budgeted sales mix?
4 Is it possible for the business to double its profit if the budgeted sales mix changed to two SQs being sold for every HL?

Review questions

1 Define variable and fixed costs.
2 Define contribution.
3 Explain the relationship between contribution, fixed costs and net profit.
4 Define breakeven point.
5 Draw traditional and contribution breakeven charts.
6 Define the margin of safety.
7 Explain operational gearing.
8 Draw a profit–volume chart.
9 Discuss the assumptions and limitations of breakeven analysis.

The answers to all these questions can be found in the text of this chapter.

Short-term decisions using variable costing

Introduction

Suppose you were a director of a well-known international passenger airline whose main route was London–New York. You operate this route with a fleet of several large aircraft, each with a capacity to carry 450 passengers. However, due to the number of competitors flying the same route, there is much surplus capacity and your aircraft often fly with more than 100 of their seats empty. Your standard return fare is £500, which is based on the total cost of £400 per available seat plus a 25% profit margin. The £400 total cost includes items such as depreciation of aircraft, fuel, on-board food and drink for passengers, rent of airport facilities, staff pay, training and administration costs.

Unexpectedly, a well-known holiday company offers to purchase 50 seats on every one of your flights for the next six weeks but is only willing to pay £100 a seat – only one-quarter of the total cost! What would your response be? Would you, politely but firmly, inform the holiday company that its offer is far too low or would you accept gladly and get the contract signed as soon as possible?

To solve this problem, you need to think about how your net income would change if you accepted the offer. Obviously, your revenue would increase by £100 for each of the 50 seats. But what about your costs? Which of the costs listed in the previous paragraph would increase? Most of them would not change at all! Only the cost of the on-board food and drink for passengers would increase. If this costs £10 per person, you would be increasing your net income by £90 a seat or £4,500 per return flight. If there were 100 flights during the six-week period, the net income from the contract would be £450,000. This is the case even though each seat is sold at £300 less than total cost. This is because most of the costs are 'fixed' and only the food and drink are 'variable' (see Chapter 1 on cost behaviour if you do not understand this). Your positive decision to accept the offer is based on your knowledge of variable costing and your company is nearly half a million pounds better off because of it! An understanding of variable costing will enable you to make similar, good, profitable decisions in your business career.

Note that this use of variable costing for short-term decision making is also known as contribution analysis.

Learning objectives

Having worked through this chapter you should be able to:

- advise whether or not to cease certain activities;
- advise on the order of production when one of the resources used is scarce;
- advise whether or not to accept one-off contracts;
- advise whether to produce or buy in components used in your products;
- discuss the limitations of decision making using variable costing.

Cessation of activities

The previous chapter dealt with the application of variable costing to breakeven analysis. We will now concentrate on commercial decision making in the short term, i.e. the immediate future. This aspect of variable costing is also known as *contribution analysis*. Four typical situations will be considered.

The first situation is where a financial analysis shows that a product line or profit centre is making a net loss and a proposal is made to close it down. A contribution analysis is performed to confirm or deny this course of action.

Provided the selling price of a product is greater than its variable cost, each sale will create a positive contribution towards the organization's fixed costs. This is so even when the product is making a net loss. Cessation of that product would mean that fewer of the fixed costs were covered **and the loss would be greater than before**. Remember that fixed costs are, by definition, costs which do not change with the level of activity, even if that level falls to zero. In other words, fixed costs cannot be eliminated **in the short term**.

Take the example of the Top Ski Holiday Company, which offers specialist skiing holidays in Norway, Spain and Italy. A financial analysis of last season in which 3,000 holidays were sold (1,000 for each country) shows the following:

	£000			
	Norway	**Italy**	**Spain**	**Total**
Total cost	950	700	450	2,100
Sales revenue	700	650	800	2,150
Net profit	(250)	(50)	350	50

The company would like to increase its selling prices but believes this to be unwise as its competitors are offering very similarly priced holidays in those countries. Alternatively, it has been suggested that if the Norwegian and Italian holidays for next season were withdrawn (starting in the near future) Top Ski would increase its profits from £50,000 to £350,000 by eliminating the losses for those two countries. This is based on the reasonable assumption that 1,000 holidays will continue to be sold for Spain.

A more detailed examination of the financial analysis reveals that the total fixed costs for last season were £600,000. These were for items such as brochures, advertising, directors' salaries and head office administration costs. These fixed costs were spread evenly over all the holidays. As 3,000 holidays had been sold, fixed costs of £200 (£600,000/3,000) were absorbed into each holiday. A contribution analysis of the above figures reveals the following:

		£000			
		Norway	**Italy**	**Spain**	**All**
	Total cost	950	700	450	2,100
Less:	Total fixed costs	200	200	200	600
	Variable cost	750	500	250	1,500
	Sales revenue	700	650	800	2,150
	Contribution	(50)	150	550	650
Less:	Total fixed costs				600
	Net profit				50

If the Norwegian and Italian holidays did cease, the analysis would change as follows:

		£000			
		Norway	**Italy**	**Spain**	**All**
	Contribution	0	0	550	550
Less:	Total fixed costs				600
	Net profit/(Loss)				(50)

So, instead of the profit increasing by £300,000, it would actually decrease by £100,000 to give a net **loss** of £50,000. The situation would be much worse than if no action had been taken and the Norwegian and Italian holidays sold as before.

The contribution analysis shows that, although the Italian holidays are making a loss, they are still making a positive contribution to the company's fixed costs. However, the Norwegian holidays are making a negative rather than positive contribution. Every time one of these is sold the company loses money it otherwise would not lose. Thus, it does seem a good idea to cease the Norwegian holidays.

If this happened and the Italian holidays continued, the analysis would be as follows:

	£000			
	Norway	**Italy**	**Spain**	**All**
Contribution	0	150	550	700
Less: Total fixed costs				600
Net profit				100

The rule is, in order to improve profitability, cease activities with negative contributions. (This assumes that these negative contributions cannot be made positive in the short term.)

Of course, **in the long term**, maybe the fixed costs could be reduced or maybe an alternative holiday venue could be found. In the long term **anything** is possible. However, for short-term decisions, the correct course of action comes from a contribution analysis. Although a sudden cessation of the Norwegian and Italian holidays seemed a reasonable proposition at first sight, it would have been a disaster for Top Ski Holidays if they had both been withdrawn.

From a business point of view, other aspects of the situation should always be taken into account. In particular, are the products interrelated? Consider a company selling three products: a basic food processor, a grating attachment and a coffee grinding attachment. Suppose the company stops making the coffee grinder because the accounting system shows that it is making a loss while the other two items are making a profit. Those potential customers who would have bought the processor and the grinder will not now do so. As the products are interdependent, sales of related items will be lost. Suppose it was the processor making the loss instead of the grinder. Anyone suggesting that production of the processor should cease should be asking themselves if they are in the right job.

Try the following question for yourself (answer at the end of the chapter).   **Self-assessment question S6.1**

The V&A Group is made up of four operating subsidiaries: A, B, C and D. Its corporate accounting system has produced the following figures which show the group has made a loss of £1,000. Analyse them and state which operations (if any) you would recommend for closure in order to return the group to profitability.

Summarized profit and loss accounts for last year (£000)

	A	**B**	**C**	**D**	**Group**
Sales	180	420	500	900	2,000
Raw materials	41	95	202	370	708
Direct labour	62	89	37	105	293
Direct cost	103	184	239	475	1,001
Gross profit	77	236	261	425	999
Total overheads	90	210	250	450	1,000
Net profit	(13)	26	11	(25)	(1)

Note: Fixed overheads have been apportioned according to the amount of sales revenue from each operation. Overheads are considered to be 90% variable and 10% fixed.

Tasks:

a) State which operations you recommend closing and why.
b) What would the group's profit be if your recommendations were actioned?
c) What would the group's profit be if A and D were closed?

Scarce resources

The usual factor limiting an organization's activities is the number of products it can sell. However, occasionally, a shortage of something it uses in its operations means that it cannot sell as many items as it otherwise would have. The item in short supply is known as a *scarce resource*. It is usually either a raw material or a particular type of specialized labour. For example, if there were an unforeseen shortage of crude oil due to some international dispute, the refining companies would not be able to make as much petrol as they could normally sell. In this case, in order to maximize profits, they would concentrate on the products which gave them the largest amount of contribution per barrel of oil.

The highest contribution might come from high-octane kerosene for jet engines. When the refining companies had produced all the aviation fuel that they could sell, they would concentrate on the product with the next-highest contribution per barrel, which might be unleaded petrol for cars. If there were any crude oil left after this, they would choose the next-highest-contribution product, and so on. In this way, they would ensure that they made the best use of every barrel of crude oil, i.e. every unit of their scarce resource. Here is a numerical example.

The following information has been extracted from the budget of Lonestar Petroleum:

	Contribution per 000 litres (£)	Barrels of crude per 000 litres	Sales forecast for month 5 (000 litres)	Quantity required (barrels)
Unleaded petrol	15.00	4.0	35,000	140,000
Diesel	12.00	3.0	18,000	54,000
Kerosene	20.00	4.0	8,000	32,000
Paraffin	8.00	5.0	7,000	35,000
				261,000

Due to an unexpected worldwide shortage of oil, the quota of crude oil available to Lonestar for month 5 has been set at 200,000 barrels.

Obviously, Lonestar will not be able to make all it planned to in month 5; it is 61,000 barrels short. One answer is to cut back production of all products pro rata but this would not maximize its profits. As crude oil is scarce, it needs to maximize the profit from each barrel. This is done by producing the highest-contribution-**per-barrel** product first, then the next highest, etc. **Lonestar needs to put its products into order according to their** *contribution per unit of scarce resource* **and produce in this order.**

Care must be exercised here for the contributions shown in the budget information are per thousand litres of finished product, not per unit of scarce resource which is a barrel of crude oil. To solve the problem, the contributions per barrel of crude oil must be calculated for each of the four products.

	Contribution per 000 litres (£)	Order	Barrels of crude per 000 litres	Contribution per barrel (£)	Order
Kerosene	20.00	1	4.0	20/4 = 5.00	1
Unleaded petrol	15.00	2	4.0	15/4 = 3.75	3
Diesel	12.00	3	3.0	12/3 = 4.00	2
Paraffin	8.00	4	5.0	8/5 = 1.60	4

So, the order of production would be kerosene, diesel, unleaded petrol and paraffin, until the quota of crude oil was all used up. Production in this new order gives the following results:

	Order	Quantity required (barrels)	Cumulative quantity (barrels)	Actual quantity (barrels)	Contribution/ barrel (£)	Total contribution (£)
Kerosene	1	32,000	32,000	32,000	5.00	160,000
Diesel	2	54,000	86,000	54,000	4.00	216,000
Unleaded petrol	3	140,000	226,000	114,000	3.75	427,500
Paraffin	4	35,000	261,000	–		–
		261,000		200,000		803,500

It is clear from the cumulative column that not all the unleaded petrol and none of the paraffin will be able to be produced. The total contribution for month 5 is £803,500. After the kerosene has been produced in full, any other order of production will give a smaller total contribution (and so a smaller profit). To prove this, the following table shows the result of producing in the incorrect order of contribution per thousand litres of output:

	Order	Quantity required (barrels)	Cumulative quantity (barrels)	Actual quantity (barrels)	Contribution/ barrel (£)	Total contribution (£)
Kerosene	1	32,000	32,000	32,000	5.00	160,000
Unleaded petrol	2	140,000	172,000	140,000	3.75	525,000
Diesel	3	54,000	226,000	28,000	4.00	112,000
Paraffin	4	35,000	261,000	–		–
		261,000		200,000		797,000

This total contribution is £6,500 lower than before.

The decision-making rule here is to produce in the order of the highest **contribution per unit of scarce resource** until it is used up.

From a business point of view, other aspects of the situation should always be taken into account. Are the sales of the products related? Would the lack of paraffin cause any customers to purchase their petrol or diesel elsewhere? These are not easy questions to answer but in-depth knowledge of the customers should go a long way in arriving at the correct answers.

Try the following question for yourself (answer at the end of the chapter).

Your company manufactures three products, Alpha, Beta and Gamma. The following information refers to next month:

	Alpha	Beta	Gamma
Sales demand (units)	50	150	200
Raw materials/unit	£100	£150	£80
Direct labour hours/unit	5	10	2
Fixed overheads/unit	£30	£60	£12

Direct labour is paid at £3.00 per hour. Variable overhead is equal to 10% of the cost of materials. Fixed overheads are attached to the products at the rate of 200% of the total direct labour cost. The selling price is calculated by doubling the prime cost (= total direct cost).

Tasks:

1 Calculate the contribution per unit for each product and rank them.
2 Using the ranking from the previous answer, prepare a forecast of the profit for each product and in total for next month if only 1,650 direct labour hours are available.
3 Calculate the contribution per direct labour hour for each product and rank them.
4 Using the ranking from the previous answer, prepare a forecast of the profit for each product and in total for next month if only 1,650 direct labour hours are available.
5 Quantify the difference between the answers to tasks 2 and 4 and comment on your findings.

One-off contracts

Occasionally, in addition to their 'normal' business, organizations are offered work which is of a 'one-off' nature. Take the example of Goodtime Holiday Centre plc (GHC) whose normal business is to provide package holidays in the UK at its custom-built holiday village in Cornwall. All accommodation, meals and entertainment are included in the holiday price, which averages £350 per person per week. The centre can accommodate a maximum of approximately 500 people and holidays are offered between the beginning of May and the end of September. The winter months are taken up with maintenance and new projects. GHC has been approached by an international charity to provide a one-week holiday for 500 refugee children during the last week of April. The charity is willing to pay a total of £50,000 (£100 per child). In deciding whether to accept the offer, GHC must bear in mind its duty to its shareholders to maximize their wealth.

The following information is from GHC's management accounting system and is used to determine its holiday prices.

Annual costs	£000	£000
Marketing and advertising	600	
Depreciation of equipment, vehicles, etc.	538	
Administration staff (permanent)	132	
Insurance	80	
Local rates	90	
		1,440
Holiday season* costs		
Other staff (temporary)	470	
Food and drink	310	
Other holiday running costs	120	
		900
Total		2,340

* The holiday season lasts for 20 weeks.

The total cost of providing one week's holiday = £2,340,000/20 = £117,000
The price for one week's holiday offered by the charity = 500 × £100 = £50,000
It may appear that acceptance of the proposition will lead to a loss of £67,000

However, before a decision is made, GHC should calculate the **contribution** arising from this one-off proposal.

Variable costs of special holiday:

	£000	
Other staff (temporary)	470	
Food and drink	310	
Other holiday running costs	120	
	£000	
Total variable costs for 20 weeks	900	
Total variable costs for 1 week	45	(900/20)
Total sales revenue from the charity	50	
Contribution for the special holiday week	+5	(50 – 45)

GHC should accept the offer because **profit will increase by £5,000.**

This positive contribution means that GHC will not be £67,000 worse off by agreeing to the special holiday but will, in fact, be **£5,000 better off.** This is because the remaining costs of £1,440,000 are **fixed** and will occur whether the special holiday goes ahead or not. If the fixed costs do not affect the financial outcome, they should not be used to make the decision. The fixed costs are absorbed into, and recovered by, the sales revenue from the 'normal holidays'.

The decision-making rule for one-off propositions is that **they should be accepted if they have a positive contribution and rejected if they do not.**

From a business point of view, other aspects of the situation should always be taken into account. For example, if the contract is a trial for a possible much larger order to follow, it should be made clear to the customer that the price is also a one-off and will not be sustainable in the long term. Also, any possible effects on normal sales should be considered. If a regular customer finds out that you have produced and sold a very similar product to the one it purchases from you but at a lower price for someone else, the customer may insist on renegotiating the price. The customer may even place future orders with a competitor.

<table>
<tr><td>**Self-assessment question S6.3**</td><td>

Try the following question for yourself (answer at the end of the chapter).

a) Abacus Inc. is a small one-product firm which plans to make and sell 1,000 ornamental abacuses a year at a price of $250 each. How much profit does Abacus expect to make in a year if the standard cost of one abacus is as follows?

	$/unit
Materials	100
Direct labour	25
Variable overheads	20
Variable cost	145
Fixed cost (based on a budget of 1,000)	75
Total cost	220

b) An export order is received for 200 abacuses modified by the addition of some semi-precious stones. The effect of this is a 30% increase in the cost of materials and a 40% increase in the cost of direct labour. Also, special export insurance will cost $5 for each modified abacus shipped. However, the customer is not willing to pay more than $44,000 in total for this large order. Should Abacus Inc. accept this order?

</td></tr>
</table>

Make or buy

Products and services are often made up of several component parts. A CD-player consists of an amplifier, motor, speakers, laser and casing. A holiday may consist of travel, accommodation, courier, food and drink. Businesses have a choice of creating these components themselves or buying them in from outside. Some very successful companies buy a significant proportion of their components from 'outside' companies. For its aero engines, Rolls-Royce buys in about 75% of parts included in its turbine-driven engines, enabling it to concentrate on the technology-critical areas. When reviewing their costs, organizations should compare the cost of making each component with that of buying it in. Sometimes, they are offered the chance of buying a component instead of making it. How should they decide?

Take the example of a meals-on-wheels service run by a local authority. It provides 100,000 meals a year from kitchens also used to prepare school dinners. Its costings for the meals-on-wheels service are as follows:

	£
Depreciation of kitchen equipment*	20,000
Depreciation of delivery vehicles	30,000
Catering staff wages*	30,000
Drivers' wages	90,000
Food and drink	50,000
Vehicle running costs	80,000
Total cost	300,000

* Based on proportion of total time used for meals-on-wheels.

An independent firm of caterers has offered to cook all the meals on its own premises and provide them to the authority for £0.90 each.

The cost of preparing the meals is:

	£
Depreciation of kitchen equipment	20,000
Catering staff wages	30,000
Food and drink	50,000
Total cost	100,000

As 100,000 meals are provided a year, each one costs £1.00 (£100,000/100,000). This is £0.10 more than the price being offered by the outside caterers, whose offer looks very attractive in this light. However, in order to make the best decision, the **variable** costs should be determined as they will be the only ones that change if the offer is accepted.

Assuming the number of part-time catering staff and the hours they work can be easily adjusted, the variable cost of meals-on-wheels is:

	£
Catering staff wages	30,000
Food and drink	50,000
Total variable cost	80,000

As 100,000 meals are provided a year, each one has a variable cost of £0.80 (£80,000/100,000). The fixed cost of kitchen depreciation will now have to be borne in full by the school dinners.

If the authority accepts the offer, it will be £10,000 worse off than before. This is because the offer price is £0.10 greater than the variable cost per meal. So the authority should not accept the offer.

The decision rule for make-or-buy situations is that **a component should be bought in only if its price is below the variable cost of producing it.**

From a business point of view, other aspects of the situation should always be taken into account. Will the supply of components be adequate and reliable? Will the quality of components be satisfactory? Will the price of components escalate in future? How easy would it be to start making the components again if the buying-in arrangement goes wrong?

Self-assessment question S6.4

Try the following question for yourself (answer at the end of the chapter).

Vendco manufactures a variety of vending machines which have a number of common components. As part of a cost review, Vendco has found an external supplier who will supply it with one of these parts (which has a standard cost of £90 – see below) for £75.

	£
Direct labour	25
Direct materials	30
Variable overheads	5
Fixed overhead	30
Standard cost	90

Advise Vendco whether it should continue to make this part or to buy it in at £75.

Limitations of short-term decision making using variable costing

All the above decision-making techniques have been used strictly within the confines of the variable costing model. This is the accounting part of decision making. It provides a good basis for solving the problem. However, do not forget that making decisions is essentially a management function. The role of accountancy is to provide good information to help managers make the right decisions. Remember, the reality of the situation being faced is always more complex than the assumptions from which the financial model is constructed.

The next chapter, on relevant costing, builds on what you have learnt in this chapter. It, also, is about making decisions but its context is widened to include any other effects caused by those decisions. For example, your contribution analysis may indicate that you should stop making one of your products. However, this may cause a significant number of redundancies to be made at a cost of hundreds of thousands of pounds. Whereas the variable costing model would not take this into account, relevant costing would include the redundancy costs because its boundary of cause and effect is so much wider. To find out more, have a look at the next chapter.

The manager's point of view (written by Nigel Burton)

Like most manufacturing concerns, my chemical company carried out periodic business reviews to consider withdrawing products which were no longer generating a satisfactory profit. There are many reasons why profitability might be in decline on individual items – perhaps a mature product has reached the end of its natural life, and been superseded by new technology, or fierce competition from Far Eastern suppliers has caused prices to fall to uneconomic levels. Management had to decide whether there was any course of action which would bring these products back into profitability, or whether they should be terminated, to allow the company to concentrate its resources on the newer, more profitable products.

The decision often hinged on the impact of a product's withdrawal on the recovery of fixed overhead. If a product is making a marginal loss (i.e. its variable cost is greater than its selling price) and therefore making no contribution to fixed overhead, the decision is simple. But if the product is making a marginal profit, although not enough to cover all the overheads attributed to it by the costing system, the decision is rather more complicated. If it is terminated, and there is no accompanying reduction in fixed overhead, the contribution will be lost and the company will be worse off. The fixed overhead attributed to the product will simply be reallocated to the next product. This may then become unprofitable as well, and be terminated in its turn, and so it goes on, until the domino effect wipes out the business! In the short term, fixed overheads cannot easily be reduced, so it may well be wise to persevere with the product until longer-term actions can be taken.

In this situation, variable costing is clearly crucial in preventing you from making inappropriate short-term decisions, although you will still have uncovered a problem which needs resolution in the longer term, probably by fixed overhead reductions. The decision to terminate a product is a long-term issue, which will change the future shape of the business. However, variable costing is also valuable in assessing the appropriateness of temporary actions, as a situation in our chemical factory demonstrates.

One of our plants made a high-volume product for use in the paper industry. The plant had been built in the 1970s, and despite one or two capacity improvements, the demand had grown so much by the late 1980s that we were unable to cope, even with continuous shift working. At this point, we were faced with two options: we could increase capacity by building a second plant, or we could concentrate our existing resources on the most profitable pieces of business. An analysis of the business showed that some of the sales generated a relatively low marginal income, and that, by eliminating these and accepting only the higher margin business, the profitability of the group would continue to rise.

This strategy was successful in the short term, and profitability improved. But it was an unsatisfactory way to run a business. Nobody likes to turn away business. It alienates the customer and sends them to the competition. The rejected business may have been at a lower margin, but it was still making a reasonable contribution to profit. The problem was that, at the time, there was insufficient business available to justify the cost of building a new plant. Fortunately, this changed over a period of time, and the growth in demand of both high- and low-margin business reached a point where the numbers started to add up. Accordingly, a new plant was built, doubling the capacity.

Now we had another problem. We had too much capacity for the present demand, and our sales projections showed that we would not be able to fill the plant for several years. At this point we had an enquiry from a large paper company, which needed a volume of product which roughly equated to 30% of our new plant's capacity. The margin on this product was lower than we would normally have accepted, but after much debate, we concluded that it did indeed make a positive contribution towards both fixed overheads and labour, which would otherwise have remained idle. We therefore accepted the business.

Such decisions are not as easy to make as they may seem. There are both quantifiable and unquantifiable issues to take into account. For instance, how fixed is the labour? If we do not accept this business, can we switch the labour on to cheaper single shifts, or is the volume of other business sufficient to require continuous shift working anyway? What is the impact on the cover provided by other departments, such as maintenance, quality control or the canteen? What about the level of raw material and finished goods stocks that will be needed, with the consequent warehousing and interest costs? Are we happy that the product costs on which we are basing this significant decision are sufficiently accurate in the first place? We certainly do not want to discover too late that the new business is actually draining profit from the company. And there are also the less quantifiable issues to consider, such as the extent of management input required, or the impact on the company's ability to accept unexpected, but more profitable, orders that may arise in the near future.

Once you have decided that it is in your company's interests to accept low-margin business, it is imperative that all parties are fully aware of the implications. Our American parent used marginal income percentage as one of the key measurements of our group's performance. The inclusion of a substantial piece of low-margin business naturally caused the marginal income percentage to decline, so it was important to ensure that the parent understood both the rationale and the effect of it, and that, if we chose not to do the business the following year, the parent would understand the reasons for a fluctuating sales line.

Such business should always be regarded as a one-off, separate piece of business which is outside the normal course of the company's activities. The business does not cover its share of the overheads, and is therefore technically unprofitable. We only consider accepting it when the overheads are already covered by other more profitable business. If there were a temptation to repeat this low-margin business year after year, perhaps a more advantageous course of action for the company would be to pursue a reduction in the level of fixed overheads.

There is also a risk in accepting low-margin business, in that it might encourage salespeople to chase more and more of it. After all, isn't any sale with a positive marginal income making a contribution towards overhead? Well, maybe, if you are a supermarket, where high sales volumes may well compensate for low margins and be sufficient to generate a satisfactory return. In manufacturing companies, however, capacity constraints will tend to limit the opportunity for substantial volume increases, so primary concentration on high-margin business is essential.

Summary

- Cease activities only if there is a negative contribution.
- Produce in the order of 'contribution per unit of scarce resource'.
- Decide whether to accept one-off contracts on the basis of their contribution.
- Buy in components if their price is less than the variable cost of manufacturing.
- Do not forget to take into account the factors outside the variable costing model. (The next chapter looks at this in greater depth.)

Further reading

Horngren, C., Bhimani, A., Datar, S. and Foster, G. (2002) *Management and Cost Accounting*, 2nd edition, Prentice Hall Europe, Harlow. See Chapter 8, 'Cost–volume–profit relationships'.

Upchurch, A. (2003) *Management Accounting, Principles and Practice*, 2nd edition, Financial Times/Prentice Hall, Harlow. See chapter 'Cost/volume/profit analysis'.

Weetman, P. (2002) *Management Accounting, an Introduction*, 3rd edition, Financial Times/Prentice Hall, Harlow. See chapter 'Profit measurement and short-term decision making'.

Answers to self-assessment questions

S6.1 V&A Group

	A	B	C	D	Group
Total overheads	90	210	250	450	1,000
Variable overheads (90%)	81	189	225	405	900
Fixed overheads (10%)	9	21	25	45	100
Variable costs					
Raw materials + direct labour	103	184	239	475	1,001
Add: Variable overheads	81	189	225	405	900
Variable costs	184	373	464	880	1,901
Sales income	180	420	500	900	2,000
Contribution	(4)	47	36	20	99

(a) Close factory A only

If A is closed:

	A	B	C	D	Group
Contribution	–	47	36	20	103
Less: Fixed costs					100
(b) Net profit					3

If A and D are closed:

	A	B	C	D	Group
Contribution	–	47	36	–	83
Less: Fixed costs					100
(c) Net loss					(17)

S6.2 Alpha, Beta, Gamma

	Alpha	Beta	Gamma	Total
Direct costs:				
Raw materials	100	150	80	
Direct labour	15	30	6	
Prime cost	115	180	86	
Variable overhead	10	15	8	
Variable cost	125	195	94	
Fixed overhead	30	60	12	
Total cost/unit	155	255	106	
Fixed overhead/unit	30	60	12	
Sales demand (units)	50	150	200	
Total fixed overhead	1,500	9,000	2,400	12,900

1	Selling price	230	360	172 (200% of prime cost)	
	Variable cost	125	195	94	
	Contribution/unit	105	165	78	
	Ranking	2	1	3	

2		Alpha	Beta	Gamma	Total
	Labour hours/unit	5	10	2	
	No. of labour hours	150	1,500	–	1,650
	No. of units sold	30	150	–	
	Contribution/unit	105	165	78	
	Total contribution	3,150	24,750	–	27,900
	Less: Fixed costs				12,900
	Net profit				**£15,000**

3	Contribution/unit	105	165	78
	Labour hours/unit	5	10	2
	Contribution/labour hour	21.0	16.5	39.0
	Ranking	2	3	1

4					Total
	Labour hours/unit	5	10	2	
	No. of labour hours	250	1,000	400	1,650
	No. of units sold	50	100	200	
	Contribution/unit	105	165	78	
	Total contribution	5,250	16,500	15,600	37,350
	Less: Fixed costs				12,900
	Net profit				**£24,450**

5 Using the contribution per direct labour hour ranking gives £9,450 more profit than the contribution per unit ranking. So, using the contribution per unit of scarce resource does give the highest profit.

S6.3 Abacus Inc.

(a) Normal activity

	$
Sales price	250
Variable cost	145
Contribution	105/unit

Total contribution = 1,000 × $105 = 105,000
Less: Fixed costs = 1,000 × $75 = 75,000
Net profit = **$30,000**

(b) Export order

	$
Materials	130 ($100 + 30%)
Direct labour	35 ($25 + 40%)
Variable overheads	20
Export insurance	5
Variable cost	190/unit
Sales price	220 ($44,000/200)
Contribution	+30/unit

Total contribution = +$6,000 (200 × $30)

Recommend acceptance of the export order as it has a positive contribution.

S6.4 Vendco

Compare the relevant variable costs of manufacture with the buying-in cost. Remember that fixed overheads will still have to be paid for in the short term so these are irrelevant to the decision.

	£
Variable production costs	
Direct labour	25
Direct materials	30
Variable overheads	5
Total	60
Buy-in price	75

Therefore, buying in is not recommended (in the short term).

Sara Wray Enterprises

Sara Wray lives in the Cotswolds, an area of outstanding natural beauty in central–south-west England. She started her working life as a teacher of French and art but, after several years, she gave this up to have a family. As her children grew older, she went back to work on a part-time basis, not as a teacher but as an administrator of a local art gallery. Her children are now adults with jobs of their own and Sara is the driving force behind a successful business offering language tuition and cultural holidays to non-UK residents.

Her business actually started seven years ago when she decided to gain a Teaching English as a Foreign Language (TEFL) qualification. Having achieved this, she provided English language tuition to foreign students in the summer months. Two students would come to stay in her home at any one time, receiving formal tuition in the morning and going out for visits to local places of interest in the afternoon and evenings with Sara. During her first summer season, she had a total of nine students, eight staying for two weeks and one staying for one month. This was a total of 20 student-weeks' tuition. She established a good reputation and the number of students grew each year.

After a few years, Sara branched out by offering one-week Tours of the Cotswolds for groups of approximately 16 adults without any formal language tuition element. Her success with these tours is based on her organizational ability and her experience of arranging local trips for her language students. As well as general tours, she now offers two specialized ones: English Gardens and Arts and Crafts. Sara still sees her English language courses as the basis of her operations as many of her tours include some people who have been students of hers or have been recommended by them. However, most of her tour customers come from her advertisements in France, the Netherlands, Germany, Italy and Spain.

Current demand for her TEFL courses is such that she now employs seven other qualified teachers, each taking two students at a time. The students live in the teachers' homes and are taught there in the mornings but join together for the visits and eat out together each evening at a different venue. For these outings, Sara hires an 18-seater minibus and driver for her 12-week season (mid-June to mid-September). Her non-tuition tours start in May and finish in October but do not take place every week. These tour customers stay in local hotels which are block-booked in advance by Sara. She hires the same type of minibus and driver for her tour parties and she also hires a guide to accompany them.

Up to now, there has been no difficulty finding guides of the right quality. Unfortunately, her regular garden tour guide, Rose, is about to move to Paris due to her partner's unexpected relocation and will no longer be available to guide these tours. However, one of the TEFL teachers, Mary, is also an expert gardener and has volunteered her services as garden tour guide. As Mary speaks reasonably good French, Spanish and German, she would be an ideal choice for this job. But the two planned garden tours are scheduled to take place during the TEFL season and Sara would have to find a replacement teacher for those weeks. Most of the other good TEFL teachers living in the area have contracted with the many English language schools based in nearby Oxford and Sara is finding it impossible to find a suitable replacement. As the season is just about to start, it looks as though Sara will have to cancel either two teacher-weeks of English tuition or two one-week garden tours. She is unsure whether to use Mary as a TEFL teacher or a garden tour guide.

While she is pondering this dilemma, Sara receives a letter from one of her previous students, Michael, who lives in Munich. Michael wants Sara to arrange a one-week 'Beer and Brewing' tour to include five beer-related visits for himself and 15 of his friends. When he was brushing up his English last year with Sara, he was very impressed with several local beers he tasted in the Cotswold area. He is offering to pay Sara £5,600 (16 @ £350 per person) for local accommodation, food, transport, brewery visit fees and knowledgeable guide. He will organize the travel between Munich and the Cotswolds.

Sara's friend, David, is a member of the Campaign for Real Ale (CamRA) and says that he would be willing to give up a week of his holidays to guide this tour for £500. Sara estimates admission fees at £650 and other costs the same as for a general or gardens tour. She does not see any reason why this tour should not go ahead. The only thing concerning her is that the price offered seems so low that the tour will make a loss. The lowest cost of her other tours is £6,000 (see below). She thinks she will probably have to contact Michael and refuse his offer.

As well as all this, she notices that the financial analysis prepared by her accountant shows that, although the general and gardens tours are profitable, the arts and crafts tours are making a loss (see below). Although they are more costly to run, she is reluctant to drop them but, on the other hand, does not want to run any of her activities at a loss. She is reluctant to increase her prices as she is aware of a firm in nearby Oxford which offers very similar arts tours at the price of £385 per person.

Sara wants to increase her profit next year by at least £3,000 by expanding either the English teaching or the tours but she is unsure what she needs to do to achieve this.

Financial analysis of TEFL activities

Maximum activity for season is 8 teachers for 12 weeks = 96 teacher-weeks
Each teacher has two students each week. Each student pays £400/week
Fixed costs (minibus hire, insurance, advertising, etc.) for TEFL total £19,200

For one teacher-week	£
2 hours' tuition/day for 5 days = 10 h @ £15/h =	150
Agent's commission, 2 students @ £25 =	50
Accommodation, 5 nights @ £20 × 2 students =	200
Evening meals, £5 × 2 students × 5 days =	50
Admission fees, £5 × 2 students × 5 days =	50
Total variable cost =	500
Fixed cost (£19,200/12 weeks/8 teachers) =	200
Total cost =	700
Sales revenue (2 @ £400) =	800
Net profit =	100

Financial analysis of tour activities

Tours planned: 3 general, 2 gardens and 2 arts and crafts
Maximum of 16 per tour, each person paying £400
Fixed costs (administration, insurance, advertising, etc.) for tours total £12,810

Per tour (16 people)	General/Gardens £	Arts and Crafts £
Minibus and driver	800	800
Guide fees	350	500
Hotel, bed, breakfast & evening meal	2,620	2,620
Admission fees	400	800
Total variable costs	4,170	4,720
Fixed costs	1,830	1,830
Total cost	6,000	6,550
Sales revenue (16 × £400)	6,400	6,400
Net profit	400	(150)

Tasks:

Advise Sara on the decisions facing her:

1 Is it better to use Mary as a garden tour guide or English teacher for two weeks?

(25 marks)

2 Should she decline Michael's offer of £5,600 for a Beer and Brewing tour?

(25 marks)

3 Should she stop offering the Arts and Crafts tours?

(25 marks)

4 Next year, should she expand the English teaching or the tours?

(25 marks)
(Total 100 marks)

Questions

An asterisk * on a question number indicates that the answer is given at the end of the book. Answers to the other questions are given in the Lecturer's Guide.

Q6.1* Burgabar Corporation

Burgabar Corporation owns and operates a range of fast food outlets throughout the East End of London. A summary of next year's budget (before head office costs are taken into account) is given below:

Branch	Sales revenue £	Variable costs £	Salaries & wages £	Fixed costs £
West Ham	100,000	20,000	32,000	30,000
Hackney	120,000	24,000	32,000	30,000
Forest Gate	120,000	24,000	34,000	32,000
Mile End	140,000	28,000	34,000	34,000

The administrative head office of Burgabar Corporation is at Epping. Its running costs of £96,000 a year are apportioned to branches on the basis of sales revenue.

Concern is being expressed about the West Ham branch as it is showing a loss (after head office costs have been deducted). One director has suggested that the branch is closed as soon as possible and a new branch opened, possibly in the Ilford area. However, it would take approximately 12 months to open a new branch. The closure of the West Ham branch would reduce head office costs by £10,000 p.a. with immediate effect. Also, although West Ham's salaries and wages bill would disappear immediately, redundancy pay of £8,000 would be payable.

Task:

Advise the directors of Burgabar Corporation.

Q6.2* Profoot Ltd

Profoot currently makes and sells two types of protective shoe, model P1 and model P2.

	P1	P2
Annual sales demand (pairs)	14,000	10,000
Selling price	£40	£40
Variable costs per pair:		
Materials	£15	£15
Labour – Machining (£8/hour)	£2	£2
– Assembly (£7/hour)	£3.50	£3.50
– Packing (£6/hour)	£0.50	£0.50

Annual total fixed costs are currently £300,000.

For the next financial year, Profoot intends to keep model P1 as it is but to upgrade model P2 by the use of better materials. The materials cost for P2 is expected to be £20 a pair (an increase of £5 a pair) and its new selling price will be £50 a pair. Also, the amount of time spent machining P2s will double and the cost of this will increase to £4 a pair.

Also, next year, Profoot intends to introduce the PDL, a top-of-the-range model with a selling price of £65. Labour costs for machining will be £4 a pair, assembly £7 a pair and packing £0.50 a pair. Materials will cost £32.50 a pair.

Demand for the P1, P2 and PDL next year is predicted to be 14,000, 7,000 and 5,000 pairs respectively. Annual fixed costs are expected to increase by 2% next year.

Tasks:

1 Calculate the annual net profit for the current year.
2 Calculate the annual net profit for next year assuming the predicted demand is met in full.
3 If the maximum number of machine hours available next year is 8,500, create a production plan to maximize net profit. (Clearly show the quantity of each model produced and calculate the net profit.)
4 Profoot could purchase an additional machine costing £420,000 which would last for 10 years and have no residual value at the end of that period. This machine could be used for a maximum of 1,750 hours a year. How would the purchase of this machine affect next year's net profit?

Q6.3* King & Co.

The current annual budget for King & Co., makers of baseball caps, is summarized as follows:

	£000
Sales (1 million caps @ £5 each)	5,000
Less manufacturing cost of caps sold	3,000
Gross margin	2,000
Less sales and administration expenses	1,500
Operating income	500

King's fixed manufacturing costs were £2.0 million and its fixed sales and administration costs were £1.0 million. Sales commission of 5% of sales is included in the sales and administration expenses. The company is approaching the end of the current financial year and looks as though it will exceed its budgetary targets.

King's has just been asked by its local First Division football club to make a special order of 50,000 caps in the club colours to celebrate the club's promotion to the Premier League; the club is willing to pay £4 a cap. However, a special badge of the club's emblem would have to be made for each cap.

Even though King & Co. has the necessary capacity to produce the order, the managing director has decided to reject the club's offer of £200,000 for the 50,000 caps. He explained his decision by saying,

> *The club's offer is too low. I know we would save the sales commission but the badges alone will cost twice as much as that, and it costs us £4.50 to make our ordinary caps. I'm willing to cut our usual 10% profit margin to 5%, or even less, to get this order but I'm not prepared to do it for nothing and I'm certainly not prepared to make a loss on the deal.*

Task:

Comment on the managing director's decision.

Q6.4 Parfumier Jean-Paul

Jean-Paul Cie (J-P) is a world-famous haute-couture fashion house based in Paris. It also manufactures a range of perfumes, all made from secret recipes. Only one ingredient called 'maylarnge', a mixing agent, is used in all their products. Maylarnge is obtained from SML Laboratoire in Brussels and the quantity used varies with the particular perfume recipe.

Due to temporary processing difficulties, SML has informed J-P that it can supply only €13,100 worth of maylarnge over the next three months.

The budget below relates to the quarter in question under normal circumstances. The shortage of the mixing agent means that the budget will have to be revised.

Perfume	Passion	Entice	Magique	Exotique
Sales volume (50 ml bottles)	6,000	5,500	6,500	4,500
Variable costs per bottle	€	€	€	€
Maylarnge	1.00	0.80	1.20	0.60
Ingredients (as per recipe)	2.00	3.10	2.60	1.90
Selling price	12.90	15.70	16.10	14.50

Fixed costs for the quarter amount to €133,300 (including all wages and salaries).

Tasks:

1 What would the quarter's profit be if there was no shortage of maylarnge?
2 Calculate the profit for this period of shortage if the perfumes were manufactured in the order of their contribution per bottle until they ran out of maylarnge.
3 Calculate the revised sales budget and profit assuming J-P wishes to maximize its profit for this period of shortage.

Q6.5 MPB Ltd

Marie and Peter Bridge run a business manufacturing and selling sets of the popular French game, boules. The boules are turned from aluminium, packaged in a neat carrying case and sold for £22 a set. The raw materials cost £8 a set and each set takes 20 minutes of turning by skilled operatives who are paid £9.00 an hour. The fixed costs of the business are £480,000 a year. This year, MPB plans to produce 80,000 sets.

Tasks:

1 Calculate:
   a) the variable cost of a set of boules;
   b) the absorption cost of a set of boules;
   c) the breakeven point;
   d) the profit or loss if 80,000 sets are sold.

2 A large French champagne house has asked MPB Ltd if it will produce 5,000 boule sets for a worldwide promotion. Each set has to be engraved with the French company's logo and the carrying case must bear its brand name. The extra work involved in this will cost £2.50 a set. It has offered to pay a total of £75,000 for the order. Should MPB accept this offer?

3 A Chinese company has proposed to MPB that it could manufacture the finished boule sets in China and supply them to MPB for £14 delivered. This price would apply to the first 50,000 sets, but after this it would reduce to £10 a set. MPB appreciates that this would change its function to trading only and it would be able to eliminate its manufacturing facilities, saving £180,000 a year.
   a) Advise MPB whether or not it should accept this proposition.
   b) List the points MPB should consider carefully before accepting this proposition.

Q6.6

BBQ Ltd manufactures two types of barbecue – the Deluxe BBQ and the Standard BBQ. Both undergo similar production processes and use similar materials and types of labour. However, a shortage of direct labour has been identified and this is limiting the company's ability to produce the required number of barbecues for the year ending 31 May 2002. Labour capacity is limited to 235,000 labour hours for the year ending 31 May 2002 and this is insufficient to meet total sales demand.

BBQ Ltd has stated that the standard selling price and standard prime cost for each barbecue for the forthcoming year are as follows:

	Deluxe BBQ	Standard BBQ
Selling price	£100	£50
Direct material	£50	£11
Direct labour (rate £5 per hour)	£25	£20
Estimated sales demand (units)	10,000	50,000

It has been company policy to absorb production overheads on a labour hour basis. The budgeted information for the year ending 31 May 2002 is as follows:

Fixed production overhead	£188,000
Variable production overhead	£2 per direct labour hour

Non-production costs for the year ending 31 May 2002 are estimated to be:

Selling and distribution overhead:
Variable	10% of selling price
Fixed	£35,000

Administrative overhead:
Fixed	£50,000

Required:

a) Calculate the production plan that will maximize profit for the year ending 31 May 2002.
(7 marks)

b) Based on the production plan that you have recommended in part (a), present a profit statement for the year ending 31 May 2002 in a marginal costing format.
(9 marks)

c) Discuss two problems that may arise as a result of your recommended production plan.
(4 marks)

d) Explain why the contribution concept is used in limiting factor decisions.
(5 marks)
(Total = 25 marks)

CIMA Foundation: Management Accounting Fundamentals, May 2001.

Review questions

1 Explain how to tell whether or not to cease certain activities.
2 Explain how to determine the order of production when one of the resources used is scarce.
3 Explain how to tell whether or not to accept one-off contracts.
4 Explain how to tell whether to produce or buy in components used in your products.
5 Discuss the limitations of decision making using variable costing.

The answers to all these questions can be found in the text of this chapter.

Short-term decisions using relevant costing

Introduction

Managers should take decisions that result in maximum benefit for the organization **as a whole**. This means taking into account **indirect** effects as well as the direct ones. Suppose that a lawn mower manufacturer decides to buy in a particular component, e.g. the motor, instead of making it, the justification being that the £15 purchase price of the motor is less than its £17 variable cost of manufacture. If the company uses 10,000 motors a year then the annual saving should be £20,000.

This looks like a good decision. But suppose that one indirect effect of this was to make five jobs redundant in the motor production section. If the average redundancy pay was £12,000, it would take three years before the total redundancy pay of £60,000 was covered by the savings made!

The point is that **all** the known quantifiable effects of a decision should be part of the analysis, not just the obvious ones. Relevant costing is particularly appropriate for managers as they are more likely to be aware of the indirect effects than the accountants. This applies even more so to the consideration of the qualitative factors involved. The voice of the manager should be paramount in these decisions.

Learning objectives

Having worked through this chapter you should be able to:

- describe relevant costing;
- distinguish between relevant and irrelevant costs;
- identify avoidable costs, opportunity costs, sunk costs, committed costs, non-cash costs and opportunity benefits;
- quantify the relevant cost of decisions;
- discuss the importance of qualitative factors;
- give good advice based on relevant costing.

Definition of relevant cost/revenue

Relevant costs/revenues have three criteria. They are **always**:

- **avoidable** – they are caused by a positive decision and would not happen if the decision was negative;
- **future** – costs/revenues that have already happened cannot be altered by a decision not yet taken;
- **cash** – the net change in cash (not profit) is used to measure the decision's effects.

All three criteria must be fulfilled. If only one or two criteria are met, the cost/revenue is not relevant.

The topic of 'relevant costing' is really about **relevant cash flows** (which would be a better title due to its descriptive nature). These relevant cash flows can be 'in' (revenues) or 'out' (costs).

Types of relevant cost

The two main types of relevant costs are *avoidable costs* and *opportunity costs*.

Avoidable costs

These will only be incurred if a certain course of action is followed, otherwise they will not occur. If a positive decision means that a new lorry will be purchased for £22,000 then a negative decision means that expenditure of £22,000 will be **avoided**.

Opportunity costs

These are a measure of the net cash **benefit** foregone from the next most desirable alternative course of action. Even though these do not appear on the profit and loss account, they are real and relevant for decision making.

For example, if some **scarce** specialized labour (like a high-level relational database programmer) is reassigned due to a positive decision, the opportunity cost will be the net cash benefit sacrificed due to the discontinuation of the programmer's current assignment. If there are plenty of these programmers in the organization, the opportunity cost will not arise as both projects can be performed at the same time.

Types of irrelevant cost

The three main types of irrelevant costs are sunk costs, committed costs and non-cash costs.

Sunk costs

These relate to the proposal under consideration but are incurred **prior** to the decision being made. A good example is the cost of market research undertaken to help make decisions about a new product. Sunk costs are also known as 'past costs'.

Committed costs

These are costs that have not been paid at the time of making the decision but a legal obligation exists to pay them at some time in the future; for example, lease payments of premises for the project under consideration if that lease is already in existence but the premises are currently unoccupied. As the lease payments must be made whether the decision is positive or negative, these costs are also called 'common costs'. (They are common to both the 'yes' and 'no' decision as to whether the project goes ahead or not.)

Non-cash costs

The most usual example of these is the depreciation charged in the profit and loss account. Depreciation is a legitimate cost; indeed the net profit figure would be incorrect if depreciation had not been deducted from gross profit together with the other overheads. However, depreciation does **not** cause any movement of cash and therefore cannot be a relevant cost.

**Example
7.1**

Relevant costing

Frank Jeffery Limited is a manufacturer of reproduction antique furniture. Three months ago it tendered for a one-off order from English Heritage to make a copy of a four-poster bed that was once slept in by Queen Elizabeth I. The cost of preparing this tender was estimated to be £250. The specification would use 5 cubic metres ('cubes') of English oak, a timber in regular use in the factory. Its current price is £400 a cube. There are three cubes in stock at the moment, which were bought in at £375 a cube.

Business is good and the factory is working at full capacity. To make the bed would need three skilled craftworkers for two weeks each. The company operates a 40-hour week and pays skilled craftworkers at the rate of £10 per hour. It is estimated that the normal work lost due to this order would produce a net cash contribution for the company totalling £3,000.

The machinery involved would depreciate by £400 in the two weeks and the cost of electricity to run the machines would be £80. The machines would be in continual use whether or not the tender was successful. Fixed production overheads are absorbed at the rate of £25 per direct labour hour.

One month ago, a new advanced type of hand-held router was purchased at the cost of £750 as it would be very useful if the bid was selected by English Heritage. (This was a bargain introductory offer for last month only; its price is now £899.) The company's policy is to write off in full hand tools costing less than £1,000 to the profit and loss account in the year of purchase.

What is the relevant cost to Frank Jeffery Limited of making the four-poster bed?

Solution

Item	Avoidable	Future	Cash	Note	Amount	Relevant
Tender preparation			X	1		–
English oak	X	X	X	2	5 cubes × £400	2,000
Craftworkers' pay		X	X	3		–
Cash contribution lost	X	X	X	4		3,000
Machine depreciation		X		5		–
Machine electricity		X	X	6		–
Fixed production overhead		X		7		–
New router			X	8		–
					Relevant cost	**£5,000**

Notes:
1 Sunk cost.
2 As oak is in regular use, 5 cubes will need to be replaced at the current price.
3 Craftworkers are assumed to be permanent employees paid on a time basis.
4 Opportunity cost of next-best alternative.
5 Depreciation is not a **cash** cost. It is a book entry not causing any cash to flow.
6 Common cost. The machines will be running irrespective of the tender.
7 Overhead absorption is a book entry. It does not change the overheads **incurred**.
8 Sunk cost.

Try the following question for yourself (answer at the end of the chapter).

Welgrow Ltd is a manufacturer of garden seed compost. At the moment, it makes six different types and is considering adding a new basic compost to its range. Initially, it will make a batch of 10,000 kg and has listed the following costs involved:

1 Exclusive use of the company's mixing machine will be needed for one week. The depreciation of this machine is included as a production overhead at £520 per year.
2 The trial batch will need 7,000 kg of vermiculite. Welgrow does not use this material and does not have any of it in stock at present; its market price is £1.00 per kg.
3 Several years ago Welgrow bought a large quantity of black sand at £0.10 per kg for a special project. A left-over surplus of 3,000 kg is currently in stock as it has proved impossible to resell. Welgrow has no alternative use for this surplus other than as an ingredient in the new compost.
4 To ensure successful marketing of this new product at the right time, a contract for advertising space with a total cost of £500 has been signed. A deposit of 20% has been paid and the balance is due one month before launch next spring.
5 An aluminium storage bin, which was due to have been offered for sale at the realistic price of £100, will be used for the new compost.

Consider each item and state why you think it is relevant or not. Calculate the relevant cost to Welgrow of the decision to go ahead. Also, calculate the breakeven selling price of the new compost.

Opportunity benefits

These benefits, or savings, may be created by taking a positive decision to go ahead with a project. For example, some redundancy costs which were about to be incurred may be avoided by going ahead.

The avoidance or prevention of a cash cost is equivalent to cash income.

Opportunity benefits are relevant to the decision and must be taken into account.

Relevant cost of materials

The relevant cost of a material is not what it cost to buy it in the first place, i.e. a sunk or committed cost. If a material is in regular use, its relevant cost is its **replacement** cost. This is the **future, avoidable, cash flow** caused by the decision to use it.

But if the material was already owned and would not be replaced if used (i.e. it was not in regular use) its relevant cost is the **greater** of:

a) its current realizable value (i.e. the amount received from selling it); and
b) the value obtained from alternative uses.

You should recognize this as its opportunity cost.

Relevant cost of materials

Example 7.2

Birch Brothers is a low-volume, high-specification bicycle manufacturer based in South Yorkshire. It has been requested to quote for producing a special pedal-powered vehicle for promoting bicycle use in the UK. The vehicle has four pedalling positions at the front and four at the rear. In between these is a three-dimensional platform structure for advertising the various benefits of cycling. It is approximately the size of a small lorry.

Birch Brothers is currently short of work and is operating at well below its maximum capacity. Unfounded rumours of possible redundancies are circulating among the 20-strong workforce and morale is not good. No additional labour or overtime would be needed to build this 'promotional platform'. This order would provide some very welcome work for the business.

However, the contract would need the following materials:

a) New materials not normally used, e.g. a trailer chassis for the central advertising platform. These would total £5,000.
b) Materials currently in regular use and in stock, e.g. wheels, pedals, etc. These have a book value of £1,780 but would cost £2,000 to buy now.
c) 80 metres of stainless steel tube: Birch Brothers has 60 metres of this disused item in stock left over from a discontinued model. This stock has a resale value of £500 but it is planned to use it all for an export order commencing in four months' time in place of a very similar specification tube which would cost £12.50 a metre. The current price of stainless steel tube is £20 a metre.
d) 95 square metres of aluminium sheet: it has just this amount in stock. It was left over from the manufacture of a batch of bike-trailers, a product that was unsuccessful for the company. Birch Brothers has tried reselling these sheets but not a single buyer was found. The sheeting is taking up a lot of workshop space and it was decided last week to pay £200 to have it removed in the near future.
e) 8 sets of brakes: the company has 20 sets of old-fashioned brakes that are perfectly functional although there is no demand for them. The original cost of these was £12 a set. Whatever is left of this stock item will be thrown in the bin at the financial year-end stocktake.

Solution

Item	Avoidable	Future	Cash	Note	Amount	Relevant
a) New materials	X	X	X	1	£5,000	5,000
b) Regular materials	X	X	X	2	£2,000	2,000
c) 60 m st. steel tube	X	X	X	3	60 m × £12.50	750
d) 20 m st. steel tube	X	X	X	4	20 m × £20	400
e) Aluminium sheet	X	X	X	5	£200	(200)
f) Old-fashioned brakes				6	–	
					Relevant cost	£7,950

Notes:
1　At current buying-in market price (= replacement cost).
2　At replacement cost.
3　First 60 metres at opportunity cost (= cost saved by use for export order).
4　Next 20 metres need to be bought in (at current replacement price).
5　This is an opportunity **benefit**. By using the sheeting, the company is saving the cost of its disposal.
6　No cash flows of any sort are caused by using these brakes.

Note also that there are no relevant labour costs. The labour force would be paid whether the contract is obtained or not. This is a common cost.

Self-assessment question S7.2

Try the following question for yourself (answer at the end of the chapter).

Tilly Ltd has been approached by a customer who wants a special job done and is willing to pay £20,000 for it. The job would require the following materials:

Material	Total units required	Units in stock	Book value of units in stock (£/unit)	Realizable value (£/unit)	Replacement cost (£/unit)
A	1,000	0	–	–	6
B	1,000	600	2	2.5	5
C	1,000	700	3	2.5	4
D	200	200	4	6	9
E	500	500	5	–	–

Material B is regularly used by Tilly Ltd in the manufacture of its standard products.
　Materials C and D are specialist materials, in stock due to previous overbuying. No other use can be found for material C. However, the stock of material D could be used in another job as a substitute for 300 units of material M. Tilly has no stock of material M at present but it can be purchased locally at £5 a unit.

Since the stock of material E was acquired, its sale has been banned by the government (although previously acquired stocks are allowed to be used up). It is a toxic chemical and Tilly is expecting to pay £500 in the near future for its safe disposal as it has no other use for it.

Task:

To help Tilly Ltd decide whether or not to accept the job, calculate the relevant cost of materials needed.

Qualitative factors

Although relevant costing is a numerical or quantitative analysis technique, only a poor manager would ignore the non-numerical or qualitative factors involved in a decision. These are just as important, if not more so, and should be given serious consideration before the decision is made.

Take the case of an advertising agency that currently handles the Mars UK account being offered the chance to pitch for the business of Cadbury's Chocolate. Before doing so, it should think very carefully about the reaction of Mars UK to its acting for a major competitor. Would Mars UK see it as a conflict of interests and take its business elsewhere?

Although no **definite** numerical answers are attainable in such cases, organizations should be aware of the possible risks involved and act accordingly.

Limitations of decision making using relevant costing

The context of relevant costing is broader than that of variable costing (discussed in the previous chapter). This lack of artificial boundaries makes it much more realistic. It also makes it more useful, as decisions usually have indirect consequences which should be included in the decision-making process. The main limitation of relevant costing is the difficulty in foreseeing all the indirect consequences arising from the decision in question.

Take the example used in the 'Limitations' section of the previous chapter on variable costing. This described the decision, based on an analysis of product contributions, to cease manufacturing one of several products. The indirect consequence of multiple redundancies and associated payments occurring had been foreseen and taken into account in the cessation decision. However, it may be that the dropping of that particular product would enhance the market's perception of the company as the product was considered to be outmoded and unattractive. Cessation may improve the 'positioning' of the company in the eyes of its customers and sales may increase accordingly. This particular indirect effect is much more difficult to foresee than the ensuing redundancies but its consequences are just as real.

This emphasizes the point that making decisions is essentially a management, rather than an accounting, function. The role of accountancy is to provide good information to assist managers make the right decisions. But the manager always has a limited time frame in which to make the decision. During that short time, it is impossible to foresee **all** the consequences of the decision. Even when you have made the best decision you possibly could, events may yet overtake you. Being aware of this will make you a wiser and better manager.

The manager's point of view (written by Nigel Burton)

Business decisions need to be taken in the round, giving thought to all the relevant factors and potential consequences of any actions taken. The decisions based on variable costing, as discussed in Chapter 6, would in practice never be taken on the arithmetic alone, but on their total impact on the business. While some of this will be quantifiable, much of it will not, and will require the input of judgement, inspiration and informed guesswork. Nevertheless, the starting point for most decisions remains the arithmetic. The way in which the quantifiable factors are handled in practice is perhaps best illustrated by the Capital Investment Appraisal procedures adopted by our company.

In every capital investment decision, the fundamental issue is: What is the total impact on my business of making this investment? To answer this question from a financial standpoint, we have to compare the consequences of making the investment with the consequences of not making it. Our capital appraisal model required a 'Before Case', which consisted of a 10-year income statement showing the results which would be expected if no capital investment was made, and an 'After Case', which showed the forecast position after the investment had been made. The 'Before Case' might, for example, see a flat sales line due to capacity constraints, or perhaps a declining sales line if perseverance with the old plant results in increased downtime for maintenance. Perhaps the old plant has been condemned for environmental reasons, so without the investment sales will be reduced to nil, and redundancies will ensue. All the costs and quantifiable implications of refusing the investment are considered here, including committed costs and opportunity costs, the latter being opportunities which would have been seized but for the project.

The 'After Case', on the other hand, might reflect continued sales growth arising from increased capacity, or reduced marginal costs due to more process automation, larger batch sizes or higher yields. Also shown here are the expected fixed overheads following the investment, including any changes to areas such as selling and administration. In producing these two sets of figures, the principles of relevant costing are regularly utilized. Is a particular cost directly attributable to the project, or would we have incurred it anyway? Many costs will be incurred regardless of the project, and therefore will appear in both cases.

Then, by deducting the 'Before Case' numbers from the 'After Case' numbers, we arrive at the 'Incremental Case'. This represents exactly the expected impact of the initial investment on each line of the income statement for each of the next 10 years, i.e. the net increase in sales, the net reduction in marginal costs, the additional selling expenses, and so on. From this basic data, we can calculate both the rate of return and the number of years needed to pay back the initial investment, two of the key indicators used by management to assess the viability of the project.

This Capital Investment Appraisal procedure neatly captures and displays the quantifiable elements of an investment decision. These elements may tell a good financial story, but it may well be non-quantifiable issues which cause management ultimately to approve or reject the investment proposal. Another example from my chemical business illustrates the kinds of issues which may have an influence on the decision.

One of our products had been used for many years by both the petroleum and plastics industries. It had always been profitable, not least because none of our competitors had quite managed to duplicate it, despite the fact that the patents had expired many years previously. Cheaper, but inferior, alternatives had become available on the market, but our business maintained its competitive edge.

The plant, and the technology on which it was based, was some 40 years old. Over the years, there had been many repairs and part replacements, but eventually the time came when a number of considerations, among them environmental concerns, brought us to the point when substantial changes were necessary. Failure to improve the environmental performance was ultimately likely to result in the plant's closure, although the timescales involved in this were indeterminate. We were also aware that the demand for the product from the petroleum companies might decline at some stage in the future as alternative technologies became available, although sales to the plastics industry were likely to continue. The timing of any decline was again largely a matter of guesswork.

Our options were: (a) to do nothing, and subcontract manufacturing when the plant was closed; (b) to patch up the plant once again, with a view to temporarily satisfying the environmental concerns, until such time as the petroleum business died a natural death, then sub-contract; or (c) to build a new plant, incorporating state-of-the-art technology. The financial implications of each of these scenarios were reasonably easy to establish. The 'Before Case' represented option (a), and included the costs of closing down and decommissioning the plant, as well as the redundancy costs of surplus staff. It also reflected the additional cost of buying in the material from a sub-contractor, for which role the most likely candidates were in India and China. Our first 'After Case' scenario (option (b)) was clearly the cheapest, but would provide us with only a short-term solution to our environmental problems. If the petroleum business did not decline within five years, a further patching-up project would almost certainly be required. Moreover, if the product turned out to have a much longer life than we anticipated, we might end up putting up a new plant anyway. Our second 'After Case' scenario (option (c)) was a high-cost, high-risk strategy, because if the petroleum demand turned out to be short term, we could find ourselves left with a relatively new but largely redundant plant. It would, however, solve all our environmental issues at a stroke.

Interestingly, neither of the capital investment scenarios (options (b) and (c)) produced a satisfactory 'Incremental Case' when compared against option (a). This was not because either of the proposals themselves were non-viable, but because the cost of contracting out manufacture turned out, rather unexpectedly, to be much less than expected. The additional cost of buying in from a sub-contractor was substantially offset by overhead and labour savings, so a satisfactory level of profitability could more or less be maintained without any capital investment. The financial advantages offered by the two 'After Case' scenarios were therefore relatively small, and did not appear to justify the capital outlays. The financial arguments clearly pointed towards sub-contracting as a solution to our plant problem, but here the non-quantifiable aspects came into play. Did we really want to divulge our company secrets to a third party? Could we trust any confidentiality agreement signed by the sub-contractor? Was it worth the risk? After all, the product might yet have many years of life left with the petroleum industry and would anyway still be in demand from the plastics companies.

So we had to balance the risks of losing control of our know-how, and then possibly finding our business under threat from our own product coming in cheaply from the East, against the possibility of a white elephant of a plant if the petroleum companies converted in the near future. After much deliberation, we decided to carry out the full plant renewal (option (c)). Our 'Before Case' was changed to reflect our new assumption that we would lose business to the Eastern threat, and on this basis the figures showed an acceptable return and payback period. Now, several years later, the petroleum companies are still using the product, the capital outlay has already been paid back and the environmental problems are a thing of the past. There is still talk that the petroleum companies may soon discontinue their use of the product, but the new plant has already justified its existence.

So our gamble has paid off, but we hit upon the right solution not because we followed the direction pointed out by the financial information, but because we took our decision in the light of wider business considerations. The financials, however, built up on relevant costing principles, provided an essential basis for further decision making. Sound financials, plus informed judgement, experience, and a little bit of luck, can minimize risk, and bring you to the correct conclusion.

Summary

- Relevant costing is a financial model to aid managers with decision making.
- Its objective is to maximize future net cash inflows to the business.
- It considers the indirect, as well as direct, effects of decisions.
- Its method is to identify the relevant costs and benefits **caused by** the decision.
- Relevant costs are avoidable **and** future **and** cash.
- The two types of relevant cost are *avoidable* and *opportunity* costs.
- The three types of irrelevant cost are *sunk, committed* and *non-cash* costs.
- Opportunity benefits must be taken into account.
- Qualitative factors are important and should be seriously considered.
- Relevant costing is more realistic than variable costing but it is not perfect.

Further reading

Balakrishnan, R. and Sivaramakrishnan, K. (2002) 'A critical overview of the use of full-cost data for planning and pricing', *Journal of Management Accounting Research*, Vol. 14, 3–31.

Drury, C. (2004) *Management and Cost Accounting*, 6th edition, Thomson Learning, London. See chapter 'Measuring relevant costs and revenues for decision making'.

Horngren, C., Bhimani, A., Datar, S. and Foster, G. (2002) *Management and Cost Accounting*, 2nd edition, Prentice Hall Europe, Harlow. See chapter 'Revenues, costs and the decision process'.

Upchurch, A. (2003) *Management Accounting, Principles and Practice*, 2nd edition, Financial Times/Prentice Hall, Harlow. See chapter 'Relevant costs and benefits for decision making'.

Answers to self-assessment questions

S7.1 Welgrow Ltd

Item	Avoidable	Future	Cash	Note	Amount	Relevant
1 Mixing machine		X		1		–
2 Vermiculite	X	X	X	2	7,000 @ £1	7,000
3 Black sand				3		–
4 Advertising space			X	4		–
5 Storage bin	X	X	X	5		100
					Relevant cost	**£7,100**

Notes:
1 Depreciation is a non-cash expense.
2 Vermiculite needs to be bought in at replacement cost.
3 Sunk cost with no alternative use.
4 The 20% deposit is sunk and the 80% remainder is committed.
5 Opportunity cost.

For the batch of 10,000 kg, the breakeven selling price is **£0.71 per kg**.

S7.2 Tilly Ltd

Item	Avoidable	Future	Cash	Note	Amount	Relevant
Material A	X	X	X	1	1,000 × £6	6,000
Material B	X	X	X	2	1,000 × £5	5,000
Material C	X	X	X	3	700 × £2.50	1,750
Material C	X	X	X	4	300 × £4	1,200
Material D (200 units)	X	X	X	5	300 × £5	1,500
Material E	X	X	X	6	£500	(500)
					Relevant cost	**£14,950**

Notes:
1 All 1,000 units need buying in at replacement cost.
2 600 units from stock need replacing and 400 need buying at replacement cost.
3 Opportunity cost = resale value.
4 Remaining 300 units bought in at replacement cost.
5 Opportunity cost is greatest of resale value of £1,200 (200 × 6) and saving the purchase of 300 units of M, £1,500 (300 × £5).
6 Opportunity **benefit**: using the stock of E in production avoids disposal costs of £500.

Roverco plc manufactures and markets a house-cleaning robot. At present, it is in the middle of a project to develop a voice-controlled robot from a laboratory prototype. The prototype was built from a patent which the company acquired for £50,000. The inventor agreed to accept payment in five equal instalments, three of which have now been paid.

At a recent board meeting, it was revealed that sales of Roverco's standard product had taken an unforeseen downturn and that this would have a knock-on effect on profitability and liquidity. This situation is partly due to increased competition from Housemouse Ltd, a dynamic new entrant to the market which specializes in the application of the very latest technology to its products. Also, Roverco's two long-established rivals, Cleanbot plc and Nomess plc, have been competing on price for the last year or so. Roverco decided against joining in the price war, hoping that it would soon be over. However, the market has responded positively to the price reductions, with increased orders going to Cleanbot and Nomess, causing Roverco to lose market share.

During the meeting, there was a heated discussion concerning the voice-controlled robot project. The project manager presented a financial statement (shown below) and reported that progress was slower than expected due to snags with the voice-recognition system. In connection with this, he recommends that a specialist electronic engineer be employed for the duration of the project, which he estimates will now continue for the next 18 months. The salary would be £28,000 p.a. on a fixed-term contract basis. Without this additional appointment, it is very doubtful that the project will be completed.

Project manager's financial statement

		£
Costs to date		42,000
Estimated costs for completion of project:		
Final payment for patent	20,000	
Gross salaries of two development engineers	75,000	
Gross salary of new engineer	42,000	
Materials and equipment (including M4411)	19,000	
Overheads	65,000	
		221,000
Total cost of project		263,000
Budgeted cost of project		218,000
Requested increase in budget		45,000

Following this, the finance director shocked the meeting into silence by proposing that the project be abandoned. She justified this course of action by pointing out that Roverco's share price had been falling slowly but steadily for the last three months and that in her regular meeting with share analysts from the big City firms, scheduled for next month, she feels it would be wise to issue a profits warning. The effect of this would be a steeper fall in the share price which, in turn, would make the company more vulnerable to a takeover bid. However, to avoid this, she believes the downward profit trend can be quickly reversed by abandoning the voice-controlled project and putting the savings of £191,000 into price cuts on the existing product range.

The chairman is not sure what to do. He postpones the discussion for one week and asks you for advice. You ascertain the following information:

1 Market research costing £35,000 was commissioned for the project. This predicted that the optimum price/volume relationship was a selling price of £999, creating sales of 6,000 robots a year. The product life cycle was estimated as four years, at which point a major redesign would be needed to remain competitive.

2 Roverco's accountant has estimated that the new production facility fixed assets for the voice-controlled robot will cost £900,000 and will have a resale value of £400,000 after four years. Other fixed overhead costs of £340,000 p.a. will be incurred; these are caused solely by this product and include depreciation of £90,000 p.a. for the production facility. The variable cost of producing each robot will be £917.

3 A special miniature hydraulic mechanism will be used in the robot's production. Roverco has a stock of 9,000 of these left over from a previous product. They were originally bought at a 'bargain price' of £9 each (the current market price is £15 which is included in the £917 total variable cost). They could probably be sold as a job lot for £45,000. Roverco has no other use for these items.

4 If the project is abandoned, two development engineers will have to be made redundant at a cost to Roverco of £18,000 each.

5 Some specialized voice-control testing equipment could be sold for £8,500 in its present condition, or for £2,500 at the end of the project. The rest of the equipment has no resale value.

6 A £6,000 order (order no. M4411) for bespoke electronic components was placed last month for delivery in two months' time; three months' credit is normally allowed by the supplier. A legal contract was signed for this order which Roverco is not able to cancel.

7 The project overheads of £65,000 include £15,000 for depreciation of the buildings used for product development and a general administration charge of £3,000 (nominally for services from the rest of the company). They also include £17,000 as a proportion of the project manager's pay.

Task:

Identify the relevant cash flows and advise the chairman whether, on purely financial grounds, the project should continue or be abandoned. Support your calculations with clear statements as to why particular items have been included or excluded and state any assumptions that you make.

Questions

An asterisk * on a question number indicates that the answer is given at the end of the book. Answers to the other questions are given in the Lecturer's Guide.

Q7.1* Burton Brothers

Burton Brothers manufactures machine tools for metal-based industries. One of its customers, Wey Ltd, has placed a £590,000 order for a machine, including £10,000 for delivery and installation. Wey paid a deposit of £180,000 and has since paid instalments totalling £150,000. Unfortunately, Burton Brothers has received a letter from a solicitor informing it that Wey Ltd has gone into liquidation and is unlikely to be able to pay any of its debts. This project has incurred the following costs to date:

	£
Engineering design	70,000
Materials	129,000
Direct labour (760 hours @ £10/h)	7,600
Production overheads (760 hours @ £88/dlh)	66,880
	273,480

The production overheads are all fixed costs and it is company policy to absorb them on the basis of direct labour hours (dlh).

Another customer, Bridge & Co., has expressed an interest in the machine, provided some additions are made to the specification, and is willing to pay a price of £400,000. To complete the machine to the original specification, it is estimated that a further 2,000 direct labour hours (at £10/hour) and a further £204,000 of materials will be needed. Contracts for £24,000 of these materials have already been signed but no money has yet been paid. The contract provides for a cancellation fee of £6,000 provided cancellation is confirmed in the next 11 days. These materials are components made especially to order for this machine and have no other use or value. The rest of the materials are in regular use by Burton Brothers. Twenty-five per cent of the £204,000 of materials are currently in the stores.

The additions requested by Bridge & Co. will need a further £45,000 of materials and 400 hours of direct labour. Some of these additional materials, which have an estimated purchase price of £13,500, could be replaced by similar material currently in the stores. This was left over from a previous contract and has no other use. It originally cost £9,500, which is its current stock valuation, but if it were to be sold on the open market it would fetch £12,000.

Burton Brothers is itself in a precarious position as it has no new orders on its books. If this job is abandoned, its direct workforce will be put on standby, which means they will be sent home and paid a rate of £4 an hour to retain their services. However, if this were to happen, the directors believe that some of these skilled workers would find permanent work elsewhere and would leave the company.

If no customer is found for the machine, it will be sent for scrap; this is expected to produce £6,000 income.

Task:

Burton Brothers is unsure whether or not to accept the offer from Bridge & Co. Consider each of the above items and advise the company accordingly.

Q7.2* Eezikum

Eezikum is a duo of rap artists currently touring the UK. They still have 11 venues remaining when they are asked to fill in at short notice on a tour of the USA, starting in two days' time. They will be the first act on stage to warm up the audience in preparation for the big American star whose tour it is. They know that this could establish them in the lucrative North American market but are not sure of the financial implications. There is a cancellation fee of £10,000 for each abandoned concert. Each time they perform in the UK they are paid a fee of £15,000 and their out-of-pocket expenses amount to £2,500. At present, they have no future work commitments once the UK tour is over.

If they join the tour of the USA, they will need to buy new equipment compatible with the US electricity supply and safety standards. The cost of this is estimated at £100,000 but it could be sold for £40,000 at the end of the nine-month tour, on their return to the UK. The money is not a problem as they currently have more than £1 million in a deposit account earning interest of 12% a year.

The US tour consists of 125 performances, each paying fees of £10,000 and having associated out-of-pocket expenses of £2,000. The airfare for the whole entourage, including a considerable amount of luggage, is £14,500 each way. Additional health insurance will cost £6,000 for the duration of the tour. Travel insurance is £9,000 (three-quarters of their existing annual worldwide policy, which carries a premium of £12,000).

Task:

Calculate the relevant benefit/cost of accepting the US tour.

Q7.3* Carbotest Corporation

Carbotest Corporation manufactures equipment to test for the presence of carbon monoxide in confined spaces. It has just been offered a contract to build some specialized monitoring equipment to test for the presence of carbon dioxide in the freight containers of lorries and railway wagons. The contract offers to pay £152,000 for 1,000 sets of testing equipment, which must be delivered in six months' time. Carbotest has looked into this opportunity and has produced the following information.

Materials

The contract will need 40,000 components which Carbotest does not currently use; these cost £3 each. However, it could use up old stock of 5,000 components that it recently tried to sell without success. But £1 will need to be spent on each of them to make them into suitable replacements for 5,000 of the 40,000 components needed. This old stock originally cost £20,000 but now has a scrap value of only £1,000. Each testing set also needs a carrying harness identical to those used for the carbon monoxide testing equipment. Carbotest has 600 of these currently in stock, valued at their cost price of £8 each. The suppliers of this harness have just increased their price to £9, which Carbotest will have to pay for future orders.

Labour

The contract will use five skilled operatives full time for six months. These operatives are paid £1,400 a month gross and are presently employed on the carbon-monoxide-testing production. They will have to be redeployed from this work to the new contract. Their combined output for the six-month period is estimated to have a sales revenue of £60,000, a variable cost of £48,000 and to absorb £8,000 of fixed overheads. It is thought that one of the factory supervisors (currently with a light workload) could manage the project for 50% of his time. His annual gross pay is £24,000. Carbotest is working at full capacity and has enough orders to keep it busy for 15 months.

Machinery

Three years ago, Carbotest bought a machine for a similar project, which had to be abandoned after two years. It cost £25,000 and was estimated to have a useful life of five years, with a zero residual value. (Carbotest uses the straight-line method of depreciation for all its fixed assets.) The machine has been 'mothballed' for the last 12 months and has been stored out of the way. Carbotest was just about to advertise it for sale at the very reasonable price of £5,000. It is thought that this intensive contract will effectively wear it out. To meet the six-month deadline, Carbotest plans to lease an identical machine for six months at a cost of £500 a month.

Accommodation

Employees have to park their cars on the road outside the factory. As the company is located in a busy area, this is often difficult, with cars having to be parked some distance away. Carbotest is just about to convert a rough piece of land in one corner of its site into an employees' car park. It hired a professional firm of surveyors to obtain planning permission for this and their invoice for £2,200 has recently been received but not yet paid. The cost of building the car park is £28,000. But if the contract is accepted, this land will have to be used for a temporary building to house the necessary machinery. The construction of this building will cost £8,000 and when the contract is completed, it will be demolished at a cost of £2,000. The car park will then go ahead.

Fixed overheads

Carbotest's absorption costing system attaches fixed overheads to production on a machine hour basis. The contract is expected to absorb £10,000 of fixed overhead.

Tasks:

State whether each of the above items is relevant or irrelevant to Carbotest's acceptance of the contract and explain your reasoning. Advise it whether or not to accept the contract. Discuss any other factors the company should take into consideration when making this decision.

Q7.4 Murray Polls

Murray Polls Limited recently contracted to conduct an opinion poll concerning global warming and its causes. Its costing for this job is shown below:

		£
Planning	100 hours @ £12	1,200
Questioning	800 hours @ £7	5,600
Travel and subsistence		4,800
Telephone	30,000 minutes @ £0.02/min	600
Analysis of results & report	60 hours @ £12	720
Fixed overheads	800 hours @ £25	20,000
Total cost		32,920
Profit @ 20% mark-up		6,584
Price to client		£39,504

(Overheads are absorbed on the basis of questioning hours.)

The client paid a deposit of £5,000 and contracted to pay the remainder within one month of receiving the report. Unfortunately, Murray has just been informed that its client has gone into liquidation and is not expected to be able to meet any of its debts.

At this point, Murray has completed all the planning and 75% of the questioning; travel and subsistence so far total £3,700 and 50% of the telephoning has been completed. No analysis has yet been done. If the poll is abandoned, two of the ten researchers involved will have to be paid a cancellation fee of £200 each.

The managing director of Murray immediately suspends all work on the contract and decides to attend an international conference on the environment, taking place in Stockholm next week. He is hopeful of finding another client for this project as he will be able to offer the completed poll and report at a greatly reduced price. His airfares, hotel bills and out-of-pocket expenses for the five-day Stockholm trip are expected to be £2,200. His rate of pay works out at £400 a day.

Task:

Calculate the lowest price the managing director can quote without making his firm worse off and advise him accordingly. State your reasons for including or excluding the above factors in your calculation.

Q7.5 Eldave Advertising Agency

The Eldave Advertising Agency has been working on a campaign for Greenpoint Leisure Limited for the last four months. The campaign is for Greenpoint's eco-friendly holidays in South America and uses both TV and Sunday-paper magazines. The adverts have almost been completed and the campaign launch date is in six weeks' time. The estimated cost of completion is £2,400 (two people @ £400/week for three weeks). Greenpoint has signed a contract to pay Eldave £50,000 (for advert production) plus media space at cost.

Eldave has just received a letter from a firm of solicitors stating that Greenpoint has ceased trading with immediate effect and that its creditors are unlikely to receive any of the money they are owed. Fortunately, Eldave has received a non-returnable deposit of £25,000 (50% of the production fee) from Greenpoint but a summary of its account reveals an overall balance owing of £61,000 for work to date. This includes a general fixed overheads charge of £6,000 apportioned on the basis of total direct cost.

In order to minimize Eldave's losses, Eloise Thompson, the partner in charge of the Greenpoint account, has contacted three other travel firms specializing in the South American market. She has shown them the adverts and tried to persuade them to take over the work-in-progress for the special price of £25,000. One of these three, Trek Hols Limited, has offered £12,000 for the appropriately modified and completed adverts on condition that the campaign starts in two weeks' time.

Eldave has provisionally booked advertising space for eight consecutive weeks starting in six weeks' time. The cost of this is £30,000 a week, for which it has paid £12,000 (a 5% non-returnable deposit included in the £61,000). It has also booked a one-quarter-page colour space in the *Independent on Sunday* magazine for the same eight weeks. Each of these spaces costs £9,000 but, although a contract has been signed, no money has yet been paid (not included in the £61,000). The contract allows for a 50% reduction if cancellation occurs less than four weeks before publication. This reduction increases to 75% if cancellation occurs more than four weeks before publication. Although Trek Hols is happy to take over Greenpoint's media slots, it also wants the same weekly coverage for the four weeks immediately prior to the original launch date. Trek Hols insists the campaign must start in two weeks' time and agrees to pay for all the media space in full, at cost.

In order to complete the adverts for launch in two weeks' time, Eldave will have to redeploy two of its employees (gross pay £400 a week each) for one and a half weeks, at the end of which the adverts will be delivered to the media. As a result of this, the job these two are currently doing will be one and a half weeks late and Eldave will incur a financial penalty of '£1,000 a week or part-week'.

Tasks:

Identify the **relevant costs and income** and advise Eldave as to whether it should accept Trek Hols' offer. Your calculations must clearly show the reasons why each of the above items has been included or excluded. State any assumptions that you make.

Q7.6 MOV plc

MOV plc produces custom-built sensors. Each sensor has a standard circuit board (SCB) in it. The current average contribution from a sensor is £400. MOV plc's business is steadily expanding and in the year just ending (2001/2002), the company will have produced 55,000 sensors. The demand for MOV plc's sensors is predicted to grow over the next 3 years:

Year	Units
2002/03	58,000
2003/04	62,000
2004/05	65,000

The production of sensors is limited by the number of SCBs the company can produce. The present production level of 55,000 SCBs is the maximum that can be produced without overtime working. Overtime could increase annual output to 60,500, allowing production of sensors to also increase to 60,500. However, the variable cost of SCBs produced in overtime would increase by £75 per unit.

Because of the pressure on capacity, the company is considering having the SCBs manufactured by another company, CIR plc. This company is very reliable and produces products of good quality. CIR plc has quoted a price of £116 per SCB, for orders greater than 50,000 units a year.

MOV plc's own costs per SCB are predicted to be:

	£	
Direct material	28	
Direct labour	40	
Variable overhead	20	(based on labour cost)
Fixed overhead	24	(based on labour cost and output of 55,000 units)
Total cost	112	

The fixed overheads directly attributable to SCBs are £250,000 a year; these costs will be avoided if SCBs are not produced. If more than 59,000 units are produced, SCBs' fixed overheads will increase by £130,000.

In addition to the above overheads, MOV plc's fixed overheads are predicted to be:

Sensor production in units:	54,001 to 59,000	59,001 to 64,000	64,001 to 70,000
Fixed overhead:	£2,600,000	£2,900,000	£3,100,000

MOV plc currently holds a stock of 3,500 SCBs but the production manager feels that a stock of 8,000 should be held if they are bought in; this would increase stockholding costs by £10,000 a year. A purchasing officer, who is paid £20,000 a year, spends 50% of her time on SCB duties. If the SCBs are bought in, a liaison officer will have to be employed at a salary of £30,000 in order to liaise with CIR plc and monitor the quality and supply of SCBs. At present, 88 staff are involved in the production of SCBs at an average salary of £25,000 a year: if the SCBs were purchased, 72 of these staff would be made redundant at an average cost of £4,000 per employee.

The SCB department, which occupies an area of 240 × 120 square metres at the far end of the factory, could be rented out, at a rent of £45 per square metre a year. However, if the SCBs were to be bought in, for the first year only MOV plc would need the space to store the increased stock caused by outsourcing, until the main stockroom had been reorganized and refurbished. From 2003/04, the space could be rented out; this would limit the annual production of sensors to 60,500 units. Alternatively the space could be used for the production of sensors, allowing annual output to increase to 70,000 units if required.

Required:

a) Critically discuss the validity of the following statement. It was produced by Jim Elliot, the company's accountant, to show the gain for the coming year (2002/03) if the SCBs were to be bought in.

Saving in:	£
Manufacturing staff – salaries saved: 72 staff × £25,000	1,800,000
Purchasing officer – time saved	10,000
Placing orders for SCB materials: 1,000 orders × £20 per order	20,000
Transport costs for raw materials for SCBs	45,000
Cost saved	1,875,000
Additional cost per SCB: (£116 – £112) × 58,000 units	232,000
Net gain if SCBs purchased	1,643,000

(10 marks)

b) i) Produce detailed calculations that show which course of action is the best financial option for the three years under consideration. (Ignore the time value of money.)

(12 marks)

ii) Advise the company of the long-term advantages and disadvantages of buying in SCBs.

(3 marks)

(Total = 25 marks)

CIMA Intermediate: Management Accounting – Decision Making, May 2002

Review questions

1 Describe relevant costing.
2 Distinguish between relevant and irrelevant costs.
3 Explain the terms: avoidable costs, opportunity costs, sunk costs, committed costs, non-cash costs and opportunity benefits.
4 Discuss the importance of qualitative factors.

The answers to all these questions can be found in the text of this chapter.

CHAPTER 8

Capital investment appraisal for long-term decisions

Chapter contents

Introduction

Imagine that you are a director of a large business which urgently needs to replace one of its large old machines. Preliminary investigation has narrowed down your choice to two alternatives.

The first machine costs £3.2 million, is guaranteed for three years, is four times as productive as the present machine and can be sold back to its supplier for £0.5 million after five years. The second machine costs £2.5 million, is guaranteed for one year, is three times as productive as the present machine and cannot be sold back to its supplier. How do you decide which machine is the best one to buy?

Capital investment appraisal is the decision-making process used by businesses to decide which fixed assets to purchase. Vehicles, machines and buildings can be very expensive so it is important to make the best decision possible from the information available at the time.

Correcting a bad capital investment decision can be very costly. Consider a company that has a choice between buying a large piece of plant from either Atlas Ltd or Tyrell & Co. If it spends £3.2 million on an Atlas machine and three months later finds out it would have been better to buy a Tyrell machine, correcting this decision will entail significant extra costs. For a start, the Atlas machine will now be second-hand and will have lost value. There may not be a ready market for this type of machine and the price will have to be reduced further to sell it. Also, there is the cost of uninstalling and removing it. And how about the lost production caused by this change?

Because of the importance of these long-term decisions, managers normally seek help from their management accountants. Over the years several methods for determining the best choice have been established. This chapter looks at the four most popular of these (see Figure 8.1). Note that one uses profits but all the others use cash flows.

For each of these methods it is necessary to **estimate** future profits or cash flows arising from the new investments. However, when we do this, we usually get it wrong. The quality of the investment decision will depend on the quality of these estimates. You may think it is not worth bothering if the answers will probably involve such significant errors but the alternative is to make these decisions by tossing a coin. It is better to attempt some analysis than none at all. Often, the objective is to choose between alternative fixed assets. As the same assumptions are made for each alternative, the results become more valid.

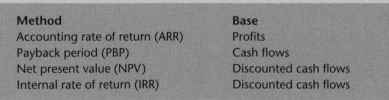

Method	Base
Accounting rate of return (ARR)	Profits
Payback period (PBP)	Cash flows
Net present value (NPV)	Discounted cash flows
Internal rate of return (IRR)	Discounted cash flows

Figure 8.1 **Summary of capital investment appraisal methods**

Having worked through this chapter you should be able to:

- calculate the accounting rate of return (ARR);
- convert profits to cash flows;
- justify the exclusion of working capital from cash flows;
- reconcile cash flows with profits over the lifetime of a project;
- calculate the payback period (PBP);
- discount future cash flows to today's values;
- calculate the net present value (NPV);
- calculate the internal rate of return (IRR);
- discuss the limitations of the four methods;
- compare NPV with IRR;
- criticize the discounted payback approach;
- discuss the choice of available methods;
- appreciate the usefulness of sensitivity analysis in managing risk;
- explain why the financing decision is excluded from the investment decision;
- discuss the importance of relevant qualitative factors.

Method 1: accounting rate of return (ARR)

The ARR attempts to express the return on the investment as an annual percentage of the cost of that investment. This is similar to comparing interest-bearing bank and building society accounts with each other when deciding where to invest your money. Businesses using this method usually set a minimum threshold rate which must be equalled or exceeded by the ARR. For example, a company may be earning an average of 18% a year from all its current activities. It may use this as a threshold or target rate for any new investments. If the calculations for a possible new investment showed its ARR to be only 15%, the investment would not go ahead. This is because, if it were adopted, it would **reduce** the 18% currently achieved by the company as a whole. On the other hand, if the potential ARR was 20%, the investment would be considered further.

If Maniff plc (threshold ARR = 24%) had to choose between machines M1 (ARR = 29%), M2 (ARR = 22%) and M3 (ARR = 33%), it would disregard M2 and further consider M1 and M3. If ARR was the only technique it used, it would choose M3 as it produces the greatest return on investment (i.e. the greatest profitability).

Unfortunately, there are several ways of calculating the ARR. However, as there is very little to choose between them, we will use the least complicated. The formula used in this book is as follows:

$$ARR = \frac{\text{average annual profit}}{\text{initial investment}} \times 100$$

(see e.g. Figure 8.2). Note that sometimes the **average** investment is used instead of the **initial** investment.

Cost of capital project = £200,000   Profit in Year 1 = £43,000
                                      Profit in Year 2 = £56,000
                                      Profit in Year 3 = £41,000
                                      Profit in Year 4 = £20,000

$$ARR = \frac{(43,000 + 56,000 + 41,000 + 20,000)/4}{200,000} \times 100$$

$$= \frac{160,000/4}{200,000} \times 100 = \textbf{20\%}$$

Figure 8.2 Example of an ARR calculation

Self-assessment question S8.1

Try the following question for yourself (answer at the end of the chapter).

You have the chance to open a manicure parlour in your local shopping centre at an initial cost of £25,000. For each manicure, the sales price will be £10 and the direct cost £6. The annual total of indirect costs (i.e. overheads) is estimated to be £16,000. Market research has estimated demand for manicures to be:

Year 1	5,000 units
Year 2	6,000 units
Year 3	7,000 units
Year 4	8,000 units
Year 5	6,500 units

What is the ARR for the project?

Limitations of ARR

One reservation concerning profit-based ARR is that profits can vary much more than cash flows. Remember that the profit figure depends on many subjective estimates such as depreciation, stock valuation and provision for doubtful debts. On the other hand, the cash figure is theoretically measurable and therefore more objective. Thus, the ARR tends to be less reliable than the cash-flow-based methods.

Converting profits to cash flows

Having considered the ARR, we will now look at the other three methods. These are all based on the relevant cash flows (not profits). A relevant cash flow is one **caused by the project**. If a cash flow will still occur whether we go ahead or not, it is not caused by the project, and so it is not relevant to our decision. Exclude irrelevant cash flows from your calculations.

Very often the starting point in these calculations is a profit and loss account rather than a cash flow forecast. In this case the first thing we have to do is to convert the profits to cash flows. This is done by **adding back any non-cash expenses** to the net profit. The most common of these is depreciation, see Figure 8.3. (If you are not sure about this, have a look at Chapter 2 on the difference between profit and cash.)

A company is considering launching a new product requiring the purchase of new plant and machinery costing £5.5 million. The additional profits resulting directly from this five-year project are as follows:

Year	Profit/(Loss)
1	(0.5)
2	1.0
3	4.0
4	5.0
5	2.0

The company uses straight line depreciation and expects to be able to sell the plant for £0.5 million at the end of the project. What are the project's cash flows?

Answer

$$\text{Annual depreciation charge} = \frac{\text{Fall in value over project's lifetime}}{\text{Lifetime in years}}$$

$$= \frac{£(5.5 - 0.5)\text{m}}{5} = £1.0\text{m a year}$$

Year	Profit/(Loss)	Annual depreciation	Other items	Cash in/(out)flow
0	0.0	0.0	plant purchase (5.5)	(5.5)
1	(0.5)	1.0	0.0	0.5
2	1.0	1.0	0.0	2.0
3	4.0	1.0	0.0	5.0
4	5.0	1.0	0.0	6.0
5	2.0	1.0	sale of scrap 0.5	3.5
	11.5			11.5

N.B. 'Year 0' is the equivalent of *now*, i.e. the start of the project.

Figure 8.3 Example of converting profits to cash flows

Try the following question for yourself (answer at the end of the chapter).

A building company is considering branching out into the mobile crane hire business. It is thinking of buying a 42-tonne model similar to ones it has often hired in the past. This will cost £190,000 and should last for nine years, after which time it will have an estimated scrap value of £10,000. The profits from this venture are expected to be as shown below. Calculate the associated cash flows.

Year	Profit (£)	Year	Profit (£)	Year	Profit (£)
1	10,000	4	30,000	7	30,000
2	18,000	5	35,000	8	20,000
3	24,000	6	38,000	9	10,000

Reconciliation of cash flows with profits

Over the whole lifetime of a project, the total of profits will equal the total of cash flows. (Note that this is **not** true for any one year within the lifetime.) This enables you to check the accuracy of your cash flow calculations. Look at Figure 8.3 to check this; the lifetime total is £11.5 million.

Beware of situations where fixed assets are sold for more or less than their written-down value. This will give a 'profit or loss on disposal' which must be included in the profit of the disposal year for the above statement to be true.

Method 2: payback period (PBP)

This calculates how long it will take for the business to recover the initial **cash** outflow to purchase the fixed asset. The answers are given in units of time, usually years. If the investment decision was a choice between several alternative capital projects, the one with the shortest PBP would be recommended. Most people agree that uncertainty increases the further you go into the future. Thus, choosing the project with the shortest PBP is a way of minimizing risk. An example of a PBP calculation is shown in Figure 8.4.

Note that we have assumed the cash to flow **evenly** throughout the year. For example, an annual net cash flow of £120,000 is assumed to occur at the rate of £10,000 a month. In reality, this is most unlikely, especially for seasonal businesses. However, unless we can forecast more accurately, this is the assumption we have to make.

Try the following question for yourself (answer at the end of the chapter).

Calculate the payback period for the manicure parlour project in S8.1 if the only non-cash expense included in the annual fixed costs was depreciation of £2,000.

Initial cash outflow (i.e. project cost) = £240,000

Year	Net cash in £	Cumulative £
1	93,000	93,000
2	107,000	200,000 Payback not reached
3	120,000	320,000 Payback occurs in year 3
4	80,000	400,000

$$PBP = 2 + \frac{\text{amount still needed}}{\text{total inflow in payback year}}$$

$$PBP = 2 + \frac{(240,000 - 200,000)}{120,000}$$

$$= 2 + \frac{40,000}{120,000}$$

$$= 2.33 \text{ years}$$

or = **2 years 4 months**   (0.33 years × 12 months/year = 4 months)

Figure 8.4 **Example of a payback period calculation**

Limitations of PBP

One limitation of this technique is that it takes no account of the cash flows occurring after the payback point has been reached. Project A in Swindon may be chosen in preference to project B in Oxford because it has a shorter PBP. But the total of net cash inflows over the projects' lifetimes may be much greater for project B than for project A.

Thus, choosing project A may be the wrong decision for the business. It depends on how risky the project is perceived to be. If it is thought to be a high-risk investment, then project A may be the best decision after all as it is more likely to recover its initial cost. One reason for the relative popularity of the PBP method is that many business decisions are considerably risky. Another reason is that the concept is easy to understand.

Discounting cash flows

The time value of money

If I were to offer you either £900 now **or** £900 in 12 months' time, which would you choose? I suspect you would choose the £900 now.

Alternatively, if I were to offer to give you either £900 now **or** £945 in 12 months from now, which would you choose? This is a more difficult choice. To help you with your decision, you are told that the bank interest rate is currently 5% a year. If you accepted the £900 now and invested it for 12 months at 5% a year, it would be worth £945 in a year's time. This implies that the two alternatives are really the same, provided interest rates remain constant for the year.

The significance of this is that the value of money changes with time because it is possible to invest and earn interest on it over a period. Check your understanding of this by considering the following question.

If the interest rate changed to 3% a year and I offered you either £945 in 12 months' time or £900 now, which would you choose? The answer is that £900 invested now at 3% gives £927 in 12 months' time. So, on this occasion, it is worth waiting for the £945.

A sum of money **now** has a greater value than the same sum in a year's time because it can be invested for that year to earn interest.

Thus, a £ in one year is *not* worth the same as a £ in another year.

This concept is known as the 'time value of money'.

When looking at cash flows over a number of years, **to be sure of comparing like with like,** future amounts should be reduced by the business's interest or 'cost of capital' rate. In simple terms, it can be thought of as the overall rate of interest applying to a business. It is also referred to as the *discount rate*. The discounted cash flow technique is

All future cash flows should be discounted to *present values*.

Compounding and discounting

Compounding is the effect of repeatedly adding interest earned to the lump sum invested so that interest will be paid on larger and larger amounts as time passes (see Figure 8.5).

Self-assessment question S8.4	*Try the following question for yourself (answer at the end of the chapter).* If £500 is invested at 7.5% p.a. compound, how much is it worth at the end of four years?

Discounting (Figure 8.6) can be viewed as the opposite process to compounding (see Figure 8.7). If the interest rate was 10% p.a. (as in Figure 8.5), instead of multiplying by 1.10, you divide by 1.10 (see Figure 8.6).

An alternative method of obtaining discount factors is to use a present value table. These show the factors for different discount rates for a number of years. Their disadvantage is that they may not include the rate or the number of years you wish to use.

What is the value of £751 invested at 10% p.a. for 3 years?
(To increase a number by 10%, multiply it by the decimal 1.10)

Year 1   £751 × 1.10 = £826
Year 2   £826 × 1.10 = £909
Year 3   £909 × 1.10 = £1,000

The answer is £1,000.

Figure 8.5 Example of a compounding calculation

You own a machine which will produce a cash income of £1,000 p.a. for each of the next three years. What is the present value of this income stream if the discount rate is 10% p.a.?

Year	Cash	10% Discount factor	Present value
1	1,000	1.0000/1.10 = 0.9091	909
2	1,000	0.9091/1.10 = 0.8264	826
3	1,000	0.8264/1.10 = 0.7513	751
		Total present value =	£2,486

Figure 8.6 Example of a discounting calculation

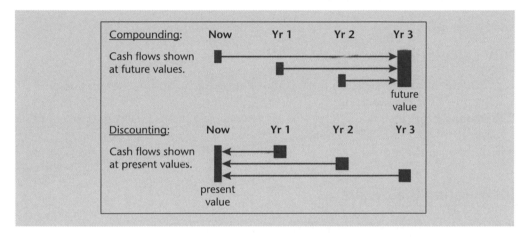

Figure 8.7 Diagrammatic illustration of compounding and discounting
Source: after P. Atrill and E. McLaney (1994) *Management Accounting: An Active Learning Approach*, Blackwell Publications Ltd, Oxford, with permission.

A present value table has been included at the end of this chapter. Practise using it by finding the factor for year 9 at a discount rate of 17%. You should find 0.243. Now try finding the factor for year 18 at a discount rate of 12.5%.

Try the following question for yourself (answer at the end of the chapter).

Discount the cash flows of the manicure parlour (see answer to S8.3) to the present time using a rate of 3% p.a. What is the total of these present values?

Self-assessment question S8.5

Method 3: net present value (NPV)

The NPV is the *sum total* of all the present values of all the cash flows caused by the project (see Figure 8.8).

A vending machine costs £2,500. It will produce positive net cash inflows of £1,000 a year for each of the next three years (residual value = nil). What is the NPV if the discount rate is 10% p.a.?

Year	Cash in/(out)	10% discount factors	Present value
0	(2,500)	1.0000	(2,500)
1	1,000	1.0000/1.10 = 0.9091	909
2	1,000	0.9091/1.10 = 0.8264	826
3	1,000	0.8264/1.10 = 0.7513	751
			NPV = £(14)

Figure 8.8 Example of an NPV calculation

NPV calculation procedure

1 Calculate the annual **net cash flows** (inflows are positive, outflows are negative).
2 Determine the discount rate.
3 Discount future cash flows to present values (calculate the factors or use present value tables).
4 Combine all the annual present values to give the NPV for the whole project period.

Interpreting the results

- If NPV is positive, accept the project.
- If NPV is negative, reject the project.
- If several projects are being considered of which only one can be accepted (mutually exclusive projects), accept the project with highest positive NPV.

Self-assessment question S8.6

Try the following question for yourself (answer at the end of the chapter).

You are considering investing in production facilities for a new product with an estimated life span of four years. The fixed assets will cost £49,500 and the net cash inflows will be £20,000 for each of the first two years and £10,000 for each of the last two years. If the company's cost of capital is 10% p.a., what is the NPV of the project? Would you recommend going ahead? (Use three decimal places for your PV factors.)

Annuities

When projects have a long lifetime and their net cash flows are the same each year, the concept of an annuity can be used to make the NPV calculation easier. An 'annuity' is defined as a fixed periodic (e.g. annual) cash flow which continues for a defined period of time (or until a specified event occurs). Consider the following example.

Eastshore Airport, NPV calculation

Example
8.1

Eastshore Airport is considering installing 50 'iris-recognition' devices to improve its security. These devices will cost a total of £2,500,000 and will have the effect of making 25 jobs redundant. The annual cost of each of these employees is £22,000. Fifteen of these employees will be redeployed and the average redundancy payment for the others is estimated at £30,000 each.

It is thought that these devices will have an effective life of 20 years before being replaced with more up-to-date technology. Their collective residual value in 20 years' time will be £250,000. Annual running costs will be £1,000 per device for the first half of their life but this will increase to £3,000 for the second half due to the increase in maintenance required.

Assuming Eastshore's cost of capital is 15% a year, calculate the NPV of this project. (Use the Cumulative present value factor table (annuities) to determine the appropriate discount factors.)

Solution (£000)

	Years 1–10	Years 11–20
Annual savings	$25 \times 22 = 550$	$25 \times 22 = 550$
Less annual running costs	$50 \times 1 = 50$	$50 \times 3 = 150$
Net annual savings	500	400

Determine the discount factors needed by reading the annuities table at the end of this chapter. A single factor can be used for years 1 to 10 as the annual savings (equal to relevant income) are £500,000; this is a 10-year annuity. Look at the 15% column and read off the factor of 5.019 for year 10. (Check this by adding up the 10 annual factors in the 'normal' single-value table for years 1 to 10.)

For years 11 to 20, the factor cannot just be read from the table as this would also include years 1 to 10. To obtain the correct factor, in the 15% column, deduct the 10-year factor from the 20-year factor, $6.259 - 5.019 = 1.240$.

	Year	Cash in/(out)	15% factors	Present values
Equipment	0	(2,500)	1.000	(2,500.00)
Redundancy	0	(300)	1.000	(300.00)
Net savings	1–10	500	5.019	2,509.50
Net savings	11–20	400	1.240	496.00
Residual value	20	250	0.061	15.25
				NPV = **220.75**

Note that 18 lines of calculation are avoided by making use of the annuity factors.

Self-assessment
question S8.7

Try the following question for yourself (answer at the end of the chapter).

The New English Wine Company is considering automating its operations by investing in some new bottling plant. It has a choice of two machines, A and B. Machine A costs £40,000 and will have a residual value at the end of its 10-year life of £1,000. Machine B costs £20,000 and will have a residual value at the end of its 10-year life of £500. Machine A will save £10,000 a year in labour costs but machine B will only save £6,000 a year. If the company's cost of capital is 20% a year, which machine would you advise the company to buy?

Limitations of NPV

For NPV calculations, all cash flows (except for the initial project cost outflows) are assumed to occur **on the last day of the year**. This is due to discounting being the opposite of compounding **once a year**. In reality, this means cash flows throughout the year, not just at its end. This is a weakness of the model.

A further weakness is that the cost of capital is assumed to remain constant over the whole lifetime of the project. The longer the time period involved, the less likely this is to be true.

Method 4: internal rate of return (IRR)

The IRR is the average annual rate of return that the project is expected to produce; it is calculated using cash flows adjusted for the time value of money. It is expressed as a percentage and is determined by calculating the discount rate that gives the project an NPV of zero.

When organizations use IRR to evaluate capital investment proposals they set a threshold or 'hurdle' rate (usually equal to or higher than their ROCE). This is the minimum acceptable IRR for the project to go ahead. In theory, this threshold is set equal to the organization's cost of capital or discount rate. In other words, the cash **generated** by the project must be at least equal to the cost of financing the project. In practice, to allow for risk and inherent approximation in the IRR calculations, the threshold may be set at a rate greater than the cost of capital.

If several mutually exclusive projects are being considered, the one with the greatest IRR is chosen. An example of an IRR calculation is shown in Figure 8.9. This mathematical technique is known as **interpolation**.

Procedure for calculating the IRR

1 Perform the NPV process using your best guess of the discount rate which will give an NPV of zero.
2 If your NPV is positive, repeat the process using a higher discount rate in order to give a negative NPV. (If first NPV is negative, try a lower rate to find a positive NPV.)
3 When you have one positive and one negative NPV, use *interpolation* to find the rate giving NPV = 0.

A project costs £28,000 and produces net cash flows as shown. What is the IRR?

Year	Cash inflow	60% factor	PV	61% factor	PV
0	(28,000)	1.0000	(28,000)	1.0000	(28,000)
1	18,000	0.6250	11,250	0.6211	11,180
2	21,000	0.3910	8,211	0.3858	8,102
3	24,000	0.2440	5,856	0.2396	5,750
4	18,000	0.1530	2,754	0.1488	2,679
			71		(289)

IRR = 60% + [71/(71 + 289) × 1%] = 60% + [71/360]% = 60.2%

60%	IRR	gap = 1%	61%
+71	0	gap = 360	(289)

Figure 8.9 Example of an IRR calculation

Note that this is an **iterative** technique using **trial and error**. Most spreadsheets and some calculators have dedicated functions to calculate PV, NPV and IRR but they do the calculations using the same method.

Try the following question for yourself (answer at the end of the chapter).

Find the IRR of the project detailed in S8.6.

Self-assessment question S8.8

Inherent approximation

Interpolation assumes that the NPV changes linearly with the discount rate. Mathematically, this is not true because the relationship is correctly represented by a curve rather than a straight line. Figure 8.10 illustrates this as follows.

Line B interpolates between NPVs of +325 (at 10%) and −125 (at 30%) and gives an IRR of 27%.

Line A interpolates between NPVs of +95 (at 15%) and −105 (at 25%) and gives an IRR of 21%.

The actual IRR is 19%.

Limitations of IRR

Consider two alternative projects, one in Sheffield and the other in Lincoln. The Sheffield project may have an IRR of 25% and the Lincoln project may have an IRR of 50%, so the Lincoln project would be chosen. But which project produces most money? Clearly, 25% of £800,000 is greater than 50% of £300,000! IRR is a **relative** measure. (In contrast, NPV is an **absolute** measure giving monetary answers rather than percentages.)

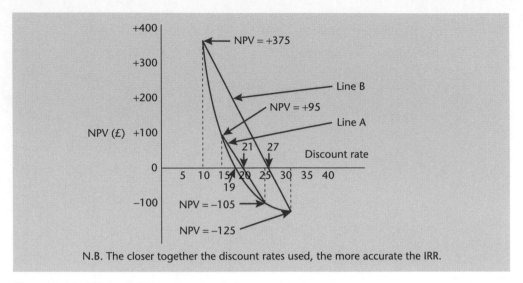

N.B. The closer together the discount rates used, the more accurate the IRR.

Figure 8.10 Effect of discount rate choice

Also, due to the mathematics involved, if any of the cash flows after year 0 are net outflows, there may be **more than one value** of the IRR. (This is similar to the square root of 9 having two answers, +3 and −3.)

Comparing NPV with IRR

Suppose a business has a choice between the Arundel project (A) and the Brighton project (B). What guidance can it gain from calculating their NPVs and IRRs? Assuming that they have different cash flows, the situation is represented in Figure 8.11 as follows:

- The Brighton project has the higher IRR (Z%).
- At a discount rate of 25%, Brighton has a higher NPV than Arundel.
- At a discount rate of 5%, Arundel has a higher NPV than Brighton.

To the right of the crossover point (X%), IRR and NPV will both recommend adopting the Brighton project. However, to the left of this point, IRR and NPV will conflict and recommend different projects.

Note that if the IRR decision conflicts with the NPV, the NPV decision should be used as it is technically more sound. Remember that IRR is a **relative** measure but NPV is an **absolute** measure (see 'Limitations of IRR' above).

Capital rationing and the profitability index

At any point in time, an organization may have identified several projects in which it is worthwhile investing as they each have a positive NPV. Unfortunately, it may not be able to raise sufficient funds to invest in all of them. This situation is referred to as 'capital

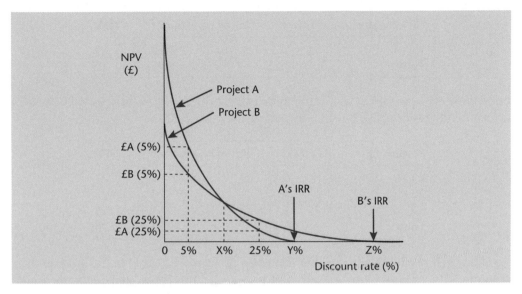

Figure 8.11 Mutually exclusive projects

rationing' and the problem it poses is how the business decides in which of the available projects to invest.

A good way of approaching this decision is to calculate the 'profitability index' (PI) of each project. This is defined by the formula

$$PI = \frac{\text{present value of future cash inflows}}{\text{initial investment}}$$

This is effectively a 'benefit to cost' ratio. (The present value of future cash inflows excludes the initial investment, year 0 in NPV calculations.)

The decision rule is for the company to accept the projects with the greatest PIs until the funds run out. (This assumes all PIs are greater than 1.0, which means they have a positive NPV.) Consider the following example of a company with a maximum of £200,000 of funds to invest in the five different projects shown in the table below. (All figures are in £000.)

Project	Initial investment	PV of future cash inflows	NPV	PI	PI ranking	NPV ranking
A	78	105	27	1.35	2	3
B	55	70	15	1.27	3	4
C	200	250	50	1.25	4	1
D	66	94	28	1.42	1	2
E	72	79	7	1.10	5	5

If projects are ranked according to the size of their NPVs, only project C is able to be undertaken, which has a total NPV of £50,000.

NPV ranking	Project	Initial investment	NPV
1	C	200	50
Total		**200**	**50**

But if projects were ranked according to their PIs, projects D, A and B would be undertaken and the resulting NPV would increase by 40% to £70,000.

PI ranking	Project	Initial investment	NPV
1	D	66	28
2	A	78	27
3	B	55	15
Total		**199**	**70**

A suboptimal result is normally obtained when projects are ranked in the order of their absolute NPVs. This is because the largest projects tend to be selected due to their high individual NPVs. However, their combined NPV is usually lower than that of those projects selected by their PI ranking.

Self-assessment question S8.9

Try the following question for yourself (answer at the end of the chapter).

Invest Quest plc has a maximum of £700 million to invest in new capital projects. Advise which of the following five projects should be chosen. (All figures are in £m.)

Project	Initial investment	PV of future cash inflows
A	185	269
B	197	260
C	81	137
D	210	299
E	282	352

Discounted PBP?

It may have occurred to you that it is possible to discount the cash flows used in payback calculations. The effect of this is to lengthen the period and so show more caution in the estimate of the time needed for the project to pay for itself.

At first sight this approach may seem an improvement on the basic PBP. However, the simplicity of PBP, which is one of its main attractions, is significantly diminished by it. Also, as PBP concentrates on the early years of a project, the benefit of discounting is limited.

More importantly, PBP assumes cash to flow evenly throughout each year but discounting assumes the annual cash flow to occur on the last day of the financial year. These two **contradictory assumptions** render this financial model theoretically unsound and its use inadvisable.

Choice of method

Having four methods of appraising capital investments at your disposal, how do you choose which one to use? Fortunately, you do not have to answer this question because you do not have to use only one method. Indeed, it is preferable to employ a variety of approaches to see how much consensus they produce. After all, each method tells you something different.

ARR tells you the percentage profit return on your investment. PBP tells you how long it will take to recoup your initial investment. NPV tells you the current cash value of the project measured in today's money. IRR tells you the average annual growth rate of your cash investment. As a starting point to your final discussion and recommendation, it is helpful to create a summary table of the results from all the methods employed. This makes the comparison of the findings relatively easy.

However, it is important not to overlook the limitations of the techniques you have used. Will the assumptions of the various methods impinge more on some projects than others or is the effect likely to be the same for all of them?

Finally, you should think more as a manager than an accountant. There will always be some qualitative factors to consider. Factors such as the availability of skilled labour, the ease of distribution to the market and the enhancement of the product range should not be ignored.

Sensitivity analysis

Sensitivity analysis is used to evaluate the risk from each of the factors involved in the project. Once the non-starters have been eliminated and only the possible projects remain, each factor can be analysed to see how much it would need to change before the project would no longer be viable (NPV = 0). Even where one single project has been chosen, it is wise to perform a sensitivity analysis to identify the factors which need to change least to cast doubt on the viability of the project. Sensitivity analysis is illustrated in the following example.

Sensitivity analysis

Example 8.2

The Freeway Driving School is considering expanding its operations by employing one further instructor and car. The car will cost £15,000 (including the addition of dual controls), will be used for three years and then scrapped (for zero value). Fixed costs such as insurance, vehicle licence duty, servicing, etc., will be £4,600 a year and the annual cost of the instructor is £20,000. Instructors are expected to give a maximum of six lessons a day for five days a week and to work for 50 weeks a year. However, it is estimated that the take-up rate for lessons will be 90% of the maximum, i.e. 27 lessons a week ($5 \times 6 \times 90\%$). The selling price of each lesson is £32 and the petrol cost is £5. Freeway has calculated that its cost of capital is 12.5% p.a. Calculate the net present value (NPV) of this three-year project and perform a sensitivity analysis to identify the relative sensitivity of the factors involved.

Suggested solution

Contribution/lesson = lesson price − petrol cost = 32 − 5 = £27
Annual contribution = weeks worked × lessons/week × contribution/lesson
= 50   × 27   × 27   = £36,450
Fixed cost   = insurance etc. + salary = 4,600 + 20,000 = £24,600
Annual net cash Inflow   = £11,850

Note that depreciation is ignored as it is a non-cash cost; NPV uses only cash flows.

NPV calculation

Year	Annual cash contribution	Initial & fixed costs	Net cash in/(out) flow	12.5% discount factors	Present value
0	0	15,000	−15,000	1.000	−15,000
1	36,450	24,600	11,850	0.889	10,533
2	36,450	24,600	11,850	0.790	9,363
3	36,450	24,600	11,850	0.702	8,323
					NPV = 13,219

If all assumptions prove to be correct, NPV = £13,219.

Sensitivity analysis – annual cash contribution

Year	Annual cash contribution	Initial & fixed costs	Net cash in/(out) flow	12.5% discount factors	Present value
0	0	15,000	−15,000	1.000	−15,000
1	30,900	24,600	6,300	0.889	5,600
2	30,900	24,600	6,300	0.790	4,987
3	30,900	24,600	6,300	0.702	4,425
					NPV = 2

By trial and error, it is found that the annual cash contribution must reduce to £30,900 for the NPV to equal zero. (An NPV of 2 is considered to be effectively equal to zero as the NPV model makes some significant assumptions which cause its numerical answers to be estimates rather than 100% accurate figures.)

Sensitivity of 'annual cash contribution' factor = (36,450 − 30,900)/36,450
= 0.15226 = 15%

However,

Annual contribution = weeks worked × lessons/week × contribution/lesson and

$$\text{Reduced annual contribution} = 0.85 \times \text{weeks worked} \times \text{lessons/week} \\ \times \text{contribution/lesson}$$

So the 15% factor applies to each of these three components (taken in isolation). This means that the weeks worked/year would have to fall to 42.5 (50×0.85) for NPV = 0, or the number of lessons given a week would have to fall to 23 (27×0.85) for NPV = 0, or the contribution/lesson would have to fall to 23 (27×0.85) for NPV = 0.

However, contribution/lesson can be analysed by lesson price and petrol cost:

Contribution/lesson = lesson price − petrol cost			
Base position:	=	32 − 5	= 27
Lesson price:	=	28 − 5	= 23
Petrol cost:	=	32 − 9	= 23
Lesson price:		$[(32 - 28)/32] \times 100 = (4/32) \times 100 = 13\%$	
Petrol cost:		$[(9 - 5)/5] \times 100 = (4/5) \times 100 = 80\%$	

Sensitivity analysis – fixed costs

Year	Annual cash contribution	Initial & fixed costs	Net cash in/(out) flow	12.5% discount factors	Present value
0	0	15,000	−15,000	1.000	−15,000
1	36,450	30,150	6,300	0.889	5,600
2	36,450	30,150	6,300	0.790	4,978
3	36,450	30,150	6,300	0.702	4,425
					NPV = 2

The fixed costs have to increase to £30,150 for NPV = 0, so the sensitivity factor is

$$[(30{,}150 - 24{,}600)/24{,}600] \times 100 = 22.561 = \mathbf{23\%}$$

Sensitivity analysis – discount rate

Year	Annual cash contribution	Initial & fixed costs	Net cash in/(out) flow	59.5% discount factors	Present value
0	0	15,000	−15,000	1.000	−15,000
1	36,450	24,600	11,850	0.627	7,429
2	36,450	24,600	11,850	0.393	4,658
3	36,450	24,600	11,850	0.246	2,920
					NPV = 8

The discount rate has to increase to 59.5% for NPV = 0, so the sensitivity factor is

$$[(59.5 - 12.5)/12.5] \times 100 = \mathbf{376\%}$$

Sensitivity analysis – initial cost of car

Year	Annual cash contribution	Initial & fixed costs	Net cash in/(out) flow	12.5% discount factors	Present value
0	0	28,219	−28,219	1.000	−28,219
1	36,450	24,600	11,850	0.889	10,533
2	36,450	24,600	11,850	0.790	9,363
3	36,450	24,600	11,850	0.702	8,323
					NPV = 0

For NPV = 0, the initial cost of the car would have to increase by £13,219 (the NPV at year 0) to £28,219. The sensitivity factor of this is

$$[(28,219 - 15,000)/15,000] \times 100 = (13,219/15,000) \times 100 = 88\%$$

Summary table of changes needed to produce a negative NPV (most sensitive factors listed first)

Factor	Change
Lesson price	13%
Weeks worked/year	15%
Lessons given/week	15%
Fixed costs	23%
Petrol cost	80%
Initial cost of car	88%
Discount rate	376%

Findings

As this table shows, the lesson price is the most sensitive factor and the discount rate the least sensitive. The assumptions and forecasts underlying the most sensitive factors should be carefully checked and reconsidered. (In this example above, the lesson price, the number of weeks worked a year and the number of lessons given a week should be carefully scrutinized.) To reduce the investment risk involved, managers may think it wise to take a more pessimistic view of these factors in order to re-evaluate the validity of the capital investment project under consideration.

The financing decision

Project loans and interest payments

Obtaining a bank loan is one way of financing a capital investment project. All the cash flows associated with the loan (initial sum, interest payments and final repayment of sum) should be **excluded** from the cash flows used in capital investment appraisal. This is because the decision on how to finance a project is separate from the decision whether or not to accept the project. The decision to accept or reject a project should be made first. Only if this is positive will the choice of finance need to be made. (The financing decision is outside the scope of this book.)

If the effect of interest charges is not eliminated from the cash flows for discounted cash flow purposes, double counting will occur. This is because the discounting process automatically allows for the time value of money, which is firmly based on the ability of money to earn interest.

To eliminate the effect of interest from the calculations, the annual interest charges are added back to profits to give the **cash flows before interest.**

Note that, in the 'Reconciliation of cash flows with profits' subsection we looked at earlier in this chapter, the position is modified as follows. **Over the whole lifetime of a project**, the total of profits (**before interest**) will equal the total of cash flows (**ignoring loans, interest and repayments**). (Note also that this is not true for any one year within the project's lifetime.)

Qualitative factors

The management accountant's role is to provide the calculations and a recommendation. The manager's role is to apply experience and knowledge of the industry, weigh up the risks involved and make the decision. The work of the management accountant is important but it is only the starting point of the appraisal process. Other factors, many of which are not numerically quantifiable but still affect the decision, should be taken into account. Remember, the final decision should be a management decision, not an accounting one.

Limitations of capital investment appraisal techniques

The limitations of the four techniques have already been discussed at the end of each of their sections. However, it is worth pointing out that all capital investment appraisals are only as good as the forecasts of profit or cash flow on which they are based. The long-term nature of capital investment appraisal compounds this weakness. The further into the future the forecast goes, the less reliable it becomes.

Also, these techniques cannot tell companies when, and in what, they should be investing. For example, the oil company Shell announced record profits of £9.8 billion in 2004, an all-time record for a European company at that time! But Shell's stated total of oil reserves was only nine years which compared badly with its rivals BP and Exxon, both of which had each identified sufficient oil to keep them in business for the next 14 years. This was an excellent opportunity to plough as much of the 'excess' profit as possible back into the company to finance increased exploration activities or research into alternative energy sources. After all, if Shell did not find any more oil or develop new products, it would be out of business in less than 10 years. However, Shell decided that it would spend its 'windfall' profits on paying a one-off special dividend to shareholders and buying back its own shares on the stock market in order to keep its share price high rather than invest in its long-term future.

The manager's point of view (written by Nigel Burton)

Capital investment decisions are among the most challenging issues faced by management. The sums of money involved can be very large, and the decision to invest or not to invest can have a profound influence on the future of the business. Large projects are often turning points in the life of a company. Success can raise the business on to a new plane. Failure can bring it down altogether. Moreover, the decision has to be taken largely on the basis of estimates of what might happen in the future. Different assumptions about future circumstances will lead to different patterns of projected profits and cash flow. Management has to decide on the most likely outcome of the project, and ensure that the proposed level of capital expenditure is compatible with this outcome. Capital appraisal techniques are designed to rationalize all the relevant information and present management with a reasonable comparison between the options available.

Preparing a capital expenditure proposal is an iterative process. It is rather like budgeting. All the contributors to the process – the engineer, salesperson, raw material purchaser, production and technical representatives, etc. – draw up proposals relating to their areas, but without seeing the overall picture. As in budgeting, therefore, everyone starts by specifying their requirements with their own particular agendas in mind, while preparing to make concessions only if it is found that the figures do not ultimately add up. For instance, engineers will tend, perhaps rightly, to aim in the first instance for state-of-the-art technology, as they feel this will keep the company in the forefront of the industry. Salespeople, being optimistic by nature, may have a tendency to overestimate what their talents can achieve, so their projected sales levels may appear to support the high capital expenditure proposals. A decision to go for expensive plant under these circumstances would be very tempting, but it may be based on a false assumption of future cash flows and could in fact be quite the wrong option for the company.

A similar pattern of optimism and aspiration is likely to be repeated throughout the departments involved, so that, when all the figures are put together for the first time, the initial view may be completely distorted. It is likely to be quite different from the final article when the iterative process is complete. Every number in the financial statements must be challenged. Are the proposed sales volumes reasonable? Will the competition bring a better product to the market during the life span of the project? Are the proposed selling prices supportable? Will the increased capacity in the marketplace, created by the project itself, have an impact on prices? And so on. For every question asked, there will be a variety of inconclusive answers, more like statements of probabilities. But every discussion will give you a better feel for the robustness of a particular number. In the end, you can only go with one set of figures, but it is useful to bear in mind the best-case and worst-case scenarios, so that you develop an understanding of the risks inherent in the project.

Throughout the iterative process, the capital appraisal techniques outlined in this chapter provide a common point of comparison between the different financial scenarios which each set of circumstances throws up. They will help you to answer critical questions such as: 'Will the business support a full replacement of the plant, or is refurbishment the more viable option?' and 'Is it worth going for the expense of a bigger expansion now, so that we do not have to put up with the upheaval of a further expansion project in three, five or ten years' time?' The internal rate of return calculation takes into account the cash flows for the whole of a project's life span, and reduces it to a single figure which can be compared not only with alternative options, but also with the company's required benchmark.

Cash is a scarce commodity for many companies, so the payback period is also a critical measurement. If we make the capital investment today, how many years of cash inflow will it take to get our money back? In other words, how soon will we be making a genuine profit on our investment? If the profit arrives a long way into the future, we could be better off by simply keeping our funds on deposit. At the very least, we should consider alternative projects which give a quicker return.

For some years, my corporation's strategy had been aimed at raising the company's overall return on capital employed to 20%, a high target, but an attainable one for a speciality chemical business. In order to achieve this, the company set a minimum IRR of 20% and a maximum payback period of three years for all capital expenditure proposals. Any project with better returns than these had a good chance of success. Since it was a multinational corporation, however, competition for capital funds was always intense. If we submitted our project at a time when other subsidiaries were putting forward even better proposals, we could find ourselves being either turned down or deferred. There was always a temptation, therefore, to go forward with optimistic figures, and while optimism is fine, there is always the risk that it may spill over into fantasy land, with disaster following closely behind.

One of our fellow subsidiaries had proposed a major expansion to one of its plants. The engineers determined that the capital cost would be $9.6 million. This included a number of specific pieces of plant for which firm quotations had been obtained, but the majority of it was based on estimates. In view of these uncertainties, it is common to add a general contingency into the cost, usually amounting to 10%. This contingency, at $960,000, was therefore completely non-specific. Yet this amount alone was larger than most other capital projects routinely undertaken by the subsidiary, all of which were subjected to the normal, detailed capital appraisal scrutiny. Much concern was expressed at the time over how this amount was to be controlled, but the engineers insisted that it represented only a buffer amount, and very little of it would actually be used. However, due to inaccurate estimating in the first place, and inadequate control during the installation process, especially over subcontractors, the actual capital cost of the project spiralled, finally amounting not to $9.6 million, but $12.3 million. If this level of cost had been incorporated into the original financial appraisal, the IRR and payback would have been insufficient, and the project would never have been approved. As it was, the problem emerged too late for any remedial action to be taken. The business group concerned was left to carry an enormous burden, which severely inhibited its profitability for several years, and might well have caused the business to collapse.

This story demonstrates how critical the capital appraisal process can be to the well-being of the business. It will result in the business making a substantial commitment, not only in terms of capital, which can be significant, but also in respect of its future, strategic direction. Once the decision is made, the die is cast. It is critical, therefore, that the optimism inherent in capital proposals is tempered with a good dose of realism, or at least an element of conservatism. This is where the sensitivity analyses described earlier play an important part. They will demonstrate the robustness of the project if specific estimates, such as capital cost or sales levels, prove to be inaccurate.

When the project is approved and under way, it is also important that all the managers contributing to the appraisal process are held to account for their commitments. Post-completion audits are a good way to focus their minds. These can take place at any time in the life of a project, but usually occur after a period of several years, when the pattern of the business has been established. Although the threat of audit can sharpen the minds of managers, the disadvantage is that they happen so far after the event that any problems unearthed will almost certainly be beyond rectification. There is no substitute therefore for detailed analysis and testing of the basic assumptions underlying the capital appraisal, followed by close control of the project at every stage of its development. The potential risk to the business of unsound assumptions is simply too great to permit the slightest lack of rigour in the management review process.

Summary

- There are four alternative ways of appraising large investments in fixed (or capital) assets: ARR, PBP, NPV and IRR.
- They all use cash flow except ARR, which uses profit.
- Cash flows can be calculated by adding back depreciation to profits.
- Due to the long time periods involved, it is appropriate to discount future cash flows to present values for NPV and IRR.
- Discounting is the opposite process to the compounding of interest.
- Several methods should be used to aid decision making as each one considers a different aspect of the project.
- Each method is based on assumptions and has its limitations.
- The interpolation process for calculating IRR contains inherent approximations.
- It is possible for the NPV and IRR decisions to contradict each other. If this occurs, it is preferable to use the NPV recommendation.
- Sensitivity analysis helps to identify the major risk factors.
- The cash flows arising from the financing decision should **not** be included in the calculations.
- The final decision should take account of qualitative factors as well as the quantitative results of the methods used.
- Each method has its own limitations/weaknesses.
- All capital investment appraisal is limited by the inaccuracy of the cash flow/profit forecasts used.

Further reading

Atkinson, A., Banker, R., Kaplan, R. and Young, S. (2001) *Management Accounting*, 3rd edition, Prentice Hall, Harlow. See chapter 'Using management accounting information for investment decisions'.

Borgonovo, E. and Peccati, L. (2004) 'Sensitivity analysis in investment project evaluation', *International Journal of Production Economics*, Vol. 90, Issue 1, July.

Boston, J. (2002) 'Purer speculation', *Financial Management* (CIMA), March.

Cohn, E. (2003) 'Benefit-cost analysis: a pedagogical note', *Public Finance Review*, Vol. 31, Issue 5, September.

Horngren, C., Bhimani, A., Datar, S. and Foster, G. (2002) *Management and Cost Accounting*, 2nd edition, Prentice Hall Europe, Harlow. See Chapter 13, 'Capital investment decisions'.

McDermott, T., Stainer, A. and Stainer, L. (2002) 'Environmental sustainability and capital investment appraisal', *International Journal of Environmental Technology & Management*, Vol. 2, Issue 4.

Otley, D. (1987) *Accounting Control and Organisational Behaviour*, Heinemann Professional Publishing, Oxford. See Chapter 8, 'Capital budgeting'.

Pogue, M. (2004) 'Investment appraisal: a new approach', *Managerial Auditing Journal*, Vol. 19, Issue 4, April.

Upchurch, A. (2003) *Management Accounting, Principles and Practice*, 2nd edition, Financial Times/Prentice Hall, Harlow. See chapter 'Capital investment appraisal'.

Weetman, P. (2002) *Management Accounting, an Introduction*, 3rd edition, Financial Times/ Prentice Hall, Harlow. See chapter 'Capital budgeting'.

Answers to self-assessment questions

S8.1

Year	Units	Profit before fixed costs	Fixed costs	Net profit
1	5,000	20,000	16,000	4,000
2	6,000	24,000	16,000	8,000
3	7,000	28,000	16,000	12,000
4	8,000	32,000	16,000	16,000
5	6,500	26,000	16,000	10,000

$$\text{ARR} = \frac{(4+8+12+16+10)/5}{25} \times 100$$

$$= \frac{10}{25} \times 100$$

$$= 40\%$$

S8.2

$$\text{Annual depreciation charge} = \frac{\text{fall in value over project's lifetime}}{\text{lifetime in years}}$$

$$= \frac{(190,000 - 10,000)}{9}$$

$$= £20,000$$

(Figures shown in £000)

Year	Profit/(loss)	Annual depreciation	Other items	Cash flow in/(out)
0	0	0	(190) buy crane	(190)
1	10	20	0	30
2	18	20	0	38
3	24	20	0	44
4	30	20	0	50
5	35	20	0	55
6	38	20	0	58
7	30	20	0	50
8	20	20	0	40
9	10	20	10 sell scrap	40
	215			**215**

S8.3

Year	Profit	Depreciation	Cash flow	Cumulative
1	4,000	2,000	6,000	6,000
2	8,000	2,000	10,000	16,000
3	12,000	2,000	14,000	30,000
4	16,000	2,000	18,000	48,000
5	10,000	2,000	12,000	60,000

$$\text{Payback period} = 2 + \frac{(25-16)}{14} = 2 + \frac{9}{14} = 2.64 \text{ years} = 2 \text{ years } 8 \text{ months}$$

S8.4

£500 invested for 4 years at 7.5% p.a. compound:

Year	Amount	Factor	Total
	£		£
1	500.00	1.075	537.50
2	537.50	1.075	577.81
3	577.81	1.075	621.15
4	621.15	1.075	**£667.73**

S8.5

Discounting cash flows at 3% p.a.:

Year	Cash flow	3% discount factor	Present value
	£		£
1	6,000	1/1.03 = 0.97087	5,825
2	10,000	0.97087/1.03 = 0.94260	9,426
3	14,000	0.94260/1.03 = 0.91514	12,812
4	18,000	0.91514/1.03 = 0.88849	15,993
5	12,000	0.88849/1.03 = 0.86261	10,351
	£60,000		Total **£54,407**

S8.6

Year	Cash in/(out)	10% factors	Present value
0	(49,500)	1.000	(49,500)
1	20,000	0.909	18,180
2	20,000	0.826	16,520
3	10,000	0.751	7,510
4	10,000	0.683	6,830
			NPV = (460)

Recommendation: Do not go ahead with project.

S8.7

Machine A

Year	Cash in/(out) £	20% factor	Present value £
0	(40,000)	1.000	(40,000)
1–10	10,000	4.192	41,920
10	1,000	0.162	162
			NPV = 2,082

Machine B

Year	Cash in/(out) £	20% factor	Present value £
0	(20,000)	1.000	(20,000)
1–10	6,000	4.192	25,152
10	500	0.162	81
			NPV = 5,233

Machine B appears to be a much better investment than machine A.

S8.8

Year	Cash in/(out)	10% factor	PV	9% factor	PV
0	(49,500)	1.000	(49,500)	1.000	(49,500)
1	20,000	0.909	18,180	0.917	18,340
2	20,000	0.826	16,520	0.842	16,840
3	10,000	0.751	7,510	0.772	7,720
4	10,000	0.683	6,830	0.708	7,080
			NPV = (460)		NPV = 480

By interpolation:

$$\text{IRR} = 9\% + \frac{480}{(480 + 460)} \times 1\% = 9.51$$

9%	9.51%	10%
+480	0	(460)

S8.9

Calculate the NPV, PI and rankings for all projects.

Project	Initial investment	PV of future cash inflows	NPV	PI	PI ranking	NPV ranking
A	185	269	84	1.45	2	2
B	197	260	63	1.32	4	4
C	81	137	56	1.69	1	5
D	210	299	89	1.42	3	1
E	282	352	70	1.25	5	3

If projects are ranked according to the size of their NPVs, projects D, A and E are undertaken giving a total NPV of £243m.

NPV ranking	Project	Initial investment	NPV
1	D	210	89
2	A	185	84
3	E	282	70
Total		677	243

But if projects were ranked according to their PIs, projects C, A, D and B would be undertaken and the resulting NPV would increase by £49m to £292m.

PI ranking	Project	Initial investment	NPV
1	C	81	56
2	A	185	84
3	D	210	89
4	B	197	63
		673	292

Based on the figures alone, IQ plc should consider investing in projects A, B, C and D.

Nufone

Nufone plc is considering the launch of a new product, the latest in its range of mobile phones. Its major selling point is a modified microwave technology which will significantly improve the quality of the voice output and the robustness of the connection. Its inventor has approached Nufone plc with a view to selling it the patent and has given the company one week before he offers it elsewhere. The patent will cost £5 million. The profit estimates below are based on a market research survey for a similar concept which Nufone commissioned four months ago from an independent bureau.

If the project goes ahead, a new factory will have to be built at a cost of £2 million plus £6 million for machinery. The company is currently negotiating for a suitable site on which to build; it expects to have to pay £3 million for it. Nufone plc's depreciation policy is to use the equal instalment (straight-line) method with residual values always assumed to be zero. Patents are decreased in value (amortized) in the same way but land is not depreciated. It is assumed the patent will have no value in 10 years' time.

It is estimated that the product will have a life of 10 years, at the end of which time it will be obsolete. It is also assumed that the factory building will then be demolished. The cost of the demolition will be exactly covered by the sale proceeds of the 10-year-old machinery. Also, the land will be sold for an estimated £3 million.

The financing of the project will be assisted by a bank loan, which will incur interest of £300,000 p.a., payable in arrears at the end of each year. The working capital (stock, debtors and creditors) needed to run this project is estimated to be £1.2 million.

The profits shown below are **after** charging depreciation, interest on the bank loan and launch costs (£1.5 million, all in year 1).

Year	Profit/(loss) £m	Year	Profit/(loss) £m
1	(2.3)	6	10.0
2	1.5	7	8.0
3	6.0	8	6.0
4	8.0	9	4.0
5	10.0	10	2.0

(The project detailed above will be known as project T.)

Having seen the above project proposal from the technical director, the financial director suggests that they should lease an existing factory instead of building one. She estimates that the lease will cost £1.4 million to purchase (payable in advance) followed by 10 annual payments of £800,000 (payable in arrears). The machinery will still have to be purchased as before. (This alternative project will be known as project F.)

The sales director has come up with a third alternative. This is to go ahead with a new design of phone with a modified casing. In this case it would not be necessary to purchase the patent. As less new technology is involved, the production could take place in the present factory by putting on a night shift. However, £4 million would still need to be spent on new machinery, although the bank loan would be unnecessary. Working capital would be reduced to £0.8 million. The profits from this phone, after charging depreciation on the new machinery, are estimated as follows:

Year	Profit/(loss) £m	Year	Profit/(loss) £m
1	2.1	6	2.6
2	3.6	7	2.6
3	3.6	8	1.6
4	3.6	9	1.6
5	2.6	10	0.6

(This alternative project will be known as project S.)

Notes:

1 Nufone plc's cost of capital (or discount rate) is 12.5% p.a.
2 Work to the nearest £000 when performing your calculations.
3 You are expected to use a word processor and a spreadsheet for this assignment.
4 When performing your calculations, **show your workings** and do not use the dedicated functions for PV, NPV and IRR provided by spreadsheets and some calculators.

Tasks:

1 For each of the three alternatives, calculate the following:
   a) the cash flows;
   b) the accounting rate of return (using the initial cost);
   c) the payback period;
   d) the net present value;
   e) the internal rate of return (using the 'interpolation' method).

(50%)

2 Create an executive summary report for Nufone plc's board of directors, appraising the capital investment decision facing them. Justify any recommendations you make and discuss any reservations you have concerning the application and interpretation of the techniques used. *(Any work in excess of the first two pages will be ignored.)*

(50%)
(Total 100%)

The Private Healthcare Group (PHG) was started nine years ago by three doctors previously employed by the National Health Service. It is based in London and specializes in cosmetic surgery. It now operates four clinics: two in London, one in Bristol and one in Cardiff. It is considering opening a new clinic in the Birmingham area.

An initial feasibility study has been carried out and several alternative ways forward have been identified. The two most likely are to erect a new building and to convert an existing one. The conversion is likely to be cheaper to build but more expensive to run.

The study was based on a clinic with a capacity of 20 beds open for business seven days a week. A new building would be operational for 50 weeks a year but a converted building for only 48 weeks a year due to the additional amount of building maintenance work needed on a regular basis. Any improvement work thought necessary could also be carried out during this shutdown period.

However, the fee to be charged to the clients (on a daily basis) and the annual occupancy rate are more difficult to determine due to the price elasticity of demand. A market research report, commissioned as part of the feasibility study, is shown below (see Table A). It predicts annual bed occupancy rates at various fee levels.

PHG thinks that the considerable entry barriers, such as high initial building costs, will result in a relatively low competitive environment for about five years. Competitors are likely to be offering equivalent treatments by then so PHG will probably sell the business and pursue other more profitable ventures. PHG has calculated that its accounting rate of return (ARR) for the whole group was 21.4% in the previous financial year.

The cost of building the clinic from scratch is estimated at £6.0m. A suitable existing building has been identified and is on the market at £3.0m but a further £2.2m would need to be spent to convert it to meet the clinic's building specification. In addition to this, in both cases, specialized medical equipment would need to be purchased and installed at a cost of £2.8m. PHG has been advised by an independent professional property company that the resale value of the new building in five years' time will probably be 10% lower than its initial cost and that the converted building should maintain its value of £5.2m over the same period.

PHG's accounting policy on depreciation is to use the straight-line method, buildings over 25 years and equipment (including vehicles) over five years, assuming all residual values to be zero. The variable costs, such as food and drink, are estimated to be £40 per client per day. A schedule of fixed costs (excluding depreciation) has been drawn up by the group accountant (see Table B).

The chief executive officer of PHG has decided to ask for some calculations to be done regarding this project. Having had his fingers burned in a similar situation a few years earlier, he is particularly concerned about the reliability of answers resulting from the application of accounting techniques.

As most of the funding for this project would be provided by a debenture, PHG estimates that the cost of capital for the new clinic will be 16.5% a year. PHG's current approach to capital projects is to stipulate that their IRRs must equal or exceed a 'hurdle rate' of 24% a year.

Table A: Market research data

Daily fee (£)	Annual occupancy rate (%)
500	94
600	91
700	82
800	77
900	67
1,000	55

Table B: Annual fixed costs other than depreciation

Item	New build (£)	Conversion (£)
Medical salaries	1,320,000	1,320,000
Admin salaries	170,000	170,000
Building maintenance	50,000	120,000
Heat, light and air conditioning	70,000	100,000

Tasks:

1 Calculate the annual operating contribution and profit for each of the price/occupancy rate combinations in the market research report and identify the 'maximum' profit for a) a new building, and b) a converted building.

(20 marks)

Note: For the following tasks, use only the price/occupancy rate combination which gives the maximum profit for a) a new building, and b) a converted building (as identified in task 1 above).

2 Calculate the first year's return on capital employed for a) a new building, and b) a converted building. (Use **initial** capital employed.)

(6 marks)

3 Calculate the payback period of the project for a) a new building, and b) a converted building.

(10 marks)

4 Calculate the net present value (NPV) of the project for a) a new building, and b) a converted building.

(14 marks)

5 Calculate the internal rate of return (IRR) of a) a new building and b) a converted building. Show your workings; do **not** use the automatic IRR function on a calculator or computer.

(14 marks)

6 For the new building option only, perform a sensitivity analysis on the following three factors: end value of building, number of operational weeks and discount rate.

(12 marks)

7 Advise the PHG directors on proceeding with the new clinic.

(15 marks)

8 Justify to the chief executive officer (who is a medic with only a little knowledge of accountancy) why PHG should use Capital Investment Appraisal. *(A discussion of CIA's limitations or a comparison of methods is not required.)*

(9 marks)

(Total 100 marks)

Questions

An asterisk * on a question number indicates that the answer is given at the end of the book. Answers to the other questions are given in the Lecturer's Guide.

Q8.1* Frynas & Co.

Frynas & Co. are considering buying a mobile drilling rig to expand the range of services the company provides for the water, gas and oil industries. The rig would cost £620,000 and last for four years, at the end of which it would be sold for £20,000. The estimated profits for each of the four years are shown below. (The company uses the straight-line method of calculating depreciation. Its latest set of accounts showed its return on capital employed to be 11.1%.)

Year	Profit/(loss)
	£
1	(50,000)
2	50,000
3	150,000
4	50,000

Tasks:

1 Calculate and comment on the accounting rate of return (using the initial investment).
2 Calculate the payback period.
3 Calculate the net present value if Frynas's cost of capital is 10.0%.
4 Calculate the internal rate of return.
5 Comment on your findings.

Q8.2* Binley Blades Ltd

Binley Blades specializes in the manufacture of rotor blades for helicopters. It has just spent £50,000 developing a new type of blade based on a mixture of carbon fibre and naturally occurring resins. These blades can withstand 80% more stress than the company's standard blades but will cost approximately 50% more to manufacture. It now has to decide whether to go ahead and build a new production facility for its new blades. Unfortunately, the net present value analysis (reproduced below) indicates that it would be most unwise to go ahead with this project.

Year	0	1	2	3	4	5
COSTS (£000)						
Plant & equipment	2,000	0	0	0	0	0
Research & development	0	10	10	10	10	10
Materials usage	0	500	500	500	500	500
Direct labour	0	200	200	200	200	200
Indirect labour	0	20	20	20	20	20
Working capital	150	0	0	0	0	0
Depreciation	0	200	200	200	200	200
Production overheads	0	40	40	40	40	40
Sales & administration						
Overheads	0	60	60	60	60	60
Finance overhead	0	200	200	200	200	200
Total costs	2,150	1,230	1,230	1,230	1,230	1,230
REVENUES (£000)						
Sales revenue	0	1,450	1,450	1,450	1,450	1,450
Disposal of plant & equipment	0	0	0	0	0	1,000
Total revenue	0	1,450	1,450	1,450	1,450	2,450
NET TOTAL REVENUE	−2,150	220	220	220	220	1,220
10% discount factors	1	0.9	0.8	0.7	0.6	0.5
Present values	−2,150	198	176	154	132	610
NET PRESENT VALUE	**−880**					

Notes:

1 It is company policy to write off research and development costs over the lifetime of the product.

2 It is company policy to use straight-line depreciation over 10 years, with a zero residual value, for plant and equipment.

3 The company is currently developing an even stronger blade which uses a very different technology. Binley thinks it will take a further five years before it is ready for production. Thus, Binley considers that the carbon fibre/resin project will have a life of five years, at the end of which the plant and equipment will be sold off at 25% of its original cost.

4 The necessary plant and equipment will be purchased for £2 million, financed in full by a bank loan for this amount, bearing interest at 10% a year (shown above as 'Finance overhead').

5 The working capital consists of carbon fibre and resin material stocks.

6 Only half of the indirect labour costs will be actually caused by this project. The other half is a redistribution from standard blade production.

7 Only 12.5% of the production overheads will actually be caused by this project. The remainder is a redistribution from standard blade production.

8 Binley believes that its current marketing and administration departments will be able to cope with any increased workloads. The overheads shown are a redistribution from standard blade production.

Task:

Redraft the above schedule, correcting any mistakes you find. Comment briefly on your results.

Q8.3* Stobo plc

Stobo plc is a well-known national chain of high-street chemists. Its traditional markets of pharmaceuticals and beauty products are becoming increasingly competitive due to the aggressive entry of certain supermarkets. To counter this, it is considering expanding its services to the public. It plans to make more effective use of some of its retail space and storerooms by introducing some sort of personal healthcare service. A few stores have been chosen in specially selected locations for a five-year pilot scheme. Stobo intends to choose one of the three following alternative possibilities:

SR	Stress relief, including aromatherapy, massage and reflexology
OHC	Oral hygiene and chiropody
PF	Personal fitness using multigym equipment

Each of these would involve an initial cash outlay on appropriate equipment and the employment of specialist personnel. Market research and a financial analysis have been carried out for each alternative; an extract of the findings is shown below.

(All figures in £000)	SR	OHC	PF
Initial cash outlay	44	40	44
Net cash flow:			
Year 1	16	8	12
Year 2	14	10	12
Year 3	12	12	12
Year 4	10	14	12
Year 5	8	16	12
	60	60	60
Internal rate of return	13%	13%	11%

Tasks:

1 Calculate the payback period for each alternative.
2 Calculate the net present value of each alternative if Stobo's cost of capital is 10%.
3 Advise Stobo which of the three alternatives it should concentrate on.

Q8.4 Fiesole Ltd

Fiesole Ltd is considering the selection of one of a pair of mutually exclusive capital investment projects. Both would involve the purchase of machinery with a life of five years. Fiesole uses the straight-line method for calculating depreciation and its cost of capital is 15% per year.

Project 1 would generate annual net cash inflows of £400,000; the machinery would cost £1,112,000 and have a scrap value of £112,000.

Project 2 would generate annual net cash inflows of £1,000,000; the machinery would cost £3,232,000 and have a scrap value of £602,000.

Tasks:

1 For each project, calculate:
   a) the accountancy rate of return (using the initial investment);
   b) the payback period;
   c) the net present value.
2 State which project, if any, you would recommend for acceptance.

   Give your reasons.

Q8.5 The Adaptor Company

The Adaptor Company has recently invested £40,000 in a market research survey to determine the demand for its new product, the AdaptAll. The bill for this survey has not yet been paid. Adaptor is encouraged by the survey and now has to decide whether or not to go ahead.

The AdaptAll cost £50,000 to develop and if it goes ahead will need a further £10,000 spent on packaging development before it can be put on the market. The equipment needed to produce it will cost £180,000.

The product will only have a four-year life. In years 1 and 2, annual sales will be 30,000 units, falling to 20,000 units in year 3 and 10,000 units in year 4. The selling price will be £12 per unit.

The costs of producing the AdaptAll are as follows:

Materials – One unit of AdaptAll requires one unit of raw material. The company has 15,000 units of material in stock. This material originally cost £2 per unit but could be sold immediately for £3 per unit. The material could not be used by the Adaptor Company for any other of its products. If the AdaptAll project does not go ahead, the material will be sold. The current market price of the material is £4 per unit.

Labour costs are £2 for each AdaptAll.

Fixed overheads – The company will need to rent a new factory unit to produce the AdaptAll, at a cost of £50,000 per annum. It does not advertise its products individually but sends out a company catalogue every two months with details of all its products. The catalogue incorporates details of all existing and new products, including the AdaptAll. The catalogue costs £1,000,000 per annum to produce and distribute, and it is company policy to allocate an equal share of this cost to each of its products. AdaptAll will therefore bear its share, amounting to £10,000 a year.

Variable overheads amount to £1 for each AdaptAll.

At the end of the four years the machinery will be sold for £20,000. The company uses straight-line depreciation for all its assets.

The company has a cost of capital of 10%, although projects are normally expected to achieve an IRR hurdle rate of at least 20%.

Tasks:

1 Calculate the net present value (NPV) of the AdaptAll project.
2 Estimate the effect on NPV of a reduction in sales volume of 10% per year, and use this to assess the % fall in volume that will reduce the NPV to zero.
3 Advise the company on whether or not it should proceed with the AdaptAll project, raising any other issues you feel should be considered in the decision. Your advice should incorporate comments on the use of the 20% hurdle rate as a decision rule.

Q8.6 MN plc

MN plc has a rolling programme of investment decisions. One of these investment decisions is to consider mutually exclusive investments A, B and C. The following information has been produced by the investment manager.

	Investment decision A £	Investment decision B £	Investment decision C £
Initial investment	105,000	187,000	245,000
Cash inflow for A: years 1 to 3	48,000		
Cash inflow for B: years 1 to 6		48,000	
Cash inflow for C: years 1 to 9			48,000
Net present value (NPV) at 10% each year	14,376	22,040	31,432
Ranking	3rd	2nd	1st
Internal rate of return (IRR)	17.5%	14%	13%
Ranking	1st	2nd	3rd

Required:

a) Prepare a report for the management of MN plc which includes:
   - a graph showing the sensitivity of the three investments to changes in the cost of capital;
   - an explanation of the reasons for differences between NPV and IRR rankings – use investment A to illustrate the points you make;
   - a brief summary which gives MN plc's management advice on which project should be selected.

(18 marks)

b) One of the directors has suggested using payback to assess the investments. Explain to him the advantages and disadvantages of using payback methods over IRR and NPV. Use the figures above to illustrate your answer.

(7 marks)

(Total = 25 marks)

CIMA Intermediate: Management Accounting – Decision Making, November 2001

Q8.7 CAF plc

CAF plc is a large multinational organization that manufactures a range of highly engineered products/components for the aircraft and vehicle industries. The directors are considering the future of one of the company's factories in the UK which manufactures product A. Product A is coming to the end of its life but another two years' production is planned. This is expected to produce a net cash inflow of £3 million next year and £2.3 million in the product's final year.

Product AA

CAF plc has already decided to replace product A with product AA which will be ready to go into production in two years' time. Product AA is expected to have a life of eight years. It could be made either at the UK factory under consideration or in an eastern European factory owned by CAF plc. The UK factory is located closer to the markets and therefore, if product AA is made in eastern Europe, the company will incur extra transport costs of £10 per unit. Production costs will be the same in both countries. Product AA will require additional equipment and staff will need training; this will cost £6 million at either location. 200,000 units of product AA will be made each year and each unit will generate a net cash inflow of £25 before extra transport costs. If product AA is made in the UK, the factory will be closed and sold at the end of the product's life.

Product X

Now, however, the directors are considering a further possibility: product X could be produced at the UK factory and product AA at the eastern European factory. Product X must be introduced in one year's time and will remain in production for three years. If it is introduced, the manufacture of product A will have to cease a year earlier than planned. If this happened, output of product A would be increased by 12.5% to maximum capacity next year, its last year, to build stock prior to the product's withdrawal. The existing staff would be transferred to product X.

The equipment needed to make product X would cost £4 million. 50,000 units of product X would be made in its first year; after that, production would rise to 75,000 units a year. Product X would earn a net cash flow of £70 per unit. After three years' production of product X, the UK factory would be closed and sold. (Product AA would not be transferred back to the factory in the UK at that stage; production would continue at the eastern European site.)

Sale of factory

It is expected that the UK factory could be sold for £5.5 million at any time between the beginning of year 2 and the end of year 10. If the factory is sold, CAF plc will make redundancy payments of £2 million and the sale of equipment will raise £350,000.

CAF plc's cost of capital is 5% each year.

Required:

a) Prepare calculations that show which of the three options is financially the best.

(15 marks)

b) The directors of CAF plc are unsure whether their estimates are correct. Calculate and discuss the sensitivity of your choice of option in (a) to:
   i) changes in transport costs;

(3 marks)

   ii) changes in the selling price of the factory.

(3 marks)

c) Briefly discuss the business issues that should be considered before relocating to another country.

(4 marks)

(Total = 25 marks)

CIMA Intermediate: Management Accounting – Decision Making, May 2002

Review questions

1 Define the accounting rate of return (ARR).
2 Justify the exclusion of working capital from cash flows.
3 Define the payback period (PBP).
4 Explain why future cash flows should be discounted to today's values.
5 Define the net present value (NPV).
6 Define the internal rate of return (IRR).
7 Discuss the limitations of ARR, PBP, NPV and IRR.
8 Compare NPV with IRR.
9 Criticize the discounted payback approach.
10 Describe the usefulness of sensitivity analysis in managing risk.
11 Explain why the financing decision is excluded from the investment decision.
12 Discuss the importance of relevant qualitative factors.

The answers to all these questions can be found in the text of this chapter.

Present value factor table

This table is used to calculate the present value of an amount received a number of years in the future, discounted at a given percentage rate.
Example 1: at the discount rate of 5%, a sum of £1 received in 25 years' time is currently worth £0.295.
Example 2: at the discount rate of 5%, a sum of £1,000 received in 25 years' time is currently worth £295.00.

Discount rate Years	1%	2%	3%	4%	5%	6%	7%	8%	9%	10%	11%	12%	13%	14%	15%	16%	17%	18%	19%	20%
1	0.990	0.980	0.971	0.962	0.952	0.943	0.935	0.926	0.917	0.909	0.901	0.893	0.885	0.877	0.870	0.862	0.855	0.847	0.840	0.833
2	0.980	0.961	0.943	0.925	0.907	0.890	0.873	0.857	0.842	0.826	0.812	0.797	0.783	0.769	0.756	0.743	0.731	0.718	0.706	0.694
3	0.971	0.942	0.915	0.889	0.864	0.840	0.816	0.794	0.772	0.751	0.731	0.712	0.693	0.675	0.658	0.641	0.624	0.609	0.593	0.579
4	0.961	0.924	0.888	0.855	0.823	0.792	0.763	0.735	0.708	0.683	0.659	0.636	0.613	0.592	0.572	0.552	0.534	0.516	0.499	0.482
5	0.951	0.906	0.863	0.822	0.784	0.747	0.713	0.681	0.650	0.621	0.593	0.567	0.543	0.519	0.497	0.476	0.456	0.437	0.419	0.402
6	0.942	0.888	0.837	0.790	0.746	0.705	0.666	0.630	0.596	0.564	0.535	0.507	0.480	0.456	0.432	0.410	0.390	0.370	0.352	0.335
7	0.933	0.871	0.813	0.760	0.711	0.665	0.623	0.583	0.547	0.513	0.482	0.452	0.425	0.400	0.376	0.354	0.333	0.314	0.296	0.279
8	0.923	0.853	0.789	0.731	0.677	0.627	0.582	0.540	0.502	0.467	0.434	0.404	0.376	0.351	0.327	0.305	0.285	0.266	0.249	0.233
9	0.914	0.837	0.766	0.703	0.645	0.592	0.544	0.500	0.460	0.424	0.391	0.361	0.333	0.308	0.284	0.263	0.243	0.225	0.209	0.194
10	0.905	0.820	0.744	0.676	0.614	0.558	0.508	0.463	0.422	0.386	0.352	0.322	0.295	0.270	0.247	0.227	0.208	0.191	0.176	0.162
11	0.896	0.804	0.722	0.650	0.585	0.527	0.475	0.429	0.388	0.350	0.317	0.287	0.261	0.237	0.215	0.195	0.178	0.162	0.148	0.135
12	0.887	0.788	0.701	0.625	0.557	0.497	0.444	0.397	0.356	0.319	0.286	0.257	0.231	0.208	0.187	0.168	0.152	0.137	0.124	0.112
13	0.879	0.773	0.681	0.601	0.530	0.469	0.415	0.368	0.326	0.290	0.258	0.229	0.204	0.182	0.163	0.145	0.130	0.116	0.104	0.093
14	0.870	0.758	0.661	0.577	0.505	0.442	0.388	0.340	0.299	0.263	0.232	0.205	0.181	0.160	0.141	0.125	0.111	0.099	0.088	0.078
15	0.861	0.743	0.642	0.555	0.481	0.417	0.362	0.315	0.275	0.239	0.209	0.183	0.160	0.140	0.123	0.108	0.095	0.084	0.074	0.065
16	0.853	0.728	0.623	0.534	0.458	0.394	0.339	0.292	0.252	0.218	0.188	0.163	0.141	0.123	0.107	0.093	0.081	0.071	0.062	0.054
17	0.844	0.714	0.605	0.513	0.436	0.371	0.317	0.270	0.231	0.198	0.170	0.146	0.125	0.108	0.093	0.080	0.069	0.060	0.052	0.045
18	0.836	0.700	0.587	0.494	0.416	0.350	0.296	0.250	0.212	0.180	0.153	0.130	0.111	0.095	0.081	0.069	0.059	0.051	0.044	0.038
19	0.828	0.686	0.570	0.475	0.396	0.331	0.277	0.232	0.194	0.164	0.138	0.116	0.098	0.083	0.070	0.060	0.051	0.043	0.037	0.031
20	0.820	0.673	0.554	0.456	0.377	0.312	0.258	0.215	0.178	0.149	0.124	0.104	0.087	0.073	0.061	0.051	0.043	0.037	0.031	0.026
21	0.811	0.660	0.538	0.439	0.359	0.294	0.242	0.199	0.164	0.135	0.112	0.093	0.077	0.064	0.053	0.044	0.037	0.031	0.026	0.022
22	0.803	0.647	0.522	0.422	0.342	0.278	0.226	0.184	0.150	0.123	0.101	0.083	0.068	0.056	0.046	0.038	0.032	0.026	0.022	0.018
23	0.795	0.634	0.507	0.406	0.326	0.262	0.211	0.170	0.138	0.112	0.091	0.074	0.060	0.049	0.040	0.033	0.027	0.022	0.018	0.015
24	0.788	0.622	0.492	0.390	0.310	0.247	0.197	0.158	0.126	0.102	0.082	0.066	0.053	0.043	0.035	0.028	0.023	0.019	0.015	0.013
25	0.780	0.610	0.478	0.375	0.295	0.233	0.184	0.146	0.116	0.092	0.074	0.059	0.047	0.038	0.030	0.024	0.020	0.016	0.013	0.010

Cumulative present value factor table (annuities)

This table is used to calculate the present value of future, consecutive, equal, annual amounts, all discounted at the same percentage rate.
Example 1: at the discount rate of 5%, a sum of £1 received each year for 25 years is currently worth £14.094.
Example 2: at the discount rate of 5%, a sum of £1,000 received each year for 25 years is currently worth £14,094.00.

Discount rate Years	1%	2%	3%	4%	5%	6%	7%	8%	9%	10%	11%	12%	13%	14%	15%	16%	17%	18%	19%	20%
1	0.990	0.980	0.971	0.962	0.952	0.943	0.935	0.926	0.917	0.909	0.901	0.893	0.885	0.877	0.870	0.862	0.855	0.847	0.840	0.833
2	1.970	1.942	1.913	1.886	1.859	1.833	1.808	1.783	1.759	1.736	1.713	1.690	1.668	1.647	1.626	1.605	1.585	1.566	1.547	1.528
3	2.941	2.884	2.829	2.775	2.723	2.673	2.624	2.577	2.531	2.487	2.444	2.402	2.361	2.322	2.283	2.246	2.210	2.174	2.140	2.106
4	3.902	3.808	3.717	3.630	3.546	3.465	3.387	3.312	3.240	3.170	3.102	3.037	2.974	2.914	2.855	2.798	2.743	2.690	2.639	2.589
5	4.853	4.713	4.580	4.452	4.329	4.212	4.100	3.993	3.890	3.791	3.696	3.605	3.517	3.433	3.352	3.274	3.199	3.127	3.058	2.991
6	5.795	5.601	5.417	5.242	5.076	4.917	4.767	4.623	4.486	4.355	4.231	4.111	3.998	3.889	3.784	3.685	3.589	3.498	3.410	3.326
7	6.728	6.472	6.230	6.002	5.786	5.582	5.389	5.206	5.033	4.868	4.712	4.564	4.423	4.288	4.160	4.039	3.922	3.812	3.706	3.605
8	7.652	7.325	7.020	6.733	6.463	6.210	5.971	5.747	5.535	5.335	5.146	4.968	4.799	4.639	4.487	4.344	4.207	4.078	3.954	3.837
9	8.566	8.162	7.786	7.435	7.108	6.802	6.515	6.247	5.995	5.759	5.537	5.328	5.132	4.946	4.772	4.607	4.451	4.303	4.163	4.031
10	9.471	8.983	8.530	8.111	7.722	7.360	7.024	6.710	6.418	6.145	5.889	5.650	5.426	5.216	5.019	4.833	4.659	4.494	4.339	4.192
11	10.368	9.787	9.253	8.760	8.306	7.887	7.499	7.139	6.805	6.495	6.207	5.938	5.687	5.453	5.234	5.029	4.836	4.656	4.486	4.327
12	11.255	10.575	9.954	9.385	8.863	8.384	7.943	7.536	7.161	6.814	6.492	6.194	5.918	5.660	5.421	5.197	4.988	4.793	4.611	4.439
13	12.134	11.348	10.635	9.986	9.394	8.853	8.358	7.904	7.487	7.103	6.750	6.424	6.122	5.842	5.583	5.342	5.118	4.910	4.715	4.533
14	13.004	12.106	11.296	10.563	9.899	9.295	8.745	8.244	7.786	7.367	6.982	6.628	6.302	6.002	5.724	5.468	5.229	5.008	4.802	4.611
15	13.865	12.849	11.938	11.118	10.380	9.712	9.108	8.559	8.061	7.606	7.191	6.811	6.462	6.142	5.847	5.575	5.324	5.092	4.876	4.675
16	14.718	13.578	12.561	11.652	10.838	10.106	9.447	8.851	8.313	7.824	7.379	6.974	6.604	6.265	5.954	5.668	5.405	5.162	4.938	4.730
17	15.562	14.292	13.166	12.166	11.274	10.477	9.763	9.122	8.544	8.022	7.549	7.120	6.729	6.373	6.047	5.749	5.475	5.222	4.990	4.775
18	16.398	14.992	13.754	12.659	11.690	10.828	10.059	9.372	8.756	8.201	7.702	7.250	6.840	6.467	6.128	5.818	5.534	5.273	5.033	4.812
19	17.226	15.678	14.324	13.134	12.085	11.158	10.336	9.604	8.950	8.365	7.839	7.366	6.938	6.550	6.198	5.877	5.584	5.316	5.070	4.843
20	18.046	16.351	14.877	13.590	12.462	11.470	10.594	9.818	9.129	8.514	7.963	7.469	7.025	6.623	6.259	5.929	5.628	5.353	5.101	4.870
21	18.857	17.011	15.415	14.029	12.821	11.764	10.836	10.017	9.292	8.649	8.075	7.562	7.102	6.687	6.312	5.973	5.665	5.384	5.127	4.891
22	19.660	17.658	15.937	14.451	13.163	12.042	11.061	10.201	9.442	8.772	8.176	7.645	7.170	6.743	6.359	6.011	5.696	5.410	5.149	4.909
23	20.456	18.292	16.444	14.857	13.489	12.303	11.272	10.371	9.580	8.883	8.266	7.718	7.230	6.792	6.399	6.044	5.723	5.432	5.167	4.925
24	21.243	18.914	16.936	15.247	13.799	12.550	11.469	10.529	9.707	8.985	8.348	7.784	7.283	6.835	6.434	6.073	5.746	5.451	5.182	4.937
25	22.023	19.523	17.413	15.622	14.094	12.783	11.654	10.675	9.823	9.077	8.422	7.843	7.330	6.873	6.464	6.097	5.766	5.467	5.195	4.948

PRODUCT COSTING AND PRICING

Part 4 comprises

There are four major reasons why it is essential to know the cost of your products. First, they are an essential prerequisite for the creation of the financial accounts. The profit and loss account needs a valuation of the opening stock and the cost of sales. The balance sheet must show the value of closing stock. This is based on the production or buying-in cost of the business's products or services.

Second, every so often managers have to make decisions regarding products and activities. For example, a customer may ask you to produce some non-standard items on a one-off basis but at a lower price than your normal selling price. In order to decide whether to accept, you need to be aware of the different product cost models and which one will help you make the right decision.

Third, in order to control costs, you need accurate information as to how much your products actually cost. If you do not know how much something costs, how do you know if you are paying too much or too little for it? Marketing and selling are vital business activities but profits created by them will soon disappear if costs are not kept under control.

The fourth reason is to avoid setting your selling prices too low. The last chapter in Part 2 describes the various ways in which prices can be set. This is another crucial management task. If prices are set too high, demand will fall and profits will reduce or disappear completely. If prices are set too low, sales revenue may not be sufficient to cover costs and losses will occur rather than profits. To avoid this happening, you need to know what your costs are.

Also, there is the problem of how to set the selling price of goods sold by one division of a company to another division of the same company. The buying division will want it to be as low as possible but the selling division will want it to be as high as possible! These intra-group prices are known as 'transfer prices' and there are several different ways of calculating them. Group directors at head office need to be very careful about their choices in these matters as there is much scope for demotivating divisional managers and so diminishing overall group profits. Thus, transfer pricing is inextricably linked to the management of divisional performance.

Many large organizations adopt divisionalized structures in order to keep control over a business that may be involved in many different products and services in many different countries. However, divisionalization implies a significant degree of autonomy being given to each business unit and, therefore, a lack of head office control. The question is, 'how much authority should be delegated to ensure optimal performance?' Then there is the problem of how divisional performance should be evaluated. Which of the alternative measures should be used?

CHAPTER 9

Product costs using absorption costing

Introduction

At some stage in your career, you may find yourself responsible for controlling costs. The object of this exercise is to minimize the costs of your products, which should enable you to keep their selling prices competitive. Hopefully, the result of this will be increased numbers of items sold and good levels of profit. Cost control is an important activity for all organizations. So how is it achieved?

The first step is fundamental. In order to control a cost, you have to have an accurate measurement of it, i.e. you need to know exactly how much the cost is. Without this information your task is impossible.

Another good reason for determining product costs is that, from time to time, you may be required to make decisions concerning your products. For example, if you do not know the cost of a product when setting its selling price, you may unknowingly set the price lower than cost. The obvious consequence of this is that you will trade at a loss rather than at a profit.

A further important reason for knowing your product costs is that they are used to value the cost of sales and stock in the periodic accounts of organizations. Indeed, the second international accounting standard (IAS 2) prescribes that production and stock must be valued at the 'absorption' production cost for accounts which are accessible to owners and other interested people **outside** the organization. In effect, if this is not done, the Companies Act is breached and the company is acting illegally and should expect to suffer the adverse consequences.

Note that this chapter applies to those organizations which perform work on their raw materials to convert them into finished products. It does not apply to merchanting or trading companies which buy at one price and sell for a higher price without changing the products in any way.

Learning objectives

Having worked through this chapter you should be able to:

- explain the difference between direct and indirect costs;
- list the constituent parts of an absorption cost;
- allocate and apportion overheads to cost centres;
- calculate overhead absorption rates using a variety of different bases;
- use overhead absorption rates to attach overheads to products.

Direct and indirect costs

(This section first appears in Chapter 1 but is repeated here for your convenience.) The absorption cost of a product is based on the assumption that costs can be analysed into their 'direct' and 'indirect' components which are defined as follows.

Direct cost

This is expenditure which can be economically identified with, and specifically measured in respect to, a relevant cost object or product. Consider an advertising agency specializing in the production of television adverts. The cost of hiring a celebrity to appear in one such advert is a measurable direct cost of that advert. Similarly, if the company is a furniture manufacturer, the cost of materials used to make a chair and the pay of the operative assembling it are measurable direct costs of that chair.

Indirect cost (or overhead)

This is expenditure on labour, materials or services which cannot be economically identified with a specific saleable cost unit or product. There are many, many different overheads, including supervisors' pay, depreciation of fixed assets, business rates and insurance. Remember,

$$\text{Total absorption cost} = \text{direct cost} + \text{indirect cost}$$

Try the following question for yourself (answer at the end of the chapter).

Macframe Ltd makes photograph frames and sells them to national retail chains. The following costs are incurred in connection with its manufacturing process. Decide whether each cost is direct or indirect and give your reasons.

1 Picture frame moulding.
2 Pay of assembly department's supervisor.
3 Heating oil used for cutting department.
4 Pay of employees assembling frames.
5 Dab of glue put in each corner joint of frame.

Self-assessment question S9.1

The absorption cost of products

The way the product cost is determined in absorption costing is illustrated in Figure 9.1. This shows that as well as the total of direct costs (prime cost) the production overheads

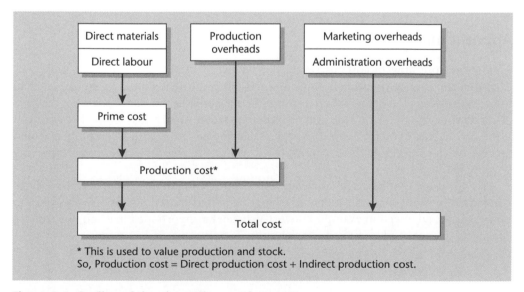

Figure 9.1 Outline of the absorption costing system

are included in the production cost (in accordance with IAS 2). Stock of finished goods is unsold production so it is logical to value it at production cost. Note that all other overheads, although part of the total cost, are excluded from the production cost. These other overheads are treated as 'period' costs and are listed in the profit and loss account as deductions from the gross profit.

The objective of absorption costing is to ensure that both the direct and indirect costs of production are included in the production cost. The CIMA *Management Accounting Official Terminology* (2000) describes absorption costing as 'a method of costing that, in addition to direct costs, assigns . . . production overhead costs to cost units by means of . . . overhead absorption rates'.

Determining the direct production costs is relatively simple as the amount of them in each product can be measured. But how do we know how much of the production director's pay, depreciation of equipment, etc., to include in the cost of a specific product or service? These indirect costs cannot be measured so there has to be some other mechanism for attaching them to products. This is achieved by allocation, apportionment and absorption of overheads.

Attaching overheads to products

Allocation

This is the assigning of **whole** items of cost, or revenue, to a single cost unit or centre. For example, in a company making furniture, an invoice for 50 kilograms of sausage meat can be safely allocated **in total** to the canteen cost centre. However, if the company produced processed foods, further investigation would be necessary. If the sausage meat was an ingredient of one of the company's products, it would be a direct cost and not an overhead.

Apportionment

This is the spreading of costs or revenues over two or more cost centres or units. For example, the invoice total for flu injections for all employees should be spread over all the cost centres in the organization. But how is this done? In this particular case, the total could be spread in the same ratio as the number of people in each cost centre. For example, if the invoice was £500 for 500 people, the dispatch cost centre with 12 employees would receive twice the amount (£12) apportioned to the site security cost centre employing six people (£6).

An apportionment base should have a logical connection to the nature of the overhead concerned. It should have a rationality of some kind but it need not give as 'accurate' an answer as the flu injection example above. Costs can be apportioned in a 'fair' way to cost centres by means of physical or financial units. For example,

Costs	Basis of apportionment
Personnel department	Number of employees
Business rates	Area
Heating and lighting	Area **or** volume
Insurance	Net book value **or** cost of assets
Maintenance	Number of machines
Central stores	Value of production **or** number of stores issues
Production planning	Value of production

Absorption

This is the attaching of overheads to products or services by means of overhead absorption rates (OARs) using some measure of activity. For example,

£/direct labour hour	% of total labour cost
£/machine hour	% of prime cost

Overhead attachment procedure (illustrated in Figure 9.2)

Step 1

Allocate or apportion the overheads to the production and service cost centres (by reasonable bases of apportionment).

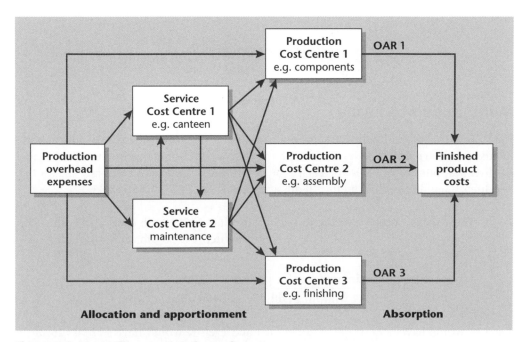

Figure 9.2 Production overhead attachment

Step 2

The total cost of the service centres is apportioned first to other service centres which use their service, and second to the production centres so that all overheads end up in production centres.

Step 3

The total amount of each production centre is divided by some measure of activity (e.g. machine hours) to derive the overhead absorption rate (OAR).

Note that production overheads are absorbed only from production cost centres or departments. All service centre overheads must be transferred into production cost centres. Where service cost centres service each other, the easiest way of dealing with this is to determine the order in which it happens and transfer the costs in that order. It may not exactly reflect reality but, unless the overheads involved are a very large proportion of total overheads, it will do the job. Remember that the nature of apportionment leads to estimates rather than perfect 'accuracy'.

Single- and multi-product companies

To illustrate these two alternative scenarios, a fork-lift truck driver's pay of £200/week is used as an example of a production overhead.

Single-product company

If a factory makes only one product, and makes 40 of them each week, the overhead absorption rate is

$$\text{OAR} = \frac{\text{estimated pay for period}}{\text{number of items made}} = \frac{200}{40} = £5/\text{unit}$$

Multi-product company

If a factory makes several different products, a different method is needed to absorb overheads into each product on an equitable basis. One way of doing this is to use the number of direct labour hours (dlh) for each type of product. Suppose a company makes two products, G and K, each G taking 10 dlh and each K taking 25 dlh to make.

If estimated weekly production = 30 × product G @ 10 dlh each = 300 dlh
4 × product K @ 25 dlh each = $\underline{100}$ dlh
$\underline{\underline{400}}$ dlh

$$\text{OAR} = \frac{\text{estimated pay for period}}{\text{output in dlh}} = \frac{£200}{400\ \text{dlh}} = £0.50/\text{dlh}$$

Each G would have £5 (10 dlh × £0.50/dlh) and each K would have £12.50 (25 dlh × £0.50/dlh) of the fork-lift truck driver's pay attached to it.

This approach is then extended to include all overheads. If these totalled £6,000 a week, then

$$OAR = \frac{\text{estimated total overhead cost for period}}{\text{output in dlh}} = \frac{£6,000}{400} = £15/\text{dlh}$$

In a machine-intensive, automated manufacturing environment, machine hours would probably be used instead of direct labour hours. (Remember that other factors may be used for OARs, such as multiples of the material cost or wages cost.)

Overhead attachment

Example 9.1

Maykit Ltd manufactures plastic chairs. It has two production departments (Moulding and Assembly) and one service department (Canteen). The following information is taken from this year's budget:

	Moulding	Assembly	Canteen
Direct labour hours	10,000	50,000	–
Machine hours	15,000	5,000	–
Direct labour pay (£)	100,000	200,000	–
Indirect labour pay (£)	3,030	5,220	4,000

Fixed factory overheads (per year)

	£
Rent and rates	15,000
Depreciation of machinery (straight line)	7,200
Heat and light	4,800
Protective clothing	6,500

Other information

	Moulding	Assembly	Canteen
Number of employees	2	8	3
Area (square metres)	3,000	5,000	2,000
Cost of machinery (£)	60,000	36,000	24,000

Tasks:

1 Calculate the total overhead cost for each department.
2 Attach the service department overhead to the production departments.
3 Calculate the most appropriate overhead absorption rate for each production department.
4 What value of production overheads would be absorbed by a batch of chairs taking two machine hours to mould and three direct labour hours to assemble?

Solution

Apportionment of rent and rates (total cost £15,000):

Most rational basis of apportionment is 'area'. Total area 10,000 sq. m.

	Moulding	Assembly	Canteen	Total
Proportion	3,000	5,000	2,000	10,000
	10,000	10,000	10,000	10,000
	= 3/10	= 5/10	= 2/10	= 10/10
Overhead cost	£15,000	£15,000	£15,000	£15,000
Apportionment	**£4,500**	**£7,500**	**£3,000**	**£15,000**

Apportionment of protective clothing (total cost £6,500):

Most rational basis of apportionment is 'number of employees' = 13.

	Moulding	Assembly	Canteen	Total
Proportion	2/13	8/13	3/13	13/13
Overhead cost	£6,500	£6,500	£6,500	£6,500
Apportionment	**£1,000**	**£4,000**	**£1,500**	**£6,500**

1	Moulding	Assembly	Canteen	Total
Indirect pay	3,030	5,220	4,000	12,250
Rent and rates (area)	4,500	7,500	3,000	15,000
Depreciation of machinery (cost)	3,600	2,160	1,440	7,200
Heat and light (area)	1,440	2,400	960	4,800
Protective clothing (employees)	1,000	4,000	1,500	6,500
Total overhead cost	**13,570**	**21,280**	**10,900**	**45,750**

2				
Canteen overheads (employees)	2,180	8,720	(10,900)	–
Service overhead attachment	**15,750**	**30,000**	–	**45,750**

3	Moulding	Assembly
Machine hours	15,000	–
Direct labour hours	–	50,000
OAR	15,750	3,000
	15,000	50,000
	= £1.05/mh	= £0.60/dlh

4			
Batch of chairs	2 mh	3 dlh	
Batch overhead	**£2.10**	**£1.80**	Total £3.90

Try the following question for yourself (answer at the end of the chapter).

Self-assessment
question S9.2

Cayten Ltd produces domestic robots to perform household chores. Its manufacturing facilities consist of three production departments and two service departments. The following information is taken from the company's current annual budget.

	Production cost centres			Service cost centres	
	PA	PB	PC	SD	SE
Indirect labour (£)	80,850	87,750	36,600	45,900	42,400
Direct labour (£)	100,000	110,000	140,000		
Direct labour hours (dlh)	90,000	120,000	90,000		
Machine hours (mh)	80,000	90,000	75,000		

Production overheads	£
Business rates	8,000
Electricity to run machines	6,000
Heating and lighting	4,800
Insurance for machinery ('like for like' policy)	2,700
Depreciation of machinery (straight line over 10 years)	19,000
Total	40,500

The following information relates to the cost centres:

	PA	PB	PC	SD	SE
Number of employees	20	35	25	12	8
Original cost of machinery (£)	60,000	70,000	40,000	20,000	–
Machinery written-down value (£)	20,000	40,000	25,000	5,000	–
Machinery power rating (joules)	350	450	250	150	–
Floor area (square metres)	12,000	8,000	5,000	3,000	4,000

Required:

a) Calculate the total overhead for each cost centre.
b) Reassign service cost centre overheads to production cost centres on the following basis:

	PA	PB	PC
SD	30%	50%	20%
SE	25%	40%	35%

c) Calculate an overhead absorption rate for each production cost centre using the following bases:

PA	machine hour basis
PB	direct labour hour basis
PC	percentage of direct pay

d) Calculate the total of production overheads absorbed by an order requiring the following resources:

	PA	PB	PC
Machine hours	7,000	2,100	900
Direct labour hours	600	9,800	2,000
Direct wages (£)	2,700	45,000	11,600

Limitations of absorption costing

Absorption costing is approximately a hundred years old. It was devised for a manufacturing era whose products relied upon direct labour much more than they do today. Volume production in the twenty-first century is based on computer-controlled automatic machinery. Compare a car production line from the 1930s with one 70 years later and the difference is quite astonishing. From a distance, the old line would look something like an ant's nest, with men scurrying about doing all kinds of job. The machinery used by them consisted to a great extent of hand-tools such as screwdrivers and spanners. The latest lines are often quite devoid of people apart from the occasional machine minder. The robotic machinery being overseen probably cost millions of pounds, which causes a commensurately large amount of depreciation (a production overhead). The trend over the last 50 years has been an increase in the importance of overheads. The proportion of overheads in the total production cost is far greater now than it was in the past.

Absorption costing was not designed for the modern automated technological environment. Overhead absorption rates are a crude device for attaching overheads to products. The absorption costing system is mathematically sound and ensures that all the production overheads are absorbed by all the production. In the days when overheads were only a small part of the total costs, it did not matter if they were not particularly accurate. Today, when overheads often represent well over 50% of total costs, it does matter. Fortunately, activity-based costing now exists to fill that gap. Having said all this, many businesses still use absorption costing. Like many aspects of business life, there is a reluctance to change from a tried-and-tested system to something new. However, the pressures of competitive marketplaces will drive the change. Absorption costing will be used less and less as time passes.

The manager's point of view (written by Nigel Burton)

No single costing system is ever likely to provide the perfect answer to a company's costing requirements. However, all systems, by providing views of the business from different angles, will produce some information of greater or lesser value to management. In certain circumstances, absorption costing may indeed prove to be the best available solution, although its inherent drawbacks will render it inappropriate for many companies.

Absorption costing is essentially simple and is therefore best suited to companies with simple processes. Consider, for example, a paint blending operation, consisting of a wide range of end products being produced on a number of standard blending machines. The blending process is simple, identical for each product, and unlikely to require significant levels of overhead. In this case, the simple spreading of overhead across all products, on a volume (i.e. number of units produced) or machine hours basis, may be perfectly adequate, particularly as overhead is likely to be a relatively small component of the overall product cost.

As companies become more complex, the simple principles of absorption costing may give a distorted picture of product costs. If our paint blender were to decide to backward-integrate into paint manufacture, and, at the same time, diversify into paint can production, its previous practice of spreading overhead simply across products would clearly no longer be valid. It would need to introduce more sophistication into its costing system to match the needs of the more complicated business. As complexity grows, the problems with absorption costing become more apparent.

Imagine a large manufacturing company, with multiple production cost centres, each producing a range of products, by differing processes, on various items of plant. The absorption costing system first requires the allocation of expenses to cost centres. Consider electricity. How many companies can accurately attribute electricity usage to individual production areas, as opposed to equipment in the maintenance department, or heating in the offices, or lighting in the factory yard? Larger companies may have it all metered, but most will need to determine some kind of apportionment. This may apply not only to utilities like electricity, but also to other items such as supervisors' salaries where the supervisors work in more than one cost centre. This is a general problem, and not necessarily specific to the absorption costing method, but it does introduce a measure of inaccuracy which absorption costing compounds.

Then the service centre costs have to be reapportioned to production cost centres. These costs, which may include maintenance, quality control, waste treatment, general factory expenses, etc., can be relatively high, so the basis of apportionment is critical. Take the cost of maintaining machinery: 'number of machines' or 'machine hours' may be a reasonable basis, but the likelihood is that Machine A is continually breaking down, while Machine B runs perfectly smoothly. Some processes place much greater physical demands on the equipment than others. For example, a very corrosive process will wear out the equipment much more quickly than a non-corrosive process. So, perhaps actual time spent on these machines by the maintenance department in the past may be a better basis for reapportioning service centre costs – though not of course if the attention given to Machine A has finally fixed a long-running problem! Similar issues surround the allocation of all service departments, and have the potential to cause major distortions.

Finally, a basis is needed to attribute production cost centres to products. These cost centres now include the reapportioned service department costs, so the numbers are significant. The use of direct labour hours as a basis is very common, but this too can be troublesome. For instance, it does not take proper account of Product C, which requires a large amount of machine time (e.g. for cooling, drying or processing) but with minimum labour input. The use of direct labour hours will seriously undercost this product. On the other hand, using machine hours may substantially undercost Product D, which requires constant supervision throughout its production cycle and consequently uses a disproportionate amount of departmental resource.

A great deal of care is required in identifying the most appropriate bases of apportionment, but a similar amount of attention needs to be given to the flaws inherent in these bases. In arriving at the final cost of our products, we have had to resort to apportionments at every level. This raises some awkward questions. First, does the final product cost contain the correct overall charge for electricity? Answer: We have no idea! Second, is the product cost correct? Answer: We do not know! Third, what level of confidence do we have in the accuracy of the product cost? Answer: We are not sure!

The key to cost apportionment is to ensure that the bases are agreed and accepted as valid by all sides. For organizational reasons, many companies divide their products into logical groupings, or product lines, each with its own business manager. Each product line has its own sales department and production cost centre, but factory management and general administration remain centralized. The apportionment of overheads will have a direct impact on the profitability of individual product lines. And in a competitive world, where demands from senior management for higher returns grow ever louder, the two options available to the business manager are either to increase sales or to cut costs. The easiest way for a business manager to increase profits at a stroke is to convince the accountant that the overhead apportionments are unfair, and that some of the costs should consequently be transferred to other product lines. In my experience, this has proved to be a recurring cause of irritation, argument and management time consumption. For this reason it is essential that the cost apportionment bases are defensible. However, this is not an easy position to achieve in a conventional absorption costing environment.

Finally, while considering the impact of overhead apportionments on the profits of individual business groups, there is another area of legitimate concern for managers. In a single-business-group company, indirect expenses, such as the factory manager's salary, security and business rates, are genuinely fixed costs which do not change as sales levels grow. In a two-business-group company, these expenses will be apportioned between the businesses on the basis of, say, direct labour hours. Similarly, non-production expenses, such as general administration, will also have an arbitrary basis, perhaps sales or volume. If the two businesses grow at the same rate, the proportion of costs assigned to each will remain the same from year to year. But suppose one business ran into trouble, and its sales halved. This would result in a switch of overhead from the failing business to the successful business. Through no fault of its own, and without any increase in the overall level of expenses, the successful business will suffer a substantial increase in its fixed costs. Is this fair? I think not. It seems to me that the failing group should suffer the full impact on profits of its reduced income.

The same situation exists if the sales of the successful business forge ahead. If its apportionment of overhead were to go up proportionately, it would be tantamount to treating fixed costs as variable! Some reapportionment may well be desirable over time, but this could perhaps best be achieved by small changes over a number of years. Business group managers, and indeed all other users of financial information, are looking for consistency, fairness and clarity. Nothing is more frustrating than finding the impact of one's sales achievements being eroded by the blind application of accounting principles, which may be mathematically correct, but logically flawed. Senior managers judge businesses on their ability to produce consistent profit growth over a number of years, and the accounting principles adopted should serve to support this objective. Absorption accounting may do the job for you, but always be aware of its limitations, and treat the results with a due measure of caution.

My purpose here is not to devalue absorption costing as a valid accounting tool, but merely to highlight the potential pitfalls. These difficulties are evident in any accounting system which requires a measure of apportionment. But absorption costing can compound the margin of error through its broadbrush approach, to the point that the information provided is so inaccurate that it risks leading management into making erroneous decisions.

Summary

- The absorption cost is the sum of the direct and indirect costs.
- Absorption costing treats production overheads as product costs.
- Overheads are assigned to cost centres via allocation and apportionment.
- Apportionment uses bases which are rational but not necessarily accurate.
- Service cost centre totals are reapportioned to production cost centres.
- Overheads are absorbed into production costs via overhead absorption rates.
- Overhead absorption rates are usually different for each production cost centre.
- Absorption costing is becoming less relevant to advanced technological production.

Further reading

Atkinson, A., Banker, R., Kaplan, R. and Young, S. (2001) *Management Accounting*, 3rd edition, Prentice Hall, Harlow. See chapter 'Traditional cost management systems'.

Drury, C. and Tayles, M. (2005) 'Explicating the design of overhead absorption procedures in UK organizations', *British Accounting Review*, Vol. 37, Issue 1, March.

Johnson, H. and Kaplan, R. (1987) *Relevance Lost, the Rise and Fall of Management Accounting*, Harvard Business School Press, Boston, MA. This provides a fascinating history of traditional cost accounting and states the case for a new direction.

Lucas, M. (2000) 'The reality of product costing', *Management Accounting*, February.

Upchurch, A. (2003) *Management Accounting, Principles and Practice*, 2nd edition, Financial Times/Prentice Hall, Harlow. See chapter 'Absorption of overheads'.

Weetman, P. (2002) *Management Accounting, an Introduction*, 3rd edition, Financial Times/Prentice Hall, Harlow. See chapter 'Accounting for materials, labour and overheads'.

Answers to self-assessment questions

S9.1 Macframe Ltd

1 Picture frame moulding is a direct cost – identifiable and measurable.

2 Pay of assembly department's supervisor is an indirect cost – not specifically identifiable in product.

3 Heating oil used for cutting department is an indirect cost – not specifically identifiable in product.

4 Pay of employees assembling frames is a direct cost – identifiable and measurable.

5 Dab of glue put in each corner joint of frame is, in theory, a direct cost as it is identifiable and measurable. However, in practice, this would be treated as an indirect cost as the cost of measuring and valuing the dab of glue would be far greater than the value of the information gained. Accounting activities should always be carried out in a commercially sensible manner.

S9.2 Cayten Ltd

	PA	PB	PC	SD	SE	Total
Indirect labour	80,850	87,750	36,600	45,900	42,400	293,500
Business rates (area)	3,000	2,000	1,250	750	1,000	8,000
Power (joules)	1,750	2,250	1,250	750	–	6,000
Light and heat (area)	1,800	1,200	750	450	600	4,800
Insurance (WDV)	600	1,200	750	150	–	2,700
Depreciation (orig. cost)	6,000	7,000	4,000	2,000	–	19,000
Sub-totals	**94,000**	**101,400**	**44,600**	**50,000**	**44,000**	**334,000**
Adj. SD	15,000	25,000	10,000	(50,000)	–	–
Adj. SE	11,000	17,600	15,400	–	(44,000)	–
Total overheads	**120,000**	**144,000**	**70,000**	–	–	**334,000**

PA	PB	PC
$\dfrac{120,000}{80,000}$	$\dfrac{144,000}{120,000}$	$\dfrac{70,000}{140,000} \times 100$

= £1.50/mh × 7,000 mh = £1.20/dlh × 9,800 dlh = 50% of direct labour cost × £11,600
= £10,500   = £11,760   = £5,800

Total absorbed = £28,060 (10,500 + 11,760 + 5,800)

Travelsound Ltd was started five years ago by three friends who had just graduated from university. They had lived in the same house for two years and were all passionate about music. During their many late-night discussions they talked much about music and, as two of them were electronic engineers, they often discussed the latest equipment for sound reproduction and how it could be improved. The third person had a joint degree in finance and marketing and saw the opportunity for a business venture involving state-of-the-art sound systems.

They started out in a garage at the home of one of their parents and soon found that ideas alone were not enough to run a business. Most of their work in the first two years consisted of upgrading and constructing personal computers and laptops. Through their contacts, they also gained from their old university several one-off contracts concerned with upgrading software and hardware (a perennial occupation for universities). At this stage in their development they employed five assistants.

Towards the end of their second year they bid for a contract to manufacture small quantities of an experimental mobile phone for a European electronics group. To their delight, they were awarded the contract and have produced several versions of this phone over the last few years. By the start of their fourth year they had 27 employees. In that year they gained the right to produce, under licence, mini-disc players for a Japanese company. This contract has gone very well despite the very tight profit margins involved. In fact, the sales price was slightly below the original estimated absorption production cost. They decided to go ahead on the assumption that they would be able to reduce their costs as they gained experience of manufacturing this product. (Although they were not aware of it, this was the reason they were awarded the contract, as other more established firms had turned it down as they believed it was not profitable.) Fortunately, Travelsound had made the right decision and this work currently has a positive net profit margin of around 3%.

However, in recent months, relations with this company have deteriorated, mainly due to a change in the pound/yen exchange rate. In fact, the three Travelsound directors believe that their licence will be revoked at the next renewal date in two months' time unless they are willing to trade in euros instead of UK pounds. They are apprehensive about this as the euro/pound exchange rate has been falling consistently for over a year. It would not be difficult for this work to be moved to mainland Europe where a significant amount of overcapacity exists.

Throughout their five-year history, they maintained an active interest in the improvement of sound systems. What little spare time the two engineering directors had was spent on developing a new method of sound reproduction. They are now at the point where, with the help of an agent, they have applied for a patent on their invention. They currently employ 88 people and made a net profit last year of £45,000. Their annual production rate is now 10,000 phones and 38,000 mini-disc players. They wish to grow in size and profitability but are unsure of how to do it. As an organization, they are now approaching a crisis point. One alternative is for them to replace the mini-disc player production with a new product using their own new technology.

This product has been named the MNP, short for Music Net Phone. It combines a WAP phone with their own miniaturized sound reproduction system which is also able to play mini-discs. They have tentatively approached the European electronics group for whom they manufacture mobile phones, with a view to its marketing the MNP. The European company is very interested but needs some indication of price before taking the idea any further.

Travelsound now needs to cost the MNP using the absorption costing system. The directors decide to do this using next year's budget, which is based on continuing production of mobile phones and mini-disc players. They assume the overheads will be the same if the mini-disc player is replaced by the MNP. The following information comes from this budget.

Travelsound has three production cost centres and three service cost centres. The former are electronic components, plastic cases and assembly. The latter are the canteen, material stores and quality control. The quality controllers inspect goods received into the stores as well as the output of each production cost centre. The assembly shop uses the manufactured components, plastic cases and items from material stores to produce the finished items ready for delivery. The estimated cost for one MNP is £12.20 for materials and £9.80 for direct labour. A single materials store serves only the three production departments. The canteen is situated just inside the factory entrance.

The production overheads are shown as:

	£
Factory rent and rates	150,000
Depreciation of machinery (straight line)	89,250
Machinery insurance (like-for-like basis)	53,000
Cost centre managers' pay	80,000
Materials storekeepers' pay	19,125
Quality controllers' pay	32,000
Heating and lighting	14,000
Canteen costs	29,920
Factory security	25,000
	492,295

The managers of the components, cases and assembly cost centres earn salaries of £30,000, £25,000 and £25,000 respectively. Factory security is provided by a local firm patrolling inside and outside the factory at intervals throughout the night. One quality controller earns £20,000 p.a., spending 30% of his time on stores materials and 70% on components. The other quality controller, who works part time, earns £12,000 p.a. and divides her time equally between cases and assembly. Any quality control costs other than pay should be considered proportional to the amounts of quality controllers' pay incurred by each cost centre. All employees eat in the canteen.

Other information:

	Canteen	Stores	Quality control	Assembly	Cases	Components
Area (sq. metres)	550	600	25	1,900	795	1,130
Employees	6	3	2	36	12	29
Number of stores issues	–	–	–	51,000	10,200	2,550
Direct labour hours	–	–	–	120,309	33,410	99,281
Direct labour cost (£)	–	–	–	611,404	148,596	450,000
Machine hours	–	–	–	100,973	51,236	453,791
Machinery cost (£000)	–	–	–	340	510	1,700
Machinery WDV (£000)	–	–	–	250	350	1,400

Tasks:

1 Calculate the overhead absorption rate (OAR) for each production cost centre. The bases used should be direct labour hours for assembly, machine hours for components and a percentage of direct labour cost for cases.

(40 marks)

2 Calculate the absorption production cost for one MNP if a batch of 100 MNPs takes 9,000 machine hours in the component shop, 667 direct labour hours in the assembly shop and has a direct labour cost of £1,100 in the case shop.

(10 marks)

3 Discuss the situation and advise Travelsound Ltd on its future course of action.

(50 marks)

(Total 100 marks)

Questions

An asterisk * on a question number indicates that the answer is given at the end of the book. Answers to the other questions are given in the Lecturer's Guide.

Q9.1* Lewington Ltd

Lewington Ltd makes a variety of kitchen fittings and equipment. It uses a three-stage process involving cutting, assembly and finishing. The following figures are extracted from its budget for the current year:

	Cutting	Assembly	Finishing
Production overheads (£000)	1,600	2,000	1,400
Machine hours	40,000	25,000	14,000
Direct labour hours	10,000	40,000	20,000

The company uses an absorption costing system for calculating its costs.

A batch of 300 'DX' workstations has just been produced using £3,300 of materials, £4,500 of direct labour and the following quantities of time:

	Cutting	Assembly	Finishing
Machine hours	50	25	10
Direct labour hours	20	45	20

Tasks:

Calculate the unit production cost and the total production cost of the batch of 'DX' workstations using the following three alternative bases:

1 Departmental overhead absorption rates are calculated on a machine hour basis.
2 Departmental overhead absorption rates are calculated on a direct labour hour basis.
3 The Cutting overhead absorption rate is calculated on a machine hour basis but the Assembly and Finishing rates are calculated on a direct labour hour basis.

Comment on your findings.

Q9.2* Graham and Sara

Graham and Sara are partners in a clothes manufacturing firm. Graham manages menswear and Sara controls ladies fashions. They have just received last year's accounts which are summarized below.

	Mens £000	Womens £000	Total £000
Materials	78	26	104
Direct labour	18	30	48
Variable overheads	4	4	8
Variable production cost	100	60	160
Fixed production overheads	10	6	16
Total production cost	110	66	176
Increase in stock	2	1	3
Cost of sales	108	65	173
Marketing overheads	8	4	12
Administration overheads	4	4	8
Total cost	120	73	193
Sales revenue	118	78	196
Profit/(loss)	(2)	5	3

Naturally, Sara is pleased with the results but Graham is not so happy. On questioning their accountant he finds that the fixed production overheads have been apportioned on the basis of variable production costs. He wonders how the results would change if they were apportioned on different bases.

Tasks:

1 Redraft the above statement if the fixed production overheads were apportioned on the basis of:
   a) direct material cost;
   b) direct labour cost;
   c) variable overhead cost.
2 What do your answers tell you about the absorption costing system?

Q9.3* Stellar Showers

Stellar Showers Co. Ltd manufactures domestic electric showers. It moulds its own plastic casings but buys in the other components from a variety of sources. In addition to 54 production operatives, it employs two quality controllers and four stores operatives. The company's production facility consists of three production cost centres (moulding, assembly and packaging) and two service cost centres (quality control and material stores). Quality control inspects work in the three production centres as well as goods received into the materials store. The store services the three production centres only.

Stellar's annual budget lists the following production overheads:

	£
Electricity to run machines and equipment	40,000
Material stores running costs	80,000
Heating (oil-fired boiler)	13,000
Lighting	4,000
Supervision	65,000
Production manager	35,000
Business rates	16,000
Fire insurance	10,000
Quality controllers' pay	30,000
Depreciation (straight line)	18,000

The supervision overhead consists of an assembly supervisor (£25,000 p.a.), a moulding supervisor (£20,000 p.a.) and a packaging supervisor (£20,000 p.a.).

The following information is also available:

	Moulding	Assembly	Packaging	Quality control	Stores
Head count	12	36	6	2	4
Machine wattage	4,500	1,200	300	–	–
Stores issue notes	2,000	14,500	3,500	–	–
Area (sq. metres)	300	800	500	50	350
Volume (cu. metres)	1,200	2,100	2,000	100	1,100
Fixed assets – cost	50,000	40,000	20,000	–	10,000
Fixed assets – WDV	22,000	18,000	9,000	–	1,000
Added value (£000)	800	5,700	500	–	–
Machine hours	34,967	24,080	3,944	–	–
Direct labour hours	20,016	63,986	10,998	–	–
Quality control (hrs/wk)	6	18	6	4	6

Tasks:

1 Calculate the most appropriate overhead absorption rate for each production cost centre.

2 Calculate the unit production cost of an SS40T shower if a batch of 800 uses the following resources:

Direct materials	£16,000
Direct labour	£8,800
Machine hours in moulding	1,500
Machine hours in assembly	900
Machine hours in packaging	170
Direct labour hours in moulding	1,200
Direct labour hours in assembly	3,500
Direct labour hours in packaging	1,000

Q9.4 Medley Ltd

Medley Ltd makes dishwashers. There are three production departments: machining, assembly and finishing; and two service departments: maintenance and stores.

Costs are as follows:

	Machining	Assembly	Finishing	Maintenance	Stores
Direct materials	£240,000	£160,000	£40,000	–	–
Direct wages	£200,000	£150,000	£100,000	–	–
Indirect wages	£9,000	£8,000	£8,000	£11,000	£8,000
Indirectmaterials	–	–	–	£4,000	–

Factory overheads are:

Business rates	£30,000
Factory manager's salary	£30,000
Heat and light	£20,000
Depreciation of machinery	£40,000

Production statistics are:

	Machining	Assembly	Finishing	Maintenance	Stores
Personnel	20	15	10	4	1
Area (sq. metres)	8,000	4,000	4,000	1,000	3,000
Kilowatt hours (000)	100	40	30	10	20
Machinery cost (£000)	100	50	50	–	–
Direct labour hours (000)	40	30	20	–	–
Machine maintenance hours	850	600	200	–	–
Material issue notes	1,800	1,000	500	100	–

Tasks:

1 Calculate an overhead absorption rate based on direct labour hours for each production department.
2 A standard dishwasher uses 4, 3 and 2 direct labour hours in machining, assembly and finishing respectively. If all direct labour is paid £5.00/hour and the cost of materials for one dishwasher is £48, what is the production cost of one dishwasher?

Q9.5 Ugur Ltd

Ugur Ltd makes three different types of marine compass: Type A, Type D and Type N. Each compass passes through two production departments: assembling and finishing. Ugur absorbs its overheads on the basis of direct labour hours.

Production overheads for the next 12 months are expected to be

	£
Factory power	80,000
Depreciation	60,000
Fixed asset insurance	3,600
Supervisors' pay	40,000
Factory rent	70,400
	254,000

The following information for next year is also available:

	Assembly	Finishing
Number of direct operatives	30	20
Floor space (sq. metres)	16,000	9,000
Book value of fixed assets (£000)	60	30
Machine hours	15,000	30,000
Power (kilowatt hours used)	30,000	20,000
Supervisory staff	1	1

Times per product (hours):

	Assembly		Finishing	
	Labour	Machine	Labour	Machine
Type A	1.0	0.75	0.75	0.50
Type D	1.5	0.50	1.00	0.40
Type N	2.5	0.25	1.50	0.30

Each operative is expected to work 36 hours a week for 46 weeks a year.

Tasks:

1 Calculate the total overheads for each department.
2 Calculate the overhead absorption rate for each department (to three decimal places).
3 Calculate the overhead cost attached to each type of compass.
4 Recalculate your answers to tasks 2 and 3 if overheads were absorbed on a machine hour basis and comment on your findings.

Review questions

1 Explain the difference between direct and indirect costs.
2 List the constituent parts of an absorption cost.
3 Explain the difference between allocating and apportioning overheads to cost centres.
4 Explain the different bases that can be used by overhead absorption rates.

The answers to all these questions can be found in the text of this chapter.

CHAPTER 10

Product costs using activity-based costing

Chapter contents

Introduction

If we were to go back a few years into the last century and look at a typical manufacturing business, we would find that product costs consisted mainly of direct materials and direct labour. Indirect overhead costs would be only a small proportion of total product costs. If these overheads were attached to products in a way that was not very accurate, the consequences were not very serious. Product costs would be incorrect to a small extent, with some products slightly undercosted and others slightly overcosted.

In today's manufacturing environment, automated machinery and advanced technology often dominate the production process. At the time of writing, the British Automation and Robot Association announced record sales of robotic machinery in the UK to companies such as Toyota and BMW. The high cost of this advanced technology means high depreciation charges and high maintenance costs. As a result, the production overheads can be much larger than the direct costs. The increase in the relative importance of overheads is also due to the increased complexity of products and their related support structures the costs of which are classified as indirect. Errors in the way that overheads are attached to products are no longer insignificant. Indeed, traditional absorption costing in this high-technology environment can give grossly inaccurate product costs.

Before looking at activity-based costing (ABC) in detail, it is worth emphasizing that it is not a panacea suitable for every organization. Some businesses may be operating in stable environments, making much the same products as they were several years ago, with no sign of significant change. Here, direct costs are still much more important than the production overheads. These businesses may continue operating successfully using an absorption costing system.

However, it has to be said that this description applies to fewer and fewer companies in the twenty-first century. Tom Peters, the American management guru, expressed this well in his book *Thriving on Chaos*:

> *the times demand that flexibility and love of change replace our longstanding penchant for mass production and mass markets, based as it is upon a relatively predictable environment now vanished.*

The rate of change seems to increase incessantly in the business world, as it does in most other aspects of society. As firms customize their products more and more (smaller production batch sizes) and those products increase in complexity (compare modern computer games with older ones), absorption product costs become more and more inaccurate.

Absorption costing produces product costs which are **averages** between high- and low-volume products and between high- and low-complexity products. Figure 10.1 shows how product costs tend to be overstated for high-volume, low-complexity products but

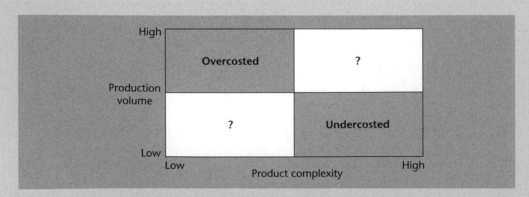

Figure 10.1 Cost distortions under absorption costing

Source: after *Cost and Effect: Using Integrated Cost Systems to Drive Profitability and Performance*, Harvard Business School Press (Kaplan, S. and Cooper, R. 1998). Reprinted by permission of Harvard Business School Press. Copyright © 1998 by the Harvard Business School Publishing Corporation, all rights reserved.

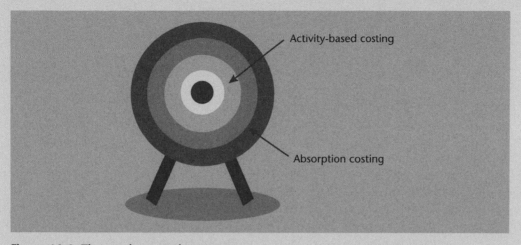

Figure 10.2 The product costing target
Source: after *Cost and Effect: Using Integrated Cost Systems to Drive Profitability and Performance*, Harvard Business School Press (Kaplan, S. and Cooper, R. 1998). Reprinted by permission of Harvard Business School Press. Copyright © 1998 by the Harvard Business School Publishing Corporation, all rights reserved.

understated for low-volume, high-complexity ones. Neither can the costs represented by the other two quadrants be assumed to be accurate, due to compensating errors.

It is easy to get carried away with the improved accuracy of ABC compared with traditional absorption costing and forget that it, too, uses estimates and approximations. The improvement in accuracy is significant, even for a basic ABC system. However, it does not give 100% accurate product costs. Figure 10.2 uses the analogy of an archery target to illustrate the comparative accuracy of the two systems.

Learning objectives

Having worked through this chapter you should be able to:

- explain the need for ABC;
- discuss how production volumes and product complexity can cause cost distortions;
- illustrate the difference in accuracy between absorption costing and ABC;
- explain the causation link between products, activities and costs;
- describe the procedure for calculating product costs using ABC;
- define the terms 'activity cost pool', 'cost driver' and 'cost driver rate';
- discuss the hierarchy of activities;
- give an overview of the ABC system in the form of a diagram;
- calculate product costs using ABC;
- explain the cross-subsidization of costs in absorption costing;
- discuss the precision, accuracy and cost-effectiveness of ABC;
- explain how ABC leads to activity-based management (ABM);
- discuss the limitations of ABC.

A new philosophy

Traditional absorption costing systems give product costs which enable production costs and stock valuations to be calculated. These valuations are an essential part of the audited financial accounts available to the public at large. The main objective is to ensure all production overheads are absorbed into the total annual production cost. This is achieved by identifying a factor whose behaviour **correlates** to the overhead costs. An example of this is the use of direct labour hours as the factor for attaching the overheads of a production cost centre to its output. (Note that the direct labour is not the **cause** of all the overhead costs involved. Also note that the correlation does not have to be particularly strong – weakly correlated factors are often used.)

This ensures that the production costs are recovered, in total, by all the different types of product made by the business. As long as this broad objective is met, there is no requirement for individual product costs to be calculated as accurately as possible. In the past, it made little difference. Today, it can make a big difference. The costs of low-volume, complex products are usually subsidized by those of high-volume, simple products when absorption costing is used (see Figure 10.1).

ABC is different. Its **main** objective is to produce an accurate cost for each product in the range. The thinking behind ABC is that, in order to control costs, it is necessary for them to be calculated **accurately**. A positive side-effect of this is that other important decisions, e.g. setting selling prices, will then be that much more effective.

ABC achieves this increase in accuracy through a simple logic:

- Products cause activities to happen.
- Activities cause costs to be incurred.

This *causation link* (see Figure 10.3) is fundamental to ABC. Note that it is **not** part of the absorption costing model.

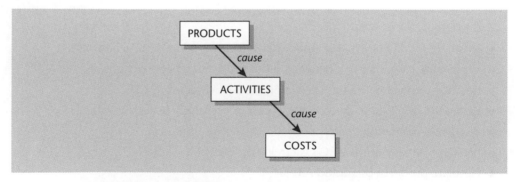

Figure 10.3 The ABC causation link

The ABC process

ABC has the following five steps:

1 Identify the different activities performed by the business.
2 Calculate the total cost of each activity over the financial period (i.e. the cost pool).
3 Identify a cost driver (i.e. a causation factor) for each activity.
4 Calculate the cost driver rate (i.e. the average cost of one occurrence of the cost driver).
5 Assign part of the cost of each activity to different products based on the extent to which each product has caused the activity to occur (i.e. apply the cost driver rate).

Storrit Ltd

Example 10.1

For instance, Storrit Ltd uses the same equipment to make two products, lever-arch files and box files. It has identified one of its activities as setting up the machinery to make a batch of one of these products. This particular activity has a budgeted annual cost of £9,000. In the year it plans to make 60 batches of lever-arch files and 30 batches of box files. A total of 90 batches gives an average set-up cost of £100 (£9,000/90). So £6,000 will be assigned to lever-arch files (60 × £100) and £3,000 to box files (30 × £100). This is based on the causation ratio of 2:1 = 60:30 = lever-arch file batches: box file batches.

The total cost of performing one type of activity in a given financial period is known as its *activity cost pool*. The mechanism for attaching accurate proportions of each activity cost pool to each product is by choosing a *cost driver* and calculating a *cost driver rate*. In the above example, Storrit Ltd:

1 The activity is setting up machinery.
2 The activity cost pool is £9,000.
3 The cost driver is the setting-up of machinery.
4 The cost driver rate is £100 a set-up (£9,000/(60 + 30)).
5 Lever-arch files are assigned £6,000 (60 set-ups @ £100/set-up).
  Box files are assigned £3,000 (30 set-ups @ £100/set-up).

Cost drivers are factors which *cause* the activity cost pool to increase. Cost drivers are causation factors. For example, the greater the number of set-ups (cost driver), the greater the total cost of setting up the machinery (activity cost pool). Figure 10.4 lists some other examples of cost pools and their cost drivers.

Sometimes, the organization will have a choice of cost drivers and must choose the one it thinks most appropriate. In the case of setting up machinery, if this was much more complicated for some products than others, 'number of set-up hours' could be used instead of 'number of set-ups'.

Activity cost pool	Cost driver
Setting up machinery	Number of set-ups
Buying raw materials	Number of purchase orders
Controlling quality	Number of quality inspections
Operating machinery	Number of machine hours
Maintaining machinery	Number of maintenance hours

Figure 10.4 Examples of activity cost pools and their cost drivers

Hierarchy of activities

It is important to understand that not all overheads increase in proportion to the number of units produced. (Traditional absorption costing assumes all overheads are volume related in this way, i.e. they all increase as output increases.)

Here are some of the categories into which activities can be analysed (examples of their cost drivers are shown in brackets):

- unit level, e.g. machining products (machine hours);
- batch level, e.g. purchasing materials (purchase orders);
- product customer level, e.g. maintenance of machinery (maintenance hours);
- facility level, e.g. site security (security hours).

Process overview

Figure 10.5 gives an overview of the ABC process. (It is worth comparing this with Figure 9.2, the equivalent diagram for absorption costing in Chapter 9.)

The Storrit Ltd example continues opposite.

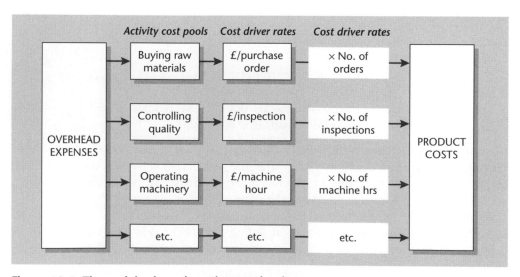

Figure 10.5 The activity-based costing mechanism

Example
10.1
continued

Storrit Ltd

Storrit Ltd makes two products, lever-arch files and box files. The annual production overhead total of £38,000 has been analysed over four activities as shown below. The cost drivers have been defined and counted. Also, the cost driver rates have been calculated.

Activity	Activity cost pool (£)	Cost driver	No. of cost drivers/year	Cost driver rate
Setting up machinery	9,000	Machinery set-up	90	£100/set-up
Buying raw materials	10,000	Purchase order	50	£200/order
Controlling quality	4,000	Quality inspection	160	£25/inspection
Operating machinery	15,000	Machine hour	10,000	£1.50/machine hour
Total	£38,000			

In the year, Storrit plans to make 60 batches of lever-arch files and 30 batches of the more complicated box files. (The metal lever-arch mechanisms are bought in, ready to attach to the folded cardboard outer. The box files are made from large sheets of flat cardboard and are fitted with a holding clip and a box fastener.) Lever-arch files are produced in batches of 200 but box files are produced in batches of 150.

Direct cost	Lever-arch file (£)	Box file (£)
Raw materials	1.05	0.90
Direct labour	0.00	0.00
Total	1.05	0.90

Note that Storrit Ltd classifies all its labour costs as fixed overheads and does not have any **direct** labour. This is not unusual as most firms have a permanent, rather than casual, labour force and do not 'hire and fire' at will.

The annual number of cost drivers is split between the two products as follows:

Cost driver	Lever-arch files	Box files	No. of cost drivers/year
Machinery set-up	60	30	90
Purchase order	12	38	50
Quality inspection	60	100	160
Machine hours	6,000	4,000	10,000

Task:

Calculate the activity-based cost for one lever-arch file and one box file.

Solution

Cost driver rate	Lever-arch files	Box files
£100/set-up	× 60 = 6,000	× 30 = 3,000
£200/order	× 12 = 2,400	× 38 = 7,600
£25/inspection	× 60 = 1,500	× 100 = 2,500
£1.50/machine hour	× 6,000 = 9,000	× 4,000 = 6,000
Total	18,900	19,100
Annual no. of files made	12,000	4,500
Production overhead per file	1.58	4.24
Direct cost per file	1.05	0.90
Production cost per file	**£2.63**	**£5.14**

Self-assessment question S10.1

Try the following question for yourself (answer at the end of the chapter).

Flatpack Industries Ltd makes many different items of household furniture in knock-down form. It has a budget for the current year which shows the total of production overheads to be £712,000. This has been analysed over five different activities as shown in the table below.

Flatpack Industries Ltd has been approached by P&Q plc to make 5,000 patio tables. The total cost of materials for this order is estimated at £70,000 and 2,000 hours of direct labour in the assembly department will be needed. The current rate of pay for assembly workers is £7.50 per hour. It is estimated that this order will cause the following production overhead activities to occur:

42 machinery set-ups	8 purchase orders raised	8,400 hours of machining
120 quality inspections	40 maintenance hours	

Activity	Activity cost pool (£)	Cost driver	No. of cost drivers/year
Setting up machinery	220,000	Machinery set-up	2,750
Buying raw materials	32,000	Purchase order	250
Controlling quality	90,000	Quality inspection	4,500
Operating machinery	330,000	Machine hour	66,000
Maintaining machinery	40,000	Maintenance hour	800
Total	**£712,000**		

Task:

Calculate the activity-based production cost of this order (a) in total, and (b) per table.

Cross-subsidization of costs

The introduction to this chapter points out that absorption costing tends to overstate some product costs and understate others (see Figure 10.1). This will now be examined in detail using the previous example of Storrit Ltd.

Let us assume that Storrit uses an absorption costing system based on machine hours.

Fixed overhead absorption rate = £38,000/10,000 machine hours = £3.80/mh

	Lever-arch files	Box files
Production overheads	3.80 × 6,000 mh = 22,800	3.80 × 4,000 mh = 15,200
Number of files produced	12,000	4,500
Production overheads/file	22,800/12,000 = 1.90	15,200/4,500 = 3.38
Direct costs/file	1.05	0.90
Absorption production cost/file	**£2.95**	**£4.28**
Compare:		
ABC production cost/file	**£2.63**	**£5.14**
Cross-subsidization	**£0.32**	**£(0.86)**

This shows that, when absorption costing is used, lever-arch files are overcosted and box files are undercosted. Lever-arch files are subsidizing box files as they are bearing some of the costs caused by box files. For the whole annual production the errors compensate each other and the correct total of overheads is attached to production for the year. But, **at the level of individual products, significantly inaccurate production costs are being used and many important management decisions are based on them**.

Many firms use costs to help them set selling prices. Consider the implications of this. If Storrit Ltd sets its selling prices at twice the level of the absorption production cost, lever-arch files will be overpriced by £0.64 (2 × £0.32) and box files underpriced by £1.72 (2 × £0.86).

Self-assessment question S10.2

Now try the following question for yourself (answer at the end of the chapter).

Assuming Flatpack Industries Ltd (see S10.1 above) uses absorption costing based on a single, fixed overhead absorption rate per machine hour, calculate the production cost of the order for patio tables (a) in total, and (b) per table. Then compare your answers with those for S10.1 and comment on the cross-subsidization of costs. Does your answer indicate that the patio table is more likely to be a complex, low-volume product line or a simple, high-volume one?

Precision, accuracy and cost-effectiveness

Absorption costing systems normally calculate their product costs to several decimal places, e.g. £8.9285. This gives the impression of a high degree of accuracy but it is really an example of mathematical precision. Because of the arbitrary correlations used by this traditional approach, it is quite possible that the first figure, i.e. the £8, is wrong (see Figure 10.2). If this is so, the calculation of several decimal places is a waste of resources, giving a misleading answer.

A traditional absorption costing system may be cheaper to operate than an ABC system but the cost of the errors resulting from its inaccuracies can be far greater. One important factor affecting the cost-effectiveness of ABC systems is the continuous fall in the price of information technology. The rapid evolution in information systems is greatly reducing their operating costs while, at the same time, greatly increasing their effectiveness.

ABC in service businesses

So far, this chapter has concentrated on production businesses and product costs. However, ABC is just as effective in service businesses such as banks, architecture, accountancy, driving schools, entertainment complexes, etc., as most of their costs are not volume related. The Co-op Bank is one example of a service provider which uses ABC.

The following example concerns the advertising agency Adage plc. Most of its work is the creation of advertising campaigns using print media such as newspapers and magazines. The agency sets its selling prices by adding 20% to total campaign costs. The following figures summarize the results for the last financial year:

	£000	£000
Sales revenue		6,600
Direct labour	2,000	
Overhead costs	3,500	
		5,500
Operating income		1,100

Adage is in the process of implementing its new ABC system but is still operating the absorption costing system it has used since its formation 30 years ago. Its old system absorbed overheads on the basis of the total cost of direct labour (e.g. copywriters, graphic artists and account managers) used for each campaign.

$$\text{Overhead absorption rate} = \frac{3,500,000}{2,000,000} = 175\% \text{ of direct labour cost}$$

During the recently ended financial year Adage completed a campaign for a product called Flamingo, a new range of bath soaps. The campaign costs were as follows using absorption costing:

	£
Direct labour	25,000
Overheads (£25,000 @ 175%)	43,750
Campaign cost	68,750
Profit margin (@ 20%)	13,750
Price charged to customer	82,500

The new ABC system involved a detailed and time-consuming identification and analysis of Adage's activities. The result of this for the current year is summarized by the following table:

Activity	Cost driver	Annual cost pool (£)	Annual use of cost drivers	Cost driver rates
Clerical support	Clerical hours	1,500,000	375,000 hours	£4.00/clerical hour
Information systems	Computer hours	1,000,000	10,000 hours	£100.00/computer hour
General management	Management hours	600,000	30,000 hours	£20.00/management hour
Photocopying	Pages of copy	200,000	1,000,000 pages	£0.20/page
Telephone	Telephone calls	200,000	200,000 calls	£1.00/call
Total		3,500,000		

The activity-based cost of the Flamingo campaign is calculated as follows:

Activity	Cost driver	Cost driver usage	Cost driver rate	Overhead attached (£)
Clerical support	Clerical hours	10,000 clerical hours	£4.00/clerical hour	40,000
Information systems	Computer hours	60 computer hours	£100.00/computer hour	6,000
General management	Management hours	800 management hours	£20.00/management hour	16,000
Photocopying	Pages of copy	2,500 pages	£0.20/page	500
Telephone	Telephone calls	1,500 calls	£1.00/call	1,500
			Total overhead	64,000
			Direct labour	25,000
			Total cost	89,000
			Profit (+20%)	17,800
			Selling price	106,800

Comparison	Campaign cost	Selling price
Absorption cost	68,750	82,500
Activity-based cost	89,000	106,800
Difference	(20,250)	(24,300)

Note that the activity-based cost is £6,500 greater than the absorption selling price! The Flamingo campaign must have been much more complex and demanding on resources than Adage's average campaign for that year as it has been significantly undercosted by the old system.

Try the following question for yourself (answer at the end of the chapter).

Self-assessment question S10.3

Gilmarsh is a large partnership of architects which currently operates an absorption costing system but is experimenting with an ABC system. The current annual budget shows the following:

	£000	£000
Sales revenue		3,120
Direct labour	1,600	
Overhead costs	800	
		2,400
Operating income		720

The architects absorb overheads as a percentage of the total cost of direct labour and their standard profit margin is 30% of total cost.

As part of their investigation into ABC, they wish to compare the two systems on a recently completed set of plans for a leisure centre. The cost of direct labour used on this job is £10,000. Their experimental ABC system is based on the following annual analysis:

Activity	Cost driver	Annual cost pool (£)	Annual use of cost drivers
Clerical support	Clerical hours	130,000	26,000 hours
Information systems	Computer hours	300,000	2,000 hours
General management	Management hours	50,000	5,000 hours
Printing and photocopying	Number of drawings	250,000	500,000 pages
Telephone	Telephone calls	70,000	35,000 calls
Total		800,000	

The leisure centre contract caused the following activities to happen:

Activity	Cost driver	Use of cost drivers
Clerical support	Clerical hours	400 hours
Information systems	Computer hours	30 hours
General management	Management hours	40 hours
Printing and photocopying	Number of drawings	3,500 pages
Telephone	Telephone calls	300 calls

Tasks:
For the leisure centre contract:

1 Calculate the absorption cost and selling price.
2 Calculate the activity-based cost and selling price.
3 Compare your findings and comment on them.

Activity-based management

In the light of this chapter so far, it is obvious that ABC can be a great help to managers in all sorts of organizations. Its major advantage is the increased accuracy in product costs, which means that costs can be controlled more effectively. It enables managers to get a better idea of the relative profitability of product lines. As a result, some products may be emphasized and others withdrawn or reduced in volume. It is even possible to rank customers according to the amount of profit they generate (something that is impossible under absorption costing). Activity-based management is discussed in detail in Chapter 18 on performance improvement techniques.

Limitations of ABC

Some costs, like heating and insurance, will apply to more than one activity cost pool. To divide them among all the appropriate cost pools, some subjective method of apportionment, as in absorption costing, has to be used. The causation link is lost at these points.

Sometimes, there is a choice of cost driver. For example, the 'setting-up machinery' cost pool could use the number of set-ups as the cost driver. Alternatively, it could use the number of set-up hours to differentiate between different types of set-up. Different cost drivers will probably give different product costs.

ABC systems are more complex than traditional absorption systems, consume more resources and cost more to operate. Also, they usually take a long time to introduce properly. This is because they involve significant change throughout the company. For some companies, the costs of introducing ABC may outweigh the benefits.

Absorption costing has been used for the best part of a hundred years, so is it really worth all the trouble of introducing ABC (and ABM and ABB)? The answer to that depends on two things. The first is the type of organization you work for. The second is the degree of effectiveness you wish to achieve in controlling the performance of your business.

The manager's point of view (written by Nigel Burton)

This is a difficult and complex area, but a rewarding one. In most areas of life, the greater the effort put in, the better the results in the end. Activity-based costing is no different. It requires a major input from almost every area of the business – factory, maintenance, purchasing, warehousing, quality control, etc., as well as finance and IT. It is a company-wide project, which may involve cultural changes, with all the management angst that that is bound to bring. It will throw new light on the production processes, and lead to a clearer understanding of resource usage in the factory. And, at the end, it will probably bring you as close to the true product cost as it is possible to get. However, as in any costing system, there are still pitfalls to trap the unwary, as I think the experiences of my own company will serve to illustrate.

The company is a large international corporation, engaged in salt production and chemical manufacture of both traditional and specialized products. These encompass a diverse range of production processes: some simple, others complex, some highly capital-intensive and others mainly laboratory-based. ABC was first introduced into the salt division, an almost perfect environment for this type of system. There are no raw material costs; salt is available in the ground, effectively for free. It requires overheads to mine it and process it, until it becomes a package on a supermarket shelf. Since salt is the second-cheapest commodity in the world after water, the control of costs throughout the production and distribution processes is perhaps more critical than in any other business. ABC provided a yardstick against which to monitor the performance not only of each activity in the factory, but also of individual items of plant. It further allowed comparisons between similar activities in different factories, thereby constituting a form of benchmarking. But above all, it provided a reliable assessment of product cost, which enabled selling prices to be set with confidence.

In view of its success in the salt division, management decided to extend the use of ABC to all other areas of the company. In the traditional chemical divisions of the group, such as mine, the nature of the products is rather different from those in the salt division. Raw materials are a significant part of the cost build-up, perhaps amounting to around 50% in a typical product. Clearly, the value of ABC in this instance is of lesser significance, although it can still play a crucial role in shedding light on the true costs of production.

The installation of ABC into my division of the group proved to be a challenging, time-consuming, but ultimately very worthwhile experience. The first stage required the production managers to examine their processes and divide them up, as far as possible, into discrete activities. Then they determined the amount of resource consumed in running those activities. In a processing activity, for instance, the resources needed may have included the number of labour hours, supervisor hours, amount of electricity required to drive the machinery, steam to heat the process up, or ice to cool it down, and so on. Once costed, these figures would constitute the activity cost pool, which would be attributed to products by means of cost drivers, in the manner already described. The factory personnel carried out this analysis work with great diligence, so everyone felt confident that the results would be accurate.

When the consumption of resources in each activity had been calculated to everyone's satisfaction, we ran them against the production budget to find out how much of each resource would be needed to carry out our annual production programme. This is where the fun started! For a number of items, the amount of resource calculated by the system bore no relation whatsoever to the actual levels historically used in the factory. Electricity was the most marked example.

The system told us that we would need 2.5 million kWh to manufacture the production budget. Yet we knew our annual consumption of electricity, taken from the monthly invoices, was 6.5 million kWh! Where was the difference? 'Not in my area,' said each of the production managers, 'I know the electricity rating of each machine in my area, and the number of hours for which each of them is used, so I know that my numbers are right!' 'But,' I replied, 'the other 4 million kWh is definitely being used somewhere!' After a short impasse, an investigation was set in motion, and gradually the true situation started to emerge. The production managers had been correct in assessing the usage of their own production areas, but electricity was also being used in a whole host of other areas outside their specific control. These included the boilers, steam pumping, effluent plant, various cooling systems, air filtering, laboratory and maintenance equipment, space heating, lighting, air-conditioning, computers, offices, etc. The pattern of our electricity usage had never been seriously considered before. We had always assumed that the direct production areas were by far the largest users of electricity, but this exercise showed that, in fact, they used barely more than a third. In the light of this new knowledge, we were able to target our energy reduction programmes more effectively, and generate significant savings.

A similar experience occurred with direct labour. The system told us that we needed only 75% of the labour we were currently using. My suggestion that, therefore, we could make 25% of the workforce redundant had the production managers scurrying off to revise their figures! The managers had simply underestimated the true level of labour input actually used by many of their activities and, again, this new information enabled them to consider whether their labour usage was really as efficient as they had believed.

Once all these anomalies had been sorted out, we had a reasonably clear picture of how and where our resources were being used and the extent to which each individual product was responsible for consuming them. The system would require honing over a number of years, as further information about the processes came to light, but even our first attempt at an ABC system gave us an insight into the true nature of our costs that no other system would get anywhere near.

And at this point, of course, another series of problems presented themselves, this time throwing the sales departments into confusion. The cost of every single product had changed. The long-established, conventional, understanding of the profitability of each product, and therefore of the structure of the business itself, was suddenly on shaky ground. Some of our mainstay products were shown to be much less profitable than we had thought. Some, indeed, were now seen to be making a loss. Conversely, others which had never been competitive had suddenly become much cheaper, and could tolerate the price reductions necessary to make them sell.

However, this was not a time for rushed decisions. The installation of ABC had been a massive exercise. How accurate were these costs? Had we made any mistakes in the installation process, either in principle, or of a clerical nature? Were there any bugs in the new IT systems? Common sense decreed that we should proceed with caution, and refrain from taking any major decisions until the system had bedded down. Some errors were subsequently unearthed and corrected, but the original message remained largely the same and, gradually, selling prices were adjusted to restore the required levels of profitability.

But what should we do with those product lines which had now become unprofitable? Simply discontinue them? Here we run up against the recurring problem of all accounting systems, that of fixed costs. For all its increased accuracy in the direct costs centres, ABC still has the problem of general, non-specific fixed overhead (plant manager's costs, security, etc.). As in absorption costing, this is apportioned to products on some kind of semi-arbitrary basis, such as machine hours. We have already seen how these apportionments can distort reality. In most companies, this will still be a significant element of the final product cost. So, we have to ask ourselves some basic questions. Can we increase the price? (Always the first question!) Are the fixed cost apportionments reasonable? If we discontinue these products, can we eliminate these overheads, or will they simply devolve on to other products, making them unprofitable? Are these products in fact generating a high marginal income (sales revenue – variable costs) which is paying for a significant chunk of general fixed overhead, albeit not quite enough to return a profit? These may be difficult questions for management to resolve, but at least, thanks to ABC, the right questions are now being addressed.

The introduction of ABC had far-reaching effects on my chemical business. In addition to the clearer view of product costs, it also provided a set of standards against which our actual performance could be monitored. And this could be done in considerable detail. For instance, if one wanted to, one could monitor actual electricity usage by production batch, by activity, and compare it with the expected usage as determined in the ABC system. In practice, of course, the capture of the actual detail on a regular basis is likely to be excessively onerous, but it demonstrates what can be done. Management have to decide the level of detail at which the ABC system will operate, but simplicity in the initial stages is strongly recommended!

ABC worked extremely well in the salt division and also proved a valuable tool in the traditional chemical manufacturing companies. But it did not work so well for every business – in particular, those where the process machinery was fairly simple. Here, the raw material costs could exceed 70% of the total cost, so that ABC-controlled overheads amounted to no more than 30%. Moreover, in some cases, the various products and processes were sufficiently similar for management to feel that simple absorption costing techniques were perfectly adequate. Nevertheless, obliged to conform to the corporate policy of global installation of ABC, they chose to adopt a simplistic approach to ABC, by identifying only a few, broadly drawn activities, and treating a large proportion of their costs as general overhead. Thus, their version of ABC was only slightly more detailed than their existing absorption system. It continued to meet all management's needs and was effectively installed without major disruption to the business.

The point here is that ABC is not a panacea for all costing problems in all companies. It is a question of 'horses for courses'. Some businesses simply do not warrant it. Others will find it a lifesaver. And once the decision to install it has been taken, there remain some very critical choices about the level of detail to be used. Insufficient detail will waste the potential of the system, while excess detail runs the risk of overburdening the staff with initial set-up work, and then swamping them with operational data which may well hide the wood among the trees. Very careful, pragmatic planning is required to avoid these pitfalls, but if the company gets the balance right, there is no doubt that the benefits accruing are well worth the initial effort. In an increasingly competitive marketplace, a clear understanding of the nature of your company's costs becomes ever more critical. ABC, in the appropriate format for your company, is very likely to be the answer.

Summary

- Advanced technology means overheads are a large part of total cost.
- Absorption costing attaches overheads to products via arbitrary correlated factors.
- Absorption costing does not give accurate product costs.
- This applies particularly to low-volume, highly complex products.
- Activity-based costing (ABC) significantly improves the accuracy of product costs.
- ABC does not give 100% accurate product costs.
- The causation link between products, activities and costs is central to ABC.
- ABC product costs are calculated by a five-stage process.
- Overhead costs are attached to products via their causation factors, i.e. cost drivers.
- Not all activity costs operate at the unit level, i.e. increase directly with output.
- Activity costs also operate at the batch, product or facility level.
- Implementation of ABC systems reveals the previous cross-subsidization of costs.
- ABC product costs are approximately right rather than precisely wrong.
- The falling price of information systems is making ABC evermore affordable.
- ABC can be equally effective in service businesses.
- ABC systems make activity-based management (ABM) possible.

- ABC and ABM make activity-based budgeting (ABB) possible.
- ABC has its limitations where accurate calculation of cost pools and choice of drivers are concerned.
- ABC systems use more resources than traditional absorption costing systems.
- ABC systems take several years to implement properly.
- ABC systems can be used alongside absorption systems.
- The main benefits are improved accuracy, cost control and management decisions.
- ABM uses process driver analysis to produce useful 'attention-directing information'.

Further reading

Atkinson, A., Banker, R., Kaplan, R. and Young, S. (2001) *Management Accounting*, 3rd edition, Prentice Hall, Harlow. See chapter 'Activity based cost management systems'.

Barlas, S. *et al.*, 'Activity-based life cycle costing', *Strategic Finance*, Vol. 87, Issue 3, p. 24.

Caplan, D., Melumad, N. D. and Ziv, A. (2005) 'Activity-based costing and cost interdependencies among products: the Denim Finishing Company', *Issues in Accounting Education*, Vol. 20, Issue 1, February.

Horngren, C., Bhimani, A., Datar, S. and Foster, G. (1999) *Management and Cost Accounting*, Prentice Hall Europe, Harlow. See Chapter 11, 'Activity based costing'.

Hughes, S. B. and Paulson Gjerde, K. A. (2003) 'Do different cost systems make a difference?', *Management Accounting Quarterly*, Vol. 5, Issue 1, Autumn.

Hussein, M. E. A. and Tam, K. (2004) 'Pilgrims Manufacturing, Inc.: activity-based costing versus volume-based costing', *Issues in Accounting Education*, Vol. 19, Issue 4, November.

Kaplan, R. and Cooper, R. (1998) *Cost & Effect: Using Integrated Cost Systems to Drive Profitability and Performance*, Harvard Business School Press, Boston, MA.

Kaplan, R. S. and Anderson, S. R. (2004) 'Time-driven activity-based costing', *Harvard Business Review*, Vol. 82, Issue 11, November.

Liu, L. (2005) 'Activity-based costing', *Financial Management* (CIMA), March.

Neumann, B. R., Gerlach, J. H., Moldauer, E., Finch, M. and Olson, C. (2004) 'Cost management using ABC for IT activities and services', *Management Accounting Quarterly*, Vol. 6, Issue 1, Autumn.

Upchurch, A. (2003) *Management Accounting, Principles and Practice*, 2nd edition, Financial Times/Prentice Hall, Harlow. See chapter 'Absorption of overheads', *sections* 'Activity based costing' and '"Traditional" absorption costing and ABC compared'.

Weetman, P. (2002) *Management Accounting, an Introduction*, 3rd edition, Financial Times/Prentice Hall, Harlow. See chapter 'The frontiers of management accounting', *section* 'Activity based costing'.

Answers to self-assessment questions

S10.1 Flatpack Industries Ltd

Cost driver rate	Order for 5,000 tables
220,000/2750 = £80/set-up	× 42 = 3,360
32,000/250 = £128/purchase order	× 8 = 1,024
90,000/4,500 = £20/inspection	× 120 = 2,400
330,000/66,000 = £5/machine hour	× 8,400 = 42,000
40,000/800 = £50/maintenance hour	× 40 = 2,000
Total production overheads	50,784
Direct cost of materials	70,000
Direct labour cost	2,000 × 7.50 = 15,000
Total production cost	**£135,784**
Production cost per table	**£135,784/5,000 = £27.16**

S10.2 Flatpack Industries Ltd

Fixed overhead absorption rate = £712,000/66,000 machine hours = £10.79/mh

	Patio table
Production overheads	10.79 × 8,400 = 90,636
Materials	70,000
Direct labour	2,000 × 7.5 = 15,000
Total production cost	**£175,636**
Number of tables produced	5,000
Absorption production cost/table	**£35.13**
ABC production cost/table	**£27.16**
Cross-subsidization	**£7.97**

This shows that, when absorption costing is used, patio tables are overcosted. Patio tables are bearing some of the costs caused by the other products in the range. This indicates that they are more likely to be **high-volume and/or simple products** (see Figure 10.1).

S10.3 Gilmarsh Architectural Partnership

1 Overhead absorption rate = $\dfrac{800,000}{1,600,000}$ = 50% of direct labour cost

Absorption costing of leisure centre contract	£
Direct labour	10,000
Overheads (£10,000 × 50%)	5,000
Absorption cost	**15,000**
Profit margin (@ 30%)	4,500
Price charged to customer	**19,500**

2 ABC of leisure centre contract:

Activity	Cost driver	Annual cost pool (£)	Annual use of cost drivers	Cost driver rates
Clerical support	Clerical hours	130,000	26,000 hours	£5.00/clerical hour
Information systems	Computer hours	300,000	2,000 hours	£150.00/computer hour
General management	Management hours	50,000	5,000 hours	£10.00/management hour
Printing and photocopying	Number of drawings	250,000	500,000 pages	£0.50/page
Telephone	Telephone calls	70,000	35,000 calls	£2.00/call
Total		800,000		

Activity	Cost driver	Contract's use of cost drivers	Cost driver rates	Overhead attached (£)
Clerical support	Clerical hours	400 hours	£5.00/clerical hour	2,000
Information systems	Computer hours	30 hours	£150.00/computer hour	4,500
General management	Management hours	40 hours	£10.00/management hour	400
Printing and photocopying	Number of drawings	3,500 pages	£0.50/page	1,750
Telephone	Telephone calls	300 calls	£2.00/call	600
			Total overhead	9,250
			Direct cost	10,000
			Activity-based cost	**19,250**
			Profit (@ 30%)	5,775
			Selling price	**25,025**

3	Comparison	Contract cost	Selling price
	Absorption cost	15,000	19,500
	Activity-based cost	19,250	25,025
	Difference	(4,250)	(5,525)

Note that the activity-based cost is only £250 less than the absorption selling price.

The leisure centre contract appears to be more complex and demanding on resources than Gilmarsh's average contract as it has been significantly undercosted by the absorption system.

Danbake Ltd is a medium-sized bakery selling mainly to supermarket chains. It produces two types of pie: pork and game. Although both pies are the same size, the pork pie has a plain crust but the game pie has a lattice-work crust and more expensive ingredients. As the bakery is highly automated, its absorption costing system uses raw materials as the only direct cost. It attaches production overheads to both products equally per batch, using the number of batches baked in total as the absorption base. Each oven firing produces one batch of pies.

Dan, the owner–manager, has noticed that last year the sales of pork pies were significantly lower than expected but the sales of game pies were significantly higher. The selling prices are arrived at by doubling the total production cost prices. But Dan is wondering if he has got his pricing right. His accountant assures him that the costing system is working correctly but one of his work-experience students has questioned the way in which the system operates. It seems illogical to her that a game pie, which is more complicated to make, receives the same amount of overhead as a pork pie. She suggests that Dan should look at something called 'activity-based costing'.

The following figures are from this year's budget:

	Budgeted output (batches)	Cost of ingredients (per batch)	Weight of ingredients (per batch)	Preparation time (per batch)	Baking time (per batch)
Pork pie	700	£120	200 kg	1.80 hours	3.00 hours
Game pie	350	£180	250 kg	2.12 hours	2.57 hours

Together with his student, Dan investigates the current cost structure and produces the following information:

Overhead activity	Budgeted cost (£)	Cost driver
Pie preparation	316,200	Weight of ingredients
Oven preparation	16,674	Number of firings
Baking	24,000	Number of oven hours
Other	126,126	Batch preparation time
Total	£483,000	

Tasks:

1 Using the current absorption costing system, calculate the production cost and selling price for one batch of each type of pie.

(10 marks)

2 Using activity-based costing, calculate the production cost and selling price for one batch of each type of pie.

(40 marks)

3 Comment on your results.

(10 marks)

4 Advise Dan whether or not he should replace his current absorption costing system with an activity-based costing system.

(40 marks)

(Total 100 marks)

Questions

An asterisk * on a question number indicates that the answer is given at the end of the book. Answers to the other questions are given in the Lecturer's Guide.

Q10.1* Hinj Ltd

Hinj Ltd manufactures and sells four products: arms, brackets, clips and D-rings. This year, for the first time, it is operating an activity-based costing system in parallel with its long-standing absorption costing system (which absorbs overheads on a machine hour basis).

The planned production activity cost pools and cost driver activity levels for all the output for the year are as follows:

Activity	Cost pool (£)	Activity level
Purchasing materials	41,500	1,000 purchase orders
Storing materials	41,600	650 issue notes
Setting up machinery	26,400	200 set-ups
Running machinery	73,000	7,300 machine hours
Total production overheads	182,500	

An analysis of actual annual production output for two of the products is as follows:

	Arms	Brackets
Units produced	1,000	500
Purchase orders	190	325
Stores issue notes	105	200
Set-ups	35	60
Machine hours	2,600	1,275
Direct materials	£8,250	£3,750
Direct labour	£46,000	£7,600

Tasks:

1 Calculate the production cost per unit for arms and brackets using the machine hour overhead absorption rate.
2 Calculate the production cost per unit for arms and brackets using the activity-based costing system.
3 Comment on your findings.

Q10.2* Numan Travel

Numan Travel plc started trading 10 years ago with its cheap airfare brand Flygo. Since then, it has expanded to offer three different types of holiday: Best Beaches, Cosy Cottages and Great Golfing. The following analysis was performed recently:

	No. of marketing staff	No. of reps per hotel	No. of hotels used	No. of customers	No. of reservations/ bookings
Best Beaches	30	1.0	192	950,000	375,000
Cosy Cottages	20	0.5	770	725,000	250,000
Great Golfing	18	0.5	192	150,000	25,000
Flygo	6	–	–	175,000	175,000
Total	74	–	1,154	2,000,000	825,000

Last year, the founder of the business relinquished the position of managing director and became executive chairman. His replacement as MD has suggested that the future of the company lies in the expanding golf sector. Also, because the cheap airfare market is becoming increasingly competitive, he suggests that the company withdraws from that sector. Further analysis reveals the following information:

£000	Best Beaches	Cosy Cottages	Great Golfing	Flygo	Total
Contribution	37,500	30,000	3,500	14,000	85,000
Advertising	15,000	15,000	2,000	3,500	35,500
Administration	18,000	12,000	1,200	8,400	39,600
Profit	4,500	3,000	300	2,100	9,900

The contribution is the sales revenue for each brand less the variable costs of operating that brand. Advertising costs are allocated directly to each brand but administration costs have been attached to brands on the basis of the number of reservations.

The chairman feels that the MD's strategy is mistaken but does not wish to appear to be heavy-handed on the basis of nothing more than an instinctive response. His last major act as MD was to instigate a pilot activity-based costing system to run in parallel with their existing absorption system. He wonders if this will provide him with a more convincing argument. So far, the pilot has produced the following activity analysis of the indirect administration costs:

	£000
Reservations/bookings	20,000
Holiday repping	10,000
Hotel liaison/contracting	6,000
Marketing	3,600
	39,600

Task:

Calculate the profit made by each brand using activity-based costing. Comment on the proposed strategy of the new MD.

Q10.3* Wilcock & Co.

Wilcock & Co. is a firm of solicitors which currently operates an absorption costing system but is experimenting with an activity-based costing system. The current annual budget shows the following:

	£000	£000
Sales revenue		2,422
Direct labour	1,384	
Overhead costs	346	
		1,730
Operating profit		692

Wilcock & Co. absorbs overheads as a percentage of the total cost of direct labour and its standard profit margin is 40% of total cost.

As part of the investigation into ABC, the solicitors wish to compare the two systems on a recently completed fraud case. The cost of solicitors' time used directly on this case is £15,000.

Their experimental ABC system is based on the following annual analysis:

Activity	Cost driver	Annual cost pool (£)	Annual use of cost drivers
Clerical support	Clerical hours	156,000	26,000 hours
General administration	Administration hours	60,000	3,000 hours
Photocopying	Number of photocopies	25,000	500,000 copies
Telephone	Telephone calls	105,000	70,000 calls
	Total	346,000	

The fraud case caused the following activities to happen:

Activity	Cost driver	Use of cost drivers
Clerical support	Clerical hours	500 hours
General administration	Administration hours	70 hours
Photocopying	Number of photocopies	1,500 copies
Telephone	Telephone calls	400 calls

Tasks:

For the fraud case:

1 Calculate the absorption cost and selling price.
2 Calculate the activity-based cost and selling price.
3 Compare your findings and comment on them.

Q10.4 Hoffman Ltd

Hoffman Ltd makes only two types of portable cooking stove, the Lightweight (LW) and the Megarange (MR). Last year it produced 4,500 LWs and 500 MRs. The direct materials cost £3.00 for one LW and £10.00 for one MR. The assembly workers who put the stoves together are all paid at the same rate of £6.30 an hour. When LWs are being produced each operative assembles nine stoves an hour and when MRs are being produced each operative assembles seven stoves an hour. This is the only labour that Hoffman classes as 'direct labour'. The factory uses automated machinery to manufacture the components which are common to both stoves. The other components are bought in. Each stove uses 15 machine hours in its construction.

For some time now, the company has been considering the introduction of activity-based costing. It has decided to recost last year's production using this method so it can compare costs with those under its current absorption costing system. The current overhead absorption rate is based on the number of machine hours. Last year's production activities have been analysed as follows:

Activity	Cost driver	Activity cost pool (£)
Purchasing	Purchase order	20,000
Training	Training hour	1,000
Setting up machines	No. of set-ups	2,250
Running machines	Machine hours	14,250
	Total	£37,500

The analysis also quantified the number of cost drivers caused by each stove:

Activity	No. of cost drivers caused by LWs	No. of cost drivers caused by MRs
Purchasing	360	40
Training	20	30
Setting up machines	60	30
Running machines	67,500	7,500

Tasks:

1 Calculate the absorption cost for each type of stove.
2 Calculate the activity-based cost for each type of stove.
3 Comment on your findings.

Q10.5 Pullman Products

Pullman Products manufactures ceramic discs for industrial use. It makes the discs in three sizes: small (S), medium (M) and large (L). Product costs are calculated using a simple absorption costing system which has only one overhead absorption rate (based on direct labour hours) for the whole manufacturing process. The following information is available:

	S	M	L
Material cost (£/disc)	6	20	72
Direct labour hours per disc	1.0	1.5	2.5
Weight of disc (kg)	1.0	3.0	11.0
Budgeted production (units)	10,000	2,000	4,000
Budgeted sales (units)	10,000	2,000	4,000

All direct labour is paid at £6/hour. The budgeted fixed production overheads total £1,380,000. Selling prices are calculated by adding 150% to the production cost.

Fierce competition from the Far East is forcing Pullman to review its selling prices, especially on its small disc. The recently appointed production manager has suggested that the use of activity-based costing may throw some light on this problem. To test the feasibility of this suggestion, a crude analysis of the firm's production overhead activities has been carried out and the results are shown below.

Activity	Cost driver	Activity cost pool (£)	Annual number of cost drivers
Clay preparation	Disc weight (kg)	180,000	60,000
Moulding	Disc weight (kg)	240,000	60,000
Firing	Kiln firing	912,000	50
Finishing	Number of discs	48,000	16,000
		Total 1,380,000	

In the budget period, there were 15 firings for small discs, 5 firings for medium discs and 30 firings for large discs.

Task:

For each disc, calculate the unit production cost and selling price using:

a) the absorption costing system;
b) the activity-based costing system.

Comment on your findings.

Q10.6 DFR

DFR operates a number of retail outlets selling a range of audio-visual products. These products range in size and value from small items such as portable radios that are easily displayed on shelves, to large and expensive equipment such as widescreen televisions. Some of these products take up considerable amounts of retail staff time advising customers at the point of sale.

DFR has a warehouse that it uses for storage of its products before they are delivered to its retail outlets using its own transport fleet. The warehouse and the retail outlets are all based in one country, but some of the outlets are significantly closer to the warehouse than others.

At present, warehousing costs are analysed between storage costs and distribution costs and these are then apportioned to retail outlets on the basis of the sales value of orders delivered. Retail outlet costs (including rent, heating and staff costs) are attributed to individual products based on their sales values.

For some time, the management of DFR has been considering the introduction of an Activity Based Costing (ABC) system. The management team has heard that this is a more accurate system of costing than that which is currently used, particularly since some of DFR's products require more involvement of staff in the retail outlets in advising customers of the meaning of the product specifications.

Required:

You have been appointed as a management accountant by DFR to introduce an ABC system. Prepare a report addressed to the Board of Directors of DFR that:

a) Explains the weaknesses of the present method used by DFR when attributing costs to products and its implications for cost control and product profitability.

(9 marks)

b) States the principles of ABC.

(4 marks)

c) Explains, with suitable examples, how DFR's warehouse storage and distribution costs and retail outlet costs could be attributed to individual products using an ABC system.

(8 marks)

d) Explains how DFR will benefit from the introduction of an ABC system.

(4 marks)

(Total = 25 marks)

CIMA Intermediate: Management Accounting – Performance Management, November 2004

Q10.7 S & P Products plc

S & P Products plc purchases a range of good-quality gift and household products from around the world; it then sells these products through 'mail order' or retail outlets. The company receives 'mail orders' by post, telephone and Internet. Retail outlets are either department stores or S & P Products plc's own small shops. The company started to set up its own shops after a recession in the early 1990s and regards them as the flagship of its business; sales revenue has gradually built up over the last 10 years. There are now 50 department stores and 10 shops.

The company has made good profits over the last few years but recently trading has been difficult. As a consequence, the management team has decided that a fundamental reappraisal of the business is now necessary if the company is to continue trading.

Meanwhile the budgeting process for the coming year is proceeding. S & P Products plc uses an activity-based costing (ABC) system and the following estimated cost information for the coming year is available:

Retail outlet costs

Activity	Cost driver	Rate per cost driver	Number each year for: Department store	Own shop
		£		
Telephone queries and requests to S & P	Calls	15	40	350
Sales visits to shops and stores by S & P sales staff	Visits	250	2	4
Shop orders	Orders	20	25	150
Packaging	Deliveries	100	28	150
Delivery to shops	Deliveries	150	28	150

Staffing, rental and service costs for each of S & P Products plc's own shops cost on average £300,000 a year.

Mail order costs

Activity	Cost driver	Rate per cost driver		
		Post £	Telephone £	Internet £
Processing 'mail orders'	Orders	5	6	3
Dealing with 'mail order' queries	Orders	4	4	1
		Number of packages per order		
Packaging and deliveries for 'mail orders' – cost per package £10	Packages	2	2	1

The total number of orders through the whole 'mail order' business for the coming year is expected to be 80,000. The maintenance of the Internet link is estimated to cost £80,000 for the coming year.

The following additional information for the coming year has been prepared:

	Department store	Own shop	Post	Telephone	Internet
Sales revenue per outlet	£50,000	£1,000,000			
Sales revenue per order			£150	£300	£100
Gross margin: mark-up on purchase cost	30%	40%	40%	40%	40%
Number of outlets	50	10			
Percentage of 'mail orders'			30%	60%	10%

Expected head office and warehousing costs for the coming year:

	£
Warehouse	2,750,000
IT	550,000
Administration	750,000
Personnel	300,000
	4,350,000

Required:

a) 1) Prepare calculations that will show the expected profitability of the different types of sales outlet for the coming year.

(13 marks)

   2) Comment briefly on the results of the figures you have prepared.

(3 marks)

b) In relation to the company's fundamental reappraisal of its business,
1) discuss how helpful the information you have prepared in (a) is for this purpose and how it might be revised or expanded so that it is of more assistance;

(7 marks)

2) advise what other information is needed in order to make a more informed judgement.

(7 marks)
(Total = 30 marks)

CIMA Intermediate: Management Accounting – Decision Making, November 2001.

Review questions

1 Explain the need for ABC.
2 Discuss how production volumes and product complexity can cause cost distortions.
3 Describe the difference in accuracy between absorption costing and ABC.
4 Explain the causation link between products, activities and costs.
5 Describe the procedure for calculating product costs using ABC.
6 Define the terms 'activity cost pool', 'cost driver' and 'cost driver rate'.
7 Discuss the hierarchy of activities.
8 Give an overview of the ABC system in the form of a diagram.
9 Explain the cross-subsidization of costs in absorption costing.
10 Discuss the precision, accuracy and cost-effectiveness of ABC.
11 Explain how ABC leads to activity-based management (ABM).
12 Discuss the limitations of ABC.

The answers to all these questions can be found in the text of this chapter.

CHAPTER 11

Comparison of profits under absorption and variable costing

Introduction

Because the annual profit figure is such an important piece of information ('the bottom line') it is advisable to monitor profit throughout the year. Knowing how things are progressing enables you to take corrective action when necessary and avoid unpleasant surprises at the financial year-end. Most organizations do this by producing monthly or quarterly management accounts.

As the idea is to help meet the annual profit target, it seems sensible to use the same rules by which the annual profit is calculated. One of these is that fixed production overheads must be treated as **product** costs and not as **period** costs (see IAS 2). In other words, annual accounts intended for public circulation are based on absorption costing. This works well for monthly accounting, provided that the pattern of trading is reasonably predictable over the year. However, for businesses whose trading pattern is difficult to predict, profits may be distorted. This also applies, to some extent, to seasonal businesses.

Distortions of profit do not help these businesses to monitor their real performance. So, it is not surprising that they sometimes decide to use a system which avoids this distortion. This alternative approach uses variable (also known as marginal) costing. Variable costing treats fixed production overheads as period costs rather than product costs. This is opposite to absorption costing used in the audited accounts **and will produce a different profit total**. However, at the end of the year, the internally reported 'variable profits' can be reconciled to the externally reported 'absorption profits'.

These two alternative financial models can be applied to a single set of commercial transactions, resulting in two different profit figures. This chapter shows you how to calculate the profits for a trading period in two different ways and how to reconcile them to each other.

Learning objectives

Having worked through this chapter you should be able to:

- explain the difference between a product cost and a period cost;
- use budget information to predetermine an overhead absorption rate;
- explain why predetermined OARs are used in preference to actual OARs;
- explain how under- and overabsorption of overheads occur;
- adjust profit and loss accounts for under- and overabsorption of overheads;
- calculate 'absorption' profit and 'variable' profit;
- reconcile 'absorption' profit to 'variable' profit;
- explain the limitations of both systems.

Treatment of fixed production overheads

As stated above, absorption costing treats fixed production overheads as production costs and variable costing treats them as period costs. A production cost is the total direct cost (prime cost) plus absorbed production overhead (see Figure 11.1a). A period cost is one which relates to a time period rather than to the output of products or services (see Figure 11.1b).

Predetermination of overhead absorption rates

The previous chapter showed how overhead absorption rates (OARs) are calculated via allocation, apportionment and an appropriate choice of the base. These OARs are used to determine the production cost and stock valuations for period-end accounts.

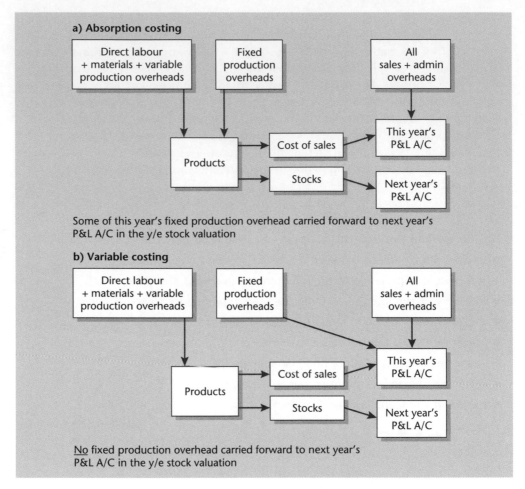

a) Absorption costing

b) Variable costing

Figure 11.1 Tracing overhead costs to the profit and loss account

The practice is to use predetermined rates rather than actual rates. After all, the actual rates could only be determined after the period has ended, so selling prices could not be based on actual absorption costs. One possibility is to use the actual rates of the last-but-one month so that rates were fairly up to date. However, this would cause monthly fluctuations in the product cost figures (see below). If selling prices were based directly on costs, they would be changed every month. Prices going up and down at each month-end would give the impression of instability and incompetence in the eyes of customers.

Annual basis:

> **Estimated annual fixed production overheads = £36,000**
> **Estimated annual volume of activity = 12,000 machine hours**
> **OAR = £36,000/12,000 mh = £3.00/mh**

Monthly basis:

	Month 1	Month 2	Month 3
Actual overheads incurred	3,000	3,520	2,500
Actual machine hours	1,000	1,100	909
Monthly actual OAR	£3.00/mh	£3.20/mh	£2.75/mh

For these reasons it is normal to calculate the OAR at the start of the year and apply it throughout. This means that the current year's production overhead cost and volume of activity used in the calculation are estimates rather than actual amounts. The major consequence of this is that the total amount of production overheads absorbed into product costs during the year is almost certainly going to be different from the amount of production overheads actually incurred. However, the profit and loss account must use the actual rather than the estimated figure. So an adjustment is necessary to change the overheads in the profit and loss account from estimated to actual amounts.

Under- and overabsorption of overheads

The first thing to note is that the overheads are absorbed by production and are in no way affected by sales volumes. Thus, if actual production volumes differ from planned volumes, either too much or too little overhead will end up in the profit and loss account. (The greater the volume of production, the greater the amount of production overheads absorbed.) If actual sales volumes differ from planned volumes, no change will be caused to the amount of production overheads in the profit and loss account.

Predetermined OAR:

> **Estimated annual fixed production overheads = £500,000**
> **Estimated annual volume of activity = 100,000 direct labour hours**
> **OAR = £500,000/100,000 dlh = £5.00/dlh**

If either of these estimates is incorrect (as they almost certainly will be) the amount of production overheads in the profit and loss account will be inaccurate:

i) Actual annual fixed production overheads = £525,000
   Actual annual volume of activity = 100,000 direct labour hours
   Overhead absorbed by production = 100,000 × £5.00
   $\qquad\qquad\qquad\qquad$ = £500,000
   Underabsorption of overheads = £25,000 (500,000 − 525,000)
   Unless this adjustment is made, profit will be overstated by £25,000.

ii) Actual annual fixed production overheads = £500,000
   Actual annual volume of activity = 112,000 direct labour hours
   Overhead absorbed by production = 112,000 × £5.00
   $\qquad\qquad\qquad\qquad$ = £560,000
   Overabsorption of overheads = £60,000 (560,000 − 500,000)
   Unless this adjustment is made, profit will be understated by £60,000.

| Example 11.1 | The Jinasy Umbrella Company |

The Jinasy Umbrella Company makes an up-market all-purpose umbrella. It produces management accounts for internal use on a quarterly basis. Its fixed production overheads are budgeted at £20,000 a quarter (£80,000 a year) and its marketing and administration overheads at £19,000 a quarter (£76,000 a year). The production plan is for 4,000 umbrellas each quarter (16,000 a year). The selling price is £20 and the variable cost of each umbrella is £8. There are 1,000 umbrellas in stock at the start of the first quarter. The actual results for last year, expressed in numbers of umbrellas, are as follows:

	Q1	Q2	Q3	Q4	Year
Sales	4,000	2,000	1,000	8,000	15,000
Production	4,000	4,000	3,000	6,000	17,000

Calculate the quarterly and annual profits (i) using absorption costing, and (ii) using variable costing. (iii) Explain why the profits differ. (Assume the total of actual overheads incurred was as forecast.)

Under both systems, stocks of finished umbrellas are valued at production cost.

	Variable costing	Absorption costing
Production cost:	variable cost	variable cost + fixed production overhead
	£8	£8 + (£20,000/4,000 units) = £13

Physical stock changes (number of umbrellas):

	Q1	Q2	Q3	Q4	Year
Opening stock	1,000	1,000	3,000	5,000	1,000
Actual production	4,000	4,000	3,000	6,000	17,000
Actual sales	4,000	2,000	1,000	8,000	15,000
Closing stock	1,000	3,000	5,000	3,000	3,000

i) Absorption costing (£000)

	Q1	Q2	Q3	Q4	Year
Opening stock	13	13	39	65	13
Add: Production cost	52	52	39	78	221
Less: Closing stock	(13)	(39)	(65)	(39)	(39)
Under-/(over)absorption	–	–	5	(10)	(5)
Cost of sales	52	26	18	94	190
Sales revenue	80	40	20	160	300
Gross profit	28	14	2	66	110
Non-production overhead	19	19	19	19	76
Net profit	9	(5)	(17)	47	34

ii) Variable costing (£000)

	Q1	Q2	Q3	Q4	Year
Opening stock	8	8	24	40	8
Add: Production cost	32	32	24	48	136
Less: Closing stock	(8)	(24)	(40)	(24)	(24)
Cost of sales	32	16	8	64	120
Sales revenue	80	40	20	160	300
Gross profit	48	24	12	96	180
Production overheads	20	20	20	20	80
Non-production overhead	19	19	19	19	76
Total fixed overheads	39	39	39	39	156
Net profit	9	(15)	(27)	57	24

iii) Reconciliation of profits (£000)

	Q1	Q2	Q3	Q4	Year
Absorption net profit	9	(5)	(17)	47	34
Variable net profit	9	(15)	(27)	57	24
Difference	–	**10**	**10**	**(10)**	**10**
Increase in stock (units)	–	2,000	2,000	(2,000)	2,000
Production overheads in stock increase (@ £5 a unit)	–	**10**	**(10)**	**10**	**10**

Annual results

The total of fixed production overheads charged in this year's 'variable' profit and loss account is the total incurred in this period, £80,000 (see Figure 11.1b). Variable profits are £24,000.

On the other hand, the net effect in this year's 'absorption' profit and loss account is that the amount of production overheads is reduced by £10,000, as follows:

> **Production overheads brought forward from last year**
> (in opening stock) into this year = 1,000 units @ £5 = £5,000
> **Production overheads carried forward from this year**
> (in closing stock) into next year = 3,000 units @ £5 = £15,000

The total of fixed production overheads charged in this year's 'absorption' profit and loss account is £70,000 (see Figure 11.2a).

The net reduction of £10,000 in production overhead charged will increase net profit from £24,000 (variable) to £34,000 (absorption).

Similar explanations and profit reconciliations can be made for each quarter (the process is summarized by Figure 11.3 below).

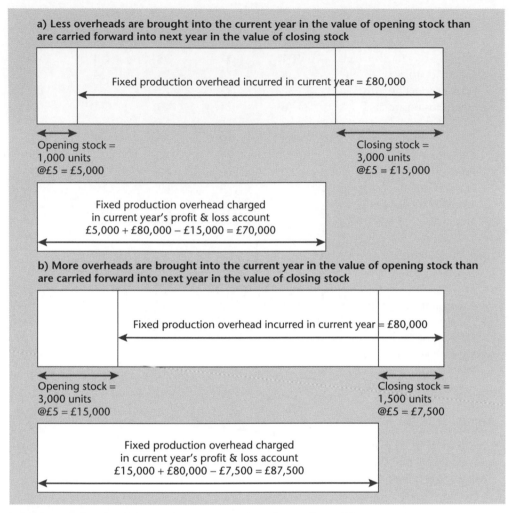

a) Less overheads are brought into the current year in the value of opening stock than are carried forward into next year in the value of closing stock

Fixed production overhead incurred in current year = £80,000

Opening stock =
1,000 units
@£5 = £5,000

Closing stock =
3,000 units
@£5 = £15,000

Fixed production overhead charged
in current year's profit & loss account
£5,000 + £80,000 − £15,000 = £70,000

b) More overheads are brought into the current year in the value of opening stock than are carried forward into next year in the value of closing stock

Fixed production overhead incurred in current year = £80,000

Opening stock =
3,000 units
@£5 = £15,000

Closing stock =
1,500 units
@£5 = £7,500

Fixed production overhead charged
in current year's profit & loss account
£15,000 + £80,000 − £7,500 = £87,500

Figure 11.2 Production overhead charged to the profit and loss account

Self-assessment question S11.1

Try the following question for yourself (answer at the end of the chapter).

Hiphoptop Ltd produces music CDs. Internal management accounts are drawn up on a quarterly basis. The company plans to produce and sell 12,000 CDs each quarter and have a stock of 2,000 CDs at the start of quarter 1. The selling price is £6 and the variable cost of each CD is £1. The production and non-production overheads are estimated at £24,000 and £30,000 a quarter respectively. The actual results for the year, expressed in numbers of CDs, are as follows:

	Q1	Q2	Q3	Q4	Year
Sales	9,000	16,000	6,000	13,000	44,000
Production	14,000	12,000	11,000	10,000	47,000

Calculate the quarterly and annual profits (a) using absorption costing, and (b) using variable costing. (c) Explain why the profits differ. (Assume the total of actual overheads incurred was as forecast.)

Limitations

Absorption profits make the realistic assumption that, in most years, most businesses will sell most of their stock. However, if the stock of finished goods brought forward into the current year proves to be unsaleable, absorption costing will bring forward overheads which should have been charged in last year's accounts.

When a seasonal business builds up stocks for next period's sales (as in quarter 3 for Jinasy) it can be argued that absorption profits avoid creating 'fictitious' losses for the build-up period. However, the greater the number of periods between production and sales (as in quarter 2 for Jinasy), the less convincing this argument becomes.

Absorption profits may be increased by producing extra units in order to increase stock levels rather than to enable sales. In certain cases, absorption profits may decrease even though the sales volume has increased. This creates some scope for the short-term manipulation of profits.

The manager's point of view (written by Nigel Burton)

Senior managers tend to be busy people who, if not financially orientated, want to spend as little time as possible poring over interim statements of account. In practice, most managers will already have a gut feeling about the current period's performance, or alternatively will have been able to obtain an indication of it from data readily available from the computer. Periodic accounts often serve only to confirm what they already know. Once again, the need for consistency, clarity and accuracy in the accounts is paramount, in order to minimize any time-consuming queries arising from them.

Unfortunately, the application of IAS 2 principles may not help in this regard. The standard requires, quite rightly, that the valuation of products in inventory should include all production costs, including overheads incurred in bringing those products to their current condition. As this is the required basis for year-end accounts, it is logical that the same basis should be used for interim internal accounts. We have already seen how absorption costing and variable costing can generate significantly different profits, and the last thing management want to see is a substantial year-end adjustment as the inventory valuation is switched from one accounting basis to the other.

But the adoption of IAS 2 in interim accounts can itself lead to confusion, particularly for periods as short as one month. Absorption costing may be precisely correct in principle, in that it matches costs to sales by transferring cost into inventory when the product goes into stock, and releasing it back into the profit and loss account when the product is sold. (This results directly from the application of the accruals or matching-up principle of accounting.) But this also means that a simple increase or decrease in the level of production will have a direct impact on the level of profitability, which is especially significant in view of that all-important yardstick, the budget.

In the vast majority of companies, the budget is the principal tool used by management to set targets and monitor performance. The budget predicts not only the levels of sales and costs, but also how these will be phased throughout the year. Unless there are special factors to consider, such as seasonal influences, it would be a reasonable assumption that, in any given month, production will match sales volumes, thus keeping inventory at a constant level. But life rarely turns out as planned. In some months, sales will exceed production, causing a net transfer of period cost out of inventory into the profit and loss account. Conversely, when production exceeds sales, there will be a net transfer of period costs out of the profit and loss account into inventory. And in an exceptionally poor sales month, profitability can apparently be improved by increasing production levels and transferring more overhead into inventory; this is probably the exact reverse of management's correct course of action, which should be to reduce production to reflect the lower demand. I stress that there is nothing wrong with these period cost transfers, which accurately reflect the movements of stock in and out of inventory. But when these movements take place against a fixed overhead monthly budget, the value of this budget as a control tool is diminished.

A solution to this problem is to use a combination of absorption and variable costing. The production overheads are fixed costs, incurred over a period of time, and it would be fair to argue that they should be written off in that period, in exactly the same way as non-production expenses such as marketing or administration. The marginal income generated by sales in the period (i.e. sales less variable costs) can then be set against the total period costs relating to that period, producing an easily understandable 'variable' net profit. The requirements of IAS 2 can be satisfied by a 'below-the-line' adjustment, transferring the necessary amount to or from inventory, before striking a final reportable 'absorption' net profit for the month. In this way, we are structuring a set of figures which achieve all our objectives: they provide data of sufficient clarity for management purposes, meet the requirements of the standard, and also highlight separately the 'accountants' adjustment', which need concern only those who understand it!

The following example relates to the Jinasy Umbrella Company illustration earlier in the chapter.

Variable costing statement:

	Q1	Q2	Q3	Q4	Year
Opening stock	8	8	24	40	8
Add: Production cost	32	32	24	48	136
Less: Closing stock	(8)	(24)	(40)	(24)	(24)
Cost of sales	32	16	8	64	120
Sales revenue	80	40	20	160	300
Gross profit	48	24	12	96	180
Production overheads	20	20	20	20	80
Non-production overhead	19	19	19	19	76
Total fixed overheads	39	39	39	39	156
Variable net profit	9	(15)	(27)	57	24
'Below-the-line' adjustment:					
Adjustment for production overheads in stock increase	–	10	10	(10)	10
Absorption net profit	9	(5)	(17)	47	34

This monthly adjustment for period cost in inventory needs to be carefully monitored. In most systems, the use of budgeted expenditure and budgeted levels of production to calculate overhead recovery rates will be quite adequate for the purposes of internal monthly accounts. But for final audited accounts, the period costs held in inventory must be valued on actual experience, rather than budget. In a normal year, where expenditure and production run close to budget, the adjustment to actual may be minimal, but, in an abnormal year, the company could be in for a nasty surprise. For instance, if the year had been going extremely well, and production had exceeded budget by 25%, the actual overhead rate would be recalculated at 20% (= 25/125) below the budgeted rate. If, at the same time, the production overhead budget was underspent by 10%, the overhead rate would decrease in total by nearly 30%. This would result in a substantial reduction of total overhead in inventory, and a corresponding increase in the charge written off in the profit and loss account. The accountants would not be popular unless this situation had been foreseen and communicated to management well in advance!

In practice, auditors will accept that the valuation of period costs in inventory should be based on normal levels of production and normal levels of expenditure. This will eliminate, or at least diminish, the impact of unusual or non-recurring events. For instance, if production had been halved in the last quarter as a result of serious plant failure, it would be wrong to double the period costs on products manufactured in that period as the situation was abnormal. The impact of such an event should be a write-off of any unrecovered overhead directly to the profit and loss account. Acceptable norms can perhaps best be established by looking at production and expenditure over a longer period of time. In my company, we used the average production over the last three years, which had the effect of smoothing out any anomalies, without discarding them altogether. We also used actual expenditure in the year, as this was usually fairly constant. The most appropriate method of establishing norms is a matter for agreement with the auditors, and may vary from company to company. But, once agreed, it will be expected that this method will be applied consistently in future years.

There is one final point to mention in connection with period cost in inventory. As one moves across a year-end into a new financial year, the overhead absorption rates will be recalculated on the basis of the new budget. Unless your system is such that you can identify the overhead costs attributed to each individual item held in stock, you will have to revalue the whole of the inventory on to the new cost basis. Otherwise you will have some products going into stock at last year's cost, and coming out at this year's higher cost, resulting in an undervaluation of inventory. The revaluation of the period cost in inventory will produce a surplus (or deficit) which will have to be written off to future profit and loss accounts, complicating the period cost in inventory adjustment line still further. In my view, therefore, it is highly desirable to isolate the adjustment below the line, where it will not confuse non-financial users of the interim accounts.

Summary

- The choice between absorption profits and variable profits only exists for internal reporting (external reporting must use absorption profits).
- No change in stock level (P = S): absorption profit equals variable profit.
- Increase in stock level (P > S): absorption profit greater than variable profit.
- Decrease in stock level (P < S): absorption profit less than variable profit.
- (where P = production volume and S = sales volume)
- The more volatile the business, the more suitable are variable profits for internal reporting.
- The less volatile the business, the more suitable are absorption profits for internal reporting.

The process by which the absorption profit is reconciled to the variable profit is shown in Figure 11.3.

It is important to note that variable profit depends solely on sales volume, but absorption profit depends on both sales volume **and** production volume. The implication of this is that absorption profits can be improved by increasing production! The effect of increasing production is to increase closing stock. Remember that absorption profits are the ones that must be used for external reporting. In the short term, profits can be manipulated upwards by this strategy **without breaking any accounting rules**. In the medium/long term, high stock levels due to excess production will return to normal and the effect on profit will be downwards.

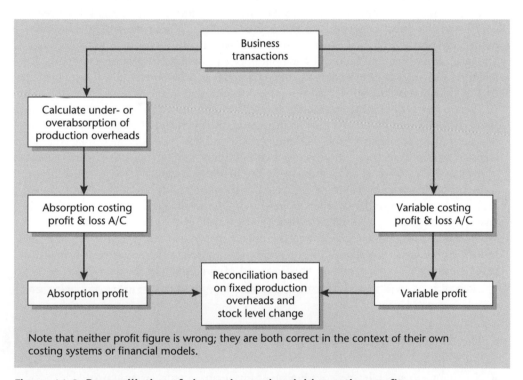

Note that neither profit figure is wrong; they are both correct in the context of their own costing systems or financial models.

Figure 11.3 **Reconciliation of absorption and variable costing profits**

Further reading

Baxter, W. T. (2005) 'Direct versus absorption costing: a comment', *Accounting, Business & Financial History*, Vol. 15, Issue 1, March.

Dugdale, D. and Jones, T. C. (2003) 'Battles in the costing war: UK debates, 1950–75', *Accounting, Business & Financial History*, Vol. 13, Issue 3, November.

Dugdale, D. and Jones, T. C. (2005) 'Direct versus absorption costing: a reply', *Accounting, Business & Financial History*, Vol. 15, Issue 1, March.

Horngren, C., Bhimani, A., Datar, S. and Foster, G. (2002) *Management and Cost Accounting*, 2nd edition, Prentice Hall Europe, Harlow. See Chapter 7, 'Income effects of alternative stock costing methods'.

Upchurch, A. (2003) *Management Accounting, Principles and Practice*, 2nd edition, Financial Times/Prentice Hall, Harlow. See chapter 'Absorption costing and marginal costing'.

Weetman, P. (2002) *Management Accounting, An Introduction*, 3rd edition, Financial Times/Prentice Hall, Harlow. See chapter 'Profit, performance and current developments', *section*: 'Absorption costing and variable costing'.

Answer to self-assessment question

1. S11.1 Hiphoptop Ltd

Under both systems, stocks of finished CDs are valued at production cost.

	Variable costing variable cost	Absorption costing variable cost + fixed production overhead
Production cost:	£1	£1 + £2 (£24,000/12,000 units) = £3

Physical stock changes (number of CDs):

	Q1	Q2	Q3	Q4	Year
Opening stock	2,000	7,000	3,000	8,000	2,000
Actual production	14,000	12,000	11,000	10,000	47,000
Actual sales	9,000	16,000	6,000	13,000	44,000
Closing stock	7,000	3,000	8,000	5,000	5,000

Under-/(over)absorption of overheads:

	Q1	Q2	Q3	Q4	Year
Planned production level	12,000	12,000	12,000	12,000	48,000
Actual production level	14,000	12,000	11,000	10,000	47,000
Under-/(over)absorption in units	(2,000)	0	1,000	2,000	1,000
Under-/(over)absorption @ £2/unit	(4,000)	0	2,000	4,000	2,000

a) Absorption costing (£000)

	Q1	Q2	Q3	Q4	Year
Opening stock	6,000	21,000	9,000	24,000	6,000
Add: Production cost	42,000	36,000	33,000	30,000	141,000
Less: Closing stock	(21,000)	(9,000)	(24,000)	(15,000)	(15,000)
Under-/(over)absorption	(4,000)	–	2,000	4,000	2,000
Cost of sales	23,000	48,000	20,000	43,000	134,000
Sales revenue	54,000	96,000	36,000	78,000	264,000
Gross profit	31,000	48,000	16,000	35,000	130,000
Non-production overhead	30,000	30,000	30,000	30,000	120,000
Net profit	1,000	18,000	(14,000)	5,000	10,000

b) Variable costing (£000)

	Q1	Q2	Q3	Q4	Year
Opening stock	2,000	7,000	3,000	8,000	2,000
Add: Production cost	14,000	12,000	11,000	10,000	47,000
Less: Closing stock	(7,000)	(3,000)	(8,000)	(5,000)	(5,000)
Cost of sales	9,000	16,000	6,000	13,000	44,000
Sales revenue	54,000	96,000	36,000	78,000	264,000
Gross profit	45,000	80,000	30,000	65,000	220,000
Production overheads	24,000	24,000	24,000	24,000	96,000
Non-production overhead	30,000	30,000	30,000	30,000	120,000
Total fixed overheads	54,000	54,000	54,000	54,000	216,000
Net profit	(9,000)	26,000	(24,000)	11,000	4,000

c) Reconciliation of profits (£000)

	Q1	Q2	Q3	Q4	Year
Absorption net profit	1,000	18,000	(14,000)	5,000	10,000
Variable net profit	(9,000)	26,000	(24,000)	11,000	4,000
Difference	**10,000**	**(8,000)**	**10,000**	**(6,000)**	**6,000**
Increase in stock (units)	5,000	(4,000)	5,000	(3,000)	3,000
Production overheads in stock increase (@ £2 a unit)	**10,000**	**(8,000)**	**10,000**	**(6,000)**	**6,000**

Canco Foods specializes in the preparation and canning of three different products: new potatoes, mincemeat and ham. The company has three divisions (one for each product), each with its own production and sales facilities. It so happens that each division has the same cost structure for manufacturing and marketing its product. For each division, the annual fixed production overheads are £200,000 and the annual fixed administration and sales overheads combined are £80,000. These are incurred evenly over the year. Also, each division has an annual budget of 20,000 cases bought and sold; all stocks are zero on 1 January. The selling price is £50 a case and the delivery costs are £2.50 a case.

The preparation and canning of new potatoes starts in February and is completed by mid-June, but sales are evenly spread over the year. Mincemeat is produced at the same rate throughout the year but sales only occur between September and December, mainly for the Christmas mince pie market. Ham is produced and sold at a steady rate with very little variation from month to month. (Stocks of all three products are zero at 1 January.)

Costs per case for each product are:	£
Direct material and direct labour	21
Variable production overhead	3
Variable production cost	24

Activity (number of cases):

		January–June	July–December	Year
Potatoes	Production	20,000	–	20,000
	Sales	10,000	10,000	20,000
Mincemeat	Production	10,000	10,000	20,000
	Sales	–	20,000	20,000
Ham	Production	10,000	10,000	20,000
	Sales	10,000	10,000	20,000

Tasks:

1 Prepare summarized profit and loss accounts for each half-year and the whole year for each division using absorption costing.

(25 marks)

2 Prepare summarized profit and loss accounts for each half-year and the whole year for each division using variable costing.

(25 marks)

3 Reconcile the profits for each of the three periods by producing a statement involving a 'below-the-line' adjustment as shown in 'The manager's point of view' section of this chapter.

(10 marks)

4 **On no more than two sides of A4**, discuss the use of absorption costing and variable costing for the periodic, internal reporting of profitability.

(40 marks)
(Total 100 marks)

Questions

An asterisk * on a question number indicates that the answer is given at the end of the book. Answers to the other questions are given in the Lecturer's Guide.

Q11.1* Clamco

Clamco makes car clamps. The following information is from January's budget, which is based on a production volume of 6,000 clamps:

	£
Opening stock of clamps	0
Fixed manufacturing overhead	72,000
Variable manufacturing overhead	18,000
Selling and administrative expenses (all fixed)	25,000
Direct labour	120,000
Direct materials used	90,000
Selling price (per unit)	64

The actual production and sales volumes for the first three months of the year were as follows:

Number of clamps	January	February	March	Quarter
Production level	6,000	5,000	7,000	18,000
Sales	4,000	6,000	7,000	17,000

Actual variable costs per unit and total fixed overheads incurred were exactly as forecast.

Tasks:

1 Calculate the profit for each month and for the quarter
   a) using absorption costing;
   b) using variable costing.
2 Reconcile the profits for each month and for the quarter. Explain why they differ.

Q11.2* Rivilin plc

Rivilin is a uni-product firm with the following budgeted amounts:

	£
Unit selling price	60
Unit variable cost	20
Fixed production overhead per month	9,600

Rivilin's planned level of production is 800 units a month. However, actual activity was as follows:

	April	May	June
Units produced	800	750	820
Units sold	800	700	850

There was no opening stock at 1 April.

The actual fixed production overhead incurred was accurately predicted at £9,600 a month.

The non-production fixed overheads are £10,000 a month.

Required:

1 A variable costing profit statement for each month.
2 An absorption costing profit statement for each month.
3 An explanation of the difference in profits between the two statements.

Q11.3* The Valley Fireworks Corporation

The Valley Fireworks Corporation manufactures special firework display kits to sell to responsible organizations only. The following information is taken from its budget for 2002:

> Opening stock of kits = closing stock of kits = 20 kits
> Quarterly production = 300 kits and annual sales = 1,200 kits

	£ per unit	£ per year
Selling price	500	
Direct materials	60	
Direct labour	180	
Variable production overhead	10	
Variable distribution overhead	20	
Fixed production overhead		96,000
Fixed non-production overhead		144,000

The actual production and sales volumes for 2002 were:

(Units)	Q1	Q2	Q3	Q4	Year
Opening stock	10	290	550	690	10
Production	300	300	200	300	1,100
Sales	20	40	60	980	1,100
Closing stock	290	550	690	10	10

The variable costs per kit and the total fixed costs were as forecast.

Tasks:

1 Prepare profit statements for each of the four quarters and the year,
   a) using absorption costing;
   b) using variable costing.

2 Reconcile the two profit figures for each quarter and prepare a summary statement in the following format:

	Qtr 1	Qtr 2	Qtr 3	Qtr 4	Year
Net profit using variable costing					
Adjustment for fixed production overheads in stock change					
Net profit using absorption costing					

3 Explain how both sets of profit figures can be useful to the management of The Valley Fireworks Corporation.

Q11.4 Nalpo Ltd

Nalpo Ltd manufactures and markets a small table that attaches to ladders. The following annual budget is based on 75,000 units made and sold:

	Per unit		Total	
	£	£	£	£
Sales revenue		5		375,000
Sales				
Production cost of sales:				
Variable	3		225,000	
Fixed	1		75,000	
		4		300,000
Gross profit		1		75,000
Selling and admin costs:				
Variable (10% of sales)		0.5	37,500	
Fixed			30,000	
				67,500
				7,500

Actual production figures for year 1 and year 2 were as follows:

	Year 1	Year 2
Opening stock	0	15,000
Production	85,000	70,000
Sales	70,000	80,000
Closing stock	15,000	5,000

Tasks:

You are required to:

1 Prepare budgeted statements of profitability on the basis of:
   a) absorption costing;
   b) variable costing.
2 Reconcile the difference in profit in the two statements produced for part 1.

Q11.5 Brafire Ltd

Brafire manufactures small, portable electric fires. It has operated an absorption costing system since it started many years ago. However, the new managing director (who is studying part time for an MBA) has recently learned of the possibility of using a variable costing system as an alternative to the company's usual approach. He decides to investigate this further by applying both systems to next quarter's budget (shown below). To provide a good comparison, the output will be shown at both a constant level and a fluctuating one.

Budget for quarter 3 (units):

	July	August	September	Total
Sales volume	3,000	3,000	6,500	12,500
Constant output	4,500	4,500	4,500	13,500
Fluctuating output	4,500	4,000	5,000	13,500

There will be 500 fires in stock on 1 July. The selling price is £30 and the cost structure is as follows:

	£/unit
Direct materials	4.00
Direct labour	1.50
Variable production overheads	0.50
Fixed production overheads*	6.00
Fixed marketing overheads*	4.00
Total cost	16.00

* These figures are based on a constant monthly production level of 4,500 fires.

Tasks:

Produce a budgeted profit and loss account for internal management reporting using the following four bases:

1 Absorption costing and constant output levels.
2 Variable costing and constant output levels.
3 Absorption costing and fluctuating output levels.
4 Variable costing and fluctuating output levels.

Comment on your findings.

Q11.6 P Ltd

P Ltd manufactures a specialist photocopier. Increased competition from a new manufacturer has meant that P Ltd has been operating below full capacity for the last two years.

The *budgeted information* for the last two years was as follows:

	Year 1	Year 2
Annual sales demand (units)	70	70
Annual production (units)	70	70
Selling price (for each photocopier)	£50,000	£50,000
Direct costs (for each photocopier)	£20,000	£20,000
Variable production overheads (for each photocopier)	£11,000	£12,000
Fixed production overheads	£525,000	£525,000

Actual results for the last two years were as follows:

	Year 1	Year 2
Annual sales demand (units)	30	60
Annual production (units)	40	60
Selling price (for each photocopier)	£50,000	£50,000
Direct costs (for each photocopier)	£20,000	£20,000
Variable production overheads (for each photocopier)	£11,000	£12,000
Fixed production overheads	£500,000	£530,000

There was no opening stock at the beginning of year 1.

Required:

(a) Prepare the actual profit and loss statements for each of the two years using:
   ● absorption costing;
   ● marginal costing

(14 marks)

(b) Calculate the budgeted breakeven point in units and the budgeted margin of safety as a percentage of sales for year 1 and then again for year 2.

(6 marks)

(c) Explain how the change in cost structure (as detailed in the budgeted information) has affected the values you have calculated in your answer to part (b).

(5 marks)

(Total = 25 marks)

CIMA Foundation: Management Accounting Fundamentals, November 2001

Review questions

1 Explain the difference between a product cost and a period cost.
2 Explain why predetermined OARs are used in preference to actual OARs.
3 Explain how under- and overabsorption of overheads occurs.
4 Explain how to reconcile 'absorption' profit to 'variable' profit.
5 Discuss the limitations of profits based on variable costs.
6 Discuss the limitations of profits based on absorption costs.

The answers to all these questions can be found in the text of this chapter.

CHAPTER 12 | Pricing your products

Introduction

One of the most important decisions that any business has to make is what prices to charge for its products and services. If it sets them too low, its profits may be insufficient for it to survive in the medium/long term. If it sets them too high, sales may be lost to competitors and profits may again be insufficient. In short, if it gets its pricing wrong it may go out of business!

So, how are selling prices calculated? Is there one best method? Or does it depend on each firm's business environment?

This chapter looks at three different points of view before attempting to integrate them into a practical pricing strategy. The viewpoints examined are those of the economist, the accountant and the marketer.

Having worked through this chapter you should be able to:

- explain the economist's pricing model;
- explain the accountant's pricing model;
- compare these by the use of charts;
- describe the optimum level of output;
- describe price elasticity of demand;
- explain cost-plus pricing;
- discuss the dangers of cost-plus pricing;
- discuss the marketer's view of pricing;
- explain the pricing strategies of skimming and penetration;
- explain target pricing as an integrating mechanism;
- discuss the limitations of pricing theory.

The economist's view

Optimum level of output

This is a simplified explanation based on economic theory. It is presented as an extension to breakeven analysis, which is covered in Chapter 5. Towards the end of that chapter there is a section detailing the limiting assumptions of that technique. Two of these limiting assumptions are that neither the variable cost, nor the selling price, change when the volume of output changes. This means that the total revenue and total cost lines on breakeven charts are **straight** and the total revenue line goes through the origin. The relationships between revenue, costs and volume are assumed to be linear (see Figures 12.1 and 12.3).

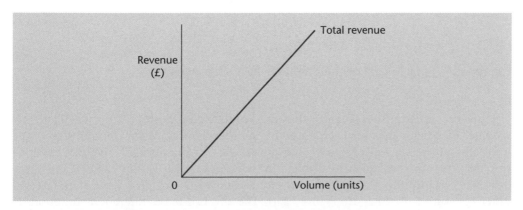

Figure 12.1 Unit selling price remains the same for all volumes

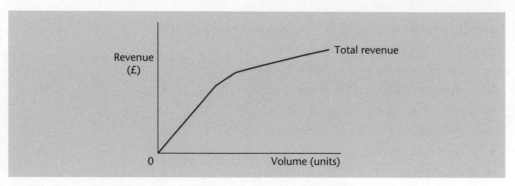

Figure 12.2 Unit selling price reduces as volume increases

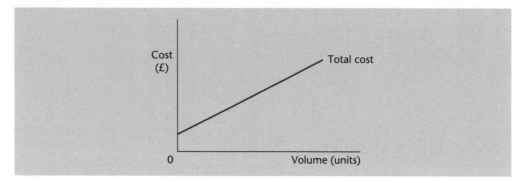

Figure 12.3 Variable cost per unit remains the same for all volumes

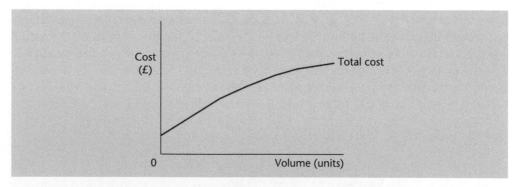

Figure 12.4 Variable cost per unit reduces as volume increases

However, economists recognize that these simple relationships do not hold for all volumes of activity. Beyond a certain point, in order to increase the volume of sales, the unit selling price has to be reduced (see Figure 12.2). Economists quantify this relationship between price and quantity through the concept of price elasticity of demand. Also, beyond a certain point, the cost per unit should reduce due to bulk-buying discounts and other economies of scale (see Figure 12.4). The effect of these different assumptions is that the lines on the charts are now curved (at least beyond a certain volume).

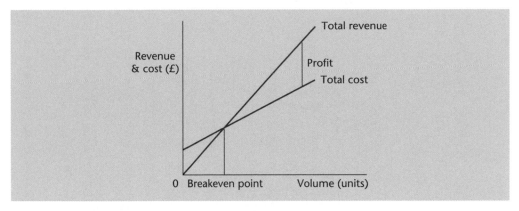

Figure 12.5 Profit continues to increase with volume

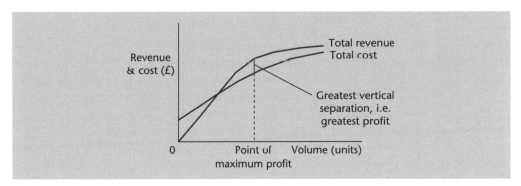

Figure 12.6 Profit is maximized at one level of activity

Combining Figures 12.1 and 12.3 gives the familiar breakeven chart shown in Figure 12.5. Combining Figures 12.2 and 12.4 gives the economist's view of the same relationships. Note the implication for profit. The accountant's version (Figure 12.5) shows profit continuing to increase with volume. However, the economist's version (Figure 12.6) shows that maximum profit is achieved at one particular volume of output and, therefore, at one particular selling price. This is how economic theory is used to determine the optimum selling price.

The major problem with this approach is that it is virtually impossible to forecast accurately the revenue and cost curves shown in Figures 12.2 and 12.4. This is an unavoidable consequence of attempting to predict the future in an ever-changing world. Economic analysis can be insightful when applied to historical data but it is of limited practical use for setting future prices. Fortunately, there are several alternative ways of approaching this problem, as you will see later in this chapter.

Try the following question for yourself (answer at the end of the chapter).

Self-assessment question S12.1

Here is a profit–volume chart as used by accountants. Redraw it, showing how it might look from an economist's point of view.

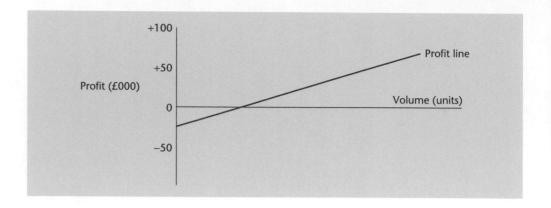

Price elasticity of demand

Another useful concept from the field of economics is that of *price elasticity of demand*. This concerns the rate at which the amount sold changes relative to the rate of change of the selling price. For products which are essentials or necessities, a large increase in price may only produce a small decrease in sales volume. For example, if petrol prices increased by 5%, the amount of petrol sold might decrease by only 2%. In this case, petrol can be described as having a 'low elasticity of demand' or being relatively 'price inelastic'. This reflects the small amount of change (or *stretching*) in demand relative to the amount of change in price. (Implicit in Figure 12.1 is the assumption that the price elasticity of demand is infinity.)

However, for other items, a small increase in price may produce a large decrease in sales volume. For example, a 5% increase in the price of coffee may produce a 10% decrease in the amount of coffee sold. In this case coffee could be described as having high elasticity of demand. The amount of coffee sold changes more than its price. One of the reasons for this is that coffee substitutes are more easily obtainable than petrol substitutes. It is easier to change from coffee to tea than to change your vehicle from petrol to diesel. When setting selling prices, it is very useful to have a reasonable idea of the product's price elasticity of demand as this will help to predict the revenue curve (see Figure 12.2). (Implicit in Figure 12.2 is the assumption that the price elasticity of demand is greater than 1.0 as total revenue continues to rise with output.)

The accountant's view

Cost-plus pricing

When setting the price of a product, the first thing an accountant usually thinks of is its cost. It is a fundamental rule of business that, in order to make a profit, prices have to be greater than costs. So, the product cost is first established and then a profit margin is added to give the selling price. But, as can be seen from earlier chapters, the concept of *product cost* is far from straightforward. There are at least three types of costing (variable, absorption and activity-based) and several specific costs within these types. So, which is the best cost to use?

Here are some of the choices:

- manufacturing cost;
- full absorption cost;
- variable cost;
- prime cost;
- activity-based cost.

The full absorption cost is often used as it is perceived to be the safest approach, but any of the others can be used if the business thinks them appropriate.

The next question is how to set the profit margin. What percentage should be added to the cost? The answer to this comes from the business's corporate plan. In this should be stated the required *return on capital employed*. This enables the required annual profit to be estimated and from this the percentage profit margin can be calculated.

For example, if Kryptomatic Limited aims to achieve a 20% return on capital employed and its latest figure of total capital is £1 million, then its annual profit needs to be £200,000. If its budget for next year shows that its total costs will be £600,000, then its total sales revenue needs to be £800,000.

Below is an extract from Kryptomatic's budget for next year:

	£000
Direct materials	150
Direct labour	50
Prime cost	**200**
Variable production overheads	25
Fixed production overheads	75
Manufacturing cost	**300**
Administration overheads	120
Marketing overheads	180
Total cost	**600**
Required profit	**200**
Total revenue	**800**

If it adopted a **prime-cost-plus** approach, the 'plus' margin added would be

$$\frac{800 - 200}{200} = \frac{600}{200} = +300\%$$

If it adopted a **manufacturing-cost-plus** approach, the 'plus' margin added would be

$$\frac{800 - 300}{300} = \frac{500}{300} = +167\%$$

If it adopted a **full-cost-plus** approach, the 'plus' margin added would be

$$\frac{800 - 600}{600} = \frac{200}{600} = +33\%$$

Self-assessment question S12.2

Try the following question for yourself (answer at the end of the chapter).

Codex Ltd has a target return on capital employed of 40% p.a. and its latest balance sheet shows its capital employed is £15 million. The following figures are from next year's budget.

Calculate the cost-plus percentage Codex should use based on (a) prime cost, (b) manufacturing cost and (c) total cost.

	£m
Direct materials	8
Direct labour	12
Prime cost	20
Variable production overheads	1
Fixed production overheads	3
Manufacturing cost	24
Administration overheads	2
Marketing overheads	4
Total cost	30

The absorption cost suicide spiral

The main drawback of cost-plus pricing is that it ignores the demand aspects of a competitive environment. It assumes that all product demand is completely price inelastic. This is very unrealistic for the vast majority of products. Figure 12.7 illustrates the potential danger of blindly following the cost-plus approach.

The amount of fixed cost attached to each unit is calculated by dividing the total of fixed costs by the planned number of units. Every time the price is increased, the volume sold goes down, which causes an increase in fixed cost per unit and, consequently, a further price increase. If this downward spiral were allowed to happen, the company would very soon cease trading.

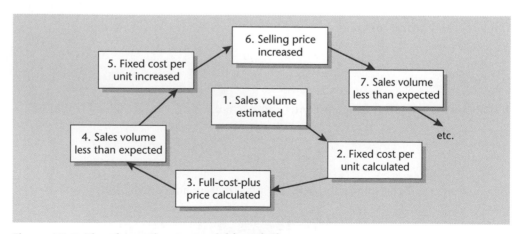

Figure 12.7 The absorption cost suicide spiral

Here is a numerical example. Blinkered Ltd produces a standard saddle. Its total annual fixed costs are £1 million and the variable cost of each saddle is £80. It prices the saddle by adding a 40% mark-up to its absorption cost.

1 Sales volume estimated at 50,000 units.
2 Fixed cost per unit = £20 (£1,000,000/50,000).
3 Absorption cost = £100 (£80 + £20); selling price = £140 (£100 + 40%).
4 Actual sales volume = 40,000 saddles.
5 Fixed cost per unit = £25 (£1,000,000/40,000).
6 Absorption cost = £105 (£80 + £25); selling price = £147 (£105 + 40%).
7 Sales volume falls to 33,000 saddles due to price increase.
8 etc.

Blinkered Ltd's profits diminish at an ever-increasing rate due to the downward spiral of sales volume. Before long, its losses will be unsustainable and it will have to cease trading.

The marketer's view

Existing products

No organization functions in isolation. Trading takes place in the competitive environment of the marketplace, which means that firms cannot charge whatever they wish for their products. They have to set their prices in relation to those set by their competitors. This is particularly true for products that have been in existence for a while. The cost-plus method may suggest a selling price of £25 but, if a competitor has a very similar product on the market for £19, it would be very risky to stick with the £25 price tag. Maybe the price should be reduced to £18 or £21; maybe the product should be discontinued. Maybe it should be altered in some way that clearly differentiates it from the competition, resulting in a perceived higher value in the eyes of the customer. If this is achieved, it may even be possible to set the selling price successfully above £25! This is an example of *product positioning* in which the selling price is an important factor. The point is that market considerations (not cost-plus calculations) should have the final say in the setting of the selling price.

New products

Occasionally, a product different enough to be called 'new' is launched into an empty or unsatisfied market. The price of new products depends on the company's marketing strategy. If it desires to recoup some of the research, development and launch costs of the product, it may decide to set the price artificially high to start with. This targets the **early-adopters** or **trend-setters** market segment. Once this segment is satisfied, the price is reduced, especially as there may be competitive products in the market by that time, encouraged by the high selling price. This marketing strategy is called *skimming* (see Figure 12.8).

The shape of the unit cost line reflects the **learning curve** concept based on the belief that during the initial period of a new process the operatives usually significantly improve

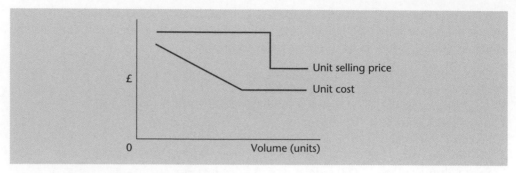

Figure 12.8 Skimming pricing policy

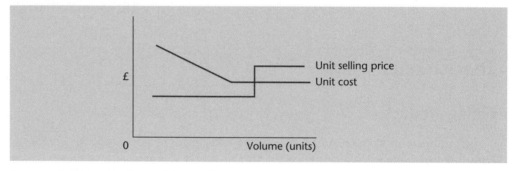

Figure 12.9 Penetration pricing policy

its efficiency. For example, in month 1, 500 items may be produced but, due to learning curve effects, 1,200 may be produced in month 2.

An alternative approach to skimming is to set an artificially low initial price to gain the maximum number of customers as quickly as possible. The object is to establish brand loyalty so that profit foregone in the introductory stage is more than compensated for by profit from repeat sales after the price has been adjusted upwards some time after launch. The object of this approach is to build market share and discourage early competition. This marketing strategy is called *penetration* (see Figure 12.9).

Target pricing and costing: an integrated strategy

The traditional approach to price setting, which starts by establishing costs and ends with the selling price decision, is turned on its head by this new approach. The first thing to be done in target pricing is to set the selling price in the context of the marketplace and its constraints. This may well involve market research, trial selling in a small geographical area and consideration of the product life cycle. In other words, determine the highest price at which the product will sell the required volume. (This sounds much easier than it actually is; the objective of the exercise is to identify and quantify customer value.) Next, calculate the desired profit margin and deduct this from the selling price. The resulting figure will be the maximum total cost allowable. The product designers then have to engineer the product so that its cost does not exceed the target cost.

This can be applied to the revamping of existing products as well as new ones. For example, cost savings may be achieved by replacing several components with one larger component which amalgamates all their functions. This will probably reduce the total material purchase cost, but even if it did not, there would almost certainly be less labour assembly time needed, resulting in a saving in labour cost. Savings may also be made in ordering and storage of components. The effects of production process learning curves are also taken into account when setting the target costs. (This may result in a contract which stipulates a **reduction** in selling price, rather than an increase, after a certain time has elapsed.) Target pricing is thought to have originated in Japan, where it is more commonly used than in other countries. However, it is now an established technique in Europe and North America. (There is an overlap between target costing and kaisen costing – see the later chapter on performance improvement techniques.)

Limitations of pricing theory

By now, you will appreciate how important it is to know the market price (i.e. the maximum price at which customers will buy the required number of items). Millions of pounds are spent every year on market research in pursuit of this information. Forecasting the quantities likely to be sold at different prices is an attempt to predict the future. It is as much an art as it is a science and is notoriously difficult to do accurately. So why do businesses spend so much on this each year?

Well, they believe that this forecasting based on current market research gives the best estimate possible. Although the figures are not accurate, they represent the best information available. However, the degree of inaccuracy can be considerable. In other words, prices are very rarely initially set at their optimum level. Businesses adjust their prices according to their experience of the market. If they have set their price too high, they will sell fewer items than desired. When they reduce the price, the opposite may happen. It is a process of trial and error. As the product becomes established, more **actual** market data is gathered and the pricing becomes more effective.

The manager's point of view (written by Nigel Burton)

Pricing is perhaps the single most crucial area in business management, and yet it is the one which is carried out amid the greatest number of unknowns. Almost every other aspect of the business can be managed from a position of knowledge. Costs, for instance, can be identified and controlled, new products developed and introduced, production processes improved, systems and procedures streamlined. But pricing is a gamble. Market intelligence will act as a guide, but in the end the setting of prices will always be accompanied by a measure of risk. What will the customers' reaction be? Will they be driven to the competition? Will they be driven to adopt different technologies? What will the competition do? These questions are at the heart of every pricing decision, and make the process of running a business so exciting.

There are few rules to apply in the setting of prices. Of course the accountants must ensure that prices are sufficiently high to produce the expected returns, and one of the cost-plus bases (preferably ABC) will enable them to do this. However, in my view, this should be seen simply as a safety net against unacceptably low pricing, and should not play an active part in the price-setting procedure itself. The correct price for a product is the highest price that the market will accept. It is, therefore, primarily a decision for the marketing department. Profits are hard enough to come by at any time, so any pricing of products below their full potential is highly undesirable. Overpricing a product may be a mistake, but it is always much easier to reduce prices at a later stage than to increase them. The use of cost information in the initial formulation of prices may inhibit the imagination of the marketing department!

Pricing is influenced by many factors other than cost. Each business, and most likely each individual product within the business, will have a different set of circumstances affecting its market position. Is there anything about the product which distinguishes it from the competition, and which will allow us to charge a premium price? Perhaps it is easier to look at the situation from the point of view of purchasers. What factors will encourage them to pay the higher price?

Brand identity is clearly one such factor. A BMW and a Ford both have the necessary equipment to get buyers to their destination, but they will pay more for the BMW, either because they perceive that they are buying a higher-quality product, or because it panders to their ego. Whatever their motivation, their perception of the product will have an impact on the market price.

Product quality will usually allow a premium price to be charged. However, the right quality can be defined as that which meets, but does not exceed, the requirements of customers. They will not pay a premium price for a higher level of quality than they need. Also, it is worth remembering that the first priority for a purchasing officer is to ensure that there is material of the right quality available at the right time for use by the production or sales department. This is more important than shaving an extra per cent or two from the price. The loss of production or sales through stock shortages will normally far outweigh any cost-saving advantage.

The quality of the supplier is another key, but often underrated, element. Purchasers need to feel confident that the supplier will always meet their delivery requirements with consistent quality material. They, therefore, may feel more comfortable dealing with a solid, blue-chip company than with a small cut-price outfit which may be here today and gone tomorrow. In the chemicals industry it has been possible for some time to source many raw materials from suppliers in India and China. Although prices are very compettive compared with the European competition, quality has not always been of a consistent standard. Moreover, the extended lead times involved inevitably limit flexibility where quick responsiveness to changing customer needs is paramount. The comfort factor of a local, reliable supplier may be worth paying extra for.

Patented products will clearly command a higher price, and can become significant profit generators if they are in the right market niche. But purchasers are always on the lookout for cheaper, unpatented alternatives, even if it means adopting different technologies or changing production processes. The higher the price, the greater the spur to customers to find cost-saving alternatives.

These are just a few of the many factors which influence the initial establishment of prices, and which will continue to cause price movements, perhaps even on a daily basis. The competition never stands still. It will react to every action taken and, as in a game of chess, the real skill in business is to anticipate the competitor's next move. The marketplace is constantly changing, and prices are being set in the light of the best information available at the time.

There are times when this feels like a leap in the dark. In the chemicals industry, there has recently been a move towards global sourcing. Accordingly, one of our major customers notified us of their intention to source their worldwide requirements for a particular range of products from a single supplier. At the time, this business was split between several suppliers, and everyone was making good profits. We were asked to quote prices for each piece of business in each country. This was a daunting prospect. Business worth millions of dollars was at stake, so, at the end of this process, there were going to be some big losers and one big winner! At what level should we pitch the prices? How much of our existing profit should we give away in order to be sure of picking up the rest of the business? How aggressive would our competitors be as they stood to lose as much as we did? We arrived at a set of prices which we calculated would give us an acceptable return, and submitted them. It was with an enormous sense of relief that we heard we had been successful in picking up the entire contract. But we were nevertheless left with a nagging doubt that perhaps we had pitched the prices too low and given away some profit unnecessarily.

As we basked in the success of this venture, we heard that another major customer was travelling down the same route, another worldwide tender, again with some very profitable business at stake. We went through the same agonizing process, and made our submission. Unfortunately, on this occasion, we had underestimated the aggression of our competitors, who were still smarting from their failure in the previous tender, and we lost the business. Well, you win some, you lose some! Overall, we came out of it just ahead on profit, although at the cost of considerable anxiety.

For both tenders, we had set up a computer model which compared our proposed prices with the underlying costs, enabling us to monitor the overall profitability while we played with different pricing options. As this product range consisted mainly of high-margin-earning products, there was plenty of scope to reduce prices without jeopardizing the minimum returns required. The underlying costs did not play a significant role in the establishment of our quoted prices; for us, the likely action of our competitors was the key factor. In this we were perhaps a good deal more fortunate than many other businesses, where costs are the overriding factor. At this latter end of the scale, I am aware of one company bidding to develop and supply automotive parts for a new range of vehicles due to come to market in five years' time. It quoted a price below today's total cost, on the assumption that advances in technology in the intervening period would generate sufficient cost savings to leave a profit. A high degree of entrepreneurship, as well as courage, is needed to do business on this basis.

You may feel that my comments in this chapter have strayed away from the main management accounting theme of this book. I make no apology for this. I wish to emphasize the point that the setting of prices is primarily a marketing, not an accounting, function. The accounting techniques described in the chapter are, of course, essential as a backdrop against which the marketing people can do their work, and it is the accountants who will monitor whether the pricing proposals will generate the overall returns required by management. But my guess is that, if the pricing of the automotive parts had been left to conservative accountants, the contract would have been lost. And if the worldwide tenders had been left to accountants, the subtle nuances in the marketplace would have been overlooked, and the bid weakened as a result. So, if there is any rule on pricing, it is 'leave it to the marketing people', while keeping a close eye on their decisions within the context of the company's overall financial objectives.

Summary

Economic theory helps us to understand the relationships between selling price, unit cost, profit and volume of activity. It tells us that there is an **optimum level of output and profit** rather than a range of continuously improving results. It also makes us aware that the demand for different products is affected by their selling prices to different extents. This is the *price elasticity of demand* concept.

The accounting approach is to establish the cost structure of products and then to increase this by a calculated percentage to give a profit margin. This is the *cost-plus* method with the amount of the 'plus' or mark-up being determined by the organization's required return on capital employed. The full cost is probably used more than any other cost as it establishes a minimum price below which products cannot be sold profitably in the long term.

When finalizing the selling price, it is critically important to consider the **competitive nature of the marketplace.** It is essential to know which products compete directly with yours and what their current prices are. Knowledge of your product's minimum price (equal to its full cost) and an understanding of its elasticity of demand enable you to decide intelligently on its selling price.

Target pricing is a strategy which integrates all three viewpoints discussed in this chapter. It starts by setting the price and then working backwards to establish the desired profit margin and the maximum allowable cost. If this cost cannot be achieved satisfactorily, the product is abandoned (unless there is good reason for its continuation). The result of this is that all the company's products should provide adequate profits, and cross-subsidization of products should be avoided.

There is no getting away from the fact that, ultimately, the price-setting process is **subjective.** The selling price will be based upon the opinions, feelings and intuition of top managers who, hopefully, have their fingers on the pulse of the marketplace.

Further reading

Ahmed, M. N. and Scapens, R. W. (2003) 'The evolution of cost-based pricing rules in Britain: an institutionalist perspective', *Review of Political Economy*, Vol. 15, Issue 2, April.

Atkinson, A., Banker, R., Kaplan, R. and Young, S. (2001) *Management Accounting*, 3rd edition, Prentice Hall, Harlow. See chapter 'Using management accounting information for pricing and product planning'.

Cardinaels, E., Roodhooft, F. and Warlop, L. (2004) 'The value of activity-based costing in competitive pricing decisions', *Journal of Management Accounting Research*, Vol. 16, Issue 1, December.

Davila, A. (T.) and Wouters, M. (2004) 'Designing cost-competitive technology products through cost management', *Accounting Horizons*, Vol. 18, Issue 1, March.

Horngren, C., Bhimani, A., Datar, S. and Foster, G. (2002) *Management and Cost Accounting*, 2nd edition, Prentice Hall Europe, Harlow. See Chapter 12, 'Pricing decisions and customer profitability analysis'.

Ingenbleek, P., Debruyne, M., Frambach, R. T. and Verhallen, T. M. M. (2003) 'Successful new product pricing practices: a contingency approach', *Marketing Letters*, Vol. 14, Issue 4, December.

Matanovich, T. (2003) 'Pricing services vs. pricing products: don't buy into the duality myth. Focus on value to the customer', *Marketing Management*, Vol. 12, Issue 4, July/August.

Swenson, D., Shahid, A., Bell, J. and Il-Woon Kim (2003) 'Best practices in target costing', *Management Accounting Quarterly*, Vol. 4, Issue 2, Winter.

Upchurch, A. (2003) *Management Accounting, Principles and Practice*, 2nd edition, Financial Times/Prentice Hall, Harlow. See Chapter 8, 'More decisions: price-setting and limiting factors', *section 5*: 'Price-setting'.

Answers to self-assessment questions

S12.1 Profit–volume chart based on economic theory

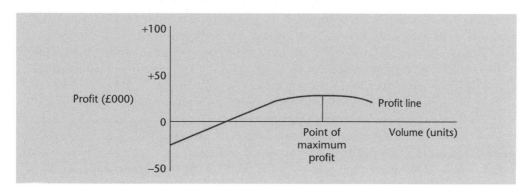

S12.2 Codex Ltd

	£m	
Direct materials	8	
Direct labour	12	
Prime cost	20	
Variable production overheads	1	
Fixed production overheads	3	
Manufacturing cost	24	
Administration overheads	2	
Marketing overheads	4	
Total cost	30	
Required profit	6	(40% of £15m)
Total revenue	36	

a) If it adopted a **prime-cost-plus** approach, the 'plus' margin added would be

$$\frac{36 - 20}{20} = \frac{16}{20} = +80\%$$

b) If it adopted a **manufacturing-cost-plus** approach, the 'plus' margin added would be

$$\frac{36 - 24}{24} = \frac{12}{24} = +50\%$$

c) If it adopted a **full-cost-plus** approach, the 'plus' margin added would be

$$\frac{36 - 30}{30} = \frac{6}{30} = +20\%$$

The Hydrogen Car Project

A well-known multinational car manufacturing company has developed a prototype small town car fuelled solely by hydrogen. It intends to market this through a subsidiary company called the Hydrogen Car Project (HCP). This vehicle is code named H1. It will carry a minimum of two passengers and have luggage space adequate for a family shopping trip. The luggage space will be convertible into two child seats, greatly enhancing the flexibility of this vehicle. Its maximum speed will be 60 mph (100 kph) and it will have a range of approximately 150 miles (240 km) from a full tank of hydrogen.

Harmful emissions from the H1 will be zero as the only waste product from running the engine will be water. Based on current energy prices, the H1's fuel cost per mile is about half that of existing equivalent-sized cars. The number of hydrogen fuelling stations, although small at the moment, is gradually increasing and it is assumed that this will have reached a sufficient level to support this type of car by the time the H1 is launched.

A comprehensive business plan has been produced to investigate the economic viability of this venture. During negotiations, the joint owners agreed that, due to the risks involved, it was essential that the return on capital employed (ROCE) should be a minimum of 15% a year. Having completed the business plan they also agreed that, due to the critical nature of the forecast sales volumes, independent market research should be commissioned to produce a demand forecast at selling prices within £1,000 of their initial estimate.

A) Extracts from business plan

The competition has been identified as those electric/hybrid cars which have been recently introduced by most of the current global car manufacturers. Initially, the H1 will be built to a single basic specification and the prices of the nearest competitors have been identified as follows:

Car 1	£11,600
Car 2	£11,300
Car 3	£11,200
Car 4	£10,700
Car 5	£10,400

The business plan adopted a selling price of £10,000 for the H1 which gave a profit margin of 20%. It also assumed a level of activity which produced a ROCE of exactly 15%. To enable HCP to produce and market its electric car, capital of £1,000 million will be needed for buildings, machinery, office equipment, IT systems and other fixed assets.

The maximum production capacity is 90,000 cars a year. HCP's best estimate for the production cost of one car is as follows:

	£
Direct materials	2,266
Direct labour	400
Prime cost	**2,666**
Variable production overheads	334
Fixed production overheads	1,000
Manufacturing cost	**4,000**

Annual non-production fixed overheads, including administration and marketing are expected to be £300 million.

B) Extract from market research report

Demand forecast:

Selling price £	Annual demand Units
11,000	44,880
10,800	53,720
10,600	59,160
10,400	62,560
10,200	64,600
10,000	68,000
9,800	71,400
9,600	74,120
9,400	78,200
9,200	85,000
9,000	94,520

Tasks:

1 Assuming the market research data to be more reliable than the assumptions made in the business plan, calculate the total contribution and total net profit for each of the 11 demand levels shown in the marketing plan. (You are expected to use a computer-based spreadsheet for this.)

(35 marks)

2 Advise HCP on its operating level and selling price. Include a discussion of the specific business risks involved. (Using succinct language, it should be possible to present your answer to this part on no more than two sides of A4 paper.)

(35 marks)

3 If HCP decided it needed to spend an extra £20 million on launching the H1, how might it achieve this **without reducing its target profit**? (Using succinct language, it should be possible to present your answer to this part on no more than two sides of A4 paper.)

(30 marks)

(Total 100 marks)

Questions

An asterisk * on a question number indicates that the answer is given at the end of the book. Answers to the other questions are given in the Lecturer's Guide.

Q12.1* Demarco

Demarco makes miniature mobile generators and has a standard profit margin of 20% for all its products. Its annual budget includes marketing, administration and production overhead allowances of £60,000, £20,000 and £50,000 respectively. It also shows that the company intends to use £18,000 of materials and pay direct wages of £32,000. Marketing and administration overheads are all fixed but 10% of production overheads are considered to be variable. Demarco uses the cost-plus method of setting its selling prices.

Task:

Calculate the cost-plus percentage if the base was:

a) variable cost;
b) production cost;
c) full cost.

Q12.2* Wizkid

WSM Enterprises introduced the Wizkid in 1991 to compete with Action Man. Although the peak demand for these products occurred several years ago, sales have stabilized and WSM sells 15,000 Wizkids a year.

The recommended retail price is £24.99 and the current wholesale price is £10.00. However, the managing director wishes to increase the return on this product and has proposed a 100% mark-up on total variable costs.

WSM has an annual output of 15,000 Wizkids. The fixed costs related to this product are £40,000 and the variable (or marginal) costs are £6.00 per unit.

Tasks:

1 What is the breakeven volume of this product if a selling price of £10.00 is charged? What is the profit at this price?
2 What price would the MD like to charge? What would the resulting net profit be if there were no change in demand?
3 The marketing director has forecast a 10% drop in orders if the price is raised as suggested. What would WSM's profit be if this were to happen?
4 Discuss the other factors the MD should take into account when deciding on the selling price of Wizkids.

Q12.3* Ride-on Lawn Mowers

Ride-on makes and sells a mini-tractor lawn mower called the Luxon. The company is just about to start its new financial year for which the budget (recently approved by its holding company) shows the following:

	£000
Total capital employed	4,000
Total sales revenue	2,800
Total fixed costs	1,104
Net profit before tax	800
Return on capital employed (ROCE)	20%
Number of Luxons sold	1,120

Its holding company requires it to achieve a ROCE of at least 20% and Ride-on's directors are awarded annual bonuses if they succeed in this.

Yesterday, Ride-on's main competitor released details of a new product in direct competition to the mower. The Luxon has a selling price of £2,500 but its new rival has been priced approximately £300 below this. After a hastily convened meeting, Ride-on's top managers have decided to reduce the Luxon's price to £2,150 with immediate effect. They also feel that their forecast sales revenue now looks optimistic.

Tasks:

Advise them how they might maintain their forecast return on capital employed (ROCE) at 20% now that the Luxon's price has been reduced:

a) if total sales revenue is maintained at £2.8 million; and
b) if total sales revenue decreases to £2.5 million.

Q12.4 Theory questions

a) What is meant by 'price elasticity of demand'?
b) Create a numerical example of the 'absorption cost suicide spiral'.
c) Explain the differences between the accountant's and the economist's approach to pricing.
d) Why is pricing really a marketing function?
e) List the stages involved in target pricing.

Q12.5 Brightwell Shades

Brightwell Shades Ltd has developed a new kind of sunglasses, the Shadewell, whose strength can be manually adjusted. The variable cost of one pair is £50 but the firm is unsure what the selling price should be. During a lengthy board meeting it was decided to commission some market research into the new product's price elasticity of demand. The results of the market research survey have just been received and are summarized as follows:

Sales price (£)	60	70	80	90	100
Sales volume (units)	16,000	13,000	10,000	7,000	4,000
Sales revenue (£)	960,000	910,000	800,000	630,000	400,000

It is estimated that when output is equal to, or greater than, 12,000 units the variable cost per unit will reduce to £45. Also, additional fixed costs of £50,000 will be incurred if production exceeds 8,800 units.

Task:

Advise the board on the selling price of the Shadewell.

Review questions

1 Explain the economist's pricing model.
2 Explain the accountant's pricing model.
3 Compare these two models by the use of charts.
4 Discuss the economist's optimum level of output.
5 Explain the concept of price elasticity of demand.
6 Explain cost-plus pricing.
7 Discuss the dangers of cost-plus pricing.
8 Discuss the marketer's view of pricing.
9 Compare the pricing strategies of skimming and penetration.
10 Describe target pricing as an integrating mechanism.
11 Discuss the limitations of pricing theory.

The answers to all these questions can be found in the text of this chapter.

chapter 13

Divisional performance and transfer pricing

Introduction

At some time in your life you may find yourself working for a company that is actually a conglomeration of several companies, an amalgamation of separate 'strategic business units'. For example, Rolls-Royce Group plc has five separate business divisions; their performance for 2003 is shown in the extract from its annual review for that year (see Figure 13.1). Similarly, the BG Group plc (commonly known as British Gas) shows a segmental analysis in its annual review for 2003 (see Figure 13.2). Both these companies operate internationally but there are also many divisionalized firms which operate mainly within national boundaries.

If you worked for the group head office, you would be interested in knowing how each of your constituent divisions was performing. The answer to this seems very straightforward: why not simply list the divisions in the order of their profits? Unfortunately, there are several reasons why this is too simplistic and would give a misleading picture. What about the amount of capital invested in each division? What return is it earning in percentage terms? The return on capital employed ratio may well order the divisions differently. Also, how much say does the division have about the amount of capital invested in it? And to what extent can each division influence the decisions on which assets are purchased?

What about the costs incurred by each division? Does it have complete control of all these or are some of them beyond its control? For instance, one division may be told by head office that it must operate from a certain site because the group cannot sell that

	Group turnover £m	Profit before interest £m
Civil Aerospace	2,694	82
Defence	1,398	132
Marine	927	32
Energy	584	30
Financial Services	42	(6)
	5,645	270

Figure 13.1 The performance of Rolls-Royce Group plc for 2003

	Group turnover £m	Total operating profit £m
Exploration & Production	1,794	959
Liquefied Natural Gas	945	77
Transmission and Distribution	678	116
Power Generation	184	129
Other activities	3	(30)
Less: Intra-group sales	(17)	
	3,587	1,251

Figure 13.2 The performance of BG Group plc for 2003

site to any third party. This site may have outdated facilities or be in a location which is preventing the organization from being competitive. The division may want to move to a different site with better transport links in order to reduce its costs. Is it wise to judge the division on its return on capital employed when it does not have control over the capital invested? Is this potentially misleading information worse than having no information at all?

All the divisions in a group benefit from the services provided by their head office and the cost of providing these services is usually significant. However, the head office does not create any sales revenue of its own against which these costs can be offset. It is logical for these costs to be divided among its operating divisions, but what basis should be used for this distribution? The choice of bases includes sales revenue, contribution, operating profit, profit after interest, gross assets, net assets, book value of fixed assets, and so on. Or the head office may attempt to arrive at a 'fair' distribution of its costs based on the relative use of its services made by each division. Also, it may be that the amount of tax paid by the group as a whole can be reduced by the way in which head office costs are allocated to divisions.

This brings us to the related problem of 'transfer pricing', the amount for which goods and services are sold by one division to another division in the same group. If you look at the performance summary of the BG Group plc shown above, you will see the item 'Intra-group sales' of £17 million. These sales must be deducted if the figure for the group turnover is to reflect accurately the amount of sales to customers outside the group. Again, this seems straightforward at first sight; a simple application of arithmetic should give us the true picture. However, a little thought will reveal the true complexity of the situation.

Should the transfer price charged by the selling division be the price it normally charges to outside customers? If it charges different prices to different customers, which one should be used? Will the buying division feel exploited because it knows that the selling division has not had to incur the normal amount of marketing expenses connected with third-party sales? Is it fair to expect a 'group' discount? Or should transfers be made at cost? After all, these divisions are all part of the same group and it is the group's combined results that matter in the end. If this approach is adopted, which cost should be used – variable cost or full cost? If variable cost is used, the selling division has no incentive whatsoever to make the sale. All it gets back is what it has had to pay out. What is the point of getting involved in activities for which you get no return? If full cost is used, the buying division may feel it is being asked unfairly to contribute to the overheads of the selling division. After all, these overheads tend to be fixed costs so they are not increased by internal transactions.

The measurement of divisional performance and the setting of transfer prices will now be discussed in detail.

Having worked through this chapter you should be able to:

- explain the different bases of divisionalization;
- state the advantages of a divisional structure;
- list the roles played by head office;

Learning objectives

- distinguish between the different types of responsibility centres;
- evaluate the use of different types of profit to measure performance;
- calculate a division's return on investment;
- calculate a division's residual income;
- compare and contrast return on investment with residual income;
- explain what a 'transfer price' is;
- explain how 'ideal' transfer prices are calculated;
- describe the four different approaches to 'practical' transfer pricing;
- calculate transfer prices using alternative methods;
- explain how 'international' transfer prices can be used to avoid paying tax;
- discuss the limitations of divisional performance measurement;
- discuss the limitations of transfer pricing.

Bases of divisionalization

The two annual review extracts shown at the beginning of this chapter both show an analysis of a company's activities according to its major product lines. However, some companies analyse their activities not by product but by geographical area; the Volkswagen group is one of these (see Figure 13.3).

Region	2001	2002	2003
Europe/Rest of World	3,398	3,365	2,454
North America	1,664	1,287	(50)
S. America/S. Africa	(45)	(359)	(390)
Asia/Pacific	407	469	432
Total group	5,424	4,761	2,346

Figure 13.3 Volkswagen GmbH's profit/(loss) by geographical area (€m)

Advantages of divisionalization

As companies grow they tend to diversify their product range. Although this increased complexity consumes extra resources, it can be advantageous in an uncertain world. If one product line unexpectedly loses its popularity and its sales plummet, the company will be protected from the financial consequences by its other products. The organization can be thought of as an investor holding a *portfolio* of products. So, in this way, it can minimize the risk posed by downturns in specific markets.

Another advantage of divisionalization is that its inherent managerial autonomy increases the motivation of its managers. Of course, this depends on the degree of autonomy granted by the head office; the higher it is, the higher the motivation will be. It is generally accepted that most managers rise to the challenge of increased independence and responsibility.

Then there is the question of specialized knowledge. If all the decision making were retained by the head office of Rolls-Royce plc, its directors would have to be experts in such diverse markets as civil aircraft and marine power. The directors of British Gas would have to be experts in both exploration and power generation. The complexity of modern business dictates that it is unreasonable to expect such a wide degree of expertise in a very small number of people. Head office boards of directors realize that it is far more effective to concentrate specialized product and market knowledge in the top management of each division. This should result in better decisions which should translate into improved performance.

This also has the advantage of allowing the head office to get on with its own unique role of reviewing group strategy and co-ordinating inter-divisional activities. A useful side-effect of minimizing head office involvement in operational activities is that there will be fewer opportunities for misunderstandings and wasted effort to arise. Communication should be more effective due to the avoidance of information overload and improved communication usually results in improved performance.

Role of head office

In addition to the co-ordinating role mentioned above, the head office should set corporate policies, goals and objectives. For example, it may decide that all divisions should be in the top three of their respective industry's league table. Very often, the head office has the responsibility of raising the funds for capital investment in the divisions. After all, it is in a much better position to do this as the investors see the group as a single entity with pooled resources.

Also, in addition to setting long- or medium-term plans, it is standard practice for the head offices to set annual financial targets for divisions. For example, a return on capital employed of 18% a year may be required of one division but another division (considered to be more risky) may be required to produce 24%. Depending on the degree of autonomy, the head office may also set targets regarding sales revenues/volumes, market share, cash generation, etc.

Degrees of responsibility

The level of independent financial responsibility varies from group to group and sometimes within groups. The following are standard types of responsibility centres:

	£m
Sales revenue	1,100
Variable costs	695
Contribution	**405**
Controllable fixed costs	189
Controllable profit	**216**
Non-controllable fixed costs	44
Profit before head office charges	**172**
Head office charges	93
Divisional pre-tax profit	**79**

Figure 13.4 The choice of profits

Cost centre – responsible for costs only.
Revenue centre – responsible for revenue only.
Profit centre – responsible for costs and revenue, i.e. profit.
Investment centre – responsible for capital investment and profit.

In reality, hybrids of these four standard types also exist. For example, a cost centre may be responsible for most, but not all, of its costs.

Profit centres

Consider the example in Figure 13.4 where four different profits are shown (in bold print). For which specific profit should a profit centre be responsible?

If *contribution* is used, managers may manipulate this by increasing operational gearing (increasing fixed costs and reducing variable costs, e.g. automation).

Controllable profit is a good measure of the **manager's** performance. However, to calculate this it is assumed that differentiation between controllable and non-controllable costs is possible. In reality, the distinction is sometimes blurred. Take petrol costs as an example: the amount of mileage covered is within the control of the division but the price of petrol is not. Is it worth splitting costs like this down into their controllable and non-controllable elements?

Profit before head office charges is a good measure of the **division's** performance rather than the manager's. It takes all the costs into account irrespective of whether they are controllable or not.

Divisional pre-tax profit is not useful for measuring divisional performance as head office charges have been deducted. These charges can be calculated in any way the head office chooses and do not have to be logical or 'fair'.

Investment centres

Investment centres may simply decide which investments to make or they may also have the added responsibility of raising the funds. The performance of these profit centres with additional responsibility for capital investment is usually measured by either 'return on investment' or 'residual income'.

Return on investment (ROI)

The ROI is similar to the return on capital employed ratio; it is a relative measure, expressed as a percentage. Its objective is to give an idea of how well the investment has performed compared with other investments or its own pre-planned performance. Here are three versions of the ROI formula:

$$\frac{\text{Profit before interest and tax (PBIT)}}{\text{Capital employed in the division}}$$

$$\text{or} \quad \frac{\text{Profit before interest and tax (PBIT)}}{\text{Value of operational net assets}}$$

$$\text{or} \quad \frac{\text{Sales revenue}}{\text{Net assets}} \times \frac{\text{PBIT}}{\text{sales revenue}}$$

The ROI depends in part on the measurement of profit and the valuation of operational assets. Unfortunately, profit can be relatively easily manipulated (legally or illegally) and, if profit is unreliable, so is the ROI. Also, in a divisional structure, sales and purchases between divisions tend to distort the profit measure. 'Transfer pricing' between divisions is the subject of the second part of this chapter. The basic problem is that transfer prices can be set in any way the head office decides; it does not have to be rational, logical or fair and may vary from division to division.

To complicate things further, there are several alternative ways in which the asset base can be measured. Should 'historical cost' be used? After all, it is objective and auditable. But this will distort the ROI ratio by ignoring depreciation, which reflects technical obsolescence and inefficiencies caused by age or wear and tear; the older the assets, the greater the distortion. Perhaps 'current cost' should be used. This gives an equitable basis for comparison but it is difficult to determine and is prone to subjectivity.

So, is 'net book value' (also known as 'written-down value') the answer? Well, this too has its drawbacks. If profit were to remain constant over two consecutive periods, ROI would increase due to the effect of depreciation; this would be misleading.

Residual income (RI)

This is an absolute measure expressed in monetary terms (not as a percentage). The formula used to calculate it is

RI = profit after interest but before tax − notional interest charge on equity capital

This is an attempt to reflect the fact that, if the division were not part of a group of companies, it would have to bear the cost of providing funds to buy its fixed assets. These funds are often provided by the head office without any specific charge to the division for them. The idea is to give a more realistic view of the division's performance as a 'stand-alone' unit.

The notional interest charge is partly determined by the division's cost of capital. This can be measured accurately on a historical basis but there is no guarantee that this will not change for the present year. The interest charge is also determined by the value of the asset base. Ideally, this should be calculated using the 'current cost' of assets but this is subjective. Alternatively, if 'net book value' or 'historical cost' is used, the RI is distorted for the same reasons given above for the ROI. So the RI measure is also far from perfect.

Which measure should be used: ROI or RI?

Consider the example of division C which, last year, produced £900 million controllable profit on capital invested of £6,000 million. This gave an ROI of 15% (900/6,000). This year, the division is considering a new capital project requiring an investment of £80 million. The estimated profit before head office charges is £10 million a year, giving an ROI of 12.5% (10/80). The division is reluctant to go ahead with the project because, assuming an equivalent performance to last year on its existing assets, its average ROI will be reduced. Due to a relative downturn in the ROI percentage, the project will probably not go ahead.

But what will the RI calculation show for the same project? First of all, a 'notional income charge' must be calculated at a rate decided by the head office. If this rate were 10%, the interest would be £8 million (£80 million × 10%) and the RI £2 million (£10 − £8 million). This significant positive outcome indicates that the group would benefit from going ahead as its wealth would increase by £2 million. To summarize the conflicting advice:

> ROI – reduced from 15.0% to 12.5% – abandon project
> RI – £2 million increase in wealth – proceed with project

Would you rather receive an extra £2 million or avoid a reduction in a percentage measurement? This is a very strong argument for recommending the RI.

Of course, the two measures can, and often do, recommend the same course of action. For example, if the cost of capital had been 14% the notional interest charge would give a negative RI and both measures would recommend abandoning the project.

(If you have already studied capital investment appraisal, you will probably recognize a similarity in the comparison of net present value (NPV) and internal rate of return (IRR). NPV, which gives an absolute measure in money, is considered superior to IRR, which expresses its answers in percentage terms.)

Self-assessment question S13.1

Try the following question for yourself (answer at the end of the chapter).

The Dominion Distillery Group is considering building a new industrial alcohol production facility in south-west France at a cost of 30 million euros. The annual fixed costs are 20 million euros including 6 million which are not considered controllable by the division. Sales revenue is estimated at 156 million euros and variable costs at 134 million euros.

　　Using 'profit before head office charges' calculate:

1　the ROI;
2　the RI using an interest rate of 5% a year;
3　the interest rate required to make RI = 0.

What justification might the group have for using profit before rather than after head office charges?

A note on Economic Value Added (EVA)

(EVA is a trademark of Stern Stewart & Co.)

EVA is discussed in greater detail in the later chapter on performance improvement techniques. It is a similar concept to the RI in that it deducts a charge for the *opportunity* cost of equity capital. However, EVA is solidly based on economic theory rather than accountancy theory. Many adjustments (up to 160!) can be made to the profit figure in an attempt to show the economic profit rather than the normal accounting one. For example, the cost of training is capitalized and appears on the balance sheet instead of being written off in the profit and loss account. This reflects the nature of training as an investment in the future of the business; it is treated as a long-term intangible asset which is depreciated over a number of years. Also, it may be that there are good reasons not to make identical adjustments to each division. This makes it even more difficult to compare the performance of one division with another.

　　A further difficulty arises when the valuation of a division depends partly on discounting future cash flows of capital investment projects to their present-day value.

　　The NPVs of these capital investment projects should use discount rates specific to the divisions pursuing them. In practice, it is not unusual for head office to apply the same discount rate (that of the group as a whole) to all divisions. Individual divisions should use different discount rates to reflect their riskiness; it is very unlikely that these will be identical. For example, consider a group made up of two divisions of very similar size and performance. The group's overall discount rate may be 10% but division A's risk-adjusted rate is 6% and division B's is 14% (giving a weighted average cost of capital of 10%). If the 10% rate is used to compare them, errors of valuation will occur. Also, if A was considering a project with a return of 9%, it would be incorrectly turned down as it is less than the group's 10% threshold rate.

　　Alternatively, division B may erroneously accept a project returning 11% as it clearly exceeds the 10% threshold but is actually significantly below its risk-adjusted rate. However, in order to avoid a diminution of wealth, this high-risk division should be applying 14% as its threshold. If the project was accepted on the basis of calculations using a rate of 10%, it will result in a decrease in wealth for both the division and the group.

Of course, companies are entitled to use EVA to evaluate divisional performance if they so wish. But they should take into account that it is significantly more complex than the RI, is more difficult to understand, will need more resources to produce mathematically correct answers and is inherently more error prone. None of the three methods discussed will give a totally accurate answer and, due to the margin of error emanating from the assumptions made by each technique, there is a strong case for using the relatively simple RI approach rather than the complex EVA one.

Transfer pricing

The *transfer price* is the monetary value for which goods and services are exchanged between different responsibility centres of the same organization. If the responsibility centres are in different countries, the exchange value is referred to as the *international transfer price.*

Ideal transfer prices

About 50 years ago, an academic by the name of Hirschleifer produced an economic theory for establishing ideal transfer prices between divisions or fellow subsidiaries of a company. The value of this theoretically optimum price is found by calculating the *opportunity cost* to the supplier of the goods or services.

However, in practice, ideal transfer prices are not always used. Other considerations, such as the privacy of information and inter-divisional bargaining, encourage the use of non-ideal transfer prices. For example, sometimes the ideal price is the variable cost, but this means the supplying division earns zero contribution which is potentially demotivating as the division receives no reward for its effort.

Determination of transfer prices

The rules for determining transfer prices are drawn up by each organization without reference to any external accounting-body guidelines. The extent to which the prices cover costs and contribute to internal profits is a matter of company policy. As these prices are internal to the company, it can set them in whatever way it chooses. The practical objective of setting transfer prices is to influence the behaviour of divisional managers – in particular, to avoid demotivating them.

We will now consider four alternative ways in which transfer prices can be set:

- market-based;
- cost-based;
- negotiated;
- administered.

Market-based transfer prices

Where identical products or services are being offered by other companies in the open market, it is possible to set the transfer price at the market price. This is the opportunity cost to the selling division (assuming it is operating at full capacity and can sell all it makes on the open market). By selling within the group, the division foregoes receiving the market price from an outside company. But if the transfer is made at market price, the selling division does not lose any income.

However, when inter-divisional transfers are made, these sales do not usually involve any marketing activity by the selling division. For this reason, the buying division may expect to pay less than the market price. This will increase the buying division's profits but will reduce those of the selling division. So, it is not unusual for inter-divisional conflict to arise as a result of transfer pricing policy, especially if the managers are remunerated, at least in part, by profit-related pay.

Cost-based transfer prices

When the selling division is operating at below full capacity it would be inappropriate to sell to another division at market price as it is not losing any profit on the transaction. In this situation the ideal transfer price is the *variable cost* (which is the opportunity cost to the selling division). But this gives no incentive to the selling division as its earnings are zero. Sometimes, to get round this, a nominal contribution margin is added. However, this could increase the selling price of the group's end product offered on the open market and may make it less competitive.

If *full cost* is used to determine the transfer price, the position is made worse. Sometimes a nominal profit margin is added on top of this to give an incentive to the selling division. The effect on the competitiveness of the final product on the open market will be aggravated.

It is worth noting that a cost-based approach does not give any incentive to the management of the selling division to control costs as these can be passed on to the buying division.

Negotiated transfer prices

Transfer prices can be set by negotiation between the managers of the selling and buying divisions. This works best where there is an active external market for the products as the external market price will significantly influence the transfer price by acting as a reference point.

Where there is no external market, negotiations usually lead to conflict. The 'selling' manager will want the price to be as high as possible but the 'buying' manager will want it to be as low as possible.

Administered transfer prices

Transfer prices can be set by an individual or committee of head office employees, none of whom are directly connected to the divisions involved. The head office administrator will follow corporate policy to determine the transfer prices. For example, the transfer price could be equal to variable cost plus X%, full cost plus Y% or market price less Z%.

There are two advantages of this approach: one is objective consistency and the other is the reduction of conflict. The disadvantages are the probable suboptimal economic performance of the group as a whole and the undermining of divisional autonomy and its consequent demotivating effect.

Example 13.1

Financial data for product X

	£
Materials	11
Direct labour	2
Variable overhead	1
Variable cost	14
Fixed overhead	5
Full cost	19
Profit margin	8
Sales price	27

If operating at full capacity, the *ideal transfer price* is £27.

If operating at less than full capacity, the *ideal transfer price* is £14.

If operating at full capacity, the profit margin may be shared between supplying and buying divisions, so the practical transfer price may be £23 [19 + (50% × 8)].

If operating at less than full capacity, full cost may be used, giving the supplying division a contribution to its fixed overheads. The practical transfer price would be £19, giving a positive contribution of £5.

Self-assessment question S13.2

Try the following question for yourself (answer at the end of the chapter).

Division S sells one of its products, an electric motor, to division B in the same group. One motor costs £36 in materials, £9 in direct labour, £5 in variable overhead and is assigned £15 of fixed overhead. The division sets its profit margin equal to 40% of its variable cost.

What is the ideal transfer price if the division is operating at (a) full capacity, and (b) less than full capacity? Suggest practical transfer prices if the division is operating at (a) full capacity, and (b) less than full capacity.

International transfer pricing

International transfer pricing is usually nothing more than a device to minimize the amount of tax paid in total by international organizations. Although divisional profitability may be distorted, this is normally perfectly legal. The group arranges its accounts so that most of its profits are declared by its divisions in low-tax areas. (For example, at the time of writing, the Republic of Ireland has a corporation tax rate of 12.5% which is approximately half that of the average European Union rate of 23%. This attracted major companies such as WPP and Shire to relocate to Eire.) However, it is not difficult to see how losses and liabilities could be hidden by doing this. The tax avoidance possibilities encourage organizations to set up offshore subsidiaries in areas which demand little, if any, disclosure of corporate information.

Unfortunately, this secrecy can encourage false accounting and fraud as in the Parmalat scandal of late 2003 where billions of dollars of assets reported in a Caribbean subsidiary's accounts were found to be non-existent. Parmalat was based in Parma, Italy, and had extensive operational divisions in South America. But this sort of activity also happens much closer to home.

In 2004, company 'V' was being investigated by the UK tax authorities concerning transactions valued at hundreds of millions of dollars shown in the accounts of its Jersey-based subsidiary, 'J'. Company V buys coffee beans from growers in developing countries and sells them to international coffee- and chocolate-making companies in developed ones. The difficulty seems to be that, although the vast bulk of V's profits are shown in the accounts of its Jersey subsidiary, the coffee beans never physically pass through the island. The company paid no tax on its multi-million-dollar profits reported in the offshore tax haven of Jersey. Apparently, the subsidiary J does not exist in the normal sense of the word and is merely a 'postbox' operation with only a handful of administrative staff. This is very likely an example of transfer prices being used to avoid paying tax.

Limitations

Most of the limitations have already been discussed above. Measuring divisional performance involves choosing between alternative profits. The profits most often used are the 'profit before head office charges' and 'controllable profit'. The first is a good measure of the division's performance but the second is a better measure of the manager's performance. Also, profit is used rather than cash flow so the ROI and RI are both subject to the distortions caused by creative accounting.

When determining inter-divisional transfer prices, some degree of behavioural psychology is usually involved. The objective is to avoid demotivating the divisional managers involved. But it is far from possible to please everybody all the time, especially when managers are remunerated by bonuses based on profit performance.

The manager's point of view (written by Nigel Burton)

It makes obvious sense to divide up a company into manageable units and let each one operate with a measure of independence. There is nothing more energizing for lower-level managers than to be given responsibility for a business area, provided they are granted sufficient authority and freedom of action. But how much autonomy should be devolved down to divisional managers? On one hand, 'interference' from head office can be seriously demotivating. On the other, senior managers do retain ultimate responsibility for the overall performance of the company, and would be negligent if they did not impose some level of supervision over the divisional activities.

The balance between head-office control and freedom of action for divisional managers is a common point of debate. Head office needs regular feedback from the divisions, so that they can spot any signs of underperformance at an early stage; but, with modern computer systems able to provide a wealth of information about the performance of every nook and cranny of the company, the temptation for senior management to micro-manage is very great. Divisional managers can find themselves spending ever more time responding to queries from head office, instead of concentrating their energies on managing the front end of the business.

Head office may consider, and rightly so, that some elements of the company can be more effectively managed from the centre. An obvious example is IT, where it makes sense for all divisions to be using the same software, so that all data is produced on a comparable basis and further program developments need only be done once. Insurance is another area, where senior management must ensure that appropriate cover is in place to protect the company as a whole (and not least the senior management themselves). There is also a trend towards global purchasing agreements, where economies of scale across divisions can bring benefits to the company as a whole, even if individual divisions may feel they have lost out on more effective, local purchasing deals.

All of these elements serve to undermine the autonomy of the divisional manager. So how should his or her performance be judged? Should the profit calculations include a series of cost items over which the divisional manager has no control, or should they be excluded from the divisional accounts? How wise is it to contemplate the profitability of a business which has no IT or insurance costs charged to it? The elimination of 'uncontrollable' material purchasing costs could lead to some very peculiar, and possibly inappropriate, pricing decisions.

In my view, management is about running a business profitably, so managers should focus at all times on the true bottom line. Head-office charges are always unwelcome, but they do represent genuine costs. Divisional managers may have a legitimate grouse that the distance of head-office departments from the front line means that there is less incentive for them to pare down costs. After all, at the sharp end, we tend to think about the number of sales needed to pay for a particular item of expenditure, an angle rarely considered by head-office spending departments. But, in the end, the true costs, as far as one can ascertain them, should always be reflected against the sales revenue. Head-office costs will at least be budgeted. One of the tasks of management is to achieve the profit target in spite of uncontrollable factors affecting the business. If the cost of petrol rises unexpectedly, cover it by making savings elsewhere, or by generating more sales. 'Uncontrollable' costs have to be dealt with in just the same way as 'controllable' ones.

As discussed in the chapter on absorption costing, managers can attempt to increase the profitability of their own areas of responsibility at a stroke, by arguing for a reduction in overhead allocations. The same is true of head-office charges. Another subtle way of increasing your profits is to argue for a change in the level of transfer prices. In all these cases, if you argue successfully, your division will benefit instantly at the expense of its rivals. These arguments can consume a large amount of time and energy, without generating a single extra penny for the company.

Transfer pricing is a can of worms. There is no right or wrong way to fix transfer prices, so the issue is always a bone of contention. Fortunately, within a UK group, transfer prices have no external effect, so management have a free rein to play whatever motivational games they like. UK companies are taxed on a group basis, so it does not matter where the profits are located. It is an entirely different matter in an international situation.

International companies have plenty of opportunity to divert profits into low-tax areas, thereby increasing their overall net income. Simply increasing or decreasing the transfer prices will have a direct impact on the bottom line. However, the tax authorities around the world are not stupid, and are well aware of this type of manipulation. In fact, they tend to assume that the principal objective of international companies is to rob them of their due, and as a result always pay very close attention to transfer pricing policies. There is a big risk to international companies here. For instance, if the UK tax authorities consider that the UK selling company is charging too low a transfer price for its goods to a French sister company, they will raise an assessment on the notional profit which they deem should have been earned. Meanwhile, the French authorities could come to the conclusion that the same transfer price had been too high, and similarly raise an assessment on the notional profit missed. The company could end up paying tax twice, on profit which never existed in the first place.

So how does a company avoid this situation? The tax authorities want to see a transfer pricing policy that is transparently objective and consistently applied. They take the simple view that intercompany sales should be carried out at arm's length. This may be fairly straightforward, if the product is also sold on the open market and a clear market price can be established. But this is not always the case. Market prices can vary considerably from one country to another, depending on a myriad of local factors, such as competition, exchange rates, local taxes, etc. The variation in the price of cars around Europe in recent times is a classic example of this. If the receiving company is simply selling on into the local market, the best option will be to allow it to make a profit equating to a commission, so a transfer price of ultimate selling price, less say 20%, is probably most appropriate.

But what if there is no market price? My company used to make a product in the UK which was shipped to Holland for incorporation into a different product, which was then shipped to our French company for onward sale to customers there. So where do we start? There were no real external market prices to refer to, either for the UK product, or for the Dutch product, and no real competition for this specialized product in France. In such cases, our policy was to use total cost plus 10% for each transfer, ensuring that each company in the line was receiving a fair reward for its contribution to the end product, and that the ultimate selling price did not become uncompetitive. Incidentally, in my view, fixed overhead should always be included in such cost calculations, as there is no reason why intercompany sales should not carry their full burden of cost.

Our total-cost-plus-10% policy was never applied blindly. We still had to make variations when it produced a clearly inequitable result. For instance, we manufactured a product for use in the cosmetics industry which had been very expensive to develop, but which now commanded a high price. There being no independent market for this, the cost-plus-10% basis would normally have been used, but this would have left considerably more profit in the receiving company than in the manufacturing company, which still had the developmental costs to recover. Similarly, we had another line of products which fell into the high-volume, low-price category, where the cost-plus-10% basis left insufficient profit in the receiving company. In these cases we had to move away from the standard policy in order to achieve an equitable split of profit. It was vitally important to document the reasons for this variation, so that the decision could be justified to the sceptical tax authorities.

So, for international companies, a transfer price based on market price remains the safest policy but, where this is not feasible, select another basis, and stick with it as far as you can. The overriding principle is that the transfer price should be demonstrably fair to all parties; the adopted policy should be consistently applied and any variations adequately documented. The tax authorities will certainly examine this area of your business, and you manipulate profit for tax avoidance purposes at your peril.

For companies operating solely within the UK, the issues are far less severe, but the principle of fairness still seems to me to be the overriding factor. There are far more productive uses for management time than the settling of internal disputes about transfer prices.

Summary

- Divisionalization can be based on product type or geographical area.
- Divisionalization reduces risk for the group.
- Divisionalization encourages specialization of management.
- Divisionalization allows the head office to concentrate on strategy and fund raising.
- There are four types of responsibility centre: cost, revenue, profit and investment.
- There are four types of profit to measure divisional performance.
- Return on investment (ROI) is a relative percentage measure.
- Residual income (RI) is an absolute monetary measure.
- Transfer prices (TPs) are used for inter-divisional sales.
- The 'ideal' TP is the *opportunity cost* to the supplier of the goods or services.
- TPs can be determined in four ways: market-based, cost-based, negotiated and administered.
- Whether the division is working at full capacity or not can affect the TP.
- International TPs are often used to avoid tax.
- Divisional performance and transfer pricing have their limitations.

Further reading

Aggarwal, R. K. and Samwick, A. A. (2003) 'Performance incentives within firms: the effect of managerial responsibility', *Journal of Finance*, Vol. 58, Issue 4, August.

Arnold, J. and Turley, S. (1996) *Accounting for Management Decisions*, 3rd edition, Prentice Hall, Harlow. See Chapter 18.

Atrill, P. and McLaney, E. (2004) *Management Accounting for Decision Makers*, 4th edition, Financial Times/Prentice Hall, Harlow. See Chapter 10.

Drury, C. (2004) *Management and Cost Accounting*, 6th edition, Thomson Learning Business Press, London. See chapters on divisional profitability and transfer pricing.

Horngren, C., Foster, G. and Datar, S. (2002) *Cost Accounting*, 11th edition, Prentice Hall International, Harlow. See Chapter 22.

Przysuski, M., Lalapet, S. and Swaneveld, H. (2005) 'Multinational business strategies and transfer pricing in a global marketplace', *Corporate Business Taxation Monthly*, Vol. 6, Issue 5, February.

Vaysman, I. (1998) 'A model of negotiated transfer pricing', *Journal of Accounting & Economics*, Vol. 25, Issue 3, June.

Answers to self-assessment questions

S13.1 Dominion Distillery Group

	€m
Sales revenue	156
Variable costs	134
Contribution	**22**
Controllable fixed costs	14
Controllable profit	**8**
Non-controllable fixed costs	6
Profit before head office charges	**2**

1 $\text{ROI} = \dfrac{2}{30} = 6.7\%$

2 RI: Notional interest charge = 30 × 5% = 1.5 million euros

Profit before head office charges − notional interest charge = 2.0 − 1.5

= 0.5 million euros

3 **New interest rate:**

Notional interest charge = 2.0

New interest rate = 5% × (2.0/1.5) = **6.7%**

The group may justify using profit **before** rather than **after** head office charges if the charges do not increase because of the new distillery. The same total head office cost would be distributed differently among the divisions with no increase to the group as a whole.

S13.2

	£
Materials	36
Direct labour	9
Variable overhead	5
Variable cost	50
Fixed overhead	15
Full cost	65
Profit margin	20
Sales price	85

If operating at full capacity, the *ideal transfer price* is £85.

If operating at less than full capacity, the *ideal transfer price* is £50.

If operating at full capacity, the profit margin may be shared between supplying and buying divisions, so the *practical transfer price* may be £75 [65 + (50% × 20)].

If operating at less than full capacity, full cost may be used, giving the supplying division a contribution to its fixed overheads. The *practical transfer price* would be £65 giving a positive contribution of £15.

VT Ltd

VT Ltd is one of several subsidiaries in the GP group of companies. It manufactures electronic control units and sells them both on the open market and to fellow subsidiaries. Recent market research has produced the following figures regarding the elasticity of demand of its TX9 controller:

Selling price	£6	£7	£8	£9	£10
Demand	30,000	25,000	21,000	16,000	13,000

The standard cost for the TX9 is as follows:

		£
Direct labour	0.20 hours @ £6/h	1.20
Direct materials:	1 multi-switch @ £2.50	2.50
	1 microchip @ £0.50	0.50
	Other components	0.20
Overhead	0.1 machine hours @ £4/mh	0.40
Total cost		4.80

Overheads are 90% fixed and 10% variable.

The multi-switches and microchips are supplied by fellow subsidiaries SGN Ltd and MLF Ltd respectively. All the other components are sourced outside the GP group. Cost and pricing data for these two components are as follows:

Unit costs	SGN Ltd Multi-switch	MLF Ltd Microchip
Direct labour	0.45	0.20
Direct materials	1.15	0.05
Overhead	0.40	0.10
Full cost	2.00	0.35
Internal transfer price	2.50	0.50
External market price	3.50	0.80

SGN is operating at full capacity and has a backlog of orders to fulfil. MLF is short of orders and, if more are not received soon, it may have to make some redundancies.

Tasks:

1 Based on the market research data, which price–volume combination will maximize the total **contribution** made by the TX9 controller for VT Ltd?

(30 marks)

2 Assuming the proportion of fixed and variable overheads is the same for all GP's subsidiaries, determine the ideal transfer prices which will maximize profits for the **GP group** as a whole.

(20 marks)

3 **Based on your answers to task 2,** determine the price–volume combination to maximize the total **contribution** to VT Ltd.

(20 marks)

4 Discuss the alternative ways that transfer prices can be calculated and comment briefly on the fact that 'ideal' transfer prices are not being used within the GP group.

(30 marks)

(Total 100 marks)

Questions

An asterisk * on a question number indicates that the answer is given at the end of the book. Answers to the other questions are given in the Lecturer's Guide.

Q13.1* RI v ROI

The table below shows the annual results for the four divisions of a group company.

	£000			
Division	A	B	C	D
Sales revenue	156	445	3,014	2,036
Variable costs	134	400	2,642	1,781
Contribution	**22**	**45**	**372**	**255**
Controllable fixed costs	14	35	298	211
Controllable profit	**8**	**10**	**74**	**44**
Non-controllable fixed costs	6	7	50	30
Profit before head office charges	**2**	**3**	**24**	**14**
Head office charges	1	1	6	4
Divisional pre-tax profit	**1**	**2**	**18**	**10**
Capital employed	30	60	450	240

Tasks:

1 Calculate the return on capital employed for each of the four divisions and rank them accordingly.
2 Calculate the residual income for each of the four divisions using an interest rate of 5% and rank them accordingly.
3 Comment on your findings.

Q13.2* Gorgon Group plc

Gorgon Group plc is a manufacturer with a divisional structure. The Odeen division makes a single product which it sells outside the Gorgon Group as well as to the Trey division. Odeen's product has a variable cost of £17 a unit and its total annual fixed costs are £480,000. It sells 30,000 units externally at £40 each and 10,000 to Trey at £34 each. For its internal profit calculations, Odeen allocates 20% of total fixed costs to Trey and 80% to external sales.

Trey has been approached by an external supplier, Hexup Ltd, which is offering a virtually identical product to that currently purchased from Odeen at a price of £30 each.

Tasks:

a) If Trey refuses Hexup's offer, calculate Odeen's annual profit and analyse it between intra-group and external activities.

b) If Trey buys its total requirement from Hexup and Odeen cannot replace the lost sales, what will be the effect on the profits of (1) Odeen and (2) Gorgon?

c) If Odeen refuses to match Hexup's price and Trey buys its total requirement from Hexup, how many extra external sales would Odeen have to make to avoid any reduction in its profit?

d) If Trey decides to purchase half its requirement from Hexup, what effect will this have on Gorgon's profit?

e) If Odeen agrees to match Hexup's price of £30 provided Trey still buys 100% of its requirement from it, what effect will this have on Gorgon's profit?

f) Advise Gorgon Group regarding this situation.

Q13.3 MCP plc

MCP plc specializes in providing marketing, data collection, data processing and consulting services. The company is divided into divisions that provide services to each other and also to external clients. The performance of the divisional managers is measured against profit targets that are set by central management.

During October, the Consulting division undertook a project for AX plc. The agreed fee was £15,500 and the costs excluding data processing were £2,600. The data processing, which needed 200 hours of processing time, was carried out by the Data Processing (DP) division. An external agency could have been used to do the data processing, but the DP division had 200 chargeable skilled hours available in October.

The DP division provides data processing services to the other divisions and also to external customers. The budgeted costs of the DP division for the year ending 31 December 2002, which is divided into 12 equal monthly periods, are as follows:

	£
Variable costs:	
Skilled labour (6,000 hours worked)	120,000
Semi-skilled labour	96,000
Other processing costs	60,000
Fixed costs:	240,000

These costs are recovered on the basis of chargeable skilled labour hours (data processing hours) which are budgeted to be 90% of skilled labour hours worked. The DP division's external pricing policy is to add a 40% mark-up to its total budgeted cost per chargeable hour.

During October 2002, actual labour costs incurred by the DP division were 10% higher than expected, but other costs were 5% lower than expected.

Required:

a) Calculate the total transfer value that would have been charged by the DP division to the Consulting division for the 200 hours on its AX plc project, using the following bases:
   i)   actual variable cost;
   ii) standard variable cost + 40% mark-up;
   iii) market price.

(6 marks)

b) Prepare statements to show how the alternative values calculated in answer to requirement (a) above would be reflected in the performance measurement of the **DP** division **and** the Consulting division.

(12 marks)

c) Recommend, with supporting calculations, explanations and assumptions, the transfer value that should be used for the 200 hours of processing time in October. Your answer need not be one of those calculated in your answer to requirement (a) above.

(7 marks)
(Total = 25 marks)

CIMA Intermediate: Management Accounting – Performance Management, November 2002

Q13.4 CTD Ltd

CTD Ltd has two divisions – FD and TM. FD is an iron foundry division which produces mouldings that have a limited external market and are also transferred to TM division. TM division uses the mouldings to produce a piece of agricultural equipment called the 'TX' which is sold externally. Each TX requires one moulding. Both divisions produce only one type of product.

The performance of each divisional manager is evaluated individually on the basis of the residual income (RI) of his or her division. The company's average annual 12% cost of capital is used to calculate the finance charges. If their own target residual income is achieved, each divisional manager is awarded a bonus equal to 5% of his or her residual income. All bonuses are paid out of head office profits.

The following budgeted information is available for the forthcoming year:

	TM division TX per unit £	FD division Moulding per unit £
External selling price	500	80
Variable production cost	*366	40
Fixed production overheads	60	20
Gross profit	74	20
Variable selling and distribution cost	25	**4
Fixed administration overhead	25	4
Net profit	24	12
Normal capacity (units)	15,000	20,000
Maximum production capacity (units)	15,000	25,000
Sales to external customers (units)	15,000	5,000
Capital employed	£1,500,000	£750,000
Target RI	£105,000	£85,000

* The variable production cost of the TX includes the cost of an FD moulding.
** External sales only of the mouldings incur a variable selling and distribution cost of £4 per unit.

FD division currently transfers 15,000 mouldings to TM division at a transfer price equal to the total production cost plus 10%.

Fixed costs are absorbed on the basis of normal capacity.

Required:

(a) Calculate the bonus each divisional manager would receive under the current transfer pricing policy and discuss any implications that the current performance evaluation system may have for each division and for the company as a whole.

(7 marks)

(b) Both divisional managers want to achieve their respective residual income targets. Based on the budgeted figures, calculate:
   (i) the **maximum** transfer price per unit that the divisional manager of TM division would pay.
   (ii) the **minimum** transfer price per unit that the divisional manager of FD division would accept.

(6 marks)

(c) Write a report to the management of CTD Ltd which explains, and recommends, the transfer prices that FD division should set in order to maximize group profits. Your report should also:
   ● consider the implications of actual external customer demand exceeding 5,000 units; and
   ● explain how alternative transfer pricing systems could overcome any possible conflict that may arise as a result of your recommended transfer prices.

Note: your answer must be related to CTD Ltd. You will not earn marks by just describing various methods for setting transfer prices.

(12 marks)
(Total = 25 marks)

CIMA Intermediate: Management Accounting – Decision Making, November 2002

Q13.5

M Ltd has two divisions, X and Y. Division X is a chip manufacturer and Division Y assembles mobile phones. Division X currently manufactures many different types of chip, one of which is used in the manufacture of the mobile phones. Division X has no external market for the chips that are used in the mobile phones and currently sets the transfer price on the basis of total cost plus 20% mark-up.

The budgeted profit and loss statement for Division Y for next year shows the following results:

Mobile phone range	P	Q	R
	£000	£000	£000
Sales	10,000	9,500	11,750
Less: Total costs	7,200	11,700	9,250
Profit/(loss)	2,800	(2,200)	2,500
Fixed costs	2,000	5,400	5,875

The total costs shown above include the cost of the chips.

Division Y uses a traditional absorption costing system based on labour hours.

M Ltd operates a performance measurement system based on divisional profits. In order to increase profit for the forthcoming year, Division Y has asked permission to buy chips from an external supplier.

The accountant of M Ltd has recently attended a conference on activity-based costing (ABC) and has recommended that the divisions should implement an ABC system rather than continue to operate the traditional absorption costing system.

Required:

a) A presenter at the conference stated that 'ABC provides information that is more relevant for decision making than traditional forms of costing'. Discuss this statement, using Division Y when appropriate to explain the issues you raise.

(8 marks)

b) The management team of M Ltd has decided to implement ABC in all of the divisions. Discuss any difficulties which might be experienced when implementing ABC in the divisions.

(6 marks)

c) (i) Discuss the current transfer pricing system and explain alternative systems that might be more appropriate for the forthcoming year.

(7 marks)

(ii) Explain the impact that the introduction of an ABC system could have on the transfer price and on divisional profits.

(4 marks)
(Total 25 marks)

CIMA Intermediate: Management Accounting – Decision Making, May 2003

Review questions

1 Explain the different bases of divisionalization.
2 Discuss the advantages of a divisional structure.
3 List the roles performed by head office.
4 Distinguish between the different types of responsibility centres.
5 Evaluate the use of different types of profit to measure performance.
6 Describe how to calculate a division's return on investment.
7 Describe how to calculate a division's residual income.
8 Compare and contrast return on investment with residual income.
9 Explain what a 'transfer price' is.
10 Explain how 'ideal' transfer prices are calculated.
11 Describe the four different approaches to 'practical' transfer pricing.
12 Explain how 'international' transfer prices can be used to avoid paying tax.
13 Discuss the limitations of divisional performance measurement.
14 Discuss the limitations of transfer pricing.

The answers to all these questions can be found in the text of this chapter.

Part 5 comprises:

'If you do not know where you want to go, you will probably end up somewhere else!' A foolish statement or a recommendation for planning? Budgets are a kind of route map: they detail a series of activities which will lead to a certain position at a certain time. Almost every organization uses budgets to help it achieve its objectives.

The budgetary control process consists of two main activities. The first is the creation of the budget and the second is using the budget to control operations. Both of these activities take up large amounts of managers' time and other corporate resources. If you are a manager, it is highly probable that you will be involved in the budgetary control process to a greater or lesser extent. This being so, you will benefit from an understanding of how budgets are constructed and how they are used. Budgets can help you to achieve your management objectives.

However, the last decade has witnessed a growing discontent with traditional budgetary control systems. Out of this has grown the 'Beyond Budgeting' movement which advocates a new paradigm for the way in which organizations are managed. Almost always, organizations adopting this new model find that their traditional budgetary control systems hinder, rather than help, their performance. Hence, they are abolished and replaced with several 'adaptive processes' which are more in tune with the new management model.

Another new way of managing business is the balanced scorecard, which is now about 20 years old. This has been much more readily adopted than 'Beyond Budgeting', probably because it does not advocate getting rid of any existing management devices; it can be added on to existing systems (although there are dangers of doing this). It has broken the monopoly of financial ratio analysis in the assessment of business performance. It is a feed forward system that uses a majority of non-financial (rather than financial) information to guide and assess business performance.

The formal discipline of management accounting is approximately 100 years old and, not surprisingly, it has changed and developed over its lifetime. Managers have come to understand that management accounting techniques can be adapted to become agents for change. They can act as media through which organizations can achieve their objectives. New developments such as the 'balanced scorecard' (including non-financial performance indicators) and activity-based management (including activity-based budgeting) are modern tools to tackle the managerial problems of the twenty-first century. Managerial accounting is no longer confined to the roles of costing, control and decision making. It is now in the front line of business performance management.

Further to this, a plethora of techniques/models/systems designed to improve business performance has evolved over the last 40 years or so. In addition to those mentioned above, there are also lean production, six sigma, value analysis, benchmarking, performance dashboards and strategic management accounting. In all, 14 of these paradigms are described and discussed in the last chapter. Management accountants are playing an ever-increasing role in improving the performance of the organizations they work for. After all, if this function was not within their remit, they would be no more than the 'cost and works accountants' they were at the mid-point of the twentieth century. Performance improvement is of critical importance to each and every one of the businesses that make up our economy.

CHAPTER 14 | Budgets and their creation

Introduction

If you were one of the top managers in an organization, e.g. a director of a company, you would be expected to have a vision of where the organization should be a few years from now. Knowing where you are going is one important aspect of leadership. However, although having a vision is very important, it is not sufficient in itself. You need to know how to go about realizing that vision. First, you need to be able to **make the plans** which will get you to where you want to be. Second, you need to know the best way to **use those plans**. Armed with this knowledge you stand a fair chance of achieving your goals. Without it, you are much less likely to succeed. This chapter is all about how to make those plans, how to create a budget.

Note that although budgets are just as important to service industries as they are to manufacturing industries, their preparation is illustrated in this chapter using examples of manufacturing. Budgets for service organizations are prepared in just the same way but, obviously, without the manufacturing schedules.

Learning objectives	**Having worked through this chapter you should be able to:**

- explain what a budget is;
- explain how it fits into the corporate planning context;
- list the positive attributes of budgetary control systems;
- differentiate between fixed and flexible budgets;
- differentiate between incremental and zero-based budgeting;
- create functional budgets;
- create a budgeted profit and loss account, balance sheet and cash flow forecast;
- create flexible budgets;
- define standard cost;
- discuss the issues about the setting of standards;
- discuss the limitations of budgets.

Budgets and their context

A budget is a predictive model of organizational activity, quantitatively expressed, for a set time period. In plain English, a budget is a plan of operations and activities for the next year (or month, etc.), stated in monetary values.

The organization's strategic plan, not the annual budget, is the master plan of the organization. This strategic plan should state the long-term organizational objectives and

STRATEGIC CORPORATE PLAN
– long-term organizational objectives
– policies through which goals are to be achieved

ANNUAL BUDGET
Master budget – profit and loss account, balance sheet and cash flow forecast,
Functional budgets – for departments or processes,
e.g. purchasing, marketing, material usage, etc.

Figure 14.1 The budget in context

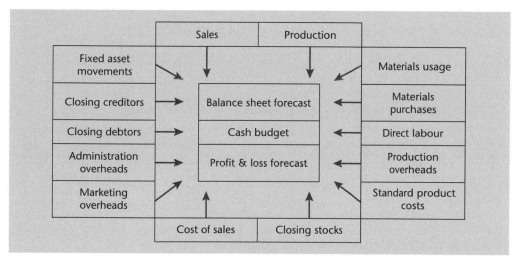

Figure 14.2 Budget relationships

the policies through which these goals are to be achieved. The annual budget is created within the context of the strategic plan (see Figure 14.1).

The relationships between the various constituent budgets are illustrated in Figure 14.2.

Functional budgets

The primary budget

Where to start? Does it matter which budget is created first? The answer to this last question is 'yes'. Start with the activity that determines all the other activities. In the vast majority of businesses, this is sales. The amount of goods or services that it is realistically considered can be sold in the budget period will influence all the other activities. This primary budget can be thought of as a limiting factor. (However, if titanium components were being manufactured for jet engines and there was a sudden unforeseen shortage of this material, then the limiting factor might be the availability of titanium. In this unusual case, the raw material budget would have to be the first one prepared.)

The sales forecast is the responsibility of the sales and marketing section and, because it is so crucial, it would have to be approved at the highest level in the organization. The management accountant would have little, or no, input into this primary budget.

The production volume budget

To plan the production volume for a period it is necessary to know the stock levels of finished goods at the beginning and end of that period. These may be determined by a policy such as 'opening stock is to be equal to one-half of the next month's sales'. So, if it is planned to sell 100 items in March and 120 items in April, the stock will be 50 items on 1 March and 60 items on 1 April. As the sales volume is already known, the number of items to be made is determined by the following formula:

$$\textbf{Production = sales + closing stock – opening stock}$$

Self-assessment question S14.1	*Try the following question for yourself (answer at the end of the chapter).*
	The sales of Minnow Ltd are planned to be: April 100, May 140, June 120 and July 160 items. Stock levels are planned to be one-quarter of the next month's sales. What are the planned production budgets for April, May and June?

The raw material purchasing budget

To calculate this, it is necessary to know how much raw material will be used as well as knowing the policy on raw material stock levels. It may be that, due to the unreliability of supplies, the policy of a particular firm is to have sufficient stock at the start of a month for that month's production. The production volume budget will determine the amount of raw material usage and raw material purchases are therefore calculated as follows:

$$\textbf{Purchases = usage + closing stock – opening stock}$$

(This formula applies to both quantities and values.)

Self-assessment question S14.2	*Try the following question for yourself (answer at the end of the chapter).*
	Minnow Ltd plans to spread its production of 1,800 items evenly throughout the year. Each item uses five units of raw material. Minnow expects to start the year with 80 units of raw material in stock but to reduce this by 25% by the end of the year. If each unit of stock costs £6 to buy in, what is the company's raw material purchasing budget for the year?

The cost of sales budget

For a manufacturing organization, the cost of sales is calculated by the following formula:

Cost of sales = opening stock + production cost − closing stock

(All the items in this equation relate to finished goods only.)

Try the following question for yourself (answer at the end of the chapter).

If Minnow Ltd's stock of finished goods is valued at £30,000 on 1 January and £27,000 at 31 March and the cost of production is £20,000 a month, what is the cost of sales for the quarter?

The cash receipts budget

In order to prepare the cash budget, it is essential to know the amount of money planned to be received in each period. For sales made on 'cash terms' (i.e. transfer of goods and payment for them take place at the same time), the total receipts equal the total sales revenue. For sales made on 'credit terms' (i.e. payment takes place at a later time than the transfer of the goods), the picture is more complicated. The total of receipts in a period depends on the amount of debtors at the start and finish of the period as well as the amount sold on credit terms during that period. Thus

Receipts = opening debtors + credit sales − closing debtors

Try the following question for yourself (answer at the end of the chapter).

Minnow Ltd plans to sell 2,400 items for £10 each evenly through the year, half on cash terms and half on credit terms of one month. If its opening debtors were £1,300, what would be the planned total of receipts from all sales during the year? (Assume all debtors pay on the due dates.)

The cash payments budget

In order to prepare the cash budget, it is also essential to know the amount of money planned to be paid out in each period. When goods and services are paid for immediately they are received, the total of payments equals the total of purchases. However, when purchases are made on credit terms, the total of purchases must be adjusted by the amount of creditors at the start and finish of the period to give the total amount of payments. Thus

Payments = opening creditors + credit purchases − closing creditors

Try the following question for yourself (answer at the end of the chapter).

Minnow Ltd buys 1,600 items at £5 each evenly through the year, one-quarter on cash terms and three-quarters on two months' credit. If the company's opening creditors were £750, what would be the total of its payments for the year?
(Assume all creditors are paid on the due dates.)

Master budgets

The cash budget or cash flow forecast

This budget is of particular importance to all organizations. If there is insufficient cash to pay all the bills due at a certain time, then the organization may be forced out of business even though it is trading profitably (see Chapter 2).

The summary cash budget for the period is simply

Opening balance + receipts − payments = closing balance

However, it is normal to create a detailed cash budget for each month in order to monitor and control the organization's cash resources. It is also useful to know the net result of monthly cash flows. Is more money coming in than going out (i.e. a net inflow) or is more going out than coming in (i.e. a net outflow)? Once this is known, the net cash flow can be combined with the opening balance to give the closing balance:

	Cash in
Less:	Cash out
	Net cash flow
Add:	Opening balance
	Closing balance

It is conventional to give net inflows a positive sign and net outflows a negative sign (shown below by the use of brackets).

The following is an example of a simple cash budget in summary terms:

		Jan	Feb	Mar	Total
	Cash in	45	49	54	148
Less:	Cash out	37	53	41	131
	Net cash flow	8	(4)	13	17
Add:	Opening balance	850	858	854	850
	Closing balance	858	854	867	867

Note that the opening balance for a month must be the same as the closing balance for the previous month. This is only to be expected as exactly the same money is being referred to by each of the two balances.

The illustration below shows these summary figures in bold type together with some of the detailed items that help to make them up.

	Jan	Feb	Mar	Quarter
Receipts:				
Credit sales	32	37	41	110
Cash sales	11	12	12	35
Other	2	–	1	3
Total	**45**	**49**	**54**	**148**
Payments:				
Purchases of materials	25	27	25	77
Wages	8	8	8	24
Expenses	4	4	5	13
Other	–	14	3	17
Total	**37**	**53**	**41**	**131**
Net in/(out)flow	**8**	**(4)**	**13**	**17**
Opening bank balance	**850**	**858**	**854**	*850*
Closing bank balance	**858**	**854**	**867**	*867*

Be careful of the two numbers (in italics) at the bottom right-hand corner. They are **not** found by adding across (like all those above them) but by **copying** the opening balance for the quarter (850) and then working down the 'Quarter' column. The resulting number (867) in the extreme bottom right-hand corner should be exactly the same as that on its immediate left. After all, they should both show the balance on 31 March.

The figures above show the months when the cash actually moves, i.e. comes in or goes out. For sales and purchases made on credit terms, this date will always be later than the point of sale or purchase. The cash budget may be dangerously misleading if these timing differences are not taken into account.

Note that the balances on the bottom two lines of the cash budget can be negative as well as positive. This shows that the organization has a bank overdraft rather than a positive balance, a very common business situation.

When referring to cash budgets, use the terms *net inflow*, *net outflow*, *surplus* or *deficit* but **never** *profit* or *loss*.

The cash flow forecast is a very important management tool. It is used to:

● ensure that sufficient cash will be available to carry out planned activities;
● give a warning of the size of overdraft or loan needed;
● plan for investment of surplus cash.

Try the following question for yourself (answer at the end of the chapter).

Self-assessment question S14.6

Using the pro forma below, create (in pencil?) a cash budget from the following information: Opening balance is £150 *overdrawn*; credit receipts are £100 per month, cash receipts are £30 per month and other receipts are £70 in Feb.; purchases are £100 per month, wages £25 per month, expenses £35 per month and other payments are £15 in Jan.

Cash budget for quarter ended 31 March				
	Jan	Feb	Mar	Quarter
Receipts:				
Credit sales				
Cash sales				
Other				
Total				
Payments:				
Purchases of materials				
Wages				
Expenses				
Other				
Total				
Net in/(out)flow				
Opening bank balance				
Closing bank balance				

The budgeted profit and loss account and balance sheet

These budgets are compiled from information on the functional budgets or provided from elsewhere in the organization. This is best appreciated by working through the case study at the end of this chapter.

Types of budget and budgeting methods

Fixed budget

This is a budget based on one predetermined level of activity. Its main function is to act as a master plan for the following year.

Flexible budget

This is a budget which, by recognizing different cost behaviour patterns, is designed to change as the volume of activity changes. It can be thought of as several fixed budgets, each at a different level of activity, shown side by side.

Incremental budgeting

This approach to budget creation assumes that there will be little change in activity for next year compared with the current year. So, the numerical amounts (known as *allowances*) are arrived at by taking last year's amount and adding an increment for any known changes and for inflation.

Zero-based budgeting

This is a method of budgeting which requires each cost element to be specifically justified, as though the activities were being undertaken for the first time. Without approval, the budget allowance is zero.

Flexible budgets

Shown below is a flexible budget for a firm which expects to sell about 1,400 items a year. However, its market tends to fluctuate year to year and so it also produces budgets for sales of 1,200 and 1,600 items. These are its estimates of the minimum and maximum annual sales.

Flexible budgeted profit and loss account for y/e 31 December

Sales (units)	1,200	1,400	1,600
Sales revenue (£000)	600	700	800
Materials	300	350	400
Labour	120	140	170
Factory overhead	20	21	27
Total	440	511	597
Gross profit	160	189	203
Marketing costs	16	18	20
Admin costs	30	30	30
Total	46	48	50
Net profit	114	141	153

This shows that net profit does not increase in direct proportion to sales volume. At maximum sales the net profit increases by only £12,000 for the extra 200 units sold over the expected number. But at minimum sales (200 units less than expected) net profit decreases by £27,000. This type of situation arises due to the way in which costs behave (see Chapter 2). Remember that many costs have both fixed and variable elements. For example, the marketing costs above have a fixed component of £4,000 and a variable component of £10 a unit. Sometimes, fixed costs step up. Weekend working had to be introduced to produce the extra 200 items needed for maximum sales. This caused extra labour costs at an overtime premium of 50% and additional factory overheads.

Understanding cost structures is essential for the creation of flexible budgets. If you are asked to create one involving stepped fixed costs you will have to be told both the activity level at which the step happened and the size of the step. But you would probably be expected to calculate the semi-variable costs (such as marketing in the above example) for yourself. One way of going about this is known as the 'high–low method' (also covered in Chapter 1, on cost behaviour).

Example
14.1

Illustration using the semi-variable cost of water supplies

For the first six months of the year the monthly invoices for the use of water by the business were:

Month	Usage	Total cost (£)
1	520	12,080
2	570	12,310
3	600	12,400
4	510	12,040
5	540	12,160
6	500	12,000

Using only the highest- and lowest-usage months, the cost structure can be determined as follows:

Highest (month 3)	600 units	£12,400
Lowest (month 6)	500 units	£12,000
Difference	100 units	£400

Variable cost per unit produced = £400/100 = £4
Variable cost of 500 units   = 500 × £4 = £2,000
Fixed cost (at 500 units)   = total cost − variable cost
                  = £12,000 − £2,000
                  = £10,000

This can be checked by substituting these values in the other month. In month 3:

$$£$$

Variable cost = 600 × £4 = 2,400
Fixed cost   = 10,000
Total cost   = 12,400

When performing this check, be sure to use **only** the other occurrence used in the original calculation (month 3 in this case). Note that many costs do not behave as predictably as water bills.

As this method uses the two extreme values of the variable, it is advisable to check that these are representative of the normal cost behaviour. This can be done by sketching a scattergraph which will show up any 'outliers' or unrepresentative values.

Self-assessment question S14.7

Try the following question for yourself (answer at the end of the chapter).

The monthly costs of machine maintenance have been recorded during the past few months as follows. (During July the machine maintenance team were redeployed to assist on emergency repairs to the factory building.)

Month	Machine Maintenance hours	Total cost
October	155	2,013
September	122	1,723
August	135	1,902
July	69	280
June	157	2,073
May	149	1,937

If the machine maintenance hours for November are planned to be 180, estimate the machine maintenance cost for that month.

Standards and how they are set

A *standard* is the physical and financial plan for **one unit** of output.

> The standard cost *is the planned unit cost of the products, components or services produced in a period.*
> *(CIMA, Management Accounting Official Terminology)*

Example standard cost data for one plastic wheel (type KR2)

Category	Item	Quantity	Price	Cost
Materials:	Plastic beads	1.2 kg	£2.00/kg	2.40
Labour:	Type A	0.25 h	£4.00/h	1.00
	Type D	0.10 h	£5.00/h	0.50
Variable overhead		0.35 h	£2.00/h	0.70
Variable cost				4.60
Fixed overhead (@ 900 wheels/week)		0.35 h	£4.60/h	1.61
Standard cost				£6.21

Bases for setting standards

There are three common sources for setting standards:

1 Performance levels of a prior period – these are based on recent experience.
2 Estimates of expected performance – these are based on recent experience and knowledge of any imminent changes.

3 Performance levels to meet organizational objectives – these are calculated from set targets; particularly useful if 'target costing' is used.

Approaches to standard setting

Standards are usually set at either *ideal* or *attainable* levels:

- *Ideal standards* make no allowances for any inefficiencies. They are achievable only under the most favourable conditions and represent the theoretical maximum outcomes. It is not possible for actual performance to exceed ideal standards and their use may demotivate many employees.
- *Attainable standards* are set at high but achievable levels; they represent a challenge. They make allowances for normal working conditions and are achievable by operating efficiently. They are capable of being exceeded and, therefore, can be used to motivate the workforce.

However, it is worth considering who decides what is the attainable level of performance. This decision is normally, at least partially, subjective. Top managers may have a different viewpoint from the budget holders charged with executing the budget.

This potential conflict of interests has led to *participative budgeting* where budget holders are involved in creating their own budgets. Management accounting staff help them to create their budgets, which then have to be agreed at a higher level of management. Two important points arise from this.

First, budget holders gain 'psychological ownership' from being involved in creating their own budget. It becomes 'their' budget rather than someone else's imposed upon them. They have a greater commitment to the success of their budget, which leads to improved performance. Non-involvement leads to a lack of interest in its success.

Second, as budget holders know they will ultimately be held responsible for meeting the budget, they have a natural tendency not to set their own targets too high. The technical term for these 'safety' or 'buffer' factors is *budgetary slack*. This is defined as 'the intentional overestimation of expenses and/or underestimation of revenues in the budgeting process' (CIMA *Management Accounting Official Terminology*).

The final decision on the contents of the budget belongs to senior management. However, this form of centralized control is potentially demotivating. To counteract this, the budget holder is usually given a high degree of responsibility for **how** the budget is achieved. He or she makes the day-to-day operating decisions and decides the tactics for meeting the corporate objectives. This bipartite approach effectively defuses the potential conflict between delegation and centralized control.

Importance of accurate standards

Badly set standards cause misleading variances whose investigation wastes both time and resources. Variances caused by poor standards are known as *planning variances*. One way to avoid these is by the systematic reviewing and updating of all standards.

Another aspect of accuracy is the question of how the budget allowance is arrived at for discretionary costs. How do you set the budget for items such as advertising or training? This type of cost may vary significantly from year to year. There is no easy answer to this question but managers should be aware of the problems posed by this type of cost.

Limitations of budgets as plans

In the 1970s, most large UK companies had a planning department employing a significant number of people. The wisdom of that era was that good planning for the next 5 to 10 years would enable the business to operate efficiently by anticipating and being prepared for future changes. Some also had outline plans for the next 15, 20 or 25 years. Many resources were tied up in the planning process. Forty years later, at the beginning of the twenty-first century, the proportion of resources allocated to this process is far smaller.

The main reason is that the rate of change in the business environment has greatly accelerated during those years and shows no sign of slowing down. To plan in detail for the next 10 years is considered to be a waste of time. The organization may be supplying different products and services in different markets by then. It may have been taken over or it may have acquired other organizations to take it in new directions. The stock markets of the world operate globally and faster than ever before. The amount of uncertainty in the business environment is much greater than it was before. Long-term planning is not seen as an effective use of resources. It is common to produce detailed plans only for the next year, and outline plans for the next three years only.

The manager's point of view (written by Nigel Burton)

Almost every field of human endeavour can be improved by a little advance planning. This is particularly true of businesses, which are complicated operations consisting of numerous disparate activities and disciplines. Planning is crucial to ensure that all these disciplines are moving forward in the most efficient way for the enterprise as a whole.

In the vast majority of businesses, the most important driving force is the strategic sales plan. The sales department, with its close knowledge of the market in general and of individual customers' needs in particular, is best placed both to determine the growth potential of existing products and to identify marketing opportunities for new products. Its view of what can be achieved, given the right products and supported by the right infrastructure, will provide the pattern of the company's direction for the foreseeable future.

The activities of all other departments in the company will be directed towards supporting the strategic sales plan. The technical department will develop new products to meet the customer requirements specified by the salesforce. Production will gear themselves up, through new equipment or plant modifications, to meet the sales forecast. Purchasing will identify reliable sources for any new materials required. Even Personnel and Administration will provide an infrastructure designed to support the overall plan.

It is then helpful to pull together the plans of all the departments into a long-range company plan. This should not be a detailed document, but should give an outline of the way the company might look over the next few years. In particular, it should ensure that the timing of any specific initiative is properly co-ordinated. For instance, is the development work for new products being started early enough? How long will it take to get approval for the capacity expansion project? Are we developing our people quickly enough to support the expanding business? All this will also lead to profit and cash forecasts, allowing the viability of the overall plan to be established at an early stage.

This should only be an outline document because the circumstances surrounding it will be constantly changing. Such is the pace of change in all fields now, in production and product technology, in IT and information flow, in increasing competition from all corners of the world, that plans can no longer be rigid. Ideally, they would change as every new circumstance emerged. It may not be practical to keep the company plan regularly updated, but the fact remains that managers must constantly be aware of the impact of external factors on their businesses, in both the short and long term.

The annual budget, however, is quite different. It is a working document, full of important detail, which enables the business to be controlled on a day-to-day basis. In my chemicals company, the establishment of the budget was always the biggest exercise of the year. Although everyone traditionally complained about the amount of time it consumed, there is no doubt that the examination of the detail meant that all managers developed a profound understanding of the dynamics of the business. It was the only time in the year that the elements of the profit and loss account were closely examined, allowing cost/benefit issues to be questioned and cost-saving opportunities to be identified. For the rest of the year, the detailed budget became a yardstick against which actual performance could be confidently and easily measured.

If your company has a relatively stable customer base, it is highly desirable to set up a detailed sales budget by customer and product. A computerized sales reporting system will then be able to highlight with ease the areas where targets are not being met, so that early corrective action can be taken by the sales department. If your business consists of one-off contracts, it is clearly less easy to set up such a monitoring procedure, but it is still important to set up some appropriate measurement to provide an early warning of sales shortfalls.

The same principle applies to both direct costs of production and overheads. The budgeting process provides the opportunity to re-evaluate every aspect of cost. Are the standards used in product costing still accurate? Can we justify the level of expenditure we are proposing for, say, travel or advertising? Are there any new or one-off items we want to budget for in the current year? Or any items incurred last year which we do not expect to be repeated next year? This is why, in my view, zero-based budgeting should be used wherever possible.

In my company, managers were required to justify the whole of their budgeted expenditure each year. Travelling expenses, for instance, were always frighteningly large, as our salesforce used to travel all over the world, but, by breaking this lump sum down into individual trips for each salesperson, it was possible to carry out a realistic review. Is it really necessary to have three trips to the Far East, or will two be enough? The sales manager has to provide a convincing justification. However, not all expense headings lend themselves easily to this type of analysis. Repairs to plant, for instance, was another large sum, which consisted of a mass of generally small items. The problem here is that, despite the use of sophisticated maintenance planning systems, there will always be a large number of unforeseeable repair costs. Moreover, the piece of equipment which incurred costly repairs last year is perhaps unlikely to break down again next year, so there is never an identifiable pattern to repairs. For this type of expense, therefore, we were obliged to adopt the incremental approach, taking average expenditure levels in recent years, and adding or subtracting amounts for known changes. In doing this, however, we accepted that we would be unable to exercise the same level of control as in many other areas of expenditure.

Incremental budgeting is a crude tool which allows inaccuracies and inefficiencies to be built into the system. Take salaries as an example. The actual salaries bill for last year is not the sum of the annual salaries of your employees. Staff turnover will inevitably mean that there are unfilled vacancies at times during the year. Replacement staff may have higher or lower salaries than the previous incumbents. There may have been promotions during the year, with accompanying salary increases. Temporary staff may also have been employed, at a much higher cost than permanent staff. Will overtime patterns be the same next year? As you can see, there are many occurrences which can have an impact on the total salary costs. When you come to budget for the following year, you have two options. You can assume that the same situations will occur again next year, so simply take last year's cost and add on a percentage for inflation. Alternatively, you can construct a detailed budget based on actual salaries and projected overtime levels, perhaps ignoring the impact of staff turnover, as it is impossible to forecast where in the company this will occur. Any savings arising from staff turnover can then be taken as favourable variances next year. My preference would always tend towards the latter option. If the managing director asks you why your department's salaries are over budget, you will be able to give a precise answer if you have a firm, detailed budget. If you have to answer 'Well, I think it's because we were understaffed last year', your credibility will undoubtedly suffer!

A detailed, well-constructed budget will also enable you to understand where there is some slack in the system. This is important for the inevitable moment when you receive an instruction from senior management to find more profit. It is a feature of budgeting that, when the proposals of all the departmental managers are put together, the resulting profit figure is never high enough! You will be asked to find more sales volumes, increase prices, or cut down costs, so it would be an unwise manager who did not leave a little slack in his or her initial numbers. If you work for a large corporation with multiple subsidiaries, the same phenomenon will occur at the higher level, when the budgets of all the businesses are added together. The profit is never high enough to meet the shareholders' expectations, and the instruction will come down to increase your local profit by a further factor. With a detailed budget, you can reflect these amendments by specific changes to your plans, e.g. by deferring the recruitment of new staff till later in the year. With a poorly constructed budget, however, this reiterative process will further distance your numbers from reality, and render the budget even less useful as a yardstick.

Summary

- Budgets are medium-term organizational plans expressed in monetary terms.
- They are intended to help the achievement of corporate, strategic long-term goals.
- Detailed functional or departmental budgets are prepared first.
- The summary master budget is prepared last; the process is bottom up.
- Budgets can be fixed or flexible.
- They are usually created incrementally, sometimes by a zero-based approach.
- Standards can be set in different ways and are subjective.
- Their main limitation is that they cannot be easily adjusted for unforeseen changes.

Further reading

Horngren, C., Bhimani, A., Datar, S. and Foster, G. (2002) *Management and Cost Accounting*, 2nd edition, Prentice Hall Europe, Harlow. See chapter 'Motivation, budgets and responsibility accounting'.

Langford, B. N. (2000) 'Production budgets, simplified', *Folio: The Magazine for Magazine Management*, Vol. 30, Issue 1, 1 January.

Otley, D. (1987) *Accounting Control and Organisational Behaviour*, Heinemann Professional Publishing, Oxford. See Chapter 7, 'Budgetary systems design'.

Upchurch, A. (2003) *Management Accounting, Principles and Practice*, 2nd edition, Financial Times/Prentice Hall, Harlow. See chapter 'Budgetary planning'.

Weetman, P. (2002) *Management Accounting, an Introduction*, 3rd edition, Financial Times/Prentice Hall, Harlow. See chapter 'Preparing a budget'.

Answers to self-assessment questions

S14.1

		April	May	June	July
	Sales	100	140	120	160
Add:	Closing stock	35	30	40	
Less:	Opening stock	25	35	30	40
	Production	**110**	**135**	**130**	

S14.2

$$\text{Purchases} = \text{usage} + \text{closing stock} - \text{opening stock}$$
$$= 9,000 + 60 - 80$$
$$= 8,980 \text{ units of raw material @ £6}$$
$$= £53,880$$

S14.3

		£
	Opening stock	30,000
Add:	Production	60,000
Less:	Closing stock	27,000
	Cost of sales	**63,000**

S14.4

		£	
	Opening debtors	1,300	
Add:	Credit sales	12,000	$(2,400 \times 10 \times 0.5)$
Less:	Closing debtors	1,000	
		£	
	Receipts from debtors	12,300	
	Receipts from cash sales	12,000	$(2,400 \times 10 \times 0.5)$
	Total receipts for year	**24,300**	

S14.5

		£	
	Opening creditors	750	
Add:	Credit purchases	6,000	$(1,600 \times 0.75 \times £5)$
Less:	Closing creditors	1,000	$(200 @ £5)$
	Payments to creditors	5,750	
	Payments on cash terms	2,000	$(1,600 \times 0.25 \times £5)$
	Total payments for year	**7,750**	

S14.6

Cash budget for quarter ended 31 March

	Jan	Feb	Mar	Total
Receipts:				
Credit sales	100	100	100	300
Cash sales	30	30	30	90
Other	–	70	–	70
Total	130	200	130	460
Payments:				
Purchases of materials	100	100	100	300
Wages	25	25	25	75
Expenses	35	35	35	105
Other	15	–	–	15
Total	175	160	160	495
Net in/(out)flow	(45)	40	(30)	(35)
Opening bank balance	(150)	(195)	(155)	(150)
Closing bank balance	(195)	(155)	(185)	(185)

S14.7

It is obvious from the question that July is not a representative month and it should be excluded from your calculations. The scattergraph below confirms this:

High month:	**June**	157	2,073
Low month:	**September**	122	1,723
		35	350

Variable cost per hour = 350/35 = £10

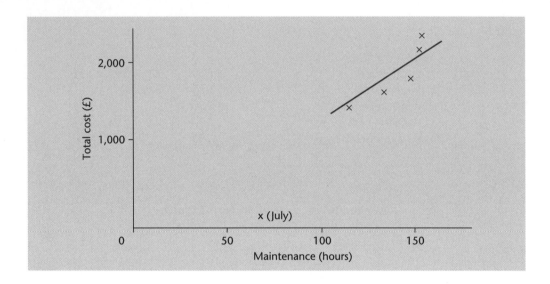

Calculate by using the highest month (June):

$$\text{£}$$

Total cost	= 2,073
Total variable cost = 157 h × £10/h	= 1,570
Total fixed cost	= 503

Check by using the lowest month (September):

$$\text{Total cost} = \text{total fixed cost} + \text{total variable cost}$$
$$= 503 + (122 \times 10)$$
$$= \underline{\text{£1,723}}$$

So, the best estimate for maintenance expenditure in November is

$$\text{Total cost} = \text{total fixed cost} + \text{total variable cost}$$
$$= 503 + (180 \times 10)$$
$$= \underline{\underline{\text{£2,303}}}$$

The Omega Document Case Company

Omega is a long-established firm which used to make many different kinds of leather goods. However, in 2012 it made a loss for the first time in over 20 years. This was due to fierce competition, mainly from the Far East. In response to this, it has slashed its product range to its best-selling and most profitable items. It is hoping to benefit from economies of scale and now plans to make only two types of document case: the Delta and the Alpha.

Task:

From the following information, using the pro formas provided, you are required to create a budget for the year ending 31 December 2013.

Sales forecast

	Delta	Alpha
Number of cases sold	4,000	2,500
Selling price per case	£60	£55

Standard production data

Omega has only two production departments: Cutting and Stitching.
  Unit costs:

Direct labour rates		Raw materials	
Cutting	**Stitching**	**Leather**	**Zip fasteners**
£6.00/h	£7.00/h	£3.00/unit	£1.00/unit

Product content

	Delta	Alpha
Leather	2 units	4 units
Zips	1 unit	2 units
Cutting dept labour	2 hours	1.5 hours
Stitching dept labour	1 hour	0.5 hour

Production overheads

	Cutting Department		Stitching Department	
	Fixed	**Variable**	**Fixed**	**Variable**
	£	**£**	**£**	**£**
Indirect labour	7,000	–	3,000	–
Indirect materials	–	3,000	–	9,000
Maintenance	2,000	1,000	500	500
Business rates	6,000	–	1,000	–
Depreciation	8,000	–	2,000	–
Electricity	1,000	2,000	500	1,000
	24,000	6,000	7,000	10,500

Marketing overheads

	£
Salaries	28,000
Advertising	24,000
Other	2,000
	54,000

Administration overheads

	£
Salaries	32,000
Telephone	5,000
Other	4,150
	41,150

Stocks forecast

	Raw materials		Completed cases	
	Leather	**Zips**	**Delta**	**Alpha**
	(units)	**(units)**	**(units)**	**(units)**
Opening stock	6,000	1,000	100	1,000
Closing stock	8,000	2,000	1,100	500

Debtors and creditors

Raw materials, labour, all overheads and debenture interest will be paid in full through the bank and cash accounts. Debtors and creditors at 31 December 2012 will pay and be paid during 2013. Debtors and creditors at 31 December 2013 are expected to be £25,000 and £10,000 respectively. One year's interest on the debenture is paid during the year.

Fixed assets

There are no disposals expected during 2013 but some new equipment will be acquired, on cash terms, for £20,000 just before the end of 2013.

Expected balance sheet as at 31 December 2012

	Cost	Depreciation provision	NBV
Fixed assets	£	£	£
Buildings	40,000	40,000	–
Machinery	200,000	50,000	150,000
	240,000	90,000	150,000
Current assets			
Raw material stock	19,000		
Finished goods stock	40,000		
Total stock		59,000	
Debtors		15,000	
Bank and cash		10,000	
		84,000	
Less: Current liabilities			
Creditors		8,000	
Net current assets			76,000
			226,000
Less: Long-term liabilities			
10% debenture 2021/22			120,000
			106,000
Financed by:			
Shareholders' capital			£
Ordinary shares			82,000
Retained profit			24,000
			106,000

Pro formas

1   Sales budget y/e 31 December 2013

	Units	Selling price	Revenue
		£	£
Delta	....	....	....
Alpha	....	....	....
		Budget revenue	_____

2 Production budget y/e 31 December 2013

	Delta (units)	Alpha (units)
Planned sales	....	....
Desired closing stock finished goods	....	....
Total required	....	....
Less opening stock finished goods	....	....
Budgeted production	....	....

3 Direct materials usage budget y/e 31 December 2013

	Delta			Alpha		
	Material content (units/case)	Production (cases)	Usage (units)	Material content (units/case)	Production (cases)	Usage (units)
Leather	....	....	....	....	....	....
Zips	....	....	....	....	....	....

	Cost/unit £	Total usage	Cost of materials used £
Leather	....	....	....
Zips	....	....	....
		Budgeted material cost	_____

4 Direct materials purchases budget y/e 31 December 2013

	Leather	Zips
Desired closing stock	.... units	.... units
Units needed for production	.... units	.... units
Total required	.... units	.... units
Less opening stock	.... units	.... units
Purchases needed	.... units	.... units
Cost per unit	£.........	£.........
Budgeted purchases cost	£.........	£.........

5 Direct labour budget y/e 31 December 2013

	Labour content in product (hours)	Cases produced	Total labour hours	Rate per hour £	Total labour cost £
Cutting Dept	....	....	....	....	....
Delta	....	....	....	....	....
Alpha	....	....	....	....	....
Stitching Dept	....	....	....	....	....
Delta	....	....	....	....	....
Alpha	....	....	....	....	....
Budgeted labour hours and cost			_____		_____

6 Production overheads budget y/e 31 December 2013

| | Cutting Dept (expected 13,000 direct labour hours) | | Stitching Dept (expected 6,000 direct labour hours) | |
	Fixed costs	Variable costs	Fixed costs	Variable costs
	£	£	£	£
Indirect labour	....	....	....	....
Indirect materials	....	....	....	....
Maintenance	....	....	....	....
Business rates	....	....	....	....
Depreciation	....	....	....	....
Electricity	....	....	....	....
Budgeted overhead costs	_____	_____	_____	_____
Overhead absorption rate per direct labour hour	_____	_____	_____	_____

7 Standard budgeted unit cost of manufacturing y/e 31 December 2013

| | | Delta | | Alpha | |
	Unit cost	Units in product	Cost	Units in product	Cost
	£		£		£
Leather	....	....	....	....	....
Zips	....	....	....	....	....
Direct labour:					
Cutting	....	....	....	....	....
Stitching	....	....	....	....	....

| | | Delta | | Alpha | |
	Unit cost	Units in product	Cost	Units in product	Cost
	£		£		£
Production overheads:	....	....	....	....	....
Cutting – Fixed	....	....	....	....	....
– Variable	....	....	....	....	....
Stitching – Fixed	....	....	....	....	....
– Variable	....	....	....	....	....
Standard cost of product			_____		_____

8 Closing stock budget at 31 December 2013

	Units	Unit cost £	Total cost £	£
Direct materials:				
Leather	....	....	....	....
Zips	....	....	....	....
Finished products				
Delta	....	....	....	....
Alpha	....	....	....	....
Budgeted closing stock				_____

9 Cost of sales budget y/e 31 December 2013

	£	£
Direct materials usage (3)	....	
Direct labour (5)	....	
Production overheads (6)	....	....
Add: Opening stock finished products		....
Less: Closing stock finished products		....
Budgeted cost of sales		....

10 Marketing and administration expenses budget y/e 31 December 2013

	£	£
Marketing expenses:		
Salaries	....	
Advertising	....	
Other	....	....
Administrative expenses:		
Salaries	....	
Telephone	....	
Other	....	....
Budgeted selling and administrative expenses		....

11 Budgeted profit statement y/e 31 December 2013

	£
Sales (1)	....
Less: Cost of sales (9)	....
Gross profit	....
Less: Marketing and admin expenses (10)	....
Budgeted net profit	....
Less: Interest on debenture	....
Profit after interest	....

12 Cash budget y/e 31 December 2013 (summary form)

	£	£
Opening cash balance		....
Add receipts		....
Total cash available		....
Less payments:		
Purchases	....	
Direct labour (5)	....	
Factory overheads less depreciation (6)	....	
Marketing and admin expenses (10)	....	
Debenture interest	....	
Fixed asset purchases	....	....
Budgeted closing cash balance		....

13 Budgeted balance sheet of Omega Manufacturing as at 31 December 2013

	£ Cost	£ Depn provn	£ NBV
Fixed assets			
Buildings	....	....	....
Machinery	....	....	....
	....	....	....
Current assets			
Stocks:			
Finished goods	....		
Raw materials	....	....	
Debtors		....	
Bank and cash		....	
Less current liabilities			
Creditors		....	....
Net current assets			....
Less long-term liabilities			
10% Debenture 2021/22			....
			£_____
Financed by:			
Shareholders' capital			
Ordinary shares			....
Retained profits			....
			£_____

Questions

An asterisk * on a question number indicates that the answer is given at the end of the book. Answers to the other questions are given in the Lecturer's Guide.

Q14.1* Kellaway Ltd

Kellaway Ltd makes aluminium junction boxes for the electrical industry. It makes the boxes in three different sizes: small, medium and large. The following details are taken from next quarter's budget:

	Large	Medium	Small
Sales volume (units)	4,000	5,000	3,500
Direct labour:			
Fitters and turners (hours/unit)	1.25	0.90	0.80
Assemblers and packers (hours/unit)	0.40	0.25	0.20
Direct materials:			
Aluminium strips per unit	2.5	1.0	0.5
Packaging materials (metres)	1.25	0.75	0.5
Stocks:			
Finished goods opening stock (units)	300	400	200
Finished goods closing stock (units)	400	300	150

Rates of pay for fitters/turners and assemblers/packers are £10.00/hour and £6.00/hour respectively. Aluminium strips cost £3 each and packaging is £1/metre. Kellaway plans to have opening material stocks of 220 aluminium strips and 80 metres of packaging. The closing material stocks are 150 aluminium strips and 50 metres of packaging. The quarter's fixed production overheads of £31,700 are attached to product lines on a direct labour hour basis.

Tasks:

1 Create the production budget for the quarter.
2 Calculate the unit production cost of each type of junction box.
3 Create the materials usage budget in quantities and value.
4 Create the materials purchases budget in quantities and value.
5 Create the direct labour budget in hours and value.

Q14.2* Pierce Pommery

Pierce Pommery specializes in the manufacture of dry cider. The 1-litre bottles sell for £3.00 each, with 25% of sales on cash terms and 75% on one month's credit. The budget shows the following sales volumes:

Month	Litres
August	400,000
September	340,000
October	300,000
November	260,000
December	320,000
January	250,000

The company's policy is for opening stock of cider to equal one-fifth of each month's sales, but the stock of cider on 1 September was actually 80,000 litres. For stocks of apples, the policy is for opening stock to equal 50% of each month's usage. On 1 September, the stock of apples was actually 2,200 tonnes.

On average, 15 kilograms of apples are needed to produce 1 litre of cider (1 tonne = 1,000 kg). The cost price of apples is £50/tonne in September and October but £150/tonne in November and December as they have to be imported. Direct labour is paid in the month it is incurred and costs £0.20 a litre. Fixed overheads are £30,000 a month (including £5,000 for depreciation). Payment for apples is made two months after purchase but all other expenses are paid for one month after being incurred.

Tasks:

1 For the months of September, October, November and for the quarter as a whole, prepare the production budget (in litres) and the purchases budget (in tonnes and £).
2 For November only, prepare the cash budget. (Assume the bank balance on 1 November is £495,900 overdrawn.)

Q14.3* Norman Ropes

The sales budget for next year for a particular type of rope manufactured by Norman Ropes is as follows:

Period	Metres	Period	Metres
1	3,000	7	8,000
2	4,000	8	7,000
3	5,000	9	6,000
4	4,000	10	5,000
5	6,000	11	4,000
6	6,000	12	3,000

The stock of finished rope at the start of each period is to be equal to 25% of the sales estimate for the period. (Norman Rope's policy concerning finished product stock levels is to have a quantity of rope in stock approximately equal to one week's sales.) Exceptionally, at the beginning of period 1 there will be 1,500 metres of rope in stock. There is no work-in-progress at the end of any period.

This type of rope uses only one material, a nylon cord known as ARN. Many lengths of this cord are twisted together to form the rope. The budget assumes that each metre of rope uses 100 metres of ARN and that each metre of ARN will cost £0.04.

Materials equal to 25% of each period's usage are to be on hand at the start of the period. Exceptionally, the stock at the start of period 1 will be 125,000 metres of ARN. (Norman Rope's policy concerning raw material stock levels is to have a quantity of material in stock approximately equal to one week's usage.)

Tasks:

For the first six periods, prepare:

a) the production budget (in metres of rope);
b) the materials usage cost budget;
c) the materials purchases cost budget.

Q14.4 Bishop & Co.

Bishop & Co. manufactures vinyl pond lining for the water-garden industry. The company buys vinyl beads by the tonne and heats and rolls them into large sheets which are then cut to the required sizes. One tonne of beads produces 10,000 square metres of liner. Bishop & Co. is uncertain of demand for next year and decides to produce a flexible budget covering five activity levels from 400,000 square metres to 600,000 square metres in steps of 50,000 square metres.

The vinyl beads cost £800/tonne for purchases of up to and including 50 tonnes per year. Bishop & Co.'s supplier offers it the following bulk-purchase incentive. For annual purchases exceeding 50 tonnes, the cost of every tonne in addition to the first 50 is £750.

The direct labour cost is made up of an annual lump sum of basic pay plus a volume-related bonus operative on all production output.

The present annual capacity of the manufacturing plant is 450,000 square metres. For production above this, a new machine will have to be purchased at a cost of £500,000. (No additional labour will be necessary to operate this highly automated machinery.) Bishop & Co.'s policy on depreciation is to write off machinery in equal instalments over 10 years, assuming a zero residual value.

The cost of insurance cover is a fixed amount up to a production level of 500,000 square metres. Beyond that, there is an additional cost per unit.

Bishop & Co. is currently one of the market leaders (in terms of sales volume) in the vinyl pond liner market although it is very competitive. Bishop & Co. sets its selling price per square metre on a cost-plus basis by adding a 300% mark-up to the total production cost. This covers marketing and administration expenses and leaves a little left over for profit.

Tasks:

1 Complete the following production department budget for next year:

000 sq. m	400	450	500	550	600
	£	£	£	£	£
Vinyl beads	32,000				47,500
Direct labour	80,000				90,000
Electricity	8,000				10,000
Depreciation	22,000				34,000
Insurance	11,000				11,250
Other production costs	139,000				139,000
Total	**292,000**				**331,750**

2 If demand were to exceed 500,000 square metres and the new machinery was purchased, what effect might this have on Bishop's overall performance? What advice would you give regarding the purchase of the new machinery?

Q14.5 Chinkin Corporation

The Chinkin Corporation produces surfboards. Its sales have been 300 a month for the last few months but it is about to launch an expansion strategy aimed at increasing sales by 50% over the next four months, April to July. Sales in April are expected to be 300 boards but to increase by 50 units a month until 450 units are sold in July and each subsequent month.

The selling price of the boards is £50 and half the customers pay in the month following purchase. One-quarter take two months to pay and the other quarter pay cash on delivery, taking advantage of a 5% cash discount.

Chinkin has planned an advertising campaign for the months of April, May and June, costing a total of £40,000. Half this amount is payable in April and the remainder in two equal instalments in May and June.

To facilitate the increase in production, new plant and equipment costing £18,000 have been ordered for delivery in April, with payment in three equal monthly instalments, commencing in May. The cost of commissioning this machinery is estimated at £2,000 and will be paid to the outside contractors in April.

To lessen the impact of acquiring these fixed assets, Chinkin plans to arrange a three-month loan of £20,000 from its bank and expects to pay interest at the rate of 10% per annum. The interest will be paid in one amount on the same day as the capital sum is repaid. The money is to be transferred into its account on 3 April.

Raw materials cost £20 a unit and are paid for one month after purchase. Chinkin plans to have a monthly opening stock of raw materials equal to each month's production requirements. Similarly, its policy regarding stocks of finished boards is to have a monthly opening stock equal to each month's total sales.

Monthly fixed costs, including depreciation of £600, total £6,200 and are paid for in the month incurred.

The opening bank balance for April is expected to be £11,400 positive. Chinkin's current overdraft limit is £25,000.

Task:

Create Chinkin's monthly cash budget for the four-month period April to July and for the four-month period as a whole (work to the nearest £). Advise the corporation accordingly.

Q14.6 T Ltd

T Ltd is a newly formed company that designs customized computer programs for its clients. The capital needed to fund the company will be provided by a venture capitalist who will invest £150,000 on 1 January 2002 in exchange for shares in T Ltd.

The directors are currently gathering the information needed to help in the preparation of the cash budget for the first three months of 2002. The information that they have is given below.

Budget details

The budgeted sales (that is, the value of the contracts signed) for the first quarter of 2002 are expected to be £200,000. However, as the company will only just have commenced trading, it is thought that sales will need time to grow. It is therefore expected that 15% of the first quarter's sales will be achieved in January, 30% in February and the remainder in March. It is expected that sales for the year ending 31 December 2002 will reach £1,000,000.

Clients must pay a deposit of 5% of the value of the computer program when they sign the contract for the program to be designed. Payments of 45% and 50% of the value are then paid one and two months later respectively. No bad debts are anticipated in the first quarter.

There are six people employed by the company, each earning an annual gross salary of £45,000, payable in arrears on the last day of each month.

Computer hardware and software will be purchased for £100,000 in January. A deposit of 25% is payable on placing the order for the computer hardware and software, with the remaining balance being paid in equal amounts in February and March. The capital outlay will be depreciated on a straight-line basis over three years, assuming no residual value.

The company has decided to rent offices that will require an initial deposit of £13,000 and an ongoing cost of £6,500 per month payable in advance. These offices are fully serviced and the rent is inclusive of all fixed overhead costs.

Variable production costs are paid in the month in which they are incurred and are budgeted as follows:

January   £1,200   February   £4,200   March   £8,000

A marketing and advertising campaign will be launched in January at a cost of £10,000 with a further campaign in March for £5,000, both amounts being payable as they are incurred.

Administration overhead is budgeted to be £500 each month: 60% to be paid in the month of usage and the balance one month later.

Tax and interest charges can be ignored.

Required:

(a) Prepare the cash budget by month and in total for the first quarter of 2002.

(15 marks)

(b) Identify and comment on those areas of the cash budget that you wish to draw to the attention of the Directors of T Ltd, and recommend action to improve cash flow.

(7 marks)

(c) Briefly explain three advantages for T Ltd of using a spreadsheet when preparing a cash budget.

(3 marks)

(Total = 25 marks)

CIMA Foundation: Management Accounting Fundamentals, November 2001

Q14.7 ST plc

ST plc produces three types of processed foods for a leading food retailer. The company has three processing departments (Preparation, Cooking and Packaging). After recognizing that the overheads incurred in these departments varied in relation to the activities performed, the company switched from a traditional absorption costing system to a budgetary control system that is based on activity based costing.

The *foods* are processed in batches. The budgeted output for April was as follows:

	Output
Food A	100 batches
Food B	30 batches
Food C	200 batches

The number of activities and processing hours budgeted to process a batch of foods in each of the departments are as follows:

	Food A **Activities per batch**	**Food B** **Activities per batch**	**Food C** **Activities per batch**
Preparation	5	9	12
Cooking	2	1	4
Packaging	15	2	6
Processing time	10 hours	375 hours	80 hours

The budgeted departmental overhead costs for April were:

	Overheads **$**
Preparation	100,000
Cooking	350,000
Packaging	50,000

Required:

(a) For food A ONLY, calculate the budgeted overhead cost per batch:
   (i) using traditional absorption costing, based on a factory-wide absorption rate per processing hour; and
   (ii) using activity based costing.

(6 marks)

(b) Comment briefly on the advantages of using an activity based costing approach to determining the cost of each type of processed food compared with traditional absorption costing approaches. You should make reference to your answers to requirement (a) where appropriate.

(4 marks)

(c) The actual output for April was:

	Output
Food A	120 batches
Food B	45 batches
Food C	167 batches

Required:

Prepare a flexed budget for April using an activity based costing approach. Your statement must show the total budgeted overhead for each department and the total budgeted overhead absorbed by each food.

(10 marks)

(d) Discuss the advantages that ST plc should see from the activity based control system compared with the traditional absorption costing that it used previously.

(5 marks)

(Total 25 marks)

CIMA Intermediate: Management Accounting – Performance Management, May 2004

Review questions

1 Explain what a budget is.
2 Explain how budgets fit into the corporate planning context.
3 List the positive attributes of budgetary control systems.
4 Differentiate between fixed and flexible budgets.
5 Differentiate between incremental and zero-based budgeting.
6 Define standard cost.
7 Discuss the issues about the setting of standards.
8 Discuss the limitations of budgets.

The answers to all these questions can be found in the text of this chapter.

Using budgets to control operations

Introduction

Having learned how to create a budget, you will have some idea of the complexity of this task. The budget in the case study at the end of the previous chapter comprised 13 schedules; a real organization will probably have many more. Creating a budget uses a great deal of time, effort and money. So it is understandable for the people involved to heave a sigh of relief when the completed budget is accepted by top management. It must be tempting to file it away and get on with some other work. But if the budget is now forgotten about, all the resources that went into it will have been completely wasted!

The creation of the budget means that the plan is now ready to be put into action. This chapter is all about how budgets are **used** to control the activities of organizations, to take them towards their chosen destination.

<table>
<tr><td>Learning
objectives</td><td>

Having worked through this chapter you should be able to:

- explain the basic theory of budgetary control systems;
- state the common formulae for cost variances and sub-variances;
- flex the budget to the actual level of production;
- calculate cost variances and their sub-variances;
- produce a profit reconciliation statement;
- illustrate the relationships between variances;
- discuss the additional benefits of budgetary control systems;
- manage the operating cost of budgetary control systems;
- comment on the problems of 'responsibility accounting';
- discuss the limitations of budgetary control systems;
- list 10 points for good budgetary control.
</td></tr>
</table>

The budgetary control system

The basic principle of budgetary control systems is very simple and is best thought of as a cyclical four-step process (see Figure 15.1).

Although the budget is an annual statement, it is usually divided into 12 monthly periods. This is because, if something starts to go wrong, an attempt to put it right needs to be made as soon as possible to minimize the negative effect. For example, if an underground water pipe cracked in month 2, causing the cost of the metered water supply

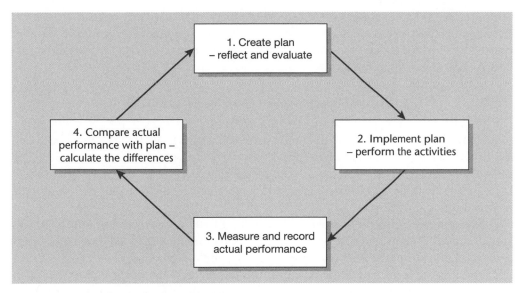

Figure 15.1 The budgetary control loop

unexpectedly to treble, a comparison of the actual and planned cost at the end of that month would reveal this and corrective action could be taken quickly. If the comparison was not made until the end of the year, the unnecessary extra cost would be much greater. The comparisons need to be made frequently if effective control is to be exercised.

Variances

Variances are the increases or decreases in profit which occur when things do not go according to plan. Variances are the differences referred to in step 4 of the budgetary control process (see Figure 15.1).

$$\text{Profit} = \text{sales revenue} - \text{total costs}$$

If sales revenue changes, then the profit will change. If total costs change, then profit will change.

A *variance* is a change in *profit* caused by changes in either sales revenue or costs from their budgeted levels.

Variance formulae and raw material variances

For every item of cost, e.g. raw material, the cost variance is calculated by the following formula:

$$\text{Cost variance} = \text{budgeted cost} - \text{actual cost}$$

Suppose the budget showed that 80 kg of material was to be used at a price of £15 per kg: the budgeted cost would be £1,200 (80 × 15). If the actual production record showed that only 65 kg of material had been used and that each kilogram cost only £10, then the actual cost is £650 (65 × 10).

$$\text{Cost variance} = 1{,}200 - 650 = +£550 = £550 \text{ F}$$

Note that the answer to this calculation is positive; it is **plus** £550. If the formula had been the other way round, it would have given a negative answer (650 − 1,200 = −550). The formulae are carefully designed so that a positive answer means that the variance will increase profit. This is described as a *favourable* variance and the plus sign is usually replaced by a capital 'F'.

In the above example, it was planned to spend £1,200 on material but only £650 was actually spent. This means that actual profit is £550 more than planned. On the assumption that the more profit the better, this result is 'good' or 'favourable'.

If the answer turns out to be negative, this means that the profit will be less than expected. This type of variance is 'bad' or '*adverse*' and the minus sign is usually replaced by a capital 'A'. (Sometimes 'U' for 'unfavourable' is used.)

Sub-variances

It is worth saying at this point that the words 'cost' and 'price' are often used to mean the same thing in colloquial English. However, in variance analysis these words are used in a precise sense to mean two different things. To avoid confusion in the calculation of variances it is a good idea to understand this clearly from the start.

'Price' refers to one item only. 'Cost' refers to the total expenditure for several items. For example, if 10 kilos of flour are bought at a *price* of £2 a kilo, the *cost* of the purchase is £20.

$$\text{Cost} = \text{price} \times \text{quantity}$$

Having got this distinction clear, the cost variance can now be analysed into its two component variances:

$$\text{Cost variance} = \text{price variance} + \text{quantity variance}$$

This enables us to find out how much of the profit change is due to a change in purchase **price** and how much is due to a change in the **quantity** used. This information may enable us to take corrective action to improve the profit or it may identify areas for further investigation.

Price variance

$$\text{Price variance} = (\text{budgeted price} - \text{actual price}) \times \text{actual quantity}$$
$$= (\text{BP} - \text{AP}) \times \text{AQ}$$

In the above example,

$$\text{Price variance} = (15 - 0) \times 65 = +325 = 325 \text{ F}$$

It is conventional always to calculate price variances at actual quantities used. This gives the difference in cost **due to price changes only.** (It is not distorted by any change in quantities used.)

Quantity variance

$$\text{Quantity variance} = (\text{budgeted quantity} - \text{actual quantity}) \times \text{budgeted price}$$
$$= (\text{BQ} - \text{AQ}) \times \text{BP}$$

In the above example,

$$\text{Quantity variance} = (80 - 65) \times 15 = +225 = 225 \text{ F}$$

It is conventional always to calculate quantity variances at budgeted prices. This gives the difference in cost **due to changes in quantity only.** (It is not distorted by any change in price.)

Reconciliation of variances

	Price variance	325 F
Add:	Quantity variance	225 F
	Cost variance	550 F

These relationships are illustrated by Figure 15.2.

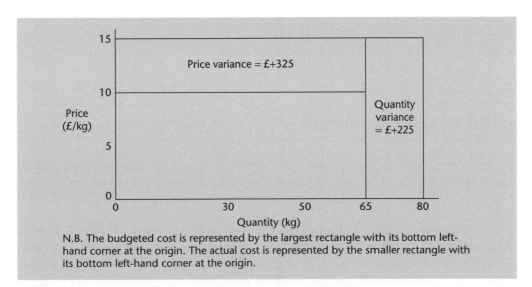

N.B. The budgeted cost is represented by the largest rectangle with its bottom left-hand corner at the origin. The actual cost is represented by the smaller rectangle with its bottom left-hand corner at the origin.

Figure 15.2 Cost variance analysed into price and quantity elements

Terminology

There are two other types of variable cost: direct labour and variable overheads. They can also be analysed into their constituent price and quantity variances. However, these sub-variances are known by different names, as follows:

	Price variance (BP – AP)AQ	Quantity variance (BQ – AQ)BP
Raw materials	Price variance	Usage variance
Direct labour	Rate variance	Efficiency variance
Variable overheads	Expenditure variance	Efficiency variance

Observe that the same basic formulae are used for each of these cost types. It is possible to calculate all six variances named above if you can remember the two formulae shown at the top of the columns.

Note that, in this context, the word 'standard' can be used instead of 'budget'.
So,

$$\text{Standard price} = \text{budgeted price}$$

and

$$\text{Standard quantity} = \text{budgeted quantity}$$

Self-assessment question S15.1

Try the following question for yourself (answer at the end of the chapter).

Roach Ltd planned to use 100 kg of material at £5 per kg for last week's output. Although its production output was exactly as planned, it used 110 kg of material and paid only £4 per kg for it. Calculate the material cost, price and usage variances.

Direct labour variances

The price of labour is the rate at which it is paid, e.g. £9 per hour. The quantity of labour (the number of hours) needed to do a particular job is a measure of the efficiency of the workforce. This is why the sub-variances are known as the *rate variance* and the *efficiency variance*.

Here is an example. SUB Ltd estimates that one particular order will need 30 hours of grade A labour, which is paid at the rate of £10 per hour. After the order has been completed, the records show that only 28 hours were taken, but these were paid at £11 per hour due to a new incentive bonus. What are the direct labour rate, efficiency and cost variances?

$$
\begin{aligned}
\text{Rate variance} &= (\text{BP} - \text{AP}) \times \text{AQ} \\
&= (\text{budgeted} - \text{actual rate}) \times \text{actual hours} \\
&= (10 - 11) \times 28 \\
&= -28 \\
&= 28 \text{ A}
\end{aligned}
$$

$$
\begin{aligned}
\text{Efficiency variance} &= (\text{BQ} - \text{AQ}) \times \text{BP} \\
&= (\text{budgeted hours} - \text{actual hours}) \times \text{budgeted rate} \\
&= (30 - 28) \times 10 \\
&= +20 \\
&= 20 \text{ F}
\end{aligned}
$$

$$
\begin{aligned}
\text{Cost variance} &= \text{budgeted cost} - \text{actual cost} \\
&= (30 \times 10) - (28 \times 11) \\
&= 300 - 308 \\
&= -8 \\
&= 8 \text{ A}
\end{aligned}
$$

Self-assessment question S15.2

Try the following question for yourself (answer at the end of the chapter).

Roach Ltd has a small finishing department employing two people. The budget showed they were expected to work for a total of 4,000 hours during the year just ended. The standard rate of pay used was £6.50 per hour. The payroll shows they actually worked a total of 4,100 hours and were paid a total of £26,650 to produce the budgeted output. Calculate the direct labour cost, rate and efficiency variances.

Idle time variance

Consider the following situation:

$$
\begin{aligned}
\text{Budget} &= 100 \text{ direct labour hours @ £5/h} = £500 \text{ cost} \\
\text{Actual} &= 108 \text{ direct labour hours @ £4/h} = £432 \text{ cost}
\end{aligned}
$$

Variance calculations:

$$
\begin{aligned}
\text{Labour rate} &= 108(5 - 4) &&= 108 \text{ F} \\
\text{Labour efficiency} &= 5(100 - 108) &&= (40) \text{ A} \\
\text{Labour cost variance} &= 500 - 432 &&= \underline{68} \text{ F}
\end{aligned}
$$

Note that the £40 labour efficiency variance is shown in brackets as well as being followed by the capital 'A'. These brackets signify that this is a negative number.

The analysis shows that the workforce were paid less than planned for each hour worked but that the number of hours needed to complete the work was eight more than planned. It indicates that the operatives were inefficient.

But what if the 108 hours included 10 hours that were paid normally but during which no work could be done? Suppose there had been a power cut, preventing operators from using their machines? This 10 hours of idle time means that only 98 hours were actually worked although 108 hours were paid. To get a better analysis of the situation, the variance caused by the idle time needs to be isolated and shown separately.

Amended variance calculations:

Labour rate	$= 108(5 - 4)$	$= 108$ F
Labour efficiency	$= 5(100 - 98) =$	10 F
Idle time	$= 5(98 - 108) =$	$\underline{(50)}$ A
Total labour variance		$\underline{68}$ F

This more detailed analysis shows that, far from being inefficient, the workforce were efficient. They took only 98 hours to complete work estimated to need 100 hours.

Idle time occurs only occasionally, but when it does it is important for its effects to be separated from the other variances. Otherwise the operatives may be unnecessarily demotivated by being identified as inefficient when they are actually efficient. When idle time occurs, the variance formulae are modified as follows:

Labour efficiency variance = (budgeted hours − actual hours worked) × budgeted rate
Idle time variance   = idle hours × budgeted rate

Note that the idle time variance is always adverse and that the labour rate variance does not change.

Self-assessment question S15.3

Try the following question for yourself (answer at the end of the chapter).

Roach Ltd has a direct labour budget for June's planned output of 2,000 hours at £10 per hour. Early in July it is found that the planned output for June was achieved but 2,100 hours were paid for at £11 per hour. However, no work could be done for 300 of the hours paid due to a failure in the just-in-time stock control system. Calculate the appropriate variances.

Variable overhead variances

Variable overheads are expenses indirectly associated with production activity. Two examples are lubricants for, and maintenance of, the production machinery. The more the machinery is used, the more these items cost. They increase or decrease as activity increases or decreases.

In Chapter 9, we saw that some mechanism is needed to include a 'fair' proportion of these indirect expenses in the product cost. One method often used is to spread these expenses out among products in the same proportion as they use direct labour hours.

So, if each product A takes 8 dlh and each product B takes 4 dlh to complete, this means that not only will A have twice the labour cost of B, it will also have twice the variable overhead cost.

Using the example given above of SUB Limited, its variable overhead absorption rate is £3.00 per direct labour hour (dlh). This means that, for the particular order involved, it planned to spend £90 (30 dlh × £3.00/dlh) on variable overheads. The order was actually completed in 28 dlh and the actual cost of the variable overheads was £79.80. Calculate the variable overhead cost, expenditure and efficiency variances.

$$
\begin{aligned}
\text{Cost variance} &= \text{budgeted cost} - \text{actual cost} \\
&= 90.00 - 79.80 \\
&= +10.20 \\
&= 10.20 \text{ F}
\end{aligned}
$$

$$
\begin{aligned}
\text{Expenditure variance} &= (\text{budgeted absorption rate} - \text{actual absorption rate}) \times \text{actual dlh} \\
&= (\text{budgeted abs. rate} \times \text{actual dlh}) - (\text{actual abs. rate} \times \text{actual dlh}) \\
&= (£3.00 \times 28) - (£79.80) \\
&= 84.00 - 79.80 \\
&= +4.20 \\
&= 4.20 \text{ F}
\end{aligned}
$$

$$
\begin{aligned}
\text{Efficiency variance} &= (\text{BQ} - \text{AQ}) \times \text{BP} \\
&= (\text{budgeted dlh} - \text{actual dlh}) \times \text{budgeted absorption rate} \\
&= (30 - 28) \times 3.00 \\
&= +6.00 \\
&= 6.00 \text{ F}
\end{aligned}
$$

Note that the combination of the expenditure and efficiency variances should give the cost variance.

Try the following question for yourself (answer at the end of the chapter).

Self-assessment question S15.4

Building on the example of Roach Ltd in S15.1–3 above, it was planned to spend £4,400 on variable overheads, giving a budgeted absorption rate of £1.10/dlh. At the end of the year it was found that the actual amount spent on variable overheads was £4,592. Calculate the variable overhead cost, expenditure and efficiency variances.

Fixed overhead variances

Fixed overheads are those indirect expenses which do **not** vary with output. This section on fixed overhead variances is covered in two parts:

(i) in a variable costing system; and
(ii) in an absorption costing system.

Variable costing treats fixed costs as period costs but absorption costing treats them as product costs. The earlier chapter of this book entitled 'Comparison of profits under absorption and variable costing' discusses the differences between the two systems in detail.

Variable costing systems

As fixed production overheads are **not** included in the product cost, the volume of goods produced has no effect. The only variable to measure is the amount of money actually spent on the fixed overheads. Therefore, a single cost variance (called 'expenditure') is calculated as follows:

$$\text{Fixed overhead expenditure variance} = \text{budgeted fixed overhead} - \text{actual fixed overhead}$$

For example, Budgeted fixed overhead   = £300,000
Less: Actual fixed overhead   = £321,000
           Fixed overhead expenditure variance = £(21,000) A

Self-assessment question S15.5	Try the following question for yourself (answer at the end of the chapter).

Roach Ltd expects its total annual expenditure on fixed overheads to be £180,000 and decides to spread this evenly over its 12 accounting periods. If the amount actually spent on fixed overheads in month 8 is £16,100, what is the fixed overhead expenditure variance for that month?

Absorption costing systems

For the 'production' activity, all absorption costing systems use predetermined fixed overhead absorption rates (FOARs). For example, the budget for next year may show total fixed production overheads to be £5,500,000 and the total of direct labour hours to be 11,000. This gives a predicted FOAR of £500 per direct labour hour. This is the rate at which fixed production overheads will be attached to next year's actual activity.

These FOARs depend on two factors:

1 The total amount of expenditure on fixed overheads.
2 The total quantity of the chosen activity base (e.g. direct labour hours).

It is extremely unlikely that the predetermined rate will equal the actual rate. For that to happen, both of the factors shown above would have to be predicted with 100% accuracy. The difference between actual and budgeted expenditure causes the **fixed overhead expenditure variance**. The difference between actual and budgeted volume of activity (e.g. direct labour hours) causes the **fixed overhead volume variance**. *For the period, the total variance of fixed production overhead cost equals the total of fixed production overhead under- or over absorbed.*

Because the FOAR is based on the original budget, the fixed overhead variance formulae use some figures from the original budget as well as the flexed budget. However, the total fixed overhead cost variance follows the same pattern as the material, labour and variable overhead cost variances:

Fixed overhead (FO) total cost variance = flexed budget (FB) cost − actual cost

This can be analysed as follows:

$$FB \text{ cost} - \text{act. cost} = (FB \text{ cost} - OB \text{ cost}) + (OB \text{ cost} - \text{act. cost})$$
$$\text{TOTAL} = \text{VOLUME} + \text{EXPENDITURE}$$

Also, the volume variance can be further analysed as follows:

$$(FB \text{ cost} - OB \text{ cost}) = (FB \text{ hrs} - OB \text{ hrs})FOAR$$
$$= (FB \text{ hrs} - \text{act. hrs})FOAR + (\text{act. hrs} - OB \text{ hrs})FOAR$$
$$\text{VOLUME} = \text{EFFICIENCY} + \text{CAPACITY}$$

The efficiency variance is concerned with 'output per hour' or the *rate* of producing. The capacity variance is concerned with 'total hours used'. (Note that the idea of 'capacity', in the sense of the **total volume** that the production facilities are capable of producing, is inappropriate and misleading.)

For example, if the operatives are working below the planned rate (i.e. the efficiency variance is adverse), the actual number of hours worked would have to be greater than planned *in order to achieve the planned total output*. In this case the efficiency variance would be *adverse* but the capacity variance would be *favourable*. In other situations the efficiency variance could be favourable and the capacity variance could be adverse or they could both be favourable or both adverse.

Figure 15.3 illustrates the relationships between the fine variances discussed immediately above.

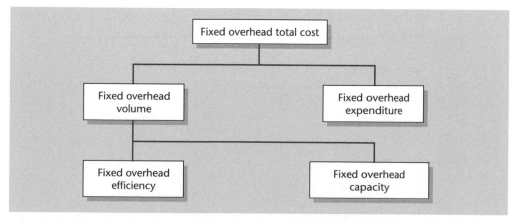

Figure 15.3 Fixed production overhead variance relationships under absorption costing

Comparison of systems

Note that the volume variance only occurs where a standard absorption costing system is used. Where a business adopts a standard variable costing system, no volume variance arises because fixed production overheads are treated as period costs and are debited directly to the profit and loss account. So, for variable costing systems, the 'fixed overhead total cost variance' will always equal the 'fixed overhead expenditure variance'.

Under standard absorption costing systems, fixed overheads are treated as a product cost and are attached to products. For unsold products, they are included in the *inventory valuation* on the balance sheet; for products sold in the period, they are included in *cost of sales* on the profit and loss account.

To summarise:

	FO expenditure variance	FO volume variance
Variable costing system	Yes	No
Absorption costing system	Yes	Yes

Example 15.1

FO variance calculations in standard absorption costing

Scaatefour Plc makes only one product, the Skylon, and never has any work-in-progress at the end of a production period. It operates a standard absorption costing system which uses direct labour hours as a base for its fixed overhead absorption rate (FOAR). The management accountant had calculated all the other variances before she was unexpectedly admitted to hospital as an emergency case. In order that the monthly variance analysis report can be completed, you are required to use the following data for month 11 to calculate the five fixed overhead variances.

The budgeted output for this month was 12,000 Skylons, each one budgeted to use 10 direct labour hours in production. The predetermined FOAR was calculated at £6.70 per direct labour hour. The actual production data are

Units produced	11,200
Number of direct labour hours worked	110,000
Expenditure on fixed overheads	£824,000

Solution

i) FO total cost variance

$$= \text{flexed budget cost} - \text{actual cost}$$
$$= (11,200 \times 10 \times 6.70) - 824,000$$
$$= 750,400 - 824,000$$
$$= £73,600 \text{ A}$$

Sub-analysis of FO total cost variance using labour hours

ii) FO expenditure variance

$$= \text{OB cost} - \text{act. cost}$$
$$= (12,000 \text{ units} \times £67 \text{ per unit}) - 824,000$$
$$= 804,000 - 824,000$$
$$= £20,000 \text{ A}$$

iii) FO volume variance

$$= \text{FB cost} - \text{OB cost}$$
$$= (11,200 \text{ units} \times £67 \text{ per unit}) - (12,000 \text{ units} \times £67 \text{ per unit})$$
$$= (11,200 - 12,000)67$$
$$= (-800)67$$
$$= £53,600 \text{ A}$$

Sub-analysis of FO volume variance using labour hours

iv) FO capacity variance

$$= (\text{act. hrs} - \text{OB hrs})\text{FOAR}$$
$$= (110,000 - 120,000)6.70$$
$$= (-10,000)6.70$$
$$= £67,000 \text{ A}$$

v) FO efficiency variance

$$= (\text{FB hrs} - \text{act. hrs})\text{FOAR}$$
$$= (112,000 - 110,000)6.70$$
$$= (2,000)6.70$$
$$= £13,400 \text{ F}$$

Try the following question for yourself (answer at the end of the chapter).

Self-assessment question S15.6

Blackpack Limited makes only one product, the darkbox, and never has any work-in-progress at the end of a production period. It operates a standard absorption costing system which uses direct labour hours as a base for its fixed overhead absorption rate. Use the following data for month 5 to calculate the five fixed overhead variances.

The budgeted output for this month was 24,000 darkboxes, each one budgeted to use 5 direct labour hours in production. The predetermined fixed overhead absorption rate was calculated at £15 per direct labour hour. The actual production data is as follows:

Units produced	20,000
Number of direct labour hours worked	132,000
Expenditure on fixed overheads	£765,000

Appendix: the algebraic basis for the FO variances in standard absorption costing

There is no need or requirement for students to know or understand the algebra presented below but many students of accountancy have good mathematical skills and will not find it difficult to grasp. However, an understanding of the underlying algebra may help students to derive the correct formulae when needed, during an examination for example.

Let

$$S = \text{flexed budget cost}$$
$$T = \text{actual cost}$$
$$N = \text{original budget cost}$$
$$P = \text{predetermined FOAR}$$
$$J = \text{flexed budget hours}$$
$$R = \text{actual hours}$$
$$K = \text{original budget hours}$$

Then the following formulae can be derived:

FO total cost variance

$$S - T = S - N + N - T$$
$$= (S - N) + (N - T)$$

FO volume variance
   If $S = JP$ and $N = KP$, then

$$S - N = JP - KP$$
$$= JP - RP + RP - KP$$
$$= (J - R)P + (R - K)P$$

FO expenditure variance

$$= N - T$$

FO efficiency variance

$$= (J - R)P$$

FO capacity variance

$$= (R - K)P$$

The importance of the flexed budget

Suppose you were the manager responsible for a large production facility. For the year just ended, your budget for raw material costs was £9 million but your actual expenditure was only £8 million. Do you deserve a bonus?

It appears you have made a saving of £1 million, but this may not be so. There is not enough information to provide a clear answer. The £9 million budget was to achieve a certain level of production. If that level was achieved, then a bonus is probably deserved. But what if the production output was only half of what was planned? This means that only £4.5 million **should** have been spent on materials, not the £8 million actually spent! In this case, a bonus seems rather inappropriate.

To get meaningful answers when calculating the variances for the variable costs (materials, labour and variable overheads) the actual amounts must be compared with a budget which has been revised to the actual level of output. This revised budget is called the *flexed budget*; it is created **after** the actual figures are known. The effect of using the flexed budget instead of the original budget is that the variances will now show the differences between the actual costs and what those costs **should have been** for the output actually achieved. This is useful information. Variable cost variances based on the original budget will almost certainly be misleading.

	Example 15.2

Illustration with raw materials (manufacturing wheels from raw plastic)

Original budget: 10,000 wheels using 5 kg of plastic each @ £2.00/kg
                       Cost = 10,000 × 5 × 2 = £100,000
Actual expenditure: Total cost of plastic used in period was £74,880.
                          Thus, saving on budget £25,120

Is the production manager to be congratulated on this favourable variance?

Yes, congratulations are in order if 10,000 wheels were actually produced.

But what if only 6,000 wheels were actually produced (each using 5.2 kg @ £2.40/kg = £74,880 cost)?

Flex the budget to the actual level of activity:

Flexed budget: 6,000 wheels using 5 kg plastic @ £2.00 = £60,000 cost
Material price variance = (2.0 − 2.4) × 31,200 = (12,480) A
Material usage variance = (30,000 − 31,200) × 2 = (2,400) A
Actual cost of materials = £74,880

Congratulations are not appropriate in this case.

As you can see from this example, flexed budgets use the same standard amounts as the original budget (1 wheel uses 5 kg of plastic costing £2/kg). The only thing that changes is the level of output or production volume. More often than not, the actual output differs from that planned. **When calculating variances, the first step is to create the flexed budget.**

This does not mean to say that the difference between the original and flexed budget is ignored. This difference is accounted for elsewhere by the sales volume variance (see below).

Try the following question for yourself (answer at the end of the chapter).

During week 32, Maykit Ltd planned to produce 50 plastic boxes using two hours of direct labour for each box, paid at the standard rate of £10 per hour, giving a budgeted cost of £1,000. At the end of that week, it was found that 55 boxes had been produced, using 105 hours of labour paid at £10 per hour and costing £1,050. As there is no labour rate variance and the labour cost for the week was £50 greater than planned, is it accurate to say that the labour force must be working inefficiently?

Sales variances

As sales are concerned with income rather than cost, the sales price variance will differ from cost variances in the following way. If the actual sales price achieved is greater than the budgeted price then the profit will increase, giving a **favourable** variance. So the prices inside the brackets will be the opposite way round (**actual** – **budget**).

Sales price variance

Sales price variance = (actual price – budget price) × actual quantity
For example, Sales budget = 20,000 items @ £10; actual = 20,000 items @ £11
Sales price variance = (11 – 10) × 20,000 = 20,000 F

Sales volume variance

Sales volume variance = flexed budget profit – original budget profit

This is consistent, with the only difference between the original and flexed budgets being the level of activity. The number of items produced is assumed to be the same as the number of items sold and the situation one of making to order and not for stock.

Try the following question for yourself (answer at the end of the chapter).

The following data refers to Pike Ltd for the month of May. The original budget showed 400 items sold at £25 each, resulting in a profit of £2,000. The actual performance was 300 items sold at £26 each, resulting in a profit of £1,663. When the budget was flexed, it gave a revised profit of £1,650. Calculate the sales price variance and the sales volume variance.

The profit reconciliation statement

When the variance analysis exercise is complete, the original budget should be reconciled to the actual results to summarize the findings of the investigation. As the flexed budget is an important part of the analysis, it should be included in the reconciliation. An example of a profit reconciliation statement is shown below.

Pike Ltd: profit reconciliation statement

			£	£
Original budget profit				**2,000**
Sales volume variance				(350) A
Flexed budget profit				**1,650**
Sales price variance				300 F
Material variances:	Usage	(140) A		
	Price	20 F		
	Cost		(120) A	
Labour variances:	Efficiency	75 F		
	Rate	(25) A		
	Cost		50 F	
Variable overhead variance:	Efficiency	56 F		
	Expenditure	(24) A		
	Cost		32 F	
Fixed overhead expenditure variance			(249) A	
Actual profit			**1,663**	

Note that the adverse variances are shown in brackets. This is not compulsory but it may help students to arrive at the correct answers, especially during exams. The capital 'A' or 'F' is compulsory.

Try the following question for yourself (answer at the end of the chapter).

Self-assessment question S15.9

From the following information (all figures in £000) produce a profit reconciliation statement. Fixed overheads cost 24 less than expected; variable overhead expenditure variance = 5 F and variable overhead efficiency variance = 1 A; labour variances are rate = 14 F and efficiency = 2 A; sales price variance = 18 A; material variances are usage = 39 F and price = 27 A; original budget profit = 400 and flexed budget profit = 431; there is also an idle time variance of 12.

Variance relationships

Figures 15.4 and 15.5 illustrate the interrelationships of variances.

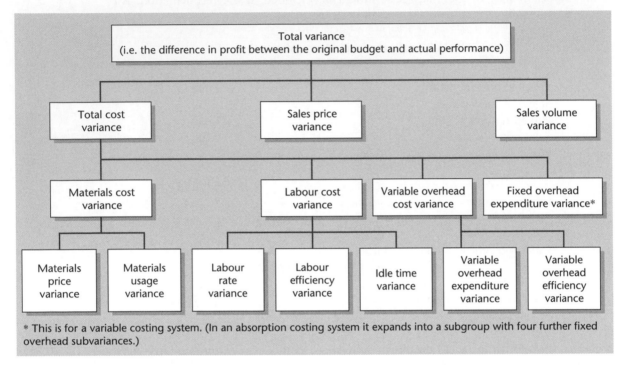

Figure 15.4 Variance family tree

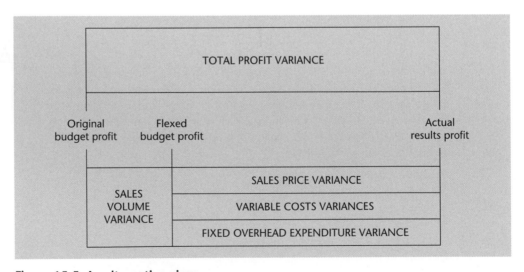

Figure 15.5 An alternative view

Additional benefits of the budgetary control system

As well as appropriately recording and evaluating performance, budgetary control systems have the following positive effects:

1 They communicate organizational aspirations. The annual organizational plan is distributed to budget holders who are then aware of what is expected of them.
2 They co-ordinate complex activities. For example, if there is no opening stock of finished goods and the company plans to sell 200,000 items next year, it must budget to produce at least 200,000 items.
3 They authorize budget holders. For example, if the purchasing budget shows that £1 million of materials are to be bought every month, the purchasing manager does not have to seek permission to spend this amount. The purchasing budget itself authorizes this spending.
4 They motivate budget holders. Budgets can also be used as targets. The performance levels (known as *standards*) in a budget are often set high but attainable in order to encourage improvement.

Managing the cost of the system

The process of variance investigation is time consuming and has a cost of its own. Organizations need to control this activity. The usual approach is that of 'management by exception'. If operations are going more or less as planned and the variances are small, no follow-up activity takes place. However, where the variances are significant, they are investigated. But how do you know if a variance is significant or not?

This decision is inherently subjective and may vary from business to business. Someone has to decide **in advance** what the significance levels of their organization are going to be. A percentage difference between budget and actual is determined in advance, subject to a minimum amount. For example, a given company may investigate all variances that are at least 5% different from budget provided they are at least £250 in amount. This approach is both relative and absolute. But another company may have a policy of 10% difference with a threshold of £10,000.

Responsibility accounting

Budgetary control works through people. Functional budgets are delegated to the lowest practical level, where an appropriate person is made the 'budget responsible manager'. For this to work effectively, the lines of authority must be clearly defined. This can be a problem, especially in those organizations operating a matrix approach to their management structure. Where two people are responsible for an item of income or cost, there is always room for dispute as to who should take the credit or accept the blame.

Responsibility accounting usually supports the payment of rewards, such as cash bonuses, to budget-responsible officers for meeting their targets. The theory is that the company will benefit from their increased motivation and a 'win–win' situation will occur. For this to happen, the accounting mechanisms must be structured in the same way as the responsibilities. For example, if the regional sales managers are responsible for the value of sales in their areas, the budgets and reporting mechanisms must be analysed over these areas. A single set of aggregated figures for the whole country would not allow the individual responsibilities to be defined or monitored.

This allows companies to achieve their goals through 'management by objective' (MBO) as well as 'management by exception' (MBE). A good example of the latter is the investigation of variances only when they are significant. If actual performance is not very different from budget, things are considered to be going to plan, i.e. no exceptions have occurred.

Another aspect of responsibility accounting is that of **uncontrollable** costs. Not all costs are completely within the control of management. For example, the business rates for the factory may be one item on the production manager's budget. If the cost of these rates is completely outside that person's control, he or she is likely to be demotivated when held responsible for an adverse variance. To avoid this, either the situation should be made very clear in the variance analysis reports or the uncontrollable items should be extracted and isolated in a budget of their own. Unfortunately, problems still arise from some costs that are **partially** controllable. For instance, the cost of running the computerized management information system may be partly based on the manager's ability to retain experienced staff (temporary IT staff are expensive). But it is also based on the rates of pay in the marketplace. The manager may be responsible for the first but not for the second. In this case, it would be up to that manager to justify any adverse variances arising, if he or she can.

Limitations of the budgetary control process

For many, many years, most organizations have operated a budgetary control system. This management accounting technique has been enormously successful. Yet, during the last few years there have been signs of firms moving away from traditional budgeting. IKEA (furniture), Asea Brown Boveri (engineering), Svenska Handelbanken (banking) and Borealis (petrochemicals), all huge multinational organizations based in Europe, are examples of this trend. They believe that there is more to measuring and controlling business performance than can be expressed by a traditional budget. The main influence on their thinking is the accelerating rate of change in the business environment. Many organizations are finding that their environment is not only constantly changing but changing faster and faster as time moves on.

Budgets tend to reinforce the 'old' way of doing things. Budget managers have many other responsibilities pressing on them when the budget creation deadline is imminent. To reflect changing circumstances, changes may need to be made concerning which data is shown. Consequently, the layout of the form would need to be changed, but this would have to be approved at a high level, which would take considerable time and effort. The normal 'efficient' approach to this situation is to use the same form as last year, meet the deadline and get on with the next task. Over the years, the budget format becomes more and more divorced from reality and less effective in improving performance.

Having said this, budgets are still very effective and necessary instruments of control for the vast majority of organizations. If budgets were removed without something better being put in their place, the organization would almost certainly start to deteriorate.

The manager's point of view (written by Nigel Burton)

As discussed in the previous chapter, the first major objective of budgeting is to complete a detailed review of the business, and set up a budget framework which ensures that the company is progressing down its designated strategic path. The second objective is to monitor performance against that budget, but with the minimum amount of time and effort.

The main advantage of a detailed budget is that it provides a sound basis for management by exception. Once the budget is agreed, all departmental managers know exactly what is expected of them, in terms of the level of sales to be achieved, or the amount of cost they can incur. Subject to the normal safeguards, they are authorized to spend the amount budgeted in furtherance of their departmental objectives. Moreover, the managing director knows that he or she has nothing to worry about, providing managers are performing within the budgeted parameters. The MD simply reviews the numbers for any significant variances, and then gets on with the job of running the business.

The key to effective management by exception is the IT system. Information must be presented in such a way as to minimize any further analysis work. My company, for instance, used a simple but effective system for monitoring sales. This showed orders due out this month, by volume, sales value and marginal income (contribution), set against the budget for the month. Initially, it summarized these items for the whole company, but there was a feature which allowed the user to 'drill down' through the layers of product group and product line, to individual customer/product level. It took a matter of moments, therefore, on arriving at the office each morning, for me to update myself in detail on the progress of this month's sales. I knew exactly which customers and which products had so far failed to meet expectations. I was so familiar with our performance at all times that the monthly management accounts served merely to confirm what I already knew. Not only did this allow me to spend my time more productively, but also it gave me a detailed knowledge of our current situation from which to answer the regular stream of questions from our head office in the USA.

We had a similar 'drill down' system with which to interrogate previous months' results. By the simple expedient of ranking sales on the basis of variance from budget, an analysis of the causes of shortfalls and overachievements was the work of a few minutes. By presenting the information in the right format, all the traditional, painstaking sales analysis work was completely eliminated. It should be borne in mind that users at different levels in the company, e.g. managing director, sales manager or sales executive, may need the information in a different format, so a cleverly designed system should address the needs of all.

Analysis of manufacturing variances is another case in point. As we have seen above, each production batch will generate at least six variances. In any given month, the factory will produce hundreds of batches, so an enormous amount of variance information is produced. Each batch's variances will tell a slightly different story. In chemicals manufacturing, no two batches are ever the same. The raw materials may have slight differences in specification, the chemical reactions might not work in precisely the same way, and even atmospheric temperatures and humidity might play their part. As a result, processes may need a further input of materials, or perhaps more reaction time or a longer cooling period. Each divergence from the standard generates manufacturing variances. How much time should be spent analysing it all? While a manufacturing process is at the development stage, the production staff will clearly wish to examine all the information in detail, looking for clues which will help them to improve the efficiency of the processing. Once the process has stabilized, however, the production staff will, for the most part, ignore small variations on batches, and look for regular trends which indicate that a process change is required. They will only look at individual batches where there is either a significant variance or a complete batch failure.

Standards may sometimes be set as targets, in order to encourage greater efficiency in the factory. This can be a two-edged sword. The standards are incorporated in the product costs, so, if they are drawn too tightly (showing low costs), there is a risk that the salespeople might be misled into thinking that they can reduce their selling prices. Production's failure to achieve the standards will emerge as adverse manufacturing variances on the profit and loss account, but will be seen as a local production problem, rather than an issue for the whole of the company. Conversely, if the standards are drawn too slackly (showing high costs), production will have a nice, comfortable time. However, the resultant higher costs might discourage salespeople from quoting more competitive prices and generating more business. In my view, standards should always be set at expected performance and not at 'target' levels. However, if there is still a requirement for a target, production can always be asked to produce at a specified level which will result in favourable variances. If they achieve this consistently, it can then be transferred into the product costs, and everyone is happy.

As in many areas of management accounting, the secret of success is to keep it simple but effective. When setting up new systems, there is a natural tendency to over-elaborate. One wants to feel that a thorough and professional job has been done, and perhaps too little thought is directed at the practical aspects of managing the system when it is up and running. I have already described some of the benefits and pitfalls of the activity-based costing system, which my US head office decided to install throughout the organization (see Chapter 10, on activity-based costing). One of the more complex aspects of this system was variance reporting. Normal standard costing principles were used, so the normal manufacturing variances described earlier in this chapter were generated. However, to make the product costs more accurate, and therefore of greater value to the salesforce, the standards were changed every three months. Actual performance was then monitored against the new standards, but, as the original standards were still the basis of the budget, we had another set of variances capturing the difference between the original and revised standards. Somehow, for every batch produced, the number of variances had grown to 16! The monthly variance printout was three-quarters of an inch thick. We were swamped with information and, as a result, gave less attention to this area than we might otherwise have done.

A similar example of overkill occurred with our performance-monitoring reporting. We had developed a simple graphical representation of eight key measurements which we felt reflected our overall performance as a company on a monthly basis. These included the percentage of batches achieving specification without rework, the percentage of orders dispatched on time, and the number of customer complaints received. By combining these eight measurements, we arrived at a single company performance indicator. It was crude, perhaps, but effective, as it helped to focus the minds of employees throughout the company on the need for high-quality performance. Our head office was quite taken with this concept, and decided to adopt it throughout the organization. However, head office increased the number of measurements to 30, some of which were rather dubious as performance monitors. Purchase price variance was one example. Does a favourable PPV reflect a good performance by the purchasing department? Not necessarily. If the market price was coming down, perhaps the variance should have been twice the size. Conversely, a 10% adverse variance could be a fine performance if the market price had actually gone up by 20%. So the selection of performance monitors should be done with a great deal of care. Nevertheless, we duly submitted our data (a time-consuming exercise in itself), and the worldwide results were published in a vast monthly tome. This contained so much information, much of it flawed or inconsistent, that no one ever bothered to look at it, and the motivational impact was completely lost.

A really good information system, whether it is performance monitoring or budgetary control, will tell the users exactly what they need to know, nothing more, nothing less. And it will do so with the minimal amount of input from the users. Experience will help in deciding the right level, although even experienced managers can fall into the trap of immersing themselves in excessive amounts of data. It is one of the features of this technological age that there is more information available than the human mind can reasonably assimilate, and one of the most important business skills is the ability to specify exactly the information you want and the format in which you want it. Another significant business skill is obtaining the necessary programming time in the IT department, but that is another story!

Summary

- The budgetary control process is a continuous closed-loop system.
- It consists of planning, recording, comparing, evaluating and acting.
- The differences between budget and actual are known as variances.
- Cost variances can be analysed into their constituent price and quantity variances.
- The budget should be flexed before the cost variances are calculated.
- Fixed overhead variances are different in absorption and variable costing systems.
- Sales volume variance is the difference in the original and flexed budget profits.
- Profit reconciliation statements give a complete summary of the variance analysis.
- Spin-offs include communication, co-ordination, authorization and motivation.
- System operating costs are controlled by a 'management by exception' approach.
- Budget holders can be demotivated if held responsible for non-controllable costs.
- Budgetary control systems do not measure the effect of missed opportunities.
- A few large successful organizations claim to have recently abandoned budgeting.
- The vast majority of organizations still operate budgetary control systems.

Ten points for good budgetary control

1 Areas of responsibility are clearly defined.
2 Budgets are held at the lowest practical management level.
3 Non-controllable items are clearly identified.
4 Reporting system is routine/automatic.
5 Reporting periods are short.
6 Reports are produced soon after the period end.
7 Variance significance levels are pre-established.
8 Significant variances are always investigated.
9 Corrective action is taken where possible.
10 Senior management exemplify the importance of the budgetary control system.

Further reading

Atkinson, A., Banker, R., Kaplan, R. and Young, S. (2001) *Management Accounting*, 3rd edition, Prentice Hall, Harlow. See Chapter 11, 'Using budgets to achieve organisational objectives'.

Budding, G. T. (2004) 'Accountability, environmental uncertainty and government performance: evidence from Dutch municipalities', *Management Accounting Research*, Vol. 15, Issue 3, September.

'FA kicks off new budget control system' (2004) *Computer Weekly*, 30 November.

Horngren, C., Bhimani, A., Datar, S. and Foster, G. (2002) *Management and Cost Accounting*, 2nd edition, Prentice Hall Europe, Harlow. See chapters on 'Flexible budgets, variances and management control 1 & 2'.

Merchant, K. A. (1998) *Modern Management Control Systems: Text and Cases*, Prentice Hall, Englewood Cliffs, NJ.

Otley, D. (1987) *Accounting Control and Organisational Behaviour*, Heinemann Professional Publishing, Oxford. See Chapters 5 and 9, 'Performance appraisal' and 'Accounting for effective control'. (Other chapters concentrate on the 'human' aspects of budgetary control.)

Player, S. (2003) 'Beyond the budget games', *Intelligent Enterprise*, Vol. 6, Issue 16, 10 October Supplement.

Shim, J. and Siegel, J. (2005) *Budgeting Basics and Beyond*, 2nd edition, Wiley, Hoboken, NJ.

Upchurch, A. (2003) *Management Accounting, Principles and Practice*, 2nd edition, Financial Times/Prentice Hall, Harlow. See chapters 'Budgetary control' and 'Analysis of variances'.

Weetman, P. (2002) *Management Accounting, an Introduction*, 3rd edition, Financial Times/Prentice Hall, Harlow. See chapters 'Standard costs' and 'Performance evaluation and feedback reporting'.

Answers to self-assessment questions

S15.1

$$\text{Budget: 100 kg @ £5/kg = £500 cost}$$
$$\text{Actual: 110 kg @ £4/kg = £440 cost}$$

$$\text{Price variance} = (BP - AP) \times AQ$$
$$= (5 - 4) \times 110 = 110 \text{ F}$$

$$\text{Usage variance} = (BQ - AQ) \times BP$$
$$= (100 - 110) \times 5 = (50) \text{ A}$$

$$\text{Cost variance} = \text{budget cost} - \text{actual cost}$$
$$= 500 - 440 = 60 \text{ F}$$

Note: The combined price and usage variances should equal the cost variance.

S15.2

$$\begin{aligned}
\text{Rate variance} &= (\text{budgeted rate} - \text{actual rate}) \times \text{actual hours} \\
&= (\text{BR} \times \text{AH}) - (\text{AR} \times \text{AH}) \\
&= (6.50 \times 4{,}100) - 26{,}650 \\
&= 26{,}650 - 26{,}650 \\
&= \text{zero (The actual rate paid must also} = £6.50/\text{hour.)}
\end{aligned}$$

$$\begin{aligned}
\text{Efficiency variance} &= (\text{budgeted hours} - \text{actual hours}) \times \text{budgeted rate} \\
&= (4{,}000 - 4{,}100) \times 6.50 \\
&= (-100) \times 6.50 \\
&= -650 \\
&= 650 \text{ A}
\end{aligned}$$

$$\begin{aligned}
\text{Cost variance} &= \text{budgeted cost} - \text{actual cost} \\
&= (4{,}000 \times 6.50) - 6{,}650 \\
&= 26{,}000 - 26{,}650 \\
&= -650 \\
&= 650 \text{ A}
\end{aligned}$$

Note: As the rate does not vary, the efficiency variance should equal the cost variance.

S15.3

$$\begin{aligned}
\text{Rate variance} &= (\text{budgeted rate} - \text{actual rate}) \times \text{actual hours paid} \\
&= (10 - 11) \times 2{,}100 \\
&= -2{,}100 \\
&= 2{,}100 \text{ A}
\end{aligned}$$

$$\begin{aligned}
\text{Efficiency variance} &= (\text{budgeted hours} - \text{actual hours worked}) \times \text{budgeted rate} \\
&= (2{,}000 - 1{,}800) \times 10 \\
&= +2{,}000 \\
&= 2{,}000 \text{ F}
\end{aligned}$$

$$\begin{aligned}
\text{Idle time variance} &= \text{idle hours} \times \text{budgeted rate} \\
&= 300 \times 10 \\
&= -3{,}000 \\
&= 3{,}000 \text{ A}
\end{aligned}$$

$$\begin{aligned}
\text{Labour cost variance} &= \text{budgeted cost} - \text{actual cost} \\
&= (2{,}000 \times 10) - (2{,}100 \times 11) \\
&= 20{,}000 - 23{,}100 \\
&= -3{,}100 \\
&= 3{,}100 \text{ A}
\end{aligned}$$

S15.4

$$\text{Cost variance} = \text{budgeted cost} - \text{actual cost}$$
$$= 4{,}400 - 4{,}592$$
$$= -192$$
$$= 192 \text{ A}$$

$$\text{Expenditure variance} = (\text{budgeted absorption rate} - \text{actual absorption rate}) \times \text{actual dlh}$$
$$= (\text{budgeted abs. rate} \times \text{actual dlh}) - (\text{actual abs. rate} \times \text{actual dlh})$$
$$= (1.10 \times 4{,}100) - (4{,}592)$$
$$= 4{,}510 - 4{,}592$$
$$= -82$$
$$= 82 \text{ A}$$

$$\text{Efficiency variance} = (\text{BQ} - \text{AQ}) \times \text{BP}$$
$$= (\text{budgeted dlh} - \text{actual dlh}) \times \text{budgeted absorption rate}$$
$$= (4{,}000 - 4{,}100) \times 1.10$$
$$= -110$$
$$= 110 \text{ A}$$

Note: The combination of the expenditure and efficiency variances should give the cost variance.

S15.5

Fixed overhead monthly budget = 180,000/12	= 15,000
Less: Actual expenditure in month 8	= <u>16,100</u>
Fixed overhead expenditure variance	= −1,100
	= 1,100 A

S15.6

Solution to Blackpack Limited

i) FO total cost variance

$$= \text{flexed budget cost} - \text{actual cost}$$
$$= (20{,}000 \times 5 \times 15) - 1{,}465{,}000$$
$$= 1{,}500{,}000 - 1{,}465{,}000$$
$$= £35{,}000 \text{ F}$$

Sub-analysis of FO total cost variance using labour hours

ii) FO expenditure variance

$$= \text{OB cost} - \text{act. cost}$$
$$= (24{,}000 \times 5 \times 15) - 1{,}465{,}000$$
$$= 1{,}800{,}000 - 1{,}465{,}000$$
$$= £335{,}000 \text{ F}$$

iii) FO volume variance

$$= \text{FB cost} - \text{OB cost}$$
$$= (20{,}000 \times 5 \times 15) - (24{,}000 \times 5 \times 15)$$
$$= (1{,}500{,}000) - (1{,}800{,}000)$$
$$= \pounds300{,}000 \text{ A}$$

Sub-analysis of FO volume variance using labour hours

iv) FO capacity variance

$$= (\text{act. hrs} - \text{OB hrs})\text{FOAR}$$
$$= (132{,}000 - 120{,}000)15$$
$$= (12{,}000)15$$
$$= \pounds180{,}000 \text{ F}$$

v) FO efficiency variance

$$= (\text{FB hrs} - \text{act. hrs})\text{FOAR}$$
$$= (100{,}000 - 132{,}000)15$$
$$= (-32{,}000)15$$
$$= \pounds480{,}000 \text{ A}$$

S15.7

As the actual output is different from that planned in the original budget, the first step is to **flex the budget** to the activity level of 110 items.

Flexed budget (activity level = 55 items):

$$\text{Cost} = 55 \text{ units} \times 2 \text{ hours/unit} \times \pounds10\text{/hour} = \pounds1{,}100$$

$$\text{Labour cost variance} = \text{budgeted cost} - \text{actual cost}$$
$$= 1{,}100 - 1{,}050$$
$$= +50$$
$$= 50 \text{ F}$$

$$\text{Labour efficiency variance} = (\text{budgeted hours} - \text{actual hours}) \times \text{budgeted rate}$$
$$= (110 - 105) \times 10$$
$$= +50$$
$$= 50 \text{ F}$$

$$\text{Labour rate variance} = (\text{budgeted rate} - \text{actual rate}) \times \text{actual hours}$$
$$= (10 - 10) \times 105$$
$$= 0$$

These results show that the workforce are working **efficiently**; the statement made in the question is not accurate.

S15.8

$$\text{Sales price variance} = (\text{actual price} - \text{budgeted price}) \times \text{actual quantity sold}$$
$$= (26 - 25) \times 300$$
$$= +300$$
$$= 300 \text{ F}$$

$$\text{Sales volume variance} = \text{flexed budget profit} - \text{original budget profit}$$
$$= 1,650 - 2,000$$
$$= -350$$
$$= 350 \text{ A}$$

S15.9

Profit reconciliation statement

		£000	£000	
Original budget profit			400	
Sales volume variance			<u>31</u>	F
Flexed budget profit			431	
Sales price variance			(18)	A
Material variances:	Usage	39 F		
	Price	(<u>27</u>) A		
	Cost		12	F
Labour variances:	Efficiency	(2) A		
	Idle time	(12) A		
	Rate	<u>14</u> F		
	Cost		0	
Variable overhead variance:	Efficiency	(1) A		
	Expenditure	<u>5</u> F		
	Cost		4	F
Fixed overhead expenditure variance			<u>24</u>	F
Actual profit			<u>**453**</u>	

Anomira Ltd

Anomira Ltd is a wholly owned subsidiary of an industrial conglomerate. It produces one standard size of sealing compound used in the motor vehicle industry. As the new management accountant of this company, you have been asked to explain why the actual results differed from the budget for the year just ended. You ascertain the following information.

The budget was for a volume of 100,000 units produced and sold, each using 2 kg of material at £3.00 per kg. The total of variable overheads was expected to be £100,000 and the fixed overheads £250,000. Total sales revenue was planned to be £1,500,000 and the 50,000 direct labour hours planned were expected to cost £250,000. The variable overhead absorption rate is £2.00 per direct labour hour.

The actual performance for last year showed production of 90,000 units and no change in stock levels over the year. Sales revenue was £1,440,000 and 196,000 kg of material were used, costing £529,200. Variable overheads were £94,500 and fixed overheads £255,000. The total cost of direct labour was £232,750 for 49,000 hours. However, 1,000 of these hours were completely non-productive due to a breakdown of the heating system during exceptionally bad winter weather causing the factory to be temporarily closed.

Tasks:

1 Perform a variance analysis (in as much detail as the information will allow) reconciling the actual profit to the budgeted profit.

(40 marks)

2 Suggest possible explanations for any significant variances you have found.

(20 marks)

3 Discuss budgetary control and responsibility accounting in organizations. Include comments on any dangers/limitations inherent in this technique.

(40 marks)
(Total 100 marks)

Windsurfers of Perth Limited

Windsurfers of Perth Limited makes and sells windsurfing boards in the UK. It buys the board already made (complete with all fittings) but it manufactures the sails and assembles the finished product. It operates a **standard variable costing system** and performs variance analysis on a monthly basis.

	Standard variable cost for one windsurfer
Sailcloth	60 square metres at £7.00 per square metre
Labour	20 hours at £8 per hour
Board	£400
Variable overheads	£50

Windsurfers Limited budgeted to sell 90 units in May at a price of £1,500 each. It estimates that its fixed overheads are £240,000 a year (incurred evenly throughout the year). Variable overheads are absorbed per windsurfer (not per direct labour hour). Opening and closing stocks were zero for May.

The actual performance for May was as follows:

Item	Detail
Sales	81 windsurfers
Revenue	£109,350 total
Sailcloth	4,800 square metres, costing £38,400
Labour	1,540 hours, costing £13,860
Board	£420 per windsurfer
Variable overheads	£3,240 total
Fixed overheads	£21,000 total

Tasks:

a) Perform a variance analysis for May in as much detail as the information will allow. Produce a profit reconciliation statement and comment on your findings.

(70 marks)

b) Windsurfers of Perth Limited holds the purchasing department responsible for the price at which materials are purchased and the manufacturing department responsible for the quantities of materials used. Comment on this policy.

(15 marks)

c) Sometimes, managers blame adverse variances on poor standard setting. Explain how accurate standards can be set and describe the dangers of setting inaccurate standards.

(15 marks)

(Total 100 marks)

Questions

An asterisk * on a question number indicates that the answer is given at the end of the book. Answers to the other questions are given in the Lecturer's Guide.

Q15.1* Welco Ltd

Welco Ltd manufactures one type of hydraulic jack. The labour force, who are all paid at the same rate, assemble and finish two bought-in components. Each jack uses two metal castings and one rubber seal. The jacks are very popular and Welco sells all it can make. It budgets to make a profit of £4,400 each month.

The budget is as follows:

	Standard (1 item)		Budget (1,100 items)
		£	£
Rubber seals	(1 @ £2)	2	2,200
Metal castings	(2 @ £3)	6	6,600
Direct labour	(10 minutes)	1	1,100
Fixed overhead		7	7,700
		16	17,600
Sales revenue		20	22,000
Profit		4	4,400

The £7 fixed overhead consists of production, marketing and administration overheads. It is based on production and sales of 1,100 jacks (the budgeted activity level for each month).

Last month, the actual results were as follows:

Number of jacks made and sold	1,050
	£
Rubber seals (1,060 @ £1.95)	2,067
Metal castings (2,108 @ £3.25)	6,851
Direct labour (190 hours @ £5.90)	1,121
Fixed overhead incurred	7,600
	17,639
Sales revenue (1,050 @ £19)	19,950
Actual profit	2,311

Tasks:

1 Flex the budget to the actual level of activity.
2 Analyse the variances in as much detail as the figures will allow.
3 Create a profit reconciliation statement.

Q15.2* Stanley & Co.

Stanley & Co. manufactures door frames from a bought-in wooden moulding. The budget for one door frame has costs of £20 for materials and £6 for labour. Each frame has a standard usage of 5 metres of wooden moulding at a standard price of £4.00 per metre. Each frame has a standard time of 0.50 hours and the standard rate of pay is £12.00 per hour.

The budget for April was for 2,200 frames with a material cost of £44,000 and a labour cost of £13,200.

However, 2,100 frames were actually produced in April, taking 1,000 hours to make at a total labour cost of £13,000. Also, 11,550 metres of wooden moulding were used at a total cost of £43,890.

Tasks:

1 Calculate the cost, quantity and price variances for materials and labour in April.
2 Suggest possible reasons for these variances.
3 If 50 of the 1,000 hours paid were during a power cut which prevented work continuing, what changes would you make to your answers to tasks 1 and 2?

Q15.3* Ivanblast computer game

Bigcheque Ltd has created a new computer game called Ivanblast. It knows it will only have a five-week period from launch in order to market this successfully before pirating will reduce its sales to virtually zero. The budget for this period is

				£
Sales:	25,000 games	@ £50	=	1,250,000
Production materials:	25,000 blank CDs	@ £1.10	=	27,500
Variable overheads:	25,000 games	@ £0.50	=	12,500
Fixed overheads:			=	800,000
Net profit			=	410,000

(Note that, like many firms with highly automated production facilities, Bigcheque Ltd considers its production labour to be all fixed in nature. So, **all** labour costs are included in the fixed overheads.)

The actual results for the five-week period are shown below (no stocks of raw materials or finished computer games were left over at the end of the period).

				£
Sales:	30,000 games	@ £45	=	1,350,000
Production materials:	30,250 blank CDs	@ £1.00	=	30,250
Variable overheads:			=	15,000
Fixed overheads:			=	850,000
Net profit			=	454,750

Tasks:

1 Prepare a variance analysis for the period in as much detail as the figures allow.
2 Produce a statement reconciling the budgeted profit with the actual profit.
3 Comment on your findings.

Q15.4* Flipside Limited

Flipside Ltd manufactures a single-size lubrication unit for use in wind turbines etc. It operates a standard absorption costing system and uses variance analysis to control its operations. The figures below refer to the year just ended.

Production costs:	Standard costs (1 item)	Original budget (10,000 items) £	Actual results (11,000 items)
Material A	5 kg @ £2.00/kg	100,000	66,000 kg @ £1.50/kg
Material B	10 kg @ £4.00/kg	400,000	99,000 kg @ £5.00/kg
Direct labour	2 hrs @ £15.00/dlh	300,000	20,900 dlh @ £16.00/dlh
Variable overhead	2 hrs @ £3.00/dlh	60,000	20,900 dlh @ £3.00/dlh
Fixed overhead	2 dlh @ £7.00/dlh	140,000	20,900 dlh @ £7.50/dlh

The standard selling price used in the original budget is £150. However, due to increased competition, this was reduced to £139 with effect from the first day of the year. (This revised price remained in operation throughout the year.)

Tasks:

1 Calculate all possible variances from the above information in as much detail as possible.
2 Create a statement reconciling the original budget profit (before all other overheads, e.g. marketing, administration) to the actual profit.
3 Comment on your findings.

Q15.5 Elbo Ltd

Elbo Ltd makes roof tiles. It has two production departments: moulding and packing. It makes two different sizes of tile, the Handi and the Jiant. The following table shows the standard costs of labour per pallet of tiles (one pallet contains 144 tiles):

Department	Labour type	Standard hourly rate £	Standard production hours per pallet Handi	Jiant
Moulding	A	5.00	4	6
Moulding	C	4.00	5	8
Packing	A	5.00	1	2
Packing	B	4.50	2	3

During October, 400 pallets of Handis, and 150 pallets of Jiants were actually produced and the following labour hours and costs were incurred:

Labour type	Moulding department		Packing department	
	Actual hours worked	Actual pay (£)	Actual hours worked	Actual pay (£)
A	2,600	12,480	695	3,336
B	–	–	1,250	5,875
C	3,180	12,720	–	–
Totals	5,780	25,200	1,945	9,211

Tasks:

For the month of October:

1 Create the labour budget (hours and £) for (a) Handis, and (b) Jiants.
2 Calculate the budgeted direct labour cost of one pallet of Handis and one pallet of Jiants.
3 Calculate the budgeted total labour cost of each department and of the whole factory.
4 Calculate the direct labour cost variance for each department and for the factory.
5 For each department and labour type, analyse the cost variances into their rate and efficiency variances.
6 Comment on your findings.

Q15.6 Fablus Limited

Fablus Limited makes a single product, the NL. It operates a standard absorption costing system. The budget for 2012 shows sales of 500,000 NLs at £0.25 giving a profit of £12,500.

Standard absorption cost for one unit of NL:

		£
Materials	1 kg plastic @ £0.05/kg	0.050
Direct Labour	15 minutes @ £0.50/h	0.125
Variable Overheads	15 minutes @ £0.10/h	0.025
Fixed Overheads	15 minutes @ £0.10/h	0.025
Standard cost of production		**0.225**

Actual results for 2012:

Number of NLs actually made = 452,000 which were sold at £0.30 each.

Item	Details	Cost £
Materials	480,000 kg	18,000
Direct labour	100,000* hours @ £0.55/h	55,000
Variable overheads		12,000
Fixed overheads		12,000

* Due to a power cut, only 95,000 hours were actually worked.

Required:

Assuming there were no opening or closing stocks, calculate as many variances as the information will allow and present them in the form of an operating statement reconciling the actual and budget profits.

Q15.7* Triform Limited

Triform Limited operates a standard absorption costing system. During last month, it made only one product, the TR2. Using the following information, you are required to calculate as many variances as possible, discuss their causes and reconcile the budgeted profit with the actual profit.

Standard cost card (for one unit of TR2)

		£
Direct materials	4 kg @ £5/kg	20
Direct labour	3 hours @ £7/hour	21
Variable overhead	3 hours @ £3/hour	9
Fixed overhead	3 hours @ £4/hour	12
Standard cost		62
Standard profit margin		14
Standard selling price		76

Budgeted output and sales for last month = 800 units of TR2

Actual results for last month (700 units of TR2 produced and sold)

		£
Sales revenue	700 @ £79	55,300
Direct materials used	3,100 kg @ £4.25/kg	13,175
Direct labour hours worked	2,350 hours @ £6.40/hour	15,040
Variable overhead incurred		6,700
Fixed overhead incurred		9,200

Q15.8 JK plc

JK plc operates a chain of fast-food restaurants. The company uses a standard marginal costing system to monitor the costs incurred in its outlets. The standard cost of one of its most popular meals is as follows:

		£ per meal
Ingredients	(1.08 units)	1.18
Labour	(1.5 minutes)	0.15
Variable conversion costs	(1.5 minutes)	0.06
The standard price of this meal is		1.99

In one of its outlets, which has budgeted sales and production activity level of 50,000 such meals, the number of such meals that were produced and sold during April 2003 was 49,700. The actual cost data was as follows:

		£
Ingredients	(55,000 units)	58,450
Labour	(1,200 hours)	6,800
Variable conversion costs	(1,200 hours)	3,250
The actual revenue from the sale of the meals was		96,480

Required:

(a) Calculate
  (i) the total budgeted contribution for April 2003;
  (ii) the total actual contribution for April 2003.

(3 marks)

(b) Present a statement that reconciles the budgeted and actual contribution for April 2003. Show all variances to the nearest £1 and in as much detail as possible.

(17 marks)

(c) Explain why a marginal costing approach to variance analysis is more appropriate in environments such as that of JK plc, where there are a number of different items being produced and sold.

(5 marks)

(Total = 25 marks)

CIMA Intermediate: Management Accounting – Performance Management, May 2003

Q15.9 TBS

TBS produces two products in a single factory. The following details have been extracted from the standard marginal cost cards of the two products:

Product	S3 £/unit	S5 £/unit
Selling price	100	135
Variable costs:		
Material X (£3 per kg)	30	39
Liquid Z (£4.50 per litre)	27	45
Direct labour (£6 per hour)	18	24
Overheads	12	16

TBS uses a standard marginal costing system linked with budgets.

Budgeted data for the month of October included:

	S3	S5
Sales (units)	10,000	10,000
Production (units)	12,000	13,500
Fixed costs:		
Production		£51,000
Administration		£34,000

Actual data for the month of October was as follows:

	S3	S5
Sales (units)	12,200	8,350
Production (units)	13,000	9,400
Selling prices per unit	£96	£145
Variable costs:		
Material X	270,000 kg costing	£786,400
Liquid Z	150,000 litres costing	£763,200
Direct labour	73,200 hours costing	£508,350
Overheads		£347,000
Fixed costs:		
Production		£47,550
Administration		£36,870

Required:

a) Calculate the budgeted profit/loss for October.

(2 marks)

b) Calculate the actual profit/loss for October.

(3 marks)

c) As a management accountant in TBS you will be attending the monthly management team meeting. In preparation for that meeting you are required to:

(i) Prepare a statement that reconciles the budgeted and actual profit/loss for October, showing the variances in as much detail as is possible from the data provided.

(15 marks)

(ii) State, and then briefly explain, the main issues in your profit reconciliation statement.

(5 marks)
(Total = 25 marks)

CIMA Intermediate: Management Accounting – Performance Management, November 2004

Review questions

1 Explain the basic theory and cyclical nature of budgetary control systems.
2 State the common formulae for cost variances and sub-variances.
3 Discuss the importance of flexing the budget to the actual level of production.
4 Describe the purpose of a profit reconciliation statement.
5 Give examples of the possible relationships between variances.
6 Discuss the additional benefits of budgetary control systems.
7 Explain how the operating costs of budgetary control systems can be managed.
8 Comment on the problems of 'responsibility accounting'.
9 Discuss the limitations of budgetary control systems.
10 List 10 points for good budgetary control.

The answers to all these questions can be found in the text of this chapter.

Budgets, behaviour and beyond budgeting

Introduction

Have you ever thought of starting a business of your own? You may have thought carefully about how you were going to do this; you may even have committed your plans to paper. However, even with the help of meticulously detailed plans, there is no guarantee that you will be able to fulfil your ambitions. Even if you are one of the few who does manage to 'achieve' your idea, it is almost certain that the reality of what you have created will be different, to some extent, from your original idea. It may be better or worse than you expected or just different. To quote John Lennon, 'Life is what happens to you whilst you are making plans!'

The point is that making things happen is not just down to you. Every aspect of the world around you will have an impact on your actions; on many occasions you will have to modify your ideas and intermediate objectives. If you do not, your chances of success will diminish. Business activities do not happen in a vacuum; they are influenced by their many different environments: economic, social, legal, cultural, political, technological, etc. Businesses are also affected by the behaviour of their competitors, employees, suppliers and government. In the modern age, these factors are changing increasingly quickly. Is it possible for a CEO alone to react to these continual changes as they impact on the various elements of his or her business? Or is it more sensible to delegate a measure of control to individuals who have direct responsibility for the affected areas?

In many companies, the instinct of the senior management is to maintain tight controls over the activities of the business. After all, everything that happens in the company is their legal responsibility. In the industrial age, this approach worked because companies dominated their markets (i.e. suppliers not customers were in charge). As a result, *efficiency* was the critical success factor. These conditions led to the development of the command and control management model with functional hierarchies, budgetary control systems and centralized decision making.

This traditional approach is a *deterministic* way of managing. However, in recent years there has been a distinct power shift in the marketplace. Due to the increased speed and scope of communications, typified by the Internet, the customer is more in charge than the supplier. In the twenty-first century, business needs to replace its traditional deterministic model with a *systemic* one. To succeed on a long-term basis in their complex, highly-competitive markets, they need to satisfy the interests of all of their stakeholders: customers, suppliers, employees, shareholders, government and society.

In the past, budgets were the primary mechanism for command and control. These days, advancing technology and communications provide management with alternative methods of imposing this control. Yet, budgets are still widely used for setting annual targets, and forming the basis for bonus calculations. Employee financial incentive schemes are a form of 'fixed performance contract' consisting of predetermined, unchangeable targets based on budgets, balanced scorecards, etc. Remuneration is offered to employees dependent on the achievement of these targets. These devices are referred to alternatively as 'bonus schemes', 'employee incentive schemes' and 'share option schemes'. Employee targets are based on figures in the original budget *which is fixed*.

They are based on a prediction and used in a deterministic way. Predictions, as Jan Wallander (former CEO and Chairman of Handelsbanken) pointed out, are mainly of two types: *'same weather tomorrow as today'* and *'something really abnormal'*. In coping with the first type, budgets are trite and of limited use, being merely an extension of the historical trend adjusted for minor known changes. However, in the case of the second type they will almost certainly be wrong because the timing and impact of large changes are difficult to predict. If they are followed, e.g. by building up or reducing stocks or staffing, the probable outcome is that some corporate value will be destroyed. Strengthening the fixed performance contract by tying incentives to the achievement of (likely to be wrong) targets aggravates the problem.

Even without financial inducements, managers have a positive desire to achieve the budget figures, not least because they are partially responsible for creating those figures. The participatory budget creation process is deliberate and designed to give managers psychological ownership of the business plan. If the plan is not achieved, it reflects badly on the manager who consequently 'loses face' in the eyes of his or her colleagues. There is a lot of pressure on managers to 'make their numbers'.

The trouble with this is that it encourages managers to play budget games (see below). Where people's personal remuneration is concerned, their imaginations become very 'creative', resulting in the manipulation of activities, the distortion of information and an increase in their personal rewards. Due to the prevalence of these activities, a significant body of people now believe that fixed performance contracts have become part of the problem of poor business performance rather than its solution.

This is usually the context in which people first encounter the 'Beyond Budgeting' philosophy. Its title has become synonymous with the abolition of budgets. This is unfortunate as managing without budgets is not Beyond Budgeting's main idea; rather, it is a consequence of it.

Dissatisfaction with traditional budgeting has grown to the extent where opposition to it is mainly co-ordinated under the single umbrella movement of 'Beyond Budgeting'. This international movement operates a Beyond Budgeting Round Table (BBRT) with its own website (www.bbrt.org). The BBRT describes itself as a collaborative organization that offers shared learning, performance management research and consulting support to its members.

Two of the leading lights of this movement are the late Jeremy Hope and Robin Fraser. They have written a book entitled *Beyond Budgeting – How Managers Can Break Free from the Annual Performance Trap*, published by Harvard Business School Press in 2003. In their summary at the end of Chapter 4, they conclude that:

> *By removing the budgeting process and fixed performance contract, firms are able to change the attitudes and behaviors of people at every level of the organization. In particular, they are likely to eradicate the undesirable behaviors that result from setting a fixed target that must be met even though the outcome is highly uncertain.*

Learning objectives

Having worked through this chapter you should be able to:

- describe the weaknesses of traditional budgetary control systems;
- define and describe the various types of 'budget game';
- explain the exacerbating nature of employee cash incentive schemes;
- describe mechanisms for moving future sales to the present;
- describe mechanisms for moving present sales to the future;
- evaluate the utility of budgetary control systems;
- describe the 'Beyond Budgeting' management model;
- list the six principles of 'devolved leadership';
- list the six adaptive processes recommended to replace budgeting;
- describe the management model used by Svenska Handelsbanken;
- describe the management model used by the Toyota production system;
- explain the difficulties in the adoption of the 'Beyond Budgeting' philosophy;
- state the arguments against the 'Beyond Budgeting' model;
- list some of the findings of the 'Better Budgeting' open forum in 2004.

The weaknesses of traditional budgeting

The 'tried-and-tested' method of controlling corporate performance is budgeting; it is used by almost every business in existence. (The creation and use of budgets is covered in previous chapters of this book.) In brief, it can be seen as a cyclical four-stage process (see Figure 15.1):

1 Create plan.
2 Implement plan.
3 Measure performance.
4 Compare plan with performance and evaluate differences.
5 Create next plan.
6 Etc.

Of course, actual performance rarely, if ever, turns out to be identical to the original budget. Unforeseen events and unplanned internal changes occur at various times throughout the financial year. Managers respond to these deviations from plan as they arise and set new directions/objectives appropriate to the new situation. In this way, the annual performance of the business should at least resemble the last revision of the budget. So why does the traditional budgetary control system often produce disappointing results? What are its weaknesses?

First, unlike the business environment, budgets do not change. The rate of change in the environment is continuously increasing but the budgetary control system was designed almost a century ago when things changed much more slowly. For instance, in the 1920s, if you wanted to hold an important face-to-face meeting with a business associate in the USA, it would take you at least a week to travel there! It is now possible to travel there and back in the space of a day. The modern technological environment allows for vastly increased speeds of communication; examples include video-conferencing and IP communications which allow voice-, video- and data-sharing as well as real-time drawing on virtual whiteboards (e.g. Skype and MS Messenger).

Today, speed is a key factor, but this is not just a technological issue. The business world has become so much more competitive that if companies do not respond fast they really suffer. Today, it is essential that businesses respond fast and change continually. *The world has changed but the way we manage has not*. This idea is the main theme of Professor Gary Hamel's 2007 book, *The Future of Management*, in which he exhorts managers to revolutionize their practices to meet the radically changed business environment of the twenty-first century. He says:

> *Contrary to popular mythology, the thing that most impedes [management] innovation in large companies is not a lack of risk taking. Big companies take big, and often imprudent, risks every day. The real brake on [management] innovation is the drag of old mental models. Long-serving executives often have a big chunk of their emotional capital invested in the existing strategy.*

Any single change in a business activity may have repercussions on many other activities and affect many other people. The introduction of a new product by a competitor may cause you to want to change your sales plan. But any such change will impact on purchasing, manufacturing, administration, marketing, etc. These areas are controlled by different budget-responsible officers who will need to agree the changes which will then be referred to senior management for authorization.

Most organizations are bureaucratic because they have functional structures and centralized decision making. They need to be more decentralized and more organized around their processes (i.e. activities that create value for customers) in order to respond faster and do things in a less costly way. The organizational structure and processes need to be continually reassessed. A possible downside of this is that the amount of work may stifle innovation. In extreme cases, in the cause of self-preservation, managers may learn to respond negatively to innovative ideas even though they may be good for the business.

Also, the widely adopted practice of giving cash bonuses to managers based on their actual performance measured against budget is detrimental to many companies. These personal incentive schemes may be expressed in 'narrow' terms which ignore their effects on other parts of the business. Also, the achievement of their individual budget targets can become more important to managers than acting in the best interests of the company **as a whole**. Budget-responsible officers often exhibit what is known as 'gaming behaviour'.

Budget games: definition and types

The term 'budget games' refers to certain behaviours exhibited by budget-responsible managers. Some games involve their making their budget figures easier to achieve than they actually expect; others involve some form of manipulation and/or misrecording of their actual performance. The object of playing these games is to create some benefit for the employee, *even if the company suffers as a result.*

Managers may appear to act in the best interests of their organization, e.g. reaching or exceeding income targets but not exceeding expenditure allowances. However, in reality, their actions may well result in the organization performing worse than it otherwise would have. Also, an unfortunate side-effect of these games is that misinformation is introduced into the management information systems and future decisions based on this will tend to be less effective than they otherwise would have been.

Managers prefer to be seen by their peers to be in control of their budgets and to be thought of as being 'on top of things' and good at their job. This desired respect from their peers encourages them to play these games. However, their motivation for playing them is greatly increased when their personal remuneration is linked to meeting targets based on budget figures. The fact that annual bonuses are often based on budget targets results in the playing of these games being very common.

There are several different types of budget game but the most common is where managers build 'slack' into their targets. The budget is constructed by negotiation between the budget holder and senior management (possibly with the technical support of a management accountant). The idea is that the budget holder is more likely to achieve his or her 'own' target than one imposed from above. But because the bonus depends on meeting his or her targets, the budget holder will be tempted to make them easier to achieve. So revenues tend to be underestimated and expenses overestimated.

Over the years, most executives have experienced their budget estimates of expenses being cut back in the name of efficiency. However, if they expect their estimates (known as 'allowances') to be cut back, they may well overestimate them in the first instance to avoid any reduction. If they expect an overall (or blanket) cutback of 10% they may inflate their suggested allowances by an appropriate amount and end up with the number they originally wanted.

'Virement' is another game played as the year progresses. This is the recording of an expense under the wrong heading. For example, if the budget allowance for travel has already been reached before the end of a budget period, further travel expenses in that period may be incorrectly classed as training or some other item that has not used up all its allowance. This makes budget holders appear to be better at controlling expenditure than they actually are by hiding their overspending.

If, towards the end of a budget period, it looks as though an expense allowance will be underspent, it is common for the budget holder to go on a 'spending spree', buying items not strictly necessary at that time. These items would not have been bought had the budget expense allowance been lower. Note that this unnecessary spending behaviour may perpetuate the error in future years. In the eyes of the budget holder, it helps to avoid cutbacks in that particular expense budget in the next period; better to have the money available just in case it is needed than not to have the 'buffer' it creates.

Salespeople are often paid partly by commission on the sales they make. If the commission is triggered by sales reaching a certain value and the salespeople think they are not going to reach this threshold, they may attempt to bring forward 'regular' sales from the next period into the current one. Of course, these brought-forward sales will create a problem regarding the commission earned next period, but increased sales to other customers may more than compensate for these brought-forward sales. Most people prefer 'jam today' rather than 'jam tomorrow'.

On the other hand, in a good period, the salespeople may have sold well over estimate and reached the amount where the commission payments are capped at a maximum level (this is normal corporate practice). It may be that the salespeople could sell even more before the end of the period but why should they? They will not earn anything extra for doing so and these 'additional' sales will go towards next period's bonus. The effect of this on the business is that sales **and their resulting cash flow** will be delayed.

The effect of the budget games identified above is to feed misinformation into the budgetary control system (which is an important part of the management information system). In turn, this will cause poor decisions to be made throughout the organization, resulting in suboptimal performance. As all budget schedules are interdependent, incorrect figures in one area will cause incorrect figures in other areas. Activities throughout the organization will be based on misleading information!

This offers an insight as to why traditional budgetary control systems are not as successful as they should be. Their theoretical strength is always undermined to some extent by *normal self-centred* human behaviour.

The effect of employee cash incentive schemes

Before looking at the last two games in more detail, we will look at how these employee incentive schemes operate, particularly those offering cash bonuses. First of all, employees are offered additional pay for reaching targets based on their budgets. However, companies acknowledge that the business environment may be better or worse than assumed for the creation of the original budget. To compensate for this, the threshold figure triggering the payment of a bonus is set below the budget allowance, say at 80% of that amount. From the company's point of view, this ensures a significant amount of the target is met before any bonus is paid.

Once the threshold has been reached, the activity will continue and the bonus will increase accordingly. However, companies like to keep their expenditure under control and will normally place an upper limit on the amount of bonus that can be earned in any period. This upper limit may be set at, say, 120% of the budget allowance (see Figure 16.1).

To help understand the above, consider the example of a salesman whose budget states that he is to sell £50,000 of goods every month. He is on a bonus scheme which rewards him with 10% of sales value above £40,000 (80% of budget) subject to a sales cap of £60,000 (120% of budget). If he sells goods worth £40,000 or less in the period he earns zero bonus, if he sells £50,000 he earns £1,000 bonus, if he sells £60,000 he earns £2,000 bonus and if he sells £70,000 he still earns £2,000 bonus.

Imagine you are this salesman; it is approaching the end of the month and you have sold only £28,000 and you estimate that you will not sell more than £35,000. You realize it is most unlikely that you will earn any bonus this month. What effect do you think this will have on your motivation? What attitude will you adopt towards selling between

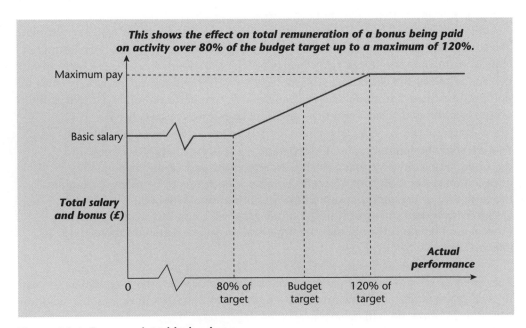

Figure 16.1 **Bonus-related behaviour**

now and the end of the month? Most people will stop making any effort to sell above the minimum and have a 'rest' before next month. After all, any sales that can be pushed forward into next month will help enhance the next bonus. This may lead to an active decision to stop selling this month.

Alternatively, if you have reached the bonus threshold before the month-end, you will be motivated to sell. You will want to take maximum advantage of this month's opportunity to earn as much as you possibly can. Every £1,000 of sales above £40,000 will earn you an extra £100. Suppose there is one week left before the month-end and it looks like you will sell a total of £57,000 in the period. Your bonus will be £1,700 (10% of 57,000 – 40,000). This is good but it could be better; you are missing out on £300 of bonus that will be lost to you for ever. Is there anything you can do to avoid this and maximize your earnings? What about next month's 'regular' sales? Is it possible to bring any of them forward into this month? This may cause a problem next month but it may be possible to make up for the 'missing' sales and at least you will have earned the maximum bonus this month.

On the other hand, with one week to go to the month-end, you may have just reached the £60,000 limit for which bonus is paid. How would this affect you? You have reached your maximum earnings for this month and have no incentive to sell for the remainder of the period. But you could help next month's bonus by recording the final sales of this month as the first sales of next month (assuming the system allows this to happen) or actually postponing further sales to then. Why shouldn't you have a rest for a week – after all, you've earned it, haven't you?

This 'personal earnings/bonus management' behaviour may be advantageous to the employee but it can be counter-productive to the business. An obvious example of this, as mentioned above, is where sales are pushed into the future **together with the related cash inflow**. However, there are more subtle ways in which the company can be damaged. These will become apparent as we look in more detail at specific ways in which sales can be *pulled forward* and *pushed back*.

Moving future sales to the present

One way of pulling sales forward from next month into the current one is to offer 'abnormal' discounts (assuming you have the authority to do so). These are discounts which are not justifiable from the company's point of view but offer an incentive to the customer to buy now rather than later. For example, offers 'only available for a limited period' could fall under this heading.

When selling to distributors/wholesalers ('intermediaries' in the supply chain) it may be possible to engage in 'channel stuffing'. This is where an excessive amount of goods are delivered to suppliers this month with the expectation that deliveries will be smaller next month or that some goods will be returned.

Alternatively, if customers are told by the salesman that he has heard 'on the grapevine' that a price increase is likely next month, it may encourage them to buy more than their normal amounts this month (and less next month). Of course, when no price increase occurs next month, they can be told the good news that this is due to the supplier's good management and that increases have been held off **for the time being**.

The ingenuity of employees to improve their bonuses can be very great. There is one documented case involving the export sale of a large, expensive machine where the trigger for the payment of the bonus to the sales team was its delivery to the customer. Because the machine was not completed in time for delivery in one month, arrangements were made for it to be shipped in kit form for later assembly. This did the trick as the technicality of the machine not being in workable order was not specified by the incentive system and the bonus was paid for the month of delivery. However, the supplier subsequently had to send an assembly team to the customer's premises involving much extra expenditure that it would not normally have incurred. This unnecessary cost had an adverse effect on company profits but the sales team got their bonuses earlier than they should have.

Pre-dating orders/invoices is another way of pulling sales forward. For example, if the goods are to be delivered on 1 August (the first day of the next period) but you can arrange for the invoice to be dated 31 July (the last day of the current period) then the associated bonus will be paid one month earlier than it should. However, it must be pointed out that this should not be possible if the company has adequate control systems in place. This is breaking the rules rather than bending them and, if employees are caught, they should be subject to disciplinary measures. Having said that, it has certainly happened in the past and, where company control systems are poor, it could happen in the future.

Moving present sales to the future

On the other hand, if it is in the employees' personal interest to push sales back into the following period, they may arrange for delivery of the goods to be delayed until then. This may be possible by giving incorrect information to the dispatch office. Alternatively, they may be able to arrange for the invoice to be post-dated to the next period. Again, corporate control systems should not allow this to happen but systems are rarely perfect.

A more subtle approach is for salespeople to voice to their customers the possibility of imminent price cuts. The spurious information is passed on under the guise of the salespeople's 'goodwill' towards their customers! Of course, the price cuts must never be guaranteed. The information is presented in the form of a rumour which may or may not turn out to be true. The 'get-out' clause is there to be used next month when no price decreases occur.

A more dangerous approach is for the salesperson to hint that there may be quality problems with the latest batch of manufactured goods and that it may be advisable for the customer to delay ordering until next month if possible. The customer would be asked to keep this information 'confidential', especially as the problem has now been corrected and the next batch out of the factory will be back to the normal standard of quality.

One further way of pushing sales into the future is for the salesperson to lie to the customer about stock availability. Again, this is a risky short-term ploy as the customer may give its business to a competitor to avoid serious delays.

The service sector is equally prone to these distortions. The 'credit crunch' of 2008 illustrates what can happen when incentives are paid to traders in the financial markets. Their bonuses caused them to follow their personal short-term interests by selling mortgages to 'sub-prime' homeowners to increase sales at the expense of long-term credit risk to their employers. This model is flawed because the traders get their bonuses in the good years but do not have to repay them in the bad years. So the system works in the favour of the employee but at the expense of the long-term interests of shareholders.

The above examples are not confined to budgetary control systems. The same can happen with **any** targets that are negotiated in advance and used as the basis of the performance contract, not just budgets. For example, *balanced scorecard games* are played wherever this management model is adopted.

The utility of budgetary control systems

There will also be other ways of moving sales backwards and forwards in time. People are nothing if not ingenious when it comes to increasing their earnings. Bonus schemes based on budget targets are very common and successful motivators of employees. Unfortunately, the resulting employee behaviour is not always in the best interests of the business.

There is a significant consensus of opinion that the way in which traditional budgetary control systems are used is part of the current corporate performance problem rather than its solution. Much of this stems from personal incentive schemes being directly linked to budget targets. The 'gaming' behaviour which this encourages often causes businesses to perform less well than they would otherwise do.

The command and control management model was designed to meet shareholders' interests. Unfortunately, when poorly administered, it may do so at the expense of employee and customer satisfaction. The 'fixed performance contract' at the heart of this model has the potential to cause dysfunctional and unethical behaviour, and destroy corporate value. Moreover, it focuses employees' attention on pleasing their bosses in the hierarchy (by meeting their individual negotiated targets) rather than focusing on what they should really do to satisfy customers (which is necessary to meet the long-term interests of shareholders).

In today's highly competitive conditions, a model is needed that meets the interests of **all** stakeholders, not just shareholders. Only a model that serves the long-term interests of customers, employees, suppliers, shareholders, government and society will create the greatest value in the long term. Companies, like Toyota, which have done this have become leaders in their industries. It took them several decades but they have laid the foundations for sustained success, and it will be hard for their competitors to catch them up unless they too adopt a new leadership model.

The 'Beyond Budgeting' philosophy

'Beyond Budgeting' advocates a new leadership model. It involves changes in organizational structure and management processes for long-term success in doing business in the twenty-first century, particularly for knowledge-based organizations. It acknowledges a shift from the production–supplier-oriented businesses of the industrial age to the

Industrial Age	Innovation Age	Success factors
Incremental change	Discontinuous change	Fast response
Long life cycles	Short life cycles	Continuous innovation
Rising prices	Falling prices	Operational excellence
Limited choice of product	Extensive choice of product	Customer intimacy
Access to capital	Access to talent	Great place to work
Passive shareholders	Intolerant shareholders	Effective governance
Manual workers	Knowledge workers	Freedom and trust

Figure 16.2 Change and success factors
Source: based on information provided by the BBRT

competitive, customer-driven, complex knowledge-based entrepreneurial ones of the innovation age. The emphasis changes from continually improving efficiency to the management of complexity. The main idea of the Beyond Budgeting movement is that the management model should be changed to support, not conflict with, the conditions of the innovation age. It achieves this by adopting a system model (i.e. '**Devolved Leadership via Radical Decentralization**') in place of the traditional deterministic command and control model.

The elimination of budgetary control systems is a consequence of this management model, **not its purpose**. Also, it is worth noting that it does not claim its ideas to be suitable for all business conditions. The main aspects of change and the appropriate success factors for this new model are shown in Figure 16.2. In the Industrial Age of the last century, by far the most important success factor was operational excellence. Now, in the Innovation Age of the current century, several other factors are considered equally important (see right-hand column of Figure 16.2).

A few decades ago, large businesses invested significant amounts of their resources into planning departments which would produce detailed plans for the next 10 or 20 years. They considered this worthwhile as environmental changes seemed to happen at a manageable pace. Today, that belief is seldom held; instead 'unpredictability' and 'constant change' are accepted as the norm. Planning for more than about five years ahead is seen as a waste of time and resources by most commercial organizations.

(However, there are some industries, such as nuclear power, that *need* to plan decades ahead; these are the exception rather than the rule. They attempt to build as much flexibility as possible into their plans but in reality there is little scope for them to do so. Because of unforeseen changes in the environment, this tends to produce solutions which do not provide the best possible results.)

The nature of work is also changing. Peter Drucker said that:

> *The knowledge worker … must lead in the information age. This leadership has to be visionary and completely different from traditional ways of leadership and management applied in the command and control model.*

Figure 16.3 summarizes the main differences between manual and knowledge workers.

Manual workers	Knowledge workers
Productivity gains	Productivity challenge
Replaced by machines	Supported by technology
Costs to be reduced	Assets to yield a return
They need employers	Employers need them
Must be supervised	Must direct themselves

Figure 16.3 Manual workers v knowledge workers
Source: based on information provided by the BBRT

Theory X *Typical of command and control*	Theory Y *Typical of devolved leadership*
Attitude People dislike work, find it boring and will avoid it if they can.	**Attitude** People need to work and want to take an interest in it. Under the right conditions, they can enjoy it.
Direction People must be forced or bribed to make the right effort.	**Direction** People will direct themselves towards a target that they accept.
Responsibility People would rather be directed than accept responsibility, which they avoid.	**Responsibility** People will seek, and accept responsibility, under the right conditions.
Motivation People are motivated mainly by money and fears about their job security.	**Motivation** Under the right conditions, people are motivated by the desire to realize their own potential.
Creativity Most people have little creativity – except when it comes to getting round management rules.	**Creativity** Creativity and ingenuity are widely distributed.

Figure 16.4 Assumptions about human nature; McGregor's theories X and Y
Source: based on information provided by the BBRT

This new breed of worker needs the freedom to be self-directing in order to be effective. McGregor's Theories X and Y (Douglas McGregor, *The Human Side of Enterprise*, 1960) are particularly appropriate here. These are summarized in Figure 16.4. In the Industrial Age, it was very common to refer to employees as 'hands'; this practice is much less common now as it is more appropriate to think of them as 'brains'!

Devolved leadership: structure and principles

The hierarchical structure adopted by most 'traditional' organizations is unsuitable for innovative knowledge-based companies. Hierarchies do not encourage fast response, continuous innovation or trust; in fact, they tend to act as barriers to these things. Devolved leadership needs a network of 'independent' business units/teams to flourish. The more autonomous the units, the more successful the business is likely to be, provided there is at the same time a strong corporate culture. Head offices will still exist but their major role will be that of creating the corporate culture and supporting their 'front-line' business units (see Figure 16.5). In contrast to the old hierarchical systems, the power is devolved to the front-line units, and the centralized services become suppliers to them. Thus, the new network organization is driven not through the hierarchy but through its customer–supplier relationships.

In a devolved network, the head office takes a 'hands-off' approach; it sets the direction in which it wants its business units to go then lets them get on with it, taking care not to micromanage them. The individual units not only decide their tactics, but also decide their strategies. A consequence of this is that two units may decide on different strategies in order to realize the direction and objectives set by head office. The justification for this is that their environments and the needs of their customers may not be exactly the same. Moreover, letting each decide what is best for them should lead to greater innovation when best practices are shared. This fundamental delegation of

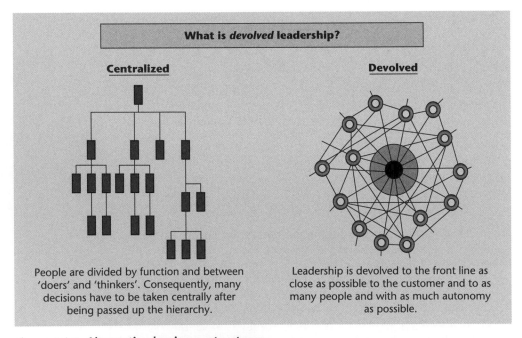

Figure 16.5 Alternative business structures
Source: from 'Beyond Budgeting Round Table' (BBRT), reproduced by kind permission of the BBRT

autonomy is described by Beyond Budgeting as 'Radical Decentralization'. This determines the essential structure of Beyond Budgeting organizations.

Devolved leadership operates through the enactment of the following **six basic principles:**

1 *Customer focus:* focus all employees on their customers – not on hierarchical relationships.
2 *Network of teams:* perform business processes via a lean network of accountable teams – not centralized functions.
3 *Empowerment:* autonomous teams given freedom and capability to act – avoid micromanagement.
4 *Responsibility:* create a culture of high responsibility at every level – not just at the top.
5 *Open information:* make information systems open/transparent to enable self-management – do not restrict information hierarchically.
6 *Culture statement:* governance via a few clear values, goals and boundaries – not detailed regulations.

Adaptive (or flexible) processes

However, organizations adopting these principles almost always find that their traditional budgetary control systems are not compatible with this new management model. The reasons for this are that budgets:

● reinforce centralized, hierarchical 'command and control';
● create a bureaucratic rather than an entrepreneurial culture;
● encourage managers to play budget games;
● are a barrier to flexibility and fast response;
● discourage teamwork by emphasizing individual contributions;
● distort information by combining forecasts and targets;
● use huge amounts of resources, especially managers' time.

This is why Beyond Budgeting recommends the abolition of budgetary control systems and their replacement by the following **six flexible/adaptive processes:**

1 *Relative goals:* corporate goals should be relative (not absolute), aiming for continuous improvement – no fixed performance contracts.
2 *Relative rewards:* reward team (not individual) success using relative (not fixed) targets.
3 *Action planning:* make planning a continuous and inclusive process – not a top-down annual event.
4 *Control:* base controls on relative indicators/trends – not variances against plan.
5 *Resources as needed:* allow teams the freedom to use their resources as they think best – hold them accountable via productivity ratios such as 'cost to income'.
6 *Co-ordination as needed:* co-ordinate interactions dynamically – not via annual planning cycles.

Each of these processes will now be discussed in more detail.

Relative goals

It is a good idea for corporate goals to be based on external benchmarks and competitor performance. For example, one company might have goals of being in the upper quartile in its industry in terms of profitability or return on equity. It would measure its performance relative to a league table of its competitors' performances ranked from the highest to the lowest, *not* against fixed targets like 20% a year. Using relative measures (if the information can be obtained) is much more effective than absolute measures because it takes into account any changes in business conditions that affect all players. Budgets are fixed measures based on assumptions decided in advance, whereas relative measures are based on the actual circumstances with the benefit of hindsight. Thus, in bad conditions an organization's good performance may be worse than budget, but it may still beat its competitors, which is the real target.

The performance of work teams (e.g. branches or sales units) may be measured relative to each other. So work teams are empowered to set their own performance targets to improve their position in the league table against their peers. Doing this themselves gives them the psychological 'ownership' to maximize their performance. Instead of creating targets based on plans, scorecards or budgets decided in advance, they strive for relative improvement. It is also important that very few, only high-level measures are used (e.g. profitability), not a host of detailed measures (e.g. the time taken to complete the sales order), because such detailed measures constrain the achievement of maximum overall performance. Senior managers trust managers to work responsibly, but they still hold them accountable for their overall performance. They will challenge them to do better and coach them, but not micromanage them.

Relative rewards

Under command and control, setting the employee cash bonus threshold at 80% of the budget target is meant to combat a harsh environment such as a level of competition greater than that envisaged by the budget. But if the difficulties faced are such that it is not possible to reach the threshold, no bonus will be earned despite the strenuous efforts made by the employees. On the other hand, if conditions are much more favourable than planned for, employees are able to earn significant bonuses without really trying. The illogicality of this is plain to see, yet this type of bonus incentive scheme is widespread. The effect of operating such schemes is to encourage employees to indulge in the dysfunctional behaviour of 'gaming' as discussed above. They give false and misleading information in order to increase the size of their bonuses. As subsequent business activities are based on this misinformation, it is no wonder that corporate performance suffers. **Financial incentives should *not* be based on predetermined budget targets.**

Hindsight should be used to help decide the amount of bonus payable. Bonuses are paid in arrears so why not take advantage of this and base the rewards more on the efforts made by employees than their achievements? After all, they are not responsible for changes in the business environment so why should they be punished for, or benefit from, them?

Team, rather than individual, bonuses encourage co-ordination of activities which should result in improved performance. For optimal company performance, the bigger the team, the better. The formula for calculating the bonus should be based not on a budget target but on a set of key performance indicators (KPIs). These should be carefully chosen to reflect the appropriate corporate objectives (e.g. profitability, growth, productivity). These objectives can be agreed with each business unit in advance, but without setting specific fixed targets for them. The actual performance of the unit would be determined after the event (e.g. yearly) relative to an agreed set of benchmarks.

Using reward schemes based on group rather than individual performance often raises the question as to whether this is really enough of an incentive. However, in the Beyond Budgeting model, these are not seen as incentives to perform but as rewards for shared success. The incentive to perform is the individual responsibility and the visibility of their results. Making the results of the performance of all units open for all to see is a far greater incentive to individuals to perform, the more so as everyone participates in the same reward pool, which creates peer pressure.

Action planning

The authority and responsibility to plan their own activities lie with the local teams. All members of the team are encouraged to participate in this. Planning becomes a continuous process, not an annual cycle. Senior management may challenge their teams to perform better, but whatever plans they make are their own. They are judged, not by their plans but by their overall results against a few key measures. Teams are encouraged to concentrate on the continuous creation of value rather than hitting fixed numerical targets.

If the organizations prepare a 'rolling forecast' every quarter for the following five quarters, it is a forecast and not a budget by another name; **a forecast is not a commitment**. Although it would not contain as much detail as a traditional budget, it would show summary figures of sales, costs, profits and cash flows. It is a realistic estimate of where the unit will be at a future time. Such a forecast helps senior managers to review the financial outlook of the business without being constrained by the corporate financial year or its effect on their own personal remuneration. Based on the position shown by these forecasts, local managers would plan the actions to improve their own performance.

Control

Actual results should be produced quickly and made available to all interested parties in the organization. This information should include trends and moving averages rather than variance analysis. Patterns and trends can be used to control performance by applying a 'management by exception' approach. Rolling forecasts and benchmarking/league tables should also be used and the actual performance against KPIs reported. Under devolved leadership, such information is produced primarily for local managers to improve their own performance, while keeping senior managers informed.

Resources as needed

Resources should be provided when required. Resource planning is still essential but it should be done as near as possible to the required date rather than a long time in advance in the original budget.

Local teams use resources as they need them based on their current requirements and up-to-date information rather than an out-of-date budget. Overall control can be exercised by a series of preset limits (e.g. a cost to income ratio of no more than, say, 35%). For small projects, more authority to use resources could be devolved to the appropriate teams.

Central services, such as Information Systems or Personnel, should operate on an internal market basis at predetermined prices. This will ensure that they will only be used when necessary; if a service is freely available, it tends to be overused. This should also bring about an increase in the efficiency of central services as they respond to the demands made upon them. (This theory is also embodied in Charles Handy's *Doughnut Principle* of management.)

Co-ordination as needed

Do not rely on annual budgets: plan more frequently by making periodic service-level agreements with other teams. Manage your short-term capacity in real time by adjusting it according to demand. The whole organization will be more efficient if other teams are seen as internal customers or suppliers. Co-ordination will be improved if teams listen to their customers and respond accordingly. This is different from viewing customer demands as part of your predetermined budget plan. What customers want may not fit in with your budget and you may try to amend their requests to make them fit. How much better it is to respond to customer demands by giving customers what they want, when they want it, instead of being constrained by an out-of-date plan.

Robin Fraser, one of the co-founders of the Beyond Budgeting movement, has described 'Beyond Budgeting' organizations as those which meet their critical success factors better than their competitors by adopting the devolved leadership management model. Two such companies will now be described.

Example 16.1	# Svenska Handelsbanken

The most frequently quoted example of a Beyond Budgeting organization is the Swedish bank, Svenska Handelsbanken (SHB). At the end of 2010, it had about 750 branches (over 100 of which are in Great Britain) in 22 countries worldwide and approximately 10,000 staff. Its operating profit for 2010 was £1.3 billion and its assets totalled £205 billion.

One function of its head office in Stockholm is to create new products in response to requests from its branches. However, each branch can decide what price to charge its customers for these products and, if they wish, they can charge different prices to different customers. The responsibility is theirs; each branch must make its own decisions and be assessed on the overall profitability that it achieves relative to its peers.

These pricing decisions are based on the high level of 'customer intimacy' the branch has with each of its customers. It does not adopt a mass-marketing, one-size-fits-all approach, it does not use central advertising and it does not issue product brochures. Each branch advertises locally to the extent it thinks appropriate and produces a branch business plan on a regular basis (primarily for its own use – no one approves it). There are no sales targets or centralized product campaigns.

Branches are responsible for their own customers, with 98% of all credit decisions being made at branch level. Each branch is a profit centre; reporting to head office is restricted to a few profit and efficiency ratios on a monthly basis. Each branch manager has the responsibility for deciding:

- how many staff to employ;
- staff skill profiles;
- how much to pay each employee;
- which customers to approach;
- what products to offer;
- what prices to charge.

This autonomy is reflected in Svenska Handelsbanken's well-used slogan, 'the branch is the bank'. This independence is reinforced by SHB's Internet banking activities. There is not just one SHB Internet banking site; each branch has its own website through which existing accounts can be operated if the customer wishes to do so. The service is free of charge and is viewed as a labour-saving benefit by the branch and, therefore, a cost minimization device. Branches adopt a 'church spire' approach to keeping their customer base local; customers should be physically visible from the top of an imaginary spire adjacent to the branch office. Branches believe this helps them to achieve a high level of 'customer intimacy', an essential requirement for their way of doing business. One result of this is the very low level of bad debts they incur.

SHB has only three management levels: president/CEO, executive vice president and branch manager. This results in a very flat structure where even the CEO is only two steps away from the customer. It is managed 'bottom up' and has no annual master plan. Its aim is 'to provide better service at lower cost' (see Figure 16.6).

For more than 30 years, the bank has had only one corporate goal, 'to achieve a higher return on equity than the average of comparable banks in its marketplace'. The direction given to branches is also very simple: each one must aim to be better than average. Of course, this means that half of them will fail! This would be very demotivating and counter-productive *if penalties were consequential*. However, penalties are not imposed and the process is seen as a learning and improvement opportunity. The high level of responsibility that a branch manager has to run his or her own business and the visibility of his or her branch's performance are the main drivers to improve.

Performance is always measured in a relative fashion. At the broadest level, taking the whole bank as a single entity, SHB is compared with other banks using return on equity as the main performance indicator. At the regional level, the various regions are compared with each other using return on equity and the cost to income ratio. At the branch level, inter-branch comparisons are made using the following: cost to

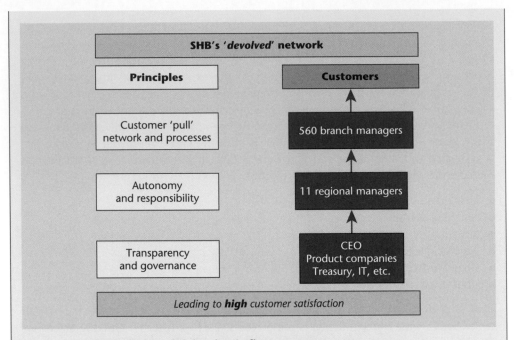

Figure 16.6 Svenska Handelsbanken's flat structure
Source: from 'Beyond Budgeting Round Table' (BBRT), reproduced by kind permission of the BBRT

income, profit per employee and the total profit figure. Branches also report on the profitability of their medium and large customers.

Internal league tables (a form of benchmarking) are created, published and made available to all employees; this information is not restricted to certain special groups but is available to **all** employees. They are created at three levels: bank, region and branch (see Figure 16.7). Branches at the top of the tables have nothing to lose by sharing their 'winning ways' with branches at the bottom, if asked to do so by them. On the contrary, the company as a whole benefits from this knowledge-sharing process and all employees benefit from this in the profit-sharing scheme.

SHB's management model is an exemplar of 'devolved leadership'. It considers budgetary control systems to be incompatible with this model and so does not use budgets (and has not done so for the past 35 years). It recognizes that budgets are the result of negotiations and static assumptions, dictating predetermined actions in a world of rapid change. SHB believes it is better to know its present position rather than make guesses about the future. It understands that 'better-than-budget' performance may not be good enough in a very competitive world. It prefers to benchmark itself against its competitors – a relative rather than an absolute measure.

It uses the following *adaptive processes* in place of budgets:

- a deeply rooted corporate culture of responsibility and genuine empowerment;
- benchmarking at three levels: company, region and branch;
- internal support-function pricing (sometimes possible to outsource if cheaper);
- ongoing discussions about self-improvement;

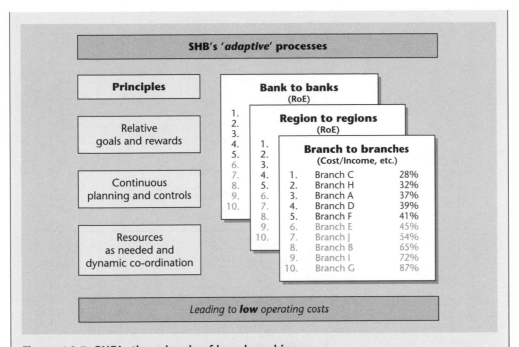

Figure 16.7 SHB's three levels of benchmarking
Source: from 'Beyond Budgeting Round Table' (BBRT), reproduced by kind permission of the BBRT

- profit-sharing model focuses minds on its overall corporate objective;
- employees are trusted.

SHB does not give annual bonuses but it does have a profit-sharing scheme which applies to all employees. One-third of annual profits (over and above the average profit of its 'basket' of competitor banks) is put into a deferred retirement income fund and invested for the long term, mostly in the bank's own shares. **The annual amount appropriated to each employee is exactly the same in monetary value.** This means that the clerks at individual branches receive the same value as the head office directors! As this money is not accessible until retirement, 'short-termism' is discouraged in employees. Also, consider the motivating effect of this; each employee, irrespective of their position in the bank, will feel as valued as the CEO. *The size of the team becomes the size of the whole organization and everybody is a shareholder and pulls in the same direction.*

In 2006, Deutsche Bank compared the performance for 2005 of 30 leading European banks using two important ratios, costs as a percentage of income and costs as a percentage of total loans. SHB came **top** in both categories (see Figure 16.8). In October 2011, SHB was rated top for customer satisfaction for the third year running, in an independent survey (by EPSI Rating) of UK banks' personal and business customers. Customer satisfaction has been consistently higher than its UK high-street competitors. In May 2011, SHB was placed second on the list of the strongest banks in the world published by Bloomberg.

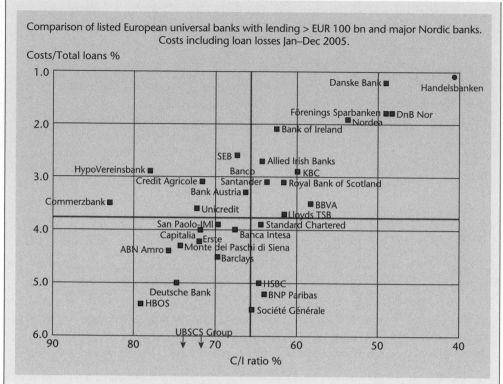

Figure 16.8 Best cost to income ratio

Source: from 'Beyond Budgeting Round Table' (BBRT), reproduced by kind permission of the BBRT

Example 16.2	# The Toyota production system

Toyota is one of the biggest and most successful companies in the world. In 2011 it had 318,000 employees, sales of 19,000 billion yen and an operating income of 468 billion yen. The following paragraphs give an insight into how this success has been achieved. However, it can be categorically stated that budgetary control systems are in no way responsible since the Toyota production system does not use them to drive performance.

Toyota takes customer satisfaction very seriously. This is reflected in the results of a J. D. Power Customer Satisfaction Index which put Toyota in first place (followed by Mazda, BMW and Volvo). It operates a 'pull' system, responding to customer orders, rather than trying to sell what it has made. As far as possible, it provides manufacturing resources as they are required through its sophisticated just-in-time system. The Toyota production system does not use budgets; it does make plans but targets are separate from them and are aspirational.

Its employees work in small self-coordinated teams and are encouraged to think of ways of improving the production system. Every single employee is encouraged to challenge the system by suggesting changes. All ideas are treated with respect, even if they only result in very minor changes saving just a few pence per car. This *kaisen* approach of continuous improvement is a fundamental part of Toyota's working practices. In just one year in its Kentucky, USA plant, 100,000 suggestions were made, approximately 90,000 of which were implemented!

As well as kaisen, Toyota encourages a *genchi genbutsu* ('go and see for yourself') approach which emphasizes the importance of experiencing problems first-hand rather than reading about them in a report. Reports tend to be abstract simplifications of reality and solutions created at a distance can sometimes miss vital aspects of the problem. (This approach is similar to the management accounting techniques discussed in this book; they are abstract models – hopefully useful ones – but can never be as rich as the reality they attempt to represent.)

Genchi genbutsu has been referred to as 'getcha boots on' and go and have a look at the problem yourself. This fits in with the devolved leadership principle of performing business processes via a lean network of accountable teams. Toyota believes that, if the processes are right, the profits will follow, a significantly different approach from keeping expenditure within predetermined budget targets.

But Toyota's aim goes well beyond making good cars. Its unique corporate philosophy is that of:

> *Seeking harmony between people, society, the global environment and a sustainable development of society through making things.*

It strives to achieve and maintain mutual trust and respect in its employee relations.

It manages by means (e.g. satisfying customers) rather than ends (e.g. meeting annual targets). It sees itself as a living system, organic rather than rigidly structured; it acknowledges change as a way of life.

Toyota believes in open, transparent information; it communicates ideas to employees using 'A3s', posters on A3-size paper. This means that the information on these has to be concise and clearly expressed, using illustrations where appropriate. These 'bite-sized' chunks of information are much more likely to be read than multiple-page instruction manuals. This is one of the tools it uses to build consensus which, in turn, allows it to exercise effective governance.

Toyota is one of the most successful companies to have adopted a management model based on the Beyond Budgeting principles. An independent opinion of the magnitude of Toyota's success is provided by Jon Ashworth's article in the 28 April 2007 edition of the magazine *The Business* – see Figure 16.9.

The late Jeremy Hope, the co-founder of the Beyond Budgeting movement, in an IBM survey of CEOs, has stated his opinion that, 'Competitive advantage will increasingly come from the choice of business management model'. Toyota Motor Corporation's Chairman, Fujio Cho, appears to agree with him saying that, 'Toyota views its culture as its most competitive weapon'. The Beyond Budgeting business model seems to be at the heart of Toyota's success even if Toyota does not call it that!

'It may only have been a matter of time but the news this week that Toyota has finally overtaken General Motors (GM) to become the world's biggest car maker marks the end of an era. Detroit, once one of the world's industrial capitals, is in irreversible decline, dragged down by its archaic cost structures and working practices. Like in all matters industrial, the power continues to shift east.

Toyota, one of the world's most efficient companies, sold 2.35 m vehicles in the first three months of 2007, beating GM's 2.26 m sales during the quarter. The Japanese car giant's quarterly sales in the US, the critical battleground for the industry, were up 9% year-on-year compared with 3% for GM. The Japanese car maker is widely expected to be the world's top seller for 2006, with global sales of 9.34 m units. GM sold 9.098 m.

Toyota's market share leapt to 15.6% in the quarter, up from 9.3% in 2000; conversely, GM, which commanded 28.1% of the US market seven years ago, saw its share slip to a miserable 23.1%.

GM is cutting North American production by 1 m units and closing 12 North American factories; conversely, Toyota has announced two new factory openings to add to its six North American sites, one in Ontario, Canada; a second in Mississippi, opening in 2010. By next year, the company will have the capacity to make 2 m vehicles a year in North America, up from 1.5 m in 2006.

Toyota's success piles fresh pain on Detroit's Big Three car makers – GM, Ford and Chrysler – which are struggling to adapt to changing consumer tastes while burdened by billions of dollars in pension and healthcare costs. These amount to $18 bn (£8.9 bn, 13 bn euros) in the case of Chrysler alone; the huge legacy costs of Chrysler's retired workers adds $1,000 to the cost of every car rolling off the production line.

American motorists are abandoning gas-guzzlers for more efficient European-style cars and vans. Toyota, having invested millions in factories and a distribution network in the US, is perfectly placed to tap into this shift: the Toyota Camry saloon is America's top-selling car; Toyota's petrol-electric hybrids, led by the Prius and a hybrid version of the Camry, broke through the 500,000 sales mark for the first time in March.

Toyota sold 61,635 hybrids in the year to end-March, a 68% increase on the previous 12 months. Pump prices in the US have risen 33% in the past 11 weeks, according to the US Energy Department.

It is no surprise that Toyota, along with Honda, Nissan and the rest, are stealing a march on Detroit. The US giants have the wrong products and find it hard to adapt. Powerful trade unions have them boxed in.

Small wonder DaimlerChrysler is exploring selling the US side of its business, in a humiliating admission that the German company's great American adventure has failed miserably.'

Figure 16.9 'Toyota motors ahead as Detroit's dinosaurs get left further behind'
Source: Ashworth, J. (2007) 'Toyota motors ahead as Detroit dinosaurs get left further behind', *The Business*, 28 April, with permission of the Press Holdings Media Group (The Spectator)

Membership of the BBRT

Organizations that support or have supported the Beyond Budgeting movement include: A C Neilsen, Aldi Supermarkets, American Express, Anheuser Busch, Barclays Bank, BT Group, BG Transco, Boots the Chemists, Cadbury-Schweppes, CIMA, Coors Brewers,

Diageo, De Beers, Deutsche Bank, IBM Business Consulting Services, Kingfisher, KPMG Consulting, Mars Confectionery, Port of Tyne Authority, Mastercard, Mencap, Sainsbury Supermarkets, Siemens, Sightsavers International, South West Airlines, Standard Life, Telecom New Zealand, Thames Water, The World Bank, UBS and Unilever. These are just some that you may have heard of; there are many more which you may not have. Not all these organizations embrace the Beyond Budgeting philosophy 100%, but they all agree that it includes some very interesting ideas worthy of adoption.

Limitations

The Beyond Budgeting philosophy is to manage in a way that supports, not conflicts with, the organization's critical success factors and the interests of stakeholders. Although this is suitable for **all** organizations, those companies working in Industrial Age conditions might find it hard to make a case for change. For example, a company producing cement powder from raw limestone based in a single location with no competitors and no difficulty in attracting and retaining suitable employees should organize itself to maximize efficiency, almost irrespective of its impact on customer service and employee morale, so that it can achieve the highest returns to shareholders.

Another interesting case is the UK Royal Mail which, until recently, had a monopoly on the delivery of non-business letters, reinforced by law with prices controlled by the national government. When this was so, there would have been no point in instigating the Beyond Budgeting approach. However, the monopoly has now been removed, regulations relaxed and competition encouraged. If the Royal Mail is to survive, it should consider adopting the Beyond Budgeting model of devolved leadership as its structure is already decentralized with many similar branches in existence. Internal competition between branches could transform not only its work practices but also its finances.

If this transformation was attempted, a huge shift in its internal culture would be essential as, at the moment, it is very much a 'command and control' type of organization. Vested interests exist on the side both of management and of the trade union. Both would have to want to achieve the necessary changes but this would entail each of them giving up a significant amount of power. It is disappointing that the Royal Mail, despite having shown significant interest in the Beyond Budgeting movement, has not adopted the devolved leadership management model.

Without doubt, it is easier to establish Beyond Budgeting practices in brand new organizations than transform established companies which have traditional hierarchical functional structures and have used traditional performance management processes (including budgetary control techniques) for many years. In 1513, the Italian scholar and diplomat Nicholas Machiavelli wrote in his book *The Prince*:

> *there is nothing more difficult to execute, nor more dubious of success, nor more dangerous to administer than to introduce a new order of things; for he who introduces it has all those who profit from the old order as his enemies, and he has only lukewarm allies in all those who might profit from the new.*

This is just as true today as it was 500 years ago. It offers an explanation as to why, if it is such a good idea, Beyond Budgeting has not been more widely adopted. But, although difficult, transformations are possible; at the time of writing, the giant Norwegian oil company, Statoil, is undertaking this huge change process. It will cost many millions in resources but it obviously thinks it worthwhile.

Robin Fraser has said that such transformations stand the greatest chance of success when it is recognized that a major change in leadership is needed, not just a change of accounting systems. He advises that the first step is to assess the 'case for change'. This involves envisaging the whole model (i.e. all 12 principles), understanding the changes required and the costs and benefits of adopting it. If urgency through dissatisfaction with the organization's performance is high enough and the case for change compelling enough, there is a good chance of success. It must be led from the top but in a way that is consistent with devolved leadership. It is not an easy transformation, but judging by the success of pioneers like Handelsbanken and Toyota, adopting the model is not a matter of whether, but when!

The counter point of view

Having read the above summary of the Beyond Budgeting philosophy, you should now consider some of the arguments against abandoning the budget. The following sub-sections present a counter point of view to each of the six 'Beyond Budgeting' adaptive processes stated above. They are the personal opinions of Nigel Burton who has written most of the 'Manager's point of view' sections at the end of each chapter. During his career he has been the accountant, financial director and managing director in an international manufacturing company, and he speaks with the authority of many years' personal experience of these issues. It is fair to say that, although he believes that the practice of budgeting needs to be continually improved, the total abandonment of budgeting would be detrimental to the vast majority of organizations.

Goals

If you want to be number one in the industry, the first thing to do is to establish the sales and profits of the current leader, and work out a strategy for exceeding them. This will give you a timescale and a required growth rate. You then need to go into the detail, to work out exactly how you are going to generate the increased sales/profits over the coming years, and how much you need to do each year. In other words, you need detailed annual budgets indicating what you need to do to achieve the long-term targets. In this way, budgets can be used as strategic tools rather than mere control mechanisms. At the same time, there is no reason why you cannot benchmark your performance against competitors as you go along, although this will always be a retrospective procedure.

Rewards

The use of hindsight to determine cash bonuses sounds exemplary but is it possible to separate internal and external business environment factors from the efforts of individuals or discrete teams to produce a monetary formula for the calculation of bonuses? Is it possible to eliminate subjectivity from the bonus calculations? Maybe the bonus should be left entirely to the discretion of the manager, who is best placed to make such a judgement, but do you really want a significant part of your remuneration to be subject to the whim of your superior, whose own bonus might be enhanced if he or she can keep costs pared down to a minimum?

Basing a bonus formula on a small group of KPIs sounds fine at first hearing but it can be difficult to find ones which are objective, quantifiable and relevant. Also, KPIs can be manipulated in just the same way as budget targets by the playing of 'KPI games'.

There is no such thing as a perfectly fair bonus scheme. External factors will always have a bearing on an individual's performance. It is his or her job to deal with them, and achieve the shareholders' requirements, notwithstanding the difficulties thrown in the way. Effort is all very laudable, but should hardly lead to a bonus if the company has made a loss.

Planning

A predetermined annual budget does not preclude any thought being given to the way the business is progressing, either long term or short term. For instance, consider an annual production budget containing details of capacity, labour requirements, material costs, etc. This does not prevent the actual monthly production plans being prepared on the basis of actual requirements at the time rather than the original production budget. The existence of a budget does not cause companies to ignore up-to-date information and stick with their original plans no matter what.

Controls

Trends and moving averages may be useful in some companies, but they can be very misleading, for instance, when a significant past event drops out of the moving average calculation. For other companies, variance analysis is perfectly suitable for assessing performance 'at a glance'.

Resources

The annual budget acts as a **guide** to future requirements. Companies do not sanction expenditure on capital projects or additional personnel just because it was included in the original budget; all such expenditure needs to be justified at the time. Similarly, management are highly unlikely to turn down a profitable activity simply because it was not included in the budget. If a business thinks there is a good chance of making a profit by doing something outside its budgeted activities, it will find the necessary resources one way or another.

Co-ordination

Co-ordination is a normal management function. Short-term planning and capacity management are part of the day-to-day functions of management. Listening to internal and external customers' requirements is a TQM idea, and a very good one. It is in no way constrained by the existence of an annual budget. Obviously, managers have to react to the real world. The budget is simply a yardstick against which to assess the impact of their actions.

Better Budgeting

In 2004 the Chartered Institute of Management Accountants (CIMA) and the Institute of Chartered Accountants in England and Wales (ICAEW) held a joint round table event called 'Better Budgeting'. There were 32 delegates in all including the BBC, GlaxoSmithKline, J Sainsbury plc, Unilever, the Beyond Budgeting Round Table, Atos KPMG Consulting and the University of Bristol.

The idea was to allow top managers from large respected companies and a select few academics and consultants to openly discuss the current state of budgeting and comment on its usefulness or otherwise. The findings of this forum were published in a report entitled 'Better Budgeting'. The text below is a highly summarized account, in bullet point form, of some of the main points arising from the open discussion:

- Budgets suffered a very bad press in recent years based on their high cost, lengthy preparation time and their associated 'gaming' behaviour.
- But most organizations thought budgets were indispensable as they provided a control framework without which management would not be possible.
- However, they admitted that formal budgetary control systems could discourage value-creating, entrepreneurial attitudes; for example, new projects may be abandoned if budgetary resources are exhausted before the year-end.
- Resources may be inappropriately concentrated on perfecting budgetary control systems at the expense of competitive awareness and agility, but, when this happens, it can be countered by a culture of openness and flexibility.
- Budgeting has significantly improved over the last 20 years; organizations are adapting, rather than abandoning, budgets. For example, rolling forecasts are now used much more often, particularly where the business environment changes rapidly such as the telecommunications industry.
- It is important to note that 'forecasts' are not the same as 'budgets'; semantics are an important aspect of this discussion. The data in forecasts is much more summarized and 'high-level' than the detailed information in budgets.
- Creating a budget forces managers from different parts of the organization to discuss things with each other; this inter-functional communication and co-ordination is very beneficial and may not otherwise happen in such depth.
- Delegates thought that a culture of trust and empowerment was necessary for modern budgeting to thrive but acknowledged that, often, the prevailing culture of budgetary control systems was one of blame and mistrust.
- Delegates agreed that the common practice of linking personal remuneration systems to budget targets often resulted in dysfunctional behaviour. (Interestingly, only a few of the delegates operated personal remuneration systems that were linked directly to budget targets.)

- Budgets are evolving incrementally rather than changing rapidly.
- The bottom-up participative approach is gaining favour compared with the top-down centralized one.

The 'Better Budgeting' report goes on to give summaries of the forum's three main presentations. The first is in favour of the continuing improvement of budgetary control systems, the second advocates the abolition of budgets and the third presents the results of a survey of attitudes towards budgeting. *Readers are strongly recommended to study the full report for themselves*; it is freely available as a *technical report* from CIMA's website (see 'Further reading').

The manager's point of view (by Gary Burmiston)

Settling down on a Friday night after another week at work and it's time to have that small glass of Chablis – a fruity little number I've been looking forward to. Bottle at the ready, glass at the ready, now where's that corkscrew? Five minutes of searching through a drawer, which is well overdue for a tidy, and corkscrew is present and correct. Attempting to remove the cork it splits, second attempt is more successful and the cork is removed but, as the wine sloshes into the glass, I notice small pieces of cork in the wine. Never mind, I'll make do and ignore the pieces. However, on sipping the wine it has a strange taste, cork taint if I'm not mistaken. I persevere but it's not what I had in mind. Ten minutes after settling down I start drinking poor quality wine.

Corks are known for being flawed and their flaws are many:

- they are known as being relatively expensive, with variable quality;
- cork dust cannot be avoided;
- cork taint (2-4-6 Trichloroanisole or TCA to be precise) has a negative effect on wine quality.

Surely there must be something better.

There is; it's called a screw cap and yet when I recall my purchasing experience I immediately bypassed the wines with screw caps as not being 'proper' wines, they surely must be somewhat inferior not to have a cork.

And it's this type of logic that's seen constantly with budgets.

Outlined in this chapter are a plethora of problems with traditional budgeting techniques and the issues outlined are not just hypothetical. As someone who has been responsible for producing a range of companies' budgets over the last 15 years, I find the issues highlighted in this chapter to be wholly consistent with my experiences.

Real examples include:

- **Time.** The time taken to produce a budget can be almost as long as the year itself; the maximum that I've experienced is over seven months. Usually this time is extended due to multiple 'sign-offs' required at various stages of the process. The sign-off process alone can sometimes take longer than the actual budget production process. This is particularly apparent when foreign parents are concerned. The budget is first produced and signed off at a departmental level. It's then consolidated and signed off at a business unit level before going on to be consolidated and signed off at a country level before being ultimately consolidated and signed off at a corporate level. Only by starting a budget process in March can it be completed in time for the following January.

- **Relevance.** Although it can take up to seven months to produce a budget the chances of its being useful are diminished because of the knowledge that has been gained in the months that followed and because of what has happened in the external environment. The starting points for many budgets are the sales and price assumptions. Many changes can happen in seven months to the point where in one organization the budget, which had taken many hours, much effort and caused huge debate in all parts of the business, was used only for January reporting and then was totally discarded as being irrelevant. A price decrease of a major product had rendered the assumptions in the budget irrelevant!

- **Game playing.** Human nature is one of self-preservation and nowhere, in an organizational environment, is this more visible than in the budget-setting process. There are many examples that could be used, but to give a flavour consider the purchasing manager who is incentivized on creating a positive purchase cost variance, i.e. how far below the standard cost he can actually procure goods for. Great in theory; which company wouldn't want to challenge the purchasing manager to get better deals? However, it is also the purchasing manager who sets the standard cost for the goods produced! So he sets a high standard cost and when his actual costs come in lower than standard, he gets a good bonus. However, the selling prices are based on the standard cost. The impact of this is that it limits the ability of the salesmen to negotiate lower prices to gain sales. They assume, incorrectly, that they would be selling the product at a loss. Therefore, as a result of the budget process, sales could be lost.

Budgets are truly and absolutely flawed. Budgets are pilloried as being out of touch with the needs of modern business and accused of taking too long, costing too much and encouraging all sorts of perverse behaviour.

And yet, like corks, we're happy to put up with their limitations. Despite people being aware of the problems, companies by and large regard the budget system and the accompanying process as indispensable.

Corks have a positive image and are seen as emotionally appealing. They are part of the wine culture and the opening of a bottle is almost a ceremony – that pop as the cork comes out of the bottle can signify the start of an event. Do budgets also hold this romanticized sense of experience for us?

The budgeting process has its limitations, and techniques such as Beyond Budgeting show, where it's been implemented, improved results. A powerful case for change and yet research claims that as many as 99% of European companies have a budget in place and no intention of abandoning it. So what is it that's stopping organizations from making the move?

Beyond Budgeting does have its limitations as highlighted within this chapter; however, the major obstacle experienced in industry appears to be taking that first step in agreeing that Beyond Budgeting is the way for an organization to move forward. Being involved with a number of organizations which have tried, and to date failed, to introduce an alternative to the budget process I have observed some common themes as to why senior managers appear reluctant to take those major steps which will drive towards a successful outcome.

First there is the issue of leadership. The success of Svenska Handelsbanken was driven initially by the vision and determination of one man, the CEO, Jan Wallender. He knew the organization had to change and it was his vision of a devolved network that permeated throughout all parts of the organization in a way that inspired people enough to change. Nowadays the decision to move to an alternative to budgeting is still taken at the highest level, but as soon as that decision is made it is often passed down to a project team to implement.

As soon as this happens the implementation is increasingly doomed to failure. All too often this top priority can fall down the list as other issues arise. It could be argued that Beyond Budgeting is just an accounting technique that can be copied and replicated in all organizations; doing A and B will result in the outcome C no matter where or who you are. In the same way David Beckham could argue that taking free kicks is just a matter of kicking the ball in the right place at the right speed. Done correctly, anyone should be able to replicate what he achieves. And yet this rarely happens.

Beyond Budgeting is not a change of technique. It is a change of culture, a change that needs to be driven from the highest level. Project teams are not able to do this. Hearts and minds need to be won over as much as, if not more than, logical intuition.

Secondly, another huge hurdle to overcome is the nature of its implementation. To achieve this successfully it is an all or nothing implementation; you cannot run both budgeting and Beyond Budgeting in parallel to test the water. As mentioned above, this is not just a technique; it is a cultural change and an organization needs to commit fully to it to reap its benefits. The analogy used by the Beyond Budgeting Round Table is that if you want to change the UK to driving on the right you wouldn't stage the implementation by saying on Monday morning buses and taxis can drive on the right and then we'll evaluate the success of the implementation before allowing cars and lorries to change from left to right. Implementation does not have a safety net to fall back on – a very scary scenario for many chief executives – highlighting the importance of strong leadership.

Finally, while there is a good case for change, there is also an excuse for no change. One of the first comments senior managers will make when presented with such a change will be, 'Show me where this has been done and the impact it has had'. Current beacons are few and far between. Svenska Handelsbanken is the leader and other organizations such as Toyota are following to a lesser extent. The critical mass of organizations which can demonstrate the benefits they are achieving through replacing the budget process has not yet been achieved. Therefore, each new company will be seen as an early adopter when many just want to be followers. Why upset the apple cart when they have something in place which works? They know it's flawed, they know it doesn't optimize performance; they know it could be better but they also know it meets their needs and are prepared to put up with the issues budgeting causes. It could be argued that no organization has ever failed due to its budget; it is the actuals that count. So why throw away everything people know for something which is unproven on a mass scale?

Of all the management accounting techniques, budgeting is the one that is used by the majority of companies. It is also the one that is most open to the vagaries of human behaviour, and the examples and issues highlighted in the chapter happen continuously in most organizations on a daily basis. The case for change is great but the people still need to be convinced by the alternatives.

Budgeting as a technique is not necessarily poor – it is how people **use** budgeting that is poor. Beyond Budgeting offers a new way of managing your business without budgets. Alternatively, if the Better Budgeting approach is adopted to make businesses work better, it will not be enough to improve the budgeting process; peoples' behaviours will have to improve.

Summary

The current disquiet with budgetary control systems is being addressed in many organizations by attempting to improve them. This is the route that the majority of businesses are taking. However, there now exists an alternative way of overcoming the acknowledged difficulties. There is a new management model called Beyond Budgeting which is particularly suitable for the twenty-first century. This is a *systemic* management model, one which should respond much better than the traditional *deterministic* model in today's highly competitive, fast-changing business environment.

Its main philosophy is devolved leadership through radical decentralization, a kind of permanent empowerment to units within a network organization rather than a functional hierarchy. Getting rid of traditional budgetary control systems is a *consequence* of this new model as the tools of command and control are incompatible with it. However, if budgets are abolished, something must be put in their place; these are the adaptive processes proposed by Beyond Budgeting. (There are six principles of devolved leadership and six adaptive processes.) In the right context, this new management model should lead to sustainable competitive advantage; Handelsbanken and Toyota are examples of this, demonstrating the value of the model.

It is pertinent that the foreword to Hope and Fraser's book, *Beyond Budgeting*, is written by one of the most distinguished management accountants of the twentieth century, Charles T. Horngren of Stanford University, USA. In his final paragraph he states the following:

Most of the solutions generally proposed for management problems involve putting something new into the organization. In this regard, Beyond Budgeting is very different. Perhaps uniquely, it proposes taking something powerful out to make room for something new and even more powerful. We have all the tools and techniques we need. What we lack is the right overall context for them to work effectively.

Further reading

'Better Budgeting – a joint report from CIMA and ICAEW'. See the CIMA website, www.cimaglobal.com/Thought-Leadership/Research-topics/Budgeting-and-planning/Better-budgeting/

Bishop, J. (2004) 'Beyond budgeting in practice', *Chartered Accountants Journal*, Vol. 83, Issue 11, December.

Bourne, M. and Neely, A. (2002) 'Cause and effect', *Financial Management*, September.

Bragdon, J. (2006) *Profit for life: How Capitalism Excels*, Society for Organizational Learning, Cambridge, MA.

Brignall, S., Fitzgerald, L., Johnson, R. and Silvestro, R. (1991) 'Performance measurement in service businesses', *Management Accounting* (*UK*), November.

Cassell, M. (2003) 'Can we budge it?', *Financial Management* (CIMA), November.

Hamel, G. with Breen, B. (2007) *The Future of Management*, Harvard Business School Press, Boston, MA.

Henschen, D. (2005) 'Amex ends budgeting as usual', *Intelligent Enterprise*, Vol. 8, Issue 4, 1 April.

Hope, J. and Fraser, R. (2003) *Beyond Budgeting – How Managers Can Break Free from the Annual Performance Trap*, Harvard Business School Press, Boston, MA.

Hope, J. and Fraser, R. (2003) 'New ways of setting rewards: the Beyond Budgeting model', *California Management Review*, Vol. 45, Issue 4, Summer.

Howard, M. (2004) 'Go figure', *Financial Management* (CIMA), March.

Hyndman, N., Jones, R. and Pendlebury, M. (2003) 'Use it or lose it', *Financial Management* (CIMA), November.

Jensen, M. C. (2001) 'Corporate budgeting is broken – let's fix it', *Harvard Business Review*, November.

Liker, J. (2003) *The Toyota Way – 14 Management Principles from the world's greatest manufacturer*, McGraw-Hill, New York.

Lynch, R. and Cross, K. F. (1995) *Measure Up! Yardsticks for Continuous Improvement*, 2nd edition, Basil Blackwell, Oxford.

Marginson, D. and Ogden, S. (2005) 'Budgeting and innovation', *Financial Management* (CIMA), April.

Prickett, R. (2003) 'Beyond budgeting case study 1, the private company', *Financial Management* (CIMA), November.

Saetre, E. and Bogsnes, B. of Statoil, 'Break with the Budget', http://www.thefinancedirector.com/contributors/contributor316/

Shim, J. and Siegel, J. (2005) *Budgeting Basics and Beyond*, Wiley, Hoboken, NJ.

Stockdyk, J., 'Budgeting a thing of the past for Statoil', http://www.accountingweb.co.uk/cgi-bin/item.cgi?id=163586&d=526&h=524&f=525Medibed

Medibed

Background

Medibed manufactures hospital beds. These are complicated mobile platforms with several moving parts. It is located on the outskirts of Bromsgrove and has good connections to the motorway system. Bromsgrove is centrally situated in the UK and has a good-quality workforce. Medibed has never experienced any difficulty in finding appropriately trained staff during its expansion over the last 12 years.

The business started when George Wright was made redundant from a firm which is now one of its rivals. As a design engineer, George had some ideas about how the hospital beds he was helping to design could be improved. However, before he had the chance to develop these, his previous firm suffered a severe cash crisis and went into administration, emerging as a much smaller operation under new ownership. George invested his £30,000 redundancy pay into his new business, Medibed, and persuaded a local bank to invest a further £70,000 (secured against his domestic residence).

Starting with only three employees, Medibed has grown gradually over the years to become a well-established, medium-sized company specializing in a single product. George is now 57 years old and has decided to step back from the operational side of the business and cut down his input to one or two days a week. Instead of being both chairman and managing director, he has retained the chairmanship but has recently appointed a new managing director, Alex Medlev, from outside the business. Alex is 43 years old and was the production manager for six years of a firm producing office furniture.

It has been a difficult year for Medibed with competition becoming much more aggressive than in previous years. These difficulties can be seen from the following extracts from a recent management meeting chaired by the managing director:

Managing director
You all know that the figures show that the labour force is working below standard. But I'm not sure I believe it. I walk round the factory every day and I don't see any slacking, the atmosphere is good and I have not seen any evidence of demotivation among the operatives. I'm not convinced our budgetary control system is telling us the whole truth.

Purchasing manager
Well, it has served us well for many years. I'm not sure we can start to ignore it just because it is telling us something we would prefer was not happening.

Production director

It's all very well for you to say that but I think Alex has a point. I realize we have to keep our costs down to remain competitive but I am not convinced sourcing a significant portion of our material components from Eastern Europe was a good idea. I reckon if we had stuck with our original UK suppliers in the first place we would have been better off all round, despite their higher prices. I suggest we reconsider our position on this as soon as possible.

Purchasing manager

I don't agree. Just look at the figures and you will see how much money we have saved on our material costs. That is what I was asked to do and I've done it.

Production manager

I admit the figures look good but we've all played budgetary games at some time or other. I think this is an area we really need to tighten up on.

Sales director

I think we should remember that the bottom line is still positive. It has been difficult since we had that quality crisis in the first quarter of the year and had to cancel our attendance at the London Trade Show. But we have managed to stay in the black. Admittedly, our volume is well below the original budget but it could have been a lot worse; our past reputation has helped greatly but we can't rely on that any longer. I hope we will soon be in a position to increase our advertising spend up to previous levels but we must maintain the quality of our product. It is absolutely vital to our long-term success. I can't stress that enough.

Managing director

I can't argue with that but I'm not convinced our traditional approach to performance and control is sufficient to help us do that and achieve our objectives in today's turbulent trading conditions. We are already facing a new wave of cheap imports from the Far East. We've got to be more proactive in improving our performance. Some well-known firms are reputed to have given up budgets and seem to be doing alright without them thank you very much. I know it is drastic but I think we have got to be prepared to be radical in our approach in order to survive. With the agreement of our Chairman, I've just commissioned a report about controlling and improving our corporate performance from the management consulting branch of our auditors. I'm expecting to receive it in the near future, just after the end of the financial year.

Medibed's current budgetary control system

Medibed operates a traditional budgetary control system on a quarterly rather than a monthly basis. The financial reporting is also done quarterly. A significant part of the remuneration for the budget-responsible officers is dependent on their achieving their budgets.

The budget responsibilities are as follows:

Operational area	Budget-responsible officer
Sales	Sales director
Materials budget	Purchasing manager
Labour budget	Production manager
Variable overhead budget	Production manager
Fixed overhead budget:	
Marketing	Sales director
Production	Production director
Administration	Managing director

The current financial year has just ended and the actual results for quarter 4 (Q4) are expected very soon. The results for the previous three quarters have been known since just before the management meeting two months ago.

Additional information

- All these budgets **have already been flexed** to the actual level of activity.
- The **original budget profit (OBP)** is £7,550,000.
- The budgeted selling price of one bed is £10,000.
- The actual selling price of one bed is £10,500.
- Variable overheads are absorbed on a labour hour basis.
- Labour operatives can earn bonuses dependent on the completion of their tasks in less than the standard times allowed.

List of attached schedules

1 Summary budget for year and by quarter
2 Materials budget for year and by quarter
3 Labour budget for year and by quarter
4 Variable overheads budget for year and by quarter
5 Marketing fixed overheads budget for year and by quarter
6 Production fixed overheads budget for year and by quarter
7 Administration fixed overheads budget for year and by quarter
8 Sales budget for year and by quarter
9 Summary of actual results
10 Extracts from materials and labour flexed budgets for Q4
11 Extracts from materials and labour actual results for Q4
12 Variance analysis for the first three quarters

1. Summary budget for year and by quarter

Item (£000)	Q1	Q2	Q3	Q4	Year
Materials	3,738	3,429	2,849	3,605	13,621
Labour	2,136	1,936	1,628	2,060	7,760
Variable ohds	534	460	407	515	1,916
Fixed ohds:					
Marketing	1,922	1,701	1,465	1,854	6,942
Production	1,602	1,453	1,221	1,545	5,821
Administration	748	645	570	721	2,684
Total costs	10,680	9,624	8,140	10,300	38,744
Sales revenue	11,890	10,990	9,100	11,550	43,530
Profit	1,210	1,366	960	1,250	4,786

2. Materials budget for year and by quarter

Item (£000)	Q1	Q2	Q3	Q4	Year
Frame	1,495	1,372	1,140	1,442	5,449
Mattress	1,121	1,028	855	1,082	4,086
Motors	523	480	399	504	1,906
Accessories	599	549	455	577	2,180
Total	3,738	3,429	2,849	3,605	13,621

3. Labour budget for year and by quarter

Item (£000)	Q1	Q2	Q3	Q4	Year
Grade A	1,142	904	843	1,090	3,979
Grade B	608	496	407	580	2,091
Grade C	386	536	378	390	1,690
Total	2,136	1,936	1,628	2,060	7,760

4. Variable overheads budget for year and by quarter

Item (£000)	Q1	Q2	Q3	Q4	Year
Assembly	232	201	187	235	855
Finishing	302	259	220	280	1,061
Total	534	460	407	515	1,916

5. Marketing fixed overheads budget for year and by quarter

Item (£000)	Q1	Q2	Q3	Q4	Year
Customer relations	495	412	340	480	1,727
Advertising	210	250	180	240	880
Salaries	910	900	945	920	3,675
Trade shows	307	139	0	214	660
Total	1,922	1,701	1,465	1,854	6,942

6. Production fixed overheads budget for year and by quarter

Item (£000)	Q1	Q2	Q3	Q4	Year
Assembly	492	476	405	506	1,879
Finishing	309	290	251	327	1,177
Materials handling	451	337	215	362	1,365
Salaries	350	350	350	350	1,400
Total	1,602	1,453	1,221	1,545	5,821

7. Administration fixed overheads budget for year and by quarter

Item (£000)	Q1	Q2	Q3	Q4	Year
Accounting	148	152	150	148	598
Heat & light	124	44	44	144	356
Site securlty	75	75	75	75	300
Directors' pay	200	200	200	200	800
General office	48	52	50	48	198
Other	153	122	51	106	432
Total	748	645	570	721	2,684

8. Sales quantity budget for year and by quarter

	Q1	Q2	Q3	Q4	Year
Number of beds	1,189	1,099	910	1,155	4,353

9. Summary of actual results

Item (£000)	Q1 + Q2 + Q3	Q4	Year
Materials	9,540	3,659	13,199
Labour	6,070	2,072	8,142
Variable ohds	1,498	512	2,010
Fixed ohds:			
Marketing	4,806	1,909	6,715
Production	4,402	1,503	5,905
Administration	2,003	684	2,687
Total costs	28,319	10,339	38,658
Sales revenue	34,075	11,632	45,707
Profit	5,756	1,293	7,049

10. Extract from materials and labour flexed budgets for Q4

Materials: Motors	2,880 @ £175 each	= £504,000
Labour: Grade C	43,333 hrs @ £9.00/hr	= £389,997

11. Extract from materials and labour actual results for Q4

Note: Due to a power failure, no work could be done during 1,155 of the 42,210 hours. The operatives used this time to have a general tidy-up of their workplaces and then had to wait in the canteen until the power was restored.

Materials: Motors	2,520 @ £200	= £504,000
Labour: Grade C	42,210 hrs @ £9.50	= £400,995

12. Nine months' (Q1 + Q2 + Q3) variance analysis

Item (£000)	Budget for Q1 + Q2 + Q3	Actuals for Q1 + Q2 + Q3	Cost variances
Materials	10,016	9,540	476 F
Labour	5,700	6,070	370 A
Variable ohds	1,401	1,498	97 A
Fixed ohds:			
Marketing	5,088	4,806	282 F
Production	4,276	4,402	126 A
Administration	1,963	2,003	40 A
Total costs	28,444	28,319	125 F
Sales revenue	31,980	34,075	2,095 F
Profit	3,536	5,756	2,220 F

Tasks:

1 **Variance analysis**
   Using the information provided:
   a) Perform a variance analysis on the Materials (Motors) budget extract for Q4.

   (6 marks)
   b) Perform a variance analysis on the Labour (Grade C) budget extract for Q4.

   (8 marks)
   c) Perform a variance analysis of all budget items for Q4 and present them in a table.

   (4 marks)
   d) Perform a variance analysis of all budget items for the year and present them in a table.

   (4 marks)
   e) Calculate the sales volume variance and the sales price variance for the year.

   (4 marks)
   f) Create a profit reconciliation statement for the year.

   (4 marks)

g) Comment on Medibed's performance for the year.

(20 marks)

Note: Perform the variance analyses in as much detail as the information given will allow.

(Sub-total 50 marks)

2 **Budget games**

Define the term 'budget games'; give six examples of these and state four negative effects they have on companies.

(14 marks)

3 **Beyond Budgeting**

If Medibed adopted the Beyond Budgeting management model and abolished its budgetary control system, state six measures you would recommend it to take to fill the resulting vacuum.

(12 marks)

4 **Balanced scorecard**

Design a balanced scorecard for Medibed utilizing three items for each of the four perspectives.

(24 marks)
(Total 100 marks)

Freeshire Hospital Trust

Background

In common with the rest of the National Health Service, Freeshire Hospital Trust is having to cope with considerable constraints on resources. To address this, a new accountant was appointed two years ago to introduce a decentralized budgetary control system to make managers more accountable for their actions. The new system gave managers full responsibility for their costs. The central overhead support costs are devolved to the departments which buy in these central services.

However, the introduction of the new budgetary control system has not gone well. The chief executive, whose skills lie in the area of managing people rather than in financial control, is perplexed by the performance of the various departments. Last year's adverse variances produced by the orthopaedics department are typical of the situation (see below).

Actual outcome compared with fixed budget (Orthopaedics)

	Actual	Budget	Variance
Annual patient days	10,000	9,000	1,000
Variable costs	£	£	£
Pharmacy	144,000	99,000	45,000 A
Laboratory	109,000	108,000	1,000 A
Meals	54,000	49,500	4,500 A
Laundry	40,000	36,000	4,000 A
Fixed costs			
Staff	310,000	300,000	10,000 A
Other	465,000	460,000	5,000 A
Total:	**1,122,000**	**1,052,500**	**69,500** A

The chief executive is outraged that every variable cost variance is adverse and is, in his view, a demonstration of completely ineffective cost control. Moreover, he is becoming increasingly concerned, not only about the failure to keep within previous budgets, but also by the new budgets for next year which are being proposed by the department managers. Mindful of his lack of financial expertise, the chief executive has decided to bring in a new financial director. The latter has been recruited to investigate the problems with the newly decentralized system and to put forward some proposals on future development. In his initial meetings with senior staff the new financial director obtained the following quotes:

Chief executive

I don't understand it. I didn't have these problems in my last organization. People understood the system and its objectives. People didn't play games, they didn't build 'fudge factors' into their budgets. I don't see any budget reductions made in the light of our cost-saving information technology investment programme. As for the new budget reports, I never know if the variances are real or just a matter of poor phasing of expenditure across the year. I also need more warning of how the year is developing. I want realistic budget figures with a little to stretch people and we have got to have a budget which fits our corporate objectives. Or maybe we should scrap the budget altogether and put one of these new balanced scorecards in its place?

Department manager

I'm not going to put another brave budget forward after last year. Last year they published a league table of performance against budget and I came bottom. This year I will be giving myself plenty of slack. Next year's budget is this year's plus 15 per cent. I am sure they will knock 5 per cent off straight away even without looking at the budget submission. As for the forms, reports and budget procedure, they just take too long. Every month I have to fill this massive form covering what I have spent and even what bills I am going to pay in the future. This is a system designed by accountants for accountants. I've got real work to do. In any case, I never get any feedback on the figures until months later.

Chief accountant

We produce monthly reports with actual spend against budget and never get any credible responses explaining the variances. All we seem to get is complaints about the way we have phased the budgets. They don't understand it's not down to us that their budgets are cut – not that it makes any difference, they never know if they are overspent or not. All levels of management have poor budgetary discipline, the budget is there to be complied with. They're always being creative; it's amazing what gets classed as training when that line is underspent! How can I stop them from messing around with my accounts? Most managers aren't rigorous enough in defining their budget assumptions, especially the board; I keep telling them it's to protect them, especially when things go wrong.

A clinical director

I am fed up with this budgetary control system, it just gives me a headache. Firstly, it's too complex. Secondly, I get the analysis of my expenditure five or six weeks after the month end. Thirdly, I get no explanation of the variances! My staff have also become adept at beating the system. I found one spending her budget on non-essentials just so it wouldn't get cut next year. Another overspent manager negotiated with a local supplier to post-date an invoice into next year. Where will it end?

Tasks:

1. Discuss the chief executive's opinion that the orthopaedics budget is indicative of a complete lack of control. Show the calculations of any figures you use to substantiate your argument.

(20 marks)

2. Explain what you understand by 'budget games'. Using the Freeshire case where possible, give examples of these games.

(28 marks)

3. State the main purpose of balanced scorecards. Also, list their subsidiary benefits/objectives. Compare the concept of lead/lag perspectives in 'for-profit' and 'not-for-profit' organizations.

(18 marks)

4. Design a balanced scorecard for use in a not-for-profit hospital. Give two goals and two performance indicators for each of the perspectives. (Do not show targets.)

(34 marks)
(Total 100 marks)

Review questions

1 Describe the weaknesses of traditional budgetary control systems.
2 Define what is meant by 'budget game'.
3 Give examples of six types of 'budget game'.
4 Explain the effect of employee cash incentive schemes on budget gaming.
5 Describe the 'Beyond Budgeting' management model.
6 List the six principles of 'devolved leadership'.
7 List the six adaptive processes recommended to replace budgeting.
8 Describe the management model used by Svenska Handelsbanken.
9 Describe the management model used by the Toyota production system.
10 Explain the difficulties in the adoption of the 'Beyond Budgeting' model.
11 State the arguments against the 'Beyond Budgeting' model.
12 List the findings of the 'Better Budgeting' Open Forum in 2004.

The answers to all these questions can be found in the text of this chapter.

Balanced scorecards

Introduction

Imagine the following conversation between two friends, Claude and Chantal, who want to go and see a Rolling Stones concert in Cologne.

Claude: *'OK, we are going to drive from Rouen to Cologne.'*

Chantal: *'Yes, but which way are we going to go?'*

Claude: *'Remember last June when we drove from Paris to Brussels?'*

Chantal: *'Yes, the Johnny Haliday concert. Let's look at how long it took us, how many wrong turnings we made, what our average speed was for each part of the journey and for the whole trip, all the costs involved, how much diesel we used and how much we had left at the end.'*

Claude: *'I'm glad we calculated all those statistics about the journey. I knew they would come in handy.'*

Chantal: *'OK, let's use them to plan our journey to Cologne. It would be good to know exactly how long it will take to get there and how much everything will cost.'*

Having made their plans, the two friends commence their journey, driving east at their predetermined speed. Unfortunately, after driving for 45 minutes, they find their road closed for repairs and have to take a diversion; this takes an additional 30 minutes before they return to their chosen route. After another hour's driving they stop for lunch at a service station. Returning to their car, feeling refreshed, they find that the driver's wing mirror has been knocked off and is lying on the floor by the side of the car. There is also a nasty scratch and dent on the front wing! They report this to a policeman in a traffic patrol vehicle parked nearby and record the details to send to their insurance company at a later date. The policeman advises that the mirror must be repaired before the journey is recommenced. This takes an extra hour but the required repairs are achieved; this cost them 150 euros that they had planned to spend on a good hotel in Cologne.

The journey continues and goes well for the next two hours. Unexpectedly, as it is now April, it then starts to snow. All traffic slows down and their average speed drops by 30 kph. Fortunately, the snowstorm only lasts for 20 minutes but the road surface remains wet and speeds increase only a little. They stop to change drivers but, when Chantal exits the passenger seat, she feels dizzy and decides she is not fit to drive. She has had a cold for the last few days but assumed she would be over it by now and has not brought any medication with her. Claude has no choice but to continue driving after a quick wash to freshen up. Two hours later, night falls and Claude feels too tired to drive any further. So, reluctantly, they stop at Aachen for the night. Acknowledging that they will not now get to the Rolling Stones concert, they book into a local motel and watch a movie they both wanted to see on the television in their room.

They do not consider their trip to be a total disaster but they certainly did not achieve their original objective. So, is there anything they could have done to help themselves get to the concert on time? How sensible was it to plan their journey based on what happened in a previous journey to a different destination at a different time? Could they have predicted the snow from available weather forecasts and allowed more time for the journey? Should Chantal have anticipated the return of her cold and bought some appropriate medicine to take with her even though she may not have had to use it?

All analogies break down at some point but this story is not too dissimilar to the way businesses typically used to make their plans for the next financial year. They used previous years' statistics such as profit margins, sales volumes and prices, rates of pay, material and expense costs; these were known from the previous year and it was assumed they would remain valid for the current year. They felt content with this approach because the information was certain and, after all, no one could accurately predict what these statistics were going to be. So the plan was made and (for companies listed on the stock exchange) independent analysts were informed of the predicted profits. Employees were strongly encouraged to meet their budget numbers, often by the use of personal financial incentives, and future changes in the environment were conveniently ignored. These may have included changes in interest rates, innovative competition, widespread flooding, a flu epidemic among employees, decreases in demand due to higher rates of VAT and even terrorist activities. Many resources had been invested in the budgeting process and there was a natural reluctance to abandon it.

However, a better way of achieving corporate objectives has been created, a method that uses more than just recent financial statistics and gives a more rounded approach to the task of managing business performance. It is called the balanced scorecard.

Learning objectives

Having worked through this chapter you should be able to:

- describe the theory and structure of the balanced scorecard;
- describe the internal 'lead' and 'lag' relationships between balanced scorecard components;
- explain the different relationships in 'for-profit' and 'not-for-profit' organizations;
- explain the advantage of involving front-line staff in balanced scorecard design and operation;
- draw a diagram to show how corporate strategy can be implemented through the balanced scorecard;
- give examples of how popular strategies would appear on the balanced scorecard;
- explain the flexibility of balanced scorecard design;
- describe the process of cascading scorecards within organizations;
- describe the process of employee involvement in the operation of scorecards;
- create a strategy map in connection with a balanced scorecard;
- appreciate how balanced scorecards are adapted for use by real companies;
- explain how the scorecard approach can help with strategy formulation;
- describe the multiple benefits of operating balanced scorecards;
- explain the role of financial incentives connected to balanced scorecards;
- appreciate the dangers of operating two different performance systems at the same time;
- describe the limitations of balanced scorecards.

Structure and internal relationships

The balanced scorecard was first proposed by Kaplan and Norton in 1992. It is a device to aid managers in their efforts to improve corporate performance in line with corporate goals and was designed to combat the short-termism of traditional accounting systems. To help managers avoid information overload it is recommended that four corporate goals or objectives are chosen for each of four 'perspectives' (or aspects) of organizational activity (16 items in total). The four perspectives are financial, customer, internal business processes and learning/innovation. Each goal (or critical success factor) is monitored by a different performance indicator and a specific target is set for each indicator. These indicators are sometimes referred to as *key performance indicators (KPIs)*. Figure 17.1 illustrates the balanced scorecard structure.

The specific targets set for each indicator should be stretch targets, high but achievable. If they are set either too low or too high, they will demotivate employees and performance will be suboptimal. So, the targets should be set very carefully. But even this is not enough to ensure success. It is good practice for the people responsible for achieving targets to create 'action plans' setting out in detail how they are going to achieve their objectives. A separate action plan should be created for each of the 16 objectives. Also, a single named employee should be designated as responsible for each plan and they should be reviewed on a regular basis at least every six months.

However, it is not essential that each perspective has exactly four objectives; the idea is to keep the amount of monitored information small and, therefore, manageable. Also, if an organization thinks it useful to have five perspectives, there is no reason why it should not do so. For example, one major European oil and gas multinational has a fifth perspective concerned with 'health and safety', which is a very important aspect of its business. Balanced scorecards are essentially flexible and should always be tailored to the requirements of the organization using them.

However, as the number of items monitored is small, it is vital that they and their performance indicators are very carefully chosen. Duplication should be avoided; for example, no indicator should be used more than once on the scorecard. The goals listed should give a broad perspective of activities rather than a narrow one. In the past, it was not unusual for managers to be expected to monitor a much larger number of individual measurements, sometimes more than a hundred! The pressing nature of their other duties meant that they could not do this effectively and strategy implementation was very difficult to achieve. *It was difficult for them to see the forest as a whole because there were so many trees in the way.*

One of the perspectives concerns 'traditional' financial measures but the other three consist of non-financial items. Taken together, the financial, customer, internal business and innovation/learning indicators give a balanced view of corporate performance. Provided the non-financial performance indicators are carefully selected, improvement in them should automatically translate into improved financial performance. This can be thought of in terms of *cause and effect* or *action and result*. Accordingly, the non-financial factors are known as 'lead' indicators and the financial factors as 'lag' indicators. See Figure 17.2. Note that a perspective in the middle of the system may be 'lag' for the one before it but 'lead' for the one after it; the terms are relative. ('Lag' indicators are examples of a 'feedback' system but 'lead' indicators are a type of 'feedforward' system.)

The financial perspective

Corporate goal	Performance indicator	Target
Survival	Liquid ratio	Increase to 0.8:1.0
Profitability	Return on capital employed	Improve by 5% over the year
Growth	Sales revenue	Increase by 4% a year above inflation
Self-funding	Interest cover ratio	Reduce interest to 10% of operating profit

The customer perspective

Corporate goal	Performance indicator	Target
Responsiveness	Sales order processing period	Reduce to 12 working days
Reliability	On-time deliveries	95% each month
Product quality	Complaints received	2% of goods delivered each month
Image	Ranking by customer	Customer's first or second choice in independent survey

The internal business perspective

Corporate goal	Performance indicator	Target
Satisfied employees	Staff turnover ratio	5% a year maximum
Production efficiency	Output per employee	Increase by 1% every 3 months
Working capital management	Cash-cycle period	Reduce by 1 day every 2 months
Production quality	Value of defective production	Reduction of 2% every 3 months

The innovation and learning perspective

Corporate goal	Performance indicator	Target
Continuing introduction of new products	Proportion of sales from new products	15% of annual sales from products launched in current or previous financial year
Employee development	Number of training hours per employee	16 hours per year minimum for each employee
Market diversification	Number of new markets served	At least one new market entered each year
Product improvement	Spending on research and development	Minimum of 10% a year of after-tax profits

Figure 17.1 The four perspectives of the balanced scorecard and examples of their application

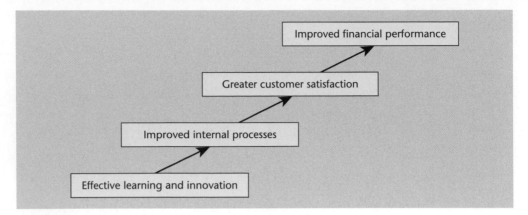

Figure 17.2 Lead and lag perspectives in a for-profit organization

The model is that:

1 Improvements in learning and innovation will automatically lead to improvements in internal business processes.
2 Improvements in internal business processes will automatically lead to improvements in customer satisfaction.
3 Improvements in customer satisfaction will automatically lead to improvements in the financial statistics (profit, return on capital employed, sales revenue, etc.) and, therefore, shareholder value.

This is fundamentally sound but somewhat simplistic as there is a considerable amount of interaction occurring between all perspectives. Note that the model described above assumes the organization to be a 'for-profit' example; in a 'not-for-profit' organization, the lead/lag relationship changes. The ultimate lag perspective becomes that of the customer/client and the financial perspective becomes the first of the lead perspectives. Income is essential for training and innovation to occur *which leads to* improved internal processes *which leads to* improved client satisfaction (see Figure 17.3).

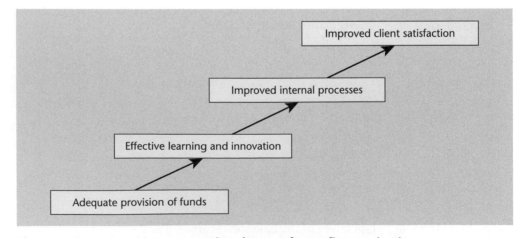

Figure 17.3 Lead and lag perspectives in a not-for-profit organization

Balanced scorecards are equally useful in both types of organization and many relevant skills are transferable between them. Peter Drucker is on record saying that it would be a good idea for not-for-profit organizations to acquire the performance management skills of commercial ones and for for-profit organizations to acquire the mission-management skills of not-for-profit ones. Whether profit is the main objective or not, all organizations can benefit from the use of balanced scorecards.

The indicators included in the scorecard are not generic; they should be reviewed periodically to reflect changes of corporate strategy made in response to the external environment. This is facilitated by a flexible management information system, possibly based on a unified relational database used to warehouse both internal and external data. In summary, the balanced scorecard is driven by organizational strategic objectives rather than a desire for operational control. It is not constrained by the financial year in the way that a budgetary control system is. Note that it is not a strategy in itself but a mechanism designed to help organizations translate their chosen strategies into reality.

To summarize the importance of measurement-based balanced scorecards, I quote Melnyk *et al.* (2004):

> *Strategy without metrics is useless; metrics without a strategy are meaningless.*

Practical application

Introducing a balanced scorecard into an organization is a demanding task and involves significant cost. But although it consumes large amounts of resources it usually turns out to be well worthwhile. After all, its basic objective is to improve business performance through effective implementation of corporate strategy.

Balanced scorecards use only a small number of key performance indicators, mostly non-financial; but who decides which ones to use? If the choice is imposed from above, the effectiveness of the initiative will be limited. On the other hand, if front-line operatives are involved in the choice of indicators, the balanced scorecard is more likely to bring about the desired improvements in corporate performance. Front-line staff, rather than higher-level managers, often know best where improvements can be made most effectively. The performance indicators selected should come out of discussions between them and their managers. Genuine consultation here will pay handsome dividends later. Like budgets, balanced scorecards are more likely to be effective if created both top-down and bottom-up.

The choice of balanced scorecard indicators is critical and deserves much thought (see Bourne and Neely's 'Cause and effect' article listed below in Further reading). **Whatever a business decides to measure, it will strive to achieve.** Kaplan and Norton, the inventors of the balanced scorecard, express this succinctly as 'You get what you measure.' For example, suppose a company chooses 'average length of sales order processing' as one of its key performance indicators in the 'customer perspective' of its balanced scorecard. If this is currently taking 18 days and the company finds out that its main competitor is taking only 16 days, it may decide to set itself a target of 14 days. If management seek to achieve this in isolation from other aspects of corporate performance and without consulting the delivery operatives, the company may experience a significant increase in the number of complaints it receives concerning the quality of goods received by customers. It may be that a different method of delivery was adopted in order to achieve the new standard of 14 days but this caused a significant increase in damage to goods in transit. For example, instead of relying on its existing delivery system, the firm may have hired outside contractors to move more goods in less time. Unfortunately, these contractors would not have been as experienced as the firm's own staff and more damage would have occurred.

If the firm's own staff had been consulted, they may have been able to point out that the policy of having only one person per vehicle means that the driver also has to do all the unloading. If there were two employees per vehicle, one hour of unloading time a day could be saved and the number of deliveries increased by 15%. Alternatively, the vehicles could be modified somehow to speed up the unloading process, e.g. the installation of a powered lift at the back of the vehicle. The drivers would be very aware of the possibilities but it is unlikely that senior managers would have any ideas in this respect due to their detachment from the unloading process.

The role of the balanced scorecard has developed over time. As well as being a mechanism for monitoring a broad range of performance indicators, it is now also seen as a strategic business tool, a mechanism for clarifying strategy and turning it into action. Because the performance indicators can be changed to suit an evolving environment or revised internal direction, the balanced scorecard can be used to implement new strategic objectives (see Figure 17.4). Where it is used throughout an organization, it not only acts as a mechanism for including employees in the strategy process but also becomes a communication medium for new strategies. This applies just as much to not-for-profit organizations such as the Royal Navy (see Woodley's 'Ship shape' article in Further reading below) as it does to profit-seeking businesses like Tesco.

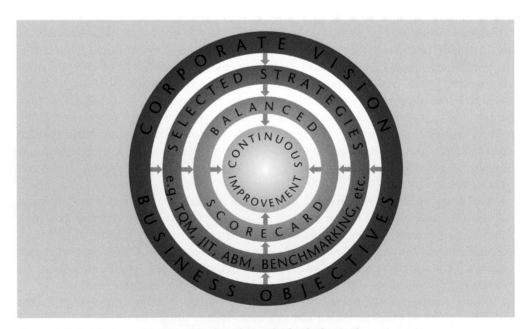

Figure 17.4 **Strategy implementation through the balanced scorecard**

Extract where JIT is an adopted strategy:

Corporate goal	Performance indicator	Target
Eliminate stock	Stock value	5% of weekly production materials used value

Extract where TQM is an adopted strategy:

Corporate goal	Performance indicator	Target
Eliminate product defects	Defective parts per million (DPPM)	Ten per million

Extract where benchmarking is an adopted strategy:

Corporate goal	Performance indicator	Target
Efficient information system	Number of independent IT systems in use	Three

Extract where ABM is an adopted strategy:

Corporate goal	Performance indicator	Target
To minimize non-value-added costs	Amount spent on factory security	10% reduction from current cost

Figure 17.5 **Examples of popular strategy implementation**

The goals and their performance indicators can come from the management techniques (e.g. JIT, TQM, benchmarking and ABM) adopted by the organization as their strategy. For example, a company adopting a JIT inventory control strategy would have a goal of eliminating stock, and 'stock value' could be one of the selected KPIs (see Figure 17.5 for examples). Most of the performance data will be available internally but sometimes it may have to be obtained via customer surveys, benchmarking, intercompany comparisons, etc. The number of indicators is limited on purpose in order to help management focus on their current priorities. (Along with 11 other strategies, TQM, benchmarking, JIT and ABM are discussed in detail in Chapter 18 'Performance improvement techniques'.)

Flexibility

One reason why balanced scorecards have been adopted so widely is their flexibility. Kaplan's standard model is an example of how they can be structured but it is not meant to be a rigid format suitable for all organizations. The four perspectives are almost always used but there is no reason why a fifth should not be added if the organization considered it useful. For example, a pharmaceutical company may decide to have a 'Research & Development' perspective as well as a perspective for employee 'Learning & Growth'. Products could be separated from people and scientists from other personnel.

There is no reason why each perspective should highlight exactly four business objectives; three or five may be preferred. Only objectives considered important should be included. However, in order to avoid information overload and the dilution of management focus, it is inadvisable for any balanced scorecard to have more than about 20 objectives in total. Similarly, only one KPI should be chosen to measure performance against objectives. There is almost always a choice of indicators and the decision as to which one to use should always be made carefully.

For example, the various KPIs concerned with the corporate goal of 'improving product quality' could include:

1 defects as a percentage of production, found by quality inspections;
2 number of customer complaints received;
3 market share (measured independently);
4 etc.

Indicator 2, 'number of complaints', will depend on the size of orders placed by individual customers. Only 10 customers may complain in one year compared with 20 customers in the previous year. This looks like a big improvement but the 20 may account for 18% of total sales volume whereas the 10 may represent 25%.

If indicator 3, 'market share', is the chosen indicator, a decrease would be interpreted as a reduction in product quality. But the decrease could be caused by other factors such as a new entrant into the market, possibly using discounts to buy its way in, or by a dent to the brand image caused by association with some sort of political incorrectness such as the use of child labour in the manufacturing process. The point is that a change in market share could have some cause other than a change in product quality.

'Defects as a percentage of production' is probably the best of the above indicators as the link between it and the objective is the most direct and influenced by few, if any, other factors than quality.

Remember, if 'what you measure is what you get' you need to be very careful in deciding what to measure.

Cascading and employee involvement

So far, we have been thinking about balanced scorecards designed for a single semi-autonomous business unit (often referred to as a strategic business unit or SBU) but large organizations often have a holding company and a number of divisions. There is no reason why balanced scorecards should not be used at each of these levels provided appropriate modifications are made. The group could have its own scorecard and each of the divisions or SBUs could have theirs. Obviously, the objectives, performance indicators and targets must be integrated so that the results achieved at any level help to achieve the targets set at the next level above (see Figure 17.6).

Also, each division may be split into a number of teams, each consisting of a number of employees. In such cases, performance improvement devices for teams and individuals can be created taking as their vision/mission the device at the level immediately above. These 'team/personal scorecards' would not look like the 'standard' balanced scorecards as described above but would be based on them; for example, they would be unlikely to have the four perspectives. These devices would consist of a list of objectives, performance measures and target levels. Titles of these devices include 'personal development matrix' and 'responsibility log' (see Figure 17.7).

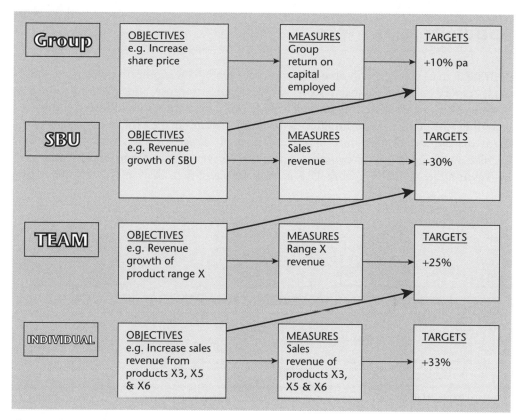

Figure 17.6 Performance improvement cascade

Process	Bread making
Responsible manager	M. Bunn (team supervisor)
Financial (F1)	**Variable cost**
Current	£124.50/100 kg
Target	£118.00/100 kg
Cause	Waste dough after mixing
Action	Improved-design containers to be purchased
by when	September 30
by whom	A. Spooner, chief mixer
Non-financial (N1)	**Productivity**
Current	310 loaves/hour/operative
Target	350 loaves/hour/operative
Cause	Oven interior rack design is inefficient.
Action	Racks to be dismantled and rebuilt. N.B.: 3-day shutdown needed.
by when	First opportunity is December 27–29.
by whom	Maintenance department plus M. Bunn and D. Nutt
etc.	

Figure 17.7 Team responsibility log (extract)

Strategy maps

A strategy map shows the interconnections between business objectives from the different perspectives of a balanced scorecard. It maps the cause and effect relationships between them, e.g. shortening the sales order processing time should lead to improved customer satisfaction. Their function is to summarize and make explicit the results of the many discussions, deliberations and decisions made concerning business strategy. They are also a very good way of communicating this to everyone in the business and help to maintain strategic focus. Figure 17.8 is an example of a strategy map with the arrows

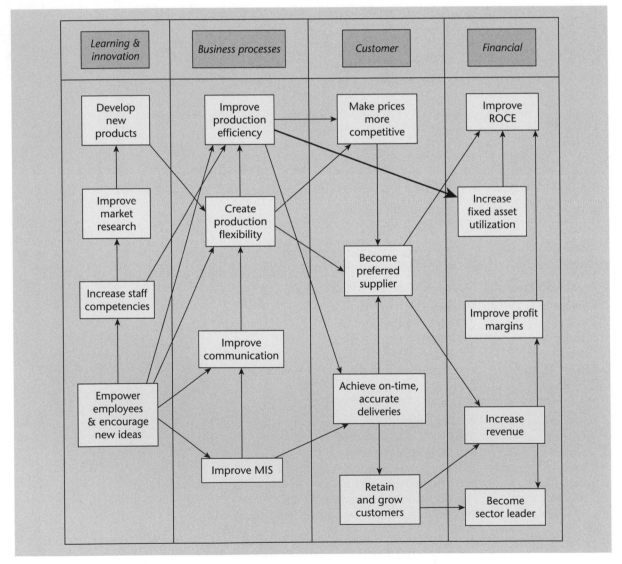

Figure 17.8 An example of a strategy map

showing the linkages; note that one of these is thicker than the others. This is to point out that, although most linkages are between adjacent perspectives, they are not restricted to this pattern. An improvement in production efficiency should lead to an improvement in the utilization of fixed assets (assuming the extra capacity created is utilized).

A multinational pharmaceutical company

Example 17.1

This example is of a real existing veterinary pharmaceutical company operating internationally in Europe with a multi-million pound turnover. The lead management team were proactive towards managing their performance and decided to investigate the possible use of balanced scorecards (BSCs). Following a pilot scheme concentrating on the customer/marketing perspective only, the company introduced a BSC whose perspectives followed the standard model. However, only two perspectives had four objectives; the other had three objectives each (14 in total). The 'master' BSC was easily displayed on one side of A4 paper; each perspective had three columns: Objective, Status and Owner (see Figure 17.9). The targets (which incorporated the KPIs) were shown on a separate page, one for each perspective. The whole thing printed out on five pages of paper.

Although this design deviates substantially from Kaplan and Norton's generic model, the main emphasis of monitoring non-financial key success factors is at the heart of the system. The status column consists of blocks of 'traffic-light' colours showing the current state of achievement for each of the key success factors. A green colour signifies that the objective is well on the way to being achieved, red indicates that there is much work still to be done and yellow means that a medium amount of progress has been achieved. Although this approach lacks sophistication, it does make it very easy to see the areas where management should focus their attention. It communicates very effectively.

The company took advantage of the inherent flexibility of the BSC management model to create a scorecard tailored exactly to its own needs. It reviews its choice of key success factors annually but the status and the target levels are updated quarterly. After operating the system described above for a year, it decided to condense the BSC from five pages to one page by showing simplified targets within the four perspectives. Also, the number of objectives was reduced to 2, 3, 3 and 4 (12 in total). The idea of this was to communicate a significant amount of key data as efficiently as possible and in a memorable form.

FINANCIALS	Status (green/yellow/red)	Owner (manager's name)
1.1 Achieve plan		
1.2 Double-digit vet products sales growth		
1.3 Price increase 3%		

INNOVATION	Status (green/yellow/red)	Owner (manager's name)
2.1 XY franchise: new EU regulations		
2.2 Food animals: no timeline slippage		
2.3 Companion animal: 2 submissions/year		
2.4 Affiliates: 3 launches per year		

ORGANIZATION & CAPABILITIES	Status (green/yellow/red)	Owner (manager's name)
3.1 Productivity improvement – Apply new business model		
3.2 Shaping environment: – No barriers to sales		
3.3 Customer service > 98%		
3.4 Regulation & business compliance – No issues		

SALES & MARKETING EXCELLENCE	Status (green/yellow/red)	Owner (manager's name)
4.1 Generics: 20% increase in market share		
4.2 Species teams		
4.3 Marketing plan targets and message kick-off		

Figure 17.9 Scorecard front page used by multinational veterinary pharmaceutical company

Example
17.2

'Tesco's steering wheel'

Source: CIMA, *Insight*, 2005

'In the 1990s Tesco was third in the UK retail market and losing market share. The recession had hit performance hard and Tesco was purely a food retailer with no operations outside the UK. Tesco subsequently turned around. It became the UK's preferred supermarket (third in the world), reporting a pre-tax profit of £2 billion for the year ending 26 February (a rise of 21 per cent) and 13 per cent growth to £7.6 billion total international sales in 2004.

'Tesco then formulated its "steering wheel" approach. This is its own customized balanced scorecard. It communicates strategy-aligned goals and manages strategic performance. It monitors progress and measures success. The organization's core purpose – "to create value for our customers and to earn their lifetime loyalty" – has been delivered on a clear and simple strategy of long-term growth.

'This strategy underpins Tesco's four operational elements:

- core UK business;
- non-food business;
- retailing services;
- international operations.

'Tesco's steering wheel framework comprises four perspectives – people, customer, financial and operations. Each is driven and monitored by demanding but achievable business targets. Throughout Tesco's retail operations, every store has its own individual steering wheel, to which all staff members' objectives are linked, and which relate strategy to day-to-day work. At every organizational level, where the KPIs are not on track and targets are not being met, the steering wheel group investigates the reasons why, and plans corrective action.

'Performance is reported quarterly to Tesco's board and a summary report is sent to the top 2,000 managers in the company to pass on to staff. Further, the remuneration of senior managers is shaped by KPIs, with bonuses based on a sliding scale according to the level of achievement on the corporate steering wheel.

'Tesco's values and priorities (concerning customers, staff, business, and compliance issues) are embedded in the steering wheel through appropriate KPIs. These values pervade operations and are instrumental in securing staff commitment to the steering wheel. It is arguable that, by embedding its values in the steering wheel, Tesco transformed its balanced scorecard from a management framework to a cohesive living strategy.'

Successful implementation of a balanced scorecard

Introducing a balanced scorecard into an organization is not merely replacing one system with another. More often than not, it involves a change in corporate culture. It involves increased communication, genuine participation, genuine empowerment, more training and increased costs. Maybe this is why many attempts to introduce balanced scorecards fail. Balanced scorecard systems seem deceptively simple so it is assumed that they are easy to implement.

Two researchers in the Netherlands, Lewy and du Mee, looked into the difficulties of implementation and produced the following 10 pieces of advice:

1 Use the scorecard as the basis for implementing strategic goals, since its visibility makes it the ideal vehicle for doing so.
2 Ensure that your strategy is in place before developing the scorecard, as ad hoc development will encourage undesirable behaviour.
3 Ensure that the project is sponsored at senior management level.
4 Run a pilot project before full implementation.
5 Scorecards should be designed to meet the specific needs of business units; the generic scorecard should not be used without appropriate adaptation.
6 Introduce the scorecard gradually to each business unit only after its design has been tailored to its needs.
7 Do not use the scorecard as a method of hierarchical control.
8 Do not underestimate the need for training and communication.
9 Do not overcomplicate the scorecard by striving for perfection. It will never be 100% right, so do not delay its implementation by searching for better indicators.
10 Do not underestimate the costs of recording, administrating and reporting.

Strategy formulation

The fundamental role of the balanced scorecard is in strategy interpretation and realization, not in strategy formulation. However, the four-perspective structure can be used as a guide in the formulation process. The four generic questions shown in Figure 17.10 demand thought about the actions necessary to achieve good business performance. They

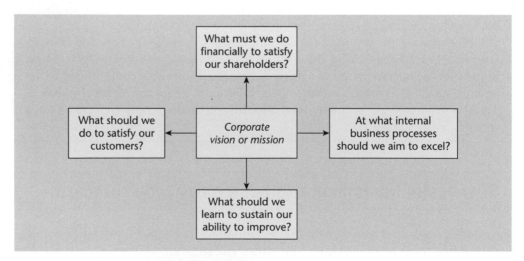

Figure 17.10 Strategy-guiding questions

should be answered in the context of the corporate vision/mission which embodies the long-term aspirations of the business. (The results recorded by the balanced scorecard will also enable the strategy formulators to reflect on the appropriateness of their choices.)

In connection with the International Federation of Accountants (IFAC), the Chartered Institute of Management Accountants has created a 'Strategic Scorecard' to help companies decide their strategy. Like the balanced scorecard, it has four perspectives/dimensions; however, they are very different in nature. They are:

STRATEGIC POSITION	*STRATEGIC OPTIONS*
STRATEGIC IMPLEMENTATION	*STRATEGIC RISKS*

The objective is to help top-level managers to ask appropriate and relevant questions which guide them to formulate effective strategy. Although very different, this links to the balanced scorecard through the 'Strategic Implementation' dimension.

Multiple benefits

As discussed above, the major objective of balanced scorecards is to align organizational and personal objectives and activities in order for the organization to achieve continuous improvement through effective strategy implementation.

However, Otley (2006) lists the following 12 areas where balanced scorecards can make a significant additional contribution to improved business performance:

1 clarifying organizational vision;
2 gaining consensus around the organizational vision;
3 communicating goals and educating employees;
4 setting goals;
5 linking rewards to performance measures;
6 setting targets;
7 aligning strategic objectives;
8 allocating resources;
9 establishing milestones;
10 articulating the shared vision;
11 supplying strategic feedback;
12 facilitating strategy review and learning.

Financial incentives

If the performance of the business is expected to improve when employees meet their personal balanced scorecard targets, it seems sensible to offer them an incentive to do so. If bonuses are awarded on this basis, management are seen to be committed to this performance management system and the degree of success is heightened. Although this sounds straightforward, in practice it can be complicated. Deciding which set of measures to use and their weighting in the bonus calculation is inherently subjective and open to criticism. The danger here is that, after all the hard work of implementing a balanced scorecard system, an employee may be demotivated if he or she thinks the treatment is unfair. However, this can be countered by operating a transparent reward system involving consultation and discussion.

An intended consequence of financial incentives is that people will strive to achieve their targets. An unintended consequence is that some will bend, or even break, the rules in order to get their cash bonuses. Human nature is such that, given a choice between behaviour beneficial to shareholders and that beneficial to themselves, most people will choose the latter. There is much evidence of this in traditional budgetary control systems where the playing of 'budget games' is common. When businesses introduce balanced scorecards, they should expect that some 'scorecard gaming' will occur. It would be naive of them to assume that the new system would change basic human behaviour. When designing the reward system, they should be careful not to make the incentives **too** attractive. Consider the words of W. E. Deming:

> *People with sharp enough targets will probably meet them even if they have to destroy the company to do so.*

A note of caution

It is not unusual for organizations to have a balanced scorecard as well as a traditional budgetary control system. This has been described by the late Jeremy Hope (co-founder of the Beyond Budgeting movement) as 'similar to driving a car with two steering wheels!' While this is not impossible, extremely high levels of driving skills are essential to avoid things going badly wrong. The risk of accidents is increased.

There are several reasons why these two different strategy implementation devices should not be used simultaneously. First, they may contradict each other, allowing managers to choose which one to follow as best suits them at any particular time. This may let them off the 'responsibility hook'. Second, when contradictions do occur, confidence in management systems will diminish and managers will be demotivated. Lastly, significant amounts of resources will be used unnecessarily, maintaining two systems attempting to achieve the same objective, and profits will be adversely affected. Unambiguous clarity of direction is a great help in improving performance.

If both systems are used simultaneously, extra care must be taken to ensure their financial metrics do not contradict each other. However, this raises the 'old chestnut' of the difficulty of using the same numbers as targets and plans. Using both variance analysis and balanced scorecards does seem to cause an excessive use of resources.

Limitations

Choice of strategy

The use of balanced scorecards concerns enabling organizations to gain competitive advantage by implementing corporate strategy resulting in constantly improved performance. This descriptive definition indicates two areas where this management model is vulnerable. The first is getting the strategy right: choosing the activities with the most potential and doing them in the most effective order. Strategy is about doing the right things in the right way. The second critical area is the quality of the information system: choosing the best performance indicators and providing accurate, timely, summarized information in a flexible form.

Getting the strategy right is a perennial problem. Even when the indications are that you have got it right and results are improving, it is dangerous to sit back and become complacent. The business environment is constantly changing and competitors are continually looking for ways of gaining competitive advantage over you. Strategy review and formulation should be a continuous activity of high-level managers. However, it is a fact of business life that they do not always get it right. Business performance depends on the quality of the chosen strategy.

Quality of the information system

Also, the quality of the management information system is crucial; it needs to be appropriate, accurate, up to date and user-friendly. The following questions should be asked on a regular basis. Is the information system's strategy appropriate for the operation of the balanced scorecard? Is the hardware network sufficient to support corporate needs? Is the data management system flexible enough to meet frequent changes in information requirements? Is the right data being collected? How reliable is the **external** data collected? Are systems maintenance and modification easy to achieve? The answers to these questions will indicate the effectiveness of the system.

Cause and effect relationships

The nature of the relationships between different perspectives and between different objectives has been described above as one of 'cause and effect'. You may be surprised to know that this is an assumption rather than a fact. Most readers will intuitively have felt comfortable with the relationships discussed earlier, e.g. that a significant shortening of the sales order processing period automatically always leads to an increase in customer satisfaction or that increased customer satisfaction automatically always leads to increased profits. However, these relationships have never been proved to be those of cause and effect; they could be based on correlation rather than causation. The achievement of corporate objectives indicates that the desired outcomes were likely to be achieved rather than 100% guaranteed.

However, if the cause and effect relationship does not actually exist, use of the balanced scorecard may lead to dysfunctional behaviour and suboptimal performance. Managers may perform inappropriate actions based on balanced scorecard information. Also, it is worth noting that, if employee reward incentive schemes are based on achieving balanced scorecard targets, any dysfunctional effects are likely to be exaggerated.

Time lags

The information on a single balanced scorecard is divided into four sections by perspective but all of it relates to the same period of time. None of the specific items in any of the four perspectives are causes or effects of specific items in any other perspective. For example, the objectives stated in the 'customer' perspective should lead to different financial performance levels from those shown in the financial perspective of the same scorecard. The latter should be a result of the 'customer' objectives on the previous scorecard.

Also, the complexity of reality may contradict the assumed cause and effect relationships. For example, to gain market share as quickly as possible, a business may adopt a market penetration strategy entailing the initial selling of products at or below variable/ marginal cost. This may result in a profit decrease in the next financial period but an overcompensating increase in the period after that.

Subjectivity

Because balanced scorecards are designed and actioned by people, the choice of objectives, performance indicators and target levels will be subjective to some extent. Designers will be influenced by their past experiences and will attempt to project these into a future which will always contain a degree of uncertainty. In other words, their assumptions will not always prove correct.

Semantics and language

It is inevitable that communication within organizations always contains some management-speak jargon. However, words can be interpreted differently by different people. To take a basic example, if an objective was stated as 'increase sales', would this refer to sales volume or sales revenue? If this was not made clear, confusion could easily occur.

Management guru ethos

Peter Drucker (himself a management guru!) said that an important part of a manager's job is to think clearly about the business and that this task was far from easy. He followed this up by saying that adopting management fads/fashions without specific justification was a common excuse for not thinking. Balanced scorecards fit this description as well as other popular management models (total quality management, business process re-engineering, etc.). Norreklit and Mitchell summarize this very well in their chapter on balanced scorecards in the third edition of *Issues in Management Accounting*:

> *The world of organizational management is not a well-ordered, rational world. Managerial actions such as introducing new techniques like the balanced scorecard may be motivated by more than the immediate search for profit. They may reflect managers' personal needs to be seen to be changing things, to resemble admirable others, to acquire legitimacy by employing the latest techniques, and to retain flexibility in the ways information is used within their organizations.*

The manager's point of view (by Gary Burmiston)

In this increasingly competitive environment, organizations introduce balanced score-cards to answer two vital questions which take up a vast amount of management time:

● What is good performance?
● How do we measure good performance?

Unfortunately, like every other management accounting technique, its 'correctness' is dependent upon how a scorecard is designed, implemented and used.

Many hours of soul searching take place throughout organizations to arrive at that brief, highly focused and insightful report that tells everyone in the company how well it is performing and identifies the areas that need to be addressed to improve performance further.

The reason that many hours are spent is because a good balanced scorecard is not easy to arrive at. Senior managers today can be presented with tomes of information on a daily, weekly and monthly basis and it is part of their job to decipher all the information and identify the key messages, enabling them to make the right decisions. But can the performance of a multinational, multi-billion pound, multi-product company really be distilled into 12 or 15 key performance indicators without losing the intricacies of performance that are important to individuals?

It could be argued that, at the highest level, ROCE should be used to measure an organization's performance and in many cases it is. But, for most people in the organization, ROCE fails on one key issue, its *relevance*.

To measure performance effectively and to expect people across an organization to respond to performance issues, they have to understand how what they do affects the results of the business. It is at this point that ROCE can begin to fall down. An operator on a production line may accept a loss rate of, say, 2% as that is what has been achieved historically and so is accepted as standard performance. But would the impact on ROCE be known if he were to reduce that loss rate to 1.7%? Similarly, would a salesperson know the impact on ROCE if she were to offer an extra discount of 5% to achieve a sale? In both cases the answer is probably 'no'.

Balanced scorecards are used to present information over a wide range of key performance indicators, financial and non-financial, to give an all-round picture of the organization's performance. By giving this all-round picture it is hoped that it becomes relevant to most people within an organization. The word 'hope' is used deliberately as there are frameworks for setting up a balanced scorecard, as highlighted earlier in the chapter, but the key to a successful scorecard is that it picks up on those indicators which truly drive an organization's performance. This is where the debate and management time should be spent.

In a number of organizations I've worked in, the introduction of a balanced scorecard has been a long and protracted affair. There is a desire to keep the performance indicators to a minimum but everyone has their favourites which they feel are important. At one organization, starting from a desire to highlight the top 20 performance indicators to the Board on a weekly basis, the discussions have moved on and the current balanced scorecard currently contains over 50! This is not what Kaplan and Norton envisaged over 15 years ago. The reasons for so many indicators are down to the types of information that is presented and the behaviours demonstrated by senior managers.

Some indicators are there just as background information. These are not needed, but even senior managers and directors like the comfort of knowing. They will argue they get too much information, but try and take information away from them and the debate will really start. Some indicators are there highlighting performance but the ability of managers to act upon and influence them over a short time horizon is limited. Again, it's not really necessary to report on a weekly basis something that takes four months to turn around and is based on an organization's strategic direction.

The best performance indicators are those that can be improved before the next report is issued. Very good balanced scorecards contain only this type of indicator. They succeed in being both relevant to individuals and also demonstrating how decisions are linked to results. Unfortunately, experience shows that such scorecards are in a minority and managers still gain a sense of comfort from too much information, even if they do complain about it.

Once the balanced scorecard has been constructed the key thing to determine is what to compare the actual performance indicators against; what results would suggest the organization is performing well?

Good performance is very subjective and down to the ambition, desires and wants of the senior leaders of an organization. Good performance could be to stand still in a difficult environment, to improve on last year's results, to beat key performance indicators of local competitors, to be seen as best-in-class in their own field or even to be judged to be a world-class company by both peers and non-peers alike.

The key to a good balanced scorecard is being able to compare actual results, in a timely manner, against expectations (whatever they may be) and ensure the right people have the ability to make decisions that can influence those results. Having this will drive improved performance. Reporting numbers which are irrelevant to individuals, who cannot influence them, will not produce any improvement in results.

It is without doubt that a balanced scorecard can be an incredibly powerful and insightful tool for reporting and improving an organization's performance. It is also true that it can be an expensive and resource-sapping total waste of time. The key to getting it right is spending the time to understand the drivers of performance in an organization and making those drivers relevant. By doing so, people at all levels in an organization will know the part they play in its success and are likely to behave in a way that contributes to that success.

Summary

Should balanced scorecards be part of a book on management accounting? After all, three of the four perspectives deal with non-financial information. To answer this question, it is necessary to ask why management accounting exists. The fundamental reason is to provide managers with relevant, timely, accurate information to help them improve company performance. The mechanism is illustrated in Figure 17.4. Why, then, is performance management still perceived by some people as not really directly concerned with **accounting**? To answer this I can do no better than to quote the last words of the seminal text *Relevance Lost: The Rise and Fall of Management Accounting* (H. T. Johnson and R. S. Kaplan, 1987, Harvard Business School Press, Boston):

> *For too many firms today, however, the management accounting system is seen as a system designed and run by accountants to satisfy the informational needs of accountants. This is clearly wrong. Accountants should not have the exclusive franchise to design management accounting systems. To paraphrase an old saying, the task is simply too important to be left to accountants. The active involvement of engineers and operating managers will be essential when designing new management accounting systems.*
>
> *Contemporary trends in competition, in technology, and in management demand major changes in the way organizations measure and manage costs and in the way they measure short- and long-term performance. Failure to make the modifications will inhibit the ability of firms to be effective and efficient global competitors.*

To finish, it is worth adding another quote to the above, this time from Charles Darwin, author of the famous theory of evolution, in his book *Origin of the Species*:

> *Those who respond quickly, thrive, those that do not, die.*

The way forward

It is in the interest of all organizations to re-examine and adapt their management systems continuously to ensure their effectiveness. Thoughtless repetition of business activities is no longer an option for successful organizations in the twenty-first century.

The management of business performance is a journey not a destination.

If you have not already done so, you will probably enjoy reading *The Goal* by Goldratt and Cox (2004). This is all about continuous improvement and is all the more interesting, being written in the form of a novel.

Fundamentally, business performance management is about continuous improvement and the best advice I can offer for achieving this is: be **open to new ideas.**

Further reading

Atkinson, A., Banker, R., Kaplan, R. and Young, S. (2001) *Management Accounting*, 3rd edition, Prentice Hall, Harlow. See chapter 'Management accounting and control systems for strategic purposes: assessing performance over the entire value chain'.

Bauer, K. (2005) 'KPIs: avoiding the threshold McGuffins', *DM Review*, Vol. 15, Issue 4, April.

Bourne, M. and Neely, A. (2002) 'Cause and effect', *Financial Management*, September.

CIMA (2005), 'Making your balanced scorecard work harder', *Insight*, June, www.cimaglobal.com/insight

Davis, S. and Albright, T. (2004) 'An investigation of the effect of balanced scorecard implementation on financial performance', *Management Accounting Research*, Vol. 15, 135–53.

DeBusk, G. K., Brown, R. M. and Killough, L. N. (2003) 'Components and relative weights in utilization of dashboard measurement systems like the balanced scorecard', *British Accounting Review*, Vol. 35, 215–31.

Dilla, W. N. and Steinbart, P. J. (2005) 'Relative weighting of common and unique balanced scorecard measures by knowledgeable decision makers', *Behavioral Research in Accounting*, Vol. 17, Issue 1.

Drucker, P. (2006) *Managing the Non-Profit Organisation: Principles and Practices*, HarperCollins, New York.

Gering, M. and Rosmarin, K. (2000) 'Central beating: succeeding with the balanced scorecard means moving on from central planning', *Management Accounting*, June.

Goldratt, E. and Cox, J. (2004) *The Goal*, North River Press, Great Barrington, MA.

Horngren, C., Bhimani, A., Datar, S. and Foster, G. (2002) *Management and Cost Accounting*, 2nd edition, Prentice Hall Europe, Harlow. See Chapter 19, 'Control systems and performance measurements'.

Kaplan, R. and Norton, D. (1996) *The Balanced Scorecard*, Harvard Business School Press, Boston, MA.

Kaplan, R. and Norton, D. (2001) *The Strategy-focused Organization: How Balanced Scorecard Companies Thrive in the New Business Environment*, Harvard Business School Press, Boston, MA.

Kaplan, R. and Norton, D. (2001) 'Transforming the balanced scorecard from performance measurement to strategic management', *Accounting Horizons*, Vol. 15, 87–104.

Melnyk, S. A., Stewart, D. M. and Surink, M. (2004) 'Metrics and performance management in operations management: dealing with the metrics maze', *Journal of Operations Management*, Vol. 22, 209–17.

Norreklit, H. (2000) 'The balance on the balanced scorecard: a critical analysis of some of its assumptions', *Management Accounting Research*, Vol. 11, 65–88.

Norreklit, H. and Mitchell, F. (2007) 'The Balanced Scorecard' – Chapter 9 in *Issues in Management Accounting*, 3rd edition, edited by Hopper, T., Northcott, D. and Scapens, R., Financial Times/Prentice Hall, Harlow.

Otley, D. (2006) 'Trends in budgetary control and responsibility accounting', Chapter 13 in *Contemporary Issues in Management Accounting*, edited by Bhimani, A., Oxford University Press, Oxford.

Prickett, R. (2004) 'Balanced Scorecard provides ROI', *Financial Management*, December/January, p. 4.

Smith, M. (1999) *Management Accounting for Competitive Advantage*, LBC Information Services, Pyrmont, Australia.

Smith, M. (2000) 'Strategic management accounting: the public sector challenge', *Management Accounting*, January.

Smith, M. (2005) 'The balanced scorecard', *Financial Management*, February.

Ward, A. (2005) 'Implementing the balanced scorecard at Lloyds TSB', *Strategic HR Review*, Vol. 4, Issue 3, March/April.

Whittle, N. (2000) 'Older and wiser', *Management Accounting*, July/August.

Williams, K. (2004) 'What constitutes a successful balanced scorecard?', *Strategic Finance*, Vol. 86, Issue 5, November.

Woodley, P. (2002) 'Ship shape', *Financial Management*, June.

Introduction

Chumpy Lighting Limited manufactures a wide variety of light bulbs which it sells to lighting shops and builders merchants through wholesale distributors. It also sells direct to the big UK supermarkets. It is situated in a small town a few miles from the city of Durham in the north-east of England where it has been making light bulbs for domestic use for more than 40 years. Five years ago, it diversified into bulbs for industrial lighting, using its wholesale distributors, in an attempt to grow its revenue. It currently employs 550 people and has an annual turnover of £125 million, making it the fifth largest producer of light bulbs in the UK.

Just over six months ago, it was taken over by a multinational electrical products company, Eindnacht GmbH, based in Germany. Since then, the new owner has been reviewing the operations of its UK acquisition. Last week, the managing director of Chumpy Lighting received a confidential report from its parent company detailing the review's findings. In summary, most comments were critical and highlighted areas where Chumpy's performance has been declining. In conclusion, Eindnacht has given Chumpy two years in which to demonstrate a significant improvement in performance. If this does not happen, the manufacturing will be transferred to other Eindnacht factories in mainland Europe.

The managing director, Harriet Thompson, summoned her fellow directors yesterday to an extraordinary management meeting to discuss the report and the demands made by their new owners.

Organizational structure of Chumpy Lighting Limited

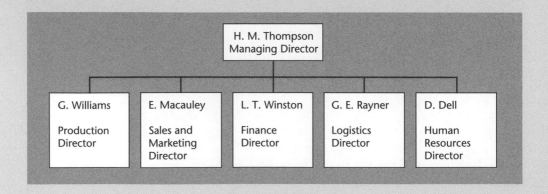

Summary of Eindnacht's report on Chumpy Lighting Limited

Products

Chumpy Lighting serves two distinct light bulb market segments, domestic and industrial. No new products have been launched in either sector in the last two years. Twelve years ago, in response to a growing market, the 'Alpha' range of 20 different low-energy long-life domestic bulbs was introduced. A significant investment in new plant and machinery was made to produce this range. The traditional tungsten filament light bulbs were phased out over two years from the introduction of the Alpha range which now accounts for 100% of domestic bulb production. The 'Beta' range of industrial bulbs was introduced five years ago in an attempt to achieve increased sales and profits. There are now 154 different bulbs in this range.

Production

On the basis of 'number of bulbs produced', the Alpha and Beta ranges account for 73% and 27% of production respectively. Production facilities are used Mondays to Fridays from 08:00 to 17:00 with operatives allowed a morning and afternoon break of 15 minutes each and a one-hour lunch break. The factory is closed for five weeks each year during which holidays must be taken.

The last new product, the 'Everlasting Halogen Spotlight' (EHS) bulb, aimed at the industrial security sector, was launched by Chumpy Lighting just over two years ago. Unfortunately, due to a manufacturing fault, the EHS was prone to overheating and had a high failure rate. On several occasions, the EHS exploded causing potential physical danger to anyone in the vicinity at the time. Fortunately, only one serious injury occurred and a damaging legal case was only avoided by a significant out-of-court settlement being made to the injured person. Although much negative publicity was avoided, negative rumours concerning product safety circulated in the industry. A product recall had to be performed and the EHS production process had to be redesigned to correct the fault. This resulted in a five-month gap before the EHS was relaunched. It is estimated that this and the attendant bad publicity caused a 5% fall in annual sales revenue from the Beta range for that year in addition to the very significant cost of the recall operation.

Marketing and sales

It is estimated that the domestic bulb market is worth approximately three times as much as the industrial bulb market.

Domestic: Apart from the last year, spending on advertising and promotion has shown very little variation in monetary terms (indicating a reduced spend in real terms). During this period, sales volumes have increased by an average of 2% a year. However, the market size of low-energy long-life domestic bulbs has increased by 8% a year on average over the same period. Selling price increases have generally matched inflation at around 2% a year except for an increase of 5% two years ago in an attempt to boost revenue. Superficial changes and new packaging were introduced at this point in an attempt to reposition the Alpha bulbs. Unfortunately, this strategy does not seem to have worked; the loss in volume caused by the price increase appears to have countered the extra revenue gained from higher prices in an increasingly competitive market.

Industrial: During the first three years of its life, the Beta range of industrial bulbs approximately doubled its sales each year until the EHS recall. Due to an increased spend on advertising and promotion, sales have now recovered to the level immediately prior to this incident. For the last decade or so, this market sector has increased by about 3% a year.

Customer satisfaction

Domestic: Retailers (via the wholesalers) say that their domestic customers think the Alpha range bulbs look dated and overpriced compared with those of their competitors. The wholesalers themselves are not too happy with the 35 days' average time it takes to deliver their orders. Apparently, there is only one other manufacturer who is slower than Chumpy so the company is not the automatic first choice of most suppliers. Sales order processing times are approximately twice as long as the 21 days taken by the company's best competitor.

Industrial: A telephone survey of 'heavy' customers showed a decrease in confidence regarding the product quality of 'Beta' bulbs over the last two years, although their prices are seen as reasonable.

Employee satisfaction

The anonymous Employee Satisfaction Survey commissioned by Eindnacht raised some issues of concern. The level of motivation is low and the staff turnover rate is currently 6% a year (5% last year).

Production efficiency is driven by the current production bonus scheme which is based on the number of bulbs produced by each operative in given time periods. Quality inspection takes place later, in the receiving area of the warehouse. Over the last three years, the proportion of rejected bulb production has increased from 3.6% to 5.4% with a commensurate increase in the cost of wastage.

Financial performance

Although sales revenues have increased for three of the last four years, operating profit has fallen slightly each year over the same period. Also, the return on capital employed has reduced from 14% to 11% a year. The ROCE required of its subsidiary companies by Eindnacht GmbH is a minimum of 18% a year.

Summary

Chumpy Lighting's present management have been given two years to meet the standards set by its parent company, in particular to reach an 18% ROCE. If this is not achieved, the UK site will face closure and production will be relocated, probably to mainland Europe. There will be an interim review after 12 months to gauge the extent of progress made.

Extracts from management meeting

Mr Winston, Finance Director

A RoCE of 18% is asking a lot! That's not far off double of last year's 11%. There's going to have to be a huge joint effort from all of us; efficiency is certainly going to have to improve significantly. And the quality of our bulbs – that's going to be fundamental.

Mr Williams, Production Director

OK, I'm already working on that. I keep trying to impress the importance of bulb quality to our workforce. They all say they understand but then they work as fast as they can to maximize their bonuses. If we scrapped the bonus scheme, the output quantities would plummet; we couldn't keep up with demand.

Ms Macauley, Sales and Marketing Director

You can't do that. We would lose sales by the thousands. Word would get round that we can't supply and we would lose even more. We've got to maintain our supplies to our customers, especially the big ones. Our quality control means that the bulbs we send out are OK; well, most of them anyway.

Mr Williams, Production Director

Most of our machinery is 12 years old or more now, breakdowns are common and maintenance costs are increasing all the time. Even more important, our technology is well out-of-date. Our best machine can only turn out 300 bulbs an hour and I know that our competitors are all using much more modern and efficient equipment. We need to invest in some new machinery. That will give us the efficiency you want – with fewer operatives – and the cost per unit should come down at the same time. That should help with our profitability.

Mrs Dell, Human Resources Director

Are you saying we will need fewer operatives? Morale is not very high at the moment and redundancies won't do anything to improve it. We've lost two of our best supervisors in the last three months; it takes time to train good people and they are a bit thin on the ground right now. When rumours of redundancies start going round, it's usually the best people who leave first.

Frankly, I think our production bonus scheme aimed at individual operatives is out of date. I'd like to introduce more team-working with teams competing against each other and league tables of performance published monthly for all to see. You would have to empower them to devise their own methods but this has the effect of boosting morale. The perceived wisdom is that this can dramatically increase productivity. It would also get round the problem of finding good supervisors as you wouldn't need them any more. You could let each team select its own leader, which would again be good for morale.

Mr Winston, Finance Director

Well, if we are going to reach 18% RoCE, we are going to have to get our costs down somehow, and quickly. What about reviewing our suppliers? I can't remember when we last had a price decrease from any of them. Except for one, they are all based in the UK; I'm sure we can get our material costs down by sourcing from China or eastern Europe.

Mr Williams, Production Director

That's all very well but what about reliability? It's no use paying less if they send you rubbish.

Ms Thompson, Managing Director

Yes, I understand that but plenty of other businesses do it. I think a review of material sourcing is a good idea. It's essential that we become more competitive. We need to act on several fronts, and with the minimum of delay. We may be able to improve our profitability by undercutting our competitors. If we can get more volume by bringing our prices down, the contribution from each extra sale is pure profit. If a 10% reduction in cost and selling price gave us a 25% increase in volume, I reckon that would add a few percentage points to our profitability right away.

Ms Macauley, Sales and Marketing Director

I'd like to agree with you but, in my experience, a 10% price reduction would soon be matched by our competitors and we would just start a price war which would do none of us any good. I think we are going to have to be more subtle than that. We need to work on our image and increase sales that way, get customers to think of us as their first choice supplier . . . and get some new customers too.

Mr Rayner, Logistics Director

We could make our wholesalers happier if we delivered in the strict order we received our sales orders in. But you know as well as me that when one of the big supermarkets places one of their huge orders, we have to give it priority or they won't come back – we know that for a fact. So all the other orders in progress are put on one side until we get theirs out of the way. It's only the relationships we've built up with the wholesalers over many years that keeps them coming back. If I were them, I'd certainly be looking elsewhere; and I think more and more of them are doing just that. Isn't there any way we could increase our productivity without increasing costs? An extra delivery lorry wouldn't do any harm either.

Mr Williams, Production Director

We looked at working a two-shifts-a-day system a few years ago and decided we couldn't justify it. Maybe we should look at it again. Perhaps we could introduce weekend working or some sort of more complex flexible working arrangements.

Ms Macauley, Sales and Marketing Director

There is one avenue we haven't explored yet – the Internet. Selling directly to the public is a very different approach. Although we would probably end up poaching some of our own sales from the supermarkets, it could give us access to many more new customers and a much bigger market. But it would need a significant investment in the necessary technology and, in view of the timescale, we would have to buy in some expertise. In the circumstances, I think this is a risk we have to take. If we do it right, it could secure our future.

Mr Winston, Finance Director

That sounds great but I am somewhat concerned about the effects of all this expansion on cash flow. Our liquid ratio is now at an all-time low of 0.7:1.0. I think we ought to get it back up to 1.0:1.0. We must avoid the overtrading trap or we really will be done for.

Ms Thompson, Managing Director
Well, if we want to stay in business, we need to do something and we need to do it soon. If the figures don't show a significant improvement in a year's time, it's going to be bad news all round.

Tasks:

1 Create a balanced scorecard for Chumpy Lighting Limited in the form of a diagram; show clearly your chosen perspectives, objectives, key performance indicators and target performance levels. Summary draft action plans should also be shown.
2 From your balanced scorecard, create a strategy map for Chumpy Lighting Ltd. Start by identifying the cause and effect relationships between the objectives.

Parnham Clarke (UK) plc

Introduction and background

Parnham Clarke (UK) plc manufactures and markets 'off-the-shelf' material fastenings (based on zips and Velcro) mainly for the clothing industry. These are mostly sold through a network of wholesalers. The company has two main sites in the East Midlands employing about 800 people. It was taken over a few years ago and is now wholly owned by the American conglomerate Spicer Lowe Inc. (listed on the New York Stock Exchange).

Parnham Clarke (UK) plc is number five in the over-the-counter material fastenings market in the UK (based on sales revenue). Its management is led by the chief executive officer, Mr D. Gamlin, who was 'head-hunted' from Clarke Fastenings (a major UK producer of Velcro-based products) nine years ago. Two years after that, Parnham Zip Fastenings Limited (as it then was) merged with Clarke Fastenings Limited to form Parnham Clarke (UK) plc. Just over four years ago, the enlarged company was taken over by a hostile bid from Spicer Lowe Inc. who are quoted on the New York Stock Exchange.

The two sites (one in Leicester and one in Nuneaton) stem from the days when the two companies were independent. For the last 18 months PC (UK) plc has been trying to persuade its American parent, Spicer Lowe Inc. to invest in a brand-new, state-of-the-art manufacturing facility part-way between Leicester and Nuneaton. However, Spicer Lowe Inc. is not happy with PC (UK) plc's current performance and is unlikely to invest in new facilities unless significant improvements occur.

Staffing

Each of the following directors reports directly to the CEO, Mr D. Gamlin:

Mr D. Stretch	Finance Director
Ms L. Jones	Marketing Director
Mrs J. de Blonde	Human Resources Director
Mr P. Martin	Production Director
Mr P. Kendall	Distribution and Materials Director

Their responsibilities are as follows:

Mr D. Gamlin, Chief Executive Officer

The CEO has overall responsibility for long-term growth and development of PC (UK) plc. He is also responsible for its long-term strategic direction in the UK market and its profitability.

Mr D. Stretch, Finance Director

The FD controls cash flow, financial resource allocation and the budgetary control system. He is responsible for the company meeting its financial targets.

Ms L. Jones, Marketing Director

The MD is responsible for all aspects of sales and marketing; this includes sales volumes and revenue as well as PC (UK) plc's marketing and public relations strategies.

Mrs J. de Blonde, Human Resources Director

The HR director is responsible for the company's strategies for recruitment, selection, training, development and the remuneration system. She is also responsible for employee satisfaction and internal communications.

Mr P. Martin, Production Director

The PD is responsible for production volume, efficiency and quality. In addition to this, he is responsible for the development of new products. He is helped in this last task by a two-person team of technicians who work from a single laboratory/office. These two 'researchers' are both nearing pensionable age and have been with the organization, in its various guises, for many years.

Mr P. Kendall, Distribution and Materials Director

The D&M director is responsible for the finished products from the time they come off the production lines to the time they reach the customers. Major aspects of this are stock storage, sales order processing and delivery logistics. However, due to the fact that the same buildings are used to store both finished products and raw materials, he is also responsible for the purchasing of raw materials.

Internal memorandum – confidential

From: D. Gamlin, CEO   To: The Directors of PC (UK) plc

Dear All,

As you know, I have just returned from my routine quarterly meeting with our parent organization, Spicer Lowe, in Seattle. Unfortunately, I have to tell you that they are seriously displeased with our performance. Off the record, CEO Jon Spicer intimated to me that unless big improvements were forthcoming in the next 12 months or so, we may be closed down and our operations transferred to our sister organization in Spain. At first, I thought this was just another exhortation for us to improve our performance but, in the present economic climate, I think we have to take it at face value.

As I was reminded, the Spanish operation outperforms us on almost all fronts; the only thing we seem to be better at is our fixed asset turnover ratio and that is only because our machinery has such a low value on the balance sheet. The Spanish manufacturing facilities are only three years old which gives them many advantages over us but we cannot go on just blaming our aging machinery. We've got to make some genuine improvements, and fast. If we don't, we could all be looking for new employment – and that may not be as easy as we would like to think!

Jon is very concerned that we have not launched any new products in the last two years. He believes this to be crucial and cites it to be the major cause of our decline in market share and sales revenue. This may also be the reason why we have slipped from third to fifth place in the recently published annual survey and market league table in our trade magazine, *Coming Together*. Indeed, there was a copy of this prominently displayed on the table where I had my 'discussion' with Jon. I can assure you that it was not a pleasant experience; I felt about two feet tall by the time he had finished.

Jon had obviously looked into this in some detail and pointed out that the two rivals who have overtaken us have not done much more in the last few years than introduce minor innovations and redesign their packaging, especially with an eye to the 'green' market. I was asked to explain why we had not adopted a similar strategy and competed more effectively.

My explanation that we have been concentrating on our cost reduction programme in order to increase our profit margin (which now stands at 6.0%) was brushed to one side. Although we have managed to reduce our fixed costs by 11% over two years, which I think is pretty impressive, I had to accept that we could have been more outward looking and proactive in the marketplace.

It was also pointed out to me that our debtors collection period is now the worst in the whole group at 79 days. The fact that a big part of this (£350,000) is caused by the dispute and impending court case with Hobbit Anoracks was not accepted as an excuse. If I did not believe we had such a strong case, I would be prepared to settle out of court. As you know, they have offered £265,000 in full settlement but I think we will get the full amount. However, if we lose, our legal costs are likely to be in the region of £50,000 (but zero if we win). The hearing is set for four months time; I just hope they do not go out of business in the meantime!

I am also aware that the extensive maintenance problems we have had with our aging machinery has not helped us to perform at the level we would have liked. The resulting downtime actually produced some temporary shortages in some product lines which must have lost us a significant amount of sales. This has caused us permanent damage with too many of our customers switching to competitors' brands. One of our first priorities must be to somehow get them back.

I pointed out, yet again, that we desperately need newer and more flexible machinery to compete effectively but Jon was quite adamant that he was not prepared to sanction any further investment in what he sees as a failing organization! I am afraid we are in a 'catch 22' situation and we have somehow got to break out of it. I do not think he is bluffing. If I were on their board, a rationalization of Spicer Lowe's European operations would probably look like a good international strategy for the group.

To be more specific, I have been told that our residual income (the measure used by head office to judge our performance as a division) must increase from this year's best estimate of £16m to £25m for the financial year just about to start. To be blunt, *we are being asked to improve our overall performance by 50% in little more than one year!*

I am calling an extraordinary management meeting for next Monday at 09:00; we can't wait until the usual meeting at the end of the month. We need to get started on our recovery plan *as soon as possible*. We have four days in which to marshal our thoughts. I expect each one of you to make a positive contribution on how we can improve our performance.

D. Gamlin,
CEO, Parnham Clarke (UK) plc

Extracts from the extraordinary management meeting

Mr. D. Stretch, Finance Director
Moving from £16m to £25m in a year is going to take some doing. We are going to have to co-operate with each other much more than we do now; and we are going to have to ditch any 'silo' mentality we may have and all work for the good of the company. If we can improve our processes and systems, and co-ordinate our activities better, we should be able to make some significant efficiency savings. I have not had chance to finalize it yet but I have started working on a plan to reduce our working capital without any detrimental effects; I hope to have this ready to show you in a couple of weeks time.

Mr P. Martin, Production Director
Funnily enough, I was thinking along the same lines, about our systems, that is. We should integrate our core processes more; product development, materials supply, production and sales order fulfilment. I am sure there are areas where we can improve, and not necessarily at great cost. Our MRP2 production control system is very out of date and occasionally leads to machinery being idle and sometimes our labour too!

Despite increased competition in the marketplace, our raw material costs seem to increase all the time. I cannot remember a period when we actually reported a reduction. We have been with some of our suppliers for a very long time and perhaps our relationships have grown too cosy. I suggest this is one area overdue for a review. There must be some deals to be done out there. I believe we could bring our direct costs down significantly.

Our customers are so much more demanding now; we need to be more flexible in our dealings with them. I have been hearing a lot about 'lean manufacturing' for the last few years. This seems to be some sort of common-sense approach (underneath the inevitable jargon) to organizing our activities so they are more efficient and flexible. I am trying to find out as much as I can about this so I can share it with you.

Mr P. Kendall, Distribution and Materials Director

I like to think we have a very good relationship with our suppliers but I have to admit that, because of all the extra work caused by rescheduling deliveries (caused by production downtime), we are not spending as much time on this as perhaps we should. There were a number of late deliveries of materials last quarter which caused some production rescheduling and all the accompanying 'knock-on' effects. I just do not have the time to keep this constantly under review. As you know, when my assistant stores manager left 10 months ago, she was not replaced in order to save money. At the time, I thought I would be able to cope with the increased work-load but, in hindsight, perhaps it was not such a good idea after all.

As for delivering our finished products to our customers, this is working very well. But this may be due to our target delivery dates being on the long side. When sales get an order, they seem to quote a delivery date two weeks after the relevant production run has finished. We do not usually have any difficulty in meeting these dates but I think it would be possible to cut this down to a week, or even less, if we wanted to. Our customers would get a much faster service which should result in more orders.

To take this even further, if we had more sophisticated production scheduling software, we could forecast product availability dates more accurately and perhaps deliver in three, or even two, days! I do not think this would entail much more risk of missing delivery dates. Of course, more trucks and drivers would also speed things up but this would need significant investment up front and the trucks would be out of use more often. I am not sure about this one.

Alternatively, we could scrap our delivery capability and use third-party logistics firms to do it for us. If you remember, we tried this (as a pilot) five years ago and it did not seem to have any significant advantages to it. However, despite its age, I estimate we could sell our present fleet of vehicles for not far short of £1m which we could put to good use elsewhere. We would also save on labour costs and release a large amount of space currently used for garaging and maintenance. The contract costs would need to produce a saving over our current costs but there are some keen transport organizations out there at the moment. Unfortunately, it would mean making our delivery staff redundant, which will cost us in redundancy pay but, at the same time, it would reduce our wage bill.

Ms L. Jones, Marketing Director

Our prices are reasonably competitive but I believe it would help our sales a great deal if we could avoid any price increases during the next year. We may even be able to actually increase our margins at the same time by reducing both our direct and indirect costs. From what has been said earlier, this does not seem to be out of the question.

If I could pick up on the 'silo' mentality mentioned earlier, the liaison between our product development section and my people is ad hoc and not really what I would call 'proactive'. If I am honest, I have to admit I have been concentrating heavily on selling; after all – no sales, no business! *I do not seem to have any time to investigate what our customers would like from us although this is obviously important.*

I suggest we set up a New Product Development Committee – or perhaps we had better call it an 'action group'; there is no point doing this unless it comes up with some new products. We also need a formal system of feedback from our customers about how we can improve their experience of us, including their ideas for product modifications and development.

Mrs J. de Blonde, Human Resources Director

You all seem to have come up with some good ideas but I need to bring you back down to Earth. The last survey we did on staff satisfaction, five months ago, showed that overall satisfaction had dropped 6 points and motivation by 8 points. Nearly one-quarter of employees said they were actively looking for work elsewhere and this is likely to be an understatement. If the economy was not so weak at the moment, I suspect our staff turnover ratio of 9% a year would be even higher.

My point is that you are more likely to successfully carry out your new schemes if you have motivated people operating them. I really think we should reconsider our approach to staff development. Last year, when I suggested more training for our operatives, it was turned down because we were trying to reduce costs; the average amount of training given to employees is currently only 2.4 hours a year. I understood the need to keep costs down but the situation has changed. We really need to have our people onside if we are going to survive. I think a small investment in this area will produce a quick return.

Also, most of our employees are paid a fixed amount each month and have no incentives to work better for the company. The annual Christmas bonus of one week's pay is seen as a right rather than something that has to be earned. And there is nothing else for them to aim at in the intervening 12 months (apart from the five sales representatives who work on monthly commission).

Incentives need not even be about money! Indeed, monetary bonuses bring many problems of their own; they do not always benefit the company because they are often badly designed.

Peer pressure in various guises can be very effective in raising people's performance. We should think about creating internal teams doing the same work but competing against each other. If we put a chart of monthly team performance levels on the canteen noticeboard for all to see, I bet our efficiency would rise dramatically. I propose we establish a working committee as soon as possible to look at working strategies and employee remuneration. As a minimum, it should consist of the CEO, myself and at least one other director, preferably the production director as he is responsible for more employees than the rest of us put together.

Mr D. Gamlin, Chief Executive Officer

Thank you all for your contributions. I am relieved and impressed that you are all giving this the attention it deserves. Personally, I am already reviewing our strategic plan; I am not sure that better or more of the same is going to be enough. We need to look at new and associated markets to make sure we are not missing any tricks. I think we are going to have to 'think outside the box' to meet the 'plus two-thirds' target we have been set for residual income. Ms Jones, I would like your help with this; between us, we need to come up with some viable ideas to take forward.

We are meeting again in two weeks and I will add 90 minutes to our regular slot to discuss our progress. I suggest we each write an initial draft report explaining our ideas, for distribution to each other. Incidentally, I am looking at a 'vehicle' which will incorporate and co-ordinate all our different performance improvement initiatives. You may have heard of it – it is called the balanced scorecard. I will explain more about it next time we meet.

Tasks:

1 Create a balanced scorecard for Parnham Clarke (UK) plc showing four corporate objectives for each of the four generic perspectives. Also choose and show one appropriate key performance indicator for each objective. Target performance levels and action plans should also be shown.

(64 marks)

2 Based on your balanced scorecard, create a strategy map for Parnham Clarke (UK) plc. To do this, you will have to identify the cause and effect relationships between the objectives.

(36 marks)
(Total 100 marks)

Review questions

1 Describe the theory and structure of the balanced scorecard.
2 Describe the internal 'lead' and 'lag' relationships between balanced scorecard components.
3 Explain the different relationships in 'for-profit' and 'not-for-profit' organizations.
4 Explain the advantage of involving front-line staff in balanced scorecard design and operation.
5 Draw a diagram to show how corporate strategy can be implemented through the balanced scorecard.
6 Give examples of how popular strategies would appear on the balanced scorecard.
7 Explain the flexibility of balanced scorecard design.
8 Describe the process of cascading scorecards within organizations.
9 Describe the process of employee involvement in the operation of scorecards.
10 Explain how a strategy map can be created from a balanced scorecard.
11 Explain how the scorecard approach can help with strategy formulation.
12 Describe the multiple benefits of operating balanced scorecards.
13 Explain the role of financial incentives connected to balanced scorecards.
14 Describe the limitations of balanced scorecards.

The answers to all these questions can be found in the text of this chapter.

chapter 18

Performance improvement techniques

Introduction

According to the Official Terminology of the Chartered Institute of Management Accountants, management accounting is:

The application of the principles of accounting and financial management to create, protect, preserve and increase value so as to deliver that value to the stakeholders of profit and not-for-profit enterprises, both public and private. Management accounting is an integral part of management, requiring the identification, generation, presentation, interpretation and use of information relevant to:

- *formulating business strategy;*
- *planning and controlling activities;*
- *decision-making;*
- *efficient resource usage;*
- *performance improvement and value enhancement;*
- *safeguarding tangible and intangible assets;*
- *corporate governance and internal control.*

This chapter concentrates on one of the above seven aspects which can be summarized as follows:

Management accounting is an integral part of management which, amongst other things, aims to improve performance (and consequently increase value).

There is a strong argument for saying that this is **the primary objective** of management accounting. The reason why this book uses the word 'managerial' rather than 'management' in its title is to emphasize management accounting's managerial function rather than its accounting one. (Over the years, management accounting came to be thought of as a branch of accounting rather than as an aid to managing; this trend has now reversed and relevance is being regained.)

A comparison of the functions of financial accounting with those of management accounting is very informative. Financial accounting looks back at what has already happened and attempts to communicate this story in annual instalments. Management accounting looks forward and attempts to assist the organization to perform better in the future.

Anyone working in an organization will have encountered ideas formulated to improve its performance. These ideas are variously described as techniques, models, paradigms, strategies, initiatives or systems. They are often referred to individually by their initials and collectively as a branch of 'management-speak'. During the course of their careers, it is the norm for managers to experience many of these techniques one after another or sometimes two or more at the same time.

From time to time, it is natural for organizations to become complacent about their performance. An initiative (such as business performance re-engineering) may operate in an organization for, say, four years before it runs out of steam. At the end of that period management may compare their current performance with that at the start and declare their satisfaction '*at a job well done*'. This is understandable. However, it is dangerous to allow these periods of positive reflection to drift into complacency. 'Standing still' is not an option for a successful business; competitors have a tendency to catch up and overtake. Continuous improvement is the recommended philosophy; it is advisable to think of organizational activity as an ongoing journey with milestones every so often rather than a final destination that can be reached and so end the story. When one initiative comes to an end, it is usually not very long before a new one is put in place in order to reinvigorate the organization's momentum.

Performance improvement initiatives are a way of business life. The remainder of this chapter explores 15 of the more popular ones, giving a **brief insight** into each. (Full expositions would probably increase the size of this book 10-fold!) The hope is that readers will be stimulated to explore for themselves, in much greater detail, those techniques that are of interest to them. There are a significant number of books dedicated to just one of the chosen techniques; some of these are listed in the 'Further reading' section at the end of this chapter.

The techniques are presented in a loose order according to the author's perception of their popularity, usefulness, importance and age. (The existence of a positive correlation between these four factors has been assumed.) The difficulty in putting them into any sort of order is that they have a tendency to overlap each other *in more ways than one*. This 'overlapping' will be explored further in the summary at the end of this chapter.

Learning objectives

Having worked through this chapter you should be able to:

- explain and give an overview of each of the 15 performance improvement techniques discussed;
- describe how they can be used in combination with each other;
- compare and contrast the operation of the 15 techniques.

Life cycle costing

(Also known as 'whole life costing'.)

When a product is costed using the traditional absorption costing system, an estimate is made of its variable costs and an amount is added for its fixed costs using a predetermined overhead absorption rate(s). These are combined to give a total product cost. If activity-based costing is used, the selected cost drivers will be used to attach individual costs to the product resulting in a more accurate product cost. However, both these methods use only current costs, those that are incurred in the current accounting year. They do not take into account any costs incurred before the product is launched or after it is withdrawn from the marketplace. These are lumped together as part of the fixed costs and spread out 'unfairly' amongst all the products. In effect, some products will cross-subsidize others.

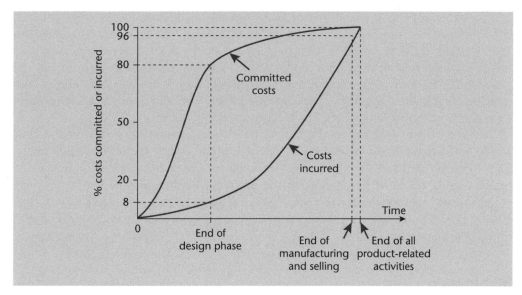

Figure 18.1 **Life cycle costs**

A business can be thought of as the collection of its products, and its performance as the sum of the net differences between **all** the costs and incomes of each product. So any costs concerning research, development and product launch should not be ignored. Similarly, any costs concerning decommissioning of plant and machinery specific to the product, and any special arrangements for continuing customer service, should be accounted for. Over its lifetime, the total revenues from the product should exceed its **total** costs.

A classic example of huge decommissioning costs is nuclear power, where the cost of producing electricity is relatively cheap until these end-of-life costs are taken into account. To calculate a 'fair' cost of the electricity generated by nuclear stations, the decommissioning costs would need to be factored in right from the start.

Life cycle costing is essentially an attention-directing device. It forces managers to think about the 'before and after' costs caused by the product and to consider their impact on manufacturing/selling costs. For example, clever design can reduce manufacturing costs without reducing the product quality and extra training can reduce wastage costs as well as improving efficiency (which in itself will lead to a further reduction of costs).

The great majority (say about 80%) of lifetime product costs will be determined at the design stage; these can be said to be 'committed'. These turn into 'incurred' costs as the product is launched, sales grow and eventually decline. This relationship is illustrated in Figure 18.1.

Criticisms

Figure 18.1 looks very neat and self-contained. It describes the incidence of costs for a product which, once launched, does not undergo any changes. However, many products are partially redesigned from time to time in response to market demand tailing off, usually due to active competition.

Take the Ford Escort, a family car made and sold in Europe for 32 years (1968 to 2000). Altogether it underwent five major modifications. The Mark 2 was launched in 1975 and lasted five years before being superseded by the Mark 3 in 1980. Also, during this five-year period several minor modifications were launched. A cosmetic update was given in 1978, with some models getting their headlights, front track, interior and exterior specification upgraded. Three special editions, the Linnet, Harrier and Goldcrest, were launched in 1979 and 1980. The Mark 6 ceased production in 2000.

Two consequence of this are that not all the design costs were incurred before 1968 and less of the total costs would be committed by the end of the initial design phase, marked by the launch of the Mark 1 in 1968. At that point, no one could know how many modifications would be needed during the product's lifetime or how much they were going to cost. In other words, the complexity of product extensions renders the life cycle costing model much less simple than it first appears. Consequently, the model becomes of less practical use.

Summary

Life cycle costing takes into account all costs from the conception of the idea to the elimination of all associated activities. It is a long-term view, not constrained by financial years. Its main benefit is that it causes managers to think about lifetime costs before they are irreversibly committed.

As a significant element of life cycle costing is the reduction of manufacturing costs by redesigning the product, this performance management technique overlaps with target costing and value engineering.

Business process re-engineering (BPR)

This approach to improving business performance was introduced in the early 1990s by Hammer, Champy and Davenport in the USA. The catalyst was the new wave of competition from Japan, China and other Pacific-rim countries which was proving to be very successful. The numerous innovations in computer hardware and management information systems offered new ways of organizing corporate processes. This also provided a golden opportunity to reassess what and how companies were doing. The prevailing structure tended to be 'functional' where a firm was divided into stand-alone departments such as production, marketing, purchasing and delivery. This 'silo' mentality had the minimum of interconnecting communications and managers concentrated on running their departments well rather than meeting the needs of customers, internal or external.

The BPR approach is to *fundamentally rethink* the existing business processes and *radically redesign* them, taking advantage of the latest available technology and information systems. When creating new processes, it can be useful to consider the five dimensions involved: organizational structure, corporate objectives, corporate strategies, technology and people. If the last of these is overlooked and adequate retraining and/or recruitment is not carried out, all the other efforts may come to nothing. It is always worth remembering that people are not 'outside operators' interacting with the system but are fundamental parts **of** the system. If they are not 'maintained' properly, the system will break down. In information systems technology, they are sometimes known as 'liveware' as opposed to hardware or software!

The idea of BPR is to achieve dramatic improvements in key aspects of performance such as product quality, customer service and costs. Rather than just improve existing processes, managers were encouraged to scrap them altogether and start from scratch with a 'clean sheet'. At the same time, there was an emphasis on the elimination of non-value-adding activities.

Typical implementation mechanism

1 Identify non-value-adding processes and rank them in order of importance.
2 Starting with the most important, design radically different processes which give added value to customers, taking advantage of the latest information technology.
3 Test these new processes and refine as necessary.
4 Implement the refined processes and eliminate the non-value-adding ones.

There are many variations of the BPR mechanism (every firm of management consultants produced their own slightly different version) but the one stated above is a typically logical approach which also includes a sensible risk management element (step 3).

Criticisms of BPR

Many large companies adopted BPR in the 1990s but it was often used as a cover for downsizing (reducing the number of employees and operations without specific justification). However, most of the companies which used it in a genuine fashion did improve their performance.

The important things that organizations do are almost always made up of smaller activities which are often carried out by several different departments. For example, product quality depends on work done by research and development, production, distribution and after-sales departments. It is quite usual for no single person to be responsible for the whole process! When responsibility is shared in this fragmented way, it can be very difficult to hold anyone to account when things go wrong.

Poor performance by a company may not be the result of poor processes, it could have many other explanations such as substitute products, market decline and a difficult national economy. Far too often, the human aspects of the inherent changes were overlooked with devastating consequences (see the discussion of 'liveware' above).

Summary

BPR always involves some *change management* activities and sometimes it will include some specific techniques from other performance management systems such as TQM and JIT; performance improvement activities are rarely exclusive. BPR is not about incremental improvements, it is about radical change; revolution as opposed to evolution. It is about leapfrogging the competition and stealing a march on the enemy. Unfortunately, when you are playing leapfrog, competitors not only catch up but usually end up in front! So standing still is not an option. Having said that, all performance management techniques are something of a fashion and fashion changes with time. BPR may have been flavour of the decade in the 1990s but it is nowhere near as popular now as it was then; it will probably have been replaced by one of the more recent models.

(BPR is also known as BP management or BP redesign but these are essentially the same idea.)

Theory of constraints

The originator of this theory, Dr Eliyahu Goldratt, described it at length in his 1984 book, *The Goal* (which is in the form of a novel). He said:

> *Every real system, such as a business, must have within it at least one constraint. If this were not the case then the system could produce unlimited amounts of whatever it was striving for, profit in the case of a business.*

A constraint is a restriction that is preventing a company achieving its goal. Constraints can be internal or external. Internal ones are usually production related whilst external ones could be supplier related, e.g. the inability to purchase sufficient raw materials. Constraints are also referred to as 'bottlenecks'. These can be departments, teams or machines which are already working at full capacity and cannot handle any extra demand. Managers are usually aware of which bottleneck is having the largest negative effect on the rate of output.

In order to ensure the identified bottleneck works at maximum efficiency, buffer stocks of work-in-progress are maintained on either side of it. This is in order to prevent the output rate decreasing and causing knock-on effects all the way down the line when any unforeseen problems arise. The buffer stocks minimize the effects of any problems elsewhere by providing time in which to put the problem right. This is one way of managing risk; managers must exercise judgement as to the quantity of buffer stocks held.

Five-Stage Process

1 Identify the leading constraint, that part of the process that, more than any other, is preventing the organization from performing better; the bottleneck is preventing the system from increasing its output capacity.
2 Identify the best way to modify ('*exploit*') the constraint; this is the solution that will increase the output rate more than any other.
3 Modify all the other processes as necessary to support this decision ('*subordinate*' the other processes).
4 Implement the modification identified above ('*elevate*' the constraint) and check to see if the planned output rate increase has been achieved or whether the constraint has just moved to another part of the system.
5 Repeat the process in the spirit of continuous or ongoing improvement.

Performance measurement system

Throughput accounting is the performance measurement system associated with the theory of constraints. It is important to note that it is not a cost accounting system; it does not attempt to attach variable and fixed costs to products. **Throughput accounting measures the speed at which throughput is generated by products.** It uses three key measures:

- **Throughput:** This is the 'money' generated by production/sales in a given time period. It is similar to the concept of 'contribution' and is calculated by deducting only *totally variable costs* from *sales revenue* (T = SR – TVC). All labour is considered to be a *fixed* cost (from the company's point of view) so TVC usually consists of raw materials only (T = SR – RM). Unless sales occur, throughput is zero; generating products for stock kept in a warehouse does not create any throughput.
- **Investment:** This is the value of the money tied up in the system. It can be represented by inventory and other net current asset items such as debtors. It may also take the form of fixed assets such as buildings and machinery.
- **Operational expenses:** This is the cost of converting raw material inventory into finished products. It covers all expenses including items such as maintenance of buildings and machinery, insurances and lease payments. Note that it also includes labour costs (specifically excluded from the throughput contribution defined above).

The theory of constraints aims to increase the throughput contribution whilst decreasing operational expenses and the amount of investment in inventory. However, it may be that businesses trading in highly seasonal markets decide to increase their finished goods inventory prior to their major selling season. This may temporarily decrease their throughput on a monthly or quarterly basis but, because none of their demand is left unsatisfied, the **annual** throughput will be increased. (A firm manufacturing the red dye used to colour winter heating oil could purposely stockpile it in the summer.) Thus, the concept of throughput accounting can be seen to be more applicable to a company with only small seasonal fluctuations in the demand for its products.

When making important decisions, managers of companies striving to meet their 'goal' should consider the following questions:

- To what extent will my decision increase throughput?
- To what extent will my decision reduce investment?
- To what extent will my decision reduce operating expenses?

When considering these questions, the following ratios can be used as key performance indicators:

- Net profit = throughput – operating expense
- Return on investment = net profit/investment
- Productivity = throughput/operating expense
- Investment turn = throughput/investment.

Criticisms

The main drawback of the theory of constraints is that only one constraint can be tackled at a time. The activities involved are carried out in serial fashion and cannot be performed in parallel. If big improvements in performance are needed urgently, this is probably not the best technique to use.

Summary

This performance improvement model concentrates on the manufacturing process. It seeks to identify the weakest link in the manufacturing chain and improve it as much as possible. When this has been done, a new weakest link will manifest itself and the model can then be applied again. This iterative process is an example of continuous improvement or *kaisen*.

Kaisen costing

Kaisen is Japanese for *continuous improvement*; '*Kai*' can be translated as 'change' and '*Zen*' as 'better'. So *kaisen costing* is a system for continually reducing costs, both product costs and process costs. It is sometimes used as part of a lean production approach along with just-in-time and six-sigma systems.

This fundamental objective contrasts with that of standard costing which strives to control costs by identifying variances to predetermined standards or targets. However, corrective action is usually only taken when the variance is adverse (actual cost higher than standard). Where the variance is favourable (actual cost lower than standard) the cost is considered to be satisfactory and no action is taken. Whereas standard costing sets out to limit or contain costs, **kaisen costing aims to reduce costs, on an ongoing basis**.

Cost reduction targets can be frequently set, usually monthly or quarterly, and production operatives are very involved in setting these. Employees are thought of as 'brains' rather than 'hands'; suggestions for improvements are usually encouraged by incentive schemes. Toyota has successfully adopted this approach for many years. It aims to reduce costs by making many small adjustments rather than a few large ones. Identified savings do not just involve materials and labour, they can also concern things such as storage, flexible working, size of work areas, inter-workstation travel time and distance.

The Boeing Commercial Airplane Company in the USA also uses kaisen costing. Boeing believes it allows it to exceed customer requirements of quality, functionality and price, thereby maintaining product competitiveness. Boeing stresses that it is not sufficient to set a clear reduction target, but that information has to be clearly communicated to the operatives involved. Also, in the spirit of responsibility accounting, individual team leaders are responsible for achieving the agreed reductions. It is claimed that the savings achieved are often in excess of the set targets.

Kaisen costing is a proactive process which involves the continual reviewing of processes to identify any 'wastage' followed by its reduction/elimination. However, it has been pointed out that the empowerment of individual employees is counterbalanced by the pressure that kaisen costing puts upon them. The technique has been referred to as an example of 'management by stress' due to the pressure on employees to come up continually with new ideas to produce savings.

Benefits of the technique, other than a reduction in costs, include improved product quality and enhanced customer satisfaction. Companies often find that employees are more motivated and consequently have an improved workrate. In addition, as kaisen costing deals with small incremental changes, the results are more immediate than when implementing a large and complicated change. This rapid feedback reinforces morale and further improves employee performance. Ongoing and continuous improvement has a positive effect on corporate performance.

Just in time

'Just in time' is a management model that aims to improve manufacturing efficiency. It began in Japan in the 1950s, an era when American workers produced approximately nine times as much as Japanese workers. Taiichi Ohno of the Toyota Motor Company visited American car manufacturers to learn how his organization could match American productivity. However, he was not impressed by what he saw. Fortunately, during that visit he was inspired by the simple operation of a drinks vending machine. Each time a customer paid for and removed a drink from the machine, a replacement drink automatically took its place. An empty receptacle triggered the appearance of new stock. Ohno built the now famous Toyota production system around this simple process.

Over the years, JIT has developed significantly. Originally it was a 'top-down' process imposed on employees by management but its current sophistication depends on the proactive interventions of an empowered workforce. Every single worker has personal responsibility for efficiency and quality; the workers are motivated by having psychological ownership of their roles and wholeheartedly endorse the philosophy of continuous improvement and personal development. It is also worth noting that one of the basic foundations of this model is 'respect for the individual worker', a fact often overlooked by students of this very important system.

The common perception of JIT is that its main objective is the elimination of stocks. Those who operate it know that it embraces much more than this. A more complete list of its objectives includes the achievement of:

- zero defects;
- zero waste;
- zero inventory;
- zero lead times;
- smooth continuous flow processes;
- flexible manufacturing.

The first four of these lend themselves to measurement by performance indicators.

JIT systems are most suitable for high-volume, repetitive manufacturing, although they can be adapted for less repetitive production. They work best when the manufacturing schedule is stable for reasonably long periods of time (months rather than days). On the production line, the system operates by each workstation requesting materials to work on from the previous workstation. This is referred to as a 'pull' system and no workstation is allowed to 'push' its output down the line to the next operation. The mechanism by which this is achieved is the 'kanban' system. Incidentally, each workstation is responsible for ensuring the quality of its outputs; no 'external' inspection teams are used.

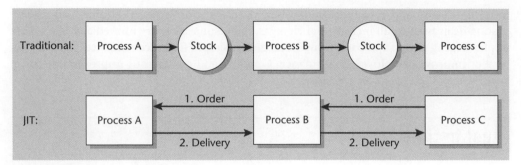

Figure 18.2 JIT poll system

A kanban is simply a request to the previous workstation for a specific quantity of its output (always the same small amount, often a single unit). The kanban often takes the form of a container **sent by** one station to the previous station and used to transport the work-in-progress to the requesting station. In this way, work is *pulled* up the line (rather than *pushed* down it). Figure 18.2 illustrates this by comparing it with a traditional system; process A is followed by process B which is followed by process C. Traditional systems concentrate on machine and labour efficiencies; for example, producing large batches which create large inventories inbetween stations. In contrast, JIT systems avoid stock by preventing anything being made by a workstation until it receives a kanban requesting its output. At times when no output has been requested, the operatives concerned are not idle; they perform maintenance operations or work on prearranged projects.

When component parts are supplied by external firms or other divisions within the group of companies, it is impossible to avoid stocks completely. It is not unusual for the supplier to deliver 3, 4, 5 or even 6 times every day, which keeps buffer stocks very small. Neither are these deliveries normally inspected for quality; if there are defects in the supplies, the problem cannot be hidden and it has to be solved immediately. The supplier would play the major role in correcting the situation. The fundamental idea is to get the right quantity of the right component parts to the right place at the right time.

A further consideration is the possibility of a disaster, such as a major fire, at the premises of a supplier. This would have the potential to shut down complete production lines, which would have serious financial repercussions. The way to get round this is to have more than one supplier; it is normal to have one major supplier and at least one minor one which would be willing to gear up its production levels, at least on a temporary basis.

Minimizing inventory has the effect of improving cash flow as less money is tied up in stocks. But very low stock levels also have another advantage: if there are any problems with the quality of the stock, they have to be addressed immediately, they cannot be put to one side to be dealt with at a later time. The cause of a production line stoppage will very quickly attract the attention of everyone affected by it. In this way, problems are not allowed to escalate or hang around.

There is a well-known saying which encapsulates this idea: 'Inventory is like water in a river, it hides problems that are like rocks'. Get rid of the water and the rocks can no longer be ignored.

This analogy compares the company with a boat sailing on deep water (high inventories) which effectively covers dangerous rocks (production problems) on the river bed. As long as the water remains deep, the rocks can be ignored *but remain in place*. If the water level is lowered (inventories reduced) the rocks (problems) must be dealt with, otherwise the boat (company) will sink. Dealing with problems as soon as they arise makes the company both efficient and effective.

JIT is active in the following four areas of manufacturing:

- product design;
- process design;
- human/organization elements;
- manufacturing planning and control.

Product design uses *value engineering* to increase the product's value to the customer without increasing costs. (Product *redesign* uses *value analysis* to achieve the same objective.) For example, by combining several components into one, the total number of components in a product may be reduced. This may lead to a reduction in the cost price which will, in turn, enable a decrease in the selling price. It builds-in achievable quality at appropriate levels. Where possible, it uses modular designs with parts common to other products and enables manufacturing to take place in flexible production cells with self-directed work teams.

Process design aims to make use of flexible manufacturing cells. It builds-in preventative maintenance schedules and reduces machine set-up times to a minimum. In common with TQM and lean production, it uses computer-aided design/manufacturing (CAD/CAM), built-in fault-detection features and automatic process controls. Stock-holding areas are eliminated so that any unrequested work-in-progress is immediately seen as a problem demanding a solution.

The human element is a holistic approach encouraging the use of **all** the employees' skills. This implies continuous training in new skills, including problem solving, and a flexible, multi-skilled labour force. The difference between direct and indirect labour is reduced – if not eliminated – and teamwork is encouraged. Employees are encouraged to use their brains as well as their bodies to achieve production goals. Computing power is made available to employees at the point of work to help them monitor their own performance and create solutions to their problems. This kaisen approach is sometimes known as *total employee involvement* or *empowerment*. Decision making is devolved to the people at the sharp end of the production process, leaving managers free to tackle more strategic issues.

Manufacturing planning and control aims at continuous, rapid-flow, small-batch manufacturing but strictly within the confines of a 'pull' system. The use of kanbans encourages paperless, visual systems to control workflow. JIT software is commonly available to assist in the production planning process and this is usually interfaced with a materials requirements planning (MRP) program. One advantage of this approach is that it reveals the costs of the 'hidden factory', i.e. those jobs and systems that are not really necessary and add no value to the products under a JIT environment. For example, in non-JIT manufacturing it is not unusual for 'progress chasers' to be employed to expedite specific orders for certain customers. This activity is unnecessary when production is planned and continuously monitored. Another very important aspect is the supplier relationship. The concept of the right-quality raw materials being delivered to the right place at the right time is central to JIT. It is common for raw materials not to be inspected on delivery. If defects do occur, the supplier is expected to rectify the situation immediately. If necessary, the manufacturer will send a team of its own employees to help with this process. It is no longer seen as essential to buy materials at the lowest possible price. The quality and reliability of supplies is more important. The two parties work together in a partnership to their mutual benefit.

This has several implications for the management accounting information system. Traditional variance analysis can actually work against the successful operation of JIT. Purchasing the cheapest materials will give the most favourable price variance, but the low price may be due to the poor quality of the materials. Asset utilization ratios can be positively misleading as they encourage continuous usage of machinery producing for stock. Direct labour hours are no longer an appropriate basis for the apportionment of overheads. New performance indicators are required to monitor and enforce the JIT system. JIT does not sit easily with traditional cost accounting practices.

A London-based company, MK Electric, allowed its customer service to deteriorate to the point where only 30% of its sales were delivered to customers within its stated 10-day time period. Consequently, its reputation was suffering and customers were looking at alternative sources of supply. When it eventually realized the seriousness of the situation, it took the opportunity to investigate and reassess its business practices. It concluded that it was producing too many products, the sales department was not liaising and co-ordinating with production control and it was manufacturing large batches of whatever products made it seem most efficient according to its traditional absorption costing system. As a result of this, MK Electric introduced *optimized production technology*, a computer software system that was based on JIT principles. Before long, deliveries within 10 days of receiving the order rose from 30% to 80% and the value of inventory held reduced by one-third.

JIT forms the basis of lean manufacturing as it concentrates on efficiency and the elimination of waste. A recent chairman of Toyota, Fujio Cho, defined waste as 'anything other than the minimum amount of equipment, materials, parts and labour which are absolutely essential to production'. Another thing JIT and lean manufacturing have in common is the idea of improving customer value which leads to improvements in their own performance.

Total quality management

TQM is associated with W. Edwards Deming more than any other person. Early in Deming's career, he worked under Walter Shewart at Bell Telephone Laboratories in the USA. Shewart developed statistical process control (SPC) which enabled operatives to detect defects and reduce/eliminate them early on in the production process; the objective was to reduce variation in the output. (SPC is a direct forerunner of six sigma; it used three sigma *or standard deviations* as a threshold action point.)

A key part of Deming's TQM model is the empowerment of operatives to use their first-hand knowledge to intervene and improve production processes. He believed that the attitude of the workers is fundamentally important to quality improvement and that a positive attitude towards quality could be fostered by respecting them. In 1950, to help rebuild the industries of Japan which had been devastated in the Second World War, Deming gave a series of lectures in that country elaborating his ideas on quality improvement. The Japanese wholeheartedly embraced his ideas and over the next two decades became the world-leader in high-quality manufactured goods, often surpassing that of American production. The 'wake-up call' was finally heard and North America, followed closely by Western Europe, widely adopted the TQM philosophy.

The following inexhaustive list gives a taste of the breadth of Deming's thinking, although not its depth (this can be found in many other books, articles and websites – see Further reading):

- The 85/15 rule: operatives can control only 15% of the problems they encounter; only management have the power to control the other 85% which are often systemic.
- The Deming cycle: 1. Plan, 2. Do, 3. Check and 4. Act.
- Deming's seven corporate diseases which inhibit good-quality output.
- Deming's 14 points to assist the effective implementation of total quality programmes.

The 14 points include the following:

- Give high priority to motivating employees and creating a high level of employee satisfaction by affording them due respect.
- Eliminate everything that undermines operatives' self- and mutual-respect (e.g. sexism, favouritism).
- Consider inputs from suppliers to be an important part of your system; do not buy on price alone.
- Use statistical monitoring to control operations wherever possible.
- Monitor 'outputs' throughout the process, not just at the final stage.
- Continually refine processes by making small improvements, not infrequent large company-changing events which are invariably disruptive.
- Eliminate all barriers to teamwork, whether physical or due to organizational structure.
- Involve both suppliers and customers in your quest for quality; send your staff to work with them on their premises to create mutual quality improvements, benefitting all concerned.
- Emphasise long-term profit sharing for teams rather than short-term profit sharing for individuals.

Another American and contemporary of Deming, Joseph Juran, also played an important role in the quality movement. His main contribution was the application of the Pareto principle to the control of quality. The Pareto principle (or 80/20 rule) states that 80% of the problems come from 20% of the possible sources. This encouraged the identification of the critical 20% and enabled managers and operatives to concentrate on improving these, leaving the other relatively benign 80% alone for the time being.

Three other 'quality gurus' also played important roles in the quality movement during the latter part of the twentieth century. Kaoru Ishikawa is best known for his 'Fishbone' diagram which has a similar appearance to that of a fish's skeleton. This is still frequently used today in various contexts (e.g. as part of a six-sigma initiative). It facilitates brainstorming sessions enabling the causes of quality problems to be identified. Philip Crosby is remembered for his pronouncement that 'Quality is Free' – the title of one of his books. His basic argument is that the cost of conforming to quality standards is less than the cost of not conforming – see Figure 18.3 for items included in both categories. Genichi Taguchi invented some new statistical techniques and refined others to further improve the quality of output. He is best known for the idea of *designing quality into the product* rather than *inspecting it out* (i.e. relying on inspections to identify defects).

The aim of TQM is to continually improve the quality of the product. 'Quality' is a difficult concept to define and several definitions exist. However, the following is one of the most useful:

> A quality product is one that meets the requirements of the customer.

This practical definition is useful in that it enables the degree of quality to be measured or estimated, *provided the customer requirements are known*. Note that, unless there are special reasons, these requirements should not be exceeded as this will cause unnecessary costs.

Of course, the operation of a TQM system has an associated cost. As much as they would like to, firms cannot spend endless amounts of money on improving quality. To help them decide how much they are prepared to spend, they need to understand the various cost elements involved.

In simple terms, the cost of quality (see Figure 18.3) consists of:

a) the cost of preventing poor quality occurring in the first place;
b) the cost of dealing with the effects of poor-quality items after they have been produced.

There is a trade-off between the costs of **prevention** and those of **cure**. The more that is spent on prevention and appraisal, the less has to be spent on putting things right, and vice versa. Many firms believe that the cost of conformance ('a' above) is likely to be less

Cost of conformance	Cost of non-conformance
Prevention costs	*Internal failure costs*
– engineering and designing of product for quality	– cost of scrap
– engineering and designing of process for quality	– cost of reworking
– training of employees	– reinspection
– statistical process control	–failure investigation
– preventive maintenance	– cost of lost production
– etc.	– etc.
Appraisal costs	*External failure costs*
– sample preparation	– loss of sales revenue
– sample testing	– warranty claims
– test reporting	– loss of future orders
– purchase and maintenance of test equipment	– loss of customer goodwill
– quality audits	– making good customer losses
– etc.	– product recalls
	– law suits
	– etc.

Figure 18.3 The component costs of quality

than that of non-conformance ('b' above). This is understandable when you consider some of the costs of external failure (i.e. failure occurring after the product has been received by the customer). These include the loss of customer goodwill and future orders. Although impossible to quantify precisely, these may be justifiably described as **potentially very significant**.

One common approach to avoiding poor quality arising in the first place is the introduction of the '**internal** customer and supplier' concept. Every team in the organization is considered to be a supplier with an internal customer, e.g. the next team in the production process. This could also apply to the accounts department; its customers are the users of the information it produces. Employees should be encouraged to consider how they might improve their service to the next in line. Also, internal customers should be encouraged to reject any input which did not conform to the set quality standards.

Unfortunately, customers are not always explicit about their requirements. This being so, the providing firm will have to judge this for itself and decide on how much to spend on quality. One way of going about this is to ascertain the combined cost of conformance and non-conformance for different degrees of quality (at a given level of production). The point at which the combined cost is at its minimum is the point of 'optimum quality', from a cost point of view, for the producing firm (see Figure 18.4). However, it should be recognized that some amount of rectification, internal and external, will probably arise when operating at the chosen quality level.

Of course, the curves drawn in Figure 18.4 are based on the assumption that all the costs are known. In reality, many of them are subjective and based on estimates. So how does a firm know if it is improving its quality? It needs to choose some performance criteria that will indicate whether or not this is so. Some of these performance indicators will be financial and others will be non-financial; Figure 18.5 lists a selection of them.

One of the principal aims of TQM in a mass-production environment is to achieve zero defects. Admittedly, this performance standard is a theoretical ideal but it does ensure that the search for quality improvement is ongoing even when significant milestones have been reached. When a firm achieves a failure rate of one item per million for

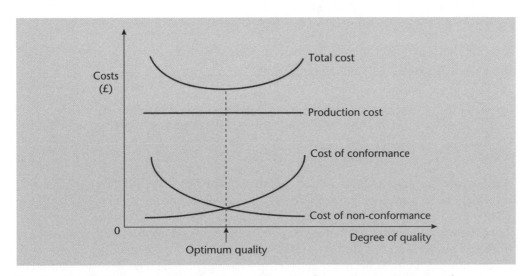

Figure 18.4 Finding the optimum degree of quality (for a given activity level)

Financial:	$\dfrac{\text{Total cost of quality}}{\text{Sales revenue}}$ %	
	$\dfrac{\text{Cost of conformance}}{\text{Total cost of quality}}$ %	
	$\dfrac{\text{Cost of non-conformance}}{\text{Total cost of quality}}$ %	
Non-financial:	Extent of computer-aided design/manufacturing (CAD/CAM)	
	Extent of built-in fault detection features	
	Extent of built-in automatic process controls	
	Quality of raw material supplies	
	Percentage of on-time deliveries by suppliers	
	Percentage of on-time deliveries by producer	
	Percentage of items returned as unacceptable	
	Number of customer complaints	
	Number of warranty claims	

Figure 18.5 Financial and non-financial indicators used in TQM

its output it can be justifiably proud of its achievement. However, it should not rest on its laurels but strive for further improvement, say, one defect per 10 million. TQM is not just a technique, it is a managerial philosophy, attitude or 'way of life' embodying the idea of continuous improvement or kaisen. However, like all management fashions, TQM is not as popular as it once was and is being been replaced by more modern incarnations such as six sigma.

Activity-based management

The Official Terminology of the Chartered Institute of Management Accountants (CIMA) defines activity-based management (ABM) as:

> *A system of management which uses activity based cost information for a variety of purposes including cost reduction, cost modelling and customer profitability analysis.*

The increased accuracy in product costs provided by activity-based costing (ABC) means that costs can be controlled more effectively. Managers are able to get a better idea of the relative profitability of their various product lines. This, in turn, encourages them to concentrate on the more profitable lines whilst reducing or even phasing out the least profitable ones.

For example, it is possible to use an ABC approach to find the relative costs of different customers and different administration procedures. This information helps managers to prioritize their time and effort. It may be that two customers, Jones Ltd and Smith & Co., buy the same value of items but Jones Ltd causes twice the amount of costs as Smith & Co. The former firm may require more visits from sales representatives, demand higher discounts and return 'unsuitable' goods more often. If this is so, an investigation into the conduct of Jones Ltd's account will probably reveal ways of reducing the cost of maintaining that particular customer. Without ABC, no one will know the extent to which this is happening.

ABC uses the causation link to measure accurately the resources used by product lines. The financial accounts, based on absorption costing, show the cost of resources provided by management. The total of resources supplied is almost always greater than the total of resources that should be consumed according to the ABC model. Financial accounting is a *resource supply* model but ABC is a *resource consumption* model. ABC identifies only the amount of resources that should be needed but absorption accounting uses the amount actually provided. The difference represents the amount of resources that add no value to products.

Some of the resources supplied are used by activities not caused by product creation – for example, production machinery being used for a building maintenance job. Also, some 'legitimate' production activities may use more resources than they should – for example, storing raw material for three weeks instead of three days. Identification of these non-value-added resources and activities enables management to eliminate or reduce them, a major objective of ABM. (The manager's point of view section at the end of Chapter 10 on activity-based costing includes a very good real-life example of this concerning factory electricity costs.)

Ultimately, in order to bring the amount of resources supplied into line with the amount consumed, the organization needs to introduce activity-based budgeting (ABB). This is only possible if there is an ABC system in operation which is detailed and well developed (see Figure 18.6). However, the adoption of ABB is a significant change in the way the business is managed and can take many months to implement successfully. ABB is one facet of ABM.

Operational ABM and strategic ABM

ABM can be thought of as a collection of actions performed by managers that are based on information provided by an ABC system. The aim is for the organization to improve its performance by reducing its total costs whilst maintaining its sales revenue.

S. Kaplan and R. Cooper (*Cost and Effect: Using Integrated Cost Systems to Drive Profitability and Performance*, 1998, Harvard Business School Press, Boston, MA, Chapter 8) divide these managerial activities into two categories: operational ABM and strategic ABM. Operational ABM is about **doing things right** and strategic ABM is about **doing the right things**. The objectives of operational ABM are to reduce the cost of activities and to increase capacity by improving efficiency. Note that capacity increases are only translated into improved performance if they are either eliminated (to reduce present costs) or used to facilitate expansion (to reduce future costs). If no action is taken, no improvement will materialize.

Operational ABM starts by identifying possible improvements to existing processes, prioritizing them and allocating resources to carry them out. The next stage involves

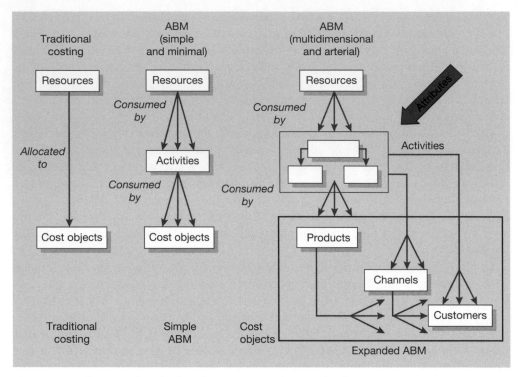

Figure 18.6 Stages of maturity of cost accounting methods
Source: Cokins, G. (2009). Reproduced with permission of John Wiley & Sons Inc.

monitoring the results of these activities to identify the extent of the actual improvements achieved. The ABC system provides the information needed to verify the reduced spending on operational activities. The variances between planned and actual resource consumption should show clearly whether the anticipated benefits have or have not materialized.

The main objectives of strategic ABM are to increase the occurrence of high-profitability activities and to decrease the occurrence of low-profitability ones. The ABC system can give information about the profitability of individual products and individual customers. This enables marketing managers to concentrate on shifting the sales mix towards the most profitable products and the most profitable customers. At the other end of the supply chain, strategic ABM can inform decisions about new product development and supplier relationships by highlighting their demands on organizational activities and resources.

Consider this actual example of a company manufacturing, amongst other things, food colourings on a worldwide basis. To follow up a 'gut feeling', the company apportioned several costs (on a causation basis) to the food colouring products which were not usually attached to individual products. These included specific freight costs, inventory holding costs, letter of credit costs, length of credit costs, export credit guarantee costs, salesmen's remuneration and travel costs. This analysis revealed that the food colouring business was barely profitable, and that the export activities were being conducted at a loss. The food colouring product group was effectively being subsidized by other, more profitable, product groups.

Value-added and non-value-added activities

Many authors encourage the practice of splitting activities into two types: value-adding and non-value-adding. They then advocate the elimination or reduction of the non-value-adding ones in order to give increased value to customers and create competitive advantage for themselves. This process is often put forward as the major objective of ABM. However attractive this may sound in theory, it is too simplistic to be universally beneficial. Implementing this basic dichotomy without careful consideration can be counter-productive.

Imagine yourself as a long-standing employee of a well-known organization. The management announce that, as part of their new ABM programme, the job you have been doing for the last 12 years has been categorized as 'non-value-added'. How would you feel about that statement? Would it motivate you, demotivate you or have no effect? The vast majority of employees would be demotivated. The statement implies that the work **you have been instructed to do** for all those years has been a waste of time. Although you have always felt yourself to be a valued member of the workforce, the implication is that this may not be the case.

Of course, this may well not be true, but, like most other people, this is probably how you would feel about it. As in many other situations, the way things are done can be more important than what is being done. In their book, Kaplan and Cooper tell how one company overcame this problem by extending the number of categories from two to four and wording each of their descriptions very carefully. The four categories are shown in Figure 18.7. Using these avoids the negative emotional overtones attached to the phrase

---

Activity categories

1 An activity required to produce the product or improve the process; the activity cannot, on a cost justification basis, be improved, simplified or reduced in scope at this time.

2 An activity required to produce the product or improve the process; the activity can be cost justifiably improved, simplified or reduced in scope.

3 An activity **not** required to produce the product or improve the process; the activity can be eventually eliminated by changing a process or company procedure.

4 An activity **not** required to produce the product or improve the process; the activity can be eliminated in the short run by changing a process or company procedure.

Figure 18.7 Four categories concerning the value of activities
Source: after *Cost and Effect: Using Integrated Costing Systems to Drive Profitability and Performance*, Harvard Business School Press (Kaplan, S. and Cooper, R. 1998).

'non-value-added activity' and greatly reduces any demotivating effect on the employees. This analysis is more helpful than the two-category one as it helps managers to prioritize their actions. Obviously, category 4 activities should be given higher priority than category 3 ones, and so on.

Note that each of the four categories in Figure 18.7 refers to **improving the process** as well as producing the product. Organizational performance can be improved by increasing the efficiency of its processes as well as reducing the costs of its products. The ABC model supports process cost drivers as well as product cost drivers. The objective is to reduce the quantity of process drivers needed for the process to take place. For managers to know if their efforts at improving process efficiency are effective, appropriate performance indicators need to be built into the management accounting information system. A good way of doing this is through the 'balanced scorecard'.

Customer profitability

Knowing which of your customers are most 'profitable' is useful information. If a business has an ABC information system, it can make a good estimate of the relative profitability of its customers. Consider the following example.

Process activity analysis for Logitree Limited

Activity	Annual cost (£)	Process driver	Annual number of process drivers	Process cost driver rate
Visit of sales representative	450,000	Visit	1,800	250 £/visit
Delivery of products*	700,000	Kilogram mile	10,000,000	0.07 £/kg mile
Product modification required by customer	50,000	Modification	25	2,000 £/modification
Order processing	48,000	Order	3,200	15 £/order
Other (phone calls, email, etc.)	35,200	Order	3,200	11 £/order

* Assuming cost of delivery is not charged directly to customers.

To help improve its performance, Logitree Limited wants to know the relative profitability of its customers. By this it means which customer costs least to support for each £ of sales. The idea is to measure the relative cost of supporting the selling *process* for each of its customers; it is a measure of their customer support efficiency.

The record of process activities for a 12-month period for two of their customers is as follows:

Customer	Sales revenue (£)	Visits	Deliveries (kg miles)	Modifications	Orders
A	594,000	25	950,000	14	104
B	571,000	4	300,000	0	12

Customer support analysis

Activity	Process driver rate	Customer A Process driver	Cost (£)	Customer B Process driver	Cost (£)
Visits	250 £/visit	25	6,250	4	1,000
Deliveries	0.07 £/kg mile	950,000	66,500	300,000	21,000
Modifications	2,000 £/modification	14	28,000	0	0
Orders	15 £/order	104	1,560	12	180
Other	11 £/order	104	1,144	12	132
		Total cost of servicing	103,454		22,312
		Activity-based product costs	300,000		298,000
		Sales revenue	594,000		571,000
		Customer 'contribution'	190,546		250,688

The 'customer contribution' is a measure of customer profitability. Although customer A's sales revenue is £23,000 more than customer B's, it earns £60,142 less in customer contribution! This gives Logitree's directors food for thought. This analysis raises such questions as:

- Can the number of visits to A be reduced?
- Can A be persuaded to purchase the same volume of goods by increasing the size of its orders and making them less frequently?
- Can A be discouraged from making product modifications?

Customer support analysis produces '*attention-directing information*' which can be used by managers to think of ways to improve the performance of their business.

When this analysis is performed for all customers, it is usual to find that some customers actually have a negative 'customer contribution'. In other words, these customers are losing the company money! Their negative effect on profitability can be shown by graphing the information – see Figure 18.8.

Note that unless the company was using an ABC costing system, this information would remain hidden. The implications of this diagram are profound: 100% of customer contribution comes from X% of customers and although there are more customers with positive contributions, these are cancelled out by those with negative ones. Application of this analysis has shown that most businesses lose money by trading with certain of their customers. This does not mean to say that all such customers should be abandoned; it may be possible to turn some of them round by changing the mix of customer support given. However, if this is not possible, these unprofitable customers should be subtly and discreetly directed towards a competitor – preferably one that does not use ABM!

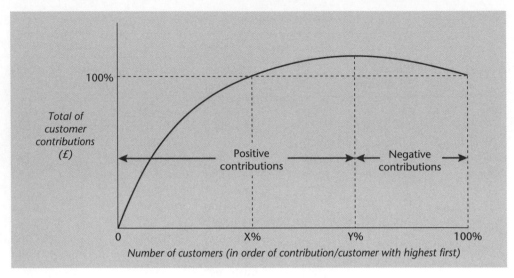

Figure 18.8 The cumulative effect of customer contributions

Benchmarking

Benchmarking is all about performance measurement and review. Its fundamental aim is the achievement of competitive advantage by learning from the experience of others. The process involves several different organizations comparing certain aspects of their performance with each other. (It can also be used for independent parts of one company.)

When considering this for the first time, firms are usually wary of participating for fear of competitors gaining access to confidential information, other participants benefiting more than themselves and company-specific factors reducing the usefulness of the exercise. However, it is possible to overcome these objections by using similar companies which are not direct competitors, concentrating on processes rather than results and looking at problems common to all the participants.

The Chartered Institute of Management Accountants' Official Terminology defines benchmarking as:

> *The establishment, through data gathering, of targets and comparators, that permits relative levels of performance (and particularly areas of underperformance) to be identified. Adoption of identified best practices should improve performance.*

Examples of similar companies not in direct competition are illustrated by the following groups:

- *Retail consumables*: toiletries/household cleaning materials/home decorating supplies/pet supplies.
- *Retail hardware*: cooking utensils/DIY tools/gardening equipment/car accessories.

- *Charities*: National Society for the Prevention of Cruelty to Children, Royal Society for the Prevention of Cruelty to Animals, Cancer Research, Royal British Legion, Royal National Institute for the Deaf, Royal Society for the Prevention of Accidents.

Topics for discussion and investigation may include the following:

- *Personnel*: roles, responsibilities, organizational structure.
- *Planning and control*: frequency and timeliness of budget reports, reporting level, thresholds for investigating variances, motivation mechanisms, committees, meetings.
- *Information systems*: user-friendliness, access levels, hardware, software, liveware, strategies for information management, e.g. using one company-wide database management system.
- *Communication channels*: briefing/cascading meetings, newsletters, appraisals, suggestion boxes, noticeboards, intranet websites, publication of short-term results.
- *Financial management*: debtors collection period, creditors payment period, stock turnover period, gross profitability, various overhead types to sales ratios.

The Xerox Corporation, USA, is believed to be the initiator of benchmarking around 1980 and Robert Camp, who worked for that organization, is perhaps the most well-known respected writer on this subject. Together with other members of its benchmarking group, Xerox looked at research and development, factory layout, quality management, marketing, distribution channels, sales order processing and information systems.

Different academics, consultants and managers have produced a variety of methodologies regarding benchmarking. There are certainly 5-, 7-, 10- and 12-stage processes in existence and there are probably even more out there. Each goes into a different level of detail. As an example, the following is a typical eight-stage process:

1 Decide on what to benchmark.
2 Thoroughly analyse how the chosen topic currently operates in your organization.
3 Identify partners with whom to benchmark.
4 Gather relevant data and information.
5 Analyse this data and information.
6 Decide your chosen level of operation.
7 Implement activities to achieve your chosen level of operation.
8 Monitor your subsequent performance and take further action as necessary.

Even when these steps have been completed, the job is not finished for benchmarking has the philosophy of continuous improvement. Of course, no organization can do everything at once and preferences have to be made, but managers should not seek to rest on their laurels. There are always improvements to be made, especially as the business environment is continually changing and new ways of doing things come online.

Take the Xerox Corporation as an example. It realized that its long sales order processing times were causing negative feedback from customers and decided to attempt to improve the situation. It looked to the mail order catalogue company, L. L. Bean, which was generally regarded as offering a fast and reliable service to customers. Bean's sales order processing time was approximately three times faster than that of Xerox. Bean kindly allowed Xerox staff to visit and examine these operations; this team found that Bean ensured that the most frequently purchased items were also the most easily accessible ones. The withdrawal of items from stock was very efficient. Bean also had a computer program that organized incoming orders so that the packers travelled the minimum distances when collecting items from the shelves. Xerox successfully adopted both these practices and its performance increased as a result. Another example of co-operative benchmarking (between companies not in direct competition with each other) is Domino's Pizza and Motorola. The following companies were also part of the same benchmarking group: Campbell Soup, Whirlpool, Boeing, Scott Paper, Apple, Digital Equipment Corporation (DEC) and Hewlett-Packard. Note that the last three of these were direct competitors for certain computer products and sensitive information would not necessarily be available. However, why should they not share information about things like the average amount of time finished products stayed in stock before being dispatched to customers? This would establish best practice and the benchmark would be quantified. If desired, it is also possible to organize the sharing of information so that only the 'leader' knows the source of the benchmark. However, this will prevent follow-up investigations.

The analysis of the information would be along the following lines:

- What things are we doing well?
- Which activities do we need to improve?
- What should we be doing that we are not doing now?

However, it is important that 'better' practices are not blindly followed without thought being given as to why they are successful in other firms. Good practices are not always directly transferable. Hopefully, different participants will obtain different benefits from this exercise. Some may gain insights into improving their information systems whilst others may become aware of possible improvements to their communication systems. Ideally, the benchmarking process will prove to be mutually beneficial. If nothing else, it usually provides the participants with a greater understanding of their external environment. Based on the common-sense approach of emulating the best, benchmarking has proved to be a popular and effective performance management technique.

Economic Value Added

(EVA is a trademark of Stern Stewart & Co.)

Economic Value Added (EVA) is a prime example of 'value-based management'. It is a measure of *economic profit* rather accounting profit. It is a fundamental measure of return that takes into account the *opportunity cost to the company of shareholder funds* (which is ignored by accountancy theory). In this respect, it is a more meaningful measure of earnings.

Accountancy theory acknowledges that an amount of investment capital has to be put into a business so that it can pay for all the things it buys in order to produce goods/ services and create sales revenue. This capital can come from either shareholders or external sources such as banks. The cost of loans from financial institutions is the amount of interest charged on their loans; this is clearly shown in the accounts as '*interest incurred*'. However, **no** such cost is shown in the accounts for the shareholders' investment capital. Yet it is obvious that this money could be invested elsewhere; in other words, it has an *opportunity cost*. One way of valuing this opportunity cost is to think of the shareholders being invested in the best alternative capital investment project available and then to calculate its net present value.

EVA's main objective is to increase shareholder value by improving corporate performance. It can be defined as follows:

$$\text{EVA} = \text{operating profit} - \text{opportunity cost of share capital}$$
$$= \text{EBIT} - \text{tax} - \text{interest on debt} - \text{opportunity cost of share capital}$$

(where EBIT = Earnings Before Interest and Tax).

The real strength of EVA is that it can be used to identify ways of *increasing* performance (i.e. economic profit). In order to achieve this, senior managers are often compensated partly by share option incentive schemes *based on EVA*. It is very important that these schemes are designed very carefully as EVA is an annual (short-term) measure and **long-term** improvement is the fundamental objective. Badly designed schemes can be manipulated to create short-term improvements at the expense of longer-term performance. Share options maturing *several years* into the future are one way of focusing managers' thoughts on sustained performance in the years ahead.

The EVA concept is very similar to that of residual income (RI) discussed in the chapter on divisional performance. The difference is that, for EVA, the operating profit is adjusted to bring it more into line with the economic theory concerning capital, expenses and investment. There are over 150 possible approved ways of amending EBIT but companies operating EVA decide for themselves which ones to apply. However, most of them apply only about one-tenth of the maximum possible, actually making between 5 and 20 modifications.

It is standard accounting practice to treat costs such as training, brand-building initiatives and some research and development costs as expenses which are deducted from sales revenue to calculate profit. Economists view such items not as expenses but as investments (long-term intangible assets) which are intended to produce positive returns in the future. They would prefer to see this type of item appearing on the balance sheet rather than on the profit and loss account. Consequently, adjustments regarding this type of item are encouraged when calculating EVA.

Note also that *goodwill* arising from mergers and acquisitions is normally written off as an expense instead of appearing on the balance sheet as the long-term investment that it is. Similarly, *restructuring costs* are normally written off in the profit and loss account rather than capitalized on the balance sheet. From the economic viewpoint of EVA, the effect of this accounting treatment is to understate the total amount of capital invested in the business and, therefore, also the cost of that capital. **Unless the total cost of capital is taken into account, the *return on capital* percentage figure will be exaggerated.**

Practicalities

Looking at the following version of the formula,

$$\text{EVA} = \text{EBIT} - \text{tax} - \text{interest on debt} - \text{opportunity cost of share capital}$$

there are four obvious ways of increasing EVA:

1 increase EBIT;
2 decrease tax;

3 decrease interest on debt;

4 decrease opportunity cost of share capital.

1 **Increase EBIT:**

Decrease the value of fixed assets – 'sweat' them (extend their lives longer than originally envisaged) by repairing rather than replacing. Annual depreciation will decrease their net book value unlike purchasing replacement assets which will increase it; repairs are usually classed as expenses and are not capitalized. The profit from the use of repaired assets will be bigger than that from newly purchased assets due to the difference in their associated depreciation charges (expenses).

Increase margins – decrease direct costs. Renegotiate contracts for raw materials or source *more* cheaply from a different supplier (but maintain quality); increase sales prices **only** if the product's elasticity of demand works favourably.

Decrease overhead costs – decrease fixed overheads (e.g. administration staff costs, power, insurances, entertaining, head office costs, etc., but be very careful about reducing the *economic investments* in long-term intangible assets mentioned above, e.g. training). Outsourcing can be another source of cost saving in certain circumstances but again, if this is not thought through properly, the decision can backfire, creating losses further down the line rather than profits.

Increase sales revenue at current margins or better – *better* advertising, *focused* sales promotions, improved incentive scheme for sales personnel, enter markets not currently served by you, devise cross-selling initiatives, etc.

Dispose of unprofitable businesses – the adoption of EVA will emphasize the effectiveness of this strategy. It is not unusual for businesses to become sentimentally attached to strategic business units that were profitable early on in the group's life but which are now in decline. It may be that the group's directors have become friends with (as well as colleagues of) the unit's directors over the years and this makes business decisions into personal ones. The imperative of EVA will help the decision to be taken on business rather than personal grounds.

2 **Decrease tax:** This is perhaps the most difficult to achieve, at least on current operations – relocation is a very expensive course of action. However, the location of new projects in low-tax geographical areas should be considered very carefully as there are usually many attendant unforeseen consequences.

3 **Decrease interest on debt:** Renegotiate current loans (if possible), shop around for new loans, repay some loans. Reduce the amount of debt – decrease working capital by reducing the debtors collection period and inventory levels whilst increasing the creditors payment period (provided this does not adversely affect supplier relationships and raw material delivery times) to reduce the amount of overdraft used.

4 **Decrease opportunity cost of share capital:** This factor does not lend itself to active intervention. Whatever alternative projects exist at the time of measuring EVA must be considered and the best one identified. The higher the return this gives, the lower EVA will be; the lower the return this gives, the higher EVA will be.

Reflection

It is not surprising if much of the above sounds familiar, even though you may not have come across the concept of EVA before. Good managers have been taking such actions intuitively for many years. What EVA does is to offer a formal framework to link all these ideas together.

However, some very successful companies have adopted EVA as a performance improvement technique and **claim** impressive results from its implementation. Perhaps the most well known of these is Coca-Cola, whose share price has increased from $3 to more than $60 since introducing EVA. Of course, there may well be other factors, such as increasing confidence in the global economy and the growth of international trade, which helped to produce this performance.

EVA encompasses many activities which were already being performed before its creation but it does have two unique points. When measuring the return received from business activities:

1 the opportunity cost of shareholders' capital should be taken into account;
2 the annual accounts should be restated on an economic basis (e.g. capitalizing brand-building costs).

Both of these improve the definition of 'performance'.

Value analysis and engineering

The main objective of value analysis is to improve customer satisfaction without incurring any costs. This is done by the identification and elimination of non-value-added features resulting in cost savings. H. Rich and M. Holweg of The Lean Enterprise Research Centre in Cardiff give the following definition followed by five points of elaboration:

> *Value Analysis can be defined as a process of systematic review that is applied to existing product designs in order to compare the function of the product required by a customer to meet their requirements at the lowest cost constituent with the specified performance and reliability needed.*
>
> 1. *Value analysis . . . is a **systematic, formal and organised process of analysis and evaluation**. It is not haphazard or informal and it is a management activity that requires planning, control and co-ordination.*
> 2. *The analysis concerns the **function of a product** to meet the demands or application needed by a customer. To meet this functional requirement the review process must include an understanding of the purpose to which the product is used.*
> 3. *Understanding the **use of a product** implies that specifications can be established to assess the level of fit between the product and the value derived by the customer or consumer.*
> 4. *To succeed, the **formal management process must meet these functional specifications** and performance criteria consistently in order to give value to the customer.*
> 5. *In order to yield a benefit to the company, the formal review process must result in a **process of design improvements** that serve to lower the production costs of that product whilst maintaining this level of value through function.*

The value analysis process is designed to be performed on existing products. However, it can also be applied, in a modified form, to new products; in this situation it is called *value engineering*. In this case, the process concentrates on pre-production activities such as concept development, design and prototyping. Companies such as Toyota, Ford, Sony and Hewlett-Packard have all attributed significant amounts of profit to their adoption of the *design review* process. Indeed, some customers insist that design reviews are carried out when commissioning new products (e.g. a government purchasing a new aircraft carrier).

Value analysis and engineering are essential techniques for companies actively engaged in total quality programmes. For these initiatives to be successful, they need to have an in-depth knowledge of:

● customer requirements
● product costs
● production process costs.

They should also be aware of the huge potential costs of product failure. In 2010, several design faults concerning the acceleration and braking systems on Toyota cars cost the company several billion dollars! For example, the cost of recalling cars from owners to correct a fault with the accelerator pedal was estimated at $1.3 billion. Toyota stated that it expected to lose 100,000 vehicle sales due to this fault alone; assuming the profit per car is $1,000, the future losses would total $100,000,000! The value of shares in the Toyota Group plummeted by more than 20% in the two weeks following the revelation of the difficulties. In addition to this, other faults concerning the braking systems etc. were revealed. It is not possible to put an exact figure on the amount of future losses caused by the fall in Toyota's reputation for quality, built up over the last half-century. However, it can be said with conviction that they will be very significant, measured in hundreds of millions of dollars.

This whole process of building quality into products is so important that manufacturers often attempt to persuade their suppliers also to adopt the same value-based approach. They offer help by seconding some of their 'quality experts' to work at suppliers' premises to train and mentor their staff. Higher-value raw materials and component parts will help both manufacturer and supplier to perform better. These supply-chain partnerships are a symptom of quality products.

For the value analysis process to be successful, managers must understand the nature of costs and value as perceived by the customer. Value comes from two sources. The first is functionality – how well does the product do what the customer wants it to? The second is how much does the product increase the customers' status in the eyes of people around them? The latter is referred to as *esteem value*. Think about buying a car for your personal use; having decided on the brand and model you want, do you buy the basic version or spend significantly more on the top-of-the-range version? In reality, many people compromise and buy somewhere in between.

On the other hand, product costs are usually understood as being the accumulation of raw materials, direct labour and factory overheads. But it is vital that managers also appreciate the potential hidden costs of poor quality such as the amount spent on future warranty claims, product recalls and lawsuits (remember Toyota). Managers should also be acutely aware of the importance of the product design phase. One of the suppositions of life cycle costing is that 80% of costs over the whole lifetime of the product are determined during the design stage, before a single product has been sold. To experience good corporate performance, it is vital at the design stage to create the best value possible.

To summarize, here are the three basic rules of value analysis as listed by Rich and Holweg:

> *No cost can be removed if it compromises the quality of the product or its reliability,* as this would lower customer value, create complaints and inevitably lead to the withdrawal of the product or lost sales.
>
> *Saleability is another issue that cannot be compromised,* as this is an aspect of the product that makes it attractive to the market and gives it appeal value.
>
> *Any activity that reduces the maintainability of the product increases the cost of ownership* to the customer and can lower the value attached to the product.

Six sigma

Six sigma has been described as 'TQM on steroids'! It has a very assertive style, likening itself to a martial art with practitioners titled 'green belts', 'black belts' and 'master black belts'. It started life in a manufacturing company (Motorola in 1985) but has since also been successfully adapted for service businesses. It can be used on its own or together with other performance management techniques such as lean production.

Six sigma uses a standardized measurement for defective production; this is the number of *defective parts per million opportunities* (DPMO). For example, a company producing microchips may currently operate at the level of 5,000 defective chips per million (equivalent to 5 per thousand) but wishes to improve this over the next year to 50 DPMO (a 100-fold improvement). To achieve this, six sigma advises the use of the following logical serial procedure, DMAIC:

Define – identify all aspects of the problem and state the project objectives
Measure – quantify the problem and describe the current performance levels
Analyse – identify the causes of the problem
Improve – eliminate the causes of the problem
Control – embed the solution into the organization's routine procedures

The microchip problem outlined above has already been defined and measured. The third step, analysis, is the identification of the *causes* of the problem. The fourth stage is process *improvement* which involves the elimination of the causes. It also includes the installation of feedforward systems to give early warning of any process degradation which may cause a reversion towards the previously unacceptable DPMO score. The fifth and final stage, *control*, is about making the new improved systems a regular part of the company's normal procedures, embedding them into everyday production activities. This involves training and giving employees confidence in the new procedures.

The DMAIC procedure is usually applied to processes that already exist but it can be modified for systems in their initial design stage, before they are implemented. The first three steps remain the same (Define, Measure, Analyse) but the last two change to: Design and Verify. However, if existing processes are deemed to have completely broken down, this modified version can also be applied to them:

Define – identify all aspects of the problem and state the project objectives
Measure – quantify the problem and describe the current performance levels
Analyse – identify the causes of the problem
Design – create a new efficient system which meets the project's objectives
Verify – implement and test the actual outcomes against the planned ones

A 'black belt' usually takes the lead in these activities with the assistance of several 'green belts' and the whole process is overseen by a 'master black belt'. This 'master' should preferably not be directly involved in the day-to-day operation of the project making it easier for him or her to stand back from it and take a dispassionate view. It is very important that the 'master' has a good understanding of statistical theory to enable him or her to correctly interpret the results of the tests, hence the high degree of training and commensurate status.

A DPMO target of 50 may have been considered very good 30 years ago but six sigma strives for the target level of 3.4 DPMO. In other words, even 4 defects per million is not good enough; the level has to diminish by at least another 0.6. The precise number 3.4 comes from statistical theory. When the results of a repetitive process are measured and recorded on a graph, they often show a 'normal distribution' (or 'bell') curve (see Figure 18.9). This shows a 'mean' (or average) with an almost symmetrical bell-shaped curve around it. Whether the bell's shape is 'short and fat' or 'tall and thin' depends on the variability of the individual scores from their mean. If there is a lot of variation, the bell is short and fat; the less variation there is, the taller and thinner the bell becomes (due to more measurements being closer to their mean). In statistical theory, the variation from the mean is measured in units of 'standard deviation'. The universal symbol used to represent this is the Greek letter 'sigma'.

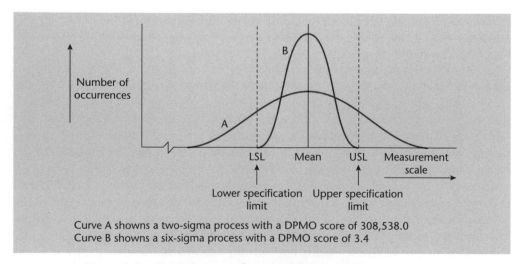

Curve A showns a two-sigma process with a DPMO score of 308,538.0
Curve B showns a six-sigma process with a DPMO score of 3.4

Figure 18.9 Normal distribution curves for repetitive processes

Upper and lower specification limits (LSL and USL)	DPMO	Percentage of defective outcomes	Percentage of good outcomes
±1 sigma	691,462	69%	31%
±2 sigma	308,538	31%	69%
±3 sigma	66,807	6.70%	93.30%
±4 sigma	6,210	0.62%	99.38%
±5 sigma	233	0.02%	99.98%
±6 sigma	**3.4**	**0.00%**	**100.00%**
±7 sigma	0.019	0.00%	100.00%

Figure 18.10 Level of defects represented by area under curve between LSL and USL

Six sigma focuses on process improvement by reducing the variability of the outcomes. It aims to reduce the long-term average of defective parts per million to a maximum of 3.4. The 'normal' curve representing this situation almost touches the horizontal axis at a distance of six standard deviations on either side of the mean. It shows that 99.99966% (= 100.00% to two decimal places) of outcomes are within the lower and upper specification limits, LSL and USL (see Figure 18.10). This is the origin of the 'six sigma' name given to this performance management technique.

A six sigma approach can be used to improve many different processes, even some not directly connected with quality. However, this performance improvement technique has not been universally adopted, perhaps because it involves collecting and analysing a lot of data, as well as needing significant amounts of employee training. Also, many people do not feel comfortable with the '*black art*' of statistics (which reflects badly on the national standard of education). The belief that there are '*lies, damn lies and statistics*', in increasing degrees of unreliability, is still prevalent in our society.

However, six sigma has been adopted by some very well-known international companies such as The Ford Motor Company, Caterpillar, General Electric, Sears, Boeing and American Express. The Dow Chemical Company reported a $1.5 billion improvement in just three years which it attributed to the implementation of six sigma and the Bank of America reported savings of $2 billion over a similar period!

On the other hand, there is some evidence of its success being over-hyped. A *Business Week* magazine article reported that creativity was stifled by its introduction at 3M and a survey of 51 large companies that adopted six sigma in the USA showed that the rankings of 91% of them went down on the Standard & Poor 500 Index rather than up.

No matter how effective six sigma can be when applied to problems within its sphere, it is not appropriate for achieving every desired business improvement. For example, it does not have the capability of creating, designing and marketing new products. Neither can it be used directly to improve a company's image as perceived by its customers.

Six sigma is not easy to implement. It almost always needs a change in organizational culture and this takes time; it cannot be done overnight. Employees' doubts and fears must be overcome; it will not work if they do not genuinely believe in it. However, there is no doubt that some organizations such as GE in the USA claim to have benefited hugely from its use.

Lean production and lean accounting

The *Oxford English Dictionary* defines the word 'lean' as 'thin, especially healthily so . . . efficient, with no wastage'. This is reflected in lean production by the use of very small batch sizes, even down to a single unit (*one-piece flow*) and the reduction of inventories to as near zero as functionally possible. It is demand-led and only the amount needed will be produced. This contrasts with traditional manufacturing which produces large volumes to minimize the fixed cost per unit.

Another important difference is that the focus is on the customer rather than the product; activities which do not create value for the customer are defined as *waste*. Any action or process that the customer is willing to pay for is said to have positive *value*. The main idea of lean production is for companies to create value for their customers by improving operating efficiency by reducing or eliminating waste. This also has the beneficial effect of freeing up some of the current capacity which can be profitably used for other activities or disposed of to save costs.

Lean accounting consists of the techniques and systems that support lean manufacturing; these include value stream cost analysis and target costing. Its aim is to provide accurate, timely and understandable cost information. The Toyota production system is usually credited as the birthplace of these ideas but service providers, as well as manufacturers, have shown increasing interest in the *lean* approach in recent years. Companies are taking more and more notice of their customers' opinions and lean manufacturing and accounting are helping them to focus on these and realize the associated benefits.

Unfortunately, the principles and application of lean accounting often contradict those of traditional absorption and ABC; it is a new approach to cost management.

> *It was not enough to chase out the cost accountants from the plants. The problem was to chase cost accounting from my people's minds.*
> *(Taiichi Ohno, founder of the Toyota production system)*

For example, under more traditional costing regimes, labour and machine efficiencies could be improved by increasing batch sizes. Unless immediate demand justified this, it resulted in increased inventories and an increase in associated costs which counteracted the effects of the improved efficiency ratios achieved. Under lean accounting, product cost accounting is replaced by value stream costing where appropriate costs are simply attached/charged to the value stream.

The heart of the conflict between traditional product costing and lean accounting is that the objective of absorption costing and ABC is to calculate the cost of individual *products* but the objective of value stream costing is to record the cost of the activities within the *processes*. Each category of activity can then be expressed as a percentage of its value stream total cost and this type of information can form the basis of decision making regarding cost control.

Lean accounting is designed around the various *value streams* of the company. A value stream encompasses all the activities, functions, assets and people involved in a defined aspect of the company's operations. The value streams of an automobile company could include engines, gearboxes, car bodies, spare parts, warranty systems and product design.

Materials & components
Site facilities
Labour
Sub-contracted processes
Machinery & equipment
Support services
Other costs of the value stream

Figure 18.11 The variety of costs attached to a value stream

All costs connected with the activities within the engine manufacturing process are charged/attached to the engine value stream (see Figure 18.11). This includes material purchasing costs, engine production line costs, etc. Most costs are not categorized as direct or indirect so there is little need for a theoretical model to apportion overheads. Note that this is a much simpler approach to costing and therefore uses fewer resources. The lean accounting information system involves less data, needs updating less frequently and is more readily understandable.

However, some facilities are used by several value streams making a degree of apportionment unavoidable. These shared costs (sometimes referred to as *monuments*) are usually apportioned to different value streams on the basis of their usage. It may appear that value stream costing is ABC in disguise but this is not so. ABC is a method of attaching overheads to products (more accurately than absorption costing does) but value stream analysis and costing aggregates them and includes them in a single figure giving the total of the value stream.

The 'analysis' part of the lean manufacturing approach is typified by the activities performed by a production review group. This is normally made up of experienced managers and engineers, some of whom are **very** familiar with the project and some **unconnected** ones who are not. This small team of 'experts' comments on and questions the way in which activities are performed, why they are performed and the order in which they are performed. The group members not familiar with the project have the advantage of being able to look at it with fresh eyes and are encouraged to ask **any** questions they wish; nothing is 'off limits'.

Group members who are familiar with the process may be aware of some of the undocumented '*process workarounds*' that front-line operatives often create for themselves. For example, a review group member might ask an operative, 'How do you get from process stage 1 to process stage 2?' and get the reply, 'Oh, we use this little spreadsheet we made up for ourselves on the laptop; it's not part of the formal process but it cuts down the time needed by at least 30 minutes every time.' This is precisely the type of activity that needs to be identified so that either the formal process is modified or the *maverick* activity (waste) is stopped.

Consider a further example. In the case of a car *final assembly* value stream, it may be observed that the spare wheel was inserted at an earlier point on the production line than the four road wheels. This means that two JIT systems for wheels must operate at two different points involving two small temporary buffer stocks of wheels. By installing the spare wheel at the same point as the four road wheels, one of these two systems

Item	Amount (£000)	Percentage (%)
Materials & components	394	51
Site facilities	201	26
Labour	33	4
Sub-contracted processes	12	2
Machinery & equipment	19	2
Support services	13	2
Other costs	2	0
Total cost	**674**	**87**
Revenues	**775**	**100**
Value stream profit	**101**	**13**

Figure 18.12 Value system income statement for period 9

can be eliminated making the value stream *leaner*, cheaper and more efficient. Small incremental improvements are typical of value stream analysis rather than a big *breakthrough* change. Under lean accounting, value stream costing replaces product costing; appropriate costs are charged to the value stream and different cost categories can be expressed as percentages of the value stream total cost. Figure 18.12 shows an example of a simple value stream income statement.

Another technique sometimes associated with lean manufacturing and accounting is target costing (discussed at length in the earlier chapter on pricing). As one of its major objectives is the improvement of customer value, this technique fits very well with the lean philosophy. However, it is worth remembering that defining and quantifying customer value is not a straightforward task. It may be wise to outsource part of this process to external agencies, such as market research companies, in order to avoid subjective bias.

Performance measurement

Lean accounting measures and communicates corporate performance on a comparative table of ratios called a *box score*. These ratios are analysed into three categories: operational, capacity and financial. Three ratios are normally shown for each performance indicator. The first states the position before the lean improvement is implemented, the second estimates the position sometime (maybe one year) after the implementation and the third estimates the position further into the future (see Figure 18.13). Note the very significant increase estimated in value stream profit in the longer term.

Also, where a reliable revenue figure exists for a specific value stream, an income statement can be prepared (see Figure 18.12). As well as expressing costs in monetary

		Current state before lean Dec 2002	Future state lean step two Dec 2003	Future state longer term including new products
Operational	Sales per person	$224,833.00	$224,833.00	$277,031.00
	Inventory turns	6.5	15	20
	Average cost per unit	$31.32	$29.88	$24.25
	First-pass yield	81%	95%	95%
	Lean time in days	25	5	2.5
Capacity	Productive	55%	52%	79%
	Non-productive	42%	12%	12%
	Available	3%	36%	9%
Financial	Revenue	$4,062,000	$4,062,000	$5,686,000
	Material costs	$1,164,184	$1,109,327	$1,552,839
	Conversion costs	$1,483,416	$1,483,416	$1,657,500
	Value stream profit	$1,414,400	$1,469,257	$2,475,661
	Value stream return on sales	35%	36%	44%
	Hurdle rate variance (40%)	−5%	−4%	4%

Figure 18.13 Box score showing the estimated financial benefits from lean improvement
Source: 'Lean Accounting: What's It All About?' by Maskell and Baggaley (2005)

amounts, they can be shown as percentages of the sales revenue. These can be compared with other periods to identify any trends, good or bad. However, revenue figures are not always available. Taking the example of a vehicle production facility, the 'design process' value stream would not have a revenue value but the 'engine' value stream probably would have one. If engines were sold to external customers, the revenue figure could be based on the selling price. Even if there were no external sales, an internal transfer price could be used provided this remained constant over reasonably long time periods. Even though transfer prices are notoriously 'flexible', they can still be used to identify trends in this way.

Summary

The effects of adopting lean production tactics are not instantaneous; in fact the full impact usually takes a number of years rather than months. Although significant new initiatives need to be championed by a top manager, most employees need convincing of the effectiveness of the changes before they buy into them and become proactive in their implementation. Indeed, it is not unusual for productivity to *decrease* immediately after implementation due to the conscious efforts needed to master the new sub-processes/ activities and the employees' lack of familiarity with them. As confidence and familiarity is gained, this 'learning curve dip' will reverse and previous levels of productivity will be surpassed.

Lean production and accounting are feedforward mechanisms. If you succeed in increasing the flow rates, reducing the quantity of data collected, getting rid of the monthly variance analysis activities, minimizing inventories, reducing wastage and adding value, it is highly likely that financial performance indicators will improve in the future, sometimes dramatically. The resulting improvements in factors such as *sales order processing time* and *new product time to market* also produce the desirable effect of motivating senior managers.

Lean production and accounting can significantly improve corporate performance, especially in a multi-production-line environment with complex product ranges. The simplification it brings eliminates many unnecessary data or physical transactions and therefore reduces costs. It also focuses on value as perceived by customers. In adopting companies, it is normal for inventories and waste to be significantly reduced, creating new capacity which should ultimately lead to genuine efficiency savings and improved profits.

Performance dashboards

Introduction

If you do not know your current performance level, how will you know whether you have improved by the end of the next period? Reliable, easily accessible, up-to-date information about your current situation is an essential prerequisite for performance improvement. The well-known phrase '*Information is power*' is very relevant in this context.

Business intelligence is the title of a management technique which became popular in the latter part of the twentieth century. The word 'intelligence' is used here in the same sense as in the phrase 'military intelligence', gathering knowledge of the situation and its environment. (It is worth noting that the information sought by military/political intelligence services is information that is **deliberately** being concealed. Not all business intelligence falls into this category but there is much that does.)

The business intelligence technique evolved in an era when corporate information was controlled to a significant extent by the IT department whose members were seen as specialist data management experts. Because demands on them were so great, they could not satisfy them all. As their 'customers' did not have the technical skills, the IT staff had to make decisions about the form and extent of information provided. Databases were in their infancy and were not nearly as powerful as those of today, so the content of IT reports was often de facto controlled by the IT staff. If individual managers were not happy with the format or contents of the reports produced, there was often little they could do about it.

As computer software systems became more user-friendly, the control of information shifted back to the business decision makers, the managers. Spreadsheets such as Excel and databases such as Access enabled managers to 'do their own thing' without being beholden to the IT department. This resulted in computer output becoming more relevant, useful and easily adaptable. However, the important thing is that accurate, current 'business intelligence' is easily accessible to managers when they need it. If it is not, performance improvement will be a matter of chance rather than design.

Semantics

Business intelligence and performance management are not the same thing. Business intelligence encompasses various systems for converting raw data into meaningful information. Business intelligence is certainly necessary for performance improvement but it is not sufficient. Performance management uses business intelligence to make better decisions, improve products and processes, increase customer satisfaction and make bigger profits. Performance management can be described as the outcome of the application of performance dashboards which use business intelligence to improve the bottom line.

Performance management would be better labelled as 'performance improvement'. In the past, management tended to give priority to maintaining their level of performance rather than focusing on improving it; management was mostly about *control* rather than *improvement*. However, it is not productive to get involved here in an argument over semantics; the following discussion will treat the two phrases 'performance management' and 'performance improvement' as interchangeable.

Consider the French term, *Tableau(x) de Bord* which translates into English as 'Dashboard(s)'. (The *Oxford English Dictionary* defines a dashboard as 'the panel facing the driver of a vehicle or the pilot of an aircraft, containing instruments and controls'.) Everything said about dashboards in this chapter also applies to French *Tableaux de Bord*. Confusion has sometimes arisen because non-French students of performance management tend to assume that French dashboards are tightly structured entities using a standard model and templates in the same way as the American balanced scorecard. This is not so; French dashboards have evolved over the last 80 years or more and the specific nature of a single example cannot be derived from its title. They vary from simple business intelligence models, limited to one aspect only of the business, to highly sophisticated company-wide systems which offer suggestions for actions based on carefully chosen '*action variables*'. *Tableau de Bord* is a general term, not a specific one.

For the purpose of clarity, this book makes a distinction between *dashboards* and *performance dashboards*. This follows the framework set out by Wayne Eckerson in his excellent book, *Performance Dashboards*, 2nd edition, 2011. This logical and helpful analysis enables us to see the big picture as well as to understand how each piece of this particular performance management jigsaw fits into it. His performance management framework diagram (see Figure 18.14) neatly summarizes the complete cyclical process. (Unfortunately, not all authors take the same approach and a certain degree of confusion permeates this complex subject.)

A basic dashboard is a business intelligence system which analyses information but does **not** automatically process it further to give a higher level of synthesized information. How the information is used, and to what extent, is left entirely to its recipients. It is even possible that the information will be ignored! In contrast to this, a performance dashboard not only provides information but also applies it to create more sophisticated information (knowledge) and/or suggested actions for managers to take in order to *achieve* performance improvement.

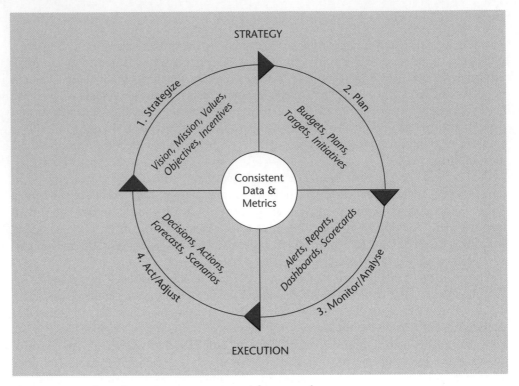

Figure 18.14 A performance management framework
Source: from *Performance Dashboards*, 2nd edition, by W. Eckerson (2011). Reproduced by permission of John Wiley & Sons Inc.

Performance dashboards

Ekerson defines a performance dashboard as:

> *a layered information delivery system that parcels out information, insights and alerts to users on demand so they can measure, monitor and manage business performance more effectively.*

- There are *three* types of performance dashboard: operational, tactical and strategic.
- They can have *three* layers (levels or types) of data: graphical, dimensional and transactional.
- They can be used to perform *three* distinct functions: monitoring, analysis and managing.

It may be helpful to think of a performance dashboard (PD) as a performance improvement system. In reality, many combinations of the above sub-categories are possible; not all PDs are the same.

Three types

Operational PDs concentrate on the monitoring of chosen performance indicators. The information they provide enables front-line operatives to take corrective action as soon as they know it is necessary. The data provided tends to be refreshed every few seconds or minutes rather than days, weeks or months. (This could also form part of a statistical process control or six-sigma process.) An example of this would be the dimensions of the cams fitted to a car engine crankshaft. If the monitoring of cam size variance shows that the tolerance levels are being exceeded, the operative should take immediate action to reset the machinery and bring them back within tolerance.

Tactical PDs are used by mid-level managers to observe and compare the performance of departments and teams. Internal benchmarking can be used to motivate 'rival' groups and improve performance by making relevant information available to them; peer-group rivalry can be a powerful stimulus. Outcomes at departmental level can also be monitored; an example of this is the number of engines produced daily or weekly by the engine manufacturing department of an automobile company. In addition, tactical PDs can be used to monitor and control the progress of one-off projects. An example of this would be the monitoring of appropriate stock levels during the introduction of a local JIT system.

Strategic PDs are used by senior managers with broad responsibilities to communicate corporate strategy and to monitor its implementation. Balanced scorecards are eminently suitable for this purpose, and therefore often used, actual performance usually being reviewed on a monthly or quarterly basis. An example of this could be the effect on productivity during the gradual introduction of automated machinery throughout a production line.

Three layers (levels or types) of data

Transactional data is the most detailed of the three layers. Its source is transactional records such as sales and purchase invoices, process time records, direct labour job times, quality inspection records and warranty payments per product per time period, etc. These masses of data are the bedrock into which managers can 'drill down' to find solutions to their current problems. For example, a 20% increase in the number of defective components produced by one process might be explained by some data analysis revealing that incorrect fastening bolts had been used for the last five weeks. The purchase invoices may show that *aluminium* bolts had been erroneously sent by the supplier in the relevant period instead of the *stainless steel* ones specified in the order. The weaker aluminium ones sheared in use, causing the increase in product failures and warranty claims.

Dimensional data is data analysed by selected criteria (dimensions). For example, sales data could be analysed by country and region; the same data could be analysed by product group and/or by sales person. Purchases could be analysed by period cost and/or by supplier; also, if working capital was under scrutiny, they could be analysed by suppliers' credit terms. This analysis and cross-analysis may also enable 'what-if' exercises to be carried out, giving management new insights into possible changes and improvements.

Graphical data is highly summarized and is usually presented in the form of graphs and charts. As well as indicating trends, it often has in-built 'alert' features to attract managers' attention when predetermined thresholds are exceeded. These alerts can take several different forms including automatically generated emails to appropriate senior managers, on-screen pop-up messages, colour-coded 'traffic light' systems (red for immediate attention, amber for early warning and green for OK). Almost always, there will be a facility to 'drill down' from one level to another, enabling executives to investigate easily any information presented to them. In other words, senior executives observing graphical data have easy access to the appropriate dimensional data and, from

Data layer	Typical number of data items	Typical users	Function	Examples
Graphical	10	Senior executives	To monitor trends 'What-if?' modelling Predictive analytics	If all suppliers allowed 90 days' credit, what would be the effect on working capital?
Dimensional	100	Middle managers	Sophisticated analysis	Sales figures by region, salesperson and product, also showing percentage changes compared with the previous period
Transactional	1000	Operatives	Take quick corrective action when necessary	Reset machinery as soon as predetermined limits of output are exceeded

Figure 18.15 Summary table of performance dashboard features

there, easy access to the appropriate transactional data if they wish to delve down to that level of detail. Compared with the data analysis techniques of the previous era, this user-friendly investigation facility is a very powerful tool, *provided it is used wisely*. (See Figure 18.15 for a summary of these data layers.)

Three functions

These are as follows:

1 **Monitoring:** One function of PDs is to monitor actual performance against some form of predetermined target data. This can be done at any of the three data layers and by any of the three PD types. For example, weights of one selected component part can be monitored, area sales volumes can be monitored and stock levels can be monitored to evaluate the implementation of a new JIT strategy. Note that monitoring at a strategic level is often performed through the mechanism of a balanced scorecard (which itself is one type of PD).

2 **Analysis:** Data at any of the three layers/levels can be analysed (and synthesized) to give more meaningful information. Transactional data can be analysed to give dimensional information by category. Dimensional information can be analysed in time series to show trends and evaluate performance against chosen corporate strategies.

3 **Management:** PDs provide an intelligent basis for decision making and for taking action in order to improve business performance. The information they provide can be used for many different purposes: for example, to change production schedules in the light of changes in demand and to identify and rectify causes of increased customer 'churn'. At the operational level, 'routine' micromanagement decisions

are made, such as when to replace an engineering die or cutter due to unacceptable production inaccuracies caused by its 'wear and tear'.

Conclusion

PDs are potentially useful to all types of organization, profit-oriented or not-for-profit, public sector or private sector. The many organizations which have adopted them include Dow Chemicals, municipal police departments, Cisco Systems and universities. All that is required is the means and the will to implement them.

Eckerson lists the following nine benefits of PDs *(these are discussed at greater length in the first chapter of his book)*:

- communicate strategy;
- refine strategy;
- increase visibility (clarify the business situation);
- increase co-ordination;
- increase motivation;
- give a consistent view of the business;
- reduce costs associated with redundant data;
- empower users;
- deliver actionable information.

Given this impressive list, it is not surprising that PDs are a very popular performance improvement mechanism. A 2009 survey by The Data Warehousing Institute found that 72% of respondents use a PD of some sort. The Institute also found that, of the 495 PD adopters, 42% said they were moderately useful and a **further 47% rated their usefulness as high or very high**. This is a very impressive vote of confidence in favour of PDs.

There are two further benefits of PDs not explicit in the above list. The first is their 'user-friendly' interface which encourages managers of all levels to engage with, and make use of, them. PDs allow users to operate in a way which is natural to them; in the past, existing dashboards were not fully utilized because of the unnatural way users were forced to interact with them.

The second benefit is the increasing ability of PDs to make reasonable predictions based on past experience. This *'predictive analytics'* function is currently being refined and will doubtless prove very attractive to senior management, further increasing the popularity of PDs.

Strategic management accounting

Definitions

The *Oxford English Dictionary* defines *strategy* in general terms as, 'A plan of action or policy designed to achieve a major or overall aim.' Further to this, in the 2nd edition of his book *Strategic Management Accounting*, 2003, Hoque refines this in a specific business context as, 'An integrated set of actions aimed at securing a sustainable competitive advantage.'

Strategic management accounting (SMA) is defined in the Chartered Institute of Management Accountant's (CIMA) Official Terminology as:

> A form of management accounting in which emphasis is placed on information which relates to factors external to the firm, as well as non-financial information and internally generated information.

Hoque goes on to describe SMA as:

> The process of identifying, gathering, choosing and analysing accounting data for helping the management team to make strategic decisions and to assess organisational effectiveness.

Origins and context

The phrase 'strategic management accounting' was first used by Simmonds in an article published in the April 1981 edition of Management Accounting (the previous title of CIMA's monthly magazine). A few years later, another writer, Tricker, commented that the:

> relationship between Business Strategy and Management Accounting has been likened to that between Military Strategy and Military Intelligence.
> (Management Accounting, December 1989)

In the 1970s and 1980s there was a significant increase in interest about formal mechanisms for gaining competitive advantage; these included such techniques as total quality management (TQM), materials requirements planning (MRP), value chain analysis, etc. This coincided with a rise in the influence of academic business schools and business research along with increased respect for business 'gurus' such as Peter Drucker, Michael Porter, Charles Handy and Robert Kaplan.

The business community acknowledged that the activities of their competitors should influence the formulation of their corporate strategy. They remembered that they did not operate in a vacuum and once more became aware of the importance of their environment; businesses can be fundamentally affected by the actions of their competitors.

When management accounting first developed, it was concerned with technical matters such as labour and product costs, progressing to capital investment appraisal. Following on from this, it has embraced the effects of human behaviour on management accounting practices. Examples of this include transfer pricing (involving compromise on price between 'buying' and 'selling' managers) and budget games (designed to maximize the budget holder's personal gain even at the expense of business performance). And now, in addition to its technical and behavioural aspects, it has also developed a strategic perspective, SMA.

Characteristics and difficulties of SMA

The CIMA definition of SMA given above emphasizes external factors. Given the importance of business competitors, information about their operations (such as pricing, product costs, sales volumes and market share) is vital to the formulation of effective competitive strategies. Benchmarking provides a different kind of external intelligence; participating organizations volunteer information about themselves in order to identify best practice.

Also, provided ABC information is available, it is possible to estimate and rank customers according to their importance to the business. This internally generated 'customer profitability analysis' is a relatively new management accounting activity (see the ABM section of this chapter). Cost reduction exercises (such as kaisen costing, value analysis and the reduction of non-value-adding activities under ABM) can also count as SMA techniques, as can value chain analysis.

All the other techniques included in this chapter are sometimes identified as part of an SMA approach. Despite the definitions given at the beginning of this section, SMA is not a tightly defined performance improvement model. It is a flexible, broad 'umbrella' term which means different things to different organizations. However, there is some agreement as to its content and this centres around its *external focus*.

Unfortunately, SMA's external nature poses problems in its execution. Other than in a benchmarking situation, businesses are understandably most unwilling to share information with their competitors. Consequently, the information has to be gathered in other ways. Suppliers of one company may also supply its competitors and it may be possible to gain some information regarding competitors from the sales personnel of their mutual suppliers. Published accounts and reports are another source of information but these are limited by the aggregated nature of their content. Newspaper articles also give little away. 'Poaching' competitors' employees is another possible way of gaining intelligence but it can be a risky and expensive tactic.

In the USA, there is an Institute of Competitor Intelligence, colleges offer degrees in the subject and it is seen as a bona fide profession. Some large companies, such as Du Pont, have competitor intelligence departments which may cost millions of dollars annually to run. This demonstrates the importance they attach to this activity. *(Industrial espionage is illegal and cannot be recommended; however, it would be naive to imagine that it did not go on.)*

One of the characteristics of SMA is the exploitation of cost reduction opportunities but this gets more and more difficult with each success. For example, moving from a defect rate of one in a million to one in 10 million is harder to achieve than moving from a defect rate of one in a hundred thousand to one in a million. Also, the removal of non-value-adding activities may result in unforeseen circumstances. Consider the closure of a subsidized works canteen; although there is no direct link to customer value, the operatives who have enjoyed this facility over the years may well be significantly demotivated by its demise. Consequently, process efficiency may diminish to an extent which reverses the envisaged savings with a net negative result on the bottom line.

There is one other important point which should be considered. This section of the chapter on SMA has assumed that external intelligence is essential to the formulation of effective strategy. But what if corporate strategy is not always formulated? Suppose it just evolves incrementally, reacting to changes internal and external to the business, over long periods of time. So, if strategy is not explicitly formulated, there is no need for any formal gathering of information about the external environment; SMA becomes unnecessary! In reality, corporate strategy is both formulated and incrementally created; companies experience both aspects of this essential function.

Conclusion

It is not unusual for SMA activities to be performed by managers other than accountants; also, these activities are often performed by organizations which do not use SMA in their management vocabulary. Managers' job descriptions and labels for the activities they perform are not important. **What is important is that SMA activities are carried out.**

> *The best foreknowledge of an opponent's condition is gained through others. It is foreknowledge that enables a brilliant ruler and excellent leader to triumph over others.*

This quotation is from *The Art of Strategy* (sometimes translated as *The Art of Warfare*) by the Chinese philosopher Sun Tzu; it was written approximately 2,300 years ago! It seems that SMA is more of a reincarnation than a new creation.

Environmental accounting

So far, in this chapter, all the performance improvement models discussed have assumed performance to mean increased profit. This implicit definition is one of the fundamental tenets of 'agency theory'; in brief, it is that managers should always act in the best interests of shareholders by increasing their wealth. However, since the mid-1970s, it has been suggested that managers should consider other 'stakeholders' in the business such as customers, suppliers, local communities, employees, local government and national government. This outlook embodies the ideas that *profit* need not be the only relevant performance indicator and that companies have a wider *social responsibility*. The term *corporate social responsibility* was coined as a succinct definition of this broader accounting perspective. This reinforces the idea that companies are an important part of the society in which they operate.

Companies listed on the stock exchange are encouraged to include (on a voluntary basis) information concerning their employees, environmental matters, social and community issues in an operating and financial review. If produced, this document should include any policies adopted by the company in these areas and give an indication of the extent to which they have been successfully implemented.

The term *sustainability* is also commonly used in connection with these ideas. The thinking behind this is that companies need to satisfy the stakeholders other than shareholders in order to survive *in the long term*; in other words, to sustain their performance. In 1996, Gray *et al.* wrote a book on *environmental accounting* called *Accounting and Accountability: Changes and Challenges in Corporate Social and Environmental Reporting*. This put forward ideas about how concerns for the natural environment (such as pollution, wastage and climate change) could be incorporated into mainstream accounting. The term *sustainability reporting* has also grown in popularity over the years.

It would be wrong to believe that the pursuit of profit is always contrary to socially responsible activities. Consider the example of excess packaging on retail goods. In the past, many products have been sold in two sets of packaging, inner and outer, where a thoughtful redesign would use only a single layer. This means that energy has been unnecessarily used in creating both inner and outer packaging, which very probably means that more carbon dioxide has been released into the atmosphere than was necessary. When companies switch to single packaging, they help to combat climate change and, in so doing, exhibit corporate social responsibility.

Now consider the effect of this action on profit and wealth creation. It is highly likely that eliminating one layer of packaging will result in cost savings for the company, directly from purchasing less packing material and indirectly from savings in storage space, labour and machine time, and the cost of operating the purchasing function. This is a good example of a win–win situation: both shareholders and society in general can benefit from activities such as packaging redesign.

When selling its products and services, an environmentally aware organization must first calculate its desired pricing level solely with regard to its market and its product cost. It can then build upon this purely financial/economic base and consider the more political factors within its social and environmental perspective. This threefold approach to accountability can be described by the phrase 'the triple bottom line', which encapsulates business success in terms of 'people, profit and planet':

- People – the organization's most important resource; they create the success. Many organizations reward their employees by sharing their success with them.
- Profit – all organizations need a certain level of 'profit' to ensure survival and continuous development.
- Planet – many organizations are moving towards more sustainable industry practices. This is a consequence of organizations taking a genuine long-term view.

One example of putting this 'joined-up thinking' into practice is where a visitor attraction promotes its sustainable objectives by using differential pricing to offer a price reduction for visitors arriving by public transport rather than by car. Another example of how people, profit and planet are interlinked is when companies reverse the normal car mileage allowance structure so as to pay a higher rate for smaller, rather than larger, engine sizes. Organizations may decide to buy or sell a product purely for profit-related reasons, but there are often wider environmental and social issues to consider, such as the generation of pollution or the use of child labour. In practice, not-for-profit organizations may take more ethical decisions regarding these sensitive issues than commercial for-profit ones. This is not to suggest that all commercial companies behave in an unethical manner; they do not. However, it is likely that not-for-profit organizations will have a greater in-built pressure to demonstrate an altruistic form of behaviour.

Objectives

In their book entitled *The Green Bottom Line*, Bennett and James use the phrase 'environment-related management accounting' and offer the following working definition:

The generation, analysis and use of financial and non-financial information in order to optimise corporate <u>environmental</u> and economic performance and achieve sustainable business.

Regarding performance, the word 'environmental' is underlined in order to give it emphasis over 'economic'. However, economic performance cannot be ignored; indeed, it usually takes precedence where there is a trade-off between the two approaches. **The general objective of environment-related management accounting is to offer an environment-related decision-support role to mainstream business managers.**

In addition to this general objective, Bennett and James discuss the following seven specific ones:

- To demonstrate the impact of environment-related activities on the balance sheet and profit and loss account – *these can be very significant and are often underestimated. Consider BP's clean-up costs after the 2010 Deep Water Horizon disaster in the Gulf of Mexico which were in the region of $20 billion.*
- To identify cost reduction and other improvement opportunities – *Capital investment appraisals for energy efficiency and waste reduction projects often have a payback period of less than one year! Product redesign improvements can have similarly short periods due to the increased sales revenue they create.*
- To prioritize environmental actions – *under the normal situation of capital rationing, capital investment appraisals are used to prioritize alternative projects.*
- To inform product pricing, mix and development decisions – *environment-related information allows the identification of long-term poorly performing products and encourages appropriate action, such as phasing them out, to be taken.*
- To enhance customer value – *for example, removing one of two packaging layers on a product may reduce the customer's waste disposal costs.*
- To 'future-proof' investment decisions (and others with long-term consequences) – *because the benefits of sustainable environmental actions are by definition long-term, the higher the discount rates used for NPV calculations, the smaller the benefits become, the further into the future the project continues. However, improved analysis of environment-related costs and benefits together with the use of lower discount rates for environmental factors can help to alleviate this.*
- To support sustainable business – *this may require the collection of new types of environment-related data such as the amount of electricity generated by a new solar-panel installation on the factory roof. Also, end-of-product-life disposal plans should be created and costed. (In the 1970s, the UK public was persuaded that nuclear energy was the cheapest source of power available. However, despite the financial accounting requirement to state and quantify contingent liabilities, the very large disposal costs of spent nuclear fuel rods and their possible severe environmental impact were not included in any costings or accounts.* **Consequently, suboptimal decisions were made concerning the types of power stations built on a national scale and the true cost of electricity over a time period of approximately 50 years***).*

The Stern Review on the Economics of Climate Change, commissioned by the UK government, was published in 2006. It was written by the eminent economist Nicholas Stern of the London School of Economics and Leeds University. This is a very comprehensive report of approximately 700 pages. Part of the report calculates NPVs of future costs and benefits associated with carbon trading schemes and carbon taxes. In brief, he concludes that taking effective action 'now' will cost about 1% (Stern revised this figure to 2% in 2008) of global gross domestic product every year, but if action is delayed it will cost at least 5% and possibly as much as 20% a year.

Some economists have questioned the discount rates Stern used but others endorse his calculations even when larger rates are used to discount future uncertainties. The logical conclusion to draw from this is that society will be much better off if emissions of green house gases (including carbon dioxide) are reduced as much as possible as quickly as possible. Unsurprisingly, Stern's conclusions have been questioned by vested interests including the DaimlerChrysler Group's chief economist in 2007, Mr Jolissaint, who considers the effects of global warming to be unquantifiable with any degree of certainty and to be too far in the future to worry about. BBC News reported that:

> *Mr. Jolissaint was particularly scathing about the Stern Report, which urged governments to take urgent action now, [the report] arguing that it would be much cheaper to act, rather than face a $10 trillion cost of climate change of not doing anything until later.*

The Stern Report team have defended their findings and responded to their critics; amongst other things, the report stated that, 'if you judge risks to be small and attach little significance to future generations you will not regard global warming as a problem'.

There are many people besides Mr Jolissaint who depend directly or indirectly on the motor vehicle industry, including influential commentators and presenters in the press, television and other media. A significant minority of these people have joined the anti-Stern lobby. Admittedly, no one knows for certain what the future holds but these people are obviously willing to gamble with the quality of life to be experienced by the next generations. Consider the possibility that (a) their arguments prevail with little or nothing being done to combat climate change, and (b) their arguments prove to be incorrect. It is questionable whether their attitude is compatible with the concept of social responsibility, corporate or otherwise.

According to Stern, ***doing nothing* is not an option**. Serious global warming is taking place now; it needs to be arrested and, if possible, reversed. However, the window of opportunity for reversal will be firmly closed and locked in only a few years' time. But there is still time to achieve a positive outcome and accountants have a role to play in this. Prince Charles created the Accounting and Sustainability Group in 2005 and used this platform to outline this role. He said, 'A new accounting and forecasting system is needed to ensure that the longer-term and broader consequences of our actions are taken into account more effectively in decision-making.'

Conclusion

It is clear from the above that sustainability and environment-enhancing decisions need a long-term outlook to succeed. How then can the unrelenting demand (driven by the world's stock markets) for short-term profits be reconciled with the prevention of environmental deterioration? Some textbooks and research papers claim that environment-driven improvements often also produce improvements in profits and performance through 'win–win' situations (see the 'two layers of packaging down to one' example above). This optimistic outlook mostly ignores the many situations where environmental improvements actually increase net costs and decrease performance *in the short term*.

Initiatives such as the Carbon Trading Scheme at least make some companies aware of their detrimental effect on the environment. Innovative technology such as the 'clean coal' carbon dioxide extraction process will earn money for its inventors and producers but its application is likely to increase electricity costs rather than reduce them. An improved environment is a benefit for society as a whole and it may be that if this benefit is to be sustained in the long term, society will have to pay the cost of stable or reduced corporate performance in the form of smaller profits, both before and after tax. Without some degree of legislation to encourage a long-term perspective, shareholders will continue to benefit more than other stakeholders but society as a whole will exist in an environment which will, at best, be stable.

However, for this legislation to be successful it will need to operate on an internationally agreed basis and that is perhaps the biggest barrier of all to be overcome. The 1997 International Conference on Climate Change produced the Kyoto Protocol which set binding targets for 37 industrialized countries and the European Community for reducing carbon emissions with effect from 2005. Each country **agreed to be committed** to the set targets.

However, due to international disagreement at succeeding conferences (especially Copenhagen in 2009) along with the belief that a compromise is better than no agreement at all, it is almost certain that the targets for Kyoto's second tranche of reductions (due to commence in 2013) will be renegotiated so that they are much weaker than originally stated. Corporate social responsibility is generally considered by the business community (including accountants) to be both legitimate and desirable. The difficulty is how to implement it on a national and international scale. Impossible? Maybe; but all our futures depend to a great extent on the degree to which this is actually **achieved** in the next few years. Politics has been described as 'the art of the possible'; the effectiveness of environmental accounting ultimately depends on the effectiveness of our politicians and the legislation they enact and enforce.

Sustainability reporting will be of little or no effect unless it helps to bring about actions which improve the environment over the coming years.

Footnote

The final few paragraphs of an article entitled 'If you want to create more jobs, don't put your faith in startups' written by John Naughton, which appeared in the *Observer* on 11 September 2011, are reproduced below. It concerns a recent interview between CNN's Candy Crowley and James Hoffa, boss of the North American Teamsters' Union. **It gives a controversial view of the meaning of corporate social responsibility.** Hoffa fails to mention the employment currently provided by giant industrial corporations or the amount they pay in taxes to the US government. Nevertheless, although the author of this book does not necessarily agree with the views of Mr Hoffa, he finds them stimulating and worthy of consideration.

> *Hoffa startled his interviewer by launching into an attack on Apple for sitting on its $78bn cash mountain and not spending it in the US. When the interviewer pointed out, mildly, that Apple was allowed to do that, Hoffa responded: 'But they are not doing anything with it. And instead of investing here, everything they do is in China or is in Asia somewhere.'*
>
> *'It's cheaper there,' explained the interviewer, at which point Hoffa exploded. 'But don't they have an obligation to America to build it in America, to put people to work?' he said. 'I think the president should challenge the patriotism of these*

American corporations that are sitting on the sidelines saying, why do we have high unemployment but I am not going to hire anybody? You know, they have an obligation just like the federal government, just like Obama. We have all got to get into the game. And I don't see that happening. So the trillions and billions of dollars that they have on the sidelines, they have money, Pfizer and General Electric, they have trillions of dollars overseas, let's start repatriating that money. Let's start a programme to get America going again.'

Now of course Hoffa is a union boss and he would say that, wouldn't he? But the point he raises is never the less sobering. Not only is patriotism a completely outmoded concept for major technology companies, but so also is the idea that these corporations have any wider **social responsibility** *to the societies which provide them with the skilled and educated people who make them so innovative and profitable.*

Overview of performance improvement techniques

When you started to read this chapter, you probably assumed you were going to read about 15 distinct methods for improving organizational performance. Now that you have got to this point, you will have noticed that there are many overlaps between the different techniques. For example, the section on ABM states that, 'The aim is for the organization to improve its performance by reducing its total costs whilst maintaining its sales revenue.' Also, the opening words in the value analysis and engineering section are, 'The main objective of value analysis is to improve customer satisfaction without incurring any costs'. These two statements are similar enough to be interchangeable.

Also, the section on ABM includes the following:

Operational ABM starts by identifying possible improvements to existing processes, prioritizing them and allocating resources to carry them out. The next stage involves monitoring the results of these activities to identify the extent of the actual improvements achieved. The ABC system provides the information needed to verify the reduced spending on operational activities.

At the other end of the supply chain, **strategic ABM can inform decisions about new product development** *and supplier relationships by highlighting their demands on organizational activities and resources.*

And if you look in the lean production section, you will find the following:

*Another important difference [of lean production to traditional manufacturing] is that the focus is on the customer rather than the product; activities which do not create value for the customer are defined as waste. Any action or process that the customer is willing to pay for is said to have positive value. **The main idea of lean production is for companies to create value for their customers by improving operating efficiency by reducing or eliminating waste.***

So, the implication is that these three techniques are broadly trying to do the same things; they have very similar objectives. In other words, their objectives overlap.

Also, it is not essential to use these techniques one after another in serial fashion; two or more of them can be applied at the same time. For example, JIT systems can be run contemporaneously with TQM initiatives. There is no reason why the six-sigma approach cannot operate at the same time as benchmarking, if management decide that this joint approach will improve performance. Admittedly, sometimes a multiple approach is adopted because the organization is in crisis, a kind of 'do-or-die' situation. Operating more than one technique simultaneously demands more management time and resolution as well as extra resources. Most firms are content to concentrate on applying one model at once; the challenges of this seem more than enough to cope with at the time.

As the introduction to this chapter said, 'Performance improvement initiatives are a way of business life.' An important skill of managers is their ability to keep employees motivated and committed to the current technique being applied. But whichever one it is, its overall objective is the same as all the others – to improve performance. This chapter uses the title 'Performance improvement techniques' because this excludes the possibility of managing and maintaining the current level of performance rather than seeking to improve it. However, different authors use different titles to describe exactly the same concept. Here is a list of some of them:

- Performance management
- Business performance management
- Corporate performance management
- Enterprise performance management
- Organizational performance management.

What something is called is not vitally important; what **is** important is **what** it does and **how** it does it. The name of the technique is not critical; carrying out the activities it involves **is**. William Shakespeare understood this for it was the master playwright himself who penned the following speech for Juliet: 'What's in a name? That which we call a rose by any other name would smell as sweet.'

Remember that no model or paradigm is as rich or complex as the reality it attempts to represent. Good managers will think carefully about which parts of a technique(s) are suitable for their organizations, combine them into a bespoke performance improvement model and implement this with confidence. It was Peter Drucker who said, 'Thinking is very hard work. And management fashions are a great substitute for thinking.' In other words, these techniques should not be applied without much thought being given to their suitability and the possible unintended consequences that may ensue. The author can think of no better way of ending this chapter than to quote one of his students, Samantha Hayes, who said, 'No accounting technique is designed to be run by people who cannot think for themselves.'

The manager's point of view (written by Gary Burmiston)

For companies to succeed it is vital that they understand their performance. Equally vital is that they understand how they can improve on their performance and identify where inefficiencies exist. The best companies do this continuously and don't wait for an event or *burning bridge*, such as a downturn in the economy, to really challenge their performance. When they do wait that long, it is often too late. This chapter has highlighted the plethora of performance management techniques that can be used to improve performance. It's worth highlighting that these are not just theoretical models and techniques. Over the course of the last 20 years in industry I have been engaged in projects which have used every one of the models explained in this chapter and continue to use some of them on a frequent basis.

The key issues for organizations concerning performance management techniques are: why are there so many? how to choose between them? and which one(s) are best in the given circumstances? At this point I need to declare a degree of cynicism. I believe an element of why there are so many techniques is to give external management consultants something to sell and to charge organizations large fees to introduce techniques that are really not that difficult to understand. Even the language of the techniques is designed to give that air of mystery and difficulty, resulting in organizations feeling they need to employ specialists to help them. There is no better example of this than Six Sigma. Firstly its name is partially Greek and it is also given an oriental martial arts feel by describing its competency levels as either green belt or black belt. Surely this must mean an organization needs external *experts* to demystify it and deliver the benefits – at a price!

One of the best ways to understand the techniques is to strip them down to the basics of what they are trying to achieve. For example, benchmarking is about comparisons, ABC is about identifying on what *activities* money is spent and Six Sigma is about trying to identify where there is waste. By stripping them down it becomes very apparent that there is a huge degree of commonality in the language and phraseology of the techniques. ABC talks about cost reduction, as does Kaizen. BPR looks to reduce non-value-adding activities which is also a stated aim of benchmarking, benchmarking also has a philosophy of continuous improvement as does Six Sigma and TQM. Six Sigma talks about *the voice of the customer*, whereas BPR talks about *meeting the needs of customers*. At their most basic level, all the techniques discussed are really just trying to achieve the same aims of eliminating waste and reducing non-value-adding activities in order to improve performance. In many ways, whilst the packaging is different for each technique, their methodologies are very similar even though they are called by different names.

Therefore a key issue for organizations is to determine which methodology they should use to **maximize** their return on the huge amounts of money invested in the business. Or is it? A key phrase used earlier in this chapter that truly underlines if an organization can successfully use one of the many performance improvement techniques is '**common sense**'. Does an organization really need to use benchmarking to determine if the cost of a process could be reduced? Does it really need to understand JIT to know that far more regular, smaller deliveries would improve its working capital and inventory levels and does it really need to use Six Sigma to know that its defect rate is unacceptably large or could it just look at its rework requirements to ascertain the same information? If the managers and employees in positions to drive improvement really want to do so, the technique they chose to use is not critical; it's their drive and desire that really counts. *The performance management methodology is merely a framework to help managers structure the identification and solution of issues.* Consultants can often be purists and insist that the techniques must be used to the 'letter' of the methodology. However, it's common sense that truly drives results and the techniques can be dipped in to and out of as required; they can even be mixed together to deliver great results.

So do the techniques work in a live environment? The answer to that is *yes, no and maybe*! It's really dependent on the extent to which people are motivated for, as mentioned above, it's not the techniques that drive the improvements, it's the people that work with the processes and the cost base. Often, the performance improvement project will come from a Board of Directors initiative saying that things need to improve. This crucial stage at the start of the project could be the beginning of an implementation failure and the waste of a large amount of money *if the people are not on board from the beginning.*

A great example of this is benchmarking. This is one of the most simple and common techniques which continues to be used today. Consultants continue to develop huge databases of the cost performance of different organizations in order to sell that information to others to allow them to compare their relative performance. However, when you talk to managers about a proposed benchmarking exercise, the underlying message could be perceived as the process and its cost base not being as good as that of a competitor. The manager could interpret this as a reprimand for underperforming. Now that could be the case or it could be explained away by lots of different reasons.

For example, you could benchmark the relative performance of two football teams – Manchester United and Mansfield Town. Success could be measured by the number of trophies and championships won and Manchester United is far ahead of Mansfield Town in both respects. However, the manager of Mansfield would immediately begin to cite reasons why the comparison is unfair. Manchester have much more investment, the training grounds and facilities are far better, they buy better quality players (raw materials) and the fan base is far higher giving more encouragement and intimidating opposition at home games. It could be argued that the manager of Mansfield isn't underperforming but his success will never be at the same level because of the reasons given.

In most benchmarking projects there is a natural assumption that all organizations are comparable (i.e. they are all Manchester United). This is not usually the case and therefore when the results of benchmarking are shared with managers the natural reaction can be to spend lots of time arguing why the comparisons are invalid and coming up with a list of reasons for the differences rather than spending time on ways to improve performance. Comparisons have to be supplemented with understanding. Failure to do so will result in the frequently used phrase, 'The results are different because . . .' Where this is the case, performance is very unlikely to improve. In any performance improvement process the impact and messages given to people have to be carefully considered to avoid them putting natural defence mechanisms in place. Understandably, people don't like being told they are not as good as someone else.

However, benchmarking can be hugely successful if used correctly. A good example is when I looked at the cost of producing one of the largest brands in the UK at two different sites. By benchmarking the raw material costs it was immediately apparent that one site was doing something different which allowed it to save money. Investigation revealed that the temperature of a liquid used in the production process was different at the two sites. When another raw material was added to the liquid, the site where the temperature was slightly higher did not need to add as much raw material as the site where the temperature was lower. This was because the increased temperature of the liquid resulted in more agitation and, therefore, more mixing of the added material. The site where the liquid was at a lower temperature had to add more as some of the raw material just sank to the bottom of the vessel. Consequently the temperature at both sites was equalized, which resulted in **a saving of raw material costs of over £2m per year!**

Without effective benchmarking this would never have been identified. The key to unlocking the saving was the **understanding** of the process. Benchmarking without understanding can be useless. On the other hand, as with all performance management techniques, benchmarking can produce exceptional results. The key is how it is used and implemented. Never forget that the *manner* in which things are done is just as important as *what* is being done; the potential for demotivating people is ever-present. The *people* aspect should never be ignored for it is people who drive improvements, not methodologies or techniques.

A further issue to consider with all performance management techniques is that they can work against each other. Consider an organization (A) that wants to implement JIT with the key aspect of zero inventory. It says to its supplier (B) that it now requires more frequent, smaller deliveries. After a while B implements ABC and finds the cost of supplying A is far greater than it costs to supply other organizations, due to not maximizing lorry capacity and making smaller, more frequent deliveries. B then asks it if can make less frequent, larger deliveries to improve the cost of its activities. Can both organizations achieve their aim of reducing costs? It's not clear that they can; a lot of thought about the situation may produce an ingenious solution but it's far from obvious and it may not be possible. Performance management cannot be used in isolation, it has to consider the environments in which it operates and in which its business partners operate.

In conclusion, the cynic in me suggests the best way for a company to improve its performance would be to reduce the amount it spends on expensive external consultants for telling it how its performance can be improved. That aside, the performance management techniques described in this chapter can be crucial weapons, helping organizations improve their performance. Scratching the surface of these techniques reveals many similarities between them. Their enduring nature indicates that they have been successfully implemented in the past and have delivered improvements. Each of the techniques can, and does, work but they can just as easily fail. The key to success in any organization is for it to clarify its specific corporate objectives and define what it wants to achieve. Then, taking a common sense approach, it should question and challenge its costs and processes to determine if there is a better way of doing things. Getting the right people engaged at the right time and with the right mindset to drive improvement will deliver results **no matter what techniques they use.**

Further reading

Aggarwal, R.K. and Samwick, A.A. (2003) 'Performance incentives within firms: the effect of managerial responsibility', *Journal of Finance*, Vol. 58, Issue 4, August.

Barlas et al., 'Activity-based Life Cycle Costing', *Strategic Finance*, Vol. 87, Issue 3, p. 24.

Bauer, K. (2005) 'KPIs: avoiding the threshold McGuffins', *DM Review*, Vol. 15, Issue 4, April.

Bennett, M. and James, P. (1998) *The Green Bottom Line: Environmental Accounting for Management*, Greenleaf Publishing, Sheffield.

Cokins, G. (2009) *Performance Management – Integrating Strategy, Execution, Methodologies, Risk and Analytics*, Wiley, Hoboken, NJ.

Collier, P. M. (2009) *Accounting for Managers: Interpreting Accounting Information for Decision Making*, 3rd edition, Wiley, Chichester.

Cooper, R. and Slagmulder, R. (2004) 'Achieving Full-Cycle Cost Management', *Sloan Management Review*, Vol. 46, Issue 1, pp. 45–52.

Coote, P. (2010) 'Value Stream Management', *Financial Management* (CIMA), October.

DeBusk, G.K., Brown, R.M. and Killough, L.N. (2003) 'Components and relative weights in utilization of dashboard measurement systems like the balanced scorecard', *The British Accounting Review*, Vol. 35, pp. 215–31.

Eckerson, W. (2011) *Performance Dashboards – Measuring, monitoring and managing your business*, 2nd edition, Wiley, Hoboken, NJ.

Goldratt, E. and Cox, J. (2004) *The Goal*. North River Press, Croton-on-Hudson, NY.

Gray, R. H., Owen, D. L. and Adams, C. (1996) *Accounting and Accountability: Changes and Challenges in Corporate Social and Environmental Reporting*, Harlow, Prentice Hall.

Hoque, Z. (2006) *Strategic Management Accounting – Concepts, Processes and Issues*, Pearson Education, Sydney.

Langfield-Smith, K., Thorne, H. and Hilton, R. (2009) *Management Accounting: Information for managing and creating value*, 5th edition, McGraw-Hill, New York.

Maskell, B. and Baggaley, B. (2005) 'Lean Accounting: What's It All About?', *Target® Magazine [online] L1–L9*, http://www.maskell.com/lean_accounting/subpages/lean_accounting/la_ppt.html

Maskell, B. and Katko, N. (2007) *Value Stream Costing: The Lean Solution To Standard Costing Complexity And Waste. Lean Accounting – best practices for sustainable integration*, edited by Stenzel, J., Wiley, Hoboken, NJ.

Melynk, S.A., Stewart, D.M. and Surink, M. (2004) 'Metrics and performance management in operations management: dealing with the metrics maze', *Journal of Operations Management*, Vol. 22, 209–17.

Plowman, B. (2010) 'Productivity Improvement', *Financial Management* (CIMA), October.

QFinance (www.qfinance.com) – a very good Internet site giving free access to much information on management issues – for example, try its 'Performance Management Best Practice' section which includes several articles on the techniques discussed in this chapter.

Rich, H. and Holweg, M. (2000) 'Value Analysis: Value Engineering', Lean Enterprise Research Centre, Cardiff, http://www.urenio.org/tools/en/value_analysis.pdf

Schifferes, S., 'Chrysler questions climate change', a BBC News article by Steve Schifferes, Economics reporter, at the Detroit Motor Show, 10 January 2007, http://news.bbc.co.uk/1/hi/business/6247371.stm

Young, R., 'Stern stuff', a publication for ACCA, 31 January 2007, http://www2.accaglobal.com/members/publications/accounting_business/archive/2007/january/

Glossary

This glossary is composed of definitions taken from *Management Accounting Official Terminology*, Revised 2000, published by the Chartered Institute of Management Accountants. I am most grateful to the CIMA for their permission to quote these definitions.

activity-based budgeting (ABB)
A method of budgeting based on an activity framework and utilizing cost driver data in the budget-setting and variance feedback processes.

activity-based costing (ABC)
An approach to the costing and monitoring of activities which involves tracing resource consumption and costing final outputs. Resources are assigned to activities and activities to cost objects based on consumption estimates. The latter utilize cost drivers to attach activity costs to outputs.

activity-based management (ABM)
System of management which uses activity-based cost information for a variety of purposes including cost reduction, cost modelling and customer profitability analysis.

activity cost pool
A grouping of all cost elements associated with an activity (CAM-I)*.

allocate
To assign a whole item of cost, or of revenue, to a single cost unit, centre, account or time period.

apportion
To spread revenues or costs over two or more cost units, centres, accounts or time periods. This may also be referred to as 'indirect allocation'.

balanced scorecard approach
An approach to the provision of information to management to assist strategic policy formulation and achievement. It emphasizes the need to provide the user with a set of information which addresses all relevant areas of performance in an objective and unbiased fashion. The information provided may include both financial and non-financial elements, and cover areas such as profitability, customer satisfaction, internal efficiency and innovation.

benchmarking
The establishment, through data gathering, of targets and comparators, through whose use relative levels of performance (and particularly areas of underperformance) can be identified. By the adoption of identified best practices it is hoped that performance will improve. Types of benchmarking include:

- *internal benchmarking*, a method of comparing one operating unit or function with another within the same industry;

- *functional benchmarking*, in which internal functions are compared with those of the best external practitioners of those functions, regardless of the industry they are in (also known as operational benchmarking or generic benchmarking);
- *competitive benchmarking*, in which information is gathered about direct competitors, through techniques such as reverse engineering;
- *strategic benchmarking*, a type of competitive benchmarking aimed at strategic action and organizational change.

budget
A quantitative statement, for a defined period of time, which may include planned revenues, expenses, assets, liabilities and cash flows. A budget provides a focus for the organization, aids the co-ordination of activities, and facilitates control. Planning is achieved by means of a fixed *master budget*, whereas control is generally exercised through the comparison of actual costs with a *flexible budget*.

budget slack
The intentional overestimation of expenses and/or underestimation of revenues in the budgeting process.

budgetary control
The establishment of budgets relating the responsibilities of executives to the requirements of a policy, and the continuous comparison of actual with budgeted results, either to secure by individual action the objectives of that policy or to provide a basis for its revision.

capital investment appraisal
The application of a set of methodologies (generally based on the discounting of projected cash flows) whose purpose is to give guidance to managers with respect to decisions as to how best to commit long-term investment funds.

cost–benefit analysis
A comparison between the cost of the resources used, plus any other costs imposed by an activity (e.g. pollution, environmental damage), and the value of the financial and non-financial benefits derived.

cost driver
Any factor which causes a change in the cost of an activity, e.g. the quality of parts received by an activity is a determining factor in the work required by that activity and therefore affects the resources required. An activity may have multiple cost drivers associated with it (CAM-I)*.

direct cost
Expenditure which can be economically identified with and specifically measured in respect to a relevant cost object.

discount rate/cost of capital (as used in capital investment appraisal)
The percentage used to discount future cash flows generated by a capital project.

discretionary cost
A cost whose amount within a time period is determined by, and is easily altered by, a decision taken by the appropriate budget holder. Marketing, research and training are generally regarded as discretionary costs. Control of discretionary costs is through the budgeting process. Also known as *managed* or *policy* costs.

factoring
The sale of debts to a third party (the factor) at a discount, in return for prompt cash. A factoring service may be *with recourse*, in which case the supplier takes the risk of the debt not being paid, or *without recourse* when the factor takes the risk.

hurdle rate
A rate of return which a capital investment proposal must achieve if it is to be accepted. Set by reference to the cost of capital, the hurdle rate may be increased above the basic cost of capital to allow for different levels of risk.

internal rate of return (IRR)
The annual percentage return achieved by a project, at which the sum of the discounted cash inflows over the life of the project is equal to the sum of the discounted cash outflows.

invoice discounting
The sale of debts to a third party at a discount, in return for prompt cash. The administration is managed in such a way that the debtor is generally unaware of the discounter's involvement, and continues to pay the supplier.

just-in-time (JIT)
A system whose objective is to produce or to procure products or components as they are required by a customer or for use, rather than for stock. A just-in-time system is a 'pull' system, which responds to demand, in contrast to a 'push' system, in which stocks act as buffers between the different elements of the system, such as purchasing, production and sales:

just-in-time production
A production system which is driven by demand for finished products whereby each component on a production line is produced only when needed for the next stage.

just-in-time purchasing
A purchasing system in which material purchases are contracted so that the receipt and usage of material, to the maximum extent possible, coincide.

net present value (NPV)
The difference between the sum of the projected discounted cash inflows and outflows attributable to a capital investment or other long-term project.

opportunity cost
The value of the benefit sacrificed when one course of action is chosen, in preference to an alternative. The opportunity cost is represented by the foregone potential benefit from the best rejected course of action.

overhead absorption rate
A means of attributing overhead to a product or service, based for example on direct labour hours, direct labour cost or machine hours:

direct labour cost percentage rate
An overhead absorption rate based on direct labour cost.

direct labour hour rate
An overhead absorption rate based on direct labour hours.

machine hour rate
An overhead absorption rate based on machine hours.

The choice of overhead absorption base may be made with the objective of obtaining 'accurate' product costs, or of influencing managerial behaviour, as where overhead applied to, say, labour hours or part numbers appears to make the use of these resources more costly, thus discouraging their use.

overhead/indirect cost
Expenditure on labour, materials or services which cannot be economically identified with a specific saleable cost unit.

The synonymous term 'burden' is in common use in the USA and in subsidiaries of American companies in the UK.

payback
The time required for the cash inflows from a capital investment project to equal the cash outflows.

period cost
A cost which relates to a time period rather than to the output of products or services.

present value
The cash equivalent now of a sum receivable or payable at a future date.

pricing
The determination of a selling price for the product or service produced. A number of methodologies may be used, including:

competitive pricing
Setting a price by reference to the prices of competitive products.

cost-plus pricing
The determination of price by adding a mark-up, which may incorporate a desired return on investment, to a measure of the cost of the product/service.

dual pricing
A form of transfer pricing in which the two parties to a common transaction use different prices.

historical pricing
Basing current prices on prior period prices, perhaps uplifted by a factor such as inflation.

market-based pricing
Setting a price based on the value of the product in the perception of the customer. Also known as perceived value pricing.

penetration pricing
Setting a low selling price in order to gain market share.

predatory pricing
Setting a low selling price in order to damage competitors. This may involve dumping, which is selling a product in a foreign market at below cost, or below the domestic market price (subject to adjustments for taxation differences, transportation costs, specification differences, etc.).

premium pricing
The achievement of a price above the commodity level, due to a measure of product or service differentiation.

price skimming
Setting a high price in order to maximize short-term profitability, often on the introduction of a novel product.

range pricing
The pricing of individual products such that their prices fit logically within a range of connected products offered by one supplier, and differentiated by a factor such as weight of pack or number of product attributes offered.

selective pricing
Setting different prices for the same product or service in different markets. This practice can be broken down as follows:

- *category pricing* – cosmetically modifying a product such that the variations allow it to sell in a number of price categories, as where a range of 'brands' are based on a common product;
- *customer group pricing* – modifying the price of a product or service so that different groups of consumers pay different prices;
- *peak pricing* – setting a price which varies according to the level of demand;
- *service-level pricing* – setting a price based on the particular level of service chosen from a range.

time and material pricing
A form of cost-plus pricing in which price is determined by reference to the cost of the labour and material inputs to the product/service.

prime cost
The total cost of direct material, direct labour and direct expenses.

production cost
Prime cost plus absorbed production overhead.

relevant costs/revenues
Costs and revenues appropriate to a specific management decision. These are represented by future cash flows whose magnitude will vary depending upon the outcome of the management decision made. If stock is sold by a retailer, the relevant cost, used in the determination of the profitability of the transaction, would be the cost of replacing the stock, not its original purchase price, which is a sunk cost. *Abandonment analysis*, based on relevant cost and revenues, is the process of determining whether or not it is more profitable to discontinue a product or service than to continue it.

relevant range
The activity levels within which assumptions about cost behaviour in breakeven analysis remain valid.

rolling/continuous budget
A budget continuously updated by adding a further accounting period (month or quarter) when the earliest accounting period has expired. Its use is particularly beneficial where future costs and/or activities cannot be forecast accurately.

semi-variable cost/semi-fixed cost/mixed cost
A cost containing both fixed and variable components and which is thus partly affected by a change in the level of activity.

sensitivity analysis
A modelling and risk assessment procedure in which changes are made to significant variables in order to determine the effect of these changes on the planned outcome. Particular attention is thereafter paid to variables identified as being of special significance.

standard
A benchmark measurement of resource usage, set in defined conditions. Standards can be set on a number of bases:

a) on an *ex ante* estimate of expected performance;
b) on an *ex post* estimate of attainable performance;
c) on a prior period level of performance by the same organization;
d) on the level of performance achieved by comparable organizations;
e) on the level of performance required to meet organizational objectives.

Standards may also be set at attainable levels which assume efficient levels of operation, but which include allowances for normal loss, waste and machine downtime, or at ideal levels, which make no allowance for the above losses, and are only attainable under the most favourable conditions.

standard cost
The planned unit cost of the products, components or services produced in a period. The standard cost may be determined on a number of bases (*see* standard). The main uses of standard costs are in performance measurement, control, stock valuation and in the establishment of selling prices.

strategic management accounting
A form of management accounting in which emphasis is placed on information which relates to factors external to the firm, as well as non-financial information and internally generated information.

strategic plan
A statement of long-term goals along with a definition of the strategies and policies which will ensure achievement of these goals.

sunk costs
Costs that have been irreversibly incurred or committed prior to a decision point and which cannot therefore be considered relevant to subsequent decisions. Sunk costs may also be termed *irrecoverable costs*.

target cost
A product cost estimate derived by subtracting a desired profit margin from a competitive market price. This may be less than the planned initial product cost, but will be expected to be achieved by the time the product reaches the mature production stage.

total quality management (TQM)
An integrated and comprehensive system of planning and controlling all business functions so that products or services are produced which meet or exceed customer expectations. TQM is a philosophy of business behaviour, embracing principles such as employee involvement, continuous improvement at all levels and customer focus, as well as being a collection of related techniques aimed at improving quality, such as full documentation of activities, clear goal-setting and performance measurement from the customer perspective.

transfer price

The price at which goods or services are transferred between different units of the same company. If those units are located within different countries, the term *international transfer pricing* is used.

The extent to which the transfer price covers costs and contributes to (internal) profit is a matter of policy. A transfer price may, for example, be based upon marginal cost, full cost, market price or negotiation. Where the transferred products cross national boundaries, the transfer prices used may have to be agreed with the governments of the countries concerned.

variance

The difference between a planned, budgeted or standard cost and the actual cost incurred. The same comparisons may be made for revenues.

variance analysis

The evaluation of performance by means of variances, whose timely reporting should maximize the opportunity for managerial action.

zero-based budgeting

A method of budgeting which requires each cost element to be specifically justified, as though the activities to which the budget relates were being undertaken for the first time. Without approval, the budget allowance is zero.

* CAM-I = Consortium for Advanced Manufacturing – International.

Answers to end-of-chapter questions

The answers to those chapter-end questions marked with an asterisk are shown below. The answers to the other chapter-end questions are given in the Lecturer's Guide.

Q3.1 Panther plc – Solution

1 Profitability

	2013	2012	2011
ROCE	$\dfrac{1,527}{6,046} = 25.3\%$	$\dfrac{837}{4,899} = 17.1\%$	$\dfrac{763}{4,570} = 16.7\%$
Asset utilization	$\dfrac{23,093}{6,046} = 3.8$ times	$\dfrac{17,931}{4,899} = 3.7$ times	$\dfrac{14,345}{4,570} = 3.1$ times
Profit margin	$\dfrac{1,527}{23,093} = 6.6\%$	$\dfrac{837}{17,931} = 4.7\%$	$\dfrac{763}{14,345} = 5.3\%$
Gross profit margin	$\dfrac{5,699}{23,093} = 24.7\%$	$\dfrac{3,359}{17,931} = 18.7\%$	$\dfrac{2,987}{14,345} = 20.8\%$

2 Working capital

Stock days	$\dfrac{2,850 \times 365}{17,394} = 60$ d	$\dfrac{2,177 \times 365}{14,572} = 55$ d	$\dfrac{1,790 \times 365}{11,358} = 58$ d
Debtor days	$\dfrac{2,711 \times 365}{23,093} = 43$ d	$\dfrac{2,260 \times 365}{17,931} = 46$ d	$\dfrac{2,356 \times 365}{14,345} = 60$ d
Purchases (CoS + CS – OS)	$17,394 + 2,850 - 2,177$ $= 18,067$	$14,572 + 2,177 - 1,790$ $= 14,959$	$11,358 + 1,790 - 1,689$ $= 11,459$
Creditor days	$\dfrac{3,216 \times 365}{18,067} = 65$ d	$\dfrac{2,980 \times 365}{14,959} = 73$ d	$\dfrac{2,474 \times 365}{11,459} = 79$ d
Cash cycle	38 days	28 days	39 days

3 Liquidity

Current ratio	$\dfrac{5,561}{4,615} = 1.2:1.0$	$\dfrac{4,437}{3,996} = 1.1:1.0$	$\dfrac{4,146}{4,254} = 1.0:1.0$
Liquid ratio	$\dfrac{2,711}{4,615} = 0.6:1.0$	$\dfrac{2,260}{3,996} = 0.6:1.0$	$\dfrac{2,356}{4,254} = 0.6:1.0$

4 Capital structure

Gearing	$\dfrac{1,564}{6,046} = 25.9\%$	$\dfrac{964}{4,899} = 19.7\%$	$\dfrac{906}{4,570} = 19.8\%$
Interest cover	$\dfrac{1,527}{93} = 16.4$ times	$\dfrac{837}{59} = 14.2$ times	$\dfrac{763}{44} = 17.3$ times

5 Suggested scenario

The only notable change in the first two years was the impressive reduction in the debtors collection period; it came down from 60 to 46 days, a 23% improvement. The company probably made a positive effort to improve its credit control in 2006. However, Panther plc improved its performance greatly in 2013.

Its ROCE went from 17.1% to 25.3% mainly due to its operating profit margin improving from 4.7% to 6.6%. The increase in gross profit margin from 18.7% to 24.7% appears to be responsible for this. But what caused these changes? Inspection of the balance sheet reveals a large increase in both debentures and fixed assets. Panther plc has raised £600 million in 2013 and invested it in new facilities (plant and equipment, buildings, etc.).

The increase in the ROCE shows that the investment has been successful. It may be that the old and inefficient plant was replaced by up-to-date machinery. On the other hand, Panther may have introduced new product lines to replace its old ones which were showing signs of obsolescence.

The length of the cash cycle has deteriorated from 28 days to 38 days (almost back to where it was in 2005). This is due to a downturn in creditor days and stock days by 8 and 5 days respectively mitigated by an improvement of 3 debtor days. Profitability would be further improved if this trend could be reversed and 2006 levels re-established.

Liquidity has been remarkably stable over the period. Gearing has increased markedly from 19.7% to 25.9% due to the new debenture. (Due to this and the increase in profitability, the shareholders have seen a significant increase in their returns.) Interest continues to be well covered at over 16 times.

Q3.2 The Wholesale Textile Company Limited – Solution

1 Liquidity

	2011	2012
Current ratio		
$\dfrac{\text{Current assets}}{\text{Current liabilities}}$	$= \dfrac{240,000}{100,000} = 2.4{:}1.0$	$\dfrac{366,000}{152,000} = 2.4{:}1.0$
Acid test ratio		
$\dfrac{\text{Current assets} - \text{stock}}{\text{Current liabilities}}$	$= \dfrac{120,000}{100,000} = 1.2{:}1.0$	$\dfrac{178,000}{152,000} = 1.2{:}1.0$

There has been no significant change in these ratios. The liquidity of the company is more than adequate at present.

2 Profitability

	2011	2012
$\dfrac{\text{Gross profit}}{\text{Sales}}$	$=\dfrac{128{,}000}{600{,}000}\times 100 = 21.3\%$	$\dfrac{152{,}000}{748{,}000}\times 100 = 20.3\%$
$\dfrac{\text{Net profit}}{\text{Sales}}$	$=\dfrac{30{,}000}{600{,}000}\times 100 = 5.0\%$	$\dfrac{34{,}000}{748{,}000}\times 100 = 4.5\%$

Both gross and net profit have fallen as a percentage of sales. One possible explanation of this is that selling prices have been reduced, which may also account for the increase in sales volume (price elasticity of demand). This shortfall of £32,000 (£780,000 − £748,000) would affect the budgeted net profit margin on each item sold as each one would have to bear a greater amount of fixed costs than planned. On the other hand, the cost of sales may have increased, possibly due to stock deterioration, obsolescence or theft. Or it may have been a combination of both of these.

Note that it is impossible to produce meaningful ratios for 2012 using the budgeted sales figure of £780,000.

Also, it is worth noting that if the extra £60,000 had been provided by shareholders instead of debentures (thus eliminating the £4,000 interest charge) then:

For 2012

$$\frac{\text{Net profit before interest}}{\text{Sales}} = \frac{38{,}000}{748{,}000}\times 100 = 5.1\%$$

Thus, the decrease in net profitability (after interest) can be explained by the source of the extra capital. This is why the operating profit (profit before interest and tax, PBIT) should be used to evaluate management performance.

Return on capital employed (ROCE)

	2011	2012
$\dfrac{\text{Operating profit}}{\text{Total operating assets}}$	$\dfrac{30{,}000}{200{,}000}\times 100 = 15.0\%$	$\dfrac{34{,}000 + 4{,}000}{294{,}000} = 12.9\%$

The new investment of £60,000 in 2012 is not yet making any improvement in profitability. Although apparently £20,000 had been spent on new fixed assets, the other £40,000 appears to be financing increased stock and debtors levels. This has resulted in the downward trend revealed by the above ratio.

3 Management effectiveness

Stock turnover period

	2011	2012
$\dfrac{\text{Year-end stock}}{\text{Cost of sales}}$	$\dfrac{120{,}000}{472{,}000}\times 100 = 25 \text{ days}$	$\dfrac{188{,}000}{596{,}000}\times 100 = 32 \text{ days}$

In order to compare 'like with like' (i.e. consistency) the year-end stock figure should be used instead of average stock.

The trend shown is disappointing. Possible explanations of this include stock levels being unnecessarily high at the end of 2012 due to deteriorating stock control. On the other hand, levels may have been purposefully increased for a good reason such as an impending strike at a manufacturing supplier.

Debtor collection period

	2011	**2012**
$\dfrac{\text{Year-end debtors}}{\text{Average daily credit sales}}$	$= \dfrac{100,000}{540,000/365} = 68 \text{ days}$	$= \dfrac{164,000}{684,000/365} = 88 \text{ days}$

Again, for consistency, year-end rather than average debtors should be used.

The possible reasons for this disappointing trend include a slackening of credit control at WTC Ltd. Alternatively, efforts in this department may have actually increased, but due to a worsening general economic climate debts have become significantly more difficult to collect.

Note that cash sales are not appropriate to this ratio.

To calculate the creditors payment period, the opening stock figure for 2011 would have to be known in order to calculate the average daily purchases. Sometimes, the cost-of-sales figure is used to approximate purchases but this assumes no change in stock value over the year.

The creditors payment period would enable the length of the cash cycle to be calculated. But even without this, the length of the operating cycle (stock days + debtor days) can be determined.

	2011	**2012**
Operating cycle	25 + 68 = 93 days	32 + 88 = 120 days

This shows a 29% deterioration in 2012. Management's effectiveness is worsening in both stock and debtor control.

4 Capital structure

Gearing

$$\frac{\text{Long-term loans}}{\text{Capital employed}} = 0 \qquad \frac{60,000}{294,000} \times 100 = 20.4\%$$

This means that 20.4% of the funding of WTC Ltd is provided by third parties. It arises solely from the debenture issue.

$$\text{Interest cover} = \frac{\text{net profit} + \text{interest charges}}{\text{interest charges}} \qquad \frac{34,000 + 4,000}{4,000} = 9.5 \text{ times}$$

Enough net profit is earned to pay the debenture interest 9.5 times over in 2012.

Q3.3 Chonky Ltd – Solution

	2011	2012	2013	2014
Profitability ratios:				
Gross profit margin	$\dfrac{160}{400} = 40\%$	$\dfrac{195}{500} = 39\%$	$\dfrac{280}{800} = 35\%$	$\dfrac{320}{1,000} = 32\%$
ROCE	$\dfrac{30}{165} = 18.2\%$	$\dfrac{40}{180} = 22.2\%$	$\dfrac{58}{230} = 25.2\%$	$\dfrac{46}{272} = 16.9\%$
Asset utilization	$\dfrac{400}{165} = 2.4$	$\dfrac{500}{180} = 2.8$	$\dfrac{800}{230} = 3.5$	$\dfrac{1,000}{272} = 3.7$
Net profit margin	$\dfrac{30}{400} = 7.5\%$	$\dfrac{40}{500} = 8\%$	$\dfrac{58}{800} = 7.25\%$	$\dfrac{46}{1,000} = 4.6\%$
Liquidity ratios:				
Current ratio	$\dfrac{57}{42} = 1.4{:}1.0$	$\dfrac{65}{51} = 1.3{:}1.0$	$\dfrac{111}{91} = 1.2{:}1.0$	$\dfrac{180}{140} = 1.3{:}1.0$
Liquid ratio	$\dfrac{33}{42} = 0.8{:}1.0$	$\dfrac{39}{51} = 0.8{:}1.0$	$\dfrac{37}{91} = 0.4{:}1.0$	$\dfrac{54}{140} = 0.4{:}1.0$
Working cap. management:				
Stock turnover period	$\dfrac{24 \times 365}{240} = 37\ d$	$\dfrac{26 \times 365}{305} = 31\ d$	$\dfrac{74 \times 365}{520} = 52\ d$	$\dfrac{126 \times 365}{680} = 68\ d$
Debtors collection period	$\dfrac{11 \times 365}{120} = 34\ d$	$\dfrac{15 \times 365}{160} = 34\ d$	$\dfrac{35 \times 365}{350} = 37\ d$	$\dfrac{54 \times 365}{500} = 39\ d$
Creditors payment period	$\dfrac{22 \times 365}{244} = 33\ d$	$\dfrac{26 \times 365}{307} = 31\ d$	$\dfrac{50 \times 365}{568} = 32\ d$	$\dfrac{92 \times 365}{732} = 46\ d$
Cash cycle	38 days	34 days	57 days	62 days
Capital structure:				
Gearing	0	0	$\dfrac{30}{230} = 13\%$	$\dfrac{60}{272} = 22\%$
Interest cover	n/a	n/a	$\dfrac{58}{3} = 19$ times	$\dfrac{46}{6} = 8$ times

Q4.1 Worthy Ltd – Solution

	2011	2012
1 ROCE		
$\dfrac{\text{PBIT}}{\text{TCE}}$	$\dfrac{350}{1,435} = 24\%$	$\dfrac{500}{1,770} = 28\%$
2 Gross profit %		
$\dfrac{\text{GP}}{\text{Sales}}$	$\dfrac{1,350}{3,000} = 45\%$	$\dfrac{1,900}{4,600} = 41\%$
3 Net profit %		
$\dfrac{\text{PBIT}}{\text{Sales}}$	$\dfrac{350}{3,000} = 12\%$	$\dfrac{500}{4,600} = 11\%$

4 Current ratio

$\dfrac{CA}{CL}$ $\dfrac{890}{1,505} = 0.6{:}1.0$ $\dfrac{2,150}{3,080} = 0.7{:}1.0$

5 Liquid ratio

$\dfrac{CA - stock}{CL}$ $\dfrac{520}{1,505} = 0.3{:}1.0$ $\dfrac{950}{3,080} = 0.3{:}1.0$

6 Stock turnover

$\dfrac{Y/E\ stock}{Av.\ daily\ CoS}$ $\dfrac{370}{1,650} \times 365 = 82$ days $\dfrac{1,200}{2,700} \times 365 = 162$ days

7 Debtors collection period

$\dfrac{Y/E\ debtors}{Av.\ daily\ sales}$ $\dfrac{440}{3,000} \times 365 = 54$ days $\dfrac{810}{4,600} \times 365 = 64$ days

8 Creditors payment period

$\dfrac{Y/E\ creditors}{Av.\ daily\ purch.}$ $\dfrac{450}{1,790} \times 365 = 92$ days $\dfrac{950}{3,530} \times 365 = 98$ days

9 Cash cycle

Stock turnover period	82	162
Debtors collection period	54	64
Creditors payment period	(92)	(98)
Cash cycle	44 days	128 days

Note: Calculation of purchases

Cost of sales	1,650	2,700
+ Closing stock	370	1,200
– Opening stock	(230)	(370)
= Purchases	1,790	3,530

Comment: Although Worthy's net profit margin has decreased from 12% to 11% (caused by a decrease in gross profit margin from 45% to 41%), its ROCE has increased from 24% to 28% due to the increase in its asset utilization from 2.1 times to 2.6 times.

However, its liquidity gives cause for concern. Both the current and liquid ratios are low and need careful monitoring. Although the current ratio has improved slightly, the liquid ratio appears very low for a manufacturer at 0.3:1.0. (Some businesses, such as Sainsbury's and Tesco, operate normally with very similar liquid ratios.)

The cause of the liquidity downturn can be identified by analysing the working capital ratios. The debtors collection period has worsened by 10 days but the creditors payment period has improved by 6 days; these changes, with a net effect of 4 days, are not the cause of the overdraft doubling from £0.9 to £1.95 million and the cash cycle increasing by 84 days from 44 to 128 days!

The major cause of concern is the stock turnover period which has doubled from 82 days to 162 days! The quantity of stock held at the year-end to support operations has increased by 200% in one year from £0.37 to £1.2 million whilst sales have only increased by 50% from £3.0 to £4.6 million. Why is so much extra stock needed compared with last year?

The reasons for this need further investigation; the increase **may be justifiable** but it is more likely to be due to a rapid deterioration in stock control. If stock levels are reduced so that they are proportional to the increase in sales, they would be £550,000 (£650,000 below the current level of £1.2 million). This change would reduce the overdraft on a £-for-£ basis to £1.3 million (£1,950,000 – £650,000), well within the original limit of £1.6 million.

However, as the sales expansion in 2012 was led by price reductions, this correction strategy may be a tall order as sales volumes will have risen by more than 50% to achieve this increase in sales revenue. Even so, it would be a good strategy to pursue; aiming high will hopefully achieve a significant improvement in stock control. At the same time, targets should also be set for improving the debtors collection period and the creditors payment period. This will further reduce the amount of overdraft needed.

Q4.2 BKZ Ltd – Solution

1 Cash budget (£000)

Month	April	May	June	July	August	September
Rev. 30%	6	12	18	30	30	30
50%	0	10	20	30	50	50
15%	0	0	3	6	9	15
Total IN	6	22	41	66	89	95
Expenses	63	53	57	63	63	63
Deprec'n	(13)	(13)	(13)	(13)	(13)	(13)
Total OUT	50	40	44	50	50	50
Net IN/(OUT)	(44)	(18)	(3)	16	39	45
Op. balance	2	(42)	(60)	(63)	(47)	(8)
Cl. balance	(42)	(60)	(63)	(47)	(8)	37

Comment: The predicted overdraft exceeds the limit imposed by the bank for each of the first four months; the worst position shows the need for an overdraft of £63,000 at the end of June. The original plan is not viable unless there is a cash injection of at least £23,000.

2 Cash budget (£000)

Month	April	May	June	July	August	September
Rev. (60–6)%	10.8	21.6	32.4	54.0	54.0	54.0
20%	0	4	8	12	20	20
15%	0	0	3	6	9	15
Total IN	10.8	25.6	43.4	72.0	83.0	89.0
Expenses	63	53	57	63	63	63
Deprec'n	(13)	(13)	(13)	(13)	(13)	(13)
Total OUT	50	40	44	50	50	50
Net IN/(OUT)	(39.2)	(14.4)	(0.6)	22.0	33.0	39.0
Op. balance	2	(37.2)	(51.6)	(52.2)	(30.2)	2.8
Cl. balance	(37.2)	(51.6)	(52.2)	(30.2)	2.8	41.8

Advice: The cash discount has improved the cash flow but the overdraft still exceeds the bank's limit in May and June by over £10,000. Also, £25,200 of profit will be lost in the period due to the cash discount ((420,000 × 60%) × 10%).

One alternative to offering a cash discount is to pay the expenses (excluding depreciation) one month after they have been incurred. The original budgeted profit would be unaffected and the cash budget would then be as follows:

A. Cash budget (£000)

Month	April	May	June	July	August	September
Rev. 30%	6	12	18	30	30	30
50%	0	10	20	30	50	50
15%	0	0	3	6	9	15
Total IN	6	22	41	66	89	95
Expenses		63	53	57	63	63
Deprec'n		(13)	(13)	(13)	(13)	(13)
Total OUT	0	50	40	44	50	50
Net IN/(OUT)	6	(28)	1	22	39	45
Op. balance	2	8	(20)	(19)	3	42
Cl. balance	8	(20)	(19)	3	42	97

If this were achievable, only half of the overdraft facility would be needed. However, it is very unlikely that a new company would be able to purchase its supplies on credit terms. A more realistic target may be for BKZ to source half its supplies on one month's credit. In this case, the cash budget would be as follows:

B. Cash budget (£000)

Month	April	May	June	July	August	September
Rev. 30%	6	12	18	30	30	30
50%	0	10	20	30	50	50
15%	0	0	3	6	9	15
Total IN	6	22	41	66	89	95
(Exps – Depn) 50%	25	20	22	25	25	25
(Exps – Depn) 50%	0	25	20	22	25	25
Total OUT	25	45	42	47	50	50
Net IN/(OUT)	(19)	(23)	(1)	19	39	45
Op. balance	2	(17)	(40)	(41)	(22)	17
Cl. balance	(17)	(40)	(41)	(22)	17	62

This shows that the bank's limit will only be exceeded by £1,000 at the end of June. By careful management of payments to creditors in June, it should be possible to postpone at least £1,000 of payments into July so that the overdraft at the end of June is no more than £40,000. Alternatively, or in addition, the bank could be asked for a temporary overdraft limit extension of £1,000 for the month of June. Also, there would be no loss of profit as there would be no need to introduce a cash discount.

Q4.3 Rogers Motor Parts – Solution

1 Calculations

	2011	2012
Mark-up	$\dfrac{50,000}{150,000} \times 100$	$\dfrac{40,000}{80,000}$
	$= 33\%$	$= 50\%$
Gross profit/sales	$\dfrac{50,000}{200,000} \times 100$	$\dfrac{40,000}{120,000}$
	$= 25\%$	$= 33\%$
Return on capital employed	$\dfrac{35,000}{50,000} \times 100$	$\dfrac{30,000}{38,000}$
	$= 70\%$	$= 79\%$
Debtor period	$\dfrac{36,000}{200,000} \times 365$	$\dfrac{12,000}{120,000} \times 365$
	$= 66$ days	$= 37$ days
Stock turnover days	$\dfrac{18,000}{150,000} \times 365$	$\dfrac{7,000}{80,000} \times 365$
	$= 44$ days	$= 32$ days
Purchases (CoGS + Cl. stk – Op. stk)	$150,000 + 18,000 - 7,000$	$80,000 + 7,000 - 5,000$
	$= 161,000$	$= 82,000$
Creditor payment period	$\dfrac{37,000}{161,000} \times 365$	$\dfrac{15,000}{82,000} \times 365$
	$= 84$ days	$= 67$ days
Cash cycle	$66 + 44 - 84$	$37 + 32 - 67$
	$= 26$ days	$= 2$ days
Current ratio	$\dfrac{54,000}{47,000}$	$\dfrac{20,000}{15,000}$
	$= 1.1{:}1.0$	$= 1.3{:}1.0$
Liquid ratio	$\dfrac{54,000 + 18,000}{47,000}$	$\dfrac{20,000 + 7,000}{15,000}$
	$= 0.8{:}1.0$	$= 0.9{:}1.0$

2 Discussion

The following points appear to be due to the reduction in selling prices:

- Sales have increased by £80,000 (67%).
- Gross profit increased by £10,000 (25%) and net profit by £5,000 (16.7%).
- Mark-up has fallen steeply (50% to 33%) as has the gross profit percentage (33% to 25%).
- Return on capital employed (based on year-end balances) is still high despite a fall from 79% to 70%.

- Increased sales may also be due to the near doubling of the credit period allowed to customers (37 to 66 days).
- This would also explain the cash balance changing from £1,000 positive to £10,000 negative.

The liquidity position at the end of 2011, as measured by both current and liquid ratios, appears satisfactory although slightly worse than 2010. However, the cash flow position is alarming. This is a classic case of 'overtrading' where the necessary additional working capital to facilitate the rapid trading expansion was not anticipated. The overdraft is right on the limit and cheques are likely to 'bounce', destroying suppliers' confidence and causing them to insist on cash terms for future purchases. This is particularly so as creditor days have increased from 67 to 84 days, resulting in more chasing by suppliers and a reduction in their confidence. Once cheques are dishonoured, word will soon get round the industry and a vicious downward spiral will follow, possibly leading to insolvency. Although Vic's strategy has increased his net profit by 17%, his business is in danger of collapsing; he is 'walking on a knife-edge' at the moment.

Vic would be well advised to tighten up his debt collection which seems to have slipped out of control. By collecting his debts earlier he will be able to return to paying his suppliers two months after delivery and reduce the threat of their withdrawing his credit. He should also take steps to reduce the number of days stock spends on his premises; this will also improve his cash position. These two actions should also enable him to reduce the amount of the overdraft used; this is essential to help prevent the vicious spiral referred to above. Vic was probably so busy due to the 67% expansion in sales that he forgot about the importance of controlling his working capital. If he does not give this his immediate attention, he may well find himself out of business!

He should also seriously reconsider his strategy of cutting prices to achieve more volume. Apart from the increased working capital requirement, he has probably doubled his sales volume. But all the extra work this involves is generating only a very modest increase in net profit. Many of his new sales probably make him no money at all!

Q5.1 Bodgit Ltd – Solution

		£	Workings	£
1 a)	Materials	15	Sales price	50
	Direct labour	8	Less: Variable cost	30
	Variable overheads	7	Unit contribution	20
	Variable cost	30		

b) BEP = fixed costs/unit contribution = 3,000/20 = 150 chairs

c) Total contribution = fixed costs + profit

$$200 \times 20 = 3,000 + profit$$

Profit = £1,000

d) Total contribution = fixed costs + profit

$$N \times 20 = 3,000 + 4,000$$
$$N = 7,000/20$$
$$= 350\ chairs$$

2 a) BEP = fixed costs/unit contribution

Workings	£
Materials	18 (15 × 1.20)
Direct labour	8
Variable overheads	7
Variable cost	33
Sales price	48
Unit contribution	15

$$= (3,000 + 1,000)/15$$
$$= \textbf{267 chairs}$$

b) Total contribution = fixed costs + profit
$$350 \times 15 = 4,000 + \text{profit}$$
$$\text{Profit} = 5,250 - 4,000$$
$$\textbf{Profit} = \textbf{£1,250}$$

c) Margin of safety = (actual − BEP)/actual
$$= (350 - 267)/350$$
$$= 83/350$$
$$= \textbf{24\% of sales}$$

d) Total contribution = fixed costs + profit
$$N \times 15 = 4,000 + 4,000$$
$$N = 8,000/15$$
$$N = \textbf{533 chairs}$$

3 The answers to these questions should be viewed as estimates because the variable costing financial model is based on several assumptions and approximations. For example, total revenue and total cost are shown as straight lines on the breakeven chart. In reality, they are curved as the selling price and total cost *per unit* tend to decrease as the volume of activity increases.

Also, breakeven charts are applicable only to single products (or constant sales mixes of several products). In reality, almost all manufacturers make more than one product. For breakeven purposes this necessitates a theoretical apportionment of the firm's fixed assets between different products. Some degree of approximation and subjectivity is unavoidable in this process.

Q5.2 Concord Toy Company – Solution

Operating Unit 1

Workings

Unit contribution = sales price − variable cost = 2.00 − 1.50 = £0.50
Sales forecast = £800,000/£2 = 400,000 pens

1 $$\text{BEP} = \frac{\text{fixed costs}}{\text{contribution/Unit}} = \frac{£150,000}{£0.5} = 300,000 \text{ units}$$

Breakeven point in £ sales = 300,000 × £2/pen = **£600,000**

2 $$\text{Margin of safety} = \frac{\text{planned sales} - \text{breakeven sales}}{\text{planned sales}} = \frac{£800,000 - £600,000}{£800,000}$$

$$= \textbf{25\%}$$

3 ROCE at 400,000 pens: Profit = total contribution − total fixed cost
$$= (400,000 \times £0.50) - 150,000$$
$$= 50,000$$

$$\text{ROCE} = \frac{50,000}{300,000} = 16.7\%$$

4 For 450,000 pens: Total contribution = 450,000 × £0.50 = £225,000

Less total fixed cost	= £150,000
Equals net profit	= **£75,000**

When a firm operates at maximum capacity, problems usually occur due to the lack of 'leeway' or safety margin if anything goes wrong. These problems affect throughput and profitability adversely.

5 Total contribution   = total fixed cost + profit

$N \times$ unit contribution = total fixed cost + profit

$$N = \frac{\text{total fixed cost} + \text{profit}}{\text{unit contribution}}$$

$$N = \frac{150,000 + 60,000}{£0.50}$$

$$N = 420,000 \text{ pens}$$

6 Possible actions to increase profitability:
- Review selling prices in the light of the effects on sales volume of the price elasticity of demand. Price reductions can lead to increased profitability if elasticity is relatively high and price increases can have the opposite effect.
- Review the potential for cost reduction in fixed overheads.
- Review the potential for cost reduction in variable costs.

Operating Unit 2

1 $\text{ROCE} = \dfrac{700,000}{3,600,000} \times 100 = 19.4\%$

2

	Buggy	Scooter	MP3 player
Selling price	20	10	10
Variable cost	6	2	4
Unit contribution	14	8	6

Working in 'bundles' of 1 buggy + 1 scooter + 1 MP3 player, the contribution of one 'bundle' = 14 + 6 + 8 = 28

$$\text{BEP} = \frac{\text{total fixed cost}}{\text{unit contribution}} = \frac{2,100,000}{28} = 75,000 \text{ bundles}$$

			£000
BEP occurs at:	75,000 buggies	@ £20 =	1,500
	75,000 scooters	@ £10 =	750
	75,000 MP3 player	@ £10 =	750
	225,000 products		**= 3,000 sales**

3	Forecast	−10%	−20%	Breakeven
	£000	£000	£000	£000
Sales	4,000	3,600	3,200	3,000
Variable costs	1,200	1,080	960	900
Contribution	2,800	2,520	2,240	2,100
Fixed costs	2,100	2,100	2,100	2,100
Profit	700	420	140	Nil

4 Unit 2 should not drop the MP3 player immediately as it has a positive contribution. If the company does drop the MP3 player, does not use the spare capacity released and fixed costs remain unchanged, its profit will be:

	£
Sales	3,000
Variable costs	800
Contribution	2,200
Fixed costs	2,100
Profit	100

i.e. it will be worse off than it is at present. The MP3 player should not be discontinued unless it can be replaced by a product or products that provide at least £600,000 contribution or unless, by dropping the product, fixed costs can be reduced by at least £600,000. For example, if the MP3 player was dropped 75,000 more scooters would have to be produced and sold to maintain profits at £700,000.

5 The danger is that this 20% price increase will cause a fall in sales volume.
New unit contribution = 12 − 4 = 8
Current total contribution = £600,000
No. of units needed = 600,000/8 = 75,000 units
If the price of the MP3 player was raised to £12, it must sell at least 75,000 units (current volume = 100,000 units) to prevent the company's profit falling below £700,000.

6 Additional information required on the new product would be:
  ● the selling price per unit;
  ● the variable cost per unit;
  ● the contribution per unit;
  ● the expected unit sales per year;
  ● the length of the contract;
  ● the cost of the new plant;
  ● the residual value of the new plant;
  ● the life of the new plant;
  ● the annual depreciation charge of the new plant;
  ● the rate of interest on the bank loan.

Q5.3 Rover's 'last chance saloon' – Solution

1 Retail price   = 22,000
    Trade price   = 16,500 (22,000 × 75%)
    Rover's total cost price   = 13,200 (16,500 × 80%)
    At BEP, total contribution   = total fixed costs
    (Unit contribution × 140,000) = total fixed costs

a) Variable cost   =   6,600   (13,200 × 50%)
      Selling price   = 16,500
      Unit contribution   = 9,900
      Total fixed costs   = **£1,386,000,000** (140,000 × 9,900)
                          = **£3,800,000/day**

b) Variable cost   =   8,580   (13,200 × 65%)
      Selling price   = 16,500
      Unit contribution   = 7,920
      Total fixed costs   = **£1,109,000,000** (140,000 × 7,920)
                          = **£3,000,000/day**

c) Variable cost   = 10,560   (13,200 × 80%)
      Selling price   = 16,500
      Unit contribution   = 5,940
      Total fixed costs   = **£832,000,000**   (140,000 × 5,940)
                          = **£2,300,000/day**

2 Total contribution = total fixed cost + profit
$$N \times 7,920 = 1,109,000,000 + 100,000,000$$
$$N = 1,209,000,000/7,920$$
$$N = 152,652 \text{ cars}$$

3   £
   Total contribution = 200,000 × £7,920 = 1,584,000,000
   Less: Total fixed cost   = 1,109,000,000
   Profit   = **£475,000,000**

4 Profit = £10,000,000,000 × 20% = £2,000,000,000
   Total contribution = total fixed cost + profit
$$N \times 7,920 = 1,109,000,000 + 2,000,000,000$$
$$N = 3,109,000,000/7,920$$
$$N = 392,551 \text{ cars}$$

Q6.1 Burgabar Corporation – Solution

£000	West Ham	Hackney	Forest Gate	Mile End	Total
Sales	100	120	120	140	480
Variable costs	20	24	24	28	96
Contribution	80	96	96	112	384
Salaries & wages	32	32	34	34	132
Fixed costs	30	30	32	34	126
Head office	20	24	24	28	96
Total fixed costs	82	86	90	96	354
Profit	(2)	10	6	16	30

If West Ham is closed and fixed costs remain unchanged (except as stated in question):

For Burgabar Group:	£000	£000
Total contribution (96 + 96 + 112)		304
Total fixed costs	354	
Less West Ham's salaries & wages	(32)	
Less reduction in head office costs	(10)	
Add redundancy pay	8	
Revised total fixed cost		320
Revised group loss for next year		(16)

Advice: The immediate closure of the West Ham branch would lose the group £46,000 in the next year. It would turn a group profit of £30,000 into a loss of £16,000.

If head office costs could be reduced by £10,000 without closing West Ham, all the branches would show a profit if sales remained the basis of apportionment for head office charges.

A positive strategy would be to aim to increase West Ham's annual sales from £100,000 to £105,000. This 5% increase would increase West Ham's contribution to £84,000 and turn its £2,000 loss into a £2,000 profit. Also, group profit would increase from £30,000 to £34,000.

The best option is to pursue a sales drive at West Ham (and possibly at the other branches at the same time) aimed at a minimum 5% improvement. The worst thing Burgabar could do is to close the West Ham branch immediately.

Q6.2 Profoot Ltd – Solution

1 Current year

	P1	P2	
Variable costs per pair:	£	£	
Materials	15.00	15.00	
Labour – Machining (£8/hour)	2.00	2.00	
– Assembly (£7/hour)	3.50	3.50	
– Packing (£6/hour)	0.50	0.50	
Total unit variable cost	21.00	21.00	
Selling price	40.00	40.00	
Unit contribution	19.00	19.00	
Annual sales demand (pairs)	14,000	10,000	
Total contribution	£266,000	£190,000	£456,000
Less: Total fixed costs			£300,000
Net profit			**£156,000**

2 Next year – full demand met

	P1		P2	PDL
	£	-	£	£
Variable costs per pair:				
Materials	15.00		20.00	32.50
Labour – Machining (£8/hour)	2.00		4.00	4.00
– Assembly (£7/hour)	3.50		3.50	7.00
– Packing (£6/hour)	0.50		0.50	0.50
Total unit variable cost	21.00		28.00	44.00
Selling price	40.00		50.00	65.00
Unit contribution	19.00		22.00	21.00
Order of preference	3		1	2
Annual sales demand (pairs)	14,000		7,000	5,000
Total contribution – per type	£266,000		£154,000	£105,000
– per total				£525,000
Less: Total fixed costs (£300,000 × 1.02)				£306,000
Net profit				**£219,000**

3 Next year – maximum of 8,500 machine hours

	P1	P2	PDL
Unit contribution	19.00	22.00	21.00
Machine hours/pair	0.25	0.50	0.50
Unit contribution/machine hour	76.00	44.00	42.00
Order of preference	1	2	3
Production*	**14,000**	**7,000**	**3,000**
Total contribution – per type	£266,000	£154,000	£63,000
– total			£483,000
Less: Total fixed costs (£300,000 × 1.02)			£306,000
Net profit			**£177,000**

* *Production workings:*

Preference	Model	Demand	Mh/pair	Total mh	Cum. mh
1	P1	14,000	0.25	3,500	3,500
2	P2	7,000	0.50	3,500	7,000
3	PDL	3,000	0.50	1,500	8,500

4 Additional machine

Shortfall in production of PDLs = 5,000 – 3,000 = 2,000 pairs
Shortfall in machine hours   = 2,000 × 0.50 = 1,000 mh

This is within the capacity of the new machine. So purchasing the machine will allow the shortfall to be eliminated.

Total extra contribution from machine = 2,000 pairs × £21 = £42,000
But, additional fixed cost depreciation = 420,000/10 = £42,000
Thus, net effect on profit   = nil

Q6.3 King & Co. – Solution

Budget

	Total cost	Fixed cost	Variable cost
	£000	£000	£000
Manufacturing	3,000	2,000	1,000
Sales & admin	1,500	1,000	500
Total	4,500	3,000	1,500

	Total	Unit
	£000	£
Sales commission (@ 5%)	250	0.25
Other variable costs	1,250	1.25
All variable costs	1,500	1.50
Sales revenue	5,000	5.00
Contribution	3,500	3.50

Contract

	Unit	Total
	£	£000
Other variable cost	1.25	62.5
Badge	0.50	25.0
All variable costs	1.75	87.5
Sales revenue	4.00	200.0
Contribution	2.25	112.5

Comment: As all fixed overheads will be recovered by the budgeted sales, the contribution from this one-off contract will translate directly into profit. The managing director's rejection of this contract will lose the company £112,500.

The breakeven price would be the variable cost of £87,500 (£1.75 a cap). So King & Co. would make a healthy profit even at a price of half the amount offered. The managing director should think again.

Q7.1 Burton Brothers – Solution

Assuming the machine is sold to Bridge & Co.

Item	Cash	Avoidable	Future	Note	Amount	Relevant in/(out)
Owing by Wey	Y	Y	N	1	(590 – 180 – 150) = 260	–
Costs to date	Y	N	N	2	£273,480	–
Completion: direct labour	Y	Y	Y	3	2,000 × (10 – 4)	(12,000)
Completion: contracted materials	Y	Y	Y	4	24,000 – 6,000	(18,000)
Completion: regularly used materials	Y	Y	Y	5	204,000/4	(51,000)
Completion: materials not regularly used	Y	Y	Y	3	204 – 24 – 51	(129,000)
Completion: production overheads	N	N	Y	6	2,000 × £88	–
Additions: materials	Y	Y	Y	5	45,000 – 13,500	(31,500)
Additions: substitute materials	Y	Y	Y	7		(12,000)
Additions: direct labour	Y	Y	Y	3	400 × (10 – 4)	(2,400)
Additions: production overheads	N	N	Y	6	400 × £88	–
Scrap value of machine as it stands	Y	Y	Y	7		(6,000)
Selling price to Bridge & Co.	Y	Y	Y	3		400,000
Net relevant cash flow in/(out)						**£138,100**

Notes:
1 This income will not now happen; it is not a future item.
2 Sunk cost.
3 Avoidable.
4 Committed cost, effectively of £6,000; other £18,000 is avoidable.
5 Replacement cost.
6 Non-cash item.
7 Opportunity cost.

Advice: Although Bridge & Co.'s offer of £400,000 is much less than the £590,000 agreed by Wey Ltd, despite the extra modifications Burton Brothers will be £138,100 better off in cash terms if it accepts it.

Q7.2 Eezikum – Solution

Item	Cash	Avoidable	Future	Note	Amount	Relevant in/(out)
UK cancellation fees	Y	Y	Y	1	11 × £10,000	(110,000)
UK lost fees	Y	Y	Y	1	11 × £15,000	(165,000)
UK out-of-pocket expenses	Y	Y	Y	2	11 × £2,500	27,500
New equipment	Y	Y	Y	1	100,000 – 40,000	(60,000)
Lost interest on deposit a/c	Y	Y	Y	3	100,000 × 9/12 × 12%	(9,000)
US fees	Y	Y	Y	2	125 × £10,000	1,250,000
US out-of-pocket expenses	Y	Y	Y	1	125 × 2,000	(250,000)
Airfares	Y	Y	Y	1	2 × £14,500	(29,000)
Health insurance	Y	Y	Y	1		(6,000)
Travel insurance	Y	N	Y	4		–
Net cash flow in/(out)						**£648,500**

Notes:
1 Avoidable cost.
2 Avoidable income.
3 Opportunity cost.
4 Sunk cost.

The net benefit of accepting the US tour is £648,500.

Q7.3 Carbotest Corporation – Solution

Item	Cash	Avoidable	Future	Note	Amount	Relevant in/(out)
Contract price		Y	Y	Y		152,000
Components – 35,000	Y	Y	Y	1	35,000 × £3	(105,000)
– 5,000	Y	Y	Y	2	5,000 × £1	(5,000)
– scrap value	Y	Y	Y	3		(1,000)
Harness	Y	Y	Y	4	1,000 × £9	(9,000)
Skilled labour – pay	Y	N	Y	5		–
– abandoned work	Y	Y	Y	6	60,000 – 48,000	(12,000)
Supervision	Y	N	Y		7	–
Machines – depreciation	N	N	Y	8		–
– resale value	Y	Y	Y	9		(5,000)
– lease costs	Y	Y	Y	10	6 × £500	(3,000)
Accommodation	Y	N	N	11		–
– planning permission						
Temporary building	Y	Y	Y	12	£8,000 + £2,000	(10,000)
Car park – construction cost	Y	N	Y	13		–
Fixed overheads	N	N	Y	14		–
Net cash flow						**£2,000**

Notes:

1 Replacement cost.
2 Modification cost.
3 Opportunity cost.
4 All at replacement cost as harness is already in regular use.
5 Unavoidable cost, will be paid irrespective of decision.
6 Lost cash contribution = opportunity cost.
7 Unavoidable, permanent employee.
8 Non-cash expense.
9 Opportunity cost.
10 Replacement cost.
11 Committed cost.
12 Construction and demolition costs.
13 Postponed, not avoided.
14 Non-cash, unavoidable.

Note that net cash inflow of £2,000 is very close to breakeven. Are the effort and risk involved worth it? Suppose unforeseen difficulties appear. To what extent will the postponement of the car park demotivate employees? On balance, I would **not** recommend acceptance of the contract.

Q8.1 Frynas & Co. – Solution

1

$$\text{Straight-line deprecation charge} = \frac{\text{original} - \text{residual value}}{\text{fixed asset lifetime}}$$

$$= \frac{£(620{,}000 - 20{,}000)}{4 \text{ years}}$$

$$= 150{,}000/\text{year}$$

$$\text{ARR} = \frac{\text{average annual profit}}{\text{initial investment}} = \frac{(200/4)}{620} \times 100 = \frac{5}{620} \times 100 = 8.1\%$$

If this project is carried out, it will lower the company's ROCE which is currently 11.1%. The size of the effect depends on the size of the investment compared with the total of all its investments.

2

Year	Trading profit/(loss)	Depreciation charge	Cash in/(out)	Cumulative cash in/(out)
1	(50,000)	150,000	100,000	100,000
2	50,000	150,000	200,000	300,000
3	150,000	150,000	300,000	600,000
4	50,000	150,000	200,000	800,000
	200,000	600,000	800,000	

$$\text{Payback period} = 3 + \frac{(620{,}000 - 600{,}000)}{200{,}000} - 3 + \frac{20{,}000}{200{,}000} = 3.1 \text{ years}$$

3 and 4 (£000)

Year	Cash in/(out)	10% factors	Present value	11% factors	Present value
0	(620)	1.000	(620)	1.000	(620)
1	100	0.909	91	0.901	90
2	200	0.826	165	0.812	162
3	300	0.751	225	0.731	219
4	200	0.683	137	0.659	132
5	20	0.683	14	0.659	13
			NPV = +12		NPV = (4)

$$\text{NPV at } 10\% = £12{,}000$$
$$\text{IRR} = 10 + (12/16 \times 1\%) = 10.75\%$$

5 The ARR of 8.1% compares badly with Frynas's ROCE of 11.1%. This project will probably reduce the company's overall ROCE to below 11.0%. The payback period is just over three-quarters is of the project's life span. This is not encouraging. Bearing in mind the assumptions and limitations of the technique, a positive £12,000 NPV on a £620,000 project should be viewed as a breakeven position. The IRR of 10.75% does not tell us anything as it is a relative measure and we do not know what Frynas's 'hurdle' rate is, although it is most unlikely to be less than its ROCE of 11.1%. This means that the IRR calculation advises against the project's going ahead.

Q8.2 Binley Blades Ltd – Solution

Year	0	1	2	3	4	5
Cash in/(out) (£000)						
Plant & equipment	−2,000	0	0	0	0	500
Research & development	0	0	0	0	0	0
Materials usage	0	−500	−500	−500	−500	−500
Direct labour	0	−200	−200	−200	−200	−200
Indirect labour	0	−10	−10	−10	−10	−10
Working capital	−150	0	0	0	0	150
Depreciation	0	0	0	0	0	0
Production overheads	0	−5	−5	−5	−5	−5
Sales & admin overheads	0	0	0	0	0	0
Finance overhead	0	0	0	0	0	0
Sales revenue	0	1,450	1,450	1,450	1,450	1,450
Net cash in/(out)	−2,150	735	735	735	735	1,385
10% discount factors	1	0.9090	0.8264	0.7513	0.6830	0.6209
Present values	−2,150	668.18	607.43	552.21	502.01	859.97

Net present value = £1,040,000

Notes:
1 Only relevant cash flows should be used for NPV calculations. Non-cash items should be excluded.
2 The disposal of plant and equipment at the end of five years gives rise to a cash inflow of £500,000. The written-down value of £1,000,000 in Binley's accounts is irrelevant.
3 Research and development costs are 'sunk' costs already incurred and not relevant.
4 Material usage and direct labour cause equivalent cash flows to occur.
5 Only half the indirect labour attached to the project is actually caused by it.
6 The working capital is released at the end of the project, equivalent to a cash inflow.
7 Depreciation is a non-cash expense and not relevant to this project.
8 Only 12.5% of the production overheads attached to the project are caused by it.
9 No additional sales and administration overheads are caused by the project.
10 Interest on the loan must not be included as it is already built into the discount rate.
11 The discount factors used were incorrect.

Comment: The corrected NPV is just over £1 million positive, strongly indicating that the project should go ahead.

Q8.3 Stobo plc – Solution

1 Payback periods

	Stobo plc Payback periods					
	Project SR		**Project OHC**		**Project PF**	
Year	In/(out)	Cumulative	In/(out)	Cumulative	In/(out)	Cumulative
0	−44	−44	−40	−40	−44	−44
1	16	−28	8	−32	12	−32
2	14	−14	10	−22	12	−20
3	12	−2	12	−10	12	−8
4	10	8	14	4	12	4
5	8	16	16	20	12	16
Payback period:						
	3.2 years		**3.7 years**		**3.7 years**	

2 Net present values

Project SR (£000)

Year	Cash in/(out)	Discount rate 10%	Present value
0	−44	1.000000	−44.000000
1	16	0.909091	14.545455
2	14	0.826446	11.570248
3	12	0.751315	9.015778
4	10	0.683013	6.830135
5	8	0.620921	4.967371
NPV = £2,929,000			NPV = **2.928985**
5-year IRR = 13%			

Project OHC (£000)

Year	Cash in/(out)	Discount rate 10%	Present value
0	−40	1.000000	−40.000000
1	8	0.909091	7.272727
2	10	0.826446	8.264463
3	12	0.751315	9.015778
4	14	0.683013	9.562188
5	16	0.620921	9.934741
NPV = £4,050,000			NPV = **4.049897**
5-year IRR = 13%			

Project PF (£000)

Year	Cash in/(out)	Discount rate 10%	Present value
0	−44	1.000000	−44.000000
1	12	0.909091	10.909091
2	12	0.826446	9.917355
3	12	0.751315	9.015778
4	12	0.683013	8.196161
5	12	0.620921	7.451056
NPV = £1,489,000			NPV = **1.489441**
5-year IRR = 11%			

3 Advice: Summary of results

	SR	OHC	PF
PBP	3.2 years	3.7 years	3.7 years
NPV (£000)	2,929	4,050	1,489
IRR	13%	13%	11%

Although stress relief (SR) has the shortest payback period, the best option is oral hygiene and chiropody (OHC) as it has the highest net present value and internal rate of return.

Q9.1 Lewington Ltd – Solution

Workings

	Cutting	Assembly	Finishing
OAR/mh	$\dfrac{1,600,000}{40,000}$	$\dfrac{2,000,000}{25,000}$	$\dfrac{1,400,000}{14,000}$
	= £40/mh	= £80/mh	= £100/mh
OAR/dlh	$\dfrac{1,600,000}{10,000}$	$\dfrac{2,000,000}{40,000}$	$\dfrac{1,400,000}{20,000}$
	= £160/dlh	= £50/dlh	= £70/dlh

1 Machine hour rates   £
Direct materials   3,300
Direct labour   4,500
Prime cost   7,800
Production overheads:
  Cutting   50 mh × £40/mh = 2,000
  Assembly 25 mh × £80/mh = 2,000
  Finishing 10 mh × £100/mh = 1,000
                        5,000
Production cost   12,800   Cost/unit = £42.67

2 Direct labour hour rates   £
Direct materials   3,300
Direct labour   4,500
Prime cost   7,800
Production overheads:
  Cutting   20 dlh × £160/dlh = 3,200
  Assembly 45 dlh × £50/dlh = 2,250
  Finishing 20 dlh × £70/dlh = 1,400
                        6,850
Production cost   14,650   Cost/unit = £48.83

3 Mixed rates   £
Direct materials   3,300
Direct labour   4,500
Prime cost   7,800
Production overheads:
  Cutting   50 mh × £40/mh = 2,000
  Assembly 45 dlh × £50/dlh = 2,250
  Finishing 20 dlh × £70/dlh = 1,400
                        5,650
Production cost   13,450   Cost/unit = £44.83

4 *Comment*: The choice of OAR makes a significant difference to the production cost (over 10% in this case). This illustrates the approximate nature of absorption costing.

Q9.2 Graham and Sara – Solution

1 a) Direct material cost

	Men's £000	Women's £000	Total £000
Materials	78	26	104
Direct labour	18	30	48
Variable overheads	4	4	8
Variable production cost	100	60	160
Fixed production overheads	12	4	16
Total production cost	112	64	176
Increase in stock	2	1	3
Cost of sales	110	63	173
Marketing overheads	8	4	12
Administration overheads	4	4	8
Total cost	122	71	193
Sales revenue	118	78	196
Profit/(loss)	(4)	7	3

b) Direct labour cost

	Men's £000	Women's £000	Total £000
Materials	78	26	104
Direct labour	18	30	48
Variable overheads	4	4	8
Variable production cost	100	60	160
Fixed production overheads	6	10	16
Total production cost	106	70	176
Increase in stock	2	1	3
Cost of sales	104	69	173
Marketing overheads	8	4	12
Administration overheads	4	4	8
Total cost	116	77	193
Sales revenue	118	78	196
Profit/(loss)	2	1	3

c) Variable overhead cost

	Men's £000	Women's £000	Total £000
Materials	78	26	104
Direct labour	18	30	48
Variable overheads	4	4	8
Variable production cost	100	60	160
Fixed production overheads	8	8	16
Total production cost	108	68	176
Increase in stock	2	1	3
Cost of sales	106	67	173
Marketing overheads	8	4	12
Administration overheads	4	4	8
Total cost	118	75	193
Sales revenue	118	78	196
Profit/(loss)	–	3	3

2 **Summary of alternative profit/(loss) (£000)**

	Men's	Women's	Total
Variable production cost	(2)	5	3
Direct material cost	(4)	7	3
Direct labour cost	2	1	3
Variable overhead cost	–	3	3

These results show the arbitrary nature of the absorption costing system regarding the internal distribution of overheads between departments/products. Note that the overall total figure is not affected.

The objective of the absorption costing system is to ensure all the production overheads are absorbed. It is **not** primarily concerned with '**accurate**' (in the sense of 'caused by') product or departmental costs.

Q9.3 Stellar Showers – Solution

Table showing apportionments and allocations

	Moulding	Assembly	Packaging	Q. control	Stores	Total
M/c electr.	30,000	8,000	2,000	–	–	40,000
Stores	–	–	–	–	80,000	80,000
Heating	2,400	4,200	4,000	200	2,200	13,000
Lighting	600	1,600	1,000	100	700	4,000
Superv'n*	20,000	25,000	20,000	–	–	65,000
Prod. mgr	4,000	28,500	2,500	–	–	35,000
Bus. rates	2,400	6,400	4,000	400	2,800	16,000
Fire ins.	4,400	3,600	1,800	–	200	10,000
QC pay	–	–	–	30,000	–	30,000
Depr'n	7,500	6,000	3,000	–	1,500	18,000
Total	71,300	83,300	38,300	30,700	87,400	311,000
Qual. con.	5,117	15,350	5,117	(30,700)	5,116	–
Total	76,417	98,650	43,417	–	92,516	311,000
Stores	9,252	67,074	16,190	–	(92,516)	–
Total	85,669	165,724	59,607	–	–	311,000

* Allocated.

1

	Moulding	Assembly	Packaging
Overhead absorption rate	$\dfrac{85,669}{34,967}$	$\dfrac{165,724}{63,986}$	$\dfrac{59,607}{10,998}$
	£2.45/mh	£2.59/dlh	£5.42/dlh

2 **Batch of 800 SS40Ts:**

Moulding	$1,500 \times 2.45 =$	3,675
Assembly	$3,500 \times 2.59 =$	9,065
Packaging	$1,000 \times 5.42 =$	5,420
Direct materials		− 16,000
Direct labour		= 8,800
		42,960

Unit production cost = £42,960/800 = **£53.70**

Workings

Apportionment of machine electricity (total cost £40,000):
Most **rational** basis of apportionment is 'wattage'. Total wattage = 6,000

	Moulding	Assembly	Packaging	Q. con.	Stores	Total
Proportion	$\frac{4,500}{6,000}$	$\frac{1,200}{6,000}$	$\frac{300}{6,000}$	–	–	$\frac{6,000}{6,000}$
	15/20	4/20	1/20	–	–	20/20
Overhead cost	£40,000	£40,000	£40,000	–	–	£40,000
Apportionment	**£30,000**	**£8,000**	**£2,000**	–	–	**£40,000**

Apportionment of production manager's pay (total cost £35,000):
Most **rational** basis of apportionment is 'added value'. Total added value = £7.0 million

	Moulding	Assembly	Packaging	Q. con.	Stores	Total
Proportion	$\frac{0.8}{7.0}$	$\frac{5.7}{7.0}$	$\frac{0.5}{7.0}$	–	–	$\frac{7.0}{7.0}$
	8/70	57/70	5/70	–	–	70/70
Overhead cost	£35,000	£35,000	£35,000	–	–	£35,000
Apportionment	**£4,000**	**£28,500**	**£2,500**	–	–	**£35,000**

Apportionment of business rates (total cost £16,000):
Most **rational** basis of apportionment is 'area'. Total area = 2,000 sq. m

	Moulding	Assembly	Packaging	Q. con.	Stores	Total
Proportion	$\frac{300}{2,000}$	$\frac{800}{2,000}$	$\frac{500}{2,000}$	$\frac{50}{2,000}$	$\frac{350}{2,000}$	$\frac{2,000}{2,000}$
	6/40	16/40	10/40	1/40	7/40	40/40
Overhead cost	£16,000	£16,000	£16,000	£16,000	£16,000	£16,000
Apportionment	**£2,400**	**£6,400**	**£4,000**	**£400**	**£2,800**	**£16,000**

Apportionment of lighting (total cost £4,000):
Most **rational** basis of apportionment is 'area'. Total area = 2,000 sq. m

	Moulding	Assembly	Packaging	Q. con.	Stores	Total
Proportion	$\frac{300}{2,000}$	$\frac{800}{2,000}$	$\frac{500}{2,000}$	$\frac{50}{2,000}$	$\frac{350}{2,000}$	$\frac{2,000}{2,000}$
	6/40	16/40	10/40	1/40	7/40	40/40
Overhead cost	£4,000	£4,000	£4,000	£4,000	£4,000	£4,000
Apportionment	**£600**	**£1,600**	**£1,000**	**£100**	**£700**	**£4,000**

Apportionment of heating oil (total cost £13,000):
Most **rational** basis of apportionment is 'volume'. Total volume = 6,500 cu. m

	Moulding	Assembly	Packaging	Q. con.	Stores	Total
Proportion	$\dfrac{1,200}{6,500}$	$\dfrac{2,100}{6,500}$	$\dfrac{2,000}{6,500}$	$\dfrac{100}{6,500}$	$\dfrac{1,100}{6,500}$	$\dfrac{6,500}{6,500}$
	12/65	21/65	20/65	1/65	11/65	65/65
Overhead cost	£13,000	£13,000	£13,000	£13,000	£13,000	£13,000
Apportionment	**£2,400**	**£4,200**	**£4,000**	**£200**	**£2,200**	**£13,000**

Apportionment of fire insurance (total cost £10,000):
Most **rational** basis of apportionment is 'WDV'. Total WDV = £50,000

	Moulding	Assembly	Packaging	Q. con.	Stores	Total
Proportion	$\dfrac{22,000}{50,000}$	$\dfrac{18,000}{50,000}$	$\dfrac{9,000}{50,000}$	–	$\dfrac{1,000}{50,000}$	$\dfrac{50,000}{50,000}$
	22/50	18/50	9/50	–	1/50	50/50
Overhead cost	£10,000	£10,000	£10,000	–	£10,000	£10,000
Apportionment	**£4,400**	**£3,600**	**£1,800**	–	**£200**	**£10,000**

Apportionment of depreciation (total cost £18,000):
Most **rational** basis of apportionment is 'fixed asset cost'. Total FA cost = £120,000

	Moulding	Assembly	Packaging	Q. con.	Stores	Total
Proportion	$\dfrac{50}{120}$	$\dfrac{40}{120}$	$\dfrac{20}{120}$	–	$\dfrac{10}{120}$	$\dfrac{120}{120}$
	5/12	4/12	2/12	–	1/12	12/12
Overhead cost	£18,000	£18,000	£18,000	–	£18,000	£18,000
Apportionment	**£7,500**	**£6,000**	**£3,000**	–	**£1,500**	**£18,000**

Apportionment of quality control (total cost £30,700):
Most **rational** basis of apportionment is 'QC work hours'. Total hours = (40 – 4) = 36

	Moulding	Assembly	Packaging	Q. con.	Stores	Total
Proportion	$\dfrac{6}{36}$	$\dfrac{18}{36}$	$\dfrac{6}{36}$	–	$\dfrac{6}{36}$	$\dfrac{36}{36}$
	1/6	3/6	1/6	–	1/6	6/6
Overhead cost	£30,700	£30,700	£30,700	–	£30,700	£30,700
Apportionment	**£5,117**	**£15,350**	**£5,117**	–	**£5,116**	**£30,700**

Apportionment of stores costs (total cost £92,516):
Most **rational** basis of apportionment is 'issues'. Total issues = 20,000

	Moulding	Assembly	Packaging	Q. con.	Stores	Total
Proportion	$\dfrac{2,000}{20,000}$	$\dfrac{14,500}{20,000}$	$\dfrac{3,500}{20,000}$	–	–	$\dfrac{20,000}{20,000}$
	4/40	29/40	7/40	–	–	40/40
Overhead cost	£92,516	£92,516	£92,516	–	–	£92,516
Apportionment	**£9,252**	**£67,074**	**£16,190**	–	–	**£92,516**

Q10.1 Hinj Ltd – Solution

1 Absorption costing

$$OAR = \frac{\text{total overheads}}{\text{total machine hours}} = \frac{182,500}{7,300} = £25 \text{ mh}$$

		Arms		Brackets
Direct materials		8,250		3,750
Direct labour		46,000		7,600
Overheads	(2,600 @ £25)	65,000	(1,275 @ £25)	31,875
		£119,250		£43,225
Per unit	[1,000]	**£119.25**	[500]	**£86.45**

2 Activity-based costing

	Cost pool (£)	Activity level	Cost driver rate
Purchasing	41,500	1,000 purch. orders	£41.50/order
Stores	41,600	650 issue notes	£64.00/issue
Set-ups	26,400	200 set-ups	£132.00/set-up
Machine running costs	73,000	7,300 machine hours	£10.00/mh

		Arms		Brackets
Direct materials		8,250		3,750
Direct labour		46,000		7,600
Purchasing	(190 × £41.5)	7,885	(325 × £41.5)	13,487.5
Stores	(105 × £64)	6,720	(200 × £64)	12,800
Set-ups	(35 × £132)	4,620	(60 × £132)	7,920
Machining	(2,600 × £10)	26,000	(1,275 × £10)	12,750
		£99,475		£58,307.5
Per unit	[1000]	**£99.475**	[500]	**£116.615**

3 *Comment:* The above shows that, under absorption costing, 'Arms' have been overcosted and 'Brackets' undercosted. One possible effect of this cross-subsidy is that 'Arms' have been overpriced and 'Brackets' underpriced. This, in turn, will affect their sales volumes in the marketplace.

Q10.2 Numan Travel – Solution

		Best Beaches		Cosy Cottages		Great Golfing
No. of reps:		(192 × 1)	+	(770 × 0.5)	+	(192 × 0.5)
	=	192	+	385	+	96
	=	673				

Admin. activity	Cost £000	Cost driver	Annual no. of cost drivers	Cost driver rate
Booking	20,000	Reservation	825,000	£24.2424/reservation
Holiday repping	10,000	Representative	673	£14,858.84/rep
Hotel contracting	6,000	Hotel	1,154	£5,199.31/hotel
Marketing	3,600	Marketing employee	74	£48,648.65/marketing employee

ABC attachment of administration overheads

£000	Best Beaches	Cosy Cottages	Great Golfing	Flygo	Total
Booking @ £24.2424	9,091	6,061	606	4,242	20,000
Repping @ £14,858.84	2,852.9	5,720.7	1,426.4	–	10,000
Hotel contracting @ £5,199.31	998.3	4,003.5	998.3	–	6,000
Marketing @ £48,648.65	1,459.5	973.0	875.7	291.9	3,600
Totals	14,402	16,758	3,906	4,534	39,600

£000	Best Beaches	Cosy Cottages	Great Golfing	Flygo	Total
Contribution	37,500	30,000	3,500	14,000	85,000
Advertising	15,000	15,000	2,000	3,500	35,500
Contribution less advertising	22,500	15,000	1,500	10,500	49,500
Admin. overheads	14,402	16,758	3,906	4,534	39,600
Profit	**8,098**	**(1,758)**	**(2,406)**	**5,966**	**9,900**
Preference	1	3?	4?	2	

Comment: ABC shows that, on a cost-causation base, Flygo makes the second-highest profit of the four brands and Great Golfing makes the largest loss. This shows the new MD's strategy to be very high risk.

Q10.3 Wilcock & Co. – Solution

1 Overhead absorption rate $= \dfrac{346,000}{1,384,000} = 25\%$ of direct labour cost

Absorption costing of fraud case:	£
Direct labour	15,000
Overheads (£15,000 × 25%)	3,750
Absorption cost	**18,750**
Profit margin (40% × £18,750)	7,500
Price charged to customer	**26,250**

2 Activity-based costing of fraud case:

Activity	Cost driver	Annual cost pool (£)	Annual use of cost drivers	Cost driver rates
Clerical support	Clerical hours	156,000	26,000 hours	£6.00/clerical hour
General administration	Admin hours	60,000	3,000 hours	£20.00/admin hour
Photocopying	Number of copies	25,000	500,000 copies	£0.05/copy
Telephone	Telephone calls	105,000	70,000 calls	£1.50/call
		346,000		

Activity	Cost driver	Contract's use of cost drivers	Cost driver rates	Overhead attached (£)
Clerical support	Clerical hours	500 hours	£6.00/clerical hour	3,000
General administration	Admin hours	70 hours	£20.00/admin hour	1,400
Photocopying	Number of copies	1,500 copies	£0.05/copy	75
Telephone	Telephone calls	400 calls	£1.50/call	600
			Total overhead	5,075
			Direct cost	15,000
			AB cost	**20,075**
			Profit (@ 40%)	8,030
			Selling price	**28,105**

3 **Comparison:**

	Cost	Selling price
Absorption cost	18,750	26,250
Activity-based cost	20,075	28,105
Difference	(1,325)	(1,855)

The current absorption costing system is undercosting this case by £1,325, which results in a shortfall in sales revenue of £1,855. This case is being subsidized by other cases, which will be overcosted and overpriced.

Q11.1 Clamco – Solution

Workings

January	
Direct labour	120,000
Direct materials	90,000
Variable production overhead	18,000
Variable cost	228,000
Fixed production overhead	72,000
Absorption cost	300,000

Variable cost/unit = £228,000/6,000 units = £38/unit
Absorption cost/unit = £300,000/6,000 units = £50/unit
Fixed production overhead/unit = £72,000/6,000 units = £12/unit

Physical stock changes (number of units)

	Jan	Feb	Mar	Qtr
Opening stock	0	2,000	1,000	0
Actual production	6,000	5,000	7,000	18,000
Actual sales	4,000	6,000	7,000	17,000
Closing stock	2,000	1,000	1,000	1,000

1 a) Absorption costing (£000) (abs. prod. cost = £50/unit)

	Jan	Feb	Mar	Qtr
Opening stock	0	100	50	0
Add: Production cost	300	250	350	900
Less: Closing stock	100	50	50	50
Under/(over)absorption	0	12	(12)	0
Cost of sales	200	312	338	850
Sales revenue	256	384	448	1,088
Gross profit	56	72	110	238
Non-production overhead	25	25	25	75
Net profit	**31**	**47**	**85**	**163**

b) Variable costing (£000) (var. prod. cost = £38/unit)

	Jan	Feb	Mar	Qtr
Opening stock	0	76	38	0
Add: Production cost	228	190	266	684
Less: Closing stock	76	38	38	38
Cost of sales	152	228	266	646
Sales revenue	256	384	448	1,088
Gross profit	104	156	182	442
Production overheads	72	72	72	216
Non-production overhead	25	25	25	75
Total fixed overheads	97	97	97	291
Net profit	**7**	**59**	**85**	**151**

2 Reconciliation of profits (£000)

	Jan	Feb	Mar	Qtr
Absorption net profit	31	47	85	163
Variable net profit	7	59	85	151
Difference	**24**	**(12)**	**–**	**12**
Increase in stock (units)	2,000	(1,000)	–	1,000
Production overheads in stock				
increase (@ £12 a unit)	24	(12)	–	12

Q11.2 Rivilin plc – Solution

Workings

	£/unit
Variable production cost	20 – variable costing production and stock value
Fixed production cost	12 – £9,600/800 units – planned absorption rate
Absorption production cost	32 – absorption costing production and stock value

Stock movements (units)

	April	May	June
Opening stock	–	–	50
Production	800	750	820
Sales	(800)	(700)	(850)
Closing stock	–	50	20
Change in level	–	+50	–30

1 Variable costing profit statement (£)

	April	May	June
Opening stock	–	–	1,000
Production (@ £20)	16,000	15,000	16,400
Less: Closing stock	–	1,000	400
Cost of sales	16,000	14,000	17,000
Sales (@ £60)	48,000	42,000	51,000
Gross profit	32,000	28,000	34,000
Less: Production overheads	9,600	9,600	9,600
Less: Non-production overheads	10,000	10,000	10,000
Net profit	12,400	8,400	14,400

2 Absorption costing profit statement (£)

	April	May	June
Opening stock	–	–	1,600
Production (@ £32)	25,600	24,000	26,240
Less: Closing stock	–	1,600	640
Cost of sales	25,600	22,400	27,200
Under/(over)recovery of fixed production overheads	–	(50 × £12) 600	(20 × £12) (240)
Adjusted cost of sales	25,600	23,000	26,960
Sales (@ £60)	48,000	42,000	51,000
Gross profit	22,400	19,000	24,040
Less: Non-production overheads	10,000	10,000	10,000
Net profit	12,400	9,000	14,040

3 Explanation of profit differences

April – no stock movement – identical profits

May – stock increase – absorption profits higher by £600 (50 × £12)

June – stock decrease – absorption profits lower by £360 (30 × £12)

Q11.3 The Valley Fireworks Corporation – Solution

Workings

Direct labour	180
Direct materials	60
Variable production overhead	10
Variable cost	250
Fixed production overhead	80
Absorption cost	330

Fixed production overhead/unit = £96,000/1,200 units = £80/unit
Underabsorption = (1,200 – 1,100) units × £80/unit fixed overhead = £8,000

Physical stock changes (number of units)

	Q1	Q2	Q3	Q4	Year
Opening stock	10	290	550	690	10
Actual production	300	300	200	300	1,100
Actual sales	20	40	60	980	1,100
Closing stock	290	550	690	10	10

1 a) Absorption costing (£000) (abs. prod. cost = £330/unit)

	Q1	Q2	Q3	Q4	Year
Opening stock	3,300	95,700	181,500	227,700	3,300
Add: Production cost	99,000	99,000	66,000	99,000	363,000
Less: Closing stock	95,700	181,500	227,700	3,300	3,300
Under/(over)absorption	–	–	8,000	–	8,000
Cost of sales	6,600	13,200	27,800	323,400	371,000
Sales revenue	10,000	20,000	30,000	490,000	550,000
Gross profit	3,400	6,800	2,200	166,600	179,000
Non-production overhead – fixed	36,000	36,000	36,000	36,000	144,000
– variable @ £20	400	800	1,200	19,600	22,000
Net profit	(33,000)	(30,000)	(35,000)	111,000	13,000

b) Variable costing (£000) (var. prod. cost = £250/unit)

	Q1	Q2	Q3	Q4	Year
Opening stock	2,500	72,500	137,500	172,500	2,500
Add: Production cost	75,000	75,000	50,000	75,000	275,000
Less: Closing stock	72,500	137,500	172,500	2,500	2,500
Cost of sales	5,000	10,000	15,000	245,000	275,000
Sales revenue	10,000	20,000	30,000	490,000	550,000
Gross profit	5,000	10,000	15,000	245,000	275,000
Production overheads – fixed	24,000	24,000	24,000	24,000	96,000
Variable non-production overhead	400	800	1,200	19,600	22,000
Fixed non-production overhead	36,000	36,000	36,000	36,000	144,000
Net profit	(55,400)	(50,800)	(46,200)	165,400	13,000

2 Reconciliation of profits (£000)

	Q1	Q2	Q3	Q4	Year
Absorption net profit	(33,000)	(30,000)	(35,000)	111,000	13,000
Variable net profit	(55,400)	(50,800)	(46,200)	165,400	13,000
Difference	**22,400**	**20,800**	**11,200**	**(54,400)**	–
Increase in stock (units)	280	260	140	(680)	–
Production overhead in stock increase (@ £80/unit)	**22,400**	**20,800**	**11,200**	**(54,400)**	–
Net profit using variable costing	(55,400)	(50,800)	(46,200)	165,400	13,000
Adjustment for fixed production overheads in stock change	22,400	20,800	11,200	(54,400)	–
Net profit using absorption costing	(33,000)	(30,000)	(35,000)	111,000	13,000

3 The profit figures derived from variable costing give a realistic view of performance for each period as they do not carry forward any fixed production overheads incurred in one period to the next. This enables managers to monitor performance and to create useful internal reports.

The profit figures derived from absorption costing are created using the basic rule for the treatment of fixed production overheads which has to be followed for external reporting purposes. It enables managers to monitor the cumulative profits which will ultimately be used by the owners of the business to judge the performance of its managers.

Q12.1 Demarco – Solution

	£000
Direct materials	18
Direct labour	32
Variable production overheads	5
Variable cost	**55**
Fixed production overheads	45
Production cost	**100**
Admin overheads	20
Marketing overheads	60
Full cost	**180**
Margin @ 20%	45
Sales revenue	**225**

a) Variable cost = 55:

$$\frac{225 - 55}{55} \times 100 = \frac{170}{55} \times 100 = 309\%$$

Variable cost plus 309%

b) Production cost = 100:

$$\frac{225 - 100}{100} \times 100 = \frac{125}{100} \times 100 = 125\%$$

Production cost plus 125%

c) Full cost = 180:

$$\frac{225 - 180}{180} \times 100 = \frac{45}{180} \times 100 = 25\%$$

Full cost plus 25%

Q12.2 Wizkid – Solution

	£
Selling price	10.00
Variable cost	6.00
Unit contribution	4.00

1 At BEP (say, at N units)

Total contribution = total fixed costs
$$N \times 4.00 = 40,000$$
$$N = 10,000$$
Thus, BEP is 10,000 units

	£
Total contribution = 15,000 × 4.00 =	60,000
Total fixed costs =	40,000
Profit =	20,000

2

	£
Variable cost	6.00
100% mark-up	6.00
Selling price	12.00

	£
Total contribution (15,000 × 6.00)	90,000
Less: Total fixed costs	40,000
Net profit	**50,000**

3 (15,000 − 10%) × unit contribution

	£
13,500 × 6.00	= 81,000
Less: Total fixed costs	= 40,000
Net profit	= **41,000**

4 **Other** factors to be taken into account include:
   - competitors' prices;
   - corporate objectives;
   - pricing strategy;
   - product life cycle stage;
   - effect on profit of lowering prices and increasing demand.

Q12.3 Ride-on Lawn Mowers – Solution

Workings

Original budget = 1,120 units

	£
Total sales revenue	2,800,000
Total profit	800,000
Total full cost	2,000,000
Total fixed cost	1,104,000
Total variable cost	896,000

Variable cost/unit = 896,000/1,120 = £800/unit

a) Total sales revenue is £2.8 million and sales price reduced to £2,150. Assume no change in fixed costs.

$$\text{No. of units sold} = £2,800,000/2,150 = 1,302$$

For the ROCE to stay at 20%, profit must stay at £800,000.

Total sales revenue	2,800,000
Required profit	800,000
Total costs	2,000,000
Total fixed cost	1,104,000
Total variable cost	896,000
Revised variable cost/unit = 896,000/1,302	= £688/unit
Original variable cost/unit	= £800/unit
Required reduction in variable cost	= **£112/unit**
112/800	= 14%

b) Total sales revenue reduces to £2.5 million and sales price is reduced to £2,150. Assume no change in fixed costs.

$$\text{No. of units sold} = £2,500,000/2,150 = 1,163$$

Profit must stay at £800,000 for the ROCE to stay at 20%.

Total sales revenue	2,500,000
Required profit	800,000
Total costs	1,700,000
Total fixed cost	1,104,000
Total variable cost	596,000
Revised variable cost/unit = 596,000/1,163	= £512/unit
Original variable cost/unit	= £800/unit
Required reduction in var. cost	= **£288/unit**
288/800	= 36%

Advice: As shown above, the budgeted full cost of the Luxon is £1,800. But as the selling price has been significantly decreased, a greater number will have to be sold to achieve the £800,000 forecast profit which is needed to maintain the ROCE at 20%.

- If total sales revenue can be maintained at £2.8 million (despite the price reduction to £2,150) and fixed costs cannot be reduced, the variable costs will have to be reduced by 14% to £688 per unit. This is a challenging target but may well be achievable.
- If total sales revenue decreases to £2.5 million in this very competitive market and fixed costs cannot be reduced, the variable costs will have to be reduced by 36% to £512 per unit. This is a huge task and is probably unachievable.

The variable costs need to be re-examined with a view to their reduction. The mower should be re-engineered. For example, is it possible to use less costly components which still meet specifications? Is it possible to replace several parts with just one that will do the job? If so, resources will be saved in ordering, inspection, storage and fitting. Even if the full amount of savings cannot be made, the greater they are, the less will be the fall in their ROCE.

The company would be well advised also to scrutinize its fixed overheads to see if any of these could be reduced. It is likely that some saving will be found, but less than the total amount needed. However, this would mean that the variable cost reduction target would diminish and so become more achievable.

The best chance of receiving an annual bonus next year is to employ the technique of *target costing/pricing* to reduce variable costs by at least 14%. Also, the selling price reduction needs to be sufficient to increase volume by 16.25% ((1,302 − 1,120)/1,120). This will maintain sales revenue, net profit, the ROCE and the annual bonus!

Q13.1 RI v ROI – Solution

Division	A	B	C	D
Profit before head office charges	2	3	24	14
Capital employed	30	60	450	240
ROCE	6.7%	5.0%	5.3%	5.8%
ROCE preferences	1	4	3	2
Notional interest @ 5%	1.5	3.0	22.5	12.0
RI (profit before HO charges – interest)	0.5	0.0	1.5	2.0
RI preferences	3	4	2	1

Comment: 'Profit before head office charges' has been used to calculate the ROCE as this is the most appropriate measure of divisional performance. Note that the two sets of rankings give different answers as to which divisions have performed better than others. Both answers are correct; which one is used depends entirely on head office.

Q13.2 Gorgon Group plc – Solution

A. **Odeen division**

	External	Trey	Total
Quantity	30,000	10,000	40,000
Sales price	40	34	
Variable cost	17	17	
Unit contribution	23	17	
Total contribution	690,000	170,000	860,000
Fixed costs	384,000	96,000	480,000
Profit	**306,000**	**74,000**	**380,000**

B. 1 **Odeen division**

Total contribution	690,000	
Total fixed cost	480,000	
Profit	210,000	
Compare	380,000	
Reduction	**170,000**	(−45%)

2 **Gorgon Group**

Trey saves 10,000 @ £4	40,000	
Odeen loses	(170,000)	
Gorgon's net loss	**(130,000)**	

C. | | | |
|---|---|---|
| Odeen loses | (170,000) | |
| External unit contribution | 23 | |
| **Extra sales = 170,000/23** | **7,391** | (25% of 30,000) |

D. Effect on total contribution and profit:

Trey's increase = 5,000 @ £4	=	20,000
Odeen's decrease = 5,000 @ £17 =		(85,000)
Gorgon Group's decrease		**(65,000)**

E. | | | |
|---|---|---|
| Odeen loses 10,000 @ £4 | = | 40,000 |
| Trey gains 10,000 @ £4 | = | 40,000 |
| **Net effect on Gorgon Group** | = | **Zero** |

F. *Advice*:

If Odeen is operating at less than full capacity, it would be advisable for it to negotiate a revised transfer price between £34 and £30. In this situation, Odeen's ideal transfer price is the variable cost of £17 so it will still be making a significant contribution of at least £13 a unit. Trey's manager will probably be very happy with a transfer price of about £32 as quality and reliability of supply will be better from its fellow subsidiary, Odeen, than from the external supplier, Hexup. Neither manager should suffer any demotivation from this.

Alternatively, if Odeen is operating at full capacity, its ideal transfer price is the market price of £40. In this situation, it is advisable for Odeen to stop supplying Trey and sell all its production externally at £40 a unit giving a contribution of £23 a unit. Also, Trey will increase its contribution by £4 a unit so this looks like a 'win–win' situation which will motivate both managers. However, this assumes that Odeen will be able to sell **all** the 10,000 units on the open market; if it cannot, it should attempt to negotiate a sales volume quota with Trey to account for the shortfall at a practical transfer price of about £32.

Q14.1 Kellaway Ltd – Solution

1 Production budget

Production = sales + closing stock − opening stock

	Large	Medium	Small
Sales	4,000	5,000	3,500
+ Closing stock	400	300	150
– Opening stock	(300)	(400)	(200)
= **Production**	**4,100**	**4,900**	**3,450**

2 Unit production costs

	Large	Medium	Small
Direct labour:			
Fitters/turners	$1.25 \times 10 = 12.50$	$0.90 \times 10 = 9.00$	$0.80 \times 10 = 8.00$
Assemblers/packers	$0.40 \times 6 = 2.40$	$0.25 \times 6 = 1.50$	$0.20 \times 6 = 1.20$
Direct materials:			
Aluminium	$2.5 \times 3 = 7.50$	$1.0 \times 3 = 3.00$	$0.5 \times 3 = 1.50$
Packaging	$1.25 \times 1 = 1.25$	$0.75 \times 1 = 0.75$	$0.5 \times 1 = 0.50$
Production overhead*	$1.65 \times 2.00 = 3.30$	$1.15 \times 2.00 = 2.30$	$1.00 \times 2.00 = 2.00$
Unit production cost	**£26.95**	**£16.55**	**£13.20**

Total dlh = 4,100(1.25 + 0.40) + 4,900(0.90 + 0.25) + 3,450(0.80 + 0.20)
  = 6,765 + 5,635 + 3,450 = 15,850
* Overhead absorption rate = £31,700/15,850 = £2.00/dlh.

3 Materials usage quantity budget

	Large	Medium	Small	Total
Aluminium	$2.5 \times 4,100 = 10,250$	$1.0 \times 4,900 = 4,900$	$0.5 \times 3,450 = 1,725$	**16,875 strips**
Packaging	$1.25 \times 4,100 = 5,125$	$0.75 \times 4,900 = 3,675$	$0.50 \times 3,450 = 1,725$	**10,525 metres**

Materials usage cost budget
Aluminium = 16,875 strips @ £3 = £50,625
Packaging = 10,525 metres @ £1 = £10,525

4 Materials purchases budget

	Aluminium (strips)	Packaging (metres)
Usage	16,875	10,525
+ Closing stock	150	50
– Opening stock	(220)	(80)
= Purchases	**16,805**	**10,495**
	@ £3	@ £1
Purchases	**£50,415**	**£10,495**

5 Direct labour budget

F/T = Fitters/Turners
A/P = Assemblers/Packers

	Large	Medium	Small	Total
F/T	$4,100 \times 1.25 = 5,125$	$4,900 \times 0.9 = 4,410$	$3,450 \times 0.8 = 2,760$	12,295 dlh
A/P	$4,100 \times 0.4 = 1,640$	$4,900 \times 0.25 = 1,225$	$3,450 \times 0.2 = 690$	3,555 dlh

F/T 12,295 @ £10.00 = £122,950
A/P 3,555 @ £6.00 = £21,330

Q14.2 Pierce Pommery – Solution

1 Production budget

Production = sales + closing stock – opening stock

000 litres	Sept	Oct	Nov	Qtr	Dec
Sales	340	300	260	900	320
Closing stock	60	52	64	64	50
Opening stock	80	60	52	80	64
Production	**320**	**292**	**272**	**884**	**306**

Purchases budget

Production = sales + closing stock – opening stock

Tonnes	Sept	Oct	Nov	Qtr	Dec
Usage	4,800	4,380	4,080	13,260	4,590
Closing stock	2,190	2,040	2,295	2,295	
Opening stock	2,200	2,190	2,040	2,200	
Purchases	**4,790**	**4,230**	**4,335**	**13,355**	
Cost/tonne	£50	£50	£150	£150	
Purchases (£)	**239,500**	**211,500**	**650,250**	**1,101,250**	

2 Cash budget

	Workings	November
Cash sales	Nov 260,000 × £3 × 25%	195,000
Credit sales	Oct 300,000 × £3 × 75%	675,000
Total in		870,000
Apple purchases	from September	239,500
Direct labour	272,000 × £0.20	54,400
Overheads (excl. depreciation)	from October	25,000
Total out		318,900
Cash in/(out)		551,100
Opening balance		(495,900)
Closing balance		**55,200**

Q14.3 Norman Ropes – Solution

Period	1	2	3	4	5	6	7
Norman Ropes – Model answer							
a) Production budget (metres of rope)							
Add: Sales	3,000	4,000	5,000	4,000	6,000	6,000	8,000
Less: Opening stock	1,500	1,000	1,250	1,000	1,500	1,500	2,000
Add: Closing stock	1,000	1,250	1,000	1,500	1,500	2,000	1,750
Production (metres)	**2,500**	**4,250**	**4,750**	**4,500**	**6,000**	**6,500**	**7,750**
b) Materials usage cost budget							
Usage (metres of ARN)	250,000	425,000	475,000	450,000	600,000	650,000	775,000
Cost (£)	**10,000**	**17,000**	**19,000**	**18,000**	**24,000**	**26,000**	**31,000**
c) Materials purchases cost budget							
Add: Cost of materials used	10,000	17,000	19,000	18,000	24,000	26,000	31,000
Less: Opening stock	5,000	4,250	4,750	4,500	6,000	6,500	7,750
Add: Closing stock	4,250	4,750	4,500	6,000	6,500	7,750	
Purchases (£)	**9,250**	**17,500**	**18,750**	**19,500**	**24,500**	**27,250**	

Q15.1 Welco Ltd – Solution

1 Flexed budget (1,050 units)

	£
Seals (1,050 @ £2)	2,100
Castings (2,100 @ £3)	6,300
Labour ((1,050/6) h @ £6)	1,050
Fixed overheads	7,700
Total costs	17,150
Revenue (1,050 @ £20)	21,000
Profit	3,850

2 Materials variances

	Seals		Castings	
Usage:				
	$(BQ - AQ)BP$		$(BQ - AQ)BP$	
	$(1,050 - 1,060)2$		$(2,100 - 2,108)3$	
	-20	= 20 A	-24	= 24 A
Price:				
	$(BP - AP)AQ$		$(BP - AP)AQ$	
	$(2.00 - 1.95)1,060$		$(3.00 - 3.25)2,108$	
	$+53$	= 53 F	-527	= 527 A
Cost:				
	Budget cost – actual cost		Budget cost – actual cost	
	$2,100 - 2,067$		$6,300 - 6,851$	
	$+33$	= 33 F	-551	= 551 A

Direct labour variances

Efficiency: (BQ − AQ)BP = (175 − 190)6 = −90 = **90 A**
Rate: (BP − AP)AQ = (6.00 − 5.90)190 = +19 = **19 F**
Cost: Budget cost − actual cost = 1,050 − 1,121 = −71 = **71 A**

Fixed overhead variance

Cost: Budget FO − actual FO = 7,700 − 7,600 = +100 = **100 F**

Sales variances

Price: (AP − BP)AQ = (19 − 20)1,050 = −1,050 = **1,050 A**
Volume: Flexed budget profit − original budget profit
3,850 − 4,400 = −550 = **550 A**

3 Profit reconciliation statement

Original budget profit				**4,400**
Sales volume variance				550 A
Flexed budget profit				**3,850**
Sales price variance				1,050 A
Materials:	Seals:	Usage	20 A	
		Price	53 F	
		Cost		33 F
	Castings:	Usage	24 A	
		Price	527 A	
		Cost		551 A
Direct labour:		Efficiency	90 A	
		Rate	19 F	
		Cost		71 A
Fixed overhead expenditure				100 F
Actual profit				**2,311**

Q15.2 Stanley & Co. − Solution

Workings

Flexed budget (for 2,100 frames)

	£
Materials:	2,100 × 5.0 m × £4.00/m = 10,500 m × £4.00/m = 42,000
Labour:	2,100 × 0.50 h × £12.00/h = 1,050 h × £12.00/h = 12,600
	Total = 54,600

Actual performance (for 2,100 frames)

Materials:	11,550 m × £3.80/m	= 43,890
Labour:	1,000 h × £13.00/h	= 13,000
		Total = 56,890

1 Variance calculations

Materials usage:	(BQ – AQ)BP	
	(10,500 – 11,550)4.00	= **(4,200) A**
Materials price:	(BP – AP)AQ	
	(4.00 – 3.80)11,550	= **2,310 F**
Materials cost:	Budgeted cost – actual cost	
	42,000 – 43,890	= **(1,890) A**
Labour efficiency:	(BQ – AQ)BP	
	(1,050 – 1,000)12.00	= **600 F**
Labour rate:	(BP – AP)AQ	
	(12.00 – 13.00)1,000	= **(1,000) A**
Labour cost:	Budgeted cost – actual cost	
	12,600 – 13,000	= **(400) A**

2 Possible explanations for variances

Materials usage = (4,200) A	– wastage from poorer-quality materials
	– wastage due to demotivated workforce
	– out-of-date standards
Materials price = 2,310 F	– lower-priced substitute material used
	– unexpected discounts achieved
	– lower prices from new supplier
	– out-of-date standards
Labour efficiency = 600 F	– motivated workforce due to pay rise
	– more highly skilled type of labour used
	– out-of-date standards
Labour rate = (1,000) A	– recent pay rise
	– some overtime at premium rates may have occurred
	– out-of-date standards

3 Amendments

The payment of 'idle time' during the power cut affects the labour efficiency variance only.

Labour efficiency:	(BQ – AQ *worked*)BP	
	(1,050 – 950)12.00	= 1,200 F
Idle time:	Idle hours × budgeted rate	
	–50 × 12.00	= (600) A
Combined (as previous)		= 600 F

It was originally thought that the operatives had worked efficiently by saving 50 hours at £12 = £600 (50/1,050 = 4.8% improvement on standard). It is now clear that they were twice as efficient as originally thought as they saved 100 hours at £12 = £1,200 (100/1,050 = 9.5% improvement on standard).

Q15.3 Ivanblast – Solution

Flexed budget: £

Sales:	30,000 games	@ £50	= 1,500,000
Production materials:	30,000 blank CDs	@ £1.10 =	33,000
Variable overheads:	30,000 games	@ £0.50 =	15,000
Fixed overheads:		=	800,000
Net profit		=	652,000

1 Variance analysis

Sales volume Variance
= flexed budget profit – original budget profit
= 652,000 – 410,000
= +242,000
= **242,000 F**

Sales price variance = (AP – BP)AQ
= (45 – 50)30,000
= –150,000
= **150,000 A**

Material quantity variance
= (BQ – AQ)BP
= (30,000 – 30,250)1.10
= –275
= **275 A**

Material price variance
= (BP – AP)AQ
= (1.10 – 1.00)30,250
= +3,025
= **3,025 F**

Material cost variance
= budgeted cost – actual cost
= 33,000 – 30,250
= +2,750
= **2,750 F**

Variable overhead cost variance
= budgeted variable overhead – actual variable overhead
= 15,000 – 15,000
= **0**

Fixed overhead expenditure variance
= budgeted fixed overhead – actual fixed overhead
= 800,000 – 850,000
= –50,000
= **50,000 A**

2 Budget reconciliation statement

	£	£
Original budget profit		**410,000**
Sales volume variance		<u>242,000</u> F
Flexed budget profit		**652,000**
Sales price variance		150,000 A
Material quantity variance	275 A	
Material price variance	<u>3,025</u> F	
Material cost variance		2,750 F
Var. ohd cost variance		–
Fix. ohd expenditure variance		50,000 A
Actual profit		<u>**454,750**</u>

3 The 10% reduction in sales price seems to have paid off as the number of games sold increased by 20%. The net effect of the sales volume and sales price variances is £92,000 favourable.

A total of 275 CDs were wasted. This could have been caused by deciding to purchase slightly inferior CDs than originally planned at the slightly cheaper price of £1.00 as opposed to £1.10. However, the favourable material price variance of £3,025 shows this was a good idea. On the other hand, the material quantity variance may be the result of simply not building normal production wastage into the budget, If so, this planning error has now been revealed and should not be repeated in future.

The adverse fixed overhead expenditure variance of £50,000 should not have occurred and should be investigated.

The net result of the period's activities is that the actual profit is £44,750 (11%) greater than originally planned.

Q15.4 Flipside Limited – Solution

Workings

Standard:	Quantity	Price	Cost (£)
Material A	5 kg	2.00 £/kg	10.00
Material B	10 kg	4.00 £/kg	40.00
Direct labour	2 dlh	15.00 £/dlh	30.00
Variable overhead	2 dlh	3.00 £/dlh	6.00
Fixed overhead	2 dlh	7.00 £/dlh	<u>14.00</u>
Production cost			100.00
Selling price			150.00
Standard profit			**50.00**

Original budget output = 10,000 units
Actual budget output   = 11,000 units

Original budget:	Quantity	Price	Cost (£)
Material A	50,000 kg	2.00 £/kg	100,000
Material B	100,000 kg	4.00 £/kg	400,000
Direct labour	20,000 dlh	15.00 £/dlh	300,000
Variable overhead	20,000 dlh	3.00 £/dlh	60,000
Fixed overhead	20,000 dlh	7.00 £/dlh	140,000
Production cost			1,000,000
Sales revenue	10,000 units	150.00 £/unit	1,500,000
Profit			**500,000**

Flexed budget:	Quantity	Price	Cost(£)
Material A	55,000 kgs	2.00 £/kg	110,000
Material B	110,000 kgs	4.00 £/kg	440,000
Direct labour	22,000 dlh	15.00 £/dlh	330,000
Variable overhead	22,000 dlh	3.00 £/dlh	66,000
Fixed overhead	22,000 dlh	7.00 £/dlh	154,000
Production cost			1,100,000
Sales revenue	11,000 units	150.00 £/unit	1,650,000
Profit			**550,000**

Actual performance:	Quantity	Price	Cost (£)
Material A	66,000 kg	1.50 £/kg	99,000
Material B	99,000 kg	5.00 £/kg	495,000
Direct labour	20,900 dlh	16.00 £/dlh	334,400
Variable overhead	20,900 dlh	3.00 £/dlh	62,700
Fixed overhead	20,900 dlh	7.50 £/dlh	156,750
Production cost			1,147,850
Sales revenue	11,000 units	139.00 £/unit	1,529,000
Profit			**381,150**

1 Variance analysis

Material A

Cost var.	110,000	less	99,000	=		**11,000 F**
Price var.	2.00	less	1.50	×	66,000	**33,000 F**
Usage var.	55,000	less	66,000	×	2.00	**−22,000 A**

Material B

Cost var.	440,000	less	495,000	=		**−55,000 A**
Price var.	4.00	less	5.00	×	99,000	**−99,000 A**
Usage var.	110,000	less	99,000	×	4.00	**44,000 F**

Direct labour

Cost var.	330,000	less	334,400	=		**−4,400 A**
Rate var.	15.00	less	16.00	×	20,900	**−20,900 A**
Efficiency var.	22,000	less	20,900	×	15.00	**16,500 F**

Variable overheads

Cost var.	66,000	less	62,700	=		**3,300 F**
Expenditure var.	3.00	less	3.00	×	20,900	**0**
Efficiency var.	22,000	less	20,900	×	3.00	**3,300 F**

Fixed overheads

Cost var.	154,000	less	156,750	=		−2,750 A
Expenditure var.	140,000	less	156,750	=		−16,750 A
Volume var.	154,000	less	140,000	=		14,000 F
Efficiency var.	22,000	less	20,900	×	7.00	7,700 F
Capacity var.	20,900	less	20,000	×	7.00	6,300 F

Sales price variance

	139.00	less	150.00	×	11,000 −121,000 A

Sales volume variance

	550,000	less	500,000	=	50,000 F

2 Profit reconciliation statement (before admin & marketing overheads)

		£	£
Original budget profit			500,000
Sales volume variance			50,000 F
Flexed budget profit			550,000
Sales price variance			−121,000 A
Material A:	Price variance	33,000 F	
	Usage variance	−22,000 A	
	Cost variance		11,000 F
Material B:	Price variance	−99,000 A	
	Usage variance	44,000 F	
	Cost variance		−55,000 A
Direct labour:	Rate variance	−20,900 A	
	Efficiency variance	16,500 F	
	Cost variance		−4,400 A
Variable overheads:	Expenditure variance	0	
	Efficiency variance	3,300 F	
	Cost variance		3,300 F
Fixed overheads:	Efficiency variance	7,700 F	
	Capacity variance	6,300 F	
	Volume variance	14,000 F	
	Expenditure variance	−16,750 A	
	Cost variance		−2,750 A
Actual profit			381,150

3 Comments

Sales

The sales price decreased from the budgeted £150 to the actual £139. The price elasticity of demand was positive and the net effect was adverse as follows:

$$
\begin{aligned}
\text{Sales price variance} \quad &= 121,000 \text{ A} \\
\text{Sales volume variance} &= \underline{50,000} \text{ F} \\
&\quad\ \underline{71,000} \text{ A}
\end{aligned}
$$

Variable costs

Material A had a favourable price variance and an adverse usage variance. This could be caused by sourcing lower-priced materials which were also lower quality causing higher wastage to occur.

Material B had an adverse price variance and a favourable usage variance. This could be caused by sourcing higher-quality materials at more expensive prices. The better-quality materials may have caused lower wastage to occur.

The adverse effect was a cost variance of £11,000 favourable for material A and £55,000 for material B.

The favourable labour efficiency variance of £16,500 may have been caused by the increase in pay from £15/hour to £16/hour. Pay rises tend to motivate operatives. However, the resulting adverse labour rate variance of £20,900 results in an adverse labour cost variance of £4,400.

Variable overheads are absorbed on a labour hour basis so their efficiency variance would follow the labour efficiency. The variable overhead expenditure variance shows a zero variance and could be caused by excellent budgeting and control. The cost variance was £3,300 favourable.

Fixed overheads

The adverse cost variance of £2,750 shows that more was spent on fixed overheads than planned. This was due to the adverse expenditure variance of £16,750. The fixed overhead absorption rate is based on direct labour hours. The favourable volume variance of £14,000 was made up of £6,300 F (capacity) due to working less hours than planned and £7,700 A (efficiency) from working at a faster rate per hour than planned.

In summary

Original budget profit	500,000
Sales variances	71,000 A
Variable cost variances	45,100 A
Fixed overhead variances	2,750 A
Actual profit	381,150

The management performance appears to have been poor. After eliminating the effect of the change in sales volume, the actual profit was £158,850 below the flexed budget profit. The increase in the sales price accounts for most of the bad performance but the adverse variance for material B is also very significant and needs to be investigated urgently. (Standards should also be checked to make sure they are up to date so as to avoid significant planning variances.)

Q15.7 Triform Limited – Solution

Standard cost card (for one unit of TR2)

		£
Direct materials	4 kg @ £5/kg	20
Direct labour	3 hours @ £7/hour	21
Variable overhead	3 hours @ £3/hour	9
Fixed overhead	3 hours @ £4/hour	12
Standard cost		62
Standard profit margin		14
Standard selling price		76

Budget for last month (800 units of TR2)

	Quantity	Price	Cost (£)
Direct materials	800 × 4 = 3,200	£5/kg	16,000
Direct labour	800 × 3 = 2,400	£7/hour	16,800
Variable overhead	800 × 3 = 2,400	£3/hour	7,200
Fixed overhead	800 × 3 = 2,400	£4/hour	9,600
Total cost			49,600
Total sales revenue	800	£76	60,800
Total profit margin	800	£14	11,200

Flexed budget for last month (700 units of TR2)

	Quantity	Price	Cost (£)
Direct materials	700 × 4 = 2,800	£5/kg	14,000
Direct labour	700 × 3 = 2,100	£7/hour	14,700
Variable overhead	700 × 3 = 2,100	£3/hour	6,300
Fixed overhead	700 × 3 = 2,100	£4/hour	8,400
Total cost			43,400
Total sales revenue	700	£76	53,200
Total profit margin	700	£14	9,800

Actual results for last month (700 units of TR2 produced and sold)

	Quantity	Price	Cost (£)
Direct materials	3,100	£4.25	13,175
Direct labour	2,350	£6.40	15,040
Variable overhead	2,350	£2.8510638	6,700
Fixed overhead	2,350	£3.9148936	9,200
Total cost			44,115
Total sales revenue	700	£79	55,300
Total profit margin			11,185

Standard hours of production (SHP) – *a measure of output*

SHP = actual number of units produced × standard labour time/unit = $700 \times 3 = 2,100$

Formulae (for a standard absorption costing system)

(FAOR = Fixed Overhead Absorption Rate = £4/hour)

Fixed overhead total cost variance

= flexed budget total cost – actual total cost

= $8,400 - 9,200 = 800$ **A**

Fixed overhead expenditure variance

= original budget total cost – actual total cost

= $9,600 - 9,200 = 400$ **F**

Fixed overhead volume variance

= flexed budget cost – original budget cost

= $8,400 - 9,600$

= **1,200 A**

Fixed overhead efficiency variance

= (flexed budget hours – actual hours worked) × standard FOAR

= $(2,100 - 2,350) \times 4 = 1,000$ **A**

Fixed overhead capacity variance

= (actual hours worked – original budget hours) × standard FOAR

= $(2,350 - 2,400) \times 4 = 200$ **A**

Sales

Sales volume variance = flexed budget profit – original budget profit

= $9,800 - 11,200$

= **1,400 A**

Sales price variance = (actual selling price – standard selling price)

× actual sales volume

= $(79 - 76) \times 700$

= **2,100 F**

Variable overheads

(VAOR = Variable Overhead Absorption Rate = £3/hour)

Total variable overhead variance

= flexed budget VO cost – actual VO cost

= $6,300 - 6,700 = 400$ **A**

Variable overhead expenditure variance

= (flexed budget VOAR − actual VOAR) × actual hours

= (flexed budget VOAR × actual hours) − (actual VOAR × actual hours)

= (flexed budget VOAR × actual hours) − actual VO incurred

= $(3 \times 2{,}350) - 6{,}700$

= $7{,}050 - 6{,}700$

= 350 F

Variable overhead efficiency variance

= (flexed budget hours − actual hours worked) × flexed budget VOAR

= $(2{,}100 - 2{,}350) \times 3$

= $(-250) \times 3$

= 750 A

Materials

Material price variance

= (flexed budget price − actual price) × actual quantity of materials

= $(5.00 - 4.25) \times 3{,}100$

= 2,325 F

Material usage variance

= (flexed budget quantity − actual quantity used) × flexed budget price

= $(2{,}800 - 3{,}100) \times 5$

= $(-300) \times 5$

= 1,500 A

Total material cost variance

= flexed budget cost − actual cost incurred

= $14{,}000 - 13{,}175$

= 825 F

Direct labour

Labour rate variance

= (standard rate − actual rate) × actual labour hours worked

= $(7.00 - 6.40) \times 2{,}350$

= 1,410 F

Labour efficiency variance

= (flexed budget hours − actual labour hours worked) × standard rate

= $(2{,}100 - 2{,}350) \times 7$

= $(-250) \times 7$

= 1,750 A

Total labour cost variance

= flexed budget labour cost – actual labour cost incurred

= 14,700 – 15,040

= **340 A**

Profit reconciliation statement

	£	£	£
Original budget profit			11,200
Sales volume variance			1,400 A
Flexed budget profit			9,800
Sales price variance			2,100 F
	Favourable	**Adverse**	
Materials price	2,325		
Materials usage		1,500	
Materials cost			825 F
Labour rate	1,410		
Labour efficiency		1,750	
Labour cost			340 A
Variable overhead expenditure	350		
Variable overhead efficiency		750	
Variable overhead total cost			400 A
Fixed overhead expenditure	400		
Fixed overhead volume efficiency		1,000	
Fixed overhead volume capacity		200	
Fixed overhead total cost			800 A
Actual profit			**11,185**

Index